A history of inequality in South Africa, 1652–2002

Sampie Terreblanche

KZN
PRESS

D1354331

review publishing

UNIVERSITY OF KWAZULU-N.

Jointly published by

University of KwaZulu-Natal Press
Private Bag X01
Scottsville 3209
South Africa
E-mail: books@ukzn.ac.za
Website: www.ukznpress.co.za

and

KMM Review Publishing Company Pty Ltd
P O Box 782114
Sandton 2146
South Africa

ISBN: 978-1-86914-022-9

Edited by Riaan de Villiers and Louis van Schaik

Layout by Shahn Irwin and Olive Hendricks

Cover design by Anthony Cuerden

Cover art by T W Bowler: Table Bay from Robben Island, 1851

USAID is thanked for their funding assistance towards the research

Printed and bound by Interpak Books, Pietermaritzburg

In memory of the late Professor Bax Nomvete

AFRICA INSTITUTE FOR POLICY ANALYSIS AND ECONOMIC INTEGRATION (AIPA)

AIPA is an independent, non-profit-making economic research entity established in July 1992. Its objective is to undertake high-level, non-partisan, inter-disciplinary economic policy analysis and research on a wide spectrum of issues relating to the promotion of economic efficiency and growth with equity in African countries, and to offer thoroughly examined and developed solutions to their problems.

While in the medium to long term AIPA will increasingly play a regional role, the immediate imperative is to address the pressing issues surrounding economic growth and the economic democratisation of South Africa.

Contents

Figures and tables

Abbreviations

AAC	All African Convention
AAC	Anglo American Corporation
AB	Afrikaner Broederbond
AHI	Afrikaanse Handelsinstituut (Afrikaans commercial institute)
AMWU	African Mine Workers Union
ANC	African National Congress
ANCYL	African National Congress Youth League
ARMSCOR	Armaments Corporation
ASSOCOM	Association of Chambers of Commerce
BA	British-American
BAAB	Bantu Affairs Administration Board
BAD	Bantu Affairs Department
BCM	black consciousness movement
BCP	Black Community Programme
BEECom	Black Empowerment Commission
BEIC	British East India Company
BER	Bureau for Economic Research
BIG	basic income grant
BLA	black local authority
BPC	Black People's Convention
BSA	Business South Africa
CBM	Consultative Business Movement
CDE	Centre for Development and Enterprise
CE	continental Europe
CM	Chamber of Mines
CNETU	Council of Non-European Trade Unions
CODESA	Convention for a Democratic South Africa
COSATU	Congress of South African Trade Unions
CPSA	Communist Party of South Africa
DEP	department of economic policy of the ANC
DP	Democratic Party
DRC	Dutch Reformed Church
EDP	economic development programme

ESCOM	Electricity Supply Commission
FCI	Federated Chamber of Industries
FDI	foreign direct investment
FMF	Free Market Foundation
FOSATU	Federation of South African Trade Unions
GATT	General Agreement on Tariffs and Trade
GDFI	gross domestic fixed investment
GDI	gross domestic investment
GDP	gross domestic product
GDS	gross domestic savings
GEAR	Growth, Employment, and Redistribution Strategy
G/NP	*Gesuiwerde* (Purified) National Party
GNU	government of national unity
ICU	Industrial and Commercial Workers' Union
IDC	Industrial Development Corporation
IFP	Inkatha Freedom Party
ILC	Industrial Legislation Commission
IM	Independent Movement
IMF	International Monetary Fund
ISCOR	Iron and Steel Corporation
ISP	Industrial Strategy Project
ISS	Institute of Security Studies
JRC	Justice and Reconciliation Committee
LP	Labour Party
MDM	Mass Democratic Movement
MERG	Macro-Economic Research Group
MK	Umkhonto we Sizwe (armed wing of the ANC)
MLL	minimum living level
NAD	Native Affairs Department
NEC	national executive committee
NEF	National Economic Forum
NEM	Normative Economic Model
NEPAD	New Partnership for Africa's Development
NGO	non-governmental organisation
NIEP	National Institute for Economic Policy
NP	National Party
NRC	Native Representative Council
NUM	National Union of Mineworkers
NUSAS	National Union of South African Students

OAU	Organisation of African Unity
OECD	Organisation for Economic Cooperation and Development
OFS	Orange Free State
OPEC	Organisation of Petroleum Exporting Countries
PAC	Pan-Africanist Congress
PFP	Progressive Federal Party
RDP	Reconstruction and Development Programme
SAAU	South African Agricultural Union
SABC	South African Broadcasting Corporation
SABRA	South African Bureau of Racial Affairs
SACOB	South African Chamber of Business
SACP	South African Communist Party
SACTU	South African Congress of Trade Unions
SADC	Southern African Development Community
SADF	South African Defence Force
SAF	South Africa Foundation
SANAC	South African Native Affairs Commission
SAP	South African Party
SASO	South African Students Organisation
SNCC	Student Non-Violent Coordinating Committee
SOE	state-owned enterprise
SSA	Statistics South Africa
SSC	state security council
TEC	transitional executive council
TRC	Truth and Reconciliation Commission
TRIPS	Trade Related Intellectual Property Rights
TUCSA	Trade Union Council of South Africa
UCM	University Christian Movement
UDF	United Democratic Front
UF	Urban Foundation
ULPP	Urban Labour Preference Policy
UN	United Nations
UNDP	United Nations Development Programme
UP	United Party
VOC	Verenigde Oostindische Compagnie (Dutch East India Company)
WHO	World Health Organisation
WTO	World Trade Organisation
ZAR	Zuid-Afrikaansche Republiek (later known as the Transvaal)

About the author

Prof Solomon (Sampie) Terreblanche is one of South Africa's most distinguished scholars. Educated at the University of Stellenbosch and Harvard University, he has spent most of his academic career at the former university, becoming professor of economics in 1968, and emeritus professor of economics in 1996.

From 1972 to 1987 he served on the board of the South African Broadcasting Corporation, the last five years as vice-chair. From 1973 to 1976 he was a member of the Theron commission of inquiry into matters concerning the coloured community. From 1979 to 1985 he served as a member of the economic advisory board of the prime minister (and state president).

In the late 1980s Professor Terreblanche was among Afrikaner academics who held numerous clandestine meetings in Britain with Thabo Mbeki and other ANC leaders to discuss a transition to democracy in South Africa.

In 1989–90 he was a founding member of and economic adviser to the Democratic Party, but is no longer active in party politics.

In 1992 he received the Stals award for economics from the South African Academy for Science and Arts, and in 2001 received honourary colours from the students' representative council of the University of Stellenbosch.

He has attended numerous international conferences, and lectured at several foreign universities. He has also been on official visits to the United States, Britain, Belgium, and the Soviet Union.

He has published eight books, mainly on economic history, the history of economic thought, and South African economic policy issues. He has also contributed to numerous scholarly journals and books, and written extensively for local and international newspapers, mainly on the political situation in South and southern Africa. He is married, and has five children.

Acknowledgements

In this book – the product of eight years of work – I have attempted to provide a systematic account of inequality in South Africa, from 1652 until the present day.

It deals with the highly unequal distribution of income, opportunities, and property that has marked South Africa for so long; however, it deals mainly with the unequal distribution of political, economic, and ideological power that has become so deeply embedded in our society, and has shaped and reshaped it in such unfortunate ways from 1652 to 2002.

Unequal power structures played a central role during South Africa's long colonial period (from 1652 to 1910). This trend continued during the period of segregation and apartheid (from 1910 to 1994), when power was entirely monopolised by whites – with devastating consequences for blacks. Unfortunately, unequal power relations and unequal socio-economic outcomes have remained defining characteristics of the post-apartheid period. Despite our transition to an inclusive democracy, old forms of inequality have been perpetuated, and some entrenched more deeply than ever before.

The idea for this book originally came from the late Professor Bax Nomvete, a highly respected South African economist who for many years played a leading role in the United Nations Economic Commission for Africa (UNECA) and other African organisations. In 1992 he established the African Institute for Policy Analysis and Economic Integration (AIPA) in Cape Town, and was its executive director until his death in July 2000.

I was greatly inspired by his enthusiasm for a truly democratic and more equitable society in the post-apartheid period. I therefore dedicate this book to his memory.

This book is an AIPA research project. I am very grateful to both Lula Gebreyesus – who succeeded Bax as AIPA's executive director – and Prof Philip Black, its research director, for their financial support and encouragement.

Moeletsi Mbeki, the co-publisher of this book, read earlier versions of the manuscript, and encouraged me to persist with my ideological and economic approach. His advice was invaluable.

I share Professor Mahmood Mamdani's conviction that the work of the Truth and Reconciliation Commission (TRC) was compromised because of the way in which it was constituted in the course of the political deals made in the early 1990s. We both believe the TRC's investigation should not have been restricted to only 34 years – especially not in a country in which the human rights of blacks had been grossly violated for almost 350 years.

I also appreciate the advice and support given to me by Colin and Margaret Legum. To Moeletsi, Mahmood, and the Legums I owe a debt which I am pleased to acknowledge. Needless to say, the defects and shortcomings in the final product are entirely my responsibility.

A sincere word of thanks to my wife, Ina, for her patience and understanding during the many years I worked on this project. My daughter Christelle also deserves my gratitude for all the research material she tirelessly sent me. I am very grateful to the department of economics at the University of Stellenbosch for supplying me with facilities without which this book could not have been written. I owe a special word of thanks to Inge Kotze and Ina Kruger, who patiently typed and retyped the manuscript.

As an Afrikaner, born and bred in the Free State, I greatly appreciate the efforts of Dr Edwin Hees, Louis van Schaik, and Riaan de Villiers to turn my Afrikaans English into proper English. A final word of thanks to Glenn Cowley of the University of Natal Press for his willingness to publish yet another book from the left of the ideological spectrum.

Part I

Power, land, and labour

Chapter 1

From systemic exploitation to systemic exclusion

'If the Past has been an obstacle and a burden, knowledge of the Past is the safest emancipation.'

Lord Acton (inaugural lecture, Cambridge, June 1895)

'People make their own history (runs a celebrated phrase), but not in a circumstance of their own choice; they act in an arena shaped by the past. Accordingly, to understand the present conjuncture in South Africa it is essential to have a sense of its history, to reflect on constraints and the possibilities created by that history.'

Colin Bundy (1993: 49)

'A radical transformation in South Africa will depend more on how the past is remembered than on how the future is plotted.'

Jacques Depelchin (1996: 94)

1.1   A new perspective, and a difficult challenge

This book is an attempt to help remember South Africa's past in a way that will inform its future. Like Colin Bundy, we are convinced that if one wishes to understand contemporary South Africa, one must have a sense of its history. The political transition of 1994 has not only liberated black South Africans from the chains of extended colonialism, stretching from 1652 to 1994, but has also liberated white South Africans from outdated, sectional, and even adulatory interpretations of this country's tempestuous history. Like Lord Acton, we are convinced that knowledge of our burdensome past can emancipate us from that burden.

With the election of 1994, and the introduction of a proper democratic system, the misguided attempts by some white South Africans – both English- and Afrikaans-speaking – to maintain a 'white' political system were finally and thoroughly defeated. Consequently, all whites (irrespective of their political orientation) have been at liberty to take stock – hopefully with as open a mind as possible – of the false trails on which they travelled for so long, and the phantoms they pursued with such conviction and enthusiasm. Of course, it has not been easy for white South Africans (or most of them at least) to acknowledge the evils of colonialism, segregation, and apartheid, and the fallaciousness of the arguments used to legitimise those forms of oppression. However, if whites do not critically re-evaluate their past, they cannot expect the victims of colonialism to accept them as trustworthy companions in building a common future. Since 1994 South Africans – especially whites – have had the opportunity to look at the country's history from a totally new perspective, and many have taken up this challenge. We are at the end of one epoch and the beginning of a new one, but the old will cast an ugly shadow over the new for a long time to come. We cannot build the new epoch without a clear understanding of the old.

Although, given the vulnerability of the South African economy in the global economy, whites are probably not in a position to fully compensate the black victims of systemic exploitation, they should at least be prepared to re-examine South Africa's past. This implies, *inter alia*, that they should acknowledge explicitly that they have benefited from colonialism, segregation, and apartheid, and that most black South Africans have been victims of these systems. White South Africans should also show an awareness of the almost insoluble nature of the problems they have bequeathed to the democratically elected government. But, unfortunately, as Hein Marais has noted, 'in many respects, [white] South Africans' vision of the future rests on foreshortened perspectives of the past. This applies centrally to the millions who engineered, administrated, and savoured the complex of exploitative practices that penetrated every aspect of lived reality – few [whites] of whom will today admit to their authorship of, or moral culpability for, the devastation they achieved' (2001: 7).

Although the transition from apartheid to an inclusive democracy did not occur without friction or loss of blood, it has been widely regarded as a political miracle. The democratic government that assumed power in 1994 inherited a rather contradictory legacy. On the one hand, it inherited the most developed economy in Africa, with a modern physical and institutional infrastructure. On the other, it inherited major socio-economic problems, including high levels of unemployment; the abject poverty of 50 per cent of the population; sharp inequalities in the distribution of income, property, and opportunities; and high levels of crime and violence. What makes these problems much more pressing is the fact that it is mainly black South Africans – and particularly Africans – who are at their receiving end.[1]

Anyone who truly understands the systemic character of these problems, and is prepared to acknowledge the social injustices inherent in them, will not be inclined to complain when they are characterised as largely the unresolved remnants of white domination and apartheid. White indignation should be rejected as unwarranted arrogance or disguised racism, and the bravado of people who have no sense of history or social responsibility towards those who have been exploited and victimised. It is indeed a precondition of nation-building and reconciliation in South Africa that whites should be honest about the multitude of power-related transgressions committed over a very long period by them and by western countries against indigenous population groups. They should also honestly acknowledge the systemic character of our socio-economic problems, and the central role the dual political-economic systems of white political domination and racial capitalism have played in creating these problems and causing such widespread social injustice.

Many whites (especially younger people) are inclined to say that they themselves did nothing wrong, and can therefore not be blamed for the effects of white domination and apartheid. However, they clearly do not understand the systemic character of colonialism, segregation, and apartheid, and their collective responsibility for what has happened. Those who are not prepared to acknowledge the evils of white domination, and accept responsibility for apartheid's residues, are usually adamant that the large-scale 'benefits' (broadly defined) that accumulated in their hands and in those of their parents and grandparents during the extended period of colonialism belong to them and them alone. But what these whites fail to realise is that these 'benefits' are 'contaminated', because they were largely accumulated by means of systemic exploitation. It is rather hypocritical of whites to claim these benefits with greedy self-righteousness but decline any responsibility (directly or indirectly) for the evil of colonialism and its ugly consequences. In as much as these problems have resulted not only from whites' obsession with power and entrenched privileges but also from their short-sightedness, greed, and reductionist individualism, white South Africans ought to realise that they cannot be effectively addressed without a willingness to make substantial sacrifices – materially and symbolically – as part of an open commitment to the restoration of social justice.

1.2   The special relationship between power, land, and labour

South Africa's history over the past 350 years is an unsavoury tale of intergroup conflict, violence, warfare, and plunder. Each of the different ethnic, racial, and/or language groups tried to enrich itself by plundering the others. If one considers the multitude of group conflicts and wars in South Africa during the past 350 years, one can distinguish certain patterns in the seeming muddle. One of the clearest patterns is that, during the long period of European colonialism and imperialism, the colonial masters were mostly the victors in group conflicts, and the indigenous population groups mostly the losers. A second pattern – closely linked to the first – is that in the post-colonial period local whites (the descendants of the settlers from erstwhile colonial Europe) were again (at least until 1974) mostly the conquerors, and therefore in a position to enrich themselves, mostly at the cost of indigenous people.

The colonial powers and white colonists did so in mainly three ways: firstly, by creating political and economic power structures that put them in a privileged and entrenched position *vis-à-vis* the indigenous population groups; secondly, by depriving indigenous people of land, surface water, and cattle; and, thirdly, by reducing slaves and indigenous people to different forms of unfree and exploitable labour. These three threads have run ominously through South Africa's modern history, from the mid-17th until the late 20th century.

Any attempt to re-examine South African history can do no better than to do so from one of the following three perspectives: firstly, the perspective of white political and economic domination; secondly, the perspective of land deprivation; and thirdly, the perspective of unfree black labour. But irrespective of which one is chosen, the other two should not be neglected.

This study sets out to explore South Africa's modern history mainly from the perspective of unequal power relations and unfree labour patterns. In this endeavour, we are – like Worden and Crais – convinced that 'much of the social and economic history of modern South Africa has been the history of unfree [black] labour'. Like them, we are also guided 'by a recognition that the history of labour in South Africa ... cannot be divorced from broader discussions of culture, ideology and polity' (1994: 3). While this study emphasises the history of unfree labour, the histories of power domination (political, economic, and ideological) and land deprivation are also central to an understanding of the unfolding drama of unfree black labour over the past 350 years.

It is axiomatic in economics that the scarcer a production factor is in relation to other factors, the more valuable it becomes. This is particularly important for the argument that South Africa's modern history has been shaped by a special relationship between power, land, and labour. Because labour was scarcer – and therefore potentially more valuable – than land, there was a continuing tendency to force black labourers into slavery, serfdom, and other repressed forms of labour. As indicated above, the colonial authorities and white colonists were mostly the victors in the relentless struggle for hegemony over land and labour. From the point of view of the white master or landowning class, it was easier to deprive indigenous people of their land than to acquire the necessary labour and to control it effectively. Given that land was abundant, and relatively easily conquered, there was a strong inclination – or an economic rationale – for the white landowning class to subjugate blacks into an unfree labour class. The choice to use unfree black labour was not a single, discrete, decision but a continuous one, as more and more land was captured. In many cases it was only possible for the white landowning class to acquire the required unfree black labour by depriving indigenous people of more of their land. The Land Act of 1913 is perhaps the best of several examples of the property class depriving indigenous people of their land in a deliberate attempt to promote their proletarianisation and impoverishment, thereby increasing the supply of unfree black labour.

A British economist, Evsay Domar, has formulated the hypothesis that, in an agricultural economy, no members of the privileged group (ie, property owners whose property rights are maintained by power or custom) would willingly work as wage labourers as long as land was freely available, and that the rest of the population (ie those not belonging to the privileged elite) would not be employed as free wage labourers but would be 'enslaved' in some form of unfree labour. If we take the three elements relevant to an agricultural economy – free land, free peasants, and a non-working landowner class – into account, then (according to Domar) any two of these elements can exist simultaneously, but never all three. If, for example, enough land is available, and the property rights of the landowning class are politically entrenched, then peasants cannot remain free – either as tenant farmers or wage labourers – but will be reduced to slaves, serfs, or other forms of unfree labour (1970: 18–32).

To illustrate his hypothesis, Domar refers to the enslavement of the European peasantry from the eighth century onwards in terms of which people were forced to become serfs within the political framework of feudalism. At that stage, Europe was sparsely populated. Although the feudal lords were not landowners in the strict sense of the word, they had enough military power and feudal privileges to force the peasants into serfdom on their manorial estates. From the 12th century onwards, peasants-cum-serfs in western Europe (ie, west of the Elbe) were gradually transformed into tenant farmers. This happened because a sharp increase in the population led to the occupation of all the available agricultural land. While labour was the scarce factor from, say, the eighth until the tenth century, from the 11th century onwards land gradually became the scarce factor. The sharp decline – from 75 to 45 million – in

Europe's population during the Black Death in the mid-14th century again created an oversupply of free land and an acute scarcity of labour. According to Domar's hypothesis, this should have resulted in peasants being re-enslaved as serfs, and the fact that this did not happen seems to refute it.

Domar is puzzled by this, because he wants to present his hypothesis as an economic necessity, and does not want to introduce too much political intervention into his formula. In fact, the fact that serfdom was not reimposed in western Europe at that time demonstrates the political bargaining power of the relatively independent tenant farmers in the decades after the Black Death.[2]

One can claim a relatively high level of universality for Domar's hypothesis: when land is widely available, landowners succeed in turning peasants into serfs. However, despite its apparently strong economic determinism, its full realisation depends in the final instance on political or military power. The weakness of the landed aristocracy and state governments *vis-à-vis* the peasantry west of the Elbe at the end of the 14th century explains why the hypothesis did not apply after the Black Death. And the weakness of the serfs *vis-à-vis* the feudal lords and state governments *east* of the Elbe is the reason why the hypothesis remains applicable to events in that part of Europe for another 500 years.

We cannot properly interpret the special relationship between power, land, and labour in South African history without focusing on the power of the colonial masters *vis-à-vis* the powerlessness of indigenous people. It would not have been possible for white colonists to become landowners if they did not have the power to turn the Khoisan and the Africans into a subservient labour force. The political, economic, and military power of the white master class has determined the nature and course of South Africa's history for almost 350 years.

1.3 From slavery through exploitation to structural unemployment

Robert Shell has applied Domar's hypothesis to the colonisation of the New World by European countries from the 16th century onwards. In all the newly colonised countries, white or European colonists became empowered as a privileged landowning class. Land was relatively easily occupied, owing to the superior military capacity of the colonial intruders and the poor epidemiological condition of the indigenous peoples. With free land available in abundance, the new colonial landowners developed an almost insatiable demand for unfree labour. In all the European colonies, including South Africa, this demand was originally met by importing slaves. In South Africa the demand for unfree labour from the early 18th century onwards was met not only in this manner but also by reducing many indigenous people – especially Khoisan – to serfdom (*lyfeienskap*). Although the Khoisan resisted their enslavement ferociously, the firepower of the *Trekboer* (pastoral farmer) commandos was too powerful. Interestingly, a free white wage-earning class emerged during the first 50 years of Dutch colonialism in the 17th century, but when an abundance of land became available in the 18th century, this class disappeared almost completely as it merged into a class of landowners. A white wage-earning class re-emerged only at the end of the 19th century when free land was no longer available (see Shell 1994a: ch 1).

When the British abolished serfdom and slavery in 1828 and 1838 respectively, these forms of unfree labour were not replaced by a free black wage-earning class. At that stage free land was still abundantly available, or could be accessed relatively easily by depriving indigenous people of their land. Consequently, the landowning class (both Afrikaans- and English-speaking) and later the British mining companies succeeded – in accordance with Domar's hypothesis – in designing, with the support of the British colonial authority, new methods of turning indigenous people into unfree wage labourers.[3]

When slavery and serfdom were abolished, the Khoisan had already been defeated and almost completely integrated into the emerging system of settler capitalism. To open up new land for occupation by mainly British settlers, and gain control over additional black labour, it became necessary for the British to defeat the Xhosa in the Eastern Cape. This proved to be quite difficult,[4] requiring three bloody frontier wars from 1834 to 1853. These wars coincided with the abolition of slavery and serfdom, but also the adoption of new methods by the white landowning class to force not only 'coloured' people (ex-slaves and ex-serfs) but also the newly conquered Xhosa into new patterns of unfree labour. This transformation of black labour into unfree labour shortly after the abolition of Khoisan enserfment and slavery is perhaps the most momentous event in South Africa's labour history. By the time diamonds were discovered in 1867, and gold in 1886, these new methods of forcing blacks into unfree labour had already been firmly institutionalised. The mines' great demand for cheap and docile African labour necessitated not only the refinement of existing methods, but also the design of additional methods of control and repression.

From an economic point of view, an important structural change in the relationship between land, labour, and the white property class took place in the late 19th and early 20th centuries. By that time almost all agricultural land had been occupied; consequently, it was no longer possible for all the members of the white elite to become landowners. On the contrary, during the period of economic modernisation initiated by the mining revolution, it became apparent that a sizeable percentage of the white landowning class (mainly Afrikaners) were farming on agricultural units that were economically unviable. These small landowners went bankrupt in great numbers (from 1880 until 1940) and either became squatters (*bywoners*) or a white, mainly Afrikaner, proletariat (*armblankes*) with no choice but to compete for jobs against the black wage-earning proletariat. This proletarianisation of a large part of the white population drastically changed the South African labour market.

For the first time since the beginning of the 18th century a formally free white wage-earning class existed in parallel with an unfree black wage-earning class. This situation had major political ramifications. During the first three quarters of the 20th century the intense competition between the free white and unfree black proletariat for the same jobs dominated political and economic developments. Because the white wage-earning class was part of the white elite, whose political rights were entrenched by the Act of Westminster of 1909, the white-controlled South African parliament enacted a multitude of labour laws from 1910 until the 1960s aimed at keeping blacks subjugated as a subservient labour force.

For more than 60 years, the white-controlled South African state – supported by the former colonial powers in the west – was strong enough to counteract black protests against these repressive and discriminatory measures. But when, after the Soweto uprising of 1976, the liberation struggle intensified, and numerous foreign countries began to support it, the white regime was thrown into a serious survival, legitimation, and accumulation crisis that ultimately led to its capitulation in the early 1990s. Although the white regime remained in place until 1994, important shifts in the balance of power between white and black occurred from the mid-1970s onwards as part and parcel of the intensification of the liberation struggle. These shifts brought about profound changes in the South African labour situation and the distribution of income and opportunities, culminating in the introduction of an inclusive democracy in 1994.

The elaborate system of proletarianism, repression, and discrimination in the labour market – institutionalised and maintained by the political systems of colonialism and white supremacy – was reluctantly dismantled from 1974 onwards. Parallel to the process of 'liberating' black labour from centuries of subjugation, South Africa has since 1970 experienced socio-economic processes that have plunged the majority of Africans into a different kind of economic bondage marked by structural unemployment and abject poverty.

A brief summary follows of the eight unfree labour patterns manifested in South Africa since 1652.

1.3.1 Slavery in mainly patriarchal households

Slaves were imported, and most of them initially owned, by the Dutch East India Company. But in time small groups – up to 20 – became part of white households. These households were organised patriarchally, with the male head in an unassailable position of power and the slaves in a subservient position of permanent minor children. Slavery was abolished in 1838. This was a system of direct forced labour (see sections 5.3 and 6.3).

1.3.2 The indentureship (inboekelingskap) of Khoisan children in the households of Trekboere in the Cape Colony during the 18th century, and of African children in the households of Voortrekkers in the two Boer republics in the 19th century

The *inboekelinge* were not slaves, and a market for *inboekelinge* did not exist. This was an adapted form of serfdom (*lyfeienskap*). The patriarchal heads of *Trekboer* or Voortrekker households also treated these *inboekelinge* as minor children until they were emancipated at age 25, as prescribed by law. This was also a system of direct forced labour (see sections 5.4, 6.2, and 7.3).

1.3.3 Lord Caledon's system of indentured labour or compulsory inboekelingskap applicable to almost all the Khoisan (1809–28)

This system of compulsory serfdom or *inboekelingskap* was applied to the Khoisan in the Cape by the 'Caledon Proclamation' of 1809. It was also a system of *direct* forced labour. It was abolished at the request of the humanitarian missionaries by Proclamation 50 of 1828 (see section 6.2).

1.3.4 A first version of black labour repression: a system designed for the employment of coloureds (formerly Khoisan and slaves) and Africans as cheap and docile contract workers in the agricultural sector (1841–1974)

The Cape colonial authority introduced this system in 1841 at the request of the British settlers. It was enacted by means of masters and servants laws, pass laws, and measures aimed at proletarianising coloureds and Africans by deliberately depriving them of their economic independence; these included frontier wars, land deprivation, anti-squatter and anti-vagrancy laws, and the abolition of coloured settlements. The social and family structures of coloureds and Africans were also severely disrupted by pestilences, the Xhosa cattle-killing episode, and tribal wars. The Native Land Act of 1913 stipulated that Africans could not practise sharecropping or squatter farming on white farms or public land. After 1948 members of an African proletariat in white rural areas were 'captured' in the white agricultural sector by means of stricter pass law and influx control measures, and an efficient labour bureau system. The masters and servants laws were abolished in 1974, and influx control in 1986. This was an *indirect* coercive system of contract labour (see sections 6.5, 7.4, 8.5, and 9.4.1).

1.3.5 A second version of black labour repression: a system designed to turn Africans still living in the native reserves into cheap and docile migrant labour for the gold mining industry (1894–1972)

This system was based on measures to proletarianise and impoverish Africans on a much larger scale by depriving them of land in the 'native reserves', and therefore their economic independence as share-croppers. The Glen Grey Act of 1894 and Native Land Act of 1913 deprived Africans of access to much of the land they had traditioinally occupied. For 60 years the Chamber of Mines played a key role in institutionalising and maintaining the migrant labour and compound (*kampong*) systems, and corrupting the collaborating tribal chiefs. Successive white supremacist governments also allowed the chamber to recruit large numbers of foreign migrant workers from neighbouring countries at exceptionally low wage rates. This was a comprehensive system of *indirect* enforced contract labour, and was based on the principle that migrant workers could be paid less than a subsistence wage because they had an agricultural subsistence base in their areas of origin. This principle was maintained until the 1970s, despite the drastic deterioration of socio-economic conditions in the overpopulated 'reserves'. In real terms, migrant workers on the gold mines earned 20 per cent less in 1960, and 8 per cent less in 1972, than they did in 1911 (see section 8.4, 8.6, and 9.4).

1.3.6 Discriminatory measures institutionalised from the end of the 19th century onwards to protect white (and mainly Afrikaner) workers against competition from the already proletarianised, and therefore cheaper, black workers (±1870–1979)

It is necessary to distinguish between black labour repression and discriminatory measures applicable to blacks. While the former decreased the costs of white employers, the latter tended to increase them. Discriminatory measures were imposed in respect of certain categories of labour, promotion opportunities, remuneration, unionisation, wage negotiations, and scholastic, skilled, and in-service training. Before 1948 discriminatory measures were imposed to improve the socio-economic position of impoverished and unemployed white (mainly Afrikaner) workers. After 1948 a multitude of additional discriminatory measures were introduced to enhance and entrench their privileged position. This was a system of direct labour coercion of blacks, and should be judged as part of the more comprehensive political and social discrimination introduced by the segregationist and apartheid regimes. Labour discrimination was abolished in 1979 (see sections 8.7, 8.8, and 9.5).

1.3.7 A third version of black labour repression: a system designed for the employment of Africans still living in 'native reserves' or 'Bantustans' as cheap and docile migrant labourers in the manufacturing industries in urban areas. This system was institutionalised during the apartheid period by the 'native' laws of Dr Hendrik Verwoerd (1952–86)

In 1952 Verwoerd introduced a comprehensive system of migrant labour for the manufacturing industries in urban areas via stricter influx control measures, pass laws (*dompas*), labour bureaux, bantu administration boards, and single-sex living quarters. The purpose of this system was to supply cheap and docile labour to emerging Afrikaner entrepreneurs without compromising efforts to keep South Africa white. To make this kind of labour even cheaper, a system of industrial decentralisation and commuter labour was also introduced in due course. This version of labour repression was also based on the principle that, despite the appalling conditions in those areas, the Bantustans provided migrant labourers and their families with a subsistence base. This was an *indirect* enforced contract labour system (see section 9.4).

1.3.8 The growing unemployment of blacks (especially Africans) in the formal sector of the economy since 1960, and their growing underemployment in the informal sector. This can be regarded as an eighth unfree labour pattern applicable to blacks

Stagflation, worsening poverty, the labour unrest during the liberation struggle, the increasing capital intensity of the economy, and a reduction in foreign direct investment (FDI) and even capital outflows all caused, from 1974 onwards, growing levels of unemployment of mainly Africans in the formal sector of the economy, and growing levels of underemployment in the informal sector. The low levels of education of many Africans have made them ineligible for employment in the tertiary sector, which has grown significantly since 1960. In 2001 about 50 per cent of African entrants to the job market could not find jobs in the formal sector. This lack of employment is a major reason for the poverty of 60 per cent of the black population. This situation of structural unemployment and poverty has a compulsory character, because it is beyond the control of the unemployed. Although they are no longer systemically exploited, the poorer 50 per cent of the population are still systematically excluded from most of the privileges of the new system of democratic capitalism (see ch 4).

1.4 The six successive systemic periods in South African history

The fact that the South African economy was sustained by slavery and serfdom for 250 years, and labour repression and discrimination for another 100, testifies to the highly unequal distribution of power between the class of white masters and employers on the one hand, and that of black servants and employees on the other. We can indeed argue that the social and economic history of modern South Africa has been one of unequal distribution of power. The country's history during the periods of colonialisation, segregation, and apartheid (1652–1994) will be discussed in part 3 (ch 5–9).

Any endeavour to explore the history of unfree black labour requires a thorough exploration of how power and authority have manifested themselves in successive systemic periods. This book is concerned with the structuring forces of colonialism, imperialism, and white political and economic domination, but more specifically with how these structuring forces deprived indigenous people of their land, and reduced them to different forms of unfree labour. Consequently, it is necessary to concentrate on the ways in which power – and especially white-controlled power – has been mobilised, maintained, legitimised, and institutionalised in different periods.

We can distinguish between the following six systemic periods in South African history:

i The mercantilistic and feudal system institutionalised by Dutch colonialism during the second half of the 17th and most of the 18th century (1652–1795). During this period the *Trekboere* created a semi-independent feudal subsystem, with its own power and labour relations. But this feudal subsystem was not fully independent, and must therefore be regarded as part of the Dutch colonial system (see ch 5).

ii and iv The systems of racial capitalism institutionalised by British colonialism and British imperialism during the 'long 19th century' (1795–1910). The legal, political, and economic patterns introduced by the British destroyed the mercantilistic, feudal, and traditional patterns of the

Dutch East India Company, the Afrikaners, the Khoisan, and the Africans in that order. After the discovery of diamonds (in 1867) and gold (in 1886), British colonialism was transformed into an aggressive and more comprehensive version of imperialism and racial capitalism. To successfully exploit South Africa's mineral resources, the British had to create a new power constellation and political and economic system. To institutionalise a system conducive to the profitable exploitation of gold, the British fought several wars at the end of the 19th century, including the Anglo–Boer War (1899–1902). The new power constellation was not only maintained but also more thoroughly institutionalised during the first half of the 20th century when political, economic, and ideological power was mainly in the hands of the local English establishment, with close ties with Britain. In our systemic analysis it is necessary to distinguish between the systemic period of colonial and agricultural racial capitalism during British colonialism (1795–±1890) and the systemic period of colonial and mineral racial capitalism during British imperialism and the political and economic hegemony of the local English establishment (±1890–1948). These two systemic periods will be discussed in chapters 6 and 8.

iii During the 19th century the Voortrekkers succeeded in creating relatively independent republics north of the Orange River, in which they adapted labour patterns that were by then regarded as illegal in the Cape. The power constellations of the two republics were precarious, but they were still independent enough of the colonial authority in the Cape to practise a separate feudal system (see ch 7).

v When the Afrikaner-oriented National Party (NP) won the general election of 1948, it used its political power to intensify unfree labour patterns. Although the NP did not drastically transform the economic system of racial capitalism institutionalised by the English establishment, it used its political and ideological power to institutionalise a new version of it. During the last 20 years of Afrikaner political hegemony (1974–94), a crisis developed surrounding the legitimacy and sustainability of white political supremacy and the profitability of racial capitalism. In the early 1990s Afrikaner political hegemony collapsed rather dramatically as a prelude to the rise of African political hegemony (see ch 9).

vi Since 1990 we have experienced a transition from the politico-economic system of white political domination and racial capitalism to a new system of democratic capitalism. Over the past 12 years a democratic political system – controlled by an African elite – has been successfully institutionalised (see ch 4). Unfortunately a parallel socio-economic transformation has not yet taken place (see ch 2, 11). An important reason for this is that the democratic part of the system of democratic capitalism is still rather weak and underdeveloped, when compared to the highly developed and powerful capitalist part of the equation. The transition to democratic capitalism was nevertheless a giant leap forward. Compared to most other countries, this transition in South Africa occurrred at a very late stage, and under difficult socio-economic circumstances.

This new politico-economic system is still unfamiliar and unclear to many South Africans. However, it is important for them to understand the true meaning of both the 'democratic' and 'capitalist' components of the system, and especially how they should interact in a country with serious socio-economic problems after almost 350 years of colonial exploitation. Hopefully, this book will contribute to such an understanding, or at least prompt a debate on the desired power relations and interaction between them in a post-colonial and post-apartheid South Africa.

Democratic capitalism is a dual politico-economic system that reached maturity, after centuries of organisational development, in the first half of the 20th century, notably in developed western countries. The 'logic' of democracy and capitalism is contradictory: while democracy emphasises joint interests, equality, and common loyalties, capitalism is based on self-seeking inequality and conflicting individual and group interests. The legal system that protects both democracy and capitalism is based on the principle of equality before the law, but maintains inequalities in the distribution of property rights and opportunities in the capitalist system. The 'logic' of capitalism – given the unequal freedoms and unequal rights upon which it is based – thus goes against the grain of the 'logic' of democracy.

Capitalism attempts to maximise efficiency and profit through merciless competition in a free market system in which the strong, skilful, and property owners win, and the weaker and less 'cunning' lose. It is the task of a democratically elected government to reconcile not only the conflicting 'logics' of democracy and capitalism, but also the 'power' with which they exert themselves in the dual system of democratic capitalism. South Africa's democratically elected government must try to bring about reconciliations that will promote the welfare of society at large. It must also rectify the unacceptable inequalities produced by capitalism.

While emphasising the conflicting 'logics' of democracy and capitalism, we are not denying the complementary relationship between them. The strength and sustainability of the system of democratic capitalism depends on the interdependence of democracy and capitalism. Democracy cannot survive without the material and/or monetary assistance of capitalism, and capitalism cannot survive without the legal and bureaucratic support of the democratic state. They also need one another in the sense that the power each exerts needs to be curtailed or 'counteracted' by that of the other in order to prevent its misuse. It is therefore important that none of the two parts is too powerful in relation to the other.

Democracy is based on the equality of rights and privileges maintained and supplied by state power, while capitalism is based on the unequal distribution of property and assets and on the state-guaranteed freedom of everyone to use his/her assets and property as he/she pleases within the prescriptions of the law (see appendix). Arthur Okun describes 'the double standards' of democratic capitalism as follows:

> A society that is both democratic and capitalistic has a split-level institutional structure, and both levels need to be surveyed. When only the capitalist level is inspected, issues concerning the distribution of material welfare are out of focus…[Democratic capitalism] profess(es) and pursu[es] [both] an egalitarian political and social system and simultaneously generate[es] disparities in economic well-being. This mixture of equality and inequality sometimes smacks of inconsistency and even insincerity…To the extent that the system succeeds, it generates an efficient economy. But that pursuit of efficiency necessarily creates inequalities. And hence society faces a trade-off between equality and efficiency…[This] is our biggest socio-economic trade-off, and it plagues us in dozens of dimensions of social policy (1975: 1–4).

This book attempts to show that the socio-economic development that took place in South Africa during the first five racist-oriented systemic periods (1652–1994) was extremely unequal, uneven, and unjust. This unfortunate state of affairs can be attributed to the fact that the 'political' component of each politico-economic system was insensitive to notions of joint interests and shared justice, while the 'economic' (and mainly capitalist) component of each system thrived recklessly on unequal freedoms and the unequal distribution of power, property, and opportunities.

It is against this background that we cannot afford to have a new politico-economic system of democratic capitalism in which the 'democratic' part – the part that has developed more recently – remains weak and underdeveloped compared to the powerful (and deeply institutionalised) 'capitalist' part, and therefore cannot address the huge inequalities and injustices that have accumulated during the five previous racially based systemic periods. Although South Africa has belatedly introduced a politico-economic system of democratic capitalism, it is unfortunately a system of democratic *capitalism*, legitimised by the ideology of liberal capitalism, which excessively empowers the 'capitalist' part of the system. Consequently, South Africa has maintained – during the first eight years of the post-apartheid period – a version of democratic capitalism that is, in many respects, dysfunctional and unable to address the dismal legacy of inequalities, inbalances, and injustices accumulated during the first five systemic periods of unfree labour.

In chapter 2 we show that the quality of life of the majority of South Africans has deteriorated during the first eight years of the post-apartheid period. We blame this partly on the legacy of apartheid and earlier colonial exploitation, and partly on the inappropriate social and economic policies of the new government. These were agreed upon during informal negotiations between key African National Congress (ANC) and business leaders before the political transformation in 1994 (see ch 4).

The compromises reached at those negotiations determined the power relations between the 'democratic' and 'capitalist' components of the new politico-economic system in the post-apartheid period. It was also decided that neo-liberalism (or the ideology of liberal capitalism) would determine economic policy, and that post-apartheid South Africa would have a free market economy.

The terms of this settlement were such that the poorest half of the population has, over the last eight years, become entrapped in a new form of oppression: a state of systemic exclusion and systemic neglect by the democratically elected government and the modern sector of the economy respectively. It is therefore not surprising that the situation of the poorest half of the population has deteriorated during the past eight years.

The elite compromises agreed upon by the ANC and business leaders will be discussed in detail in chapter 4, in order to show how the systemic exclusion and systemic neglect of the poorer 50 per cent of the population became institutionalised in our new politico-economic system. In chapter 3 we focus on the prelude to these informal negotiations to establish what was at stake as well as what the ideological orientations of the negotiating partners were before the negotiations began.

In part 3 (ch 5–9) the systemic exploitation of blacks during five successive periods of white political domination will be discussed in greater detail. In chapter 10 we summarise the apartheid regime's dismal socio-economic legacy to South Africa's new democratic government. In part 4 we plead for a social democratic approach to replace the liberal capitalist approach adopted by the new government. We also plead for another (economic) power shift, aimed at allowing the new government and its bureaucracy to act as effective 'countervailing' forces to the overpowering corporate sector. We also propose an agenda for socio-economic transformation in order to change the present neo-liberal version of democratic capitalism into a balanced, integrated, and humane system of democratic capitalism, based on the ideology of social democracy (see section 11.5).

1.5   The nature of the power shifts in South African history

To explain how new power constellations or new systems were institutionalised during each of the six systemic periods, it is necessary to concentrate on the power shifts that took place before or at the beginning of each of those periods. Alvin Toffler distinguishes between two kinds of power shifts: 'a transfer of [political] power', and 'a deep-level change in the very nature of power [that] ... transforms power' (1990: 56).

Our concern is primarily with the second. Each of the first five power shifts in our study involved not only the transfer of political and/or military power from one regime to another, but a more comprehensive transformation on three levels: firstly, the nature of *political* power and authority; secondly, the nature of *socio-economic* power (for example, changes in production methods and the legal and moral definitions of how production factors – labour, land, and capital – can be acquired and used); and, thirdly, the nature of *ideological* power (ie, changes in the value orientation and ideological arguments used to legitimise a new or emerging power constellation). The sixth power shift is still incomplete, because deep-level socio-economic and ideological trans-formations have not yet taken place.

Max Weber regarded a system as a three-dimensional social fabric or an equivalent tetrahedron: a three-sided pyramid with a political, socio-economic, and ideological side. A power shift from one system to another does not only question and undermine the legitimacy of each of the three sides of the Weberian pyramid, but is only completed when a new power constellation has been established, with a reasonable level of agreement between the new elite groups on each of the three sides of the pyramid. If the new system and new power constellation prove to be dysfunctional, and do not serve the interests of all the subgroups in society, the stability and sustainability of the new system will be threatened. In this case the new politico-economic system can be thrown into an early survival crisis.

The three power shifts brought about by Dutch colonialism (during the second half of the 17th century), British colonialism (during the first half of the 19th century), and British imperialism (during the late 19th and early 20th century) can indeed be described as three deep-level changes in the nature of power. All three were introduced by foreign powers representing power constellations that were considerably more powerful and technologically more advanced than the ones in place at the time. All three introduced not only new power constellations but also new social stratifications, new modes of production, new legal and property systems, and new ideological orientations. It is therefore not surprising that the labour patterns introduced and maintained by Dutch colonialism, British colonialism, and British imperialism differed fundamentally from the preceding ones.

In contrast with the three power shifts introduced by foreign intervention, the three that were initiated internally did not succeed in bringing about such deep-level changes in the nature of power. This is because the new power constellations were not that powerful *vis-à-vis* the power constellations that were 'defeated'. The Voortrekkers could not really effectively control the African tribes in the Transvaal and the Orange Free State (OFS). Similarly, the post-1948 NP government largely perpetuated the social stratifications, modes of production, and labour patterns of the preceding period. Although it therefore did not bring about a deep-level change in the nature of power, it did intensify the exploitative nature of the existing labour pattern, and legitimised it with new ideologies.

The sixth power shift – from whites to blacks – that began in the last quarter of the 20th century is still under way. There were expectations in 1994 that this shift would bring about a deep-level change in the nature of power – ie, that white political and economic power and whites' ideological orientation would be transformed. This has not happened. The political system institutionalised over the past eight years differs fundamentally from its predecessors, and the ideological orientation of South Africans has certainly changed; however, remnants of racism are still prevalent in white circles, while the doubtful ideology of free market capitalism has been accepted by the new governing elite but not by its large black constituency. The socio-economic transformation of the past eight years has therefore not been a deep-seated one, and has inadequately addressed the social problems inherited from the previous racially based systemic periods. Consequently, the past eight years have largely seen a continuation of the unequal power relations, unfree labour patterns, and uneven socio-economic development that characterised the long preceding period of extended colonialism.

If we take as our point of departure the dismal socio-economic legacy bequeathed to the new government in 1994 by the five racially based systemic periods described earlier, the question arises how deep and how comprehensive the change towards a new power constellation ought to be before the major problems confronting the new South Africa can be effectively addressed. We believe the political power shift of 1994 will remain ineffective not only until an ideological paradigm shift takes place towards a social democratic approach, but also until another structural shift empowers the 'democratic' part of the new politico-economic system *vis-à-vis* the 'capitalist' part. Only then will the democratically elected government and its bureaucracy be able to play a more active, constructive, and interventionist role in the socio-economic upliftment of the impoverished majority. If such a paradigm shift and power shift can be effected, we may succeed in creating a politico-economic system of democratic capitalism that will serve the needs and aspirations of the whole South African population (see ch 11).

Endnotes

1 The term 'black' is used to denote South Africans other than white, and the term 'African' to denote blacks other than coloureds and Indians.

2 In the area west of the Elbe, the landed aristocracy did try to turn the clock back and reinstate serfdom, but were not strong and united enough and did not receive the necessary support from the (then still poorly developed) nation-states. The transformation (or emancipation) of the peasantry from serfdom, and their development into economically independent tenant farmers (or peasant farmers) was almost completed west of the Elbe when the Black Death occurred. Consequently, the peasantry already had enough bargaining power at that time to resist attempts to restore their status as serfs. The peasant revolts in France and Germany during the 14th and 15th centuries are testimony to their power. East of the Elbe, however, the transition from serfdom towards tenant farming was far from complete when the Black Death caused a sharp decline in population. Consequently the landed aristocracy east of the Elbe not only succeeded – with a measure of state support – in reimposing serfdom, but also in turning it into an even more rigid form of serfdom. This spread eastwards to Russia, where it remained in place until the second half of the 19th century (see Terreblanche 1980: 63–7).

3 These measures comprised masters and servants laws, pass laws, and the proletarianisation and impoverishment of coloureds and Africans in a deliberate attempt to force blacks into unfree labour systems. If we compare South African colonial history with that of the 'new Europes' in north and south America and Australasia, perhaps the most obvious difference is that the colonial masters in South Africa made less use of imported slaves, and more use of their military power to turn indigenous people into a servile labour force.

4 If South Africa had not become a British colony, the task of defeating the Xhosas, depriving them of their land, and reducing them to an unfree labour force would have rested on the shoulders of the *Trekboere*. They would probably have failed. But the introduction of British colonialism, with its far greater military and economic capacity, and the support of a better organised and more centralised state system, meant that the Xhosas were defeated and deprived of large parts of their land (see ch 6).

PART 2

The transition and the 'new South Africa' (1990–2002)

Chapter 2

The legacy of systemic exploitation, and attempts to build a non-racial society

2.1 The legacy of apartheid

When, in 1994, a democratically elected government came to power, it inherited a contradictory legacy: the most developed economy in Africa on the one hand, and major socio-economic problems on the other. The most serious of these are high rates of unemployment; abject poverty among more than 50 per cent of the population; sharp inequalities in the distribution of income, property and opportunities; and high levels of crime and violence. What makes these problems so pressing is the fact that it is mostly blacks – and especially Africans – who are at their receiving end.

Most unemployed people are Africans; more Africans than any others live in abject poverty; the inequalities in the distribution of income, property and opportunities are mainly to the detriment of Africans; and it is largely Africans who were criminalised during the long periods of repression, discrimination, and violence, and who are now the main victims of criminality and violence.

Whites often say the socio-economic problems inherited from colonialism and white domination should not be judged in isolation; South Africa also gained a strong economy, modern infrastructure, strong educational and health services, and a sound legal system under colonialism (in a wider sense). Furthermore, it is argued, white (and western) initiative, entrepreneurship, ingenuity, perseverance, and capital accumulation all played key roles in turning South Africa into a modern and developed country. However, although the contribution of white South Africans and the western world towards developing this country should not be dismissed or minimised, it is nonetheless beyond dispute that the white colonial powers and local white establishments that ruled South Africa from the mid-17th to the late 20th centuries used their monopoly over political, military, economic, and ideological power not only to advance themselves but also to plunder indigenous people, disrupt their social structures, and turn them into exploited workers (see part 3).

Even if we take the impressive benefits of South Africa's external and internal colonial history into account, we cannot avoid the conclusion that unemployment, poverty, inequality, violence, and criminality are not only serious problems that mainly affect black South Africans, but also that they have an indisputable *structural* or *systemic* character. All of these problems have been shaped and 'created' over a very long period by the power structures on which the systems of colonialism, segregation, and apartheid were based. Given this, it is important for whites to realise – and acknowledge – that it will not be easy to resolve these problems, and that it will probably take generations to do so.

None of these socio-economic problems is incidental or temporary in nature. All of them are closely interlinked, and deeply rooted in South Africa's extended colonial history. A proper diagnosis of the true nature and root causes of these problems is a precondition for any attempt to solve them or to ameliorate their negative and humiliating effects.

Part 3 provides a historical overview of the long period of colonialism, segregation, and apartheid. In this part we distinguish between five systemic periods of white colonial control during which political and economic power was extremely unequally distributed, and various unfree and exploitative labour patterns institutionalised (see ch 5–9). Chapter 10 summarises the dismal socio-economic conditions under which many South Africans lived in 1994. Although the misery and poverty of the poorer half of the population cannot be blamed exclusively on colonialism, segregation, and apartheid, the negative effects of these 'systems' on the socio-economic conditions of the majority of blacks should not be underestimated.

Whenever the present socio-economic predicament of the poorer 50 per cent of the population is blamed on colonialism, segregation, and apartheid, many whites become indignant. Some even demand to know when these unfounded allegations are going to stop. This kind of denial is deplorable. People should realise that for decades to come it will be justifiable to blame colonialism – in the extended sense of the word – for many of the socio-economic and developmental problems confronting the 'new South Africa'. Therefore, the repressive and exploitative nature of South African society before 1994 should not be neglected. In part 3 an attempt is made to reconstruct and interpret colonial history in a way that will contribute towards a better understanding of the socio-economic legacy of the past. A proper reconstruction of all the injustices meted out to blacks during the long period of extended colonialism will hopefully help to soften the often arrogant and exculpatory attitudes of many whites.

Eight years have passed since the transition from apartheid to an inclusive democracy. This transition has been hailed worldwide as a political miracle. It is largely former president Nelson Mandela and his reconciliatory attitude that must be credited for the peaceful transition towards a non-racial dispensation in which the humanity and dignity of all South Africans are protected in a constitutional democracy. From a political and human rights point of view, South Africa is an incomparably better country in 2002 than it was before its political transformation began in 1990. While, until 1994, political power was concentrated almost exclusively in white hands, it is now firmly in the hands of a democratically elected government, and, given the composition of the population, mainly controlled by Africans.

All South Africans can be proud of the political and human rights transformations that have taken place over the past eight years. Unfortunately, a corresponding socio-economic transformation has not yet taken place. Ugly remnants of systemic exploitation and discrimination from the extended period of colonialism remain. What is really disturbing is that the precarious socio-economic situation in which large numbers of Africans and coloureds find themselves has not improved during the post-apartheid period, but has in fact become more burdensome.

This is very unfortunate, and a matter of grave concern. It should be remembered that the transition to democracy unleashed pent-up expectations of a restoration of social justice and a dramatic improvement in the living conditions of blacks. The fact that these expectations have not been realised may well lead to growing frustration and even to destructive rage, with the potential of undermining the social stability on which the newly attained democratic system depends. Even if we accept that it has not been possible – given specific economic constraints – to dramatically improve the living conditions of the impoverished majority within the first eight years, it is surely not unreasonable to have expected a tangible improvement in their living conditions. Unfortunately, their situation has not improved even marginally.

Who is to blame for this deplorable state of affairs? This question must be answered carefully. However, there is no doubt that some of the blame must be placed squarely on the shoulders of the new governing elite, whose constituency is largely drawn from the impoverished and unemployed majority. That said, there can also be little doubt that the white regimes of the past should bear most of the blame for South Africa's devastated socio-economic landscape.

Social spending (on welfare, health, education, and housing) has increased from 50,8 per cent of non-interest government spending in 1990/1 to an average of 60 per cent of non-interest spending in the period 1995/6 to 2002/3. Some of the social spending previously allocated to whites has also been 'redirected' towards blacks. The government claims that, since 1994, some 9 million more people have gained access to clean water, and about 1,5 million more households to electricity. More than 1,3 million houses have been supplied with telephone connections. More than one million houses have been built for people who had no formal shelter previously, and free medical services are now given to expectant mothers as well as children under the age of seven. Food programmes have been introduced that have reached about 5 million children. Since 1994 there has also been infrastructural development aimed at supplying rural communities with water, roads, and so on.

Given what has been accomplished, then deputy president Thabo Mbeki claimed in 1998 that 'it would be difficult to find examples elsewhere in the world where a negotiated transfer of power took place, where such progress was achieved in so short a period of time to redefine the nature of society' (1998: 4). Although there might be some merit in this hyperbolic claim from a legislative point of view, South African society has certainly not been 'redefined' from a socio-economic point of view. Unfortunately, there is a dark side to many of the bright things that have been accomplished since 1994. Many of the electricity, water, and telephone connections are cut off every month because users cannot afford to pay for them. Many of the houses built are of poor quality. In 1999 the department of water affairs admitted that many of its water provision projects had fallen into dysfunction or disrepair. The removal of farmers' subsidies as well as labour reforms and droughts in the agricultural sector have led to a decline in employment of blacks in this sector from 1,4 million to only 800 000. The improvement of health services in rural areas has led to a dramatic drop in the quantity and quality of health services in urban areas. Many of these negative results are the consequence of the government's announcement in November 1994 that government departments could only spend more on RDP projects by 'reprioritising' their spending. The HIV/AIDS pandemic has wreaked havoc, particularly among the poor, and has had an immeasurably negative effect on the quality of their lives (see Marais 2001: 190–1; Lodge 1999: 32–3; section 10.2.4).

Increased social spending on the poor represents a considerable redistribution of income from whites to blacks.[1] But despite this redistributive effect via the national budget, the structural dynamics in a situation of disrupted social structures, growing unemployment, poor health conditions, and increasing violence and criminality are such that the quality of life of the poorer 50 per cent of the population has deteriorated considerably in the post-apartheid period. With the wisdom of hindsight we now know that the legacy of colonialism, segregation and apartheid was much worse, and the pauperising momentum inherent in it much stronger, than was realised in 1994. We should also note that the South African public sector was shaped mainly to serve the interests of whites. The task of restructuring the public sector and redirecting public spending towards serving the needs of blacks, and especially the poor, is an enormously difficult one. Unfortunately, the new government does not have the bureaucratic capacity to do this effectively (see section 2.2.2).

Few countries in the world are as renowned as South Africa for the sharp contrast between extravagant wealth and luxury on the one hand, and extreme poverty and destitution on the other. While, in the past, socio-economic inequalities in South Africa had a distinctly racial character, the greatest inequality is now experienced within the African population group. As far as the total population is concerned, inequalities have now gained an obvious class character (see table 2.2). What is ultimately at stake is not only social and political stability, but also social justice after generations of systemic exploitation. The momentous importance of the political transition of 1994 was that it opened, for the first time ever, a window of opportunity for restoring social justice for blacks after centuries of social oppression, political domination, and economic exploitation. Although it is true that Rome was not built in a day, and that the injustices of centuries cannot be healed in a decade, it is certainly not unreasonable to have expected some visible progress towards greater social justice for the poor during the first eight years of democratic rule.

The main focus of part 2 is to determine why the conditions of the poor have not improved. In an attempt to identify the reasons for this deterioration, it is necessary to concentrate firstly on the nature of poverty and unemployment, or, more correctly, the nature of the remnants of systemic exploitation, and secondly on the inadequacy of the new government's economic and social policies. We will argue that the powerful corporate sector forced the new government into accepting a neo-liberal and globally oriented economic policy for the 'new South Africa' that excluded the possibility of comprehensive redistributive measures. As a result of several elite compromises negotiated between the ANC and the corporate sector, an economic system has been institutionalised that systemically excludes the poorer half of the population from mainstream economic and political activity. Although the new government has enjoyed political hegemony since 1994, economic hegemony is still in the hands of the corporate sector (see ch 4).

In section 2.2 we focus on the structural dynamics underpinning the poverty, inequality, unemployment, and violent criminality inherited from apartheid. In that section we will, *inter alia*, try to establish whether the elite groups in South African society – both white and black – understand the structural dynamics inherent in this situation. If we want to cure the illness of poverty, it must be correctly diagnosed. But this is not enough. It is also necessary to establish what it would take to heal the psychological and physical wounds inflicted on millions of blacks and on their social structures during centuries of racist exploitation.

In section 2.3 we provide a brief overview of the legislation introduced by the new government to build a non-racial South Africa. Although it has not succeeded in improving the living conditions and quality of life of the poor, it has been remarkably successful in creating a legal framework that guarantees the human rights and dignity of all South Africans.

In chapter 4 we focus on the informal negotiations from the late 1980s onwards between the corporate sector and the democratic movement, which led to elite compromises on economic and social policies. To appreciate the significance of these compromises we will focus, in chapter 3, on the policy proposals and ideological orientations brought to the informal 'negotiation table' by both parties.

2.2 The dynamics of disrupted social structures and abject poverty

Julian May refers to a considerable body of research undertaken during the last decade of the previous century on the causes of poverty and inequality. According to May, most of these studies 'provide a convincing case that many of the distortions and dynamics introduced by apartheid have the potential to become self-perpetuating'. This potential has indeed been realised to a much larger extent than anticipated. Over the past eight years the distortions and dynamics of apartheid 'continue to reproduce poverty and perpetuate inequality. *The poverty traps set by apartheid remain an important explanation for the persistence [and the worsening] of poverty in South Africa'* (May 2000: 263; author's emphasis).

We can identify at least four poverty traps inherent in the socio-economic situation of the poorest two thirds of the population, which have, since 1994, been responsible for their further pauperisation despite increased social spending by the government. They are:

i   high and rising levels of unemployment in a sluggish economy;

ii deeply institutionalised inequalities in the distribution of power, property, and opportunities between the white and black elite and the poorest half of the population;

iii disrupted and fragmented social structures and the syndrome of chronic community poverty among the poorest 50 per cent of the population; and

iv the mutually reinforcing dynamics of violence, criminality, and ill-health on the one hand and the process of pauperisation on the other.

2.2.1 The first poverty trap: high and rising levels of unemployment in a sluggish economy

In 1995 South Africa's total labour supply was 13,4 million, of whom 8,6 million were employed in the formal sector of the economy. The Bureau of Economic Research (BER) has estimated that, besides the 600 000 jobs lost in the agricultural sector since 1994, at least 500 000 jobs have been lost in the formal non-agricultural sector since 1995. In the six years from 1995 to 2001 at least 250 000 new work-seekers are added to the labour force very year. Table 2.1 compares employment in 1970, 1995, and 2001. According to conservative estimates, the labour supply (according to the extended definition) has increased from 13,4 million in 1995 to 14,9 million in 2001. This implies that structural unemployment has increased from 4,8 million in 1995 to 6,8 million in 2001, and that the percentage of unemployed has increased from 36,1 per cent in 1995 to 45,8 per cent in 2001. Although it is not possible to give a breakdown of the employment/unemployment situation for each of the four population groups (as in table 10.1), there is little doubt that African unemployment of 46 per cent in 1995 has increased to about 55 per cent in 2001.

Table 2.1:	Labour supply, employment in the formal sector, and unemployment in 1970, 1995, and 2001*					
	1970 (000)	1995 (000)	2001* (000)	Change 1995–2001 (000)	Change 1995–2001 (%)	Change 1975–2001 (%)
Labour supply	9 445	13 425	14 925	+1 500	+12,3	+58
Employment	7 543	8 585	8 085	-500	-5,8	+7
Unemployment	1 903	4 840	6 840	2 000	+41,3	+260
Unemployment (%)	20,2	36,1	45,8	–	–	–

* The 2001 figures are estimates.
Source: see Table 10.1.

Although formal sector employment has declined by at least 500 000 since 1995, there are indications that employment in the informal sector has increased quite substantially during the same period. Hard statistics are not available, but considerably more than 1 million jobs may have been created. Unfortunately, the content of these 'employment' opportunities is uncertain, and in many cases involves only part-time jobs or jobs for one or two days a week.

An important reason for the deterioration of the employment situation is the moderate growth rate attained since 1994. From 1994 to 2001 the average annual rate of growth of gross domestic product (GDP) was only 2,7 per cent in real terms, and although this represented a meaningful improvement on the average annual growth rate of only 1,6 per cent a year in the 20 years from 1974 to 1994, it was not nearly high enough to arrest the downward spiral of unemployment and poverty. The economic growth experienced during the 1990s was largely 'jobless growth', mainly due to the high – and still growing – capital intensity of the economy.[2]

The high optimism of 1994–5 that the transition towards an inclusive democracy would facilitate the reintegration of South Africa's economy into the global economy, and would greatly accelerate FDI, was unfortunately not realised. South Africa has received FDI of R5 billion a year since 1994, but needs an inflow at least four times more to sustain an annual GDP growth rate of 5 per cent.[3]

GDP per capita has increased only slightly since 1994, from R13 786 to R14 321 in 2001 (in constant 1995 prices). This represents an increase of 3,8 per cent over the six years, or an annual increase of 0,6 per cent (SARB 2002). The small annual increase in per capita income is unsatisfactory, but nonetheless represents a meaningful improvement over the annual decline of 0,7 per cent of per capita income in the 20 years from 1974 to 1994. Unfortunately, the different population and income groups did not benefit equally from this increase. While the income of the richer income groups – and especially the richer 25 per cent of black people – increased quite dramatically over the past eight years, the per capita income of the poorer two thirds of the population (mainly Africans and coloureds) has declined further – partly due to the fact that the population growth rate of the poorer 80 per cent is much higher than that of the top 20 per cent. Consequently, the gap between the income of the top 20 per cent of households and the lower 60 per cent of households has become much greater (see table 2.2).[4] It is disturbing that the increase in the income of the top 25 per cent of blacks has occurred at a time when the income of the poorer 60 per cent of blacks has declined further. The income of the poorer 60 per cent of whites has also declined over the past eight years.

The deterioration of the income of the poorest half of the population is demonstrated in table 2.2 (see also tables 10.3 and 10.4). The share of the poorest 40 per cent of households (±50 per cent of the population) of total income has declined from 5,2 per cent in 1975 to only 3,3 per cent in 2001, while the share of total income of the top 20 per cent of households (±16,6 per cent of the population) has increased from 70,9 per cent in 1975 to 72,2 per cent in 2001. After more than 25 years of poor economic growth, high inflation, growing structural unemployment, and a profound political transformation, radical shifts have taken place in the distribution of income. During this period South African society has been transformed from a rigid racially divided society into a highly stratified class society (see table 2.2 and figure 2.1).

Table 2.2: **The share of the poorest 40 per cent of households and the three other quintiles of total income in 1975, 1991, 1996 and 2001, and the changes from 1975 to 2001**

Households	Share of total income (%)				Changes (%)			
	1975	1991	1996	2001	1975–91	1991–6	1996–2001	1975–2001
Poorest 40% (±50% of the population)	5,2%	3,8%	3,4%	3,3%	-27%	-11%	-3%	-37%
41%–60% (16,6% of the population)	7,6%	7,6%	7,4%	7,3%	0%	-0,3%	-0,1%	-4%
61%–80% (16,6% of the population)	16,3%	17,6%	17,4%	17,2%	+8%	-0,1%	-0,2%	+6%
81%–100% (16,6% of the population)	70,9%	71,0%	71,8%	72,2%	+0,2%	+11%	+0,6%	+2%

Source: Estimated and projected from McGrath and Whiteford 1994: table 5.1; Whiteford and Van Seventer 1999: table 3.1, appendix.

The inequality in the distribution of income has solidified over the past eight years into five clearly identifiable classes: a bourgeois elite consisting of 16,6 per cent of the population (of which ±50 per cent is white and ±50 per cent black), receiving 72,2 per cent of total income; a petit bourgeois class consisting of 16,6 per cent of the population (of which ±15 per cent is white), receiving 17,2 per cent of total income; and a lower class consisting of ±67 per cent of the total population (of which 2 per cent is white), receiving only 10,6 per cent of total income. However, the lower class has to be divided into three subclasses: an upper lower class, consisting of 16,6 per cent of the population and receiving 7,3 per cent of total income; a middle lower class, consisting of ±25 per cent of the population and receiving 2 per cent of total income; and a lower lower class, consisting of ±25 per cent of the population, and receiving only 1,3 per cent of total income.

Despite these radical changes in the income distribution in South African society over the past 25 years, the highly stratified class society has not been cleared of its erstwhile rigid racial distribution of income, which is a legacy of colonialism and apartheid. One third of the ±15 million people in the two bourgeois classes are white, while only 2 per cent of the ±30 million people in the lower class are white.[5] Sixty per cent of Africans are poor, compared to one per cent of whites.

Most people in the poorest two subclasses (22,5 million) belong to households whose income is well below the minimum living level (MLL). In 1996 about 18 million people lived below the internationally recognised minimum income level (or poverty line) of R353 per person a month. Members of the lower lower class (±25 per cent of the population) belong to households whose income is less than 50 per cent of the MLL (see McGrath and Whiteford 1994: 20–1). In section 10.3.4 we indicate that the per capita income in real terms of the poorest half of the population in 1996 was 42 per cent lower than in 1975, and in 2001 slightly more than 40 per cent of what it was in 1975.

2.2.2 The second poverty trap: deeply institutionalised inequalities in the distribution of socio-economic power, property, and opportunities, and the persistence of racist prejudices

The political liberation of blacks in 1994 was not the first in South African history. After the slave trade was suspended in 1808, and slavery was abolished in 1838, the Khoisan and the slaves enjoyed – albeit for a short period – the same legal rights and freedoms as whites. At the time, both the Khoisan and the slaves were extremely impoverished and economically dependent, and their spirits broken after their long period of servitude. Consequently, they were simply not in a socio-economic or psychological position to benefit from their newly attained freedom and rights. With the wisdom of hindsight, we now know that the freedom given to them was too legalistic, and lacked social, economic, and moral support. Except for Andries Stockenström's Kat River scheme (see section 6.2), the required poverty alleviation and economic development programmes did not materialise.

Many black people have also experienced the political transition of 1994 as a largely legalistic emancipation. It has given them franchise rights and, in theory, equality before the law, freedom of movement, and restored human dignity. However, as Pallo Jordan pointed out in a recent article, the legal emancipation of an oppressed people is not enough; improvements in the ability to profit from opportunities are also necessary. He quoted the following extract from a speech made by the United States president Lyndon Johnson in the 1960s:

> But freedom is not enough. You do not take a person who, for years, has been hobbled by chains and liberate him, bring him up to the starting line of the race and then say, you are free to compete with all the others, and still justly believe that you have been completely fair. Thus it is not enough just to open the gates of opportunity. All our citizens must have the ability to walk through the gates... We seek not just freedom but opportunity – not just legal equity but human ability – not just equality as a right and a theory but equality as a fact and as a result (*Sunday Times*, 26 August 2001).

The political and legal empowerment of blacks since 1994 has not automatically translated into socio-economic empowerment. While political transformation has been a necessary condition for social upliftment and eradicating poverty, it is not a remotely sufficient condition for attaining these goals. Eight years after the political transition, changes in the distribution of socio-economic power have mainly benefited the ±10 million blacks in the two bourgeois classes, and has had hardly any effect on the 22,5 million blacks in the middle lower and lower lower classes. The 7,5 million in the upper lower class may have benefited only marginally (see table 2.2 and figure 2.1).

Members of the poorest half of the population are still relatively uneducated, unskilled, without formal jobs, and deprived of information about their rights and opportunities. They are unorganised, and – except in a few isolated instances – unable to exert pressure on the government. Their basic human needs remain largely unmet, perhaps even more so than in the past. Most own no property, not even household goods. They have no reserve funds at their disposal. Because of the absence of complementary assets (such as infrastructural services) and a scarcity of opportunities, they cannot take advantage of the few assets they do own. Although younger people have received (and are still receiving) much better schooling than their parents, they do not have reasonable prospects of finding formal jobs. An important reason for the powerlessness of the poor is that civil society organisations in their communities are either poorly organised or non-existent.

The economic powerlessness of the poorer half of the population should be understood against the background of the events of the past 30 years. During this time employers in the private sector have become less sensitive to the

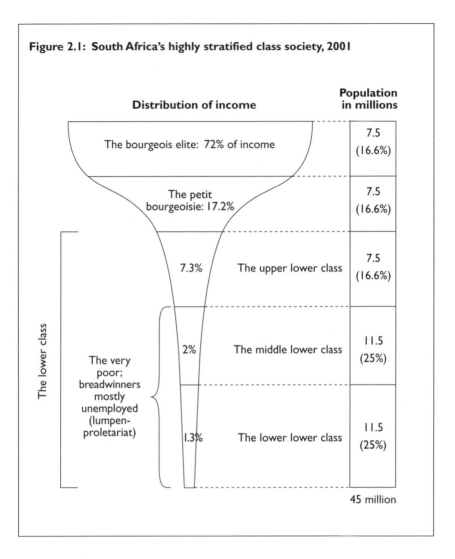

Figure 2.1: South Africa's highly stratified class society, 2001

interests of the poor, as a result, firstly, of the corporate sector's accumulation crisis, and, secondly, of the growth in the capital intensity of the modern sector of the economy. When the erstwhile insatiable demand for cheap and docile African labour petered out from 1970 onwards, a large part of the African labour force was in effect declared redundant by the mainly white employer class (see section 9.4). This trend continued after 1994. From a socio-economic point of view, the poor became more marginalised, powerless, and pauperised. It is a cruel irony that the poverty in which half of the population has to live is largely caused by their ineffective socio-economic bargaining power despite the dramatic political transition of 1994 (see section 4.4).

According to Lisa Bornstein, an important reason for the powerlessness of the poor is the fact that the 'new government's institutional basis for addressing poverty is still extremely weak' (quoted in May 2000: 203). In the course of the government's attempt to redesign the public sector, many non-governmental organisations (NGOs) have either been sidelined or commercialised to the detriment of the poor. The weakening in the capacity of the public sector, especially that of departments directly responsible for the poor, has made a disturbing contribution to the neglect of the poor and towards their further disempowerment and pauperisation. For example, a major portion of the funds budgeted for poverty alleviation over the past few years has not been spent – or has been spent belatedly – by the relevant departments.

According to May, 'it is increasingly recognised that getting institutions right is a key element in any development strategy, and that, conversely, institutional failure is a factor contributing towards the persistence of poverty' (1998: 100). It should, however, be acknowledged that the new government's failure to reform institutions (in especially rural areas) concerned with poverty relief and to create effective new institutions for this purpose is not entirely its own fault. For the best part of the 20th century the task of delivering welfare and other services to the rural population was entrusted to traditional African authorities. Many of them were caught up in apartheid engineering, and when the system of 'Bantu' authorities was implemented in the 1950s the traditional authorities were transformed into paid bureaucracies. This facilitated the creation of an African bureaucratic elite that was – as part of the apartheid bureaucracy – inclined towards self-enrichment and corruption, and disinclined to deliver services to those who needed them most. May concludes that 'institutional mayhem prevails in much of government and civil society, both in terms of structures and capacity to deliver... [Consequently,] the poor are still disempowered by the entrapping institutions and processes of the era of "total onslaught", especially in the ex-Bantustans and white-dominated farming areas ...The poor do not know where power is to be found, nor what power has on offer... because institutional structures are opaque and disempowering' (1998: 120). Early in 2001 president Thabo Mbeki announced an integrated sustained rural development programme. At the end of 2001, indications were that the strategy had become enmeshed in red tape.[6]

The situation of the urban poor is not as bad as that of the rural poor. However, before the municipal elections of December 2000 the institutions responsible for delivering services to the poor were also enmeshed in the limitations imposed by the Group Areas Act. Whether the government can transform the local authorities into institutions that will deliver services efficiently and respond to the needs of the poor is still uncertain. The supply of a certain amount of free electricity and free water to every household in urban areas will certainly improve the circumstances of millions of people. The fact is that, eight years after the political transition, most local authorities are still 'entrapping institutions' partly responsible for deteriorating conditions in many urban areas.

In the 'reshuffling' of political and economic power relations between the different income and population groups over the past 30 years – but especially over the past eight – a new 'distributional coalition' has been forged between the old white and new black elite to the detriment of less wealthy whites (mainly Afrikaners) and the poorest 50 per cent of black households. If the ideological cement that unites the old white and new black elite – ie, the ideology of neo-liberalism in the framework of global capitalism – remains intact, we can expect an alarming increase in the unequal distribution of income between the top 20 per cent and poorer 40 per cent of households. Given the extraordinary socio-economic and ideological power concentrated in the hands of the new (white and black) elite, a higher economic growth rate (even if it lasts for several years) will not – in the absence of an aggressive redistribution policy – reduce the unequal distribution of income, but will probably increase it even further between the top 20 and lower 40 per cent of households.[7] The fact that South Africa has recently been exposed to the relentless discipline of global capitalism has caused even greater inequality. Unfortunately, the tendency of globalisation to worsen inequality was not sufficiently acknowledged at the beginning of the 1990s. At the beginning of the 21st century, however, no one can claim to be unaware of the negative effects of globalisation on the distribution of income, job security, and employment (see ch 4; Michie and Padayachee 1997: 229).

The reasons for the unwillingness or inability of the new government to divert more funds and other resources from the mainly wealthy whites to the very poor (and mainly black) two thirds of the population over the past eight years will be addressed in chapter 4. The fact is that the new government has failed dismally to allocate sufficient power, property, and opportunities (including employment opportunities) to the poorest half of the population.

The tragic fact is that even if an annual economic growth rate of 5 per cent had been maintained over the past eight years, the poor would still have benefited very little. Since they are deprived of bargaining power, property, and opportunities, they have little influence over the modern sector of the economy. It is as if they are living in a different country, or rather, as if the rich and the poor are living in two different worlds: the rich in the Rich North and the poor in the Poor South, with few bridges between them. In these circumstances the notion that the benefits of market-driven economic growth will 'trickle down to the poor' is a fiction. Without aggressive redistributive intervention by the government on their behalf, the poorest half of the population will remain trapped in a situation of pauperisation.

South Africa is indeed a country of two nations – one rich, and the other poor. However, owing to the 'reshuffling' of power relations, and the new distributive coalition forged between the old white and new black elites, the one nation is no longer white and the other black. Given the unequal distribution of power, property, and opportunities between the non-racial bourgeois elite and the almost exclusively black lower class, powerful 'entrapping mechanisms' are in place that will, barring significant interventions, perpetuate these two nations for a long time to come. Income distribution in the new politico-economic system of democratic capitalism – the successor to white political domination and racial capitalism institutionalised in 1994 – is solidifying owing to the unequal distribution of socio-economic power between the 15 million people who have reached bourgeois status, and the 22,5 million people doomed to remain impoverished and marginalised. The remaining 7,5 million members of South Africa's population can either be promoted to the bourgeoisie, or degraded to the impoverished lower class.

A controversial issue is the role that racism is still playing in the power structures that deprive the poor of opportunities to escape from their bondage. Duma Goubule claims that 'if there is one common experience of everybody in the nation that is poor, it is racism. Racism has many facets: social, psychological, cultural, and economic. It is about the continuation of colonial and apartheid power relations, the exclusion of... blacks regardless of class and the virtual conditions of slavery endured by millions of farm workers, domestic workers and miners' (*Sunday Independent*, 20 May 2001). President Mbeki claims that 'many whites... have a particular stereotype of black people... It's a very negative stereotype of people who are lazy, basically dishonest, thieves, corrupt... Many [whites] carry this perception, and it informs their reading of what is happening' (*Mail & Guardian*, 1–7 June 2001).[8]

If these allegations about continued white racism are true – and there are many indications that they are – then white prejudice against blacks, and especially against blacks who are poor, is undoubtedly a serious structural impediment. White prejudice also prevents whites from acknowledging that they have been undeservedly enriched, and blacks undeservedly impoverished, by segregation and apartheid. The stubborn resistance of whites – and especially influential white business people – to higher taxes that could have enabled the government to spend more on restitution and poverty alleviation implies that racist patterns and attitudes are still an important part of the 'entrapping mechanisms' responsible for perpetuating the pauperisation of a large part of the black population (see sections 4.2 and 4.4).

2.2.3 The third poverty trap: disrupted social structures and the syndrome of chronic community poverty

The centuries-long violent conflict and unequal power struggles that mark South African history have had a very negative impact on the social structures of indigenous people. Although the 258 years of Dutch and British colonialism severly damaged family and tribal organisations, the range and penetration of exploitation during segregation (1910–48) and apartheid (1948–94) were far more destructive. During these two periods the aggressive dynamics of racial capitalism and the insatiable demand of capitalist entrepreneurs for cheap and docile labour showed little respect for the family, cultural, and social life of especially Africans. The elaborate mechanisms of proletarianisation, repression, and discrimination not only impoverished indigenous people physically, but probably did even more psychological damage. As soon as family and other social structures were disrupted, the disciplinary and civilising effect of those traditional structures were undermined. In this way a subculture – or syndrome – of poverty was institutionalised among poorer Africans and coloureds. And in this way a distinct poverty mentality, marked by deviant behaviour patterns, was inculcated into those who became captives of this syndrome.

The Commission of Inquiry into Matters Concerning the Coloured Population Group (1976) – the Theron commission – concluded that by 1976 a subculture – or syndrome – of chronic community poverty had become institutionalised among the poorer 40 per cent of coloured people. A similar syndrome had also existed for generations among poorer Africans. Over the past eight years this syndrome has acted as an important trap in perpetuating a poverty mentality, accompanied by anti-social and deviant behaviour. It will continue to act as a trap until the vicious circle of poverty has been broken by an effective and comprehensive policy of social upliftment and cultural and educational rehabilitation. Unfortunately, such a policy has not yet emerged.

The description given by the Theron commission of the poverty syndrome among the lower strata of the coloured population also applies to deviant behaviour among the lower strata of the African population. The deviant behaviour of coloureds and Africans who are indigent and powerless and have no sense of social or self-worth is not an isolated aspect of their lives; it is frequently their whole lives. Thus the total lifestyle of members of the lower strata constitutes a state of chronic community poverty. People living under these conditions are uneducated, come from broken homes, are in poor health, have poor housing, have few aspirations, and are emotionally confused. Each of these disabilities is intensified by the fact that it occurs in an embracing network of disabilities. This lifestyle exists not only in material terms, but also represents a spiritual or 'cultural' poverty defined by the fact that it constitues a backward subsociety in a modern, advanced, and progressive society.

When set against the other, materially successful, half of society, this lack of financial means, power, and a sense of social usefulness aggravates the depressing effects of the subculture of poverty, and gives rise to tension, frustration, alienation, and fatalism. Therefore, deviant behaviour largely stems from a restrictive environment, and often represents a defensive adjustment to the stresses and strains of poverty in an advanced society. Life for the individual caught in the syndrome of poverty becomes a maze of mutually reinforcing impediments and restrictions. If only one of the limiting factors were to be removed, for instance by improving household income, and the rest of the environment left unchanged, little would be gained in the long term.

Chronic community poverty has existed for generations; there are various factors that entrench this condition, and will continue to do so in future. Apart from the physical neglect of children, their spiritual, psychological, and moral neglect during their pre-school years is particularly significant. During these critical formative years children from poor families are exposed to such negative influences that they are unable, even under more favourable conditions later on, to regain lost ground. From an early age, anxiety complexes and a negative self-image take root, while defensive traits are developed to ward off the physical and psychological stresses of their disruptive social environment.

The political events involving coloured and African people during the 20th century and earlier has had important implications for the determination of their relative 'place' in the broader South African situation. Any attempt to explain the extent of poverty among coloureds and Africans and their inability to overcome this must take account of the economic system and the power relations associated with it. Chronic community poverty and its perpetuation cannot be explained without a clear understanding of the mutually reinforcing interaction between, on the one hand, processes of socialisation within these groups, and, on the other, the unfavourable economic conditions created because they are unable to measure up to the demands of the type of capitalism that existed and continues to exist in South Africa (see Theron commission 1976: paras 22.23–22.44; Terreblanche 1977).

2.2.4 *The fourth poverty trap: the mutually reinforcing dynamics between violence, criminality, and ill health on the one hand, and pauperisation on the other*

South Africa has an exceptionally violent history, and is still experiencing high levels of violence. As we will indicate in section 10.5, a subculture of criminality has developed from resistance to the violent methods used during colonialism and apartheid to dominate indigenous people. The apartheid practice that did most to ciminalise, and indeed brutalise, many African people was the migrant labour system institutionalised by Verwoerd in 1952. As many potential migrant workers in the Bantustans could not meet the stringent requirements for legal employment, they often had no option but to work illegally in urban areas (see section 9.4). Violent crime is not a recent phenomenon for most South Africans, and especially not for poor and black people. Antoinette Louw and Mark Shaw correctly claim that 'extreme levels of inequality and decades of political conflict have produced a society prone to crime. During the era of race domination, apartheid offences [by the opponents of apartheid] were classified as crimes, while those engage in "the [freedom] struggle" justified using violence against the state... In South Africa, crime and politics have been closely linked... [and] the use of violence for political and personal aims has become endemic [on both sides of the great divide]' (1997: 7).

We should not be surprised that crime and violence have escalated so spectacularly in the 'new South Africa'.[9] All the bottled-up rage and frustration among those oppressed under colonialism and apartheid were suddenly released by political liberalisation. When restrictions on freedom of movement were abolished, violent crime that had, under apartheid, been confined to the black townships spilled over into white areas. According to Shaw, 'the unbanning of the ANC and the liberalisation of politics prompted a weakening of community structures, as the common perception of threat declined' (1995: 14). The integration of South Africa into the global economy and the 'softness' of South Africa's long border created lucrative opportunities for international crime syndicates to target South Africa as 'virgin soil'. The dynamics of crime and violence in a large section of the black community should be understood not only as an extension of the struggle mentality, but also as an extension of the poverty mentality and deviant behaviour patterns that have become inculcated among the poor and destitute during generations of oppression. The dynamics of crime and violence are therefore rooted in repression, discrimination, the political struggle, and chronic community poverty.

The high levels of crime and violence in the 'new South Africa' are also the result of serious deficiencies in the criminal justice system. These deficiencies also have their roots in the apartheid period. During apartheid the police were not only tasked with combating crime, but also with implementing the multitude of apartheid laws and maintaining internal security. During the heyday of apartheid only one in ten members of the police was engaged in crime detection and investigation; the other nine were engaged in efforts to protect the apartheid regime. Police stations are also very unequally distributed among white and black, wealthy and poor neighbourhoods. In 1996 almost 75 per cent of national police stations were based in white areas, and less than 15 per cent in black urban areas. This skewed allocation of police services and their distorted orientation not only created space for crime to spread in the black townships, but also undermined the legitimacy of the police to such an extent that it will take a long time to restore. Eight years after liberation, the new government has not succeeded in reforming the criminal justice system into one capable of addressing violent criminality in a satisfactory and efficient manner. Until it does, the poor will remain the main victims of the skewed and inefficient system (see Shaw 1995: ch 4).

The co-operation and interaction between the departments of safety and security, justice, correctional services, and public works are inadequate and characterised by multiple blockages causing delays along the entire pipeline (see Louw and Shaw 1997: 51–5). The government will have to allocate considerably more resources to reforming and rebuilding the criminal justice system if it wants to attain one of its most fundamental goals, namely to create and maintain stability and order for all its citizens. Levels of violent crime are still rising, owing to a perception that crime has become a profitable career since only a small percentage of criminals are convicted.[10]

In 2000 the government announced a moratorium on crime statistics in order to improve their quality and veracity. Although those issued in June 2001 are still regarded as unreliable, they reveal that, from 1994 to 2000, some forms of violent crime have decreased and other increased, but that almost all forms of crime are at unacceptably high levels.[11] The report distinguishes between 'violent crime', 'social fabric crime', and 'property crime'. While most of the crimes in the first two categories have increased, 'property crime' has declined. But what is important is that it is mainly the wealthy who are victims of property crime, while poor people – mainly black people, women, children, and the elderly – are more at risk from personal crime, ie, both violent crime and social fabric crime.

Poor people are far more vulnerable to all three categories of crime than wealthy people. In his conceptualisation of poverty, May defines the concept of vulnerability thus: 'Poverty is not only about being poor, it is also about the risk of becoming poor or poorer in the face of change' (1998: 3). The seriousness of the crime problem and its huge pauperisation effect only become clear when we take into account that most criminals and their victims are poor – ie, the poorest two thirds of the population, who are almost exclusively black. According to Louw and Shaw, poorer communities are, however, seldom seen (at least by the rich and powerful) as the predominant victims of crime. According to these two writers, most victims of crime are poor, and for that reasons they also have fewer resources with which to cushion the cost of crime.[12]

The real vulnerability of the poor is exposed in the case of violent crimes during which bodily harm is inflicted, thus disrupting their already tenuous social fabric even further. Most of these crimes are committed within households, and are seldom reported. Women are often the victims of cruel and violent crimes that undermine not only their dignity but their ability to earn money. Children are abused, neglected, and exploited. Every new generation is trapped anew in a vicious circle of chronic community poverty and crime which is perpetuated from generation to generation, often through gang activities.

The ill health of poor people is a third element entering this mutually reinforcing dynamic. Because the poor have only limited access to health services, especially in rural areas, they are more likely to be drawn into a vicious circle of violence, ill-health, and poverty. With the advent of the HIV/AIDS pandemic, millions are being drawn into a new and appalling vicious circle of sexual promiscuity, sexual violence, AIDS, and poverty. There is great controversy about whether AIDS is the result of the HIV virus or of poverty. Whatever the case may be, the poor are more likely to be affected by the pandemic, and be further impoverished by its consequences. It is estimated that 4–6 million citizens (about 11 per cent of the population) – and a much higher percentage of the poor – are already infected.[13] When poverty in South Africa is contextualised in the historical framework of systemic exploitation, and when the vulnerability of the poor to the AIDS pandemic is considered, it comes clear that urgent comprehensive redistributive measures aimed at alleviating poverty are essential. As long as comprehensive, co-ordinated, and effective policies for alleviating poverty and preventing AIDS are not implemented, poor health and AIDS will remain an important – and ominous – poverty trap leading to the further pauperisation of especially the poorer half of the population. This is already happening, and is a vicious circle we cannot afford.

2.3   Legislation aimed at building a non-racial South Africa

In sharp contrast to the ANC government's inability to eradicate the legacy of colonialism, segregation and apartheid, it has introduced several laws aimed at laying the foundations for a non-racial society. While the government should be commended for doing so, it will not be possible to create a non-racial South Africa as long as the vast wealth gap between black and white remains intact, and as long as the government fails to alleviate poverty and rectify skewed economic structures. It is important to acknowledge that the government's inability to reduce unemployment and alleviate poverty is closely connected to the way in which racial attitudes survive among privileged whites. Although the government has laid the legal foundations for a non-racial society, it is beyond dispute that every South African (and especially the whites) still has a huge task to rid him/herself of racial prejudices, and exhort others to do the same.

In a communiqué to the Southern African Development Community (SADC) summit of 2001, the government acknowledged the need for socio-economic upliftment as follows: 'Since racial inequality in South Africa is not a set of isolated aberrations that can be corrected by the equal application of the law, or the re-education of pathological individuals, it is not sufficient to simply tamper with or reform the system. It requires instead the complete and progressive transformation of society' (department of foreign affairs 2001). The intention of the new government to create a non-racial society was confirmed in the following comment of the constitutional court on the interim constitution:

> The prohibition of unfair discrimination in the interim Constitution seeks not only to avoid discrimination against people who are members of disadvantaged groups. It seeks more than that. At the heart of the prohibition of unfair discrimination lies recognition that the purpose of our new constitutional and democratic order is the establishment of a society in which all human beings will be accorded *equal dignity and respect regardless of membership of particular groups*. The achievement of such a society in the context of our deeply inegalitarian past will not be easy, but that that is the goal of the Constitution should not be forgotten or overlooked. The Constitution also provides for numerous mechanisms to monitor and enforce the ongoing transformation of society while ensuring the protection of individual rights. These include a Human Rights Commission, a Commission for Promotion and Protection of the Rights of Cultural, Religious and Linguistic Communities and a Commission for Gender Equality.

The adoption of the final constitution in 1996 (Act 108 of 1996) represents a milestone in the history of human rights in South Africa. The preamble states that the constitution is adopted so as to:

> Heal the divisions of the past and establish a society based on democratic values, social justice and fundamental human rights; lay the foundations for a democratic and open society in which government is based on the will of the people and every citizen is equally protected by law; improve the quality of life of all citizens and free the potential of each person; and build a united and democratic South Africa able to take its rightful place as a sovereign state in the family of nations (RSA 1996: 3).

The economic and social rights recognised in the constitution include:

> Labour rights; the right to an environment that is not harmful to health or well-being; and to have the environment protected through reasonable legislative and other measures that secure sustainable development; equitable access to land; security of land tenure; and restitution of property or equitable redress for property that was dispossessed after 1913 as a result of past racially discriminatory laws or practices; the right of access to adequate housing and a prohibition on the arbitrary eviction of people from their homes or the demolition of homes; the right of access to health care services (including reproductive health care), sufficient food and water, and social security; the right against the refusal of emergency medical treatment; the right of children to basic nutrition, shelter, basic health care services and social services; educational rights; adequate accommodation, nutrition, reading material and medical treatment at state expense for persons deprived of their liberty...(ibid: 10–14).

The state's duty in relation to some of these rights is expressly qualified. For example, the sections dealing with the rights of access to housing, health care, food, water and social security, expressly state:

> The state must take reasonable legislative and other measures, within its available resources, to achieve the progressive realisation of each of these rights...[But the Constitution also entrenches] the right of everyone to have access to social security, including, if they are unable to support themselves and their dependants, appropriate social assistance (ibid).

Over the past eight years, the new government has pursued a wide-ranging legislative programme aimed at addressing the legacy of apartheid through affirmative action and special protection for the historically disadvantaged. Central to this programme is the Promotion of Equality and Prevention of Unfair Discrimination Act of 2000 (Act 4 of 2000), which requires every minister and level of government to implement measures aimed at achieving equality. These measures include the repeal of any law, policy, or practice that perpetuates inequality. Ministers are also required to draw up clear plans for eradicating inequality. The Employment Equity Act (Act 55 of 1998) is an instrument for addressing the legacy of the apartheid colour bar, which excluded black people from jobs above a basic level. Although these laws have undoubtedly helped to address the legacy of apartheid and racism in the workplace, they have benefited only the aspirant African petit bourgeois, who have jobs and are members of trade unions. Unfortunately, these laws have also increased the costs of employing labour and negatively affected the growth potential of the economy. The government should be careful not to promote – after centuries of discrimination and repression – the interests of relatively small groups to the detriment of the poorest half of the population. Its plight cannot be rectified by legislation alone. This also requires well-financed, comprehensive, and well-focused poverty alleviation programmes. Unfortunately, such programmes have not yet been implemented (see section 4.6).

A central component of apartheid was an education system designed to create an African population that would serve as 'hewers of wood and drawers of water'. Current educational programmes include implementing measures to redistribute educational resources in favour of the majority, building a culture of teaching and learning, introducing a new curriculum in line with the country's needs, and training teachers. Unfortunately, the departments of education that were institutionalised for different black population groups (and especially for Africans) during apartheid were highly inferior, poorly organised and resourced, and lacking a culture of study and dedication. Although substantial progress has been made in creating an educational system capable of underpinning a truly non-racial and prosperous South Africa, it should be acknowledged that most of the task of building such an educational system still lies ahead.

Endnotes

1 Van der Berg and Bharoot have concluded that, before the redistributive effect of the 1993 budget is taken into account, the per capita income of Africans was only 10,3 per cent that of whites. After the budget, Africans' secondary income per capita was 15,6 per cent of that of whites, due to a net gain from fiscal incidence of R895 per African person and a net loss of at least R3 421 per white person. The redistributive effect of the budget has increased considerably since 1993 (1999: 18). Unfortunately, the redistribution of income does not necessarily benefit those who need it most. The redistribution effect of the budget is no longer from white to black, but from taxpayers (both white and black) to those who pay no or little tax – who are mainly black.

2 According to the Reserve Bank, 'the structural changes in the South African economy in the 1990s left a mark on the historical relationship between changes in formal-sector employment and growth in the real gross domestic product... A given rate of economic growth has become associated with a considerably smaller change in formal-sector employment growth [than in the 1970s and 1980s] (SARB 2001: 22). Capital-intensive and labour-saving investment continued to be the rule after 1994; these included multi-billion-rand projects such as Columbus, Alusaf, the retooling of Iscor, Coega, and so on.

3 The reasons for the high dependency of the South African economy on FDI are its low levels of gross domestic savings (GDS) and gross domestic fixed investment (GDFI). From 1995 to 2000, annual average GDS and GDFI were 14 per cent and 15 per cent of GDP respectively (Bureau of Economic Research database). It is not possible to achieve a higher economic growth rate with such low levels of savings and investment. (In section 4.4 the initial projections of the GEAR strategy for 1996–2000 will be compared with what eventually materialised.)

4 According to Statistics South Africa, the Gini coefficient for the pay of Africans increased from 0,70 in 1995 to 0,81 in 1998, for the pay of coloureds from 0,57 to 0,65 in the same period, and for the pay of whites from 0,55 to 0,67. The Gini coefficient for total pay and total earnings increased from 0,73 and 0,74 in 1995 to 0,80 and 0,83 in 2000 respectively (SSA 2001: 87–8). If these shifts in Gini coefficients from 1995 to 1998 have continued in 1998–2002, this shows clearly that the rich have become much richer and the poor considerably poorer over the past eight years.

5 There is therefore merit in Mbeki's statement that 'we have [in the South African society] very deeply entrenched racial disparities. [We] have the unfortunate situation that poverty in this country is defined by colour' (Interview with Hugo Young, *Mail & Guardian*, 1–7 June 2001).

6 To reform these traditional authorities in which a rich and powerful rural African elite has attained a considerable vested interest is enormously difficult. The fact that this rural elite mostly supports the ANC or the Inkatha Freedom Party complicates matters considerably. As long as the rural elite that obtained its power from the apartheid regime remains powerful – and is even further empowered by the new government for politically expedient reasons – the majority of the rural poor will remain trapped in powerlessness and poverty.

7 The United States experienced a high economic growth rate in the 1990s, but due to the strong 'distributional coalition' among elite groups and the general acceptance of the ideology of neo-liberalism, the distribution of income became much more unequal between the top 30 per cent and the lower 70 per cent of the population.

8 Whether it is racism that informs whites' reading of what is happening (as Mbeki claims), or whether it is arrogance based on their entrenched position of wealth and privileges, is a moot point.

9 During the liberation struggle a culture of lawlessness grew in the ranks of the liberation organisations when they pursued a strategy of making the country ungovernable. Unfortunately that culture is being expressed in the new South Africa in violent crime, and some townships have become permanently ungovernable as a result. Many members of the 'lost generation' of the 1980s – people with little education, an agitated political consciousness, and poor employment prospects – are inclined towards violence and other forms of anti-social behaviour. Given that thousands of black matriculants cannot find jobs, a new 'lost generation' is being created that is destined to become derailed into a life of sophisticated criminality. Mike Nicol suggests that 'urban crime has become a replacement for the civil war that never happened' (quoted by Marais 1998: 109–10).

10 Of the 2,2 million crimes reported to the police in 1998, almost half were classified as 'undetected', implying that the evidence was insufficient or that the suspect had disappeared. Half a million more were withdrawn, leaving 524 000 cases that reached court. Of these, 203 000 (or only 9 per cent of the number reported) result in convictions. The main reason for this dismal state of affairs is the shortage of professional and well-equipped personnel (*The Economist*, 24 February 2001).

11 The murder rate has declined from 70 per 100 000 (roughly 26 800 murders) in 1994 to 49 per 1000 000 in 2000. Recorded rape (including attempted rape) increased from 110 per 100 000 in 1994 to 120 per 100 000 in 2000. Common assaults increased from 502 to 569 per 100 000, and assaults with intent to inflict grievous bodily harm from 544 to 624 per 100 000 from 1994 to 2000. Robbery with aggravating circumstances increased from 220 to 251 per 100 000 from 1994 to 2000.

12 They put the point as follows: 'The shock of being victimised by crime makes the poor more vulnerable by eroding the means available to them to withstand its effects, and to recover afterwards...[In many cases] heightened vulnerability may force victims to resort to criminal activity as a means of survival – beginning a process whereby the poor are criminalised by the desperate nature of their plight.' Louw and Shaw also quote well-documented observations 'that interpersonal violence the world over in colonial societies in particular occurs most frequently among people subject to the dual pressure of structurally entrenched economic and racial inequalities' (1997: 12, 18, 63).

13 HIV prevalence is projected to increase to 15,1 per cent by 2015 (or 6,6 million people), levelling off from about 2008 onwards. The number of people suffering from full-blown AIDS is projected to increase from 158 200 in 2000 to 518 000 by 2001 and 1,06 million by 2015. The HIV/AIDS pandemic is expected to have devastating effects on the poor, and exert huge pressure on their already meagre resources (BER 2001; see also section 10.2.4).

Chapter 3

Prelude to the informal negotiations on economic issues

3.1 The economic attitudes and ideologies of the corporate sector

Remarkably, the Cold War and apartheid ran almost concurrently: the Cold War from 1947 until 1989–91, and apartheid from 1948 until 1990–4. Whether this was coincidental or not is an interesting question, but not directly relevant to our argument.[1] What is relevant is that, during those 40 years, there was a great ideological distance between the South African corporate sector and the democratic movement in respect of economic systems. In that period the corporate sector operated within the protective framework of the capitalist-oriented western world despite the fact that the domestic system of colonial and racial capitalism recognised neither the democratic freedoms nor property rights of Africans.

Within this framework, the corporate sector was – hypocritically – neither overtly critical of the racist character of the South African dispensation, nor of the violation of the human rights of blacks. It was, however, extremely hostile towards communism, socialism, and state intervention in the economy. The democratic movement, on the other hand, was highly critical of the racist character of the South African dispensation, and, because of its close links with the South African Communist Party (SACP), and the support it received from countries in the communist bloc, favoured a socialist-oriented economic system for a liberated South Africa, to the extent of advocating the nationalisation of the gold mining and other industries.

When tentative discussions and informal negotiations between the corporate sector and the democratic movement began in the late 1980s, the ideological gap between the two parties could hardly have been greater. Given this, it is hardly surprising that both parties were initially mutually mistrustful and suspicious. However, before discussing the informal negotiations, and the elite compromises eventually reached between the two sides, we need to examine their track records and ideological 'baggage'; only then will we be able to understand what was at stake during the negotiations.

3.1.1 The corporate sector's middle-class values, and its unsympathetic attitude towards the poor

During South Africa's long colonial history, its population was always divided into a relatively small, rich, powerful, and mainly white minority, and a large, poor, powerless, and mainly black majority. The attitudes of the rich and powerful towards the poor – whether white or black – were important because they determined the degree of assistance given, or not given, to the poor. In South Africa's case, members of the white elite largely subscribed to a perspective which ascribes poverty to flaws and shortcomings in the character and personality of impoverished individuals, and/or their racial status. There is an alternative perspective that links poverty to structural factors, thus recognising that individuals become enmeshed in adverse economic and social conditions over which they have little or no control. However, the structural explanation of poverty has not enjoyed much support among members of the white and even black South African elite. The view that each poor individual must shoulder the blame for his/her poverty is typical of a prosperous bourgeoisie with a strong success ethic. In the intellectual history of the Protestant Anglo-Saxon world, poverty is often ascribed to personal shortcomings of a religious, moral, or biogenetic kind. In the religious explanation, poverty is presented as a punishment visited on children for the sins of their fathers; people are also said to be poor because they have not been elected, or because they have been ordained by providence to occupy the lower levels of social stratification.[2]

The religious explanation of poverty prevalent in the late 19th and early 20th centuries was also implicit in Herbert Spencer's doctrine of Social Darwinism, which regarded English-speaking people as superior in line with God's will, while indigenous people in the colonies were regarded as inferior and therefore doomed to poverty and even extinction. The religious explanation was also implicit – if rather awkwardly – in the mid-20th century claim by Afrikaners that they were one of God's chosen people, and that it was unfair, if not unbecoming, for so many Afrikaners to be trapped in poverty. Afrikaners' explanation of black poverty in the mid-20th century was mainly based on racist considerations, but also had a religious undertone in so far as they regarded the hierarchical social order as ordained by God, with blacks destined to occupy the lower ranks of society.

The ascription of poverty to the moral shortcomings and lack of integrity and tenacity of the poor was – and still is – popular in prosperous middle-class circles in the western world. This approach is used to justify the privileged position of the middle classes, and explain away the poverty and 'deviant behaviour' of lower-class people – ie, any behaviour that deviates from middle-class norms. In South Africa, members of the white elite often emphasise the virtue of a middle-class work ethic, and place a high value on the importance of individual initiative and achievement.

Consequently, they often strongly disapprove of people – mainly blacks – who do not appear to them to adhere to these values. For the greater part of the 20th century most whites regarded poor blacks as lazy and untrustworthy, and felt that they actually deserved their poverty as punishment for their lack of moral integrity and resolve.

According to Colin Bundy, the poverty of a large section of the Afrikaners at the end of the 19th century was either ignored or regarded unsympathetically in both English and Afrikaner middle-class circles. It was only when large numbers of Afrikaners were impoverished by the Anglo–Boer War that the poverty and social dislocation of the 'poor whites' became an ideological issue among Afrikaners (see Bundy, in Beinart *et al* 1986: 119–20). However, a strong drive for the upliftment of impoverished Afrikaners was only launched in the 1930s after the Carnegie Report had been published in 1932 and the Purified (*Gesuiwerde*) National Party formed in 1934.[3]

In South Africa a biogenetic or racial explanation of poverty was often closely linked to the moral explanation. Those favouring the biogenetic explanation assumed – explicitly or implicitly – that members of a certain racial or ethnic group were poor because they were endowed with less intellectual capacity and moral resolve, and that hereditary factors and other physical shortcomings of a biogenetic origin made 'losers' of them in the natural social order. It is simply not possible to explain the indifference of many whites towards the poverty of black people during the 20th century without taking their strong and often hidden racial prejudices into account. Or, to put it differently, the racial prejudices of many whites made it easy for them not to feel morally repentant about the poverty in which most blacks had to live. The really important question is to what extent this view still exists – whether explicitly or implicitly – today.

The approach that explains black poverty in terms of adverse socio-economic and/or political conditions received very little support in white (and probably also black) middle-class circles during the 20th century – as it does to this day (see Terreblanche 1977). The fact that most blacks did not enjoy political rights, did not own property, were deprived of educational and other opportunities for self-development, and did not effectively control their structural and institutional conditions is usually ignored.[4]

A very large percentage of whites apparently know little about the extent to which Africans were impoverished and systematically exploited as unfree labour, and even less about the extent to which the social and family structures of Africans were disrupted by the economic policies pursued during colonialism, segregation, and apartheid.[5] As long as whites remain unprepared to acknowledge the structural nature of black poverty, it is unlikely that they will regard black poverty with the necessary empathy and compassion.

Business people in South Africa – both white and black – are among those inclined to explain black poverty in terms of individual deficiencies and racial and/or biogenetic factors, while neglecting its structural explanation. These people are also strongly opposed to charity, or 'hand-outs' to the poor, on the assumption that this only leads to a dependency syndrome and further moral degeneration. They are obviously not aware of the degenerative effect of abject poverty on the poorest half of the population, trapped for generations in the vicious circle of structural poverty.[6]

When leaders of the corporate sector began negotiating with the democratic movement, they brought with them their indifference to the structural explanation of poverty as well as their inclination to explain black poverty in terms of personality deficiencies and racial and/or biogenetic factors.

3.1.2 The corporate sector's organisational structure, power and efficiency, and propensity for myth-making

The South African corporate sector has certain unique characteristics. It is concentrated in the hands of a small number of mega-corporations with formidable financial, organisational, ideological, and even political power. Its power is enhanced by interlocking directorates and by strong business organisations such as the South African Chamber of Business (SACOB), the Afrikaanse Handelsinstituut (AHI), Business South Africa (BSA), and so on. For more than a century, white supremacist governments have supported the emergence of large corporations. Protectionist policies and favouritism by both English and Afrikaner governments stimulated the growth of large conglomerates. Their growth was also stimulated by the repressive labour practices followed until the 1980s. The large surplus extracted from mineral resources, and from unfree African labour, was largely used for capital accumulation and the expansion of both the size and bargaining power of the conglomerates. Some of today's largest corporations (such as ESKOM, ISCOR, and SASOL) started as public corporations that grew into huge concerns during the governance of the NP and were recently converted, fully or partially, into private corporations.

The South African corporate sector's productive and organisational capacity, efficiency, and technological sophistication are – from an African perspective – very considerable and very impressive. We can describe the South African corporate sector as a first-world oasis in an African desert. It is often argued that the productive capacity and efficiency of the corporate sector should be regarded as one of South Africa's greatest assets, and that great care should be taken not to harm it in the course of the transition towards a new South Africa. Whatever the merits of this argument may be, it should not be used as an excuse to keep the mainly white-controlled corporate sector intact, and perpetuate white privilege. The corporate sector's enormous bargaining power and its capacity to generate propaganda – not only in the narrow economic arena, but also the broader political arena – cannot be overemphasised. Since the 1990s many of the mega-corporations have become 'internationalised' and have attained considerable additional bargaining power through the networks of global corporatism.

What is most interesting about South Africa's corporate sector is its strong propensity for myth-making and propagandising in order to legitimise its power, privileges, and alleged functionality in promoting the interests of all South Africans. This, of course, is not limited to South Africa; it is a trademark of corporate sectors in all capitalist-oriented countries, but has always been extremely strong in this country. One reason for this could be this sector's privileged position in a country in which conflict between different ethnic, colour, and language groups has been endemic, and in which privileges and opportunities have always been unequally distributed. Another is that the domestic corporate sector emerged during an aggressive phase of British imperialism, and that its tendency towards myth-making was therefore part of a more comprehensive project to justify the 'colonial construct' in South Africa. The corporate sector's propaganda has been (and still is) disseminated with great sophistication and conviction, and the 'mining' and/or mainstream media have played (and are still playing) a strategic role in doing so.

The American economist Kenneth Galbraith contends that the power of the managerial elites of the big corporations depends on their ability to create a more attractive image of their corporations than they are in reality. He describes the inclination of big corporations towards myth-making as follows:

The institution that most changes our lives we least understand or, more correctly, seek most elaborately to misunderstand. That is the modern

55

corporation. Week by week, month by month, year by year, it exercises a greater influence on our livelihood and the way we live than unions, universities, politicians, the government. There is a corporate myth, which is carefully, assiduously propagated. And there is the reality. They bear little relation to each other. The modern corporation lives in suspension between fiction and truth (1977: 257).

Capitalist-oriented corporations emerged in South Africa during the last quarter of the 19th century, largely financed by foreign shareholders. Since then corporations have played an increasingly important role in the discourse on how South Africa's political, economic, and social life should be organised, and on the privileges, powers, and freedoms that should be given to it as ostensibly the only engine of employment creation, economic growth, and prosperity. We can distinguish between two main categories of ideologies or myths propagated by South Africa's corporate sector to legitimise itself, often in very subtle and disguised ways. The first has to do with the alleged capacity of the liberal (or free market) capitalist system to promote the interests of the total population irrespective of whether or not the economic system in South Africa can credibly be described as such. The second is the contention that a high economic growth rate in South Africa will – despite deeply institutionalised inequalities – automatically 'trickle down' to the poor.

3.1.3 The ideology of liberal (or free market) capitalism

The first myth propagated by the English-controlled corporate sector for more than a century, and by Afrikaner-controlled corporations for the past 20 years, is that South Africa has a liberal capitalist economic system. If ever there was a myth that was carefully and assiduously cultivated while bearing little resemblance to reality, then this is it.

It was indeed preposterous of the corporate sector to make this claim during the first half of the 20th century when political power was monopolised by less than 20 per cent of the population, when 70 per cent of the population was prohibited from owning property in 78 per cent of the country, when 70 per cent of the labour force was subjected to repressive and discriminatory labour systems that deprived blacks of the most elementary freedoms and rights, and when economic wealth and political power were concentrated in the hands of the English establishment and a few English-controlled corporations. Given the NP government's increased intervention in the economy after 1948, the economic system during the second half of the 20th century was even less of a free market system.

The economic system in place in South Africa since the end of the 19th century – and still largely in place in the 'new South Africa' – is in fact one of colonial and racial capitalism that could not be remotely described as a system of liberal (or free market) capitalism, nor as one that advances the interests of all South Africans.

The South African economic system was deliberately moulded (by a 'compact of power' between successive white supremacist political authorities and the white-controlled corporate sector) on the basis of unfree black labour, the systemic exploitation of blacks, and the marginalisation of the majority of blacks as an impoverished proletariat without property, proper employment opportunities, and social support systems, and a reasonable chance to break out of a vicious circle of poverty and backwardness. What complicates matters further is that much economic power and property was concentrated in the hands of fewer than ten mega-corporations or conglomerates. Alarmingly, the racially based inequalities (including the inequalities in the distribution of power, property and opportunities) on which colonial and racial capitalism were based and on which they thrived for almost 100 years have become so deeply institutionalised that the economic system currently in place in South Africa, eight years after the political transition, can still not be described as a liberal or free market capitalist system, nor as one that automatically promotes the interests of all South Africans.

The unequal distribution of power, property, and opportunity apparently did not concern the dogmatic protagonists of liberal capitalism. For them the acid test of whether an economic system was a free market or liberal capitalist system was the degree of state intervention, and the number of rules and regulations that were in place. The protagonists of liberal capitalism were highly critical of the large-scale intervention or statism of the NP government from 1948 to ±1980, because they believed this interfered with the market mechanism. The 'free marketeers' claimed that the South African economic system in the first half of the century operated as if it were a system of liberal or free market capitalism, and that the corporate sector could, at the time, demand all the power, privileges, and freedom usually allocated to the corporate sector in a proper system of liberal capitalism. According to them, this would also have been the case during the NP's period in government, if it weren't for its excessive statism. But the statism of successive NP governments was not the only – and perhaps not even the most important – reason why the economic system during that party's term of power could not have been described as a liberal capitalist system.

It is important to realise that the problem in the 'old South Africa' was not only a racist political system, but also colonial and racial capitalism. The protagonists of liberal capitalism claim the moral high ground for their economic system and for the corporate sector during long periods in the 20th century, at a time when the majority of the population was ruthlessly exploited. While the white political establishment should accept full responsibility for creating and maintaining the immoral political system of white supremacy, the white business establishment should also accept full responsibility for helping to build and maintain the exploitative and equally immoral economic system of colonial and racial capitalism, and for accumulating huge wealth and power in an exploitative way. While white political supremacy was abolished in 1994, many of the racially based economic structures, property relations, and ideological orientations institutionalised during the heyday of colonial and racial capitalism still exist almost unchanged in the new South Africa.

The protagonists of liberal capitalism usually appeal to Adam Smith's 'invisible hand' to justify the alleged merits of the system of liberal, free market capitalism. According to Smith's dictum, in a system of liberal capitalism the attempts of individuals and corporations to maximise their profits will be miraculously and perfectly 'co-ordinated' by a benevolent 'invisible hand', to the benefit of all the inhabitants of the country. The fact is that Smith never formulated such a dictum, and what is usually presented in his name is nothing but a vulgarised version of his approach.[7] He did claim that if certain very strict institutional and behavioural conditions existed, all market prices would tend towards their true (or natural) value, and then – and only then – would it be as if an 'invisible hand' co-ordinated the actions of individuals pursuing their self-interest into an 'order' that would benefit all. The institutional and behavioural conditions laid down by Smith are extremely strict. They are, firstly, an open, well-organised, and civilised society in which all individuals will be disciplined and educated to pursue their self-interest with circumspection, with due regard for the interests of others, and with the necessary prudence; secondly, the existence of a sound judicial system for protecting property and contract rights and preventing all forms of fraud and corruption; and, thirdly, the existence of competitive markets in which nobody has monopolistic power to influence market prices and wages or to hamper the tendency of market prices and wages to move to their natural level or true values.

Needless to say, none of these social, judicial or market conditions laid down by Smith was even remotely present in South Africa. South African society was never open and well-organised, with all individuals disciplined or educated enough to pursue their self-interest with circumspection and prudence. On the contrary, South African society was (and still is) a divided and conflict-ridden one. It was (and still is) a 'closed' society in which whites (always less than 20 per cent of the total population) were (and still are) in a privileged position and powerful and educated enough to dominate, manipulate, and exploit the majority of people other than white. These features of domination, manipulation, and exploitation lasted for the greater part of the 20th century, but were more intense during its third quarter owing to additional repressive measures introduced by the apartheid regime. Many of these features are perpetuated in subtle ways in the 'new South Africa'.

The judicial system in place in the 'old South Africa' protected the property rights of mainly white property owners, but Africans were systematically deprived of property rights and forbidden to own property in 87 per cent of the country. Most importantly, the markets – and especially the labour market – were anything but free and competitive. For the greatest part of the last 150 years, most members of the black labour force have been powerless, impoverished, proletarianised, uneducated, unskilled, and subject to repressive and discriminatory labour patterns. In this highly imperfect labour 'market' the Chamber of Mines was granted a monopsonistic right to exploit African migrant workers – not only in South but also in southern Africa – and to keep wages at exceptionally low levels. In addition, the system of colonial and racial capitalism was characterised by all kinds of restrictions and imperfections. An important example of these imperfections was the abnormal economic, political, and ideological power concentrated in the hands of the mega-corporations (or 'commanding heights'). This power has been perpetuated almost intact – in close collaboration with the new government – in the 'new South Africa'. If anything, these corporations have become even more powerful owing to all sorts of privileges granted to them by the democratically elected government since 1994 (see section 4.5).

The corporate sector is no longer as exclusively white as it was for the greater part of the 20th century, but the property and power relations in its favour have only changed marginally since 1994. Anyone who dares to claim that the economic system in place in South Africa for the past 100 years – and effectively still in place – was a system of liberal or free market capitalism that operated automatically – or even approximately – to promote the interests of the entire population is not only propagating a myth but a dangerous economic lie.[8]

The fundamental misconception of the corporate sector and free marketeers is that South Africa has a normal, first-world economy. It is perhaps true that the modern sector of the economy – viewed in isolation – has many of the characteristics of first-world economies. But South Africa is not a first-world country; it is a developing country with a large underdeveloped sector that is extremely underdeveloped because it was recklessly exploited by the modern sector for the greatest part of the 20th century. Although those in the third-world sector cannot be exploited today as they were during segregation and apartheid, they are still 'exploited' by neglect and by the perception among members of the white and black elite that South Africa is a first-world country with a developed free market economic system.

The institutional framework in place in South Africa during the 20th century was such that all the population groups other than whites (except for a small black elite) were constantly and systemically marginalised and exploited, while the whites were constantly, systemically, and undeservedly enriched and empowered. In these circumstances it is preposterous to claim that the economic system in South Africa was a liberal or a free market capitalist system, or that such a system would have been 'created' if the government could have been convinced to introduce neo-liberal or free market-oriented economic policies. It takes much more than a neo-liberal or free market policy and an 'anti-statist' attitude to create a truly liberal or free market capitalist system.

In order to change the South African economic system into a market-oriented one that will serve the interests of all 45 million South Africans, present power, property (including human and intellectual property), and labour relations will have to be comprehensively and fundamentally restructured. This will probably not happen in the foreseeable future. But until this occurs, the state has an important role to play on behalf of the marginalised and impoverished. This is unfortunately not happening in post-apartheid South Africa; in fact, the opposite is happening, and a 'free marketeer' attitude has taken root. As Heribert Adam *et al* point out, 'the economic debate in the mainstream media reaches hysterical levels when editorials howl at anyone who even mentions that there may be a need for corrective state intervention in an unfettered market' (1997: 162).

One of the most astonishing events in the corporate sector's long history of myth-making was the establishment of the Free Market Foundation (FMF) in 1976. Several members of the managerial elite of the 'commanding heights' have had the audacity to serve as presidents and/or board members of the FMF. Even if we grant the point that this foundation campaigned for the removal of unnecessary interventionist and apartheid measures introduced by the NP government, their removal was certainly not enough to create the institutional and behavioural conditions necessary for a liberal or free market capitalist system. Also, a truly liberal capitalist economy cannot be created as long as economic power, property, and wealth remain abnormally concentrated in the hands of the 'commanding heights'. The FMF could only attain credibility if it campaigned for the abolition of the 'commanding heights', and the fundamental restructuring of South African society.

Important power shifts have taken place since 1990, but these have been mainly restricted to the political arena; in the economic sphere, most blacks remain marginalised and impoverished. It is important to realise that the propaganda of the FMF had more to do with the supposedly negative role of the apartheid state, and that it was never really concerned about the institutional and behavioural conditions that ought to be in place before we can credibly talk of a free market capitalist system. In so far as the anti-state propaganda of the FMF was responsible for the abolition of apartheid statism, this was certainly commendable. But in so far as the FMF is obsessed with rolling back the state and redefining its role in order to give the the mega-corporations more space and power, its propaganda is certainly hypocritical, misplaced, and even destructive.

In any capitalist country, capitalism is always a project in the making, and the state always has a crucial role to play in it – especially during a transformation such as that which South Africa is currently experiencing. Some economists (especially those of the classical and neo-classical schools) are inclined to regard modern capitalism as a natural construct, and its rules as akin to laws of nature. This is a dangerous misconception. Capitalism developed over almost five centuries, and is supported and defined by human institutions and attitudes; it is therefore a human or social construct, and as such a project that needs to be continuously adapted. It is beyond dispute that the state – as the embodiment of civil society – has an enormous 'restructuring' role to play before the economic system inherited from racial capitalism can operate automatically, to a reasonable degree, in the interests of all South Africans. In the meantime, the state must intervene to compensate for the dysfunctionality inherent in the system (see section 11.1).

The state not only has a crucial role to play in creating and maintaining the economic order as such, but also in making the adaptations necessary in a changing and dynamic world. *Inter alia,* the state has responsibilities as far as the nature and spread of property are concerned, as well as the power formations closely connected with property. The state also has responsibilities concerning the competitiveness of the economy, not only in consumer markets but especially in factor markets. In a developing country such as South Africa the state is undeniably responsible for ensuring that all those groups that are unemployed, 'undeveloped', 'underdeveloped', and marginalised from mainstream economic activity are included – over a reasonable period – into the main stream. The state is also responsible for ensuring that all the strata in society share in the benefits of economic activity. All these responsibilities of the state are, unfortunately, not acknowledged by the 'free marketeers' in their quest for a relatively 'stateless' society in which the mega-corporations usurp not only economic but also political power (see Hertz 2001; Klein 2000).[9]

Thus the corporate sector adopted the simplistic, unrealistic, and erroneous idea that the South African economic system is a liberal or free market economic system, and took this notion to the informal negotiations on economic matters. It was also obsessed with the idea that the state should not have an important socio-economic role to play in a democratised South Africa, and that it should be 'rolled back' as far as possible because the 'organisation' of the economy is best left to the trustworthy 'invisible hand' of the free market system.

3.1.4 The myth of a spontaneous 'trickle-down' effect in a rapidly growing economy

One of the main ideological arguments of the corporate sector – especially since the 1970s – has been that, should it be given the necessary power, freedom, and 'space' in the framework of global capitalism, it will achieve a high economic growth rate which will spontaneously lead to the creation of jobs, and 'trickle down' in other beneficial ways to the poor – if not immediately, then at least in the foreseeable future.[10] Whether economic growth automatically results in a 'trickle-down' or redistributive effect is highly controversial; this would depend, *inter alia*, on the institutional character of the economic system, and the distribution of power, property, and opportunities among different classes (and/or ethnic groups). Another important determining factor would be the nature of economic growth, ie, whether it is capital- or labour-intensive. As far as the South African system of colonial and racial capitalism is concerned, its growth record from 1890 to 1974 was quite satisfactory, but its distributive record less so. Until 1974 whites constituted only 20 per cent of the total population, but consistently received more than 70 per cent of total income. By contrast, Africans constituted almost 70 per cent of the total population, but received less than 20 per cent of total income. This huge discrepancy must be attributed to the fact that almost all property (physical and human) and almost all power (political, economic, and ideological) were concentrated in white hands, while Africans were propertyless, disenfranchised, relatively uneducated, culturally underdeveloped, and also deprived of trade union and other basic human rights as well as being the victims of unfree labour patterns (see section 10.4.1).

South Africa's economic growth and redistributive records during the 20th century did not coincide. Given the availability of cheap and docile African labour, the mining corporations achieved a remarkable mining revolution in the early part of the century that ushered in an industrial take-off in the 1930s and 1940s. During the 40 years from 1934 until 1974 an annual growth rate of 4,5 per cent was maintained, marked by a large inflow of foreign investment. However, African labour remained unfree, docile, and cheap. During the 20 years from 1974 until 1994 South Africa experienced stagflation, an outflow of foreign capital, and creeping poverty.

In sharp contrast with its growth record, the redistributive record of the South African economy during this period was unimpressive. The per capita income of all four main ethnic groups increased gradually until 1974. The only reason for this was that large-scale structural unemployment had not yet manifested itself. However, the per capita income of whites increased at a higher rate than those of black population groups, and the distribution of income between whites and blacks was more unequal in 1974 than ever before (see table 10.8). Two important distributional shifts occurred during this century, but both were brought about by political power shifts and political interventions (statism) rather than any 'trickle-down' effect of market-driven economic growth.

The first took place from 1934 to 1974, in favour of Afrikaners. This was a period of high growth, but Afrikaners would not have been enriched to the same extent if important political power shifts in their favour had not occurred. The higher growth rate benefited Afrikaner workers from the early 1930s onwards because they had protected jobs and good educational opportunities. Also, during World War 2, many Afrikaners enlisted as soldiers or were employed on lucrative terms in the industrial sector. It was, however, the NP government's pro-Afrikaner employment and spending policies and its favouritism towards Afrikaner entrepreneurs and farmers that were mainly responsible for the spectacular (and perhaps too rapid) embourgeoisement of the Afrikaners in the third quarter of the century. While, in 1948, the per capita income of Afrikaners was less that 50 per cent of that of English-speakers, it increased to 70 per cent of the (then much higher) per capita income of English-speakers in 1974. Yet, during the 40 years from 1934 to 1974, colonial and racial capitalism continued to marginalise most people other than white. While, in 1946, the per capita income of whites was 11,5 times higher than that of Africans, it was 14,6 times higher in 1975 (see table 10.8).

A second distributive shift – with both positive and negative effects – took place between 1974 and 1994. Again, political power shifts were largely responsible for both sets of effects. During this period the average annual economic growth rate was less than 2 per cent, the per capita income of the total population declined by 15 per cent, and unemployment increased from 20 per cent to 36 per cent (see table 10.1). The low growth rate and growing unemployment impoverished all those vulnerable subgroups (in all population groups) that were not powerful or organised enough to buffer themselves against the effects of creeping poverty and unemployment. These groups were mainly the poorest 60 per cent of Africans, whose income declined by almost 40 per cent from 1974 to 1994; and the poorest (and relatively unorganised) 60 per cent of whites (mainly Afrikaners), whose income declined (albeit from a much higher level) by ±35 per cent, because the NP government could not maintain – given the declining economy, and the changing political atmosphere – its favouritism towards and financial support of Afrikaners (see table 10.4).

In a situation of stagflation and creeping poverty, a positive distributive effect was brought about by the shift in extra-parliamentary power from white towards black elites from the early 1970s to 1994. The unofficial strikes by African workers in the early 1970s and the intensification of the liberation struggle from 1976 onwards enhanced the bargaining power of black elite groups considerably. The reform measures implemented by the NP government in the late 1970s and 1980s were desperate attempts to ameliorate the mounting legitimacy crisis surrounding the apartheid regime. These measures shifted extra-parliamentary power towards black elites, and increased the income of most Asians and coloureds and the top 20 per cent of Africans. From 1974 to 1994 the income of Asians increased by 30 per cent, the income of the top 80 per cent of coloured households by 20 per cent, and the income of the top 20 per cent of African households by more than 40 per cent (see table 10.4). The net effect of the negative and positive distributive shifts was to considerably widen the gap between the top 20 per cent and poorest 60 per cent of the black population. This last group remained propertyless, relatively uneducated, mostly disenfranchised, and without access to informal bargaining power. Many more Africans became unemployed, and were therefore less likely to benefit from economic growth.

The decisive role played by political power shifts and political interventions in these two distributive shifts proves that the claim of the corporate sector and the free marketeers that growth generated by the free market will automatically 'trickle down' to the poor is, in South Africa's case, nothing but ideological deception and a carefully propagated myth. The deeply institutionalised inequalities in the distribution of power, property, and opportunities between whites and the majority of blacks, and the high level of structural unemployment among Africans in particular, create institutional and socio-economic conditions under which it is simply not possible for a higher economic growth rate to have a spontaneously beneficial distributive effect in favour of those socio-economic classes that have been marginalised. The deeply institutionalised inequalities between an elite of 33 per cent and a lower class of 67 per cent have been perpetuated in the 'new South Africa'. Consequently, it is highly unlikely that a high economic growth rate alone – ie, without aggressive government intervention – will have any beneficial redistributive effect in favour of the poorer half of the population. The upper lower class (the 17 per cent between the top 33 per cent and poorer 50 per cent) might experience a 'trickle-down' effect in a situation of sustainable growth, but this is anything but certain (see figure 2.1).

Despite all this, the corporate sector took the neo-liberal dogma about the alleged merits of the liberal-capitalist economic system and the beneficial employment and redistributive effects that would result from a high economic growth rate after the political transformation to the informal negotiations, and propagated it vigorously. The distance between corporate myth and South African reality could hardly have been greater. At these negotiations, leaders of the corporate sector subjected ANC leaders to a propaganda onslaught with only one purpose in mind: to entrench and promote its vested interests, irrespective of the general interests of South African society at large.

3.2 The corporate sector, white supremacy, and the three accumulation strategies of the 20th century

After the mineral revolution at the end of the 19th century, close symbiotic relationships were forged between the corporate sector and successive white supremacist governments. Those relationships were maintained for a century, from ±1890 to ±1990. They were perhaps at their closest in the 1980s and early 1990s, when the apartheid regime experienced a serious legitimacy crisis, and the corporate sector its most serious accumulation crisis. During the preceding 100 years several mutually beneficial partnerships had come into being between the white business establishment and successive white political and bureaucratic establishments. Although these co-operative and mutually supportive relationships were often strained, the two establishments mostly worked hand in glove to protect and promote their mutual interest in the maintenance of the racist political and economic structures that secured power, privileges, and wealth for whites, and inevitably caused – as the other side of the same systemic coin – deprivation, repression, and poverty for the majority of blacks.

In 1997 almost all the representatives of the corporate sector who testified at the business hearings of the Truth and Reconciliation Commission (TRC) claimed that their corporations had not benefited from apartheid, because apartheid had raised the cost of doing business; they argued that business had really been a 'victim' and not a partner of, collaborator with, or beneficiary of the system (see TRC 1998: vol 4, ch 2, paras 7 and 8).[11] This claim is simply not true – at least not for the first three quarters of the 20th century. The corporate sector based its arguments mainly on what had happened from 1960 to 1994 – and in some cases only from 1974 to 1994 – and concentrated only on the cost-increasing effect of discriminatory labour patterns, while ignoring almost completely the more important repressive labour patterns and their cost-decreasing effect (see section 4.6 on the TRC's inability or unwillingness to uncover the 'truth' about systemic exploitation).

The corporate sector's mindset in 1997 – when it gave evidence before the TRC – was clearly one of a state of denial about its century-long symbiotic relationships with successive white supremacist governments. It was especially in denial about its partnership role in constructing and perpetuating the system of racial capitalism as well as repressive labour measures introduced to satisfy its almost insatiable demand for cheap and docile African labour. The denial was perhaps understandable in the light of the new relationship forged in the early 1990s with the democratic movement, but was – and remains – factually indefensible (see section 4.2). As we indicate in chapters 8 and 9, repressive labour patterns were designed – and periodically redesigned – in close collaboration with the corporate sector and successive white supremacist governments.

At the end of the 19th century and during the first half of the 20th century, it was mainly the gold mining companies – and more specifically the Chamber of Mines (CM) – that pressurised the colonial government and the South African Party (SAP) and United Party (UP) governments into implementing segregationist measures aimed at increasing the supply of and control over cheap migrant labour for the mining industry. The *Mail & Guardian* recently described the track record of the mining industry in the following damning terms:

For many, many years the mining industry operated in South Africa almost as a law unto itself. It has milked untold riches from the country at the expense of the impoverished majority, been allowed [by successive white supremacy governments] to conduct iniquitous labour practices, and been given free reign to hoard mineral rights (9–15 March 2001).

In their submissions to and testimonies before the TRC, neither the CM nor the Anglo American Corporation (AAC) was prepared to even acknowledge that African mine workers had been exploited and degraded.[12] This deliberate disinclination to acknowledge their role in constructing racial capitalism and exploiting African workers is deplorable. The TRC was justifiably rather critical of both these organisations in its 1998 report, and referred to the CM's 'significant formative impact on the apartheid political economy'. According to the TRC, 'the shameful history of sub-human compound conditions, brutal suppression of striking workers, racist practices and meagre wages [in the gold-mining industry] is central to understanding the origins and nature of apartheid'. It came to the damning conclusion that 'the failure of the Chamber of Mines to address [its apartheid record] squarely and to grapple with its moral implications is regrettable and not constructive' (TRC 1998: vol 4, 33–4).

The TRC was equally critical of the submission by the AAC, which did not say a single word about the extraordinarily low wages paid to African migrant workers until 1972. The TRC described the AAC's submission as 'flawed' and 'misleading', and noted that 'its most glaring failure was to sidestep the African wage issue' (TRC 1998: vol 4, 34). The submissions of the CM and AAC are prime examples of how prominent private sector institutions twist the truth in order to create an image of themselves which is more acceptable than the ugly reality of systemic exploitation.

On several occasions, the corporate sector used its symbiotic relationship with white supremacist governments to convince the latter to implement accumulation strategies that would enhance the former's profitability. We can distinguish among three broad accumulation strategies from the beginning of the 20th century, each implemented by the government of the day at the insistence of at least part of the corporate sector. The first or *segregationist* accumulation strategy, in place during the first half of the century, was implemented at the insistence of the colonial or foreign-owned mining corporations; it was aimed at solving their labour problems, and creating the political stability necessary to attract foreign capital (see section 3.1). The second or *Verwoerdian* accumulation strategy was in place during the heyday of apartheid (1952–74), and was originally implemented at the insistence of white (mainly Afrikaner) corporations (see section 3.2).

The third accumulation strategy was formulated and implemented by the corporate sector and the NP government in three phases from 1978 until 1993, in almost desperate attempts to find a formula for resolving the serious accumulation crisis that had developed from the early 1970s onwards. This crisis deepened as the liberation struggle intensified and attempts of the apartheid regime to suppress it became more relentless. We can also distinguish among three further phases in the search for a third accumulation strategy agreed upon by the democratic movement, the ANC government, and the corporate sector from 1993 until 2002. These attempts also did not succeed in placing South Africa's economy on a high growth path (see section 4.2–4.5).

In all six phases of the search for a third accumulation strategy, the corporate sector persuaded the government of the day to adopt policies that would best serve its interests, with the AAC and associated business organisations such as the Urban Foundation (UF), the Free Market Foundation (FMF), the Centre for Development and Enterprise (CDE), and the South Africa Foundation (SAF) playing particularly prominent prescriptive roles. We can therefore call the third accumulation strategy – implemented in six instalments from 1978 – the *AAC accumulation strategy*.

To demonstrate the strategic role played by the corporate sector in formulating and implementing the three successive main accumulation strategies since the early 20th century, it is necessary to give a short overview of all three.

3.2.1 The segregationist accumulation strategy (1907–48)

In the first 25 years after the discovery of gold, the mining corporations experienced a chronic accumulation crisis because the CM could not recruit enough cheap African labourers to work in the mines. An important reason for the Anglo–Boer War was that the British colonial government wanted to create infrastructural and labour conditions in the Transvaal that would be more conducive to the profitable production of gold. After the war the mining corporations informed the government that Africans could only be coerced into a wage-earning proletariat with the co-operation of the Afrikaner elite. Consequently, from 1907 onwards a remarkable *rapprochement* took place between the British and Afrikaner elite in the Transvaal. An 'alliance of gold and maize' was forged between the mining companies and the Afrikaner elite when, during the mine workers' strike of 1907, General Jan Smuts demonstrated that he clearly understood the accumulation needs of the gold mining corporations. This alliance provided the basis for unifying the four British colonies in 1910. Shortly afterwards – in 1913 – the Land Act was enacted with the deliberate aim of destroying the economic independence of a large part of the African population, and coercing them into becoming a compliant and cheap labour force on the mines and maize farms.

The segregationist accumulation strategy formulated by the 'alliance between gold and maize' was based on three pillars: firstly, the exploitation of a cheap and easily controllable African workforce with a large part of its subsistence in the 'native reserves'; secondly, the export of primary products; and, thirdly, the creation of socio-political stability in South Africa. It was, however, not easy to establish such stability. The political order created in 1910 was rather fragile; it was based on a compromise between an English-speaking and an Afrikaner elite that excluded poorer whites from active participation in policy-making. Blacks were excluded to an even greater degree. During its first 12 years the legitimacy of the new state was challenged by two serious armed rebellions (1914 and 1922), and several violently contested strikes by white and black workers. The enactment in 1924 by the Smuts government of the Industrial Conciliation Act, and the Pact victory in the same year, created a consensual order on behalf of all whites, but to the detriment of Africans (see O'Meara 1996: 471).[13] When the price of gold was increased in 1932, and a coalition formed between Hertzog and Smuts in 1933, the legitimacy of the state was finally consolidated, and very lucrative conditions for accumulation created for the mining industry.

In the early 1930s the gold mining corporations realised that gold ore reserves might become depleted. As a result, they began to diversify into other sectors of the economy, especially industy. When World War 2 created conditions conducive for an industrial take-off, the English-oriented corporate sector pressurised the Smuts government into relaxing influx control and other discriminatory measures, thus enabling manufacturing industries to employ increasing numbers of Africans in semi-skilled jobs in urban areas (see sections 8.3 and 8.6).

Immediately after World War 2 the UP government was confronted with a complex of social, political, and economic problems that could not be solved within the parameters of the 'alliance of gold and maize'. A serious accumulation crisis was threatening, as the government was incapable of restoring a favourable investment climate. The maize farmers – traditionally an important UP constituency – were in an economic predicament not only because many African workers had migrated to squatter settlements in urban areas, but also because the price of maize was too low to make farming profitable.

The new African arrivals in the urban areas could not be controlled as easily as migrant workers in mining compounds. A new cycle of resistance in the shanty towns, a growth in black trade union organisation, a growing militancy in the ranks of the ANC, and unofficial strikes all threatened the stability of the state and the profitability of the still vulnerable industrial sector. In 1948 the NP unexpectedly won a general election by exploiting the economic uncertainties of Afrikaner workers and farmers, and the fears of white voters (especially poorer Afrikaners) that they might be swamped (*oorstroom*) by African urbanisation (see section 9.2).

3.2.2 The Verwoerdian accumulation strategy (1952–86)

One of the first tasks of the NP government was to formulate a new accumulation strategy. Against all expectations, it was remarkably sensitive towards the interests of the mining industry and, to a lesser extent, the interests of the English-oriented industrial sector. The new government was put under pressure by the AHI and the Afrikaner farming community to create conditions favourable for their economic advancement. The NP resolved the crisis of a segregationist accumulation strategy by replacing the policy of segregation with the far more comprehensive and oppressive policy of apartheid. From a white entrepreneurial point of view, apartheid was – perhaps owing to its harsh and uncompromising character – successful in breaking the cycle of black resistance and in creating power relations that enabled whites to perpetuate black (and especially African) exploitation for another quarter of a century.

The immediate purpose of the apartheid policy was to gain control over all Africans outside the 'native reserves', and to suppress black resistance in urban shanty towns, trade unions, and the increasingly militant ANC. These aims were accomplished when, in 1952, Verwoerd introduced his stricter influx control and urbanisation laws. In doing so, he institutionalised a system that supplied cheap African migrant workers to industries in urban areas. At that stage, conditions in the 'native reserves' were appalling, forcing millions of Africans to look for work in urban areas. The new control mechanisms forced them to be not only docile and subservient, but also prepared to work for very low wages. In this way Verwoerd reinvented the principle of migrant labour, coupled with the notion of 'subsistence' in the native reserves, not only for employment in the mining industry but also in manufacturing. This was the one cornerstone of the Verwoerdian accumulation strategy. The other was a policy of industrialisation based on import substitution.[14]

This strategy was – from the white corporate point of view – remarkably successful. An annual economic growth rate of almost 5 per cent was maintained in the third quarter of the century. The relationship between the English-controlled corporate sector and the NP government was initially strained; the former was not in favour of the new government's overtly statist policies, its additional discriminatory measures, and its favouritism towards Afrikaners and public corporations. But as it began to benefit handsomely from the new accumulation strategy, its hostility towards the apartheid regime was replaced by an increasingly co-operative and supportive attitude.

The post-war accumulation strategy – and especially the availability of cheap and docile African labour – also created lucrative investment opportunities for foreign corporations. The large inflow of foreign investment and foreign entrepreneurship contributed substantially to the high economic growth rate, but also made the South African economy dependent on the world economy, and vulnerable to external shocks. Ironically, it was this vulnerability that the liberation movement exploited so successfully from the middle 1970s onwards via its disinvestment strategy.

Despite its economic success, the Verwoerdian accumulation strategy was incomplete (and therefore vulnerable) as long as it could not supply a credible answer to the national question – how the black population should be accommodated politically. In a desperate attempt to do so, Verwoerd announced, in 1959, his Bantustan policy. According to this policy all Africans (comprising 70 per cent of the population) were to express their political rights in the 'native reserves' (comprising 13 per cent of South Africa's territory), while forfeiting any civil rights and welfare privileges in 'white' South Africa. Although the NP government spent billions of rands on making this policy viable, it became, in due course, the Achilles heel of the Verwoerdian accumulation strategy.

After 20 years of remarkable success from the point of view of the white-controlled corporate sector, this strategy collapsed in the mid-1970s. The ensuing accumulation crisis has remained largely unresolved to this day. It was triggered in 1973 when the Organisation of the Petroleum Exporting Countries (OPEC) increased the price of oil, leading to a worldwide economic recession, and plunging South Africa's economy into almost three decades of stagflation (see section 10.2.1). An important reason for the prolonged stagflation was the liberation struggle, and the apartheid government's determined efforts to suppress it. The economic crisis therefore became inextricably linked to the political crisis, ie, the inability of the NP government to find a credible solution to black disenfranchisement.

As the accumulation and legitimacy crises deepened during the 'low-level war' between the liberation movements and the apartheid regime, stagflation and rising unemployment created an additional crisis also inextricably linked to the others: a social crisis of rising unemployment, and the further pauperisation of at least the poorest 60 per cent of the black population. This social crisis gradually deteriorated into one in which a large part of the black population was at risk of sinking into destitution and abject and dehumanising poverty.

The accumulation, legitimacy, and social (or poverty) crises that began to unravel during the last quarter of the 20th century were so interlinked that they became organic – ie, they could only be resolved if the economic, political, and social dimensions were addressed simultaneously (see Marais 2001: ch 2; Saul and Gelb 1981: ch 1).

3.2.3 The AAC-led accumulation strategy (1978–)

We can distinguish among six phases in the search for a new accumulation strategy from 1978 onwards. In each of these the AAC and associated business organisations such as the UF, FMF, CDE, and SAF played a leading role on behalf of the entire corporate sector, but mainly on behalf of the larger corporations planning to benefit from globalisation. The six phases of the AAC-led search for an accumulation strategy are briefly described below.

i   The first phase, from 1978 to 1985, coincided with the first period of P W Botha's government and was marked by the investigations of the Wiehahn and Riekert commissions into labour laws and influx control respectively, followed by some government reforms, and the Carlton and Good Hope conferences involving government and business leaders.

ii The second phase, from 1985 to 1989, coincided with the second period of Botha's government (or the 'Heunis reform' phase), marked by the abolition of influx control and the implementation of the policy of 'positive urbanisation'.

iii The third phase, from 1989 to 1993, coincided with F W de Klerk's government and included the agreement on a transitional democratic constitution, the publication of several economic scenarios by private sector think-tanks, and the agreement among the NP government, the corporate sector, and the IMF on the Normative Economic Model (NEM).

iv The fourth phase coincided with the formal political negotiations and was marked by the agreement on the transitional constitution and especially the informal or unofficial negotiations between representatives of the corporate sector and representatives of the democratic movement on economic matters that led to the first elite compromise of November 1993.

v   The fifth phase, from 1994 to 1996, coincided with the two years of the government of national unity (GNU) and was marked by formal negotiations among the GNU, the corporate sector, and representatives of global capitalism that led to the second elite compromise (the Growth, Employment, and Redistribution [GEAR] strategy).

vi The sixth phase, from 1997 to 2002, was marked by the introduction of the government's privatisation policy, the further relaxation of exchange controls, and the permission given – under severe pressure – to some of the mega-corporations to move their listings offshore, mostly to the United Kingdom. The first three of these phases resulted from close interaction between the NP government and the corporate sector, while the last three resulted from close interaction between the democratic movement, the GNU, and the ANC government on the one hand, and the corporate sector on the other (see sections 4.2, 4.4, and 4.5). As the search for a new accumulation strategy continued, emerging black-controlled corporations, with close links with the new government, played an increasingly important role. Remarkably, a *direct* resolution of the social crisis of the continuing pauperisation of the poorest 50 per cent of the population was not proposed during any of the six phases; during each of them an explicit or tacit consensus was reached between the negotiation partners to the effect that it was not necessary and also not advisable to search for a *direct* resolution of the crisis, and that the best way of resolving it (ie, the way that best suited the corporate sector) was to address it *indirectly* through sustained economic growth. The implication of this consensus was that as long as the accumulation crisis remained unresolved, the social crisis would not only remain unresolved as well, but could deteriorate into a far more serious one.

During the third phase, agreement was reached on a strategy for resolving the legitimacy or political crisis, which was successfully implemented from 1994 onwards. While, in the early 1990s, South Africa was confronted with a threefold organic crisis – ie, an accumulation, legitimacy, and social crisis – it finds itself, ten years later, in the predicament that the legitimacy crisis has been resolved, but the other two have not, and that the social crisis has become far more serious.

3.2.3.1 The first phase: the first period of P W Botha's government (1978–85)

When, in the early 1970s, the accumulation and legitimacy crises started to unfold, the government of B J Vorster was unable to address them. Vorster was not even prepared to interact with the corporate sector. In July 1997 this prompted the *Financial Mail* to call on business people to mobilise the full force of what it called 'business power' to enforce the changes it regarded as necessary for restoring corporations' short-term profitability. This was the beginning of an extraordinary politicisation of the business sector. When, in 1978, P W Botha became prime minister, a close partnership was established between the government and its securocrats and the corporate sector. This partnership was jointly responsible for Botha's reform initiatives and for putting the 'total strategy' – intended to counteract the 'total onslaught' – in place. In the 'compact of power' forged between the Botha government and the corporate sector, the ideological differences between the NP and Afrikaner-controlled corporations on the one hand and the English-controlled corporate sector on the other were removed and a broad-based agreement reached on the merits of a 'free market' approach. This was aggressively propagated by the UF and FMF, despite its inapplicability to the institutional and social conditions in South Africa after a century of colonial and racial capitalism (see section 3.1.3).

The new working relationship between the Botha government and the corporate sector was sealed at the Carlton and Good Hope conferences in 1979 and 1981. At those conferences the corporate sector was given an insti-tutionalised role, within the reorganised state sector, of formulating and implementing 'free market' economic policies. Ever since this politicisation took place, the corporate sector has regarded an active role in political decision-making as its birthright – despite the fact that this political 'usurpation' cannot be reconciled with South Africa's democratisation. Although the business sector should be commended for ending the log-jam on reform at the end of the Vorster period, its involvement in policy-making became institutionalised to an unhealthy degree. The growing involvement of the corporate sector in formulating and implementing economic policy can be described as the unfortunate 'Anglo-Americanisation' of South African society.

Whenever a corporate sector becomes too closely and too prescriptively involved in formulating economic policy, there are always four dangers that need to be kept in mind. The first is that the corporate sector will only provide advice that will advance its own interests. The second is that the corporate sector – with its often myopic vision – could be inclined to twist the trade-offs involved in favour of its own short-term profitability, to the detriment of the long-term interests of all the other interest groups in society. The third is that the corporate sector cannot be held responsible by an electorate for erroneous policy advice, while the government of the day has no option – in a well-functioning democratic system – but to take responsibility for that advice. Fourthly, in many countries – including South Africa – the media are controlled by the corporate sector, and as a result tend to portray the latter's activities in a more sympathetic light than those of the political sector.

All four of these dangers materialised quite visibly during the first phases of the search for a new accumulation strategy, but were ignored as a result of the corporate sector's persuasive power. As the search for a new accumulation strategy moved through successive phases, the dangers of the corporate sector's overly prescriptive involvement in policy formulation became more apparent, but were consistently ignored because the sector had become permanently institutionalised as a partner in policy formulation and had succeeded in convincing people of the alleged virtues of its own ideological approach. Consequently, it became increasingly politically incorrect to question its involvement in policy formulation. Under these circumstances the corporate sector not only became increasingly self-righteous, but also claimed to be morally exalted. This attitude is, however, unwarranted when judged from the perspective of the interests of society at large.

At the end of the 1970s the new partners in reform – ie the new, mainly white, 'compact of power' – decided that the NP government's labour and urbanisation policies needed to be reformed. The UF was established in 1977, at the initiative of the AAC, to improve the living conditions of urban Africans and to convince them of the alleged merits of free market capitalism. The UF played an important role in the appointment of the Wiehahn and Riekert commissions, and contributed strategically towards the ideological approach of both. The recommendations of the Wiehahn commission that all discriminatory measures in the labour market be abolished accorded not only with the corporate sector's decades-long campaign against these measures, but also with the code of employment practices published by the UF in 1977.[15] Its recommendation that Africans should be given the right to join registered trade unions – despite the fact that no political accommodation was in sight – was also made under strong pressure from the corporate sector.

The recommendations of the Riekert commission that Africans with residential rights in urban areas should be granted unrestricted freedom to move and work in any 'white' urban area, and their 'quality of life' improved by means of property rights, better housing, and higher wages, were also in line with the ideological approach of the UF and FMF. The cornerstone of the commission's approach was that a sharp distinction should be drawn between African 'insiders' in urban areas and 'outsiders' who would be firmly barricaded in the Bantustans, with increased penalties for illegal migrants and their employers. It was also in line with the UF approach that the government should concentrate on improving the living and working conditions of Africans in urban areas, rather than those of 'outsiders' in the Bantustans. The distinction between 'insiders' and 'outsiders' was based on the erroneous assumption that the South African economy was still dualistic in nature, and that the modern sector could be revitalised by granting economic freedoms and rights to 'insiders' only. It was rather hypocritical of the free market-oriented UF to plead for greater freedoms for urbanised Africans while supporting greater restrictions on the movement of 'outsiders' (see sections 9.5.3 and 9.5.4).

The first phase of the AAC-led search for a new accumulation strategy failed because it focused on the accumulation crisis in isolation, without even acknowledging that this crisis was inextricably linked to the legitimacy and social crises. In line with the AAC proposals, urbanised Africans were supposed to continue exercising their political rights in the Bantustans. After the introduction in 1984 of the tricameral parliament, the issue of the political rights of African 'insiders' became much more pressing. At the same time, the neglect of the social crisis and the continuing pauperisation of African 'outsiders' was a serious shortcoming of the attempt to formulate a new accumulation strategy.[16]

3.2.3.2 The second phase: the second period of P W Botha's government (1986–9)

Faced with an even more serious accumulation crisis by the mid-1980s, the UF again took the initiative: it launched a well-directed campaign to abolish influx control, hoping that a larger influx of Africans into the urban areas would decrease the pressure from unionised African workers for higher wages. It described its new accumulation strategy as 'positive urbanisation'. Rather than using legal measures to differentiate between 'insiders' and 'outsiders', it proposed that class differentiation among Africans should be left to market forces: those who could afford to live in the new middle-class suburbs should be allowed to do so, while those who could not (mainly the unemployed) should be accommodated in squatter settlements on the peripheries of the cities. The UF recommended new legislation and other forms of social engineering to control those living in squatter settlements. In 1986 its proposals were accepted by Chris Heunis in his capacity as minister of constitutional development and planning (see Morris, in Gelb 1991: 50–5).

The acceptance of the UF proposals for 'positive urbanisation' and the abolition of influx control represent one of the most decisive turning points in the NP government's economic policies in respect of Africans. When influx control was abolished, the final nail was hammered into the coffin of the Verwoerdian accumulation strategy of 1952 and the Stallardist urbanisation strategy of 1923. The new policy also ended the NP government's policy of 'class compression' by using the legal ceiling of apartheid to prevent class differentiation among Africans. For generations, white-controlled governments had used racist legislation as the basis for inclusion and exclusion. When the policy of 'positive urbanisation' was implemented, market forces were accepted as the alleged automotive, non-racist, and non-ideological basis for differentiating between those classes that could buy their way into privilege and those that were not productive and industrious enough – or not employed to the necessary degree. For almost a century it had been accepted that welfare services for migrant workers were provided in the Bantustans. When the policy of 'positive urbanisation' was accepted, it was decided that welfare services for Africans – for example, medical services – should be privatised: those who could pay would have access to privatised services, while those who could not would only have downgraded public services in squatter settlements at their disposal (see Morris 1993: 8).

At the end of the 1980s the corporate sector also succeeded in convincing the NP government to accept the policy of privatisation. Until then public corporations had formed an integral part of the NP's economic policies, and were regarded as an essential 'countervailing power' against the powerful, mainly English-controlled, private corporations. During the 1970s public sector investment, especially in ESKOM, ISCOR, SASOL, and ARMSCOR, was the driving force behind the economy, and was responsible for two thirds of gross investment. The economic stagnation in the 1980s was partly a consequence of the decline in public sector investment. In 1987 the NP government published a white paper in which it declared its preparedness to sell some public assets 'if it is convinced that this will be in the long-term interest of the Republic's inhabitants'.

According to Ben Fine, the NP government's *volte-face* on public corporations must be understood against the background of its closer symbiotic relationship with the English-controlled corporate sector, and the government's serious external debt crisis after P W Botha's disastrous 'Rubicon' speech in August 1985. The arguments that privatisation would enhance efficiency and stimulate accumulation in the private sector were, according to Fine, not applicable at the time, because it was the lack of government creditworthiness, in terms of its ability to raise loans, that provided the primary motive for privatisation.[17] In the last phase of the apartheid regime the NP government concentrated on commercialising a number of parastatals, including ESKOM, and corporatising others, including TELKOM (see Rix and Jardine, in Baskin 1996a: ch 4). The NP government's partial privatisation of public corporations in the late 1980s and early 1990s did not succeed in revitalising the economy.[18]

The second phase of the search for a new accumulation struggle also failed. In the latter part of the 1980s township unrest escalated, and the security forces failed to control the internal wing of the liberation movement. The new strategy failed not only because it ignored both the legitimacy and social crises, but also because it 'displaced' the social crisis spatially from rural to urban areas, augmenting it considerably in the process. Although the abolition of influx control was long overdue, it was a huge mistake to expose newly urbanised Africans in squatter settlements to 'free marketeerism' without supplying basic welfare services. When 'free marketeerism' was superimposed on the ash-heap of apartheid – ie, on structural unemployment, poverty, and an inclination towards violent crime among poor blacks – powerful socio-economic forces were unleashed that have been restructuring the basis of inclusion and exclusion ever since (see Morris 1993: 8). Those black people who had been reduced to an impoverished and vulnerable proletariat by the cruel system of apartheid were now exposed to the relentless tyranny of 'free market' forces.

When, in 1984, the tricameral parliament was introduced, coloureds and Indians were included politically and economically in the 'white' order in a somewhat awkward way. When, in 1986, influx control was abolished, about 20 per cent of Africans were economically included, and many of the rest formally acknowledged as South Africans, but were still very much *excluded* by the workings of the 'free market' economy. While, for decades, migrant workers had been shunted around by the *apparatchiks* of the Bantu administration boards, large numbers of black people were now swept into squatter settlements by the chill winds of 'free marketeerism'. These victims of apartheid were not fit – psychologically, educationally, or physically – to play the 'free market' game. They were also not equipped with even the minimum of resources and opportunities needed to make progress in a 'free market' environment. Consequently, the quality of their lives deteriorated further in the disrupted socio-economic conditions in the urban squatter settlements. While almost 16 years have elapsed since the abolition of influx control, those living in the erstwhile Bantustans and in squatter settlements are – with few exceptions – still not equipped to play the 'free market' game.

The new 'system' that was institutionalised at the insistence of the AAC and the rest of the corporate sector at the end of the 1980s is still in place. A full 16 years after influx control has been abolished, the powerful socio-economic forces that have been restructuring the basis of inclusion and exclusion have trapped the poorest 60 per cent of the black population in systemic exclusion without the necessary employment and the necessary minimum of welfare services, while the same forces have promoted the top 20 per cent of the black population to the status of a prosperous bourgeoisie (see table 2.1).

3.2.3.3 The third phase: the F W de Klerk presidency, and the agreement on the Normative Economic Model (NEM, 1989–94)

At the end of the 1980s the corporate sector realised that it would not be possible to formulate a workable accumulation strategy as long as the legitimacy crisis remained unresolved. In August 1988 the Consultative Business Movement (CBM) was launched with the express purpose of challenging South African business people to 'define the real nature of their own power, and to identify how they can best use this not inconsequential power to advance the society towards non-racial democracy' (Christo Nel, chairman of CBM, as quoted in O'Meara 1996: 387). Also in August 1988 Dr Zach de Beer (a former executive director of the AAC) replaced Colin Eglin as leader of the Progressive Federal Party (PFP), and immediately announced his determination to seek unity with the mainly Afrikaans-oriented Independent Movement, or IM (*The Star*, 7 August 1988). The Democratic Party (DP), launched in April 1989 – with considerable financial support from the AAC – consisted of the PFP, the IM, and other (mainly Afrikaner) reform-oriented groups. At its first executive meeting it decided to campaign in the election of September 1989 for a majoritarian democracy.[19]

During that election the NP conducted a rather questionable election campaign against the DP, and condemned its 'one person, one vote' proposals in the strongest possible terms. After the election, De Klerk accepted – under relentless pressure of the British prime minister, Margaret Thatcher, and the local corporate sector – many of the proposals of the DP in his speech of 2 February 1990 in which he announced the unbanning of the liberation organisations and the release of Nelson Mandela, and committed the NP government to negotiating a constitution embodying the political accommodation of black people, while also reaffirming the economic strategy of privatisation, deregulation, and 'free marketeerism'.

Although the NP became convinced in 1990 that a fundamental restructuring of the political and ideological system had become a *sine qua non* for formulating a new accumulation strategy, it embarked on this path without a strategic master plan. While the NP was still unclear about the terms under which blacks should be politically incorporated, it was adamant about constraining 'the ANC's ability to wield political power in the service of a radical agenda of socio-economic transformation' (see Marais 2001: 71). Until September 1992 De Klerk regularly assured his white constituency that he would not sign a new constitution if it did not contain a 'statutory entrenched minority [read white] veto'. After several insurrections in 1992 threatened to derail the negotiation process, the NP accepted, on 26 September 1992, the so-called 'sunset' clauses in which agreement was reached on a 'one person, one vote' system and on a period of power-sharing for five years in a government of national unity (GNU).

The preparedness of the white bourgeois establishment to enter into negotiations with the liberation movement over a new political dispensation should be judged in historical perspective. By 1990 the business sector was extremely frustrated by the fact that all attempts to formulate a new accumulation strategy had been in vain. Although, 20 and even ten years earlier, it regarded the political accommodation of Africans as inconceivable, factions of this sector were prepared, at the end of the 1980s, to risk Africans' inclusion in the political system in a desperate attempt to resolve the accumulation crisis. The fall of the Berlin Wall in 1989, which made the communist peril less threatening, may have made both the political and business establishments more inclined to negotiate with the socialist-oriented liberation movement.[20] The corporate sector's new strategy of co-option was an extension of the AAC strategy during the first two phases of the search for a new accumulation strategy, when urbanised Africans were pampered in an attempt to convince them of the virtues of capitalism.

During the five years from 1990 to 1994 the corporate sector anxiously participated in various scenario-building exercises aimed at formulating an economic strategy that would be business-friendly and would perpetuate its position of power and privilege in a fully democratised South Africa. In September 1990 SACOB published its *Economic options for South Africa*, which defended the alleged benefits of a 'free market' economy. It claimed dogmatically that 'free enterprise systems – where [they] flourish – are the remedy for poverty and ensured economic growth'. It tried to distance itself from apartheid, and claimed that the economic crisis was not the result of the failure of the free enterprise system, but of the inhibiting effects of apartheid (see Kentridge 1993: 17). In defending this point of view, SACOB conveniently concealed the fact that the South African economic system had never been a free market system but one of racial capitalism that had thrived on repressive labour patterns and unequal power relations until the mid-1970s.

During the next few years, several business and research groups published scenarios dealing with economic systems for a democratised South Africa. The purpose of these exercises was to forge an overarching social contract among the NP government, big business, the ANC, labour, and organised community groups.[21] Patrick Bond summarises these exercises as follows:

> Increasingly the scenario exercises reflected the desire of the masters [of capital] and carefully hand-picked participants [mainly from the democratic movement] to come up with a deal – rather than with good analysis. As a result, the universal characteristic of scenario planning was a failure to

grapple with problems which are very hard to resolve. Instead, the cliché-ridden scenarios became increasingly stylised and niche-marketed (1999: 57).

A core element of all these scenarios was to emphasise the vulnerability of the South African economy after almost two decades of stagflation, and to spell out the grave dangers of macroeconomic populism if a new democratically elected government were to be pressurised by its impoverished constituency into increasing social spending and the rapid alleviation of poverty. Although all the scenarios mentioned the need for alleviating poverty and redistributing economic benefits, their main thrust was to emphasise the importance of economic growth as the only feasible way of addressing poverty via the alleged 'trickle-down' effect.

However, the possibility that the deeply institutionalised inequalities in the distribution of socio-economic power, property, and opportunities made it highly unlikely that even an annual growth rate of 5 per cent would have a meaningful 'trickle-down' effect was not even considered. Instead, the corporate sector went out of its way to warn the democratic movement of the grave dangers of a comprehensive redistribution or poverty alleviation programme. In 1992 the International Monetary Fund (IMF) stated that 'neither individual proposals nor the package as a whole should result in any additional taxation or any increase in government expenditure overall' (quoted in Bond 1999: 71). Mike Morris summarises this approach of the corporations as follows:

> There was an assumption that, once the constitutional issues were sorted out, the dozing South African 'economic giant' would lumber to its feet and cart off to the land of promise. In short, the crisis was seen as primarily political, not economic... Redistribution [was] viewed as a political accessory that can be tagged onto the measures aimed at restoring economic growth; it [was] not seen as being integrally connected to – in fact part and parcel of – long-term sustainable growth (1993: 8).

It should be acknowledged that, in the early 1990s, all the factions in the corporate sector did not agree on all policy issues. The entire sector agreed on the merits of a free market economy; the need to roll back the state, privatise, and restrict taxes; and the desirability of the neo-liberal approach. But different factions demanded different adjustments that best favoured them. The large financial and mining firms (including the AAC) were keen on wide-ranging liberalisation that would allow them to globalise via joint ventures with foreign corporations as well as offshore listings. Corporations active in the manufacturing sector were ambivalent: those confident of their competitive potential favoured liberalisation, while their more vulnerable counterparts were less enthusiastic. In the end it was mainly the larger corporations that succeeded in convincing not only the NP government but also ANC leaders of their point of view (see Marais 2001: 128).

The fear of the corporate sector that the (alleged) socialist-oriented ANC alliance would be inclined to increase government spending indiscreetly and be responsible for macroeconomic populism was – strangely enough – aggravated by the sharp increase in central government deficits during De Klerk's presidency. During his tenure the government deficit increased from less than 3 per cent to 9 per cent of GDP. According to the BER, the total government debt (at current prices) increased from R91,2 billion in 1990 to R237,3 billion in 1994, or from 31,5 per cent of GDP to 49,2 per cent of GDP. Allowing government debt to escalate at such an immoderate pace was rather irresponsible; it placed a heavy burden not only on the new government, but on future generations as well. By allowing the government's debt to escalate as sharply as it did, the De Klerk government was guilty of reckless white 'plundering' in the final years of white supremacy. However, in mitigation, we should acknowledge that part of the increase represented the consolidation of the debts of the Bantustan governments. Another reason for the escalation was increased social spending on black communities, financed by increased borrowing.

The fact that public debt escalated in this manner in the delicate and uncertain period before the dramatic political transition towards a majoritarian government had an enormous psychological effect; it created the undeniable impression that the De Klerk government's irresponsible fiscal policies were a prelude to the macroeconomic populism that could be expected from a democratically elected government. It not only frightened the corporate sector, but also strengthened its argument against the dangers of macroeconomic populism. When the corporate sector entered into informal negotiations with the democratic movement, it brought with it an exaggerated conception of its own vulnerability, and an overblown obsession with the dangers of macroeconomic populism. Given the corporate sector's extraordinary capacity for ideological propaganda and myth-making, it is indeed not surprising that it 'oversold' to the democratic movement its own (alleged) vulnerability, its aversion to taxation, and the dangers of increased government spending. In its eagerness to keep the spending of a democratically elected government as low as possible, the corporate sector deliberately underplayed the need for poverty alleviation programmes. The fact that it never demonstrated any sensitivity towards the structural interpretation of poverty – ie, that poverty was caused by factors beyond the control of the poor – made it expedient for the corporate sector to ignore the worsening plight of at least the poorest half of the population.

In the early 1990s both the World Bank and the IMF published documents stating what the economic policies in a democratised South Africa should be. Both propagated a neo-liberal approach, an export-driven growth strategy, and fiscal discipline. The World Bank was critical of the capital-intensive character of industry, but still believed that labour should bear the brunt of adaptations through the reduction of real wages. The IMF document was more in line with free market and neo-liberal dogma.

The Normative Economic Model (NEM) published in March 1993 by the NP government as its official economic framework for a democratic South Africa was heavily influenced by the IMF's neo-liberal dogma and by the ideological approach of the AAC and its associates. It accepted the IMF's argument that the 'growth through redistribution' approach (popular at the time in parts of the democratic movement) should be replaced by 'redistribution through growth'. According to the NEM the South African economy should be placed on a higher growth path through fiscal constraint, lower corporate taxes, higher indirect taxation, wage restraint, higher productivity, lower inflation, budget deficit cuts, trade liberalisation (that would entail improving the export competitiveness of industry and a phased reduction in tariffs), curtailing the unions' position in collective bargaining, and, finally, corporatist relations among government, business, and labour. The poverty problem should – according to the NEM – be resolved through higher growth and the alleged 'trickle-down' effect (see department of finance 1993).

The publication of the NEM, with the enthusiastic support of the DP and the corporate sector, was, according to Mike Morris, of decisive importance in the prolonged search for a new accumulation strategy, because it was the third attempt to solve the threefold organic crisis in a non-organic manner. According to Morris, the NEM proposed only a '50 per cent solution' – ie, a solution that excluded the poorest 50 per cent – and was therefore doomed to fail. The NEM's proposals accorded with the wishes of the AAC and the rest of the corporate sector, because this sector was adamant that a solution to the poverty problem should not entail sacrifices by it. The thrust of the NEM was to resolve the accumulation crisis through a threefold strategy: firstly, ac-commodating blacks population in a majoritarian democratic system; secondly, attaining a high economic growth rate within the framework of an unrestrained free market capitalist system, marked by minimum state intervention and a neo-liberal and export-oriented economic approach; and, thirdly, avoiding an aggressive redistribution policy because the benefits of high levels of economic growth would 'trickle down' to the poor, while the government could provide some support through welfare measures and public works projects to the 'short-term' victims of the adjustment process.

The then minister of finance, Derek Keys, described the NEM as 'classical supply-side with a human face' (*Business Day*, 3 March 1993). According to this strategy the interests of the poorest 50 per cent of the population would be accommodated 'politically' through franchise rights, and 'symbolically' through the alleged 'trickle-down' effect of the high levels of economic growth envisaged, while improving the material conditions of the poor was postponed to a later date. When, in 1993, the informal negotiations between the corporate sector and the democratic movement were in full swing, an astonishing agreement was forged between the white political and corporate establishments on the advisability of a '50 per cent solution' to South Africa's organic crisis (see Morris, in Gelb 1991: 57–8; Morris 1993: 8).

3.3   The economic views and ideologies of the democratic movement

The ANC's first statement on the economy is set out in the Freedom Charter of 1955:
- The People shall share in the country's wealth.
- The national wealth of our country, the heritage of all South Africans, shall be restored to the people.
- The mineral wealth beneath the soil, the banks, and monopoly industry shall be transferred to the ownership of the people as a whole.
- All other industries and trade shall be controlled to assist the well-being of the people.

Some of these clauses lent themselves to controversial interpretations. Because of the ANC's alliance with the SACP, and its close relations with the Soviet Union, they were interpreted as prescribing a programme of nationalisation, and even the introduction of full-blown socialism.

Until 1990 the ANC and other liberation organisations paid very little attention to what the economic system and economic policy in a democratised South Africa should be. Two possible reasons can be given for this neglect. Firstly, the ANC was first and foremost a liberation organisation whose main thrust was to overthrow white domination and take over the South African state. It maintained an instrumentalist conception of the state: as soon as political power was in its hands, it would use the state to solve the socio-economic problems of unemployment, poverty, and inequality. The slogan of Kwame Nkrumah – 'Seek ye first the political kingdom, and all else will follow' – resonated in ANC circles. Secondly, the ANC believed that South Africa was an exceptionally rich country, and that the economic deprivation of the black population could easily be rectified after liberation through a state-led process of redistribution and the redirection of economic resources and activities.

Yet it must be said that the ANC was mistaken – and even naïve – on both counts. State power in a modern country is highly constrained by a multitude of pressure groups – both internally and externally – which cannot be ignored by the ruling elite. As regards its economy, South Africa may, in the 1970s, have been the most developed country with the largest production capacity in Africa, but it was still a developing economy. By 1990 its productive capacity had been seriously harmed by the 'low-level war' between the liberation movement and the apartheid regime. According to Marais, the ANC's 'historical neglect of economic policy left it prone to the counsel of business and mainstream foreign experts that set about schooling ANC leaders in the "realities of the world"' (2001: 123).

From 1955 to 1990 the ANC published no new statement on economic policy issues except to reaffirm its commitment to the Freedom Charter in its 1988 constitutional guidelines (see Nattrass 1994b: 344–6). During this period the ANC's economic thinking was strongly influenced by intellectuals such as Joe Slovo, a leader in both the SACP and the ANC. In an article written in 1976 entitled 'South Africa – no middle road', he argued that the only road open to the oppressed in South Africa was a comprehensive left-wing revolutionary one – ie, an armed liberation struggle and a socialist (economic) revolution that should be regarded as inseparable from national (political) liberation. At the time, Slovo believed the reform of capitalism was impossible because South African capitalism was inseparable from apartheid. He therefore regarded liberation as inconceivable without the overthrow of racial capitalism. According to Laurence Harris, during the 1980s these ideas were generally accepted by the ANC, the United Democratic Front (UDF), and black consciousness organisations. Although these groups rejected being labelled as socialist, 'their ideology of national liberation was one in which socialist ideas were mixed with ideals of Christian justice, nationhood, historic irredentism, and liberal human rights' (1993: 92).

The unbanning of the liberation organisations and the beginning of negotiations in 1990 created an unforeseen problem for the South African left: it had prepared itself for a revolutionary take-over of both the state and the economy, and was therefore unprepared for an evolutionary reform process. In 1992 Slovo published an article entitled 'Negotiations: what room for compromise?' which represented a conscious shift towards reform, without an immediate prospect of socialism. Slovo now acknowledged that national liberation could be achieved in an evolutionary way, that 'power-sharing' with the apartheid regime might be necessary *en route* to full democracy, and that the socialist reconstruction of the economy had to be delayed for an unspecified period. He expressed great concern about the danger of the negotiation process being derailed by counter-revolutionary forces (see Harris 1993: 97–100). Slovo undoubtedly strongly influenced the 'strategic perspective' on negotiations adopted by the ANC in November 1992 (see section 4.2).

On 11 February 1990, the day of his release, Nelson Mandela made the following statement in a speech in Cape Town: 'The white monopoly of political power must be ended, and we need a fundamental restructuring of our political and economic systems to address the inequalities of apartheid and create a genuine democratic South Africa.' This was a remarkable statement. The emphasis was still on terminating the white monopoly of political power, and his statement also reflected a realisation that the inequalities of apartheid could only be addressed, and a genuine democratic South Africa created, if both the political and economic systems were fundamentally restructured. However, both Mandela and the ANC soon abandoned their commitment to a fundamental restructuring of the economic system.

Three days after his release, Mandela declared in Johannesburg that 'the nationalisation of the mines, banks, and monopoly industry is the policy of the ANC, and a change or modification of our views in this regard is inconceivable'. This statement caused a furore in financial markets. Early in 1992 Mandela became convinced – under severe internal and external pressure – that South Africa would not be able to attract foreign investment if investors felt the 'sword of Damocles of nationalisation hanging over their heads' (see Kentridge 1993: 5). In December 1991 an important shift in ANC policy became visible when Mandela, speaking in Pittsburgh in the United States, emphasised the role of the private sector.[22] In 1992 the ANC dropped nationalisation from its policy programmes. In both cases it was acknowledged that the cost of nationalisation would be too high, and that it would create unbearable inefficiencies (see Kentridge 1993: 4–6; P G Moll 1991).

In 1990 the ANC's new department of economic policy (DEP) published a discussion document on economic policy in which the need for 'restructuring' the economy was still emphasised. According to Marais, this document was largely based on work done by the Economic Trends Group of the Congress of South African Trade Unions (COSATU), which had until then been responsible for the most substantive efforts to formulate a sustainable and progressive economic strategy. The document envisaged an active role for the state in planning industrial strategy and overcoming racial, gender, and geographic inequalities. According to the document, basic needs would not be met through 'inflationary financing', but by marshalling domestic savings and raising corporate tax rates. It also called for the unbundling of conglomerates in order to stimulate competition. The overriding theme was 'growth through redistribution', a formula 'in which redistribution acts as a spur to growth, and in which the fruits of growth are redistributed to satisfy basic needs'. Although the document acknowledged the role of market forces, it stated that the market on its own would merely perpetuate inequalities, and that state intervention would be necessary to equalise opportunities (see Marais 2001: 124–6). At the time, the corporate sector fiercely criticised the ANC's 'growth through redistribution' proposal, and branded it as ridiculous. It claimed the proposal would discourage savings, and put a damper on economic growth. Interestingly enough, the United Nations claimed in 1996 that the conventional wisdom that unequal distribution was conducive to growth was not necessarily true, and that an increase in income inequality could constrain both economic growth and human development (see UNDP 1996: 13).

The ANC document of 1990 declared that essential reforms should preferably be carried out in collaboration with the business sector, but if this was not forthcoming, a future democratic government should not shrink from its clear duty. Thus, in the early 1990s the ANC's policy approach was still permeated by socialist thinking. As could be expected, mainstream economists and the business sector sharply criticised the ANC document. Critics warned that this approach would cause a spending spree that would overheat the economy and result in macroeconomic populism and runaway inflation.

In May 1992 an ANC policy conference adopted a reworked economic policy document, entitled *Ready to govern*. In this document the term 'growth through redistribution' was not used at all, and the envisaged role of the state was scaled down considerably.[23] The state was now seen as primarily a provider of infrastructure and welfare transfers, although it would still have the task of overseeing the direction of the economy. In the document the ANC committed itself to macroeconomic balance, and called for a representative fiscal commission to investigate changes in the fiscal regime. The ANC still committed itself to 'the basic objective . . . to overcome the legacy of inequality and injustice created by colonialism and apartheid, in a swift, progressive, and principled way'. It also stated at the time that the document did not represent a rigid blueprint, but that it was only a discussion document in an ongoing process. The presence of many top ANC leaders, including Mandela, Cyril Ramaphosa, and Walter Sisulu at the discussion of economic policy was instrumental in selling its changed approach to grass-roots activists.[24] This document contained only the first shift in the ANC's ideological orientation; even more fundamental shifts took place over the next year and a half (see section 4.2).

Despite signs that the ANC and the corporate sector were moving closer to each other, the ANC's suspicion of business was still reflected in its intention to introduce anti-trust legislation. *Ready to govern* declared:

> The concentration of economic power in the hands of a few conglomerates has been detrimental to balanced economic development. The ANC is not opposed to large firms as such. However, (it) will introduce anti-monopoly, anti-trust and merger policies... to curb monopolies' continued domination of the economy by a minority within the white minority and promote greater efficiency in the private sector (ANC 1992b: 13).

In 1991 the ANC set up the Macro-Economic Research Group (MERG) to train black economists, support COSATU on economic issues, and develop a new macroeconomic model for South Africa. (MERG later became the National Institute for Economic Policy, or NIEP.) MERG was the product of an intervention by a team of foreign (mainly Canadian) economists to assess the development of economic policy-making in the ANC. According to Kentridge, the group concluded that not only was the capacity of the democratic movement on economic issues vastly inferior to that of government and business, but often also unco-ordinated. Unfortunately, tensions developed between the DEP and MERG. The DEP suspected that its own functions were being usurped by MERG. Tensions also developed between the local and foreign members of MERG (see Kentridge 1993: 55–7). MERG presented its neo-Keynesian final report, *Making democracy work*, in late 1993, at a time when its proposals were, according to Marais, well out of line with current ANC thinking (see Marais 2001: 136–8). Consequently, the report died a quick death despite the acknowledgement by Nattrass that the recommendations were 'carefully cast and situated in what appears to be a sound macroeconomic model' (Nattrass 1994a: 2).[25]

In May 1991 COSATU convened a conference to address the state of the economy and formulate an economy policy parallel to that of the ANC. At the end of 1992 it published a document entitled *Economic policy in COSATU*, which emphasised the need to address unemployment and meet housing, health, and education needs. To achieve these objectives, COSATU favoured 'growth through redistribution' and argued that redistribution could not be restricted to a transfer of income only, but also required a transfer of power, resources, and opportunities. To attain the goals of redistribution and restructuring, COSATU placed a large responsibility on the state, but on certain preconditions: the state should act democratically and not in a dictatorial way, and the state's actions should always be complemented by strong action from the mass organisations. COSATU also pleaded for an inward industrialisation strategy to produce goods that could satisfy the basic needs of the poor. It was critical of the ANC's *Ready to govern*.[26]

COSATU also pleaded for the creation of a National Economic Forum (NEF) which could take decisions on key economic issues, and in which trade unions could play an influential role. Although the NEF was launched in October 1992, it was not a negotiating body (as COSATU wanted it to be), but only a consultative structure. The task of formulating a new industrial policy on behalf of COSATU was given to the Industrial Strategy Project (ISP) of the Economic Trends Group. This group's research was only published in September 1994, ie, after important policy decisions on economic issues had already been taken by the ANC.[27]

Endnotes

1 The interesting question arises whether it would have been possible to maintain the apartheid system for 46 years if the Cold War had not existed. There are strong arguments that this would not have been possible without the economic and military support of the major western powers – at least not until 1994.

2 This approach enjoyed considerable and explicit support in puritan circles in the United States in the 18th and 19th centuries. Those who attained wordly success were even regarded as the elect, while the losers were – as the other side of the same religious coin – regarded as sinners who deserved their poverty.

3 It was only when the aggressive version of Afrikaner Christian Nationalism emerged in the 1930s, and the vote of every Afrikaner became important for the Purified National Party, that the upliftment of poor whites became a high priority. As far as the relative wealthy English establishment was concerned, Afrikaner poverty was the result of a lack of intellectual capacity (due to excessive intermarriages), and a lack of moral fibre.

4 When whites who display an indifferent and contemptuous attitude towards black poverty are confronted with the question as to what would have happened to them if they had been without property and disenfranchised, and if the same meagre amounts were spent on their education as were spent on the education of Africans,

they normally reject the question as irrelevant and speculative. In the same white circles there is little appreciation of the predicament of millions of blacks who have became unemployed over the last 30 years owing to factors beyond their control.

5 In his influential book *The other America*, published in 1962, Michael Harrington claimed that white Americans were completely ignorant of the poor living conditions of Afro-Americans who lived in separate townships or squatter areas. As a result of apartheid and the Group Area Act, whites in South Africa are also exceptionally ignorant of the living conditions of blacks.

6 Business people – both white and black – are often inclined to defend their attitude towards the poor by quoting the following Chinese proverb: 'Give a man a fish and he'll eat for a day, but teach a man to fish and he'll eat for a lifetime.' Those quoting this proverb are obviously not aware of the restrictive structural conditions of the poor in South Africa. It is of little avail to teach an unemployed and impoverished black person to fish if he does not have fishing gear, if there are not enough rivers with fish in them, and if there are also not enough fish in the rivers. If business people could ascertain for themselves the structural and restrictive nature of black poverty, and the lack of employment opportunities, they would refrain from the absurdity of quoting the Chinese proverb and display more empathy towards the predicament of the millions of blacks who are trapped in a situation of structural poverty and unemployment – a situation that was, and still is, completely beyond their control.

7 A neo-classical economist such as Joseph Stiglitz grants the point that Adam Smith's 'invisible hand' may be more like the 'Emperor's new clothes' – invisible because it is not there' (Stiglitz 1991: 12).

8 Strictly speaking, no country in the world can claim to implement liberal or free market capitalism. But many of the industrialised countries in Europe – and to a lesser degree in the British-American world – can claim that institutional and behavioural conditions at least approximate a market-oriented system that goes some way towards promoting the interests of the total population. But what is important is that all these countries have well-developed democratic systems, well-institutionalised welfare systems, and active civil societies which compensate in various ways for the dysfunction of their capitalist system (see appendix).

9 Cole *et al* argue that 'the free market system is not only regarded by social democrats as unlikely to remove glaring poverty, but [the system as such] is also suspected of being an ideological veil disguising a reality in which resources are allocated with little regard to the general social interest' (1991: 155).

10 Don Caldwell, a former associate editor of the *Financial Mail*, has asserted: 'The way to overcome the misery of apartheid and allow everyone to escape from poverty – black, brown and white – is to free the economy. The resulting high sustained growth would generate immense new wealth, which can make South Africa, within a generation, one of the richest countries in the world' (1989: 17). The propagandistic spokesperson for the AAC, Clem Sunter, expressed similar sentiments about the high growth that can be attained in a free market economy and the 'trickle-down' effect this would have for all sections of the populations. His plea for 'growth without concerted redistribution' is ideologically highly suspect, coming from somebody at the 'commanding heights' of the AAC (see Sunter 1992).

11 A rare exception was the AHI, which came closest to acknowledging that it had benefited from apartheid. It also expressed regret that it had supported the policy of separate development, and that it was not sensitive enough at the time to the hardships and suffering caused by apartheid.

12 It is true that discriminatory measures enacted by the Smuts and Hertzog governments in the 1920s restricted the extent to which the mining industry could use cheap African labour to lower its production costs. But the active support the mining companies received from the South African Party (SAP), the UP, and NP governments until the early 1970s to recruit super-exploitable migrant labour in almost all the countries of southern Africa more than compensates for the cost-increasing effect of the discriminatory measures. The fact that the real cash wages of migrant workers in 1960 were 20 per cent and in 1972 8 per cent lower than those in 1911 demonstrates the enormous influence of the mining industry over the segregationist governments in the first half of the century, and the apartheid government in the third (see table 8.1).

13 This consensual order enhanced the legitimacy of the state, but originally impeded the accumulation drive of the gold mining corporations. The additional discriminatory measures enacted by the Pact government and its industrial protection policy on behalf of Afrikaner workers prompted many foreign shareholders to sell their gold shares. At the time, mining capital was internationalised in terms of markets and capital and preferred 'free trade' policies. Agriculture and industrial capital were localised, and required state intervention in the form of subsidies and protection, financed by taxing the mining industries.

14 The export of minerals made it possible to import the capital equipment needed to expand manufacturing. The local industrialisation policy was based on protective tariffs, exchange and import controls, the development of parastatal corporations in a number of public industries (such as SASOL), and the production of durable consumer goods mainly for the white population (see Morris, in Gelb 1991: 37–40).

15 While the English-controlled corporate sector was always critical of the cost-increasing effect of discriminatory measures to protect Afrikaner workers, they not only openly supported cost-decreasing labour repressive measures, but also profited hugely from them.

16 In 1983 the United Democratic Front (UDF) was launched in protest against the government's 'power-sharing' policy with the coloureds and Indians. In 1985 the Congress of South African Trade Unions (COSATU) was launched as an overtly political trade union co-ordinating body. Both these organisations became part of the internal wing of the liberation struggle, led by the ANC. The sharp increase in African wages in the early 1980s, under pressure from the new black trade unions and the large-scale insurrections of 1984–6, deepened the accumulation crisis considerably.

17 Fine continues: 'In a sense the state, as guarantor of loans had lost its credibility. Consequently its own productive assets rather than its word in the form of government bonds were being offered as collateral. In short, the privatisation programme represented the selling-off of the family silver in order to raise the funds to finance the apartheid regime [in its hour of crisis]' (1995: 9).

18 Ben Fine concludes that, 'put in proper perspective, [the privatisation policy of the NP] can be seen to represent a continuity [of the white government] in serving the

interests of large-scale capital. State enterprises had played a major role [during the twentieth century] in building up the mining and energy sectors and much of the large-scale industry around them such as heavy chemicals and mineral processing' (1995: 14; see section 9.6).

19 At the time, the author of this book was a member of the executive and an economic adviser to the DP, and was involved in the decision to adopt majoritarian democracy as an election strategy.

20 According to Marais, 'South African capitalists hoped (in 1990) that political democratisation would serve as a grounding for structural adjustments that could inaugurate a new cycle of sustained accumulation, a process that would include efforts to cultivate and incorporate a black economic elite as junior partners within the white-run economy' (1998: 4).

21 The first scenario exercise was Nedcor/Old Mutual's Prospects for a Successful Transformation, launched in late 1990 and completed in 1993. A second one was SANLAM's Platform for Investment, published in 1993. Late in 1993 a social democratic think-tank published its Mont Fleur scenarios. According to Marais ,'the ostensibly social-democratic Mont Fleur scenario...significantly assisted the march of [economic] orthodoxy...less because of its content than its central theme and the range of progressive (including ANC) economists and union figures that were drawn into the exercise. The scenario daubed heterodox strategic options in the dread colours of macroeconomic populism. Striking was its disapproval of redistributive state spending' (2001: 130).

22 Mandela said on that occasion that 'the private sector must and will play the central and decisive role in the struggle to achieve many of [the transformation] objectives ...Let me assure you that the ANC is not an enemy of private enterprise...We are aware that the investor will not invest unless he or she is assured of the security of their investment...We are determined to create the necessary climate which the foreign investor will find attractive' (quoted in Marais 2001: 123).

23 Before the conference, Alec Erwin wrote an article in which he contrasted 'growth with redistribution' with 'growth and redistribution'. This was the first sign that the democratic movement was accepting the argument of the corporate sector about the alleged beneficial 'trickle-down' effect of a high growth rate (see Harris 1993: 95).

24 Kentridge's evaluation of ANC economic thinking in May 1992 was that 'three years and three generations of policy positions have wrought a sea change in ANC thinking indicative of a growing pragmatism in policy circles and a willingness to engage with and accommodate supporters and critics alike' (1993: 9–10; see also Nattrass 1994b: 355).

25 The MERG document pleaded for a restructuring of the economy through the labour market and through increased state intervention to improve the structure and operation of business. Should its key proposals be implemented, the MERG model predicted annual growth of 5 per cent by 2004 and the creation of 300 000 new jobs a year. Its emphasis on state intervention in social and infrastructural development and in restructuring the business sector clearly went against the grain of corporate and NP thinking.

26 COSATU claimed that the ANC document did not sufficiently emphasise the importance of job creation and the meeting of health, education and housing needs

and makes a plea for a reconstruction accord before a democratic government was elected. This plea eventually matured into the RDP of 1994 (see section 4.3).

27 The IPS favoured an export growth path, although it acknowledged that it would not be easy to accomplish this. It foresaw that it would be difficult to enter external markets because of the growth of protectionist barriers in large countries and because of heightened competition (see Kentridge 1993: 10–12; Marais 2001: 131–3; Bond 1999: 65–8).

Chapter 4

The hegemony of the African political establishment since 1993

4.1 The informal negotiations between the corporate sector and the ANC

Parallel with the negotiations on constitutional issues at Kempton Park during the early 1990s, representatives of the corporate sector and core ANC leaders also negotiated informally on economic issues. While the former talks took place in public, the latter took place mainly behind closed doors and could therefore not be publicly scrutinised, as the formal negotiations were.[1] It was alleged at the time that the ANC leaders were 'wined and dined from morning till night by the captains of mining, industry, and banking'[2]. Despite the secret nature of these informal negotiations, there was nothing obscure about them. In all modern states a clear understanding between the business sector and the government of the day is indispensable. Owing to the extraordinary nature of the power shift in the making in the early 1990s, informal negotiations were essential in order to dispel the mutual suspicion between the capitalist-oriented corporate sector and the socialist-oriented democratic movement.

At stake was not only the economic policy of a democratically elected government, but also the nature of South Africa's future economic system. Given that South Africa was the most developed country in Africa, the stakes were extremely high, and the negotiations were strategically hugely important for the corporate sector. For almost 20 years all the joint attempts of the corporate sector and the NP government to find a new accumulation strategy had been unsuccessful. After almost 20 years of prolonged stagflation, the latter was desperate to convince the core leaders of the democratic movement what the economic ideology and economic system in a democratic South Africa ought to be.

The strategy on which the corporate sector and the ANC agreed during the informal negotiations in 1993 can be described as the fourth phase of the AAC-led search for a new accumulation strategy. After the 1994 election, the corporate sector and the new government continued to negotiate over an improved accumulation strategy. We can also distinguish between a fifth and sixth phase of the search for a new accumulation strategy (see sections 4.4 and 4.5).

The main characteristic of every phase of the AAC-led search for a new accumulation strategy was that the supreme goal of economic policy should be to attain a high economic growth rate, and that all other objectives should be subordinated to this. By convincing ANC leaders to accept the AAC's approach, the corporate sector in effect persuaded – or forced – the ANC to move away from its traditional priority, namely to uplift the impoverished black majority socially and economically.

4.2 The fourth phase of the AAC-led search for a new accumulation strategy, and the pre-election elite compromise

In 1993 the corporate sector and core ANC leaders reached a hugely important elite compromise. This happened before the transitional executive council (TEC) accepted a secret $850 million loan from the IMF to help tide the country over balance of payments difficulties in November 1993.[3] Before the TEC signed the loan agreement, the corporate sector and NP government on the one hand and ANC leaders on the other signed a secret protocol on economic policy.[4] In the 'Statement on economic policies' agreed with the IMF, the TEC committed itself to a neo-liberal, export-oriented economic policy, and a 'redistribution through growth' strategy. The 'statement' contains the following passage:

> Monetary policy has carried much of the burden of SA's adjustment during the 1990s ... An easing of [the strict] monetary policy would have risked a further undermining of [international] confidence and a resurgence of inflation ... To redress social backlogs, SA's economic policies must be driven by the objective of durable [economic] growth in which all can share equitably. This will require political stability and a package of macroeconomic and structural policies that address the problems of high unemployment and weak investment, respect financial restraints, and promote [international] confidence in the country's economic management ... There is widespread understanding that increases in the government deficit would jeopardise the economic future of the country ... [and that] given the importance of maintaining a competitive tax structure ... [fiscal policy] will emphasise expenditure containment rather than rising taxes ... It

is [also] recognised that unless social needs are addressed in a responsible manner socio-political stability would be difficult to sustain... Trade and industrial liberalisation will be an important part of the restructuring of the economy (TEC, Statement on economic policies, reprinted in *Business Day*, 24 March 1994).

The 'Statement' reads like the wish list of a corporate sector desperate to resolve its 20-year-long accumulation crisis. It also reads like a curtain-raiser for the GEAR strategy announced two and a half years later. The social crisis of abject poverty, structural unemployment, and violent criminality – in which at least 50 per cent of the population was trapped – is euphemistically described as 'social backlogs'. The corporate sector's myth that economic growth would 'trickle down' to the poor is accepted as a self-evident. The notion that 'What is good for the AAC will be good for South Africa' is writ large throughout the statement despite the fact that the poorer half of the population was marginalised, socially and economically powerless, propertyless, structurally unemployed, and therefore unlikely to benefit from 'durable growth'. The promise that 'all can share equitably... in durable growth' was preposterous if we take into account the deeply entrenched inequalities in socio-economic power and property between the bourgeois elite and the impoverished majority.

By agreeing in the 'Statement' to contain expenditure, not to increase taxes, to maintain fiscal balance, and to lower the government deficit in order to prevent the danger of macroeconomic populism and attract FDI, the ANC committed itself – before the election of 1994 – to a macroeconomic and fiscal policy that clearly excluded a comprehensive redistribution policy for addressing the predicament of the poorest half of the population. Although no one could have favoured macroeconomic populism, it would have been possible to attain both fiscal balance and comprehensive redistribution by increasing both government spending and taxation. However, the sharp inequalities in the distribution of income and property were not acknowledged in the 'Statement' at all. Instead of emphasising the tax capacity of the white population – which had largely accumulated its wealth through systemic exploitation – the 'Statement' pleaded for a 'competitive tax structure'. An increase in taxation would have gone against the grain of the accumulation strategy for which the AAC and other corporations were lobbying. The corporate sector therefore categorically rejected a redistributive approach to social problems, and sought to convince the ANC to adapt a fiscal policy that would not demand any additional sacrifices from it or from white taxpayers.[5]

The joint TEC–IMF statement shows clearly that core ANC leaders must have changed their strategic and ideological thinking in important ways from mid-1992 onwards. Those in favour of making concessions in order to keep the formal constitutional negotiations on track were winning the battle within the democratic alliance, and have maintained their ascendancy ever since. The main thrust of the new approach was to make concessions on economic issues in order to ensure a political settlement in the shortest possible time. In its eagerness to reach a constitutional settlement, ANC leaders were, *inter alia*, prepared to yield to the severe pressure from the corporate sector to accept its neo-liberal and export-oriented approach. But by doing so the ANC leadership core in effect agreed that the severe social crisis (and abject poverty of the majority) would remain unresolved, and would only be addressed indirectly and in the long run via the high economic growth rate and 'trickle-down' effect promised by the 'super-salesmen' of the corporate sector. By accepting the promised high rate of economic growth as the panacea for all other problems, the ANC relinquished its traditional commitment to solve the social problem directly.[6]

This elite compromise should be regarded as one of the most decisive ideological turning points in the ANC's approach to economic issues. By agreeing to it, the ANC put in place the first cornerstone of the economic edifice of a post-apartheid South Africa. In effect, it agreed to an economic policy and system that would exclude the poorest half of the population from a 'solution' (ie, a '50 per cent solution') that was really aimed at resolving the corporate sector's long-standing accumulation crisis.

As soon as the ANC's leaders agreed to the statement, they were trapped in the formidable web of the domestic corporate sector and the international financial establishment, represented by the IMF and World Bank. The implications were far-reaching – not only for the ANC but also for the country at large. After agreeing to this elite compromise, the ANC was committed to proceeding down the road of 'free marketeerism', a competitive, outward-oriented economy, macroeconomic balance, and globalisation. In the nine years since then it has become evident that, once the ANC began to move down the prescribed road, it became more and more difficult for it to address the systemic *inclusion* of the poorer half of the population through meaningful poverty alleviation programmes.

When the ANC's leaders agreed to the statement, they effectively agreed with the powerful corporate sector that the politico-economic system that would be institutionalised after the democratic election of 1994 would be a liberal-capitalist version of democratic capitalism, in which the balance of power would be on the 'capitalist' rather than the 'democratic' side (see appendix). The implications of this decision would be more momentous than any of the parties to the agreement could have anticipated (see section 11.1).

During the formal and informal negotiations in the early 1990s, the ANC, NP, and corporate sector reached several other agreements relevant to the country's future economic policies and system. One important agreement was that South Africa would not become a parliamentary democracy, but a constitutional democracy. Although this system would curtail the new government's sovereignty, adopting it was deemed necessary given the way in which white governments had misused parliamentary 'democracy'. Other important agreements were that the South African Reserve Bank (SARB) would remain an independent institution, and that property rights would be entrenched to the extent that they could only be revoked by a 75 per cent majority in the national assembly. These decisions can certainly not be faulted.

Given the momentous importance of the elite compromise of November 1993, it is necessary to situate it in the chain of events at the time, and to highlight the major shifts in the ideological orientation of the ANC's core leaders from May 1992 to November 1993. In May 1992 the ANC accepted a policy document that revealed the first signs of a shift from a 'socialist' and redistributive approach towards macroeconomic balance and capitalist pragmatism.

In May 1992 the constitutional negotiations collapsed, and were formally suspended after the Boipatong massacre in June. From June to September there was a real danger that counter-revolutionary forces could undermine the transition. On 26 September 1992 – only weeks after the Bisho massacre – the NP government and the ANC agreed on the 'sunset' clauses and on a government of national unity, after both parties had made strategic concessions.[7] In November 1992 the ANC's national executive committee (NEC) took stock of the 'balance of forces' at that stage of the negotiation process, and concluded that its own strength was restricted by 'certain objective weaknesses'. It noted that:

> The [apartheid] regime still commands vast state and other military resources...[and] continues to enjoy the support of powerful economic forces...The counter-revolutionary violence and the growing potential of long-term counter-revolutionary instability acts as a resource for the [apartheid] regime...The ANC has established itself as a legal national organisation, it commands the support of the majority of South Africa...[It] enjoys the capacity to mobilise large-scale mass action...[but it] suffers many organisational weaknesses...[It] does not command significant

military and financial resources; it is unable to militarily defeat the counter-revolutionary movement or adequately defend the people.

It added that the 'balance of forces' could best be changed through

a negotiation process combined with mass action and international pressure which takes into account the need to combat counter-revolutionary forces and, at the same time, uses phases in the transition to qualitatively change the balance of forces in order to secure a thorough-going democratic transformation.

Although the NEC stressed that the 'balance of forces' was not 'static', the fear that South Africa could implode and become fragmented weighed heavily on the minds of the ANC leadership at that time. Consequently, it came to the important conclusion that 'the new democratic government would need to adopt a wide range of measures in order to minimise the potential threat to the [future] democracy. However, some of these measures may have to be part and parcel of a negotiated settlement' (see ANC 1992a, adopted by the national working committee on 18 November 1992).

The ideological shift on economic issues among ANC leaders from mid-1992 to the end of 1993 should be interpreted in terms of the differences in the balance of power at the formal negotiations on political issues, and at the informal negotiations on economic issues. The former strongly favoured the ANC, but the latter not. This enabled the corporate sector to take core ANC leaders in tow on economic policy and ideology. The question arises whether this happened because the ANC was too weak, or because the corporate sector was too strong. It would perhaps be more correct to claim that the 'balance of powers' favoured the corporate sector, not only because of the relative strength of the two parties but also because the ideological climate in the early 1990s – after the fall of the Berlin Wall, the implosion of the Soviet Union, and the emergence of galloping globalism – often, for the wrong reasons, strongly favoured the corporate sector.

At Kempton Park the focus was on replacing white political supremacy with a representative democracy. One of the most controversial issues was whether a minority (white) veto should be written into the new constitution, as requested by the NP. At the time the NP, as the party responsible for apartheid, had lost its legitimacy (both internally and externally), while the ANC enjoyed the moral high ground. The ANC was focusing most of its attention on a political settlement (regarded by it as the first prize), and was prepared to make strategic concessions on economic and social issues in order to attain this goal. The fact that both the corporate sector and the international community also wanted a political settlement considerably strengthened the democratic movement's position at the formal negotiations.

During the informal negotiations on economic matters, the corporate sector succeeded – undeservedly – in presenting itself as unblemished by apartheid and racism. It claimed that it had always strongly opposed apartheid because it had impeded the unfolding of capitalism. The corporate sector – and especially its English-controlled section – could indeed claim that it had opposed the discriminatory measures introduced to protect poor Afrikaners against black competition for more than a century. But it could not claim that it had opposed repressive labour and other segregationist measures. These measures were part and parcel of a racial capitalism that had strongly benefited all sectors of the white corporate sector until the 1970s. They were instituted and regularly adapted on behalf of the corporate sector by the colonial, segregationist, and apartheid governments in turn, in order to improve its profitability (see sections 8.6 and 9.4).

While the corporate sector's hands were anything but clean, its extraordinary capacity for propagandising and myth-making enabled it to convince ANC leaders that the informal negotiations and transformation process were not about racial capitalism; the economic wealth that had accumulated undeservedly in the hands of white beneficiaries through systemic exploitation; the huge economic power concentrated in white conglomerates through racial capitalism and white political domination; or the abject poverty, destitution, and socio-economic powerlessness of the victims of racial capitalism, but *only* about a transition to majoritarian democracy, and the creation of economic and political conditions conducive to accumulation. By remaining silent about its own ignoble involvement with colonialism, segregation and apartheid, and even explicitly denying such involvement, the corporate sector presented itself as the *deus ex machina* that would solve all social problems of poverty, inequality, and unemployment. It said it could do so provided three preconditions were met: first, South Africa should be democratised; second, the corporate sector (and with it also the power and property relations of the South African economy) should be left intact, and granted all the freedom (ie, all the 'free marketeerism') normally granted to a corporate sector in a genuinely liberal-capitalist system; and, third, a neo-liberal macroeconomic and export-oriented policy should be implemented in order to integrate South Africa into global capitalism. When the corporate sector succeeded in convincing the ANC on these issues, it scored an immensely important victory, with far-reaching negative implications for the poorer half of the population. Almost all its arguments were based on myths and lies, but were presented with so much conviction, sophistication, and power that the ANC leaders apparently had little choice but to accept them.

At the beginning of the 1990s the corporate sector was very much in a corner. Despite several attempts to formulate a new strategy, its accumulation crisis was still unresolved. Moreover, the country's largest conglomerates (and especially the AAC) had, according to Marais, come 'close to exhausting local avenues for expansion, having built in the process massive and unwieldy corporate empires that straddled any number of sectors'.[8] In its cornered state, the corporate sector fought hard to obtain permission to escape into 'globalism', irrespective of whether that would be in the interest of the country at large.

Unfortunately, it is not known what interaction took place between the formal negotiations on political issues and the informal negotiations on economic issues. Were the agreements reached at Kempton Park a function of agreements reached at the informal negotiations, or vice versa? We have reason to believe that the corporate sector was directly and indirectly a major player at Kempton Park, albeit behind the scenes. As soon as it was satisfied that it had 'boxed in' the ANC's leaders to the necessary degree, it pressurised the participants at Kempton Park into agreeing on political and constitutional matters. It is also possible that the NP delayed an agreement on constitutional issues at Kempton Park until the corporate sector was satisfied that it had 'boxed in' the ANC to the necessary degree. Be that as it may, in this way the ANC got its first prize – political control of South Africa – while the corporate sector got its first prize – continued control of the South African economy – to an even greater extent than before.

Another factor that tilted the balance of power in the informal negotiations towards the corporate sector was the latter's greater knowledge of economics – especially its theoretical and technical aspects. Michie and Padayachee put it as follows:

The ANC did not at the beginning of negotiations in 1990 possess a ready institutional capacity on the economic policy front to counter the power and resources available to its main opponents [ie, the corporate sector]...It simply did not have a set of new progressive ideas and strategies to counter those neo-liberal ideas so powerfully proposed by the Washington institutions, Western governments, local business interests, and the De Klerk regime...The more interventionist, Keynesian ideas and policy recommendations of MERG (December 1993) and RDP (February 1994) came too late in the transition process to stop the ANC's steady slide into neo-liberalism (1997: 228–9).[9]

Another reason for the relative weakness in the ANC's bargaining position on economic matters in the early 1990s was the difference in experience and culture among the so-called 'islanders', 'exiles', and 'inciles' in its ranks, while the sharpest differences between the ANC and its alliance partners (COSATU and the SACP) were over economic issues.[10]

However, the unequal balance of power between the corporate sector and ANC leaders have to be analysed at a deeper level by taking into account the power shifts (including ideological shifts) in the communist bloc and western world that were responsible for the implosion of the Soviet Union on the one hand, and the rise of global capitalism on the other.

During the 1970s and early 1980s the ANC and the other South African liberation organisations received support from many countries, especially countries in the communist bloc.[11] Among these, the financial and ideological support of the Soviet Union was the most important. But at the end of the 1980s this support decreased rather sharply. This may have resulted partly from the 'breakdown' of the Soviet Union, as exemplified by the Chernobyl meltdown of April 1986, and partly from the 'agreement' between presidents Ronald Reagan and Mikhail Gorbachev at Reykjavik and Washington in October 1986 and October 1987 respectively to seek negotiated solutions for world conflicts. The decline in financial support from the Soviet Union may be one of the reasons why Umkhonto we Sizwe (MK), the armed wing of the ANC, was in disarray at the end of the 1980s. Without substantial and growing support from the communist bloc, it was not possible for the liberation organisations to defeat the apartheid regime militarily. And without a military victory, the ANC's bargaining power at the negotiaitons – especially the informal talks on economic matters – was significantly reduced.[12] The white business sector was far more intact than the white political sector, and it was therefore easier for it to convince (or force) the ANC to leave key economic and financial institutions unchanged, irrespective of whether this was justifiable from a moral and socio-economic perspective. The corporate sector also promised – baselessly – that if its role in the economy were left intact it would deliver the jobs, taxes, and improvements in living standards so keenly desired by the ANC.

As, from the 1970s onwards, the countries in the communist bloc declined in economic and military terms, those in the western world grew stronger in ideological and economic terms. In the third quarter of the 20th century the industrialised countries experienced a golden age, achieving an average annual economic growth rate of 5 per cent. During the Cold War, and accompanied by a strong aversion to the command economy of the Soviet Union, a remarkable ideological consensus grew in the western world on the merits of welfare state capitalism and the necessity of a mixed capitalist system (see appendix).

The almost unanimous support in the western world for the Keynesian socio-democratic approach and for interventionist welfare state capitalism was shattered when the OPEC oil crisis not only reduced economic growth, but also caused large-scale job losses and inflation. With the Keynesian approach in disarray, the stagflation of the 1970s and early 1980s led to the revival – especially in the British-American world – of neoclassical economic orthodoxy, and a belief in the merits of unbridled free market economics. After the collapse of the Bretton Woods system, the opening up of financial markets by governments in industrialised countries led to an unprecedented global flow of goods and capital. These developments – together with the remarkable progress made in information technology – led to the emergence of global capitalism during the last quarter of the 20th century. The world became integrated into a so-called 'global village' in which all the countries in the western world became interdependent. After the fall of the Berlin Wall and the implosion of the Soviet Union, galloping globalisation engulfed almost all the countries in the world.

This was accompanied by major shifts in the power relations within and between countries. In the Bretton Woods period (1945–73) bargaining power in industrialised countries was distributed fairly equally between democratically elected governments and their bureaucracies, and private sector corporations. During this period organised labour was also strong enough to play, along with other civil society organisations, an important 'countervailing role' against the power of the state and the corporate sector. But with the rise of global capitalism and the ideology of neo-liberalism, power relations within the industrialised countries (the so-called Rich North) shifted drastically towards private sector corporations.[13] In all capitalist-oriented countries – but especially those of the Rich North – power has been concentrated in the hands of the relatively small managerial elite of large corporations which control not only huge economic and financial resources, but also formidable ideological and propaganda power. With most of this power concentrated in more than 40 000 multinational corporations (of which more than 95 per cent are based in industrialised countries), the economic, financial, and ideological power concentrated in the Rich North has also increased dramatically *vis-à-vis* that of the governments of countries in the Poor South.

These power shifts within and between countries have had important distributional effects. The income of the top 30 per cent of the populations of industrialised countries has increased relative to that of the poorer 70 per cent.[14] This tendency is stronger in the British-American world than in continental Europe. At the same time, the share of world income of the Rich North (housing 15 per cent of the world population) has increased, while that of the Poor South has declined sharply.[15]

To explain the implications of these power shifts, it is necessary to distinguish between what Susan Strange calls *relational* and *structural* power. Relational power is the power that one actor or group of actors (such as the corporate sector) wields directly against another actor or actors (such as the state). Structural power, however, is the ability of an actor or group of actors (such as the corporate sector) to shape the rules that other actors (the state and civil society) follow, thus enabling that actor to insidiously achieve its objectives without direct confrontation, since the other actors accept the new rules as norms and do not realise the true basis of structural power until later (see Strange 1994; Mytelka, in Lawton *et al* 2000: 19–38). In both developed and developing countries, governments are playing a diminishing role in determining the rules of the game. 'Governments now act as salesmen, promoting the fortune of their own [national] corporations in the hope of providing a core prosperity for their state and keeping themselves in power' (Hertz 2001: 86; see also Strange 1996).

From the mid-1970s onwards the governments of the Rich North supported the rise of global capitalism by implementing neo-liberal policies and freeing financial markets. This enabled the corporate sector in the Rich North (and especially in the United States) to change the rules of the capitalist game to its own advantage with the assistance of the IMF, the World Bank, the General Agreement on Tariffs and Trade (GATT), and other international organisations and instruments. By entrenching its own power, the corporate sector is continuously rewriting the rules of the capitalist game within countries and also between the Rich North and Poor South.[16] By consolidating their own power, the corporate sectors in all countries – but especially those in the Rich North – are tending towards usurping the powers as well as functions of democratically elected governments. Noreena Hertz describes this phenomenon in her book *The silent takeover: global capitalism and the death of democracy* (2001). According to her, the managerial elite of the multinational corporations is continuously increasing its power at the expense of the sovereignty of democratically elected nation states. This happens in all the countries of the Rich North, but to an even greater extent in those of the Poor South where those corporations have subsidiaries.[17]

The increase in power of the local corporate sector at the expense of the South African government already began in the period 1978 to 1994. As indicated in section 3.2.3, the AAC and the rest of the corporate sector took the NP government in tow in its search for a new accumulation strategy. The same happened during the informal negotiations between the corporate sector and the ANC. When, in 1993, they agreed on the 'Statement on economic policies', the corporate sector consolidated the structural power it would wield in the new South Africa. Given the balance of power on economic matters in South Africa and elsewhere, in the framework of global capitalism, it was as if the informal negotiations offered the corporate sector a *tabula rasa* on which it could inscribe – before the election of 1994 – not only future economic policies, but also what the rules of the game in South Africa's future economic system would be. At that point the 'corporatisation' – or more correctly, the 'Anglo-Americanisation' – of South Africa was firmly institutionalised.

Unfortunately, we don't know to what extent the corporate sector (and especially conglomerates such as the AAC) has used its considerable propaganda – and even greater financial – power to convince, coerce, or co-opt ANC leaders to embrace an economic policy of 'free marketeerism' and an unrestructured economic system as most appropriate for a post-apartheid South Africa.[18]

Given the balance of power at the time – both in South Africa and in global capitalism – the ANC's leaders apparently had little choice but to succumb to the duress of the corporate sector and its international partners in Washington, New York, London, and Frankfurt. What we also do not know is whether the corporate sector and the NP government *deliberately* mobilised the powerful agents of global capitalism – ie, the IMF, World Bank, GATT, the World Economic Forum, investment banks, and so on – to put additional pressure on the ANC to accept the neo-liberal and globalised rules of the game.

For the corporate sector it was very important to ensure that an ANC government would not embark on socialism, *dirigisme*, interventionism, macroeconomic populism, or large-scale redistribution and upliftment programmes. To accomplish this, the local corporate sector and its global partners probably thought it necessary to exercise their joint power to 'cleanse' the ANC of its erstwhile socialist and redistributive orientation, and convince it that 'there was no alternative' to a neo-liberal, free market, and globally oriented approach. In the joint ideological onslaught of local and global corporatism on the ANC, the corporate partners made use of two rather doubtful strategies. On the one hand, they presented an extremely optimistic scenario of the high economic growth rate, high rates of employment, and beneficial 'trickle-down' effect that would ensue from fiscal restraint and neo-liberal globalisation. On the other, they warned the ANC in no uncertain terms – and in all sorts of subtle ways – of the large outflow of capital, entrepreneurs, and professional skills that could be expected – or orchestrated – if their rules of the capitalist game were not accepted.[19]

Although almost nine years have passed since the elite compromise of November 1993, certain questions remain unanswered. Why did the leadership core of the ANC make an ideological leap from the left to the right of the ideological spectrum concerning economic systems? If it had to give up socialism, why did it not opt for the social capitalism of continental European countries based on the ideology of social democracy rather than the British-American version of capitalism grounded on the ideology of liberal or free-market capitalism? Why did it choose Thatcherism and Reaganomics (see appendix)?

The answer to these questions is probably that the South African corporate sector and the American-based global institutions are only familiar with this right-wing version of capitalism, and either pressurised the ANC – or seduced it with hyperbolic promises – into accepting the right-wing version, despite the fact that, after centuries of colonialism, segregation, and apartheid, socio-economic and institutional conditions in South Africa were anything but suitable for this version.

What is also astonishing is that as soon as the elite compromise of 1993 was reached, the leadership core of the ANC was apparently no longer concerned – as it was in May 1992 – about the 'concentration of economic power in the hands of a few conglomerates'. During the informal negotiations on economic issues, the business people involved boasted about the 'steep learning curve' which key ANC leaders had followed under their influence. But, with the wisdom of hindsight, there is also reason to be concerned about its 'steep forgetting curve' (see Bond 1999: 16). Did it forget, after agreeing to the 'Anglo-Americanisation' of South Africa, about the concentration of economic power in the hands of a few conglomerates? Did it forget about its own socio-economic powerlessness when it accepted the propaganda of the AAC and neoclassical economists that 'power does not matter'?[20] Did it forget about the strong tendency in unbridled free market capitalism for the rich to become richer and the powerful more powerful, while the poor get poorer and the powerless more powerless? We would have expected key ANC leaders to be more knowledgeable about the deeply institutionalised and racially based inequalities in the distribution of power, property, and opportunities between the top 20 per cent and the poorest 40 per cent of households, and how extremely unlikely it was that the benefits of economic growth would 'trickle down' in such circumstances – even if a high economic growth rate could be maintained.

4.3 The Reconstruction and Development Programme of the ANC Alliance as a temporary interlude (1994–6)

The Reconstruction and Development Programme (RDP) – the ANC Alliance's much-vaunted, but now virtually defunct, manifesto for the 1994 election – originally emanated from COSATU, and particularly its most powerful affiliate, the National Union of Mineworkers (NUM), which envisaged the programme as a set of socio-economic benchmarks against which the performance of a new democratically elected government would be judged. Many members of the democratic movement – including the ANC – contributed to the document, but it was mainly drafted by organisations associated with the MDM,[21] and particularly COSATU.[22] In 1993 tensions developed between the ANC and COSATU, and to ease these the parties tacitly agreed that the latter would supply the ingredients of a 'reconstruction accord' that would serve as the ANC Alliance's manifesto for the 1994 election. The RDP base document was published shortly before the election as the alliance's guidelines to overcoming the legacy of apartheid (see Lodge 1999: 2–5).

The RDP was based on several principles.[23] It also identified five major policy programmes aimed at rectifying the unbearable conditions created by apartheid among blacks. This included programmes to meet the basic needs of 'at least 17 million people surviving below the MLL', develop the neglected human resources of mainly Africans, democratise state and society, and successfully implement the RDP (see ANC 1994: 7–13; ch 2–5). The fifth programme was aimed at fundamentally restructuring the economy, said to be experiencing a deep-rooted structural crisis.[24] The RDP stated that 'the democratic government must play a leading and enabling role in guiding the economy and the market towards reconstruction and development' (ibid: 80), and warned that policies concentrating purely on promoting economic growth would accentuate existing inequalities, perpetuate mass poverty, and soon stifle economic growth. Thus the government was tasked with actively integrating economic growth with economic reconstruction and social development.

One of the main merits of the RDP document was that it clearly and comprehensively described all the distortions and injustices that had become part of South African society during racial capitalism and white political domination. After the 1994 election the RDP was – in president Nelson Mandela's own words – 'the cornerstone on which the...GNU is based', and 'the centrepiece of its socio-economic policy' (quoted in Blumenfeld 1997: 3).

In the 1994 election, the RDP helped to mobilise more than 60 per cent of the electorate behind the ANC alliance. Its symbolic importance and the consensus it created cannot be overemphasised, because it formed an important part of the nation-building and healing process after centuries of deep divisions and conflict. After the election, however, numerous problems were encountered in implementing the RDP. While it posited the alleviation of poverty and reconstruction of the economy as its main aims, it did not spell out a detailed programme for attaining them. The RDP was perhaps too broadly formulated, and ended up as a wish list for too many people. One of its important deficiencies was that it assigned a strategic role to the state in what it envisaged would be a truly developmental state – but shortly after the ANC took power it became evident that the capacity needed for a developmental state did not exist.[25] According to Blumenfeld, 'the probity and efficiency of the new administration was quickly undermined by evidence not only of bureaucratic incompetence and excessive red tape, but also by allegations of fraud and corruption in several projects'.[26]

Eight years after the RDP was published, it must be regarded as a dismal failure. In fact, its death blow was dealt early on, in the white paper on reconstruction and development published in November 1994. The white paper departed significantly from the original document. It introduced fiscal prudence not as a means of attaining RDP objectives, but as an added goal. The notion of redistribution was dropped, as the government's major role in the economy was reduced to the task of managing the transformation. A so-called RDP Fund was set up – within the parameters of the ANC's commitments during the elite compromise of November 1993 – in order to keep government expenditure constant in real terms and avoid the need to increase taxes. Given the ANC's commitment to fiscal discipline and macroeconomic balance, no fiscal 'space' was available for properly implementing the RDP and for the redistributive implications of its poverty alleviation programme and its emphasis on meeting basic needs. According to the white paper, the government's approach was one of *reprioritising* departmental budgets. All the line departments were to cut their budgets and re-apply for funds to spend on 'RDP-oriented' projects.[27] According to Blumenfeld, the RDP Fund 'was taking scarce resources away from every department, and offering them back only to those departments with procedures and priorities that conformed with those of the RDP Office' (1997: 14).[28]

It is sometimes said that the RDP was abandoned when the GEAR strategy was announced in June 1996, but a proper implementation of the RDP was never reconcilable with the neo-liberal macroeconomic policy to which the ANC had committed itself in 1993. It therefore seems as if the ANC accepted the RDP on a rhetorical level only, and used it mainly for electioneering purposes. It was only implemented marginally as far as this could be accommodated within the limits set by the ANC's commitment to not increase state expenditure or taxes.[29] Although administrative, fiscal, and ideological problems all played roles in the failure of the RDP, it was finally the lack of will within the ANC that led to its downgrading as a policy programme.

The second objective of the RDP – the need to fundamentally restructure the South African economy, given its 'deep-seated structural crisis' – was also abandoned by the new government. As indicated earlier, the ANC expressed concern about the monopolistic nature of the South African economy as late as May 1992, but no reference was made to this in the 'Statement on economic policies' of November 1993. When the RDP was accepted as the ANC Alliance's election manifesto early in 1994, the restructuring of the economy was again endorsed. Since then, however, the government has done almost nothing – apart from introducing new labour relations legislation – to restructure power relations in the private sector.[30] The idea of the RDP bringing about a 'fundamental restructuring' was born of the conviction that South African capitalism was not a 'normal' or 'social-democratic' kind of capitalism, but a remnant of colonial and racial capitalism that had been in place during the 20th century and had been sustained by white political domination, segregation, and apartheid. This version of capitalism had indeed demonstrated a deep-seated tendency towards systemic exploitation of and structural injustice in respect of people other than whites, and would maintain a tendency towards neglecting the poorest half as long as it remained 'fundamentally unrestructured'.

For decades, the power relations embedded in South African capitalism tended towards capital-intensity (ie, accumulation at the cost of employment creation and the development of blacks), and a further concentration of economic power in the hands of the 'commanding heights'. Those who compiled the RDP realised, correctly, that if the South African economic system were to remain 'fundamentally unrestructured', its systemic tendencies towards racially based inequality, unemployment, and increased pauperisation would continue,[31] as would the tendency towards the formation of large conglomerates (with extended foreign connections) and the concentration of economic power in the hands of a small corporate elite. It is rather puzzling, therefore, that the new government has refrained from restructuring the economy, because its structural crisis implies that market mechanisms cannot automatically correct the deeply institutionalised problems inherited from racial capitalism, and that deliberate intervention by the state is essential to do so (see section 11.1).

How should we explain this *volte-face*? After the symbiotic relationship forged between ANC leaders and the corporate sector at the end of 1993, and after the ANC had accepted the 'free marketeerism' for which the AAC and the rest of the corporate sector had lobbied so aggressively, the tasks of 'restructuring' the economy and solving the 'deep-seated crisis' were apparently left to the market and the high economic growth rate envisaged by the corporate sector. In mitigation of the ANC's actions, it should be acknowledged that – apart from a lack of will to restructure the economy – the ANC-in-government also discovered after 1994 that it did not have the bureaucratic capacity to accomplish such a complicated and painful task as *fundamentally restructuring* the economy. The consequence of this is that, eight years after the ANC took power, the economy remains largely 'unrestructured' (see section 11.2.3).[32]

Instead of correcting the power and wealth relations inherited from racial capitalism, the government is in fact dancing to the music of the corporate sector. Adam *et al* argue 'that the relationship between the new "socialist" power holders and the old business elite is now [in 1997] closer and better than the alleged racist alliance between apartheid and South African capitalism ever was' (1997: 169). And, according to Lodge, 'the [ANC] government has probably been better for business than any of its predecessors for a very long time…not so much through any direct assistance to business, though corporate taxation remains constrained, but rather through its evident acceptance of what businessmen perceive to be economic common sense' (1999: 9).[33] What Lodge is saying in diplomatic language is that in economic matters the ANC is caught up in the power, ideological paradigm, and economic logic of the free market-oriented corporate sector. Ben Fine has agreed by asserting that 'over at least the past 20 years, state economic policy has been driven by the interests of large-scale South African capital' (1995: 16).

Eight years after its publication in 1994, the RDP still remains the official policy framework of the ANC Alliance, although for all practical purposes the government has shunted it on to a sidetrack. The government's unwillingness to address the two main aims of the RDP – poverty alleviation, and the restructuring of the economy – has become an important reason for the continuing tensions between the ANC and COSATU. In its response to the 1998–9 budget, COSATU declared that 'it is blindingly obvious that it is not possible to have a developmental budget within an anti-developmental economic framework' (12 March 1998). Over the past eight years, the ideological differences between COSATU and the SACP on the one hand and the ANC on the other have become even more fundamental. Until now the loyalties forged in the trenches of the struggle have been strong enough to keep the alliance intact. However, the unity of the alliance will probably soon be severely tested by the seemingly irreconcilable ideological differences between them.

The points of difference between the ANC and COSATU should be seen in a historical perspective. COSATU was mainly responsible for compiling the RDP, but when the base document was published early in 1994 the ANC had already entered into an elite compromise with the corporate sector, to which COSATU had not been a party. This compromise did not allow the fiscal 'space' needed for implementing the RDP. This seems to show that the RDP was never an integral part of the new government's policy programme, but only a policy option propagated for electioneering purposes. The RDP Office lingered on until Mandela closed it in March 1996.[34] The RDP did, however, live on rhetorically as the ANC's 'election manifesto' for the 1999 election. During its campaign, the ANC declared that the RDP 'was the only relevant detailed programme to carry South Africa to freedom and social justice'. Despite this claim, the RDP is today only a state of mind, a remnant of the liberation philosophy, and a people-oriented ideology with which the new governing elite hopes to legitimise and perpetuate its power.

The RDP was born in the trenches of the struggle, and the purpose of its utopian *élan* was to unite the ideological viewpoints within the 'broad church' of the alliance. As its implementation has been sidelined, the question arises: when will it turn from a unifying force into an instrument of division? Paradoxically enough, the ANC now probably needs the RDP more than ever. Given that the government has become trapped within the restrictive parameters of neo-liberal macroeconomics and global corporatism, and given the deterioration in the living conditions of poor, it needs the RDP's rhetorical appeal and its promises of transformation to maintain the hopes of its rather divided constituency that it will deliver in the foreseeable future what the RDP promised in such lofty language. In a situation of systemic exclusion and neglect, the RDP must be kept on board to accomplish the 'rhetorical inclusion' of the mass of the poor.

4.4 The fifth phase of the AAC-led search for a new accumulation strategy, and the GEAR strategy (1993–6)

The appointment, in February 1996, of Trevor Manuel as minister of finance initially provoked a negative reaction from the business sector. Over the next four months the rand depreciated from R3,60 to the US dollar to R4,60, pointing to a lack of foreign confidence in the profitability of the South African economy and the ability of the new government – and Manuel specifically – to create conditions conducive to foreign investment. Manuel would soon announce a new initiative that would substantially change that assessment (even though the exchange rate would continue to worsen). However, in the intervening period, there were other notable developments in the debate on economic policy.

In early 1996 the continued poor performance of the South African economy and high levels of unemployment led to an extraordinarily sharp debate on macroeconomic and employment policy. In February the SAF published an aggressively worded document entitled *Growth for all* which claimed that the new government did not have a credible and comprehensive economic policy framework. It emphasised rising rates of crime and other forms of violence, and warned that this might wreak economic havoc. It strongly criticised the new government's fiscal, investment, labour, and trade policies, and rejected the RDP as unattainable. Its most controversial proposals were for a brisk privatisation programme (which, it claimed, could generate about R100 billion), and a vigorous campaign to integrate South Africa as fully as possible into the global economy. It pleaded for a two-tier labour market without prescribed minimum wages in order to absorb unemployed people into lower-paid jobs.

The SAF document also pleaded strongly and emotionally for curbs on government spending,[35] and identified social security and welfare spending, which absorbed almost 12 per cent of the non-interest government budget, as especially problematic for its 'disincentive effect on savings and the supply of labour'. Consequently, it proposed that social security and welfare spending 'should aim strictly to alleviate absolute poverty, providing subsidised services only for those who fall below an appropriately determined poverty line' (1996: 57). It warned the government that 'it should be cautious about making commitments regarding health and housing spending...[and] should free up these markets...so people can provide for themselves'. It is shocking that the document makes no attempt to analyse the nature, origin, and extent of poverty. Under the heading 'efficient government' it pleads for a social safety net for the poor that should be restricted to the 'very poor only' (not realising that this involves at least 50 per cent of the population) in order to minimise the waste of resources – as if poverty alleviation were a mechanical and efficiency issue deprived of all moral and human considerations. There is no better evidence than this document that the 50 corporations in whose name it was compiled have no awareness of the structural nature and human tragedy of South Africa's unemployment, poverty, and crime problems. The SAF is extraordinarily concerned about violence and criminality – as one might have expected from an organisation representing the white property class – but does not even consider the possibility that crime and violence may be rooted in the disrupted social structures and abject poverty resulting from generations of systemic exploitation under racial capitalism.[36]

From beginning to end, the SAF document is vintage 'Anglo-Americanism' in its most blatant form. We have reason to ask why the SAF deemed it necessary to publish such an extremely liberal and 'free market' document after the core ANC leadership had already committed itself to fiscal restraint, 'free marketeerism', and globalisation. It could be that the corporate sector – as embodied in the SAF – wanted to remind the ANC of the elite compromise which it had entered into in November 1993. It could also be that the corporate sector was uncomfortable with the RDP and with the influence of COSATU and the SACP within the alliance. But it is more likely that the SAF was propagating an extreme version of capitalism and globalisation in order to be in a position to blame the ANC government for not consistently implementing its 'growth model' in all its details. The fact that core ANC leaders had already become ideological proselytes of the AAC and the rest of the corporate sector was apparently not enough for the 50 largest corporations. In this document, the SAF revealed, more visibly than ever before, the core elements of the corporate sector's neo-liberal and growthmanship approach that it had been selling in instalments to successive governments since the late 1970s. The document also conspicuously ignores the unequal power relations, 'skewed' institutional framework, and uneven levels of human development that make it completely inappropriate to superimpose 'free marketeerism' (or Anglo-Americanism) onto the remnants of colonialism and apartheid.

In June 1996 the ministry of finance announced a new macroeconomic strategy entitled Growth, Employment, and Redistribution (GEAR). Devised by a group of 15 economists,[37] the strategy was aimed at providing the country with a comprehensive and well-integrated macroeconomic framework.[38] GEAR's point of departure is that higher levels of sustained economic growth requires a competitive, outward-oriented economy.[39] The GEAR strategy represents the fifth phase of the search for a new accumulation strategy. Its immediate aim was to reassure potential – especially foreign – investors that the government was committed to the neo-liberal orthodoxies of the 'Washington consensus'.[40] Decorated with all the trimmings of globalisation, GEAR represents an almost desperate attempt to attract FDI.

The GEAR document contained the optimistic assessment that 1,3 million additional jobs would be created up until 2000.[41] This would only materialise, it said, if the labour unions would co-operate with initiatives to reform the labour market and moderate wages, and if almost a third of the additional jobs would be created via infrastructural expansion in the public sector. GEAR's approach (in line with that of *Growth for all*) is that employment levels are largely determined by real wages and not by aggregate demand, as the Keynesian approach would have it. In their obsession with market forces, both *Growth for all* and GEAR showed little appreciation of the structural nature of unemployment.[42]

GEAR's emphasis on export-led growth must be read against the sharp decline in the real exchange rate in early 1996. This was regarded as an opportunity to stimulate exports by means of measures to counteract the inflationary impact of exchange rate adjustments. In August 1994 the department of trade and industry had already announced sharp tariff reductions in the clothing, textile, and automobile component sectors that went far beyond those demanded under GATT, despite the fact that those cuts had serious employment implications. GEAR stressed the need for market-led growth, fiscal and monetary discipline, and investor confidence. While the document paid lip-service to redistribution and poverty relief, its main concerns were the balance of payments, inflation, and FDI.

Strictly speaking, all the key elements of GEAR were already present in the 'Statement on economic policies' of November 1993. Ideologically, GEAR falls squarely within the supply-side/neo-classical paradigm. Apart from its more careful (and less aggressive) formulations, there are few differences between GEAR and the NEM, the 'Statement on economic policies', and *Growth for all*;[43] it is openly Thatcherite in content and tone.[44] Both GEAR and *Growth for all* envisage a worldwide capitalist economic system in which market forces reign supreme, rewarding those countries that obey its imperatives, and deservedly punishing those that do not (see Nattrass 1996: 25–42.) By retreating into the fantasy world of economic textbooks, the compilers of *Growth for all* and GEAR lost contact with the imperfect reality of and deep-seated inequalities in South Africa.

The strong anti-state orientation of the Reagan/Thatcher lurch to the right runs like a thread through the GEAR document. This begs several questions. If the state's role in the economy is to be drastically reduced, who will 'fundamentally restructure' it? Who will counter the power of the 'commanding heights' and other well-organised pressure groups in the private sector? Who will devise the urgently needed developmental state? If the role of the state has to be 'rolled back', who will see to it that the poorest half of the population does not remain marginalised, impoverished, and neglected?

Comparing the RDP of 1994 with the GEAR strategy of 1996 is a revealing exercise. At a conference hosted by the BER in October 1996, Manuel claimed that GEAR 'simply seeks to set out clearly and unambiguously the key economic requirements for achieving [the RDP] goals...[By launching a new growth cycle], GEAR will provide a foundation to underpin accelerated RDP delivery.' In reality, the RDP was a short interlude which ended when GEAR was announced and the neo-liberal approach, to which ANC leaders had already committed themselves in November 1993, reaffirmed. As was the case with the 'Statement' of 1993, the GEAR strategy's tax and spending policies also do not allow the 'fiscal space' needed for the redistributive implications of the RDP. Overall, GEAR limited tax-based government revenue to 25 per cent of GDP. Along with the successful efforts to drive down the budget deficit (from 9 per cent in 1994 to less than 2 per cent in 2001), the tax ceiling strictly limited the funding pool available for socio-economic spending and for adequate infrastructural development in poor areas (see Marais 2001: 188).

In his 1997 budget speech Manuel described promises by cabinet ministers to privatise state corporations, make wages more flexible, reduce the state deficit, and cut back public spending as 'deep transformation'. According to Adam *et al*, 'it indeed amounts to transformation, but it means *free market* transformation rather than the *redistributive* transformation popularised during the anti-apartheid struggle' (1997: 206).

But the most important difference between the RDP and GEAR was that, while the former expected the state to conduct a people-oriented development policy, the latter saw South Africa's economic 'salvation' in the high economic growth rate that would – as the corporate sector had promised – result from a sharp increase in private capital accumulation in an unbridled capitalist system. The government's task via GEAR was to refrain from economic intervention and to concentrate on the necessary adjustments that would create an optimal climate for private investment. GEAR presented state spending as an impediment to economic growth with the dubious argument that such spending would be inclined to 'crowd out' private investment.[45] Moreover, the document claimed rather dogmatically that increased private investment would not only lead to higher growth but also create jobs, and that the 'trickle-down' effect would bring about the necessary redistribution of income.[46] Consequently, the plan would not only deliver Growth, but also Employment and Redistribution. The possibilities that, even if higher economic growth rates were attained, this would be 'jobless growth', or that, even if the higher rates were sustained over time they would not in fact 'trickle down' to the poor, were not even considered.[47] Amid all the simplifications on which the plan was based, it said nothing about the unhealthy structural tendencies in the South African version of capitalism – ie, the tendencies towards greater economic concentration, greater capital intensity, jobless growth, growing inequality, and further pauperisation (see section 11.1).

GEAR's emphasis on macroeconomic balance and sound fiscal policies should be understood in the light of the fact that white taxpayers were not prepared to pay higher taxes. These taxpayers claim that tax rates in South Africa (especially individual income tax) are higher than in comparable middle-income countries. The top 15 per cent of income earners in the country provide no less than 30 per cent of total tax revenue – but this is the result of the extremely unequal distribution of income in South Africa (see table 2.2). Rates of tax on individual and corporate income are also higher than in comparable countries. But South Africa's history of colonialism, segregation, and apartheid means that it cannot be compared to other middle-income countries. The corporate sector used its extraordinary bargaining power – ie, its position of structural power *vis-à-vis* the new government – to convince the latter not to increase tax rates despite the obvious need for a more comprehensive redistribution policy.[48]

If the GEAR strategy is judged in terms of the targets it set for itself, it has failed.[49] The government reached three of its targets in the period until 2000 – the budget deficit was reduced to less than 3 per cent of GDP; the inflation rate was reduced to an annual average of less than 6 per cent; and imports tariffs were reduced to less than 7,6 per cent of the value of imports. Manufactured exports grew by 18,2 per cent a year in real terms, again exceeding GEAR's projection of 10,8 per cent, but this largely resulted from the continued decline in the real exchange rate. None of the other targets were reached – not even remotely. The economy grew by only 2,7 per cent a year instead of 4,2 per cent. Employment shrank instead of growing by 3 per cent (see table 2.1). Real government investment grew at 1,8 per cent instead of 7,1 per cent; and real private sector investment grew by only 1,2 per cent instead of the projected 11,7 per cent – a massive discrepancy. (In a lone reversal, investment by state-owned enterprises, or SOEs, grew by 13,6 per cent instead of the projected 7,6 per cent.)[50] In 2000 FDI amounted to less than R8 billion a year (or less than 1 per cent of GDP) instead of some R30 billion (or 4 per cent of GDP).

Gross private savings averaged 15 per cent of GDP a year, instead of 21,7 per cent (SARB 2000; department of finance budget review; department of trade and industry economics database).

The failure of the GEAR strategy to meet its targets has been attributed – by, among others, the director-general of finance – to the Asian crisis of 1998, with the argument that the targets were not really targets but just indicative figures to give a general idea of what was being aimed at. GEAR would, it was argued, deliver in the long term. While the Asian crisis was undoubtedly a setback, the second explanation is completely unsatisfactory. When a top government official uses this kind of excuse, we might in all fairness have expected that the non-delivery of employment and income redistribution would also have been acknowledged, and that alternative measures would have been implemented in the meantime to compensate for the human predicament caused by non-delivery. These explanations also do not acknowledge the serious inherent deficiencies of the GEAR document, nor, even more importantly, the fact that a conventional neo-liberal and globally oriented approach is not suited to South Africa. What is rather strange is that the corporate sector continues to support GEAR despite its poor performance. This can only be explained in terms of the fact that, despite its poor delivery record, the strategy protects white business privileges, and especially the interests of the larger and globally oriented corporations. It would indeed be inappropriate and ungrateful for the corporate sector to complain about the non-delivery of GEAR.

According to Nattrass, GEAR's poor growth performance 'is consistent with the warnings of economists across the ideological spectrum that GEAR would reduce demand, and that private investment would follow demand downwards ...It is also consistent with evidence that aggressively anti-inflationary of stabilisation packages [and the high level of the real interest rates] have undermined rather than supported growth' (2001: 4). Thus it seems as if the GEAR strategy was mainly designed to attract FDI, and underestimated the negative impact of inadequate domestic demand on private investment. With the benefit of hindsight, and knowledge of the poor ability of African countries to attract FDI, it is clear that GEAR's reliance on FDI was highly unrealistic.[51] But, despite GEAR's poor performance over the past six years, the government continues – under pressure from a faction of the corporate sector – to tailor its economic growth policy almost exclusively around globalisation and a large inflow of FDI. What is required instead is a package of measures that will stimulate the domestic economy, and create jobs.[52] International experience shows that FDI does not precede economic growth, but follows it.

Owing to its unrealistic orientation towards global capitalism, and its obsession with anti-statism – again under the influence of the corporate sector – the GEAR strategy grossly underestimated the positive role the government could have played, and should have played, in generating aggregate demand (in the Keynesian sense of the word) through not only higher rates of infrastructural investment, but also redistribution programmes. While South Africa is still in the throes of a political transition, and with its democracy yet to be consolidated, providing the disadvantaged majority with some tangible benefits should have been a very high priority. In primarily concerning itself with macroeconomic fundamentals and economic growth, the GEAR strategy is confusing means and ends (see Luiz 1998: 267). The unnecessarily sharp reduction of the budget deficit, the rigid ceiling on taxation, and the reimbursement of taxpayers have prevented substantial real increases in social spending which are desperately needed to address poverty and the legacy of apartheid. Instead of stimulating domestic demand, GEAR is built on the supposition that export markets are good for growth.

The strategy is based on the Asian model, in terms of which growth is generated via exports. Although growth in manufactured exports has exceeded expectations, this has been caused by the devaluation of the rand. What we should realise is that an export-led growth strategy depends on controlling production costs and increasing wages in line with productivity (see Nattrass 2001: 7).

To accomplish this would have required the state to play a more interventionist role, as was the case in Asian countries. But instead of playing an active role in stimulating domestic demand and strictly controlling cost increases, the ANC government – under pressure from COSATU – passed several labour laws that increased the cost of labour instead. At the end of the day, GEAR represents a version of 'free marketeerism' that cannot be applied consistently and successfully in South African circumstances. It was designed to fit the needs of the larger corporations to increase *their* net worth through liberalisation and globalisation, but without necessarily promoting the interests and net worth of the rest of the South African community.

In mitigation of GEAR's poor performance, it should be acknowledged that a commitment to moderate wage demands supported by appropriately structured wage flexibility within the collective bargaining system was supposed to be an important cornerstone of the strategy. Although the wages of highly skilled and skilled workers have increased only moderately, those of semi-skilled and unskilled workers have increased sharply despite the high levels of unemployment in those categories.[53] An important reason for labour market inflexibility since 1995 is the legislation and regulations enacted by the new government to redress some of the inequalities in the workplace inherited from apartheid.[54] The alleged inflexibility of the labour market should, however, not be overemphasised. It is not as difficult to retrench workers as is often alleged.

According to the economist Mike Schusster, workers are receiving a declining percentage of GDP, and although productivity and skills development are not what they ought to be, South Africa does not compare negatively with other developing countries (*COSATU Newsletter*, 5 November 2001).

All the new labour laws have increased employers' costs, and have undoubtedly contributed – directly and indirectly – to unemployment. Although the legislation was necessary in principle to address the legacy of apartheid, the policy of affirmative action has been driven too hard – mainly under pressure from COSATU – in order to improve the position of the emerging black elite, but especially that of the lower middle class. Consequently, these groups' socio-economic positions have been improved at the expense of the lower class, while the efficiency of the public sector has also been harmed by affirmative action. Although COSATU claims to be the champion of the poor, its actions – like those of the black bourgeoisie – are often geared towards promoting its own sectional class (or worker) interests to the detriment of other sectors of the black community.

In 2001 – at the end of its planning period – GEAR's protagonists claimed that it was not really a growth strategy but a *stabilisation* strategy, and that, after five years of implementation, sound macroeconomic fundamentals were in place. They also claimed that macro conditions in 2001 were conducive to increased FDI flows, and that growth would probably improve soon. This is a rather narrow economic perspective.

Even if we grant the point that sound macroeconomic fundamentals are now in place, this is not particularly helpful, because the governmental (or bureaucratic) and socio-economic 'fundamentals' – equally important for creating an investment-friendly climate and a higher economic growth path – are certainly not in place.[55] By implementing GEAR, the government – as in the case of the other attempts to find a new accumulation strategy – has put the cart before the horse in more than one sense. Implementing an adequate accumulation strategy presupposes a certain level of state capacity and efficiency. Unfortunately, these are conspicuous by their absence, while nepotism and corruption are rife in departments involved with the private sector and with potential foreign investors.[56] After 1994 the new government made a huge mistake in not prioritising the development of state capacity and the efficiency of the public sector.

An even more important reason for the failure of the new government to create – during the fifth phase of the search for an accumulation strategy – an investment-friendly and growth-promoting atmosphere is the continuing neglect of the social (or poverty) crisis. This crisis was ignored during each of the first four attempts to find a new accumulation strategy, from 1978 to 1994, and is again being ignored rather conspicuously by the GEAR strategy. In the present phase of South Africa's precarious transformation, the government should have tried not only to create macroeconomic stability, but also to build and develop society, including reconstructing the South African economy. What most South Africans need now is not the relentless discipline of global free marketeerism, but a greater compassion about the plight of the poor. It was indeed narrow-minded and myopic of the corporate sector to advise the new government that an investment-friendly atmosphere could be created in a country in which most people are abjectly poor and deprived, and crime and violence have become endemic. It was equally short-sighted of the business sector to think that it would be possible – after the political transformation of 1994 – to continue with 'normal business' after centuries of colonial and racial capitalism.

In a series of surveys undertaken in 1999 by the World Bank, in conjunction with the Greater Johannesburg Metropolitan Council, 94 per cent of the large firms interviewed identified crime as the most important obstacle to investment and growth.[57] If the new government had concentrated since 1994 on comprehensive and well-focused poverty alleviation and crime prevention programmes, levels of crime would certainly have been lower, and the investment climate would have been far more attractive.

The corporate sector and the government were wrong in thinking that it would be possible – after the crisis of legitimacy had been resolved via democratisation – to kick-start the modern sector of the economy with a neo-liberal and globalised accumulation strategy, and that this would be sufficient to pull the poorest half of the population out of its dismal predicament. They were also wrong to think that the poor – many of whom had been criminalised and brutalised during apartheid and the liberation struggle – would remain patient with vague promises that a high economic growth path would create, within a reasonable time frame, the sorely needed employment opportunities and a spontaneous redistribution of income.

Eight years after the political transition, and six years after GEAR's announcement, South Africa is faced with an oxymoron: the economic growth rate is unsatisfactory, the unemployment problem bigger, the distribution of income more unequal, and the poverty problem far more serious (see Luiz 1998: 310). The ANC agreed in 1993 – under pressure from the corporate sector and global financial institutions – to implement a neo-liberal policy and keep the economic system intact, in order to achieve a higher rate of economic growth. The high growth rates have not materialised, and the systemic exclusion and neglect of half of the population have been perpetuated.

4.5 The sixth phase of the AAC-led search for a new accumulation strategy: increased globalisation and privatisation (1997–2002)

In the six years since GEAR was announced the corporate sector has continued to place pressure on the ANC government to further relax exchange controls and grant them other privileges. The most important of these has been the permission given to at least seven conglomerates to shift their main listings to stock exchanges in the United Kingdom and the United States, and the repeated undertakings by the government to restructure the four largest state-owned enterprises (SOEs) – in transport, telecommunications, electricity, and armaments – by 2004. The government's decision to procure defence equipment from foreign suppliers costing R30 billion over 12 years was also taken during this period (these costs have since risen to more than R43 billion, and some analysts believe they will rise far more). We can regard the interaction between the corporate sector and the government on these issues as the sixth phase of the search for a third accumulation strategy.

The corporations that have won permission to shift their main listings to London are Billiton, the AAC, Dimension Data, SA Breweries, and Old Mutual.[58] Following the AAC's listing in London it became apparent that the overlapping shareholding between it and De Beers contravened the regulations of the London Stock Exchange. Under severe pressure from the AAC, the government therefore also allowed it to delist the giant De Beers Corporation, turning it into a private company mainly owned by the AAC.[59] The conglomerates were allowed to list overseas on the strength of promises that this would enhance their ability to mobilise FDI in South Africa. This development has, however, diminished the new government's normal controls over large and important sections of the corporate sector. It is doubtful whether it is in the long-term interests of the country as a whole.

Ironically, instead of accelerating FDI, the offshore listings have burdened the South African balance of payments with a large (and growing) foreign dividend outflow. While annual dividend payments averaged R2,636 million a year from 1994 to 1999, the figures for the second quarter of 2001 translates into an annual figure of R34,076 million (SARB 2001: 5–88, 89).[60] This increased outflow can be regarded as a major cause of the sharp devaluation of the rand during 2001,[61] and there is reason to fear that dividend outflows will remain the Achilles heel of the balance of payments. The longer-term impact of this capital outflow is indeed worrying.[62]

Therefore, all the hyperbolic (if vague) promises made by the corporate sector and global institutions have not remotely materialised. The new government should have been aware from the outset that the power structures of global capitalism were stacked against vulnerable developing countries such as South Africa. Unfortunately, the harm done to the South African economy cannot easily be undone. Globalisation has also created opportunities for large conglomerates – and especially the AAC – to 'escape' from South Africa before the impoverished majority can hold them accountable for their exploitative behaviour during segregation and apartheid.

An important aspect of the new government's economic policy – which can be regarded as part of the broader GEAR approach – is its policy on privatisation. The ANC originally favoured nationalisation and strongly opposed privatisation, and, in the early 1990s, pressurised the De Klerk government into suspending its privatisation programme. In July 1995 the new government released a document entitled 'Discussion paper on restructuring state assets'. It classified SOEs into three categories: those with an explicit role, a less obvious role, and no role in meeting basic needs. The government also announced its intention to restructure some SOEs.[63]

The ANC has advanced several reasons for privatising or restructuring some state-owned assets, the most important being that privatisation can resolve the accumulation crisis by attracting sorely needed FDI and foreign technology. The problem with this argument is that the government would probably – given the power structures of global capitalism – not get a price that would make it worthwhile to sell valuable state assets. However, given that the annual inflow of FDI over the past eight years has only equalled 1 per cent of GDP, and is only a quarter of what the country needs, the argument for partial privatisation becomes very strong indeed. It is also claimed that privatisation can be an instrument for black economic empowerment, and that it can supply the government with funds to finance RDP programmes. Although black economic empowerment is essential, the government should be very careful not to sell state assets to black elite groups on terms that will further enrich these groups without benefiting the impoverished majority (see Rix *et al*, in Baskin 1996a: 69).

According to Ben Fine, the argument that privatisation can help to finance the RDP 'is based on a fallacious perspective... [because] the reconstruction of the economy depends upon a long-term strategy and vision, not on a short-term management of a financial crisis'. He warns that the 'net effect of a privatisation programme will be to consolidate the power of large-scale corporate capital in an economy in which the larger corporations have in any case too much influence and too much power' (1995: 15–16). Those opposed to the new government's privatisation policies therefore believe that they will not 'restructure' the South African economy in the direction envisaged by the RDP, but will aggravate the deep-seated structural crisis evident at the end of the apartheid period by empowering the corporate sector and disempowering the already relatively weak ANC-controlled state.

When all the arguments for and against privatisation are considered, it becomes clear that the government should handle this issue very carefully, and ensure that South Africa's long-term interest prevails over short-term sectional interests. It should not succumb to pressures from the global corporate sector, which wants to buy government assets at bargain prices in developing countries. The government must also be on the alert for the strong tendency in the corporate world towards privatising the benefits of economic activities and socialising the disadvantages, to the detriment of society at large.

The government's arms procurement programme, which will cost at least R43 billion, can be regarded as the most bizarre state project of the past eight years. The decision to spend R3,6 billion (or more) on arms every year for at least 12 years – at a time when the case for spending R3,6 billion more every year on alleviating poverty is so overwhelming – is puzzling, to say the least. The argument that military spending will invite FDI is vague and unverifiable. The role that local and foreign corporations have played in the decision on the arms programme is unclear, but the suspicion exists that the government decided to proceed under duress from a part of the corporate sector.

4.6 The inability or unwillingness of the Truth and Reconciliation Commission to uncover the truth about systemic exploitation

The TRC has done an excellent job of discrediting the apartheid regime, and the atrocities committed under its aegis. In doing so it has identified many of the individual perpetrators of gross human rights violations, and also many of the individual victims of these violations. But, as Mahmood Mamdani points out, 'In the South African context, perpetrators are a small group, as are those victimised by perpetrators. In contrast, beneficiaries [of the *system* of apartheid] are a large group, and victims defined in relation to beneficiaries are the vast majority in society' (1996).

Unfortunately, the TRC has ignored the gross human rights violations perpetrated collectively and systemically against millions of black people under white political domination and racial capitalism. Its inability and/or unwillingness to systemically analyse South Africa's history of unequal power structures are puzzling. By only trying to uncover the 'truth' about one form of victimisation under apartheid and ignoring another (and perhaps even more important) form of victimisation, the TRC has failed dismally in its quest for truth and reconciliation.[64]

In attempting to solve this puzzle, it is again necessary to distinguish between the formal negotiations on political issues and the informal negotiations on economic issues. As indicated in section 4.2, the 'balance of forces' in the formal negotiations favoured the democratic movement, while those in the informal negotiations favoured the corporate sector. The political establishment of the apartheid regime was spectacularly defeated during the formal negotiations, and that prepared the way for the election of 1994 and the political transition from apartheid to representative democracy. In sharp contrast, the white corporate sector – which formed an integral part of the system of racial capitalism for more than a century – was not remotely defeated during the informal negotiations. It succeeded – given its wealth, its enormous power, and its capacity for propaganda and myth-making – in convincing ANC leaders that it was innocent of apartheid misdeeds. Consequently, the two parties agreed – if not explicitly, then at least tacitly – that the benefits that had accumulated (mostly undeservedly) in the hands of the corporate sector and other whites through systemic exploitation would either be forgotten or condoned. The TRC ratified this agreement, although it was not in the interests of truth-seeking and reconciliation to do so.

It is necessary to take the differences in the power play during the two sets of negotiations a step further. After a political transition had been negotiated, the new government deemed it necessary to consolidate its precarious political power by using the TRC to delegitimise the apartheid regime and its security forces. This was done rather dramatically when the TRC identified the individual perpetrators of gross human rights violations, and the individual victims of such violations. But because of the new symbiotic relationship between ANC leaders and the corporate sector, it was expedient for the new government not to pressurise the TRC into uncovering the truth about systemic exploitation, or to delegitimise the corporate sector for its part in the design and utilisation of repressive labour systems.[65]

The TRC's approach should be judged against the background of the compromises reached at the formal and informal negotiations. Ebrahim Moosa has concluded that 'the truth [of the TRC] was what the party (parties) said it was. The truth was not measured, but manufactured. To be charitable [to the TRC], we can say that truth was negotiated [in the informal negotiations]' (Moosa, in Villa-Vicencio and Verwoerd 2000: 116). Franco Barchiesi observes that the TRC had to operate within certain imperatives for the new South African state:

[T]he TRC itself is constituted by the institutional, social-economic, political and ideological imperatives of the new South Africa state... [These] imperatives have had a decisive influence in the TRC's reconstruction of the past and the recommendations for a future with regard to social citizenship as an unresolved issue for the present form of state (1999: 16).

The idea that 'truth' is often 'manufactured' by the elite in power is also reflected in Fernándo-Armesto's general statement about truth: 'We need a history of truth. We need it to test the claim that truth is just a name for opinions which suit the demands of society or the convenience of elites'.[66] Mahmood Mamdani says the following about the kind of truth produced by the TRC:

The truth of the TRC makes most sense when understood as institutionally produced truth, as the outcome of a process of truth-seeking, one whose boundaries were so narrowly defined by power [and especially corporate power] and whose search was so committed to reinforce the new power [of the ANC government], that it turned the political boundaries of a compromise into analytical boundaries of truth-seeking. By compromising a political compromise with a compromised truth... the TRC has turned a political [compromise] into a moral compromise, and obscured the larger truth. While the political compromise is justifiable, the moral and intellectual compromise is not (in Amadiume and Abdullahi 2000: 177–8).

Interestingly, in its final report the TRC itself asks a question about the kind of truth for which it was searching: 'But what about the truth – and whose truth?' In reply, it states that the commission 'was [inter alia] required to report on the broader patterns underlying gross violations of human rights, and to explore the causes of such violations. To do this... it became necessary for the Commission to adopt a social scientist's approach – making use of the information contained in its database and from a range of secondary sources.' It then quotes the following statement by Michael Ignatieff: 'All that a truth commission can achieve is to reduce the number of lies that can be circulated unchallenged in public discourse' (Ignatieff 1996, quoted in TRC 1998: vol 1, ch 5, paras 29 and 33).

The TRC was established by the Promotion of National Unity and Reconciliation Act (no 34 of 1995). Its mandate was formulated as follows:

The objectives of the Commission shall be to promote national unity and reconciliation in a spirit of understanding which transcends the conflicts and divisions of the past by establishing as complete a picture as possible of *the causes, nature and extent of the gross violations of human rights* which were committed during the period 1 March 1960 to 10 May 1994.

The definition of 'gross violation of human rights' was left vague. It was, however, stated that

> the Commission shall facilitate... *inquiries into (i) gross violations of human rights*, including violations which were part of a systematic pattern of abuse... (ii) [and shall also facilitate inquiries into] *the identity of all persons, authorities, institutions and organisations involved in such violations* [of human rights] (TRC 1998: vol 1, ch 4, para 31).

Despite its rather wide mandate, and its explicit intention to report on the 'broad patterns underling gross violations of human rights', the TRC decided to interpret its mandate far more narrowly. In its final report, it states categorically that its governing act limited its investigation to gross violations of human rights defined as the 'killing, abduction, torture or severe ill-treatment' and the 'attempt, conspiracy, incitement, instigation, command or procurement to commit such acts' (TRC 1998: vol 1, ch 2, para 19). Consequently, it concentrated almost exclusively on violations of the human rights of individual victims by individual perpetrators. By doing so, the TRC, for all practical purposes, chose to ignore violations of human rights 'which were part of a systematic pattern of abuse'. By concentrating on individual perpetrators and victims, it also chose not to 'identify all... authorities, institutions, and organisations involved in violations [of human rights]'. In addition, the TRC also chose to interpret 'human rights' as mainly 'first-generation' or legal 'human rights', while the violation of 'second-generation' human rights or 'social rights' were practically ignored. Consequently, it concentrated on 'perpetrators and victims' while neglecting the causal relationship between the beneficiaries and victims of racial capitalism and white political domination. In doing so, the TRC – according to Mamdani – made 'perhaps the greatest moral compromise... [in embracing] the legal fetishism of apartheid... [by making] little distinction between what is legal and what is legitimate [and] between law and right' (Mamdani, in Amadiume and Abdullahi 2000: 181). The TRC understood 'beneficiaries' to mean those who had gained from *corrupting* the laws and from acting illegally, but not those who had designed and implemented the immoral, corrupt, and skewed system of apartheid.

In its final report, the commission acknowledges that:

...there had been an expectation that the Commission would investigate many of the human rights violations which had been caused by the denial of freedom of movement through the pass laws, by forced removals of people from their land, by the denial of the franchise to citizens, by the treatment of farm workers and other labour disputes, and by discrimination in such areas as education and work opportunities. Many organisations lobbied the Commission to insist that these issues should form part of its investigations. Commission members, too, felt that these were important areas that could not be ignored. *Nevertheless, they could not be interpreted as falling directly within the Commission's mandate* (TRC 1998: vol 5, ch 1, para 48; author's emphasis).

This decision was probably not in accordance with its mandate, and should be deplored. It could only have resulted from pressure exerted on it by the corporate sector (and perhaps also by the new government), which realised that a broader investigation would include a systemic analysis of racial capitalism. Such an investigation would have embarrassed – and even angered – the business sector. In the end, the TRC devoted only three days of its life span of two and a half years to public hearings on the role of business in the apartheid era. Not surprisingly, the hearings were conducted in a way that obscured the systemic character of apartheid, and offered business people an undeserved opportunity to clear themselves and their corporations of any guilt in respect of or responsibility for the legacy of apartheid.[67]

According to Mamdani, the TRC 'enthusiastically embraced [the analogy] of dictatorships in Latin America' when it decided to narrow its investigation to perpetrators and victims of (legally defined) gross human rights violation. In the process, the TRC agreed that 'apartheid was no more than a harsh and cruel dictatorship, a gross denial of human rights'. But, in contrast to the Latin American situation, apartheid was also about racial capitalism and the systemic exploitation of blacks. Mamdani vividly identifies what was missing in Latin America and also in the TRC's approach as follows:

The Latin American analogy obscured what was distinctive about apartheid. For the violence of apartheid was aimed less at individuals than at entire communities and entire population groups. And this violence was not just political. It was not just about defending power by denying people rights. The point of torture, terror, death, was even more far-reaching: its aim was to dispossess people of means of livelihood. The point is that the Latin American analogy obscured the colonial nature of the South Africa context:

the link between conquest and dispossession, between racialised power and racialised privileges (in Amadiume and Abdullahi 2000: 179).

At the beginning of its chapter on the business hearings (vol 4, ch 2), the TRC notes that, from a range of perceptions of the relationship between business and apartheid, two dominant positions emerged: a 'pro-business' or 'business-as-victim' school, and a 'systemic exploitation' or 'business-as-beneficiaries-and-blacks-as-victims' school.[68] It concedes that the opposing arguments were relevant to the task facing it because they implied 'different notions of accountability' (para 8).

The report provides a reasonably good summary of the arguments of the two schools; however, its findings arising from the hearings are highly ambiguous. In paragraphs 161 to 167 (vol 4, ch 2) it states that '(b)usiness was central to the economy that sustained the South African state during the apartheid years', thus creating the impression that business was neutral towards apartheid and sustained the apartheid government only indirectly through its 'normal' business activities. What the TRC did not appreciate is that the slogan applicable to sport during the apartheid years – 'There can be no normal sport in an abnormal society' – also, and to a far greater extent, applied to business. Indeed, 'normal' business was not possible while apartheid (and racial capitalism) was in place. The simple fact that the political and economic freedom, bargaining power, property rights, and entrepreneurial opportunities of blacks were seriously restricted under segregation and apartheid, and that blacks were therefore reduced to exploitable units of labour, shows the veracity of this. The TRC thus ignored this obvious relationship between blacks and whites during apartheid in a manner unbecoming of an official commission.

There can be no doubt that the apartheid system (or, more correctly, the system of racial capitalism) was deliberately constructed and maintained on behalf of white business and through close and continuous collaboration between almost all white corporations and business organisations on the one hand, and the white political and bureaucratic establishments on the other. Racial capitalism was built and maintained for 150 years on successive phases of black labour repression. Consequently, the main issue during continuing consultations between white politicians and white business (in all sectors of the economy) during this period was how to design and redesign a multitude of repressive measures with the sole purpose of giving white business easy access to, and control over, cheap and docile black labour. The commission failed dismally to devote any attention to the long history and exploitative nature of the black labour system. What is astonishing about the TRC's superficial reconstruction of South Africa's economic and labour history is that it did not even distinguish between labour repressive measures (with cost-decreasing effects) and labour discriminatory measures (with cash-increasing effects), and simply accepted the arguments of business that apartheid was a cost-increasing system.

The finding of the commission (in vol 4, ch 2, para 166) that 'business failed in the hearings to take responsibility for its involvement in state security initiatives specifically designed to sustain apartheid rule [or white supremacy]' touches on a very important issue. It is a great pity that the commission did not explore this far more thoroughly. Many of the most respected corporations – led by a highly esteemed managerial elite – worked hand in glove with ARMSCOR during the 1980s when it was one of few going parastatal concerns. These corporations were, directly and indirectly, involved in the darkest hour of apartheid, and in the atrocities committed to perpetuate the apartheid regime.

While the TRC did not explicitly reject the 'pro-business' position, it also did not accept the 'systemic exploitation' position. In fact, it was very careful not to use the rhetoric of the 'systemic exploitation' school. When the recommendations are closely read it becomes clear that the TRC went out of its way to ensure that it did not present business (or whites) as *beneficiaries* of the economic system of apartheid, and blacks as *victims* of the same system. Consequently, it also did not portray business (or whites) as having a moral obligation to atone for past practices.

In its recommendations, the TRC appeals to business to voluntarily compensate black people for being disadvantaged under apartheid, stating that 'business could and should play an enormously creative role in the development of new reconstruction and development programmes' (vol 4, ch 2, para 159). This request has a positive ring; it sounds as if the TRC is giving advice to a valued friend. However, the exploitation of blacks did not happen voluntarily; it was based on economic and political systems embedded in a network of compulsory legislation, and justified by racist ideologies propagated as self-evident truths. To expect business to compensate black people voluntarily – and adequately – for the systemic injustices committed over 150 years is naïve.[69]

Elsewhere, the commission affirms the judgement of the international human rights community that 'apartheid was a crime against humanity' (vol 1, ch 4, para 1; see also vol 1, ch 1, para 62). However, it does not explain why it shares the 'international community's basic moral and legal position on apartheid' (para 2), and does not spell out what aspect of apartheid was a 'crime against humanity'. Was it that part (ie, racial capitalism and white supremacy) that enriched whites and impoverished blacks during three quarters of the 20th century, or was it the security system institutionalised and applied from the 1960s onwards to counteract black insurrection with deeds of atrocity? Or did the commission regard both parts of the apartheid system as a crime against humanity?

The international human rights community decided that apartheid was a crime against humanity before the notorious security system of the apartheid regime was institutionalised during the 1960s.[70] By concentrating on the 'legalistic' gross human rights violations by individual perpetrators, one gains the impression that the commission believed it was mainly (if not exclusively) the security system, and the atrocities committed by its agents, that was the really criminal part of apartheid.

During the business hearings most business representatives argued – in submissions and during evidence – that gross human rights violations would require active and deliberate participation by individual business persons, and illegal acts committed by them. Consequently, they claimed that they (and their corporations) could not be regarded as participants in gross human rights violations, despite the fact that they (or their parents or grandparents) were involved in designing and utilising immoral and exploitative systems. Thus the commission's individualistic and legalistic approach to human rights violations provided business people with a convenient means of distancing themselves from apartheid and from any individual or corporate responsibility towards its immoral and criminal nature, irrespective of the extent to which they had benefited from racial discrimination and separation, and irrespective of the extent to which apartheid had impoverished millions of blacks.

If the commission had explicitly applied the notion that apartheid was a crime against humanity to the business sector, business people could not have washed their hands in this manner. It would not have been possible to walk away from black poverty, or to embrace – as the commission did – the fallacious argument that what was legal could not have been immoral or criminal (see Mamdani, in Amadiume and Abdullahi 2000: 181). By not applying the notion of apartheid as a crime against humanity to racial capitalism, and the business sector's involvement in it, the TRC lost a golden opportunity to educate the individual and corporate beneficiaries of apartheid about their direct responsibilities for the disrupted social structures and abject poverty of the majority of blacks. If the beneficiaries had been educated about their participation in racial capitalism, they would certainly have been less arrogant, and possibly more compassionate and generous.

Another reason why the TRC failed to do justice to these issues may have been that the period of history it was instructed to investigate was too short to allow it to deal with South Africa's past in a credible manner. By focusing on only 34 of South Africa's modern history of 350 years, the commission not only interpreted this history in a one-sided way, but also distorted and compromised the 'truth'. By giving official status to this skewed interpretation, the commission not only detracted from the reconciliation process, but also placed obstacles in the way of restoring social justice, social citizenship, and social rights. In this way history-writing in South Africa was done a great disfavour, and the commission also missed an opportunity to 're-educate' South Africans – both white and black – about the true nature of the centuries-long relationship between the white master class and the unfree black working class.

Mamdani comes to the following illuminating conclusion on the TRC:

> In its eagerness to reinforce the new order...the TRC wrote the vast majority of apartheid's victims [i.e. the victims of systemic exploitation] out of its version of history. The unintended outcome has been to drive a wedge between the beneficiaries and the victims of apartheid. In doing so, the TRC has failed to open a social debate on possible futures in South Africa. To reflect on the experience of the TRC is to ponder a harsh truth, that it may be easier to live with yesterday's perpetrators who have lost power than to live with beneficiaries whose gains remain intact (in Amadiume and Abdullahi 2000: 183).

As noted earlier, Ignatieff contends that 'all that truth commissions can achieve is to reduce the number of lies that can be circulated unchallenged in public discourse' (1996: 113). It will indeed be very sad if the TRC's unwillingness or inability to properly analyse South Africa's troubled economic history spreads the following lie in the public discourse: namely, that the systems of white political domination and racial capitalism did not undeservedly enrich whites and impoverish blacks, and that the rich are therefore released from any moral, political, and/or systemic obligation to restore social justice towards blacks.

4.7 The rise of a black elite, and its tendency towards elitism and self-enrichment

One of the most remarkable developments over the past 30 years is the enrichment of the top 20 per cent of African households and the simultaneous impoverishment of the bottom 40 per cent. While the income of the top 20 per cent of African households (involving about 6 million people) increased by more than 60 per cent over this period, that of the bottom 40 per cent (involving about 18 million people) declined by almost 60 per cent. As the process of stratification among Africans was strictly suppressed by white supremacist policies until 1970, the belated process of stratification was necessary. Its pace was perhaps too rapid, while the unequal distribution of income within African society grew alarmingly (see tables 10.3 and 10.4). The end result of this dual process is the emergence of an African bourgeois elite capable of maintaining high living standards on the one hand, and an impoverished underclass or lumpenproletariat on the other.

In 1975 the income of the top 20 per cent of Africans households was eight times higher than that of the poorest 40 per cent. In 1991 it was 19 times higher, and in 1996 31 times higher (see Whiteford and McGrath 1994: table 6.3; Whiteford and Van Seventer 1999: table 3.6). At present, the income of the top 20 per cent of African households is probably 40 times higher than that of the poorest 40 per cent. More or less the same dual process of enrichment and impoverishment has occurred among coloured people, but has not resulted in such great inequalities as among Africans.[71] What we have witnessed over the past 30 years is the rise of a wealthy black elite of about 10 million people (about 4 million a bourgeoisie, and about 6 million a petit bourgeoisie), and an underclass (ie, the middle lower and lower lower classes) of about 22,5 million mainly black people who are poorer today than they were in the heyday of segregation and apartheid (see table 2.2 and figure 2.1).[72]

The black elite emerged during the last 20 years of apartheid, but has grown hugely over the past ten years. This is basically a healthy phenomenon; a new South Africa would not have been possible without it. The role played by the new black elite in the higher echelons of politics, business, the bureaucracy, and the media, and in cultural and educational activities gives definition and direction to post-apartheid South Africa. While those who now constitute the black elite were unjustly prevented under apartheid from reaching their full potential, it is heartening to witness their current progress and their contribution to the larger South African society.

However, it is unfortunate that this black elite has emerged during the same period in which the black underclass has become even poorer. Although we cannot identify a direct link between these two divergent tendencies, we can identify systemic and transformational links between them. The upward mobility of the black elite is closely connected to the political power shift from whites towards blacks since the 1970s. The downward mobility of the underclass is, in turn, closely linked to the deterioration of the economy and of employment over the same period (see ch 2 and section 10.4).

The rapid development of the black elite testifies to its successful co-option by the corporate sector. In its quest to institutionalise a neo-liberal and globally oriented economic approach in the 'new South Africa', the corporate sector was not only prepared to condone the lucrative remuneration of black politicians and bureaucrats, but also to offer the emerging black elite even more lucrative deals in the private sector. In turn, the downward movement of the large black underclass testifies to the harm done to the South African economy during the liberation struggle, and the inability of the new government to transform it. The highly successful political transition has meant that the whole population has been politically and constitutionally included. But, owing to the restricted tax and employment capacity of the economy, and the elite compromises between the ANC and the corporate sector, the new government has little capacity for effectively addressing mass poverty.

Even if we accept the economic and systemic constraints in the 'new South Africa', the question arises whether it was not possible to slow down the development of the new black upper class in order to reduce the alarming deterioration in the position of the underclass. But for such an attempt to be credible, the new government would have had to scale down the extraordinarily high living standards of the white elite (about 4 million people) whose members have been allowed to continue their 'Californian' standard of living amid a sea of poverty. This brings us to the important question of whether the new governing elite has the political will to tax the white and black elites more heavily, thus reducing their living standards and conspicuous consumption patterns, in order to do something meaningful about the plight of the poor. Before we can answer this question, we need to focus on the reasons why some upwardly mobile blacks have been sidetracked into elitism.

It is perhaps not fair to expect members of the black upper class to be more socially conscious and generous than members of the English and Afrikaner elite groups were when they were governing the country. The new black upper class can indeed argue that it has been deprived of good living for so long that it should not be denied this now. This argument would be valid if it weren't for the wretched and deteriorating conditions under which so many other black people have to live. What is perhaps more important is that the new black elite can also blame the English and Afrikaners for setting deplorable examples of elitism, not only when they governed the country but also since the transition.

During the first half of the 20th century South Africa was controlled politically and economically by the English establishment. This elite was notorious for its haughtiness and self-righteousness, typical during the heyday of Victorian colonialism, and displayed little concern for the relative backwardness and poverty of the rest of the population, including Afrikaners. It justified its position of power and privilege in terms of the alleged character deficiencies of poor Afrikaners, as well as racist ideologies. English elitism provoked a strong protest movement in the form of the Purified NP from 1934 onwards which enabled Afrikaner-oriented political parties to win the general election of 1948. However, while the English establishment lost its political hegemony, it has retained its economic hegemony and elitist self-righteousness to this day.

During the first 20 years after assuming power, the Afrikaner establishment displayed a high degree of social consciousness and generosity towards the poverty of its 'own people' (*volksgenote*). But the policies of the NP government were highly sectional, and mainly concerned with the group or 'national interest' (*volksbelange*) of the Afrikaners. In the 1960s a wealthy Afrikaner upper class emerged that has been as haughty and self-righteous as the English elite, but with all the trappings of the *nouveaux riche*. Members of the Afrikaner elite condoned – with few exceptions – the intensified exploitation of blacks under apartheid, and, like English-speakers, profited from it extensively.

The indifference of members of the Afrikaner and English elites towards the predicament of black people provoked a protracted liberation struggle that led to the political transition of 1994. The rise of a black elite over the past 30 years and the development of a black elitism that is openly indifferent towards the plight of poorer blacks should be understood against this background. The black elite and its inclination towards elitism are largely the creation of the two white elite groups that deliberately co-opted the black elite as a junior partner in order to perpetuate their own wealth and privilege, and legitimise their economic power in the 'new South Africa'. For this reason, black elitism has acquired the same systemic character in the new South Africa as white elitism in the old.

The new black elite has been deceived by the controllers of white wealth and privilege into buying into neo-liberalism and globalism, despite the fact that these ideologies and their application in South Africa are to the detriment of the poor. It is for these reasons that the new governing elite apparently does not have the will to tax the old white elite and the new black elite more heavily in order to obtain the resources it needs to improve the alarmingly poor living standards of the lower class.

Although black elitism has modelled its own extravagance and arrogance on white elitism, it can never be identical to it. The two white versions of elitism were based on racial prejudice. By contrast, the arrogance and indifference displayed by some members of the black elite towards the black underclass are not displayed towards other ethnic or racial groups but towards their 'own people'. It is therefore not a racially based but a class-based elitism. But what is even more problematic about some members of the black elite is that they are not only arrogant and indifferent to the plight of their 'own people', but also to that of people who suffered with them under segregation and apartheid and who fought with them in the liberation struggle. When viewed from this perspective, black elitism becomes deplorable.

The positive and negative factors responsible for class differentiation and the rise of the black elite during the last 20 years of apartheid will be described in section 10.4.4. Although many blacks attained their new status in a laudable manner, and against difficult odds, others benefited from nepotism. The same kind of duality is operating in the post-apartheid period. While many blacks have attained wealth and status by performing excellently in the public and/or private sectors, others have thrived in the atmosphere of corruption, nepotism, and careerism that has become a defining feature of the post-apartheid period. It is sad that the corruption that attained a structural character in the final phase of apartheid is being perpetuated almost intact in the 'new South Africa'. The manner in which this has happened is still shrouded in mystery, but it may have happened because of the negotiated nature of the transition, and the many 'deals' that were struck.[73]

Whatever the reasons for the persistence of structural corruption, it created ample opportunities for many members of the new governing elite to enrich themselves in all sorts of improper ways.[74] The policy of affirmative action in both the public and the private sectors – together with the small pool of black people with the necessary education, professional training, and experience to fill the lucrative jobs available – has lent its own momentum to the black elite's careerism and quest for material enrichment. The warnings of both the former president, Nelson Mandela, and the current president, Thabo Mbeki, against black careerism and insatiable and morally unbounded greed have seemingly fallen on deaf ears. Adam *et al* describe black elitism as follows:

> The [new black elite] that benefits most from the post-apartheid order is a fledgling black middle class. It consists of a growing number of independent entrepreneurs, a managerial aristocracy in high demand and a new political bourgeois eager to join in the consumerism of their former oppressors...Most ANC officials measure equality by comparison with the affluence of the predecessors. On top of the vast discrepancies in wealth [between the black elite and the lower sixty per cent of the black population] a thorough Americanisation [of ideological attitudes] has penetrated all segments. American habits and ostentatious consumption have become the

desired yardstick by which South African progress is measured...An unashamedly elitist self-confidence pervades the new bourgeoisie...The emulation of Hollywood lifestyle by a new Ebony resembles the silly glorification of royal titles, quaint British country culture, or English dress codes by the old colonisers. It should have been of no concern were it not for the squandering of public money amidst a sea of poverty (1997: 174–5).

Bishop Desmond Tutu once said that the gravy train had stopped only long enough for the black elite to climb on. Peter Storey has reproached the new black elite for 'betraying what the anti-apartheid struggle stood for', and has claimed that 'even if we accept that South Africa has to embrace the global market economy to make it in the big bad world, we don't have to emulate its fat cats and its naked greed' (*Sunday Independent*, 24 November 1996).

It is, however, not only some members of the haute bourgeoisie who are enriching themselves in questionable ways in the 'new South Africa'. The new petit bourgeoisie is also using its trade union power and its position in the ANC Alliance for short-term financial gain. The Labour Relations Act, Employment Equity Act, and Basic Conditions of Employment Act can be regarded as dramatic gains made by the trade union movement to improve the lives, and entrench the positions, of its members. Marais contends that 'many of the historical demands of the labour movement have acquired legislative force in these acts...[which supply] much of the *concrete basis* for the endurance of COSATU's alliance with the ANC' (2001: 240).

The protagonists of free market capitalism in South Africa are inclined to justify all three versions of elitism – ie, English, Afrikaner, and black – in terms of certain assertions about the structural determinants of the economy since the mineral revolution at the end of the 19th century. According to this argument, the savings, investment, and entrepreneurial needs of South African capitalism during the first half of the 20th century required an enterprising elite, but the economy could only sustain an elite of between 5 and 10 per cent of the population.

When South African capitalism entered its 'long boom' from 1934 to 1974, it could sustain a larger elite of between 10 and 15 per cent of the population, including some Afrikaners. And, although the economy grew at an unsatisfactory rate after 1974, socio-political events required the further expansion of the elite to 15 to 20 per cent of the population, incorporating some 3,5 million members of the black bourgeoisie and a further 6 million members of the black petit bourgeoisie. Although the protagonists of free market capitalism do not acknowledge this explicitly, this argument implies that it was only possible to include 33 per cent of the population in the upper classes by further impoverishing the lower classes (see figure 2.1).

When we accept – however reluctantly – these assumptions about the structural factors underpinning the economy, they may justify the notion of the slow expansion of the upper class. But they certainly do not justify the extravagant living standards and superior attitudes of all three elite groups. Those inclined to justify a system of developing capitalism in these terms should be aware of the fact that no capitalist system can be sustained if considerations of socio-political stability and morality are not taken into account in organising it. South Africa's socio-economic history in the 20th century clearly testifies to this. At the end of the 1940s the Afrikaner petit bourgeoisie mobilised a successful protest against the elitism and arrogance of the English establishment. In the last quarter of the 20th century the black population group launched a successful struggle against racial capitalism and white supremacy. Anyone who is inclined to use narrow 'economistic' arguments to justify the continued existence of the two white elite groups and the new black elite without any concern for the plight of the poor is skating on thin ice. If we contemplate the fact that both the English and Afrikaner elites lost their political hegemony because of their selfishness and arrogance, we have reason to ponder whether the same destiny does not await those who are presently so conspicuously guilty of black elitism. The fact that, since 1994, both the white and black elite have expressed concern about poverty but are not prepared to make the sacrifices needed to relieve the plight of the poor is disconcerting.

The coexistence of a new political system (controlled by an African elite) and the old economic system (still controlled by a neo-liberal white elite) constitutes a dual system of democratic capitalism which is morally unjust, dysfunctional, and also unsustainable. We are forced to ask: for how long can white wealth and elitism remain entrenched; for how long can the black elite continue to indulge in black elitism; and how far can the inequality between the black bourgeoisie and the black lumpenproletariat extend before the system cracks? Against this background, the possibility of a second struggle cannot be discounted. This is the last thing South Africa can afford.

South Africa has experienced a remarkable political transition. It is, however, incomplete, because a concurrent socio-economic transformation has not taken place. The systemic challenge facing South Africa's new politico-economic system of democratic capitalism – based on the ideology of liberal capitalism – will be discussed in part 4. The five successive systemic periods during which South Africa was politically and economically controlled by whites will be discussed in detail in part 3.

Endnotes

1 According to Freund, 'the [formal] negotiation process has [also] been one of discussions amongst power-brokers behind closed doors' (quoted in Hyslop 1999: 434). In the case of the negotiations on economic issues, the discussions were even more secretive, and the power brokers on the side of the corporate sector far more powerful.

2 According to Waldmeir, ANC leaders were 'bombarded with invitations to conferences, cocktail parties, and dinner engagements with local and visiting businessmen, all of whom delivered impromptu lectures on market economics. ANC officials were sent to Washington DC for a familiarisation course at the World Bank. Everywhere they heard the same message: generating economic growth is the biggest priority. Nothing must be done to jeopardise that' (1997: 255).

3 Strictly speaking, the deal was signed by the TEC, which had ANC leaders as members.

4 While, in the third phase of the search for a new accumulation strategy in the early 1990s, Derek Keys played an important role in bringing about unanimity between the NP government and the corporate sector on economic matters, he also played a key role in convincing the ANC of the merits of the NEM. Waldmeir describes Keys's role as follows, '[He] formalised the process of economic consensus building when he agreed to the launch of the National Economic Forum...It was a kind of "economic CODESA", and Keys took it very seriously...Keys confronted the ANC policy-makers with the unpleasant reality that they were not taking over a rich country with lots of surplus cash to spend on black economic upliftment. They would have tragically limited room for economic maneuver' (1997: 257).

5 In its 1994 annual report the IMF described the ideological shift that took place in November 1993 as follows: 'It was clear by late 1993 that the most immediate problems facing South Africa were confidence related. Consequently, the African National Congress, even before its election to government in April 1994, voiced its commitment [in November 1993] to eschewing policies to imperil confidence – i.e. interventionist regulations, excessive fiscal and monetary spending and confiscatory tax policies – and to strengthen market forces...[but] the most telling signal of the new government's economic ideology has been its broad advocacy of free trade' (IMF 1995: 89–90).

6 Marais summarises the ANC approach at the time as follows: 'Defining the ANC's negotiating strategy was the need to nurture compromises that would yield a [political] settlement. This meant that the ANC – only temporarily, it believed – retreated from positions necessary to establish and safeguard an institutional bedrock for a socio-economic programme that could weaken the structural foundations of the "two-nation" society. The political/ideological project of nation-building [for political purposes] became paramount and supplanted – or at least overshadowed – the socio-economic features of the crisis' (2001: 89–90).

7 Joe Slovo not only played an important role in engineering the 'sunset' clauses, but also acknowledged late in 1992 that the ANC had decided to forge a political consensus by 'retreating from certain previously held positions – which would create the possibility of a major positive breakthrough in the negotiating process without permanently hampering real democratic advance' (see Slovo 1992: 37).

8 Marais continues: '[The] inwardly based economy [forced on the country by the

anti-apartheid movement] was at odds with the liberalized, transnational routes of capital accumulation being threaded across the globe...Many local corporations faced the prospect of serious and sustained devalorization of capital...For conglomerates most active in the financial and mining sectors, economic liberalisation was essential if they were to wrestle free of a national economy that offered little scope for sustained expansion' (2001: 155).

9 Marais makes the same point by claiming that 'the ANC and its left allies were poorly equipped to wage battle on technical grounds, a direct consequence of the democratic movement's historical neglect of the social and economic spheres... [Consequently], business could successfully conduct a vigorous political and ideological struggle at a nominal technical level, deploying massive resources to great effect...[In due time] policy making increasingly became dislodged from the social and political objectives proclaimed by the ANC, and increasingly impenetrable to its activists' (1998: 158).

10 According to Freund, the ANC 'moved dramatically to the centre in 1993...[at a time when] the SACP looked increasingly divided and irrelevant [after the death of Chris Hani], [while] the relative weight of COSATU (forced to abandon strike action in response to ANC pressure in Nov 1993) rapidly diminishing in the "alliance", and Umkhontu we Sizwe on the verge of dissolution' (quoted in Hyslop 1999: 433).

11 Freund puts it as follows: 'The growing radicalisation of the struggle against apartheid was strongly buttressed in the 1970s by what appeared to be a world-wide trend to favour so-called liberation movements, and the military and diplomatic support of the Soviet Union and its allies and dependencies. By the end of the 1980s this kind of support had disappeared and virtually reversed itself (quoted in Hyslop 1999: 432–3).

12 According to Mike Morris, the negotiations were 'not about a [NP] government negotiating its surrender because it was defeated by superior force...[but] about a political struggle to forge a new nation and new alliances that [could] ensure the broadest basis of social consent. [The ANC was] not sweeping aside the old institutions of state power...[but had] to try and shape the terms on which it [was] incorporated into [the existing] state as a new ruling group...Transformation [was] on the cards, but it [could] not involve the creation of new revolutionary institutions' (1993: 8).

13 The changing views of the American political philosopher Robert Dahl on this subject are illuminating. Between 1956 and 1978 he wrote several books in which he claimed that, in a comprehensive democratic and capitalist system, power was distributed in such a way that a beneficial 'competitive equilibrium' was created by the plurality of power groups. He propagated the idea that power was effectively disaggregated and non-cumulative, and shared and bartered by numerous groups in society representing diverse interests (see Dahl 1956; Held 1987: ch 6). However, in a book published in 1985 he radically changed his point of view, concluding that that 'modern corporate capitalism tends to produce inequalities in social and economic resources [and power] so great as to bring about severe violations of political equality and hence of the democratic process' (1985: 60). According to this neo-pluralist view of Dahl and others, interest groups (such as the big corporations) cannot be treated as necessarily equal, and the state cannot be regarded as a neutral arbiter among all interest groups. According to the neo-pluralist view, the big

business corporations wield disproportionate influence over the state, and therefore become a threat to democracy and jeopardise the ability of governments to govern effectively. (See also Hertz 2001.)

14 According to Lester Thurow, the per capita income in the United States in 2000 was more than double that in 1950. But despite this huge increase in total income, the wages and salaries of the lower 60 to 70 per cent of the workforce were the same in real terms as in 1950 (see Thurow 1996: 18–24). Between 1977 and 1999 the top fifth of households in the United States increased their annual income after federal taxes by 43 per cent, while the middle fifth gained 8 per cent, and the bottom fifth lost 9 per cent.

15 While the Rich North received less than 70 per cent of world income in 1970, its share increased to 80 per cent in 2000. According to Watkins, 'poverty, mass unemployment, and inequality have grown [in the developing world] alongside the expansion of trade and foreign investment associated with globalisation. In the developing world, poverty continues to increase in absolute terms, and the gap between "successful" and "unsuccessful" countries is widening… In a world of disturbing contrasts, the gap between rich and poor countries, and between rich and poor people, continues to widen. It is increasingly apparent that this reality will not be changed through [economic] growth alone' (1997: 3). The income gap between the richest fifth and the poorest fifth in the world is widening at an alarming rate. In 1960 the richest 20 per cent of the world had incomes 30 times greater than the income of the poorest 20 per cent. In 2000 it was 80 times higher. (See UNDP 2000.)

16 A good example of how the corporate sector in the United States gained additional structural power by rewriting the rules of the game is the international agreement on Trade Related Intellectual Property Rights (TRIPS), agreed on the initiative of the United States (see May 2000).

17 Rodrick argues that 'the expansion of markets is undermining social cohesion and is inexorably leading towards a major economic and political crisis… [Consequently] the broader challenge of the twenty first century is to engineer a new balance between market and society [and between the corporate sector and the state] – one that will continue to unleash the creative energies of private entrepreneurship without eroding the social basis of co-operation' (1997: 22, 30, 36).

18 What is known about the informal negotiation process is that Mandela 'dined regularly with AAC patriarch Harry Oppenheimer, and participated in the "Brenthurst Group" (named after Oppenheimer's Johannesburg estate) of leading businessmen and opinion-formers' (Waldmeir 1997: 256). It is indeed hugely ironic that close friendships developed between core leaders of the ANC and the managerial elite of the AAC, which had profited for longer and to a larger degree than any other corporation from the systemic exploitation of African migrant workers. But what is even more astonishing is that the Brenthurst Group got the 'deal' it so desperately needed without even being pressurised by the ANC to pay a 'solidarity' or 'restitution tax' as a *quid pro quo*. The only 'return' the ANC got was that Mandela asked 20 top businessmen (including top AAC figures) for at least R1 million each to help him in the 1994 election and all but one complied (Waldmeir 1997: 258.) The AAC also agreed to sell some of its corporate assets to black empowerment groups at bargain prices. Whether the prices were indeed at 'bargain levels' is a controversial issue.

19 Anthony Holiday claims that 'the business tycoons...made it clear [early in the 1990s]...that [an economic] settlement could not be a way-stage to a socialist revolution. Any deviation from freemarket economics would be met with financial isolation on an international scale' (*Mail & Guardian*, 27 July–2 August 2001: 22). According to Adam *et al*, the change in the economic orientation of the ANC 'did not happen without some heavy prodding and outright threats' (1997: 173).

20 The proposition that 'power constellations' are irrelevant in the system of free market capitalism receives 'scientific support' from the mainstream or neo-classical school of economics. In Paul Samuelson's *Economics* – of which more copies have been sold than any other book except the Bible – the word 'power' is not listed in the 40-page index. This is so because power is apparently dispersed so equally in 'free' markets that it does not merit a mention.

21 Formed in 1989, the Mass Democratic Movement was a formation that brought together trade unions, the UDF, and certain churches in a defiance and resistance campaign against apartheid. It was aligned with the ANC when that organisation began to reconstruct itself inside South Africa from 1990 onwards.

22 COSATU's status as the ANC's labour ally was confirmed by the decision taken in 1990 to transfer the assets of the South African Congress of Trade Unions (SACTU) to COSATU. In June 1990 COSATU and the ANC held workshops in Harare to plan policies for a post-apartheid South Africa.

23 Firstly, the RDP requires integrated and sustainable policy programmes, as it recognises that the legacy of apartheid cannot be overcome with piecemeal un-co-ordinated policies; secondly, it notes that the programme must be a people-driven process based upon transparency and inclusivity; thirdly, it recognises that the process of reconstruction is conditional on peace and security; fourthly, it integrates growth, development, reconstruction, redistribution and reconciliation into a unified programme by attempting to meet basic needs and build the infrastructure; fifthly, it requires the democratisation of both society and state; and lastly, it commits itself to a process of continuous assessment and accountability (ANC 1994: 4–7).

24 The RDP states that 'the South African economy is in a deep-seated structural crisis, and as such requires fundamental reconstruction. For decades forces within the white minority have used their exclusive access to political and economic power to promote their own sectional interests at the expense of black people. Black people have been systematically exploited and oppressed economically and South Africa now has one of the world's most unequal patterns of distribution of income and wealth...The ever-changing and destabilising global economy has also adversely affected the local economy' (ANC 1994: 75).

25 According to Luiz, 'the RDP assumed state capacity, instead of prioritising the need to build this capacity' (1998: 263).

26 Blumenfeld also outlines some of the reasons for the apparent failure of the RDP. He lists conceptual uncertainties – the RDP meant different things to different people; a lack of funding – the affordability of the programme was questioned from the outset; ideological struggles – the RDP was caught up in the evolving struggles between radicals and pragmatists within the ANC, between those who viewed the RDP as a facilitating condition for the ultimate 'social transformation' of South Africa and those who were wary of creating a culture of dependency; and implementing failures

– the new government lacked the capacity to deliver on its promises, and even though only a few projects were approved, only a small proportion of these were implemented (1997: 5–18).

27 Stephen Gelb observes that 'the RDP Office was set up within the executive in a way that allowed it very restricted influence over fiscal policy, and no influence over monetary issues or other aspects of macro policy' (1998: 16).

28 Nattrass has criticised this process of taking funds away from departments with one hand and giving them back with the other under the guise of promoting the 'reprioritisation' of government spending as a pointless and counterproductive game of musical chairs (1996). It has been said that the RDP Fund and the 'reprioritisation' of expenditure was the idea of the then minister of finance, Derek Keys. If this is so, it can be regarded as a clever move by someone from the corporate sector, with close links with the NP, to nip the RDP in the bud by means of 'fiscal procedures'.

29 Marais states correctly that as soon as the RDP 'became the programme of [the new] government, [it] did not [any longer] represent a coherent strategic programme for popular transformation...[Shortly after the 1994 election] the ANC has been assimilated into a web of institutional relations, systems and practices tailored to service the interests of (in the first instance) white privilege and (in the final instance) the capitalist classes...[Consequently the new government] eviscerated [the RDP] of its original ideals [and] its *function* in the transition had been altered dramatically. In its revised form it became neither the paragon of, nor the mere sop to, the transformatory demands that had brought the ANC to power. It had mutated into something altogether different' (2001: 95–6, 239).

30 The 1995 draft paper on competition stated 'that competition policy should not break up the conglomerates as one means of advancing black economic interests. [This implies] that black empowerment, and the "unbundling" of the conglomerates may have to be pursued via separate policy mechanisms' (Michie *et al*, in Michie and Padayachee 1997: 21).

31 In its annual report for 2001, the SARB acknowledged that the continued decline in the ability of the economy to create jobs was due to its high capital-intensity.

32 The 'restructuring' that has taken place has often been at the behest of the corporate sector – the permission given to some conglomerates to move their main listings offshore being a prominent example. In as much as the government has accepted a policy of privatisation and has begun to restructure state assets, it has also strengthened the power of the private sector *vis-à-vis* the public sector. In this way the ANC government has been a partner in augmenting the 'deep-seated structural crisis'.

33 Companies' contributions to total tax revenue plummeted from 27 per cent in 1976 to 18 per cent in 1990 and 11 per cent in 1999. Over the same period, mines' contribution fell from 9 per cent to 2 per cent and less than 0,5 per cent. Meanwhile, the contribution of personal taxes soared from 25 per cent to 30 per cent to 42 per cent (COSATU, response to the 2000/2001 budget, 2000).

34 On that occasion, Mandela stated that the RDP Office had become redundant because the RDP had been successfully embedded in the line departments. This was certainly not the case.

35 The SAF accepts as a self-evident truth the dictum that the scope for private sector

development is limited by the size of the public sector, without giving any theoretical or empirical justification for this. Obsessed with the argument that government borrowing 'crowds' the private sector out of financial markets, it does not even consider the possibility that, in a developing country such as South Africa, public investment can stimulate private investment and be responsible for a 'crowding in' of private investment. In its determination to prevent the new government from embarking on a developmental state policy, the SAF 'oversells' the alleged virtues of liberal or free market capitalism.

36 It is not surprising that the SAF document does not consider social upliftment as a cure for criminality. It concludes that 'the only way of dealing with crime which will pay immediate and tangible dividends is to improve the quality, visibility and vigour of policing, backed by effective punishment via the justice and prison systems. This ought to be done as quickly as possible' (SAF 1996: 40).

37 The GEAR document was drawn up under 'somewhat secretive conditions', and was only shown to a small number of decision-makers in the ANC Alliance before being released. Despite strong opposition from COSATU and the SACP, Manuel and Mbeki declared the new policy approach to be 'non-negotiable'. Although the ANC's national executive committee endorsed GEAR, COSATU's sixth national congress rejected it, but did not demand that the government rescind it. As was the case with the 'Statement on economic policies' of 1993, the GEAR document was accepted without any democratic consultation, which went against the grain of the ANC's hallowed tradition of democratic practice (see Marais 2001: 162–3).

38 GEAR's thrust is succinctly summarised as follows: 'In brief, government consumption expenditure should be cut back, private and public sector wage increases kept in check, tariff reform accelerated to compensate for the depreciation, and domestic savings performance improved. These measures will counteract the inflationary impact of the exchange rate adjustment, permit fiscal deficit targets to be reached, establish a climate for continued investor confidence and facilitate the financing of both private sector investment and accelerated development expenditure' (department of finance 1996: 5).

39 GEAR projected an economic growth rate of 6 per cent a year and the creation of 400 000 jobs a year by 2000. It hoped that gross domestic savings would rise from 15 to 22 per cent of GDP, and that gross domestic investment would increase from 18 to 26 per cent of GDP in the year 2000. This would have required FDI equivalent to 4 per cent of GDP – ie, more or less R30 billion in the year 2000. FDI of this magnitude thus presupposes a far greater integration of the South African economy into the global economy. To attain this, the GEAR document also emphasised the need for privatisation.

40 A first step towards the 'Washington consensus' was taken in January 1995 when an agreement on trade liberalisation was signed with the World Trade Organisation (WTO). Shortly afterwards – on 10 March 1995 – the financial rand (finrand) was abolished. This started the gradual phasing out of exchange rate controls and the integration of South Africa's financial markets with international financial markets.

41 In 1996, André Roux – one of two co-ordinators of the technical team of 15 that compiled the GEAR document – addressed a seminar on GEAR at the University of Stellenbosch. Asked whether GEAR's highly optimistic projections were part of a

strategy to sell its ideological approach, he replied that it was 'ideologically neutral'. A 1996 government document on GEAR also claimed that 'there is an objective character about certain economic relations'. These remarks are naïve.

42 The thinking behind *Growth for all* and GEAR is questionable on several grounds. The large informal sector gives a flexibility to the labour market that was not acknowledged. According to Adelzadeh, most firms use temporary workers, because they are easier to dismiss or retrench (Adelzadeh 1996: 19). A year after GEAR's publication, André Roux acknowledged that more research was needed into the link between economic growth and job creation (*Business Day*, 13 May 1997).

43 Gelb states correctly that 'rather than introducing a more innovative strategy, [the GEAR] document was essentially a reaffirmation of the commitments to macroeconomic austerity, that is, to the reforms which had already been carried out together with an assembling of policy measures that government was planning or already actively implementing' (1999: 17–18).

44 At a media briefing two days after GEAR's release, Thabo Mbeki invited the media to 'call me a Thatcherite!' (*Business Times*, 16 June 1996).

45 According to Michie *et al*, 'both international experience and South Africa's post-war economic record demonstrate that public sector investments (both infrastructure and basic services) can both "crowd in" and reduce the cost of private sector investment, a possibility even admitted by the World Bank in a 1994 report on South Africa by Fallon and Da Silva' (Michie *et al*, in Michie and Padayachee 1997: 225–6).

46 Instead of awarding a redistributive task to the government, the GEAR document stated dogmatically that 'accelerated economic growth associated with stronger employment creation is the key to continued progress towards an equitable distribution of income and improved standards of living for all' (appendix 7 of the GEAR document).

47 In 1996 Adelzadeh claimed correctly, and with prophetic insight, 'that a careful reading of the GEAR proposals shows that income distribution will *deteriorate* during the course of the programme...There is a fundamental problem with an approach that assumes [that] growth leads to redistribution. The complex linkage between better income distribution and growth is completely neglected [by GEAR]' (1996: 3).

48 The new government has tried to compensate for the ceiling on taxation by redirecting its spending towards the poor. Although some success has been achieved with this 'reprioritising' strategy, the increased spending on the poor has not been nearly enough to counteract the deterioration of their position as a result of the 'poverty traps in which they find themselves' (see section 2.2).

49 Adelzadeh was entirely correct when he argued in 1996 that 'the proposed growth framework and policy scenarios [of GEAR] are analytically flawed, empirically unsupportable, historically unsuitable for this country, and if implemented, will lead to disappointment and failure in achieving the RDP objectives of fundamentally transforming the inherited patterns of inequality' (1996: 3).

50 The investment in the parastatal sector was mainly capital-intensive and labour-saving.

51 While FDI worldwide grew by a third from 1980 to 1990, Africa's share dropped from 6,8 per cent to 2 per cent (World Bank 1996). According to Lewis Jeffrey, a senior official of the World Bank, FDI in South Africa averaged less than 1 per cent

of GDP from 1994 to 2000. During the same period, FDI averaged 2,5–3 per cent of GDP in Argentina, Brazil and Mexico, 4–5 per cent in Hungary and the Czech Republic, and 3–5 per cent in Malaysia (see Lewis 2001: iv).

52 In his state of the nation address in parliament in February 2001, Mbeki acknowledged that GEAR had delivered fiscal balance and macro stability, but not economic growth. He articulated an emerging consensus that a new initiative was needed to spur growth and reduce poverty. He called for greater government intervention, including a more active and targeted industrial policy. The 2001 budget showed that, for the first time, the new South Africa had access to surplus resources, given the ceiling on taxation. The government planned to spend an additional R7,8 billion on infrastructure and maintenance projects in 2001/2 in order to broaden access to opportunities, lower the cost of transport and communication, and improve standards of living in poor communities. Given the government's lack of capacity for infrastructure planning, as acknowledged in the 2001 budget review, many of these projects – especially those on the third level of government – may not even be completed by the end of the current medium-term planning cycle. The proposals of Mbeki and Manuel are a step in the right direction, but too late and far too small to have an appreciable impact on economic growth and poverty alleviation. These kinds of projects – but on a much larger scale – should have been part and parcel of the government's programmes since 1994 (see IDASA, Budget Brief 59).

53 The real remuneration of semi- and unskilled workers in 1999 was about 280 per cent higher than in 1970, and about 40 per cent higher than in 1996. The real per capita remuneration per highly skilled worker was 90 per cent of the 1970 level, while real remuneration per skilled worker was 110 per cent of the 1970 level (Lewis 2001: 14). The sharp increases in the real remuneration of semi- and unskilled workers from 1970 onwards provides a distorted picture: workers' remuneration was exceptionally low in 1970, when the labour repressive system was at its zenith.

54 The main regulatory reforms have been the Labour Relations Act of 1996 which focuses on workers' rights to organise, conflict resolution, and hiring and firing. The Basic Conditions of Employment Act of 1997 focuses on better working conditions for all workers who are employed and workers' rights in the workplace. The Employment Equity Act seeks to correct racial imbalances through affirmative action. The Skills Development Levy of 1998 seeks to encourage firms to provide more worker training.

55 According to Luiz, 'GEAR assumes that through conservative monetary and fiscal policy and by the state disengaging from the economy, foreign investment will flow in and fill the vacuum...But...the success of policies designed to attract FDI may be limited, unless a *better environment* is created for domestic investment. FDI follows growth, and hence the impetus must be from domestic sources. The government should instead focus on crowding in private investment, by signalling to the market that it is confident in the economy, and demonstrate it through public investment... However, it soon [after 1994] realized that it did not possess [the] all-encompassing capacity [for a developmental state] and hence adopted a more neo-liberal strategy, as if to say "there is no alternative" ' (1998: 277–8).

56 The GEAR document reflects the anti-state sentiments popular in New Right circles in especially the British–American world. The anti-state attitude in these countries

only tries to 'roll back' state involvement in the economy without breaking down state capacity. In these countries the capacity of the state and the efficiency of the government remain well-developed and well-institutionalised. Unfortunately, this is not yet the case in South Africa. We are in a phase of the transformation process in which the state needs to reinvent and re-establish itself in important aspects in order to ensure that the necessary discipline and order are maintained not only in the public sector but also in society at large.

57 The cost of capital was rated second (by about 75 per cent of firms), the depression and/or volatility of the rand third (by about 70 per cent of firms), the impact of labour regulations fourth, corruption and administrative costs in government fifth, and the shortage in skilled labour sixth (Lewis 2001: 21–3).

58 The permission given to mainly English-controlled mega-corporations to shift their core operations abroad has had the (perhaps unforeseen) result that the share of JSE capitalisation of firms controlled by Afrikaners increased from 24 per cent in 1996 to 35 per cent in 1999. From this perspective, it seems as if the demise of apartheid has been good for Afrikaner business (see Marais 2001: 291).

59 Given the controversy around 'war' diamonds, it is convenient for De Beers to be a private company; as such, its activities can no longer be scrutinised by the public.

60 In the case of Dimension Data the rules were amended, and dividend outflows have to be matched by dividend inflows to South African shareholders.

61 The service and income account dividend outflows can be viewed as draining the export earnings that buoyed the trade account. Hence, export benefits have not fed through to the real economy but have been repatriated instead, leaving South Africa no better off despite enhanced export competitiveness via the weaker rand.

62 In mid-June 2001 Manuel made it clear that the government would not permit any other corporations to move their main listings offshore. He said corporations would be expected to take a more 'patriotic view' and to keep their main listing in South Africa (see *Business Day*, 21 June 2001). This policy shift has to be welcomed, but it has unfortunately come too late to curb corporations that have not shown the necessary 'patriotism'. The government's *volte face* on this issue is a first acknowledgement that it has 'opened' or 'globalised' the South African economy too much and too quickly to the chill winds and violent mood swings of global capitalism.

63 After intense discussions, government and labour signed a National Framework Agreement on Restructuring Parastatals (NFA) in February 1996. It provides for six representatives of each side to meet regularly to discuss disagreements. Since 1996, however, the government has proceeded with its restructuring plans against labour's wishes, and its privatisation policy has become a key issue endangering the ANC Alliance. It seems as if either the six-a-side forum has not met regularly, or could not agree on the details of the restructuring policy. In 1996 then president Mandela declared (to the surprise of the trade union movement) that privatisation was a 'fundamental policy' of the ANC. The restructuring would entail the total sale of some assets (ie, privatisation); the partial sale of others through securing strategic equity partners; and the corporatisation, commercialisation, and outsourcing of 'non-core' functions of other assets. COSATU opposed these proposals.

64 According to Marais, the TRC process 'did not penetrate the systemic nature of

oppression and the corresponding benefits that the minority enjoyed...The TRC function in a broader socio-economic – and ideological – context that demonstrably reinforce existing inequalities, cleavages and antagonisms...Individual remembrance was demanded, while collective amnesia [of mainly the whites] was condoned in the name of reconciliation. The evasion of moral (and legal) culpability was sanctioned, most obviously in the case of corporate South Africa whose complicity in a devastating social landscape still is rarely, if ever, noted publicly. On the contrary, corporate interest stand conflated with the "common" and "national" interest' (2001: 302).

65 The skewed approach of the TRC, under which the NP was delegitimised for its apartheid policies but the corporate sector's participation in creating and utilising repressive labour patterns was condoned, has had a strange – and perhaps unintended – effect on the NP and the DP. While the NP's electoral support declined from 22 per cent in 1994 to only 7 per cent in 1999, the DP – as successor to the PFP, and closely associated with the business sector – increased its support from less than 2 per cent in 1994 to more than 10 per cent in 1999. The TRC's double standards were a serious blow for the NP, and a bonanza for the DP. While the NP deserved its destiny, the DP and the corporate sector did not deserve to be exonerated.

66 He continues: 'We need to be able to tell whether truth is changeful or eternal, embedded in time or outside, universal or varying from place to place. We need to know how we have got to where we are in the history of truth – how our society has come to lose faith in the reality of it and lose interest in the search of it' (Fernández-Armesto 1997: 2).

67 In mitigation of the recalcitrant attitude displayed by business at the hearings, we should acknowledge that many members of today's managerial elite were not in their present positions before 1970, when racial capitalism and apartheid were most exploitative. To expect today's managerial elite to be aware of the actions of their parents and grandparents would require a historical perspective from them, which is perhaps too much to ask. Business people are inclined to look forwards rather than backwards. But what is deplorable is the inability of the TRC to put the evidence of business into a proper historical context. Two of the most blatant examples of corporate myth-making were the submissions and testimonies of the Chamber of Mines and the AAC. We have already discussed their twisted version of the truth in section 3.2.

68 It then described the two dominant positions as follows: 'One view, which sees apartheid as part of a system of racial capitalism, held that apartheid was beneficial for (white) business because it was an integral part of a system premised on the exploitation of black workers and the destruction of black entrepreneurial activity. According to this argument, business as a whole benefited from the system, although some sections of the business community (most notably Afrikaner capital, the mining houses and the armaments industry) benefited more than others did' (para 6). 'The other position, argued mainly by business, claims that apartheid raised the costs of doing business, eroded South Africa's skills base and undermined long-term productivity and growth. In this view, the impact of apartheid was to harm the economy...If apartheid placed obstacles in the path of profitability (as alleged by pro-business position), then business as a whole is cast more as a victim of the

system than as a partner or collaborator' (paras 7 and 8). The first view was supported and articulated in the submissions of the ANC, SACP, COSATU, the Black Management Forum, and the author of this book. The second view was supported in the submissions of the different business organisations, large corporations, Mike Rosholt of Barlow Rand, and Anton and Johann Rupert of Rupert International.

69 The opportunity given to businesses to pay off their 'apartheid debt' through charity has already amounted to opportunities to let them off the hook rather cheaply. Building schools and hospitals is a government responsibility, and should be financed through the normal tax system and not by charity. When opportunities are given publicly to corporations for all kinds of charity (by Mandela, for example), they are often misused not only for myth-making and image-building, but also to claim all sorts of patronage from the government in return.

70 In 1955, some 29 African and Asian countries decided at the Bandoeng conference that 'colonialism in all its manifestations [including apartheid] was an evil that should be brought to an end speedily'. In 1960 the United Nations general assembly unanimously accepted the Bandoeng declaration (with nine western countries abstaining). In 1965 the general assembly accepted a resolution that colonialism and apartheid not only threatened international peace and security, but were also crimes against humanity.

71 In the case of coloureds and Indians, the incomes of the top 20 per cent of households in 1996 was 15 and 11 times higher than those of the poorest 40 per cent (see table 10.4).

72 A similar process has occurred among whites over the past 30 years: the top 20 per cent have become richer, while the lower 60 per cent have become poorer. But white poor are not nearly as poor as the black poor, and the unequal distribution of income is also not as great among whites as among blacks. In 1975 the income of the top 20 per cent of white households was five times higher than that of the poorest 40 per cent; in 1996 it was ten times higher (see table 10.4).

73 Adam *et al* put it as follows: 'The origin of a culture of selfish opportunism probably lies with successive governments exploiting the state for special interest groups. When one party succeeds the other in power, claims for entitlements to loot likewise come naturally. If necessary, common looting of the public purse is agreed upon between adversaries' (1997: 18).

74 Nürnberger makes the point 'that because civil society is relatively underdeveloped and economically weak in peripheral countries, post-colonial elites tend to consolidate their power and their privileges in the state apparatus. The absence of effective democratic controls led to the development of institutionalised corruption. Lucrative channels of illicit income are protected rather than exposed. Lack of accountability leads to bureaucratic inefficiency, financial mismanagement, and misallocation of scarce resources for the self-aggrandisement of the rulers and their clienteles' (1998: 102). It seems as if this rather depressing scenario is also true of the post-colonial elite in South Africa.

PART 3

Colonialism, segregation, and apartheid (1652–1994)

Chapter 5

The systemic period of Dutch colonialism (1652–±1800)

5.1 The Dutch East India Company, the power constellation at the Cape, and land deprivation

During the 16th century the trade route around the Cape was monopolised by the Portugese.[1] Slave trading formed an important part of Portuguese trade – it has been estimated that, from the 16th to the 19th centuries, Portugal exported more than 5 million slaves to America, mainly from the Congo, Angola, and Mozambique. In the early 1700s the British East India Company (BEIC, established in 1600) and Dutch Verenigde Oostindische Compagnie (VOC, established in 1602) moved in to contest the Portuguese monopoly, but the latter managed to retain a significant portion of it during the 17th century.

It has been estimated that at least 1 000 Portuguese, 600 Dutch, and 400 English and French ships landed on the South African coast between 1500 and 1650. One consequence of these pre-settlement contacts by Europeans was the large-scale plundering of resources and people (Jaffe 1994: ch 3).

In 1652 the VOC established a fortified provision station at Table Bay in order to regulate the benefits that sailors had long derived from Cape stopovers. The voyage to the East took six to eight months, and was fraught with numerous dangers, including scurvy.[2]

The VOC had been formed in 1602 by uniting a number of Dutch commercial undertakings.[3] It developed into one of the largest and most successful commercial companies of the 17th and early 18th centuries, with extensive interests in India and Indonesia. Typical of commercial companies at that time, it enjoyed monopolistic privileges and powers granted to it by the Dutch government.[4] The dominance of the VOC and Holland in shipping and trade during the 17th century cannot easily be overemphasised.[5] While the Dutch were originally known for their Calvinist austerity, their lifestyle in the second half of the 17th century became marked by vanity, luxury, and corruption. Although the VOC lasted for almost 200 years, and was one of the most profitable companies of its time, it also acquired the reputation of being one of the most corrupt multinationals of all time (Kindleberger 1996: 90, 214). It declined rapidly during the second half of the 18th century, and was almost bankrupt by the time it was dissolved in 1795.

During the mercantilist period (1500–1880) the economic orthodoxy among the emerging nation states of Europe was that a specific country could only become rich if it could ensure a large inflow of gold (through plunder or trade), and if it had better trade routes and more ships for colonial exploitation than its rivals. This mercantilist mentality that justified military conflict, plunder, and exploitation as methods of enrichment was brought to the Cape by the VOC and the Dutch colonists, and was deeply engraved in their minds. It was based on the notion that whenever the economic interests of different countries (or population groups) clashed, it was justifiable for the stronger country or group to enforce its will on weaker ones, even by military or other violent means. This approach was not only adopted by the VOC and white colonists during the Dutch period, but remained the attitude of the white *Trekboere* (pastoral farmers) during the 18th and 19th centuries.

When the VOC established its post at Table Bay, a large part of the Cape was inhabited by the Khoisan. This is the collective name for two indigenous groups: the Khoikhoi, who kept cattle and sheep, and the San, who were hunter-gatherers. The Khoisan had lived in southern Africa for at least 8 000 years before the Dutch arrived.[6] The VOC originally depended on the Khoikhoi for cattle. The company was therefore anxious to avoid costly wars at the Cape. Consequently, it ordered its first commander, Jan van Riebeeck (1652–62), to treat the Khoikhoi with respect and to do nothing to disturb their cultural integrity and socio-economic stability. He originally applied this policy very strictly, but after the company had released some of its employees from their contracts and set them up as freeburghers (or independent farmers) in 1657, a little war of plunder broke out between the VOC and the Khoikhoi in 1659.

After the war, the Khoikhoi leader 'Harry the Strandloper' (or Autshumao of the Goringkaikona tribe) was banned to Robben Island. In April 1660 he was brought back for peace negotiations. Van Riebeeck told Autshumao that not enough grazing land was available for the cattle of both the colonists and the Khoikhoi.

Autshumao then asked: 'If the country is too small, who has the greater right: the true owner, or the foreign intruder?' Van Riebeeck recorded his answer in his diary: *'Ons dan haer lant, door diffencive oorlogh rechtvaerdigh als met 't swaert gewonnen, toegevallen, ende 't welck wij ook voornemens waren te behouden'* ('We have won this country in a just manner through a defensive war, and it is our intention to keep it.' Leipoldt 1938 [1999]; author's translation).

Van Riebeeck's argument is seminal. This was the beginning of a colonial process of land deprivation that continued for more than 250 years, and sparked many violent conflicts. This process culminated in the Land Act of 1913 which set aside only 8 per cent of South Africa's total land area as 'native reserves'. Although some of these land wars – especially those against the Xhosa and Zulu in the 19th century – were very bloody, the fact that the colonists introduced modern guns, horses, the commando system, and in due time the well-disciplined British army made the task of depriving the indigenous inhabitants of land and surface water relatively easy. With a few exceptions, the colonial authorities and white governments also denied indigenous people the right to own land.[7] With land available in abundance, and with a white land-owning class to own and exploit it, the scene was set for an ever increasing demand for unfree black labour.

The Cape was not a Dutch colony, but the colony – and for that matter the commercial property – of a trading company. As one of the first successful share companies in history, it received extraordinary privileges and support from the Dutch government.[8] With enormous power at its disposal, the VOC adapted all the mercantilist measures – such as tariffs, a monopoly, favouritism, patronage, corruption, slavery, dismissal without legal process, corporal punishment, and so on – to promote its business interests and entrench the privileges given to it in terms of a charter. For all practical purposes, the VOC was a law unto itself. Consequently the company – and its representatives at the Cape – could use legal and illegal, moral and immoral measures as long as its commercial interests were served.

Simon van der Stel and Willem Adriaan van der Stel were both authorised to expand the agricultural sector at the Cape, and each did so in his own way. During Simon van der Stel's governorship the number of freehold farms given to freeburghers increased from 50 in 1682 to 260 in 1705 and 435 in 1731.[9] But besides his ability to give land grants, the governor had the power to extend all sorts of privileges and favours to whomever he wished. Thus he imported 250 Huguenots and gave them freehold land and financial support on easy terms. He also gave contracts for supplying the VOC with meat, corn, and other produce to his favourite officials, members of the mercantile class, and freeburghers.

The freeburghers, who benefited from Simon van der Stel's corrupt system, initially did not complain about the fact that some of the officials (including the governor himself) were also benefiting from agricultural favouritism. In 1705 –

during the governorship of Willem Adriaan van der Stel – the colony experienced an overproduction of food and a shortage of labour. Only then did a group of prominent and wealthy burghers confront Willem Adriaan about the privileges he continued to dispense – arbitrarily – to officials and himself. After a minor freeburgher revolt, the authorities in Amsterdam decided against the governor and officials and in favour of the freeburghers. In a paradoxical way, all this wheeling and dealing created a wealthy landed gentry around Cape Town.[10]

While Simon van der Stel was the father of tillage farming, Willem Adriaan launched pastoral farming when, from 1703 onwards, he gave grazing permits and loan farms to colonists in areas far from Cape Town and allowed the *Trekboere* to barter and trade with the Khoikhoi. The permits issued for loan farms increased rapidly after the demographic collapse of the Khoikhoi in 1713.[11] As the *Trekboere* moved further away from Cape Town, it became increasingly difficult for the VOC to control the acquisition of land and the payment of annual fees.

5.2 Imported slaves and imported *knechts* as parallel labour patterns until 1717

The first group of 174 slaves imported from Angola in 1658 arrived at the Cape only one year after nine employees of the VOC had been allowed to set up independent farms. The slaves were almost exclusively used by the company and the tillage farmers in the Western Cape. Slaves were too expensive and also not suited to the extensive farming operations in the drier Eastern and Northern Cape. In 1721 the pastoral farmers started to subjugate the Khoikhoi illegally as *inboekelinge* or serfs (see section 5.4).

The VOC had experienced labour problems from 1652, but had never considered employing the Khoikhoi; they were regarded as too wild and uncontrollable.[12] In any case, the company could not enslave the Khoikhoi because the Dutch law stipulated 'that the aborigines of its colonial possessions should be left undisturbed in their liberty' (De Kock 1950: 14).

From the arrival of Jan van Riebeeck until 1717 there was an ongoing debate at the Cape on how the company's labour problems should be solved. The argument was between those who were in favour of importing slaves, and those in favour of importing wage labourers – or *knechts* – from Europe. Consequently, for the first 65 years of the settlement, both black slaves and white *knechts* were used as parallel labour forces. Contracted European wage labour was the company's first choice. Company *knechts*, originally employed as soldiers or sailors, were hired out to farmers for five years. In time the *knechts* became an independent component of the free white population at the

Cape, entering into contracts with the land-owning class. It has been estimated that, in 1687, the free wage-earning *knechts* comprised as much as 50 per cent of the entire free population in the Cape (Shell 1994a: 10–14).

Until 1703 it was not easy for the *knechts* to cast off their status as free wage labourers in order to become landowners. But when, in 1703, Willem Adriaan van der Stel started to grant grazing permits and loan farms to colonists in areas far from Cape Town, almost all the *knechts* opted to become *Trekboere*, and by 1740 their number had declined to only 5 per cent of the free population. During the rest of the century free wage-earning *knechts* were used mainly as teachers. By 1800 their numbers declined even further to less than 1 per cent of the free population. This presaged the failure of all free wage labour in South Africa until the emergence of a new white wage-earning class at the end of the 19th century, when former Afrikaner small farmers became a white proletariat (Boucher, in Cameron 1986: 66).[13]

The dispute about using either free white labour from Europe or imported slaves remained unresolved until 1717 when the council of policy[14] at the Cape decided (with one opposing vote) to give preference to importing slaves. During the debate it was said that the white *knechts* were unreliable, lazy, inclined to drunkenness, and unwilling to perform manual labour. At that stage the slave-owning landowners in the Western Cape had already developed into a relatively independent class with a vested interest in slavery. This was cheaper, and promoted their independence *vis-à-vis* the VOC. At the same time company officials were involved in importing and marketing slaves, and slave-owners and corrupt officials joined forces in turning the South Western Cape into a colony with chattel slaves as labour. This pattern was perpetuated in that region until slavery was abolished in 1838 (Boucher, in Cameron 1986: 68; Davenport 1991: 23).

We can divide the history of slavery at the Cape into three phases. The first phase lasted from 1652 until 1717 when the council of policy decided to import slaves rather than Europeans. At that stage the slave population numbered about 2 000, and was already larger than the freeburgher population.[15] Following this decision, even more slaves were imported. The second phase lasted until 1808, when the British suspended the slave trade. By then the total slave population was 29 000, and it had increased to roughly 39 000 by the time this institution was finally abolished in 1838. This final phase of slavery (from 1808 to 1838) coincided with a marked economic expansion which sharply increased the demand for and price of slaves.

From 1652 until 1808 about 63 000 slaves were imported to the Cape from the Indonesian archipelago, the Indian subcontinent, Madagascar, and

Mozambique, with each region contributing about a quarter of the total. Until 1750 most slaves had been imported from Indonesia and the Indian subcontinent. For the next 30 years most slaves came from Madagascar, and during the last 40 years most came from Mozambique (Shell, in Eldredge and Morton 1994c).

Slaves at the Cape were one of few slave populations that reproduced themselves before slavery was abolished. It reached its 'moment of creolisation' (ie, the point at which more than 50 per cent of the slave population was born locally) in the 1760s. Although this percentage dropped below 50 per cent in the 1790s, it increased again from 1800 onwards. When slavery was abolished in 1838, more than 70 per cent of slaves had been born in the colony (ibid).

As part and parcel of the creolisation process, there was extensive miscegenation between slaves and whites, and between slaves and the Khoisan. Given the preponderance of males among both the freeburgher and slave populations, this was to be expected.[16] Children born from white fathers and slave mothers were usually freed. More than 1 000 female slaves were also freed as a result. The children born from slave and Khoikhoi unions were called *Bastaard-Hottentots*. Their numbers grew so rapidly in the 18th century that they became regarded as a new category of colonial subjects. From early in the 18th century these children were illegally bound in service to their parents' masters. This was the beginning of the *inboekstelsel* ('booking-in system' – in other words, a form of indentured labour, or serfdom) which was used in due course to turn the majority of the Khoisan into unfree labour. The *inboekstelsel* only became a legal labour system in 1775 when it was decreed that not only *Bastaard-Hottentot* children but also Khoisan children could be 'booked in' until the age of 25. In the unfolding coercive labour pattern during the 18th century, using *Bastaard-Hottentot* children like slaves was a small, gradual, step in the direction of illegality, as was using (mainly captured) Khoisan children like *Bastaard-Hottentot* serfs. (The 'virtual enslavement' of a large percentage of the Khoisan population via the *inboekstelsel* will be dealt with in greater detail in section 5.4. See Penn, in Eldridge and Morton 1994c; Morton, in Eldridge and Morton 1994c)

5.3   The role of slavery in the Cape economy, and the nature of the master–slave relationship (1652–1834)

Compared to the more than 12 million slaves exported mainly from Africa to the West Indies and the Americas from the 16th to the 19th centuries, the number of chattel slaves at the Cape was relatively small. They were used mostly as labourers on wheat and wine farms in the Western Cape, and as domestic servants and artisans in Cape Town. Slaves played a huge role in building the Cape economy over a period of 180 years. Slave labour enabled a small landed gentry and a mercantile elite in and around Cape Town to maintain a luxurious colonial lifestyle for almost two centuries, and live in beautiful and spacious Cape Dutch homesteads.[17]

These economic advantages were achieved at the cost of exploiting human labour, and creating a coercive and divided social system. Slavery served as a model that easily led (first illegally, but later legally) to the virtual enslavement of *Bastaard-Hottentots* and captured Khoisan children. Although slavery was originally not extended to the frontier, its presence in the Western Cape did have important influences on the economic history of the frontier. The extension of the master–slave relationship to pastoral farmers and Khoisan servants had ramifications that reached into the second half of the 20th century. To appreciate the enduring impact of slavery on labour patterns in South Africa, one should try to imagine what the country's labour history would have been if the VOC had not introduced chattel slavery at the Cape (Crais 1992: 40–6).

In the first 40 years after the provision station was established, most slaves were owned by the VOC. After 1692 the number of slaves owned by colonists exceeded those of the company, and throughout the remainder of the Dutch period the great majority of slaves were privately owned.[18]

Most of the privately owned slaves were used as domestic and agricultural workers on wheat and wine farms in the Western Cape. Slaves were not only too expensive for the pastoral farmers, but also for smaller farmers in the Western Cape. Because of the amount of capital tied up in slaves, it was mainly the more prosperous farmers who could afford, say, 20 or more slaves. They were also in a position to exploit slave labour most profitably through a proper division of labour. Slave labour not only created a society divided along racial lines, but also a socio-economic stratification between the wealthy landed gentry and merchants in the Western Cape on the one hand, and poorer white farmers in the Western Cape and in frontier areas who could not afford slaves on the other (see Müller 1981a).

The price of an adult male slave doubled from 100 rix dollars in 1660 to 200 rix dollars in 1750. Owing to the economic upsurge during the last three decades of the 18th century – when more ships visited the Cape – the price of slaves increased to 350 rix dollars. The suspension of the slave trade in 1808 coincided with a sharp increase in the demand for slaves. The lowering of British tariffs on wine led to a boom in wine farming. As a result, slaves became three times more expensive than they had been in 1708. During this period slavery made perhaps its greatest contribution to the expansion of the Cape economy. Owing to the large profits that could be made from wine, the wine farmers were not only prepared to pay higher prices for slaves, but also tended to increase their workload out of all proportion. The exploitation of slave labour was at its worst during this period. After the British reinstated British tariffs in 1825, the Cape economy contracted. As a result, slavery became a liability for many slave owners during the last ten years before its abolition. During the last 30 years of slavery the number of slaves held in the Eastern Cape increased from 5 to 15 per cent of the total slave population. Strangely enough, at the time of its abolition, slavery was more profitable in the Eastern than the Western Cape (Crais 1992: 30–6; Cordeur, in Cameron 1986: 81–2).

In all slave societies, special strategies to manage and control slaves are needed. Those strategies are ultimately based on violence. To appreciate the strategies used at the Cape, it is necessary to focus on the authoritarian nature of the families into which the slaves were integrated. Robert Shell describes the family structure that developed at the Cape as patriarchal, owing to the authoritarian role typically played by the (usually male) head. The development of the patriarchal family partly resulted from the Roman Dutch law applicable at the Cape, partly from the VOC's attitude towards slave-owners, and partly from the abundance of free land. Roman Dutch law reinforced notions of patriarchy in which the master had to assume full responsibility for the behaviour of slaves who were not only his property but also his infant children. The VOC regarded slavery as a private matter, left the disciplining of slaves in the hands of their masters, and never seriously interceded in this relationship or challenged the masters' authority. The VOC only intervened – infrequently – when the behaviour of either slaves or masters threatened the good order at the Cape (see Shell 1994a: ch 7, 13).

This patriarchal family structure was well established on the larger wine estates at the end of the 17th century, and was extended to the frontier areas during the 18th century, where it became even more independent and the head of the family even more authoritarian. The VOC – dominated by commercial interests – was always prepared to create the legal 'space' needed by family patriarchs. During the second half of the 18th century, when the distances between Cape Town and the frontier areas became unmanageably great, the company's ability to intervene in the affairs of patriarchal families on the frontier declined dramatically. Consequently, 'in early South Africa the family was virtually *autonomous*, and it resisted any intrusion by gradually constituting a colonial state that would not (and could not) interfere with family governance but only buttress it' (Shell 1994a: 395–9). The autonomy of the patriarchal family not only determined the nature of the master–slave relationship, but also represented the institutional structure that subjugated the majority of Khoisan at the end of the 18th century (see section 5.4).

The hierarchies of status and power entrenched in the feudalistic order at the Cape ensured that chattel slaves and indentured Khoisan remained obedient. The patriarchal structure of slave-owning households at the Cape was promoted by the fact that there were no large concentrations of slaves on plantations, as was the case in the Caribbean or the American South. The slaves were widely dispersed in relatively small groups among small agricultural units. Only a handful of farms could boast more than 20 slaves. The average slaveholding varied between four to six slaves, and it was therefore possible to accommodate them in or near the homestead (see Shell, in James and Simons 1989: 29).

The fact that slaves were members of patriarchal families should not be romanticised. The slaves were the property and personal responsibility of their master, and he could use all kinds of 'domestic corrections' or 'internal discipline' to impose good behaviour and subordination. Although the slaves were owned, they were not entirely without rights. They could complain about ill-treatment, but this seldom happened. The Dutch authorities stipulated that privately owned slaves should not be whipped or chained, and that punishment should be limited to the same punishment the husband and father meted out to his wife and children. Although severe physical coercion was often used, it is perhaps more correct to say that psychological coercion – typical of the family mode of control – was more common. This type of coercion could be cruel, and cause great distress. The fact that adult male slaves outnumbered adult burgher males by four to one in the first half of the 18th century and by three to one in the second half may partly account for the burghers' fear of the slave population, and for their inclination to maintain a firm grip on a slave's every movement (see Shell 1994a: ch 13).

Although the chains of slavery were mainly psychological, and therefore fairly subtle, slavery could on occasion be relentless, violent, and cruel. The uncontrolled nature of the Cape slave system during the 17th and 18th centuries, when slaves were imported and sold by speculators at relatively low prices, may have discouraged careful and humane treatment by the slave masters. When the slave trade was suspended in 1808, one might have expected that the treatment of remaining slaves would improve, but owing to the economic expansion at the Cape in this period the demand for labour increased sharply, and slaves were probably treated more harshly then than ever before (Armstrong and Worden 1989: 151).

An important distinction was made at the Cape between imported slaves and '*Kreools*' (Creole), or locally born, slaves. Creole slaves were regarded as more valuable and more trustworthy than imported slaves, and were therefore also treated more humanely. The fact that these slaves were reared within patriarchal families implies that their level of domestic acculturation and social domination was higher than those of imported slaves.[19] Another unique characteristic of slavery at the Cape was the special treatment meted out to female slaves. Nearly all female slaves at the Cape were domestic servants, and played an important role in running households and rearing children.[20]

It would be wrong to regard the slaves at the Cape only as objects of property. Within the family the most significant aspect of slavery was perhaps the way in which the family patriarch dominated the slave's personality. Through this social domination the personality of the slave was slowly broken down, and reshaped in a pattern desired by the patriarch. The social domination of black slaves by white masters became a permanent ingredient of the labour pattern in South Africa until the 20th century, when it was still one of the most important characteristics of white employer–black employee relationships. When the patriarchal family at the frontier became a vehicle for placing the Khoisan in servitude, the proprietary or legal aspect of slavery became less important, and its social domination aspect more so. When slavery and serfdom were abolished early in the 19th century and replaced with other forms of labour repression, the proprietary aspect disappeared completely, but social domination over unfree labour remained, although it was exerted in different ways and via new legal measures. The history of unfree labour in South Africa can justifiably be described as one in which new but always effective modes of political domination, economic exploitation, and social oppression were designed for changing socio-political and economic conditions (see Shell 1994a: ch 13; see also section 5.5; Lötter 1997: 21–31).

If we consider the strict and often cruel forms of control and discipline over slaves, it is remarkable that there were no serious slave uprisings during the 186 years of slavery at the Cape. Only two minor uprisings occurred – in 1808 and 1825 – but both were easily suppressed. The fact that the slaves were scattered among a large number of agricultural units, and integrated with farmers' households, prevented the development of an independent consciousness that could have served as the breeding-ground for protest movements. What was more common was that slaves ran away and became *drosters* (absconders) who sought shelter in the mountains near Cape Town or in the Cedarberg (see Penn, in Eldridge and Morton 1994c; Armstrong and Worden 1989: ch 3).

Shell characterises slavery at the Cape as follows:

> Once begun in South Africa, slavery was difficult to stop…Only the energies of the world's most powerful empire [Britain] could check its momentum. The truly frightening aspect of South African slavery was its efficiency, its near universal deployment, its convenience for its owners, its long duration, and its suppression in historical literature. The slave period, 1652–1838, was the true gestation period of South African culture (1994a: 414–15).

Macmillan also believes that slavery institutionalised a pattern of 'unfree' labour that was perpetuated into the 20th century: 'Although slavery as an institution died in 1834 [when its abolition was announced], its legacy is the element of hubris in the conventional South African attitude to coloured races to this day' (1927: 82).

5.4   *Trekboer* partnerships with the Khoikhoi, and Khoisan enserfment by the *Trekboere* during the 18th century

The way in which the *Trekboere* placed the Khoisan in servitude via the *inboekstelsel* in the 18th century, and in which the Voortrekkers extended this form of serfdom to African tribes in the Transorangia in the 19th century – after slavery and serfdom had officially been abolished in the Cape colony – demonstrates how universal, convenient, and unstoppable (in Shell's words) slavery was in South Africa. During the almost 250 years of slavery and serfdom in at least some parts of South Africa, the engine of the enslavement process was the superior military power of whites, the growing independence of patriarchal families, the abundance of land, and the chronic scarcity of suitable labour.

From the point of view of the Khoisan, the arrival of the VOC introduced not only a completely new constellation of power, but also a new legal system, a new economy, and a new approach to the relationship between humans and the environment. The pastoral, political, and economic structures of the Khoikhoi were such that they could hardly withstand the foreign intruders. By contrast, the more mobile San resisted the *Trekboere* until the end of the 18th century.

Khoikhoi society was pastoral; however, it was not based on land ownership but on small kinship groups or clans which grazed their cattle over large areas. Some of these clans were loosely organised into chiefdoms or tribes, but these were not unified or organised into a single kingdom. Consequently, the political and economic structures of the Khoikhoi were fragile and vulnerable. Their existence centred on cattle, which were not owned by the clan or the tribe but by families and individuals. When a family became impoverished through theft, disease, or drought, this easily led to intertribal disputes and the disintegration of the social structure of clans and tribes. When the white colonists arrived with horses and firepower – their main interest being to acquire Khoikhoi cattle – these indigenous groups were ill-equipped to resist the onslaught in a concerted way (Elphick and Malherbe 1989: ch 1).

The VOC experienced problems in procuring the cattle it needed for its refreshment station. Due to the huge gap in civilisation between the Dutch and the Khoikhoi, it was not easy to build and maintain a relationship of mutual trust. After the first Dutch–Khoikhoi war of 1659, friendly relations were maintained for about a decade before the Khoikhoi became increasingly reluctant to supply the VOC with the type of livestock it needed. Given a clear clash of interests between the company and another group, the governor had no choice – in accordance with its mercantilist orthodoxy – but to give preference to the former. During the 1670s the governor launched several official military offensives against the Khoikhoi, using garrison troops, and many more followed during the governorship of Simon van der Stel (1679–99). Van der Stel conquered the Khoikhoi in the vicinity of Cape Town, and violently destroyed their socio-economic and political structures. The Khoikhoi were not subjugated by the freeburghers, but by the VOC.[21]

While the company wanted the cattle belonging to the Khoikhoi, the freeburghers wanted their land, cattle, and labour. Although Simon van der Stel was positively disposed towards the freeburghers, and spoiled them with many favours, he would not allow them to penetrate deeper into the country or barter with the Khoikhoi. He was afraid – apparently with good reason – that such concessions would bring the company and the freeburghers into conflict with each other. But this situation changed drastically at the beginning of the 18th century.

The new governor, Willem Adriaan van der Stel (1699–1707), started to issue free grazing permits and grant loan farms (at a small annual rent) to freeburghers at ever increasing distances from Cape Town. He also relaxed the company's control over freeburghers, and allowed some of them to go inland and barter with the Khoikhoi. These concessions were immediately abused. The freeburghers not only trespassed on land occupied by the Khoikhoi, but disputes developed over the ownership of cattle. To counteract the alleged theft of cattle by the Khoikhoi, the commando system – created by the company for its own purposes 20 years earlier – was now put at the disposal of the freeburghers in order to conduct punitive expeditions against the Khoikhoi. At first, only members of the company's garrison could serve in the commando, but from 1701 onwards freeburghers and *Trekboere* were also included. In this way an institution was established that came to play a central – and menacing – role in *Trekboer* and Afrikaner warfare, and became the symbol of the considerable self-sufficiency of the *Trekboere* and Voortrekkers for the greater part of the 18th and 19th centuries. At first, commandos with civilian members were commanded by VOC officials, and controlled by its regulations, and company officials often tried to protect Khoikhoi interests against the onslaught of the *Trekboere*. But from the 1730s onwards the commandos became purely civilian, and had only the interests of the *Trekboere* at heart. In 1739 service in the commandos became compulsory for *Trekboere* (Boucher, in Cameron 1986: 71–4; Keegan 1996: 30–1).

From 1701 onwards the newly composed commandos undertook several punitive expeditions against the Khoikhoi on behalf of the *Trekboere*. Many Khoikhoi were killed, and even more cattle captured. In the first decade of the 17th century the livestock holdings of the colonists increased dramatically – partly due to trade (barter), and partly as a result of theft via the commando system.[22] In 1713 the Khoikhoi received an even more serious blow when a visiting fleet brought the smallpox virus to the Cape. While hundreds of Europeans and slaves died from the virus, it had a devastating effect on the Khoikhoi, who apparently had a very low level of immunity; it is estimated that scarcely one in ten of the Khoikhoi in the South Western Cape survived the epidemic.[23]

The relationship that developed in the 18th century between the *Trekboere* and the Khoisan was changeable, dynamic, and complex. From one point of view it was a relationship of close co-operation and interdependence. From another it was one of continuous guerrilla warfare, reciprocal mistrust and hatred, cattle raids and retaliation, and the capture and enslavement of women and children. Violent clashes occurred throughout the 18th century, but escalated into open warfare in 1774, and reached a climax in the Khoisan rebellion of 1799 to 1803 when many Khoisan serving *Trekboere* joined forces with those who were not controlled by the settlers (Worden 1994b: ch 2).

During the first 30 years of the 18th century the *Trekboere* had to adapt to an unknown environment, while knowing little about how to farm sheep and cattle in a harsh climate and in semi-desert conditions. They acquired the necessary knowledge from the Khoikhoi, who had accumulated it over centuries. After the smallpox epidemic of 1713 small groups of Khoikhoi – whose tribes had become impoverished and disrupted – sought the protection of the *Trekboere* and either relinquished their remaining cattle to their new protectors or became their partners in sheep and cattle farming. In this way the Khoikhoi provided the colonists not only with land and cattle, but also with labour and knowledge of extensive farming. Some of these voluntary partnerships endured until the end of the 18th century. The way in which the colonists took the land, cattle, and knowledge of the Khoikhoi and entered into joint farming projects with them represents a unique mode of colonialism (see Elphick and Malherbe 1989: 28).

However, the protective relationship did not work in one direction only; the Khoikhoi also protected the *Trekboere* against hostile Khoikhoi and San. After the Bushman War of 1739 it also became obligatory for Khoikhoi serving *Trekboere* to serve in the commandos. When the general commando was deployed in 1774 for a major attack on hostile Khoisan groups, the governor stipulated that for every 100 Europeans at least 150 Khoikhoi should take part. Without the close co-operation between the *Trekboere* and the 'tame' Khoikhoi on sheep and cattle farming, territorial expansion, and security, the Europeans would probably not have succeeded in conquering much of the interior of the Cape colony (see Ross 1993: 86–7).

In the second half of the 18th century the *Trekboere* were no longer dependent on the Khoikhoi for farming knowledge. As they extended the colony to the east and north, they deprived the Khoikhoi of more and more land, proletarianising them in the process. The Khoikhoi had to retreat to the east and north, or enter into new relations with *Trekboere*. At that stage the *Trekboere* were far less inclined to share their stock-farming operations with the Khoikhoi, and became more interested in using them as wage labourers (with wages paid in kind), or subjugating them as serfs.[24] This led to tensions between *Trekboere* and 'tame' Khoikhoi. At the same time, the deteriorating security situation on the frontier meant that the *Trekboere* relied more heavily on the 'tame' Khoikhoi to help them fight the 'wild' Khoikhoi and the even more aggressive San. While the economic revival from 1770 onwards increased the scarcity of labour, the deteriorating security situation on the frontier increased the value of 'tame' Khoikhoi as warriors. This presented the *Trekboere* with a difficult choice: either maintain good partnerships with the 'tame' Khoikhoi because of their value as warriors, or exploit them as workers. In their eagerness to benefit from the improved economic opportunities in the 1780s and 1790s, the *Trekboere* opted for the latter, with devastating consequences.[25] During the Khoisan rebellion of 1799–1803 thousands of 'tame' Khoikhoi – who for decades had maintained a relationship of co-operation and trust with the *Trekboere* – deserted their 'masters' and joined ranks with 'wild' Khoisan and Xhosa. Together they caused havoc in large parts of the Graaff-Reinet district. This dramatically ended the co-operative relationships between 'tame' Khoikhoi and the *Trekboere* (see Newton-King, in Cameron 1986: 108–9; Elphick and Malherbe 1986: 33–5).

As the *Trekboere* appropriated more land and cattle, and bound more 'captive' Khoisan children as *inboekelinge*, the 'wild' Khoisan – ie, those not under the control of the *Trekboere* – reacted with more violent attacks and cattle raids. According to Newton-King, the violent clashes on the frontier between *Trekboere* and the Khoisan created the context in which the peculiar violence of the master–servant relationship was shaped.[26] As more land became available to the *Trekboere*, they needed more labour. They could not use slaves on the frontier, because they were too expensive and not suited to work on the large cattle farms. To solve their labour problems, farmers also started to indenture the offspring of slave men and Khoikhoi women – so-called *Bastaard-Hottentots* – for periods of 25 years. This practice was justified with the argument that the slave-owners had to carry the costs of child-rearing. From about 1721 onwards the children of Khoikhoi serving *Trekboere* were also indentured for periods of 18 years. Only a few of the children who became enserfed in this manner were actually registered, either because the practice was illegal or because it was regarded as unnecessary to register children. The registration of Khoisan children as serfs or *inboekelinge* was only legalised in 1775, by which time thousands had already been enserfed in this way. At the end of the children's period of bondage they were often so indebted to or otherwise economically dependent on their foster 'parents' that they could not leave their households, and became 'debt peons'. This strengthened the 'ownership' of servants by *Trekboere*, which often lasted for those servants' entire lives. Children born to enserfed women were also commonly enserfed as *inboekelinge*. It is unfortunately not known what the total number of *inboekelinge* was.[27]

Whether these people should be regarded as serfs or slaves is uncertain. Unlike slaves they could not be sold, but an illegal market for captive children existed, and some were indeed sold. The *inboekelinge* received food and clothing but no wages, and were therefore practically treated like slaves. After a commando raid, the captured children were divided – together with the cattle – between senior members of the commando. Like serfs, the captives were tied to their workplace; it was not possible for them to move from the farm where they were enserfed to another. When the farm was sold, they were – like slaves – passed on to the new owner.

Given that prisoners of war in the ancient world were reprieved from death by merciful victors and turned into slaves, the *Trekboere* were also inclined to justify the enserfment of captives on the grounds of war, and with the argument that they were taking care of the orphans. These arguments were dubious and cynical, because the wars were explicitly conducted to capture children, and their parents often deliberately killed for that reason. In the early 18th century Khoisan children were only taken prisoner when caught in retaliation raids. Later in the century commando raids were conducted for the sole purpose of capturing women and children (see Shell 1994a: 38).

Not only whites were involved in slave raids and in capturing women and children. Most members of the commandos were in fact 'tame' Khoikhoi men who farmed in partnership with the white *Trekboere*. These Khoikhoi regarded themselves as people of higher status than the San. 'Tame' Khoikhoi were often the chief victims of San attacks on colonial herds and flocks, some of which were their property. An added reasons for participated in 'man-hunting' was that the captives could solve their labour problems as well.

It is no accident that the *Trekboere* preferred to capture Khoisan children and – to a lesser extent – women. Within these patriarchal households, the children – and to a lesser extent their mothers – were 'repersonalised' through a process of domestic acculturation and social domination. From the point of view of the *Trekboer* patriarch, it was necessary to bind the serfs morally, psychologically and physically to the household to ensure that they could be trusted in the uncertain and dangerous circumstances on the frontier. It was even more advantageous to integrate the children of captives as household serfs (the so-called *huisboorlingen*), because they could be more successfully acculturated. In this way the *inboekstelsel* became a widely used pattern of labour exploitation which was maintained in an adapted form long after Khoisan serfdom was officially abolished by Ordinance 50 of 1828 (see Shell 1994a: ch 13).

5.5 The power constellation at the frontier, and the changing nature of the master–serf relationship

In contrast with the imported chattel slaves at the Cape, the Khoisan violently resisted their enslavement. The fact that Khoisan serfs were bound in close proximity to Khoikhoi and San tribes who still enjoyed a measure of independence made it much easier for them to become *drosters*. It was mainly Khoisan men in the service of *Trekboere* who were inclined towards *landlopery* (vagabondage). Predictably, the *Trekboere* were strongly opposed to this. All Khoisan men, whether 'tame' or 'wild', ran the risk of being apprehended as 'vagabonds' and potential stock thieves should they stray from their prescribed duties, however menial. When 'vagabonds' were captured, their punishment was usually exceptionally cruel. The master–serf relationship on the frontier was undoubtedly far more violent and associated with more bodily harm than in the South Western Cape. The serfs were also in a far weaker position than slaves, because they enjoyed no legal protection and were also not regarded as being as valuable as slaves, who personified the capital invested in them (see Guelke 1989: 96; Newton-King, in Cameron 1986: 100–11).

As noted earlier, the Cape colony experienced an economic revival after 1770 due to a marked increase in the number of ships visiting Cape Town.[28] The demand for meat rose sharply, which made cattle farming in the Eastern Cape more profitable. This further encouraged *Trekboere* to move east. The increased demand for additional land and labour brought the *Trekboere* into sharp conflict with the Khoikhoi in the Eastern Cape and the San in the Northern Cape, and even with the Xhosa. In 1778 Governor Van Plettenberg made the Great Fish River the colony's eastern boundary, and opened the Zuurveld – the area between the Sunday and Fish rivers in the Eastern Cape – for Trekboer occupation. This also brought the *Trekboere* into conflict with the Xhosa, who regarded the Zuurveld as part of their grazing land. To gain control over the new land, and acquire the necessary labour, the *Trekboere* used the commando system more aggressively than before. It was in this period that 'manhunting' became an important part of commando raids. At this stage not only San children but also Xhosa children were captured and indentured (see Elphick and Malherbe 1989: 28–35).

Isolated on the frontier, the Dutch colonists gradually assumed many of the responsibilities of government. Although the VOC did not formally delegate any of its powers to the colonists, the frontier settlers simply began to exercise their own forms of authority. As the patriarchal frontier farmers came to regard the VOC as irrelevant to their survival, they began to regard themselves as their own government, and used any means at their disposal to protect themselves and promote their interests. Isolated, and far from the colonial authorities in Cape Town, the patriarch of a large cattle farm regarded his 'domain' as a sovereign unit over which he exercised power and discipline by using his status, gun, and *sjambok*. In this way the *Trekboere* developed the mentality of reckless independence that became characteristic of the Voortrekkers. This mentality lived on until well into the 20th century (see Mostert 1992: 163–5). Isolated in their frontier districts, the European enlightment of the second half of the 18th century entirely passed the *Trekboere* by.

The VOC could exert its authority over the frontier district only in an indirect manner. It was responsible for the appointment of *heemraden* (ie, officials appointed to settle local disputes) and *landdrosten* (chief administrators). The *heemraden* and *landdrosten* were appointed from the ranks of wealthier farmers and were – especially on the frontier – regarded as the representatives of the *Trekboere*. They were therefore sympathetic to the latters' interests and independence. The *heemraden* and *landdrosten* were, in turn, responsible for apointing *veldcornetten*, tasked with organising the commandos. Appointment to one of these three formal positions endowed a *Trekboer* with considerable power, and therefore the means to dispense patronage. The incumbents of these three positions and the commandos co-ordinated the patriarchal *Trekboere* into a kind of collective entity. The commando was the vehicle for asserting authority over land and indigenous people, and constituted a separate constellation of power – or a political and economic subsystem – in frontier districts (see Trapido, in Marks and Attmore 1980: 351–2).

In any case, the financial decline of the VOC towards the end of the 18th century further reduced its capacity to exert any meaningful authority at the frontier. This vacuum was filled by the commandos. According to Keegan, the commandos became '... the single most important symbol of the cultural and social cohesion of the frontier burghers, and the chief instrument of their common interest in *dispossessing* and *subjugating* indigenous peoples... The commando [also] became both a reflection and an instrument of *stratification* among colonists [on the frontier]' (1996: 30).

'Tame' Khoikhoi warriors were relegated to the lower ranks of the commandos. They were obliged to do most of the fighting, but received smaller proportions of the cattle and children captured during raids. As noted earlier, the *Trekboere* gradually opted to exploit the 'tame' Khoikhoi as labourers rather than treating them as equal military or farming partners. By alienating the 'tame' Khoikhoi in this way, one of the important props of the power structure on the frontier was gradually eroded.

5.6 The ideological orientation of the *Trekboere* in the 18th century

A controversial issue in South African historiography is whether the racist ideologies prevalent among white South Africans in the 20th century grew out of the attitudes of the *Trekboere*. While a liberal school of historiography blames 20th-century racist ideology on the frontier traditions, a revisionist (or structuralist) school regards it as an extension of the system of racial capitalism institutionalised and legitimised by British settlers (with the support of the Colonial Office) in the mid-19th century. The revisionist school acknowledges

that the patriarchal economic order that had developed in the South Western
Cape and at the frontier during the Dutch period created a highly stratified
society, with whites in positions of power and privilege and blacks in positions
of powerlessness and dependency. What complicated matters is that in the 18th
century no sharp line could be drawn between white and black, as is evident
from the high frequency of mixed marriages and miscegenation, especially in
frontier districts. At the same time, by the end of the 18th century the division
between white patriarchal power and privileges and black powerlessness and
dependency had become so clear-cut that an explicit awareness of racial
differences is undeniable. Although the drive for white hegemony was
originally inspired by a mercantilist orthodoxy – ie, that power could be used
by the powerful to protect and promote his/her group interests against those
who were less powerful – it is also undeniable that, in due course, the 'power
struggle' took place along colour, ethnic, and racial lines.

A revisionist historian, Timothy Keegan, claims:

A pervasive *colour prejudice* was clearly present at the Cape [in the 18th
century], but did not constitute a *racial ideology*. Explicitly racial
terminology was seldom used; aversion was directed at cultural rather than
physiological traits; and people were not defined in racial terms... Class
distinctions were more permeable than race and ancestry; and legal
disabilities were increasingly laid on persons of non-European ancestry but
were not imposed on persons who were perceptibly Europeans' (1996:
24–5).

On the other hand, Shell is amazed that some historians can deny the
importance and even the existence of racial attitudes in the pre-industrial period
of South Africa. He argues that 'the first outlines of *racial and ethnic attitudes*
and colonial identities were deeply etched in the slave period' (1994a: 409).

The question remains whether the racial attitudes of the Dutch period had
already crystallised into a racial ideology before British colonialism began.
Robert Ross believes that a clear-cut ideology of racial exclusiveness did not
exist at the Cape at the end of the 18th century.[29] Like Keegan, he believes that
a well-articulated racist ideology only emerged in the mid-19th century as part
and parcel of British colonialism. During this period a new system of labour
control was developed that was not only applied to the entire Khoisan
population but was also easily imposed on the former slaves and on those
Africans who began to enter the colony as labourers from the 1820s onwards.
To legitimise this new unfree labour pattern – to which all blacks in the Cape

colony were subjected – the British articulated a well-integrated racist ideology during the 1830s and 1840s (Ross 1993: ch 3; Crais 1992; Keegan 1996; see also section 6.6).

Even if we accept the argument that a well-articulated racist ideology had not crystallised during the 18th century, it can nonetheless not be denied that a system of white domination over black slaves and Khoisan serfs existed during the Dutch period. Although not all Khoisan were enserfed, power relations were clearly such that both the VOC and the white colonists were in a position of power and privilege, and the slaves and the majority of the Khoisan in a position of powerlessness and poverty.

The social stratification among whites during the 18th century was rather peculiar, and reflected these skewed power relations. Senior company officials – who were often involved in illegal mercantile activities – were the real elite at the Cape. They believed the colony should be run at a small loss for the company, but at great personal profit. After the revolt against Willem Adriaan van der Stel in 1707, the relationship between the corrupt officials and landed gentry was strained, and social interaction minimal. The patriarchal landowners in the South Western Cape tried to consolidate their independence by distancing themselves from the company and its officials. This tendency was even stronger in the frontier districts. In 1778 the Dutch colonists started the Cape Patriot movement to demonstrate their hostility towards the company's administration. But despite this defiant attitude, the *Trekboere* became very vulnerable in the 1790s when they tried – amid an economic revival – to wring more labour power out of their Khoisan servants. These attempts prompted the Khoisan – both 'tame' and 'wild' – to rebel against the *Trekboer* hegemony (Boucher, in Cameron 1986: 67–70; Schutte 1989: 309–17).

In 1790 two developments occurred that enabled some Khoisan to escape from their growing servitude. During the 1790s and early in the 19th century the Moravian Missionary Society and the London Missionary Society established several mission stations among the Khoisan. The missionaries were to become the chief campaigners for an improvement in the living and working conditions of the Khoisan (see section 6.2). The mission stations also became sanctuaries for Khoisan who could no longer endure their terms of employment. The second development was the establishment by the VOC of the Cape Corps, or 'Hottentot Corps', of *Bastaard-Hottentots* and Khoisan in 1793. In 1806 the British renamed it the Cape Regiment. *Inter alia*, this regiment was deployed with other British units against the *Trekboer* rebellion of 1799 in the Eastern Cape. It was revived during World War 1, and again during the 1970s under apartheid.[30]

This war of 1799–1803 showed clearly that the system of *Trekboer* domination on the frontier – and the labour patterns on which it was based – was unsustainable without renewed military support from Cape Town. If the Dutch period had lasted another 20 or 30 years, the situation at the frontier would probably have descended into total chaos. The Khoisan War of 1799–1803 was, from another point of view, a desperate attempt by the Khoisan to reassert their independence.[31] When peace was arranged in 1803 during the Batavian period, they were promised freedom and equality. The British colonial authority reneged on this promise when it used new legal instruments (in the form of the Caledon Proclamation of 1809) to place the whole Khoisan population in a new state of servitude (see section 6.2).

The rebellion of 1799–1803 was a turning point in the relationship between the *Trekboere* and the (tame) Khoikhoi. For the Khoisan it became a relationship of enmity, and for the Afrikaners a relationship in which all Khoisan became members of a wage-earning proletariat with the status of serfs. After a century of interaction between the *Trekboere* and the Khoisan, the latter were a defeated people. Their social structures had disintegrated almost completely, and their independence had gone for ever. Their culture had been destroyed and replaced with the culture, religion, and language of the *Trekboere*. For the entire 18th century they had been exploited as co-farmers and co-fighters in bloody wars against the 'wild' Khoisan. Many Khoisan had become *inboekelinge*. All of them had been humiliated and impoverished, and their numbers had declined. Their survival as a people was at stake. The arrival of British colonialism did not bring relief. On the contrary, during the first three decades of British rule, their status as a servile labour force deteriorated even further. Thereafter their position improved somewhat, but they remained – at least in the agricultural sector – part of an unfree labour force until well into the 20th century (see Elphick and Malherbe 1989: 35–43).

Endnotes

1 The Portuguese 'armadas' were mainly financed by German capital from Augsburg and Nurnberg. Consequently Portuguese colonialism can be branded as 'hidden German colonialism' (Jaffe 1994: 33).

2 It is estimated that from the 16th until the 18th century between 30 and 40 per cent of all sailors did not return. In these circumstances a refreshment station that could supply ships with fresh water, meat, and vegetables was highly necessary.

3 The VOC was formed with Dutch, Flemish, and German capital. The company enjoyed the support and protection of the seven United Provinces of the Northern Netherlands, dominated by Holland. The VOC can be regarded as one of the first

multinationals. It was a real ' octopus' with tentacles in international trade, piracy, the slave trade, and colonialism.

4 The VOC made huge profits during the first 80 years of the 17th century. These profits were not only the result of lucrative commercial opportunities in the east, but also of plundering on the open seas in accordance with the economic philosophy of mercantilism. During the Eighty Years War (1588–1648) and the Thirty Years War (1618–48), the ships of the VOC plundered the Spanish silver fleet and the company became rich through 'wins op't vyand' (profit on the enemy).

5 In 1660 Holland possessed 16 000 sea-going vessels against the 4 000 of England and the 600 of France. During the Thirty Years War (1618–48) the VOC succeeded in taking over both the monopoly of the Portuguese in the spice trade as well as the profitable slave trade, or *asionto*.

6 It is uncertain how big the Khoisan population was, but it is estimated that 50 000 Khoikhoi lived in the South Western Cape in the mid-17th century (Elphick and Malherbe 1989: 4–7; Elphick 1985). The total Khoisan population might have been as high as 200 000.

7 In the 17th and 18th centuries, only one Griqua, Adam Kok, registered land with the VOC authorities in Cape Town (Shell 1994a: 3). The right to own land was only given to the Khoisan by Ordinance 50 of 1828, but few could make use of the opportunity.

8 The Dutch statesmen – being merchants themselves, and steeped in the merchant tradition – were perfectly aware of how much the VOC could contribute to the power and wealth of the Dutch republic.

9 Each settler received a *de facto* land allocation equivalent to about 8 square kilometres, including both an individual's freehold/land and his share of VOC pasture land (see Guelke 1989: ch 2).

10 This landed gentry – a mere 7 per cent of the free settler population in 1731 – developed, together with a small mercantile elite, into a prosperous, powerful, and influential colonial bourgeoisie at the Cape (see Crais 1992: ch 2; Schutte 1989: ch 6).

11 In return for a small annual fee, the holders of loan farms could exploit an area of land of about 6 000 acres for 12 months, at which time the farmer was supposed to renew the lease.

12 Ross puts it as follows: 'During the first decade of colonial settlement [the Europeans] discovered that the force necessary to subject the Khoikhoi and require them to work on farms was far too great to make it a paying proposition' (1993: 86). This situation changed early in the 18th century when it became possible and even obligatory for the *Trekboere* to employ the Khoikhoi. In 1653 Van Riebeeck described the Khoikhoi as a 'dull, stupid, lazy, stinking people' (Jaffe 1994: 39).

13 Shell puts it as follows: 'Except in the first 30 years of settlement, wage labour was not important in the economy of the Cape households. Families relied, at first, on their own labour, then supplemented that with slaves and, later, serfs; by the nineteenth century, slaves and serfs were the primary labour force. Family labour, while it never died out, remained a temporary phase in an individual free person's life and was nearly always rewarded with expectations of inheritance of not only a farm but also a way of life' (1994a: 25).

14 The Council of Policy was the highest decision-making body at the Cape, and consisted of the governor and senior company officials.

15 In 1713 there were 1 794 slaves and 1 699 Europeans at the Cape. In 1795 the slaves numbered 16 839, and the Europeans 14 952. In 1806 slaves still outnumbered Europeans by 29 861 to 26 268 (Müller 1981a: 52–3, 153).

16 Miscegenation between white men and slave women was quite common during the 17th century when there were very few white women at the Cape. Most of the company's slaves were housed in a slave lodge. This became the settlements chief brothel, and a large proportion of the children living in the lodge were the bastard offspring of white fathers. Miscegenation between white men and slave women continued during the whole period of slavery as female slaves (and Khoisan serfs) lived in their masters' households, and the latter regarded the bodies of slave women as their property which they could use as they wished.

17 From 1652 until 1808 – when the slave trade was abolished, and the price of slaves increased sharply – slave labour was cheap, and provided good profits to their owners. As soon as slavery was well-established, the wages for free labour fell, and it became difficult to obtain white immigrants willing to work at the going wage rate. Müller states that '[before 1795] the supply of slaves was extremely flexible and elastic'. Whenever 'shortages of labour occurred, the colonists exerted pressure on the authorities to import more slaves. Up to the end of the 18th century, the ability of supply to adjust to increases in demand resulted in the average prices being maintained at a relatively low level' (1981a: 53).

18 The slaves owned by the VOC never exceeded 1 000, and in 1795 only 3 per cent of 17 000 slaves at the Cape were owned by the company. In the first half of the 18th century about one quarter of privately owned slaves were used in Cape Town as unskilled and semi-skilled workers. The urban slaves increased to one third at the beginning of the 19th century due to the growing role of Cape Town in the Cape economy. Urban slave-owners profited from hiring out their slaves and could earn quite a large return on their investment (see Armstrong and Warden 1989: 136–43).

19 Many slave-owners were not prepared to sell house-born slaves, because this was regarded as dishonourable. In cases where these slaves were marketed, they attained prices 50 per cent higher than those of imported slaves.

20 In many cases an intimate relationship – often of a sexual nature – developed between a female slave and the male members of the white patriarchal family. This intimate relationship was perpetuated in frontier patriarchal families between captured female serfs and white male members of the family (see Shell 1994a: ch 13).

21 Elphick and Malherbe put it as follows: 'By 1700 many (but not all) Western Cape Khoikhoi had become partially or totally dependent on the colony for their livelihood and security. *The Company, not the settlers, had triggered the processes leading to this new dependence.* It was the Company which consumed large numbers of Khoikhoi cattle, *subordinated* and *humiliated* the Khoikhoi chiefs, *assimilated* Khoikhoi into its legal systems, and *instigated* the expansion of the colony into Khoikhoi pastures. Only at the last stage did the freeburghers' role become decisive – in providing employment for impoverished Khoikhoi' (Elphick and Malherbe 1989: 18; author's emphasis).

22 During the eight years from 1700 until 1708 the colonists' cattle increased from 3 700 to 8 800 and their flocks of sheep from 5 400 to 35 000 (Elphick and Malherbe 1989: 21).

23 During the rest of the 18th century many Khoisan were killed in land, cattle, and slave raids and by the epidemics of 1715 and 1767. The fact that the Khoisan population shrank from an estimated 200 000 in 1650 to fewer than 20 000 in 1800 is an indication of how devastating the wars and the epidemiological disasters had been (see Elphick and Malherbe 1989: 18–22).

24 In 1798 Khoikhoi on 'white' farms still owned an average of five cattle and 23 sheep each. Some were treated by the *Trekboere*, if not as equals, then at least as respected subordinates. But at that time their independence was under threat (see Ross 1993: 86–9).

25 In clashes between the Great Commando and the Khoisan between 1786 and 1797, some 2 504 Khoisan were killed and 669 captured on the Graaff-Reinet frontier alone. The real toll was probably far higher, for these figures do not take account of the many unreported sorties by individual farmers and their associates (see Newton-King, in Cameron 1986: 109).

26 Thus she states: 'Every stage of the long process of European expansion into the hinterland of the Cape met with fierce and bitter resistance from both Khoikhoi and San... It was from these disturbed frontier communities that there emerged a *sporadic but ferocious resistance to the expansion of the colony... It can be argued that it is within the context of this long history of resistance that the peculiar violence of master-servant relations in the South African interior can best be understood'* (Newton-King, in Cameron 1986: 106–7; author's emphasis).

27 It was not only home-born children (*huisboorlingen*) that became *inboekelinge*. Fred Morton contends that no fewer than 30 slave raids aimed at capturing indigenous children were held from 1731 until 1869 in an area from near Cape Town to the Zoutpansberg in the Northern Transvaal. According to him, almost 6 000 people – mainly women and children – were captured. However, the total number of indigenous people who became *inboekelinge* or household serfs was far higher (see Morton, in Eldridge and Morton 1994c: ch 10.) According to Newton-King, 'war captives (sometimes explicitly called *krijgsgevangenen* in the records) made up a significant proportion of the total labour force in frontier districts. It is nearly impossible to make an exact assessment of their numbers [because] *Veldwagmeesters* ...sometimes omitted to mention the taking of captives, listing only the number of "Bushmen" killed' (Newton-King, in Warden and Crais 1994: 233).

28 Foreign ships visiting Cape Town increased from an average of fewer than 30 a year in the first half of the century to an average of 90 a year during the last three decades (see Guelke 1989: 88).

29 Ross puts it as follows: 'There was no racial *ideology* [during the Dutch period], either secular or disguised ... Stereotypes had not yet become functional within the colony... because the economy had not yet forced the whites to incorporate *all* Khoisan as workers in exchange for a steadily decreasing remuneration... No rigid line... existed between 'white' and so-called 'coloured' but rather a variety of status variations based on many different criteria, and by no means congruent one with another... [Consequently]... social life... was still open and social mobility, in both

directions and with little concerns for 'race', still fully possible...*At the end of the eighteenth century the way was theoretically open for society in the Cape Colony, and in South Africa as a whole, to develop in a direction radically different from that which, in the end, it took'* (1993: 72, 74, 90; author's emphasis).

30 This regiment was expanded by the British in the early 19th century, and continued to offer alternative employment opportunities to small numbers of Khoisan. The Khoisan Regiment participated in all the frontier wars fought by the British against the Xhosas, except the Eighth Frontier War of 1851–3 (see Elphick and Malherbe 1989: 35–43).

31 According to Worden, the Khoisan rebellion was not simply intended to stem the territorial expansion of the *Trekboere*, but 'aimed to overthrow settler society from within'. For the first time 'the rebels made common cause with Xhosa chiefs who were resisting colonial advances...with considerable success' (1994b: 10). During the rebellion the British intervened for the first time in a decisive manner.

Chapter 6

The systemic period of British colonialism (±1800–±1890)

6.1 British colonialism and the advent of a new power constellation at the Cape

Britain took over the Cape colony in 1795, in order to safeguard its lucrative trade with India. The Netherlands had become a French satellite during the Napoleonic wars, and Britain assumed control of the Cape in order to prevent the French from doing so. Between 1795 and 1814 the Cape changed hands three times; from 1803 until 1806 the Dutch were in control once again during the Batavian period. This transitional period ended when the Dutch ceded the Cape to Britain in 1814.

Britain's direct colonial involvement in South Africa lasted from 1795 until 1910. During this 'long 19th century' British colonialism was imprinted on every corner of the country and on each of its wide variety of population groups – whites, Khoisan, slaves, and Africans. Over 115 years Britain's economic, political, and legal systems, culture, and ideologies were deeply embedded in this country, displacing feudal, patriarchal, and communal systems and attitudes.

From a domestic perspective, the arrival of this formidable new power constellation was not only traumatic but also exceptionally disruptive. It led to long and bitter conflicts, largely revolving around the legal, moral, and economic redefinition of the three key factors of production: labour, land, and capital. Britain redefined these factors in a way calculated to promote its own economic interests and its power as the centre of a global empire (see Keegan 1996: ch 3; Worden and Crais 1994: introduction).

At the beginning of the 19th century Britain was the leading industrial country in the world. In order to pioneer the first industrial revolution at the end of the 18th century, it needed to break down mercantilism and the monopoly of the merchant monopolists. Britain accomplished this important transition on the strength of Adam Smith's doctrines of the alleged merits of economic liberalism, self-regulating markets, atomistic individualism, and the sanctity of property rights.

One can hardly visualise a sharper contrast than that between Britain's new economic approach and the views reigning among the different groupings at the Cape. VOC officials were still ruled by the obsolete ideas of mercantilism. The idea of a labour market was incomprehensible to the patriarchal landowners, because they controlled their labour force directly by coercive means. And indigenous people were still communally organised; their economies centred on redistribution, and notions of private property and individual self-interest were completely foreign to them.

The all-embracing power of British colonialism revolutionised the way in which power, race relations, and labour patterns were structured at the Cape. This did not happen immediately, and did not affect different domestic groupings at the same time. It occurred in instalments, so to speak, and affected different groups at different periods and to varying degrees. Britain tried to promote its own – and British settlers' – sectional interests amid sharp conflicts between the economic, political, and cultural interests of Afrikaners and those of indigenous people.

To understand the unfolding of British colonialism in South Africa, it is not enough to concentrate only on domestic events. The nature of British colonialism – especially its aggressive military and economic policies, and its overtly racist character – was continuously shaped by events in Britain and the British empire during a century when British colonialism and imperialism dominated the world in what was called – rather euphemistically – the Pax Britannica. Perhaps one of the most momentous events in Britain during the 19th century was the adoption of the Reform Act in 1832. This constitutional reform shifted the balance of power in parliament from the old landed gentry to the emerging industrial bourgeoisie who favoured the Ricardian ideas of international free trade and merciless competition in labour markets, allowing wages to be determined at subsistence levels. These events consolidated not only the political and economic power of the industrial bourgeoisie, but also entrenched bourgeois ideologies of the class and racial superiority of the governing elite, not only in Britain but also in its extended colonial world (see section 6.6).

To understand labour patterns in South Africa during the 'long 19th century', and the power relations that shaped them, it is useful to distinguish among four phases of British colonialism. During the first – from 1795 until 1814 – it was not yet certain whether the colony would be transferred to Britain. Consequently, the latter's approach in this phase was hesitant, influenced by fears that the Dutch colonists would stage an uprising. Eager to relieve the labour problems of the white colonists – especially after Britain had abolished the slave trade in 1808 – the third British governor, the Earl of Caledon, issued the 'Hottentot Proclamation' in 1809, which allowed the Khoisan to be legally indentured. Also, in order to protect the *Trekboere* in the Eastern Cape against Xhosa encroachment, Cradock ordered British troops to march against the Xhosa in 1812. Both these events resonated through the first half of the century (Freund 1989: ch 7; see also section 6.2).

During the second phase of British colonialism – from 1814 until 1840 – that country consolidated its military and economic presence at the Cape. All ten British governors from 1814 until 1852 were senior military officers who had served in Britain's Peninsula War against Napoleon. All of them, but especially Lord Charles Somerset and the last one, Harry Smith (1847–52), were typical military people who thought all problems could be resolved by military means, and used military campaigns to bolster their own status. Their military aggression can be regarded as an important cause of the four bloody frontier wars fought against the Xhosa from 1818 to 1853. The Xhosa were thoroughly defeated, and deprived of much of their land and cattle in favour of British settlers. But what is more important from a labour point of view is that the military and economic assault on the Xhosa set off a process of deliberate proletarianisation aimed at integrating them into the colonial economy as unfree wage labourers (see Mostert 1992: ch 12, 13; Worden and Crais 1994: 4–5; see also section 6.5).

From an ideological point of view the most important event during the second phase of British colonialism was the campaign, driven by the evangelical humanitarian movement in Britain and at the Cape, to abolish the enserfment of the Khoisan as well as chattel slavery. These goals were accomplished in 1828 and 1838 respectively. During this phase the initially friendly relations between Afrikaners and the British colonial authorities turned sour. The abolition of serfdom and slavery deprived the Afrikaners of their compliant labour force. Serious controversies also arose in the Eastern Cape between the British and the Afrikaners over the registration of property rights and the protection of whites against Xhosa encroachment (see Le Cordeur in Cameron 1986: ch 6; see also section 6.3).

During the third phase of British colonialism – from 1840 until about 1890 – the fierce resistance of the Xhosa was finally broken, and large numbers of Xhosa were proletarianised and turned into unfree labour. Two important political and economic events took place during this period. In 1854 the Cape was granted a representative parliament, and in 1872 'responsible government', which enabled white settlers – both English and Afrikaans-speaking – to play an important role in governing the colony. But what is perhaps more important is that the white property class (and especially the settlers in the Eastern Cape) succeeded in establishing a system of agricultural capitalism based on a repressive labour system. When slavery and serfdom were abolished, the white land-owning class succeeded – in close co-operation with the colonial state – in designing new forms of labour repression, to which former slaves and serfs and large numbers of Xhosa were subjected. In this way unfree labour patterns were maintained despite the abolition of slavery and serfdom.

To legitimise the emerging system of racial capitalism, the ideology of evangelical humanitarianism was replaced almost completely from 1840 onwards with the racist idea that Africans could only be wrenched away from 'barbarism' and saved for 'civilisation' through direct British domination, and by forcing them to perform useful (and unfree) labour. The British propagated their ideas about the superiority of their civilisation and liberal utilitarianism with evangelical zeal. The restructuring of the population of the Cape colony into a white master and land-owning class and a black wage-earning proletariat was decisive not only for the labour patterns of the next 150 years but also for the racist political, social, and economic systems that prevailed in South Africa until the end of the 20th century (see Crais 1992: ch 7; see also section 6.5).

During its fourth phase – from about 1890 until 1910 – British colonialism was transformed into an imperialist expansionism which was far more aggressive and exploitative than the forms that had preceded it. This phase coincided with a relative contraction of the British economy as it was overtaken by Germany in industrial production, and as it lost international markets to Germany and the United States. This was also the period in which mineral discoveries in South Africa lured large British corporations to the subcontinent. To exploit the mineral wealth profitably, it became necessary for Britain to control the whole of South Africa – politically, socially, and economically. To accomplish this, several imperial wars were waged in order to conquer the African tribes that were not yet controlled by the British, as well as the two Boer republics. The gold mining companies experienced problems – before and after the Anglo–Boer War – in recruiting the required numbers of black miners at wages low enough to yield a profit. To solve the problem of the inadequate supply of black mineworkers, measures were implemented that created the pattern for the employment and exploitation of African workers for the greater part of the 20th century.

Britain legitimised its imperialist exploitation in the late 19th century with an arrogance characteristic of the heyday of Victorian optimism. It did so on the basis of segregationist policies and ideologies, and in terms of a Social Darwinism which claimed not only that the British race was superior to others, but also that it had a birthright to rule over people of a lesser breed. The discovery of gold in South Africa (1886) and the 'outbreak' of New (British) Imperialism led to a new power constellation being established not only in the Cape colony, but in the rest of South Africa. This constellation was perpetuated by the local English establishment after Union in 1910. We can therefore identify a systemic period that stretched from ±1890 to 1948. This period will be discussed in chapter 8 (see Bundy 1988: ch 4).

Under Dutch colonial rule a class of merchants developed in Cape Town which was responsible for importing slaves and exporting meat. This class was protected by monopolistic privileges, and made large profits from exploiting slave and Khoisan labour. During British colonialism, the formal monopolies of the Dutch period were abolished. This initiated a period of 'free trade imperialism' that lasted until the last quarter of the 19th century. Under British rule the merchant class was augmented by British immigration and British capital, and grew into a highly influential mercantile class with strong financial interests in London. This class exerted considerable influence over political and economic events at the Cape, and through its control of trade and credit obtained extensive interests in every sector of its economy. It is not possible to explain the power constellation in 19th-century South Africa without considering the role of the mercantile class. It was a major appropriator of the surplus extracted from the Khoisan and Xhosa – and even Afrikaners – in the exploitative colonial system that developed during that century (see Legassick, in Harris 1975: 237).

6.2 From the legal enserfment of the Khoisan in 1809 to the abolition of their subservient status in 1828

After the Khoisan Rebellion of 1799–1803, the relationship between the *Trekboere* and the Khoisan was very tense. The new British colonial authority tried to restore the peace, but did not succeed. This was only achieved in 1803 by the new Dutch governor, Lieutenant General Jan Willem Jansens. His promises to grant land to the Khoisan and improve their labour conditions remained unfulfilled. When the British reoccupied the Cape in 1806, Afrikaners were still very bitter and vengeful about the Khoisan rebellion,[1] and put pressure on the new authorities to do something about the great scarcity of labour. At the same time the missionaries strongly denounced the poor living and employment conditions of the Khoisan, and pleaded for their judicial status to be improved. To meet these conflicting demands the new British governor,

Earl Caledon, issued his infamous 'Hottentot Proclamation' in 1809. On the one hand, it was aimed at ending their misuse and maltreatment by including them under the rule of law, and the jurisdiction of the new Cape government. On the other, the proclamation sought to resolve the labour shortage – intensified by the suspension of the slave trade in 1808 – through measures for mobilising and controlling the Khoisan labour supply. These two aims proved to be irreconcilable. The end result of the proclamation was that Khoisan serving Afrikaners were immobilised and legally indentured as contract workers, while those who were not were forced into the labour market for servants for the first time (see Freund 1989: 334–9; Worden and Crais 1994: introduction).

The Caledon Proclamation required that labour contracts be drawn up in triplicate so that master, servant, and the authorities each had a record of the terms. It also laid down that every Khoisan must 'have a fixed place of abode... [and that] they should not be allowed to change their place of abode from one district to another without a certificate from the Fiscal or Landrost'. If Khoisan wanted to move to other employers after completing their contracts, they needed passes from their masters stating that they had 'duly served out' the terms of their contracts. That implied that they could not change their places of residence without the farmers' permission. It therefore became easier for farmers to keep Khoisan on at their farms.[2]

Caledon's proclamation not only seriously curtailed the movement of Khoisan, but also gave their masters legal means to control their servants far more strictly than before. An important side-effect of the proclamation was that it gave local officials (*landdrosten* and *veldcornetten*) extensive opportunities for dispensing patronage in the sphere of labour distribution. Therefore, instead of placing labour matters under the jurisdiction of the colonial authorities, the proclamation increased the power of local officials and supplied them with new legal instruments (Newton-King, in Marks and Atmore 1980: 177). The colonists accepted the extra state support they needed, and ignored those provisions that harmed their interests. But what was even worse is that all three categories of late 18th-century Khoisan – those who farmed in partnership with *Trekboere*, those who were *inboekelinge*, and those who were not controlled by the *Trekboere* – were now drawn into the legal web created by Caledon's proclamation. Moreover, the new legislation effectively controlled access to Khoisan mission stations, while the Khoisan were also excluded from land ownership. In 1812 Cradock granted Afrikaner farmers the right to 'apprentice' children for ten years from the age of eight if they had maintained the child during its first eight years.[3] In this way the *inboekstelsel* was perpetuated.[4]

The missionaries – especially Dr Johannes Theodorus van der Kemp and James Reid – were infuriated by Caledon's proclamation. In their campaign to improve the living and labour conditions of the Khoisan, they now concentrated on the alleged ill-treatment of Khoi servants by white farmers. In 1811 the governor at the time, Sir J F Cradock, instructed the new circuit court to investigate these charges. Whites were outraged by what they called the 'Black Circuit'. The idea that Khoisan servants could rightfully claim equality before the law and lay charges against their masters was completely unacceptable to Afrikaners. The missionaries hoped that at least 1 000 charges would be. laid against whites. It was, however, difficult to assemble the witnesses. In the end only eight of 62 whites charged with violence against servants were convicted (see Le Cordeur, in Cameron 1986: 82).

Afrikaners responded to Caledon's proclamation and Cradock's new circuit court with dismay. Both measures tried to improve the legal status of the Khoisan, and whites feared that this implied a diminution of their legal rights. Whites originally did not realise that Caledon's proclamation cut both ways, effectively strengthening white masters' legal control over their Khoisan servants. The real reason for the Afrikaners' dismay was that the new measures introduced a new and unfamiliar conception of state power, authority, and law. Under the patriarchal order that had developed during the Dutch period – in defiance of the VOC – the relationship between masters and slaves and masters and servants was regarded as a private household matter. The new measures turned the master–servant relationship into a public matter. While the patriarchal master regarded it as his right to punish slaves or servants for misconduct, the new British authority now stipulated that the right of punishment was an exclusively public matter that should happen strictly in accordance with legal regulations (see Shell 1994a: ch 13).

The Dutch colonists experienced the 'public' intervention of British state paternalism in their 'private' household sphere as a violation of their political cosmology. This was one of the main bones of contention during the protracted clashes between Afrikaners and the British during the 19th century.[5] These conflicting views of the role of the state – and especially its impact on labour relations– were undoubtedly an important cause of the Great Trek in the 1830s. Those who trekked to the north wanted to reconstruct the patriarchal order and the labour patterns to which they had become accustomed during the 18th century (see Mason, in Worden and Crais 1994: ch 2).

The second British occupation in 1806 led to a sustained recovery of the Cape economy, and the incorporation of the Cape colony into the dynamic system of the British Empire stimulated its diversification. An important upswing in the economy occurred when the duty on Cape wines entering Britain was reduced in 1813 to one third of what it had previously been. The new British period also led to an inflow of British capital and immigrants. The abolition of the slave trade in 1808 – amid a growing scarcity of labour – tripled the price of existing slaves. In these circumstances Caledon's proclamation made the employment of and control over Khoisan workers almost obligatory. The number of Khoisan in formal employment increased sharply. To satisfy the increased demand for Khoisan labour, commando raids against the Khoisan were continued. Caledon's proclamation and Cradock's apprenticeship regulations created a legal framework in which *inboekelingskap* and peonage could continue in the form of highly regulated contract workers. Owing to the sharp increase in demand for Khoisan labour, almost the entire Khoisan labour force was employed under the repressive contractual conditions created by Caledon's proclamation. Although the maltreatment of Khoisan servants was forbidden, patriarchal farmers were still inclined to settle labour disputes in the usual way as if these were still private household matters (see Elphick and Malherbe 1989: 43–50; Newton-King, in Marks and Atmore 1980: ch 7).

In the decade from 1810 until 1820 the missionaries tried in vain to improve the conditions of the Khoisan, or at least to increase the capacity of the mission stations to provide them with sanctuary. Lord Charles Somerset, who was interested in economic progress, was positively disposed towards the demands of Afrikaners, and therefore less inclined to consider the complaints of missionaries about the continued maltreatment of slaves and Khoisan serfs. The Khoisan gained an effective champion when the humanitarian Dr John Philip of the London Missionary Society arrived at the Cape in 1820. He identified the pass system as the main reason for the oppression and exploitation of Khoisan labour. The passes severely restricted their right of movement, and they could be charged with vagrancy if they were caught without them. Philip blamed the poor conditions of the Khoisan on the colonial system at the Cape. In the process he antagonised the landed gentry as well as Somerset (see Le Cordeur, in Cameron 1986: 81–4).

Evangelical humanitarianism was initiated in Britain at the end of the 18th century by the non-established churches, such as the Methodists, as a reaction to the disruptions brought about by the industrial revolution. It was as much a product of the new industrial age as Adam Smith's ideology of individual self-interest and free markets. The humanitarians regarded free markets as a necessary condition for the development of moral responsibility, and for the triumph of 'Christian civilisation'. They regarded free markets not only as economically gratifying, but also as morally gratifying. According to the humanitarians, people who enjoyed the freedom to enter labour markets without direct physical compulsion would also be much more productive than those who were coerced into labour. By advancing this argument the evangelical humanitarians served the interests of the new elites of industrialising Britain, who were concerned about the economic results of giving workers greater economic freedom. During the optimistic years when humanitarianism and economic liberalism joined hands in the campaign against serfdom and slavery, it was naïvely thought that the abolition of these feudal institutions would have positive moral and economic results.[6]

John Philip was an enthusiastic supporter of Adam Smith's economic liberalism and of the humanitarian idea that free labour markets would enhance not only the productivity but also the moral and Christian development of the enslaved. Philip was skilful at exploiting the powerful humanitarian networks in London, and succeeded in forging a close alliance with Cape Town's mercantile elite. This close co-operation was not coincidental. While the humanitarians were interested in the moral and religious development that would result from free labour markets, the mercantile elite was interested in the economic gains from integrating a free market economy at the Cape with a global British free market.[7]

Ordinance 50 of 1828 was adopted to 'improve the conditions of the Hottentots and other free persons of colour at the Cape'. It abolished all discriminatory restrictions on the Khoisan, and made them legally equal to whites. In particular they were no longer required to carry passes, and they could legally own land. Ordinance 50 in effect recalled Caledon's proclamation of 1809. It radically changed labour patterns at the Cape, and immediately resulted in large-scale vagrancy and crime. In the Eastern Cape Khoisan employees deserted the pastoral farms *en masse* and established peasant communities beyond the control of employers, but near enough to allow them to plunder white farms. Instead of resolving farmers' labour problems, Ordinance 50 led to large-scale disruptions and intensified the scarcity of labour for both Afrikaners and British settlers. The ordinance deprived Afrikaners of their firm grip on a subservient labour force to which they had become accustomed, and also of their most valuable – and often only – source of labour. Still imbued with the idea of a patriarchal order in which labour relations were a private matter, Afrikaner farmers in frontier districts reacted angrily to what they regarded as unjustified British interference in their private domain. These effects of Ordinance 50 were important reasons for the Great Trek of the 1830s to the north (see Keegan 1996: 103–7).

The purpose of Ordinance 50 was to grant every inhabitant of the colony (except slaves) equality before the law, and to the Khoisan 'the liberty to take their labour to the best market'. It was, however, too legalistic to bring about the moral and economic improvements promised by the evangelical humanitarian movement. It certainly came far too late for the Khoisan; at that stage their social structures and economic independence had already been destroyed, and they were already an agricultural proletariat in the true sense of the word. By then, the population at the Cape was divided into two groups – the one white, rich, and powerful, and the other black, impoverished, and powerless. Given this entrenched racial divide, the Khoisan were also too demoralised and had too negative a self-image to take advantage of their new legal freedom. The humanitarian movement's naïve optimism that legal freedom alone would be sufficient to develop the erstwhile serfs into morally and economically responsible individuals proved to be thoroughly unfounded (see Ross 1993: 94–102; Le Cordeur, in Cameron 1986: 81–4).

In their situation of economic and moral deprivation, the Khoisan had neither the opportunity nor the inclination to adopt a different lifestyle. The majority opted to stay on in their previous jobs, with little improvement of their labour conditions and wages. To heal the wounds of decades of violent oppression, exploitation and humiliation, the Khoisan in 1828 needed a comprehensive programme of moral and material upliftment as well as easy access to viable farming opportunities. But, in the framework of early 19th century liberalism, an active policy of social upliftment was inconceivable. The only attempt in this direction was the Kat River settlement established for the the Khoisan on the eastern frontier at the initiative of Andries Stockenström.[8] The freedom granted to the Khoisan by Ordinance 50 was short-lived. It was taken away by the Masters and Servants Proclamation of 1841 and – even more comprehensively – by the Masters and Servants Act passed by the Cape parliament in 1856.[9]

6.3 From the suspension of the slave trade (1808) to the abolition of slavery (1838)

The ideological and economic forces that played a role in Proclamation 50 of 1828 also resulted in the abolition of slavery by the British parliament in 1833.[10] While the serfdom of the Khoisan (in terms of Caledon's Proclamation of 1809) was a local (ie, a Cape colonial) matter, slavery was a British colonial matter. Slavery played a much more important role in the British colonies in the West Indies than at the Cape. The emergence of industrial capitalism and the decline of the mercantile system lessened the significance of the West Indies for the British economy. This also reduced the influence in London of British slave-owners with a vested interest in the West Indies. While Britain had a big stake in the slave trade to the Americas during the second half of the 18th century, the loss of 13 American colonies deprived Britain of that lucrative trade (see Keegan 1996: ch 4).

The dramatic changes in Britain's slave and trade relations with the West Indies and the United States created circumstances in which a strong anti-slavery movement could develop in both evangelical and business circles. The fact that Britain had adopted a belligerent attitude towards both France and the United States during the first decade of the 19th century created an opportunity for the British to assert the alleged superiority of their values and their liberties against the pretensions of American republicanism and the French revolutionaries. These considerations played a role when Britain abolished the slave trade in 1807.[11] According to Keegan, Britain abolished the slave trade 'not because the trade had become uneconomic – far from it – but because abolitionism was a cause that more than any other legitimated Britain's evolving ruling order, and provided the new empire of conquests with a sense of moral idealism and mission' (1996: 79).

The loss of influence of the West Indian pro-slavery lobby in the British parliament was decisive for the abolition of slavery at the Cape. In the early 1820s there was a tacit alliance between the pro-slavery lobby and the British cabinet, but the Reform Act of 1832 tilted the balance of power towards the new industrialists and abolitionists. The frequent and intense insurrections in the West Indies during the 1820s also played an important role in the abolition of slavery (Watson 1990: 198).

The evangelical humanitarians regarded slavery as inhumane because it gave too much power to slave owners, who often misused it. In due course the mission movement took on the trappings of a British establishment movement, and became more nationalist in its rhetoric and appeal. Consequently it became inclined to put greater emphasis on the supposed civilising mission of British imperialism than on the alleged humanism of Christian morality. This shift in emphasis brought the mission movement in line with the ideological orientation of the emerging industrial bourgeoisie in Britain (see Keegan 1996: 78–82). The industrialised bourgeoisie, imbued with the ideology of liberalism and material progress, wanted to replace slavery with a labour system that avoided direct physical coercion, but still ensured the dependence of workers on their employers for income and subsistence. In Britain the necessary supply of 'free' labour was achieved via the abolition of the Poor Laws in 1834. The liberals in Britain self-confidently stressed the alleged higher productivity of a 'free' labour force encouraged to work by the incentive of wages, but still 'driven' indirectly to the labour market by poverty and/or hunger. In South Africa the necessary supply of 'free' labour was accomplished from the 1840s onwards – ie, after the abolition of serfdom and slavery – by depriving the former serfs and former slaves of their access to land, by deliberately and systematically proletarianising the Xhosa and other African tribes, and by adopting masters and servants laws. Although coloureds and Africans were formally (legally) free, white employers and the white-controlled government deliberately created conditions that forced them on to the labour 'market' where they had no choice but to enter into unfavourable labour contracts.

The missionaries who were prominent when Ordinance 50 was passed in 1828 played a less significant role in the movement against slavery at the Cape than their counterparts in the West Indies. Those at the forefront of the anti-slavery drive at the Cape were the mercantile elite and especially John Fairbairn, editor of the *South African Commercial Advertiser*. The most striking characteristic of Fairbairn's discussion of slavery is the virtual absence of any moral or social condemnation of this institution.[12]

The British parliament passed the Emancipation Act in 1833. Slaves were set free on 1 December 1834, but the act provided for an 'apprenticeship' period of four years 'to make temporary provision for the continued cultivation of the soil and the good order of society, until all classes should gradually fall into the relationship of a state of freedom'. For all practical purposes the 'apprenticeship' period was an extension of slavery. No provision was made for preparing slaves for their 'freedom', or for inculcating notions of discipline and self-control. The only break with the past was the removal of the right of the former slave-holders to punish their former slaves (Worden, in Worden and Crais 1994: ch 5).

The abolition of slavery and the way in which it was done remained controversial among Afrikaners for generations. It was estimated that slave owners lost up to four fifths of the market value of their slaves (Crais 1992: 62).[13] Afrikaners regarded this as the most serious and unjustified intervention of the British authorities in their private patriarchal order. But what is often forgotten is that – as in the case of the Khoisan, when the indentureship system was abolished – the former slaves were not compensated in any way. They were set free as a proletariat, without land, capital, or other means of income.[14]

The 'freedom' of the slaves was indeed short-lived. In 1841 – only three years after their final emancipation – their freedom of movement and freedom of choice were seriously curtailed when the Masters and Servants Ordinance was issued (see section 6.5). After the abolition of slavery, farmers in the Western Cape tried to retain their former slaves as subservient labour; they still regarded their former slaves as their 'property', and viewed vagrancy as 'illegal'. The masters and servants acts passed by the Cape parliament enabled them to perpetuate 'slavery' for a considerable period. The only difference was that the 'slaves' were now poorly paid wage labourers (see Malherbe 1991: 23–4).

6.4 The expansionism of the British settlers, and the Sixth Frontier War and its aftermath (1820–40)

In 1820 the first group of 5 000 British settlers arrived in the Eastern Cape. This was perhaps the most portentious event of the first half of the 19th century, adding a completely new population group that would, in time, profoundly influence labour patterns and power relations in South Africa. They brought with them a notion of capitalist progress and imperialist expansionism that drastically redefined South Africa's political and economic landscape. During the first 30 years after their arrival, three bloody frontier wars were fought – at their insistence – between the British colonial forces and the Xhosa (see Nash, in Cameron 1986: ch 7).[15]

From 1814 until 1826 Lord Charles Somerset was governor at the Cape. One of the first problems he faced was the uncertain position in the 'Zuurveld' – the area between the Sunday and Fish rivers in the Eastern Cape. The attempt by Cradock, Somerset's predecessor, to drive 20 000 Xhosas out of the Zuurveld led to serious overcrowding in Xhosaland, and to increased cattle-raiding. In 1817 Somerset decided to abandon the traditional policy of maintaining a rigid boundary between blacks and whites. His new policy of concluding treaties with some chiefs while excluding others had failed dismally. In 1819 the Fifth Frontier War erupted when 10 000 Xhosas invaded the Eastern Cape, and caused havoc; the war lasted until the next year (see Le Cordeur, in Cameron 1986: 84–5).

This war convinced Somerset of the need for a white British settlement on the colonial side of the boundary to act as a barrier between the Xhosa and the Afrikaners. The British government granted a request along these lines, and sent 20 000 British settlers to the Cape. The first group of 5 000 arrived in 1820. They soon clashed with Somerset over several issues, the most important being their attempt to establish a free press.[16]

This project had a dual purpose: to relieve unemployment in Britain, and to supply a cheap form of defence on the colony's eastern frontier. The settlers were offered a free sea passage and land grants, and were lured to the Cape with the promise that they could become landed gentry within a few years. But the Cape government's idea of creating a closely knit tillage settlement in Albany (previously the Zuurveld) failed. After an extremely difficult four or five years, many settlers became either merchants or sheep farmers; the latter began to make large profits owing to the great demand for wool from British textile mills.[17]

The profitability of sheep farming created an almost insatiable hunger for additional land and labour. The settlers were not allowed to become slave-holders, probably out of fear that they would join the Afrikaners in 'manhunting' the San and Xhosa. The British settlers could therefore use only Khoisan serfs. When, in 1828, the then acting governor, General Richard Bourke, decided to issue Ordinance 50, he realised it would create serious labour problems not only for Afrikaner farmers but also for the British settlers. To pre-empt these problems, Bourke issued – rather cynically – Ordinance 49 three days before Ordinance 50. The former empowered farmers in the Eastern Cape to employ Xhosas provided they took out passes for the purpose. The fact that Xhosas became an unfree and pass-carrying labour force three days before Khoisan serfdom was abolished is another striking example of the permanence of unfree labour patterns. Ordinance 49 of 1828 began a series of labour and pass laws applying specifically to Africans that lasted for more than 150 years.[18]

The British settlers' eastward expansion to acquire more land and labour for their profitable sheep-farming put them on an inevitable collision course with the Xhosa moving westwards to graze their cattle. To understand the three bloody wars between the British and the Xhosa between 1834 and 1853, it is necessary to examine the difference between these two groups. The Xhosa were the southern wing of the Nguni peoples who had moved southwards along the eastern seaboard from about 500 AD. As in the case of the Khoikhoi, cattle were the focal point of Xhosa existence, although they also planted crops.[19] Although the Xhosa were, like the Khoikhoi, not united under a single king, their clans or chieftaincies were organised in such a manner that they could resist white intrusion far more effectively than the Khoisan; there was a unifying loyalty among the different clans (see Mostert 1992: ch 6).[20]

The confrontation in the Eastern Cape between the *Trekboere* and Xhosa at the end of the 18th century differed greatly from the conflict between the British and the Xhosa from the 1830s onwards. Although the *Trekboere* were equipped with horses, guns, and wagons, the Xhosa had numbers and a disciplined military apparatus. In the late 18th century the Boer commandos could no longer count on any meaningful military support from the colonial authorities in Cape Town. Without such support, it was impossible for the *Trekboere* to conquer the Xhosa in open warfare.[21]

The settler newspapers played an enormously influential role in promoting the sectional interests of the British settlers. In 1831 the *Graham's Town Journal* was established, with Robert Godlonton as editor. The main purpose of the newspaper was to convince the colonial authorities in Cape Town and the colonial office in London of the merits of the settlers' case against the Xhosa. The settler press turned out to be one of the most effective instruments for legitimising the expansion of the settlers, to the detriment of the Xhosa. Its two major themes were to justify the settlers' capitalist activities, and to besmirch indigenous people for their alleged laziness, thieving disposition, untrustworthiness, and general inability to become a civilised people (see Mostert 1992: 777, 828; see also Keegan 1996: 72–4).

By the early 1830s the British settlers had progressed remarkably in economic terms, largely by making inroads into the living patterns of the Xhosa. But by 1834 the situation in Albany had become highly unstable. The Xhosa had already been deprived of their land east of the Sunday's River, and as a result their remaining land became overpopulated. This was aggravated at the end of the 1820s when the Mfengu tribe of southern Natal was driven into Xhosaland in the *mfecane* ('the crushing') unleashed by Shaka and his Zulu *impis*. As a result, the Xhosa increased their cattle raids into Albany. For the British settlers, responding to violence meant escalating violence. In 1831 and 1833 the colonial state launched incursions into Xhosaland, destroying kraals, capturing cattle, burning fields, and pushing Xhosa across the 'boundary'. In 1833 many Xhosas were starving. In December 1834 war erupted on the frontier, shattering the Albany farmers' incipient prosperity (see Keegan 1996: 136–47).

Sir Benjamin D'Urban was governor from 1834 to 1838. When he was appointed, the influence of evangelical humanitarianism was very strong in London, and he was instructed to introduce a more conciliatory policy on the frontier based on treaties with the chiefs. But before he could implement these instructions, war broke out. During the war D'Urban was persuaded to abandon the treaty policy in favour of a policy of 'total expulsion'. In accordance with this policy, he set the boundary further east to the Kei River and proclaimed the establishment of the Province of Queen Adelaide, embracing 7 000 square miles between the Keiskamma and Kei rivers. D'Urban, by now completely taken in tow by the settler bourgeoisie, allocated large farms to prominent members of the settler community in the Eastern Cape and the mercantile elite in Cape Town. This created lucrative opportunities for land speculation. While

D'Urban was 'most pacifically inclined' towards the Xhosa when he arrived at the Cape, he described them in official pronouncements in 1835 as 'treacherous and irreclaimable savages' (quoted by Keegan 1996: 143; see also Crais 1992: 117–21).

When news of D'Urban's policy of 'total expulsion' reached London, it provoked serious protest from the humanitarians. John Philip and Andries Stockenström strongly opposed the new policy. The new secretary of state, Lord Glenelg, informed D'Urban that he had concluded that the Xhosa had 'ample justification' for invading the colony, and ordered the latter to hand Queen Adelaide back to the Xhosa. This decision shocked and embittered almost all sections of the white community at the Cape. Both the British settlers in the Eastern Cape and the mercantile elite in Cape Town were furious because Glenelg's decision deprived them of attractive opportunities for land-grabbing and land speculation already promised to them by D'Urban. The devastating Xhosa offensive in 1834–5, together with the reversal of D'Urban's decision on the settlement, profoundly changed the racial attitudes of the British settlers. Some of the missionaries – mainly Methodist – now claimed that the Xhosa could not be converted to Christianity unless they were totally conquered. The Sixth Frontier War and its negative aftermath – from the point of view of the settler bourgeoisie – fundamentally changed the relationship between whites and Africans at the Cape; this war can be regarded as one of the most decisive turning points in race relations in South Africa's history (see Mostert 1992: 776–8, 760; see also section 9.3).

6.5 Masters and servants laws, proletarianisation, and the growth of racial capitalism

At the end of the stormy 1830s, remarkable attitudinal and ideological changes took place at the Cape, which led to the formulation of new economic and labour policies over the next 50 years. At the instigation of the British settlers – supported ideologically by the missionary movement and the English newspapers – the colonial state became actively involved in shaping a new labour pattern. This period also saw the emergence of a new and powerful colonial elite – both agricultural and mercantile – which not only controlled political events at the Cape, but also consolidated their status in a repressive system of settler capitalism based on unfree black labour. But, perhaps most importantly, this period also witnessed the crystallisation of a clear-cut racist ideology to legitimise not only the racially based system of settler (or racial) capitalism, but also the newly designed repressive pattern of black labour. Many historians regard this period as the most formative one in South Africa's history, when a racial and colonial hegemonic order was created that lasted – with some modifications – for more than a century.[22]

The violence of the Sixth Frontier War and the return to the Xhosa of annexed territory up to the Kei River were traumatic experiences for the British settlers. A feeling of having being deserted and endangered by events in the South African subcontinent began to take root among all whites – Afrikaans- and English-speakers, the agricultural and mercantile elite, militarists and missionaries.[23] In this tense atmosphere the most effective spokespersons for the humanitarian movement – John Philip and John Fairbairn, and several of the missionaries – changed their perceptions about the coloureds and the Xhosa. Even Philip and Fairbairn now regarded the enforced 'civilisation' of the Xhosa as a precondition for their conversion to Christianity. This idea was eagerly grasped by the settler elite and its newspapers. 'Civilisation' now basically meant – for the missionaries as well – the opening up of western Xhosaland to land speculators and wool farmers, and the return of the 'D'Urban system' in addition to the implementation of policies that would successfully control and discipline Xhosa and Khoisan labour. With this new emphasis on state-imposed discipline, for the sake of civilisation and economic prosperity, evangelical humanitarianism was replaced almost completely by Benthamite liberal utilitarianism (see Mostert 1992: 797–805).

Ironically, the abolition of slavery marked the beginning of an economic boom that lasted until the 1860s. The money spent on the six frontier wars and the compensation paid to slave-holders (although less than the full value of the slaves) sharply increased the volume of capital at the Cape. Together with the high levels of wool exports, and an increase in the ivory trade, the higher investment and lucrative land speculation – in land evacuated by the Voortrekkers – led to a period of economic prosperity for both the settlers in the Eastern Cape and the mercantile elite in Cape Town. This economic revival created serious labour problems, especially in the Eastern Cape. After the abolition of serfdom and slavery, the majority of the former serfs and slaves in the Western Cape remained in their previous jobs. The opportunities for an alternative lifestyle in towns and mission stations were rather limited in that area, because almost all the land was already occupied.

In the Eastern Cape the situation was very different. Many Khoisan found sanctuary at the Kat River settlement, or became *drosters* (deserters), living in peasant communities beyond the control of whites. When slavery was abolished, 15 per cent of all slaves – almost 6 000 slaves – were owned by Eastern Cape farmers who had paid high prices for them. After emancipation many drifted back to the Western Cape. Amid a labour crisis in the Eastern

Cape, the influential British settler elite succeeded in convincing the colonial authorities to issue the Masters and Servants Ordinance of 1841. Although the ordinance was written in the language of class and not race – typical of the hypocritical liberal tradition at the Cape – it applied to people who 'may be inclined to lead an idle and vagabondising life' – ie, the Khoisan, former slaves, and Xhosas.[24] The ordinance bound workers to their employers, and imposed severe sanctions for breach of contract, including the subjectively determined 'crimes' of disobedience, defiance, and resistance. The slightest breach of contract by employees became a criminal offence (Worden and Crais 1994: 13–15; Ross 1993: 104–6).

This ordinance was the first in a series of masters and servants laws that remained on the South African statute books until 1974. Although these laws deprived employers of the right to punish their employees, they bound employees to employers for the duration of their contracts, and the state became an important player in labour relations – very much on the side of the employer. The repressive nature of the masters and servants laws became apparent in situations where the potential black labour force had already been proletarianised or could be forced into a state of proletarianisation, and therefore did not have an alternative but to enter into contracts with (white) employers who enjoyed state support in maintaining their workers' contractual conditions. Masters and servants laws and the deliberate proletarianisation of blacks were indeed the two cornerstones on which the impressive edifice of black labour repression was built and maintained for 133 years, from 1841 until 1974.

Barrington Moore clearly describes the causal role of repressive labour systems in the early phases of the industrialisation of several countries. In the case of Britain the enclosure movement (enacted by the gentry parliament) destroyed the structure of peasant society and created a 'wandering poor', or a reservoir of cheap labour.

This reservoir played a decisive role in launching the industrial revolution in Britain at a relatively early date. A similar system of 'labour repression' developed in Germany and Russia but not in France, owing to the fact that the peasants there were granted property rights during the early phases of the French Revolution (see Moore 1966). However, there is an important difference between the repressive labour system introduced in South Africa from 1840 onwards and those in other countries. In the latter, the social dislocation and proletarianisation caused by this system lasted for only 30 or 40 years before a section of the working population was able to command higher wages and was incorporated into social and political institutions (see Trapido 1971: 310). The only country in the western world in which this process of incorporation was extremely slow was Britain. The fact that it was an industrial pioneer may explain this.

In the case of South Africa, the system of labour repression applied mainly to Africans. By means of a process of legislative 'assault', first by the Cape and subsequently by the Union government, and as a result of a protracted rural class struggle, both the large and small estates of white *rentier* landlords were transformed into capitalist farms, while the rent-paying and share-cropping African peasants – at that stage economically relatively independent – were almost universally turned into wage labourers and/or labour tenants (see O'Meara 1983: 22–3). The system of labour repression in South Africa had several unique characteristics. Apart from its conspicuously racial character (if not originally, then eventually), the repressive measures were very harsh and were applied relentlessly. In other industrialised countries, breaches of contract were not regarded as a criminal offence to the same extent as in South Africa. These characteristics of labour repression in South Africa, as well as its longevity, can only be explained in terms of the power structures in place when the successive mining, agricultural, and industrial revolutions occurred. Thus labour repression in this country should be understood in terms of the structural interdependence of white empowerment and black proletarianisation. The power context in which the different phases of labour repression were introduced and maintained was responsible for sophisticated systems of 'plundering' that lasted until the 1970s.[25]

Amid the hardening of racial attitudes among whites during the early 1840s, the then governor, Sir Peregrine Maitland, allowed the settlers in the Eastern Cape to encroach on the area east of the Keiskamma River. This was the direct cause of the Seventh Xhosa War (1846–7). This time, in contrast with the past, no public case was made on behalf of the Xhosa, neither in the colony nor in Britain. In 1847 Sir Harry Smith was appointed as governor of the Cape.[26] Given his arrogance, military aggression, eagerness to please the settler farmers, and blatant racism towards indigenous people, the British government could hardly have appointed a less suitable person. After his appointment Smith declared that he was going to the Cape 'to re-do what Lord Glenelg so ably did undo'. His outspoken purpose was to restructure Xhosa society as thoroughly as possible. To this end he considered his first task to be to destroy the power of the chiefs, and subject them to the control and discipline of the colonial authorities. Smith immediately annexed the land between the Fish and Keiskamma rivers as the district of Victoria East, and the area between the Keiskamma and Kei rivers as the crown colony of British Kaffraria. This began a new frontier policy of annexation and direct rule by white magistrates.[27]

The Eighth Frontier War (1850–3) was the bloodiest, longest, and ugliest of all the frontier wars. British tactics involved burning huts, destroying crops, and capturing cattle. Some 16 000 Xhosa died during the war. After the war the Xhosa were deprived of large portions of their land and cattle, while thousands had no choice but to work as contracted wage earners on white farms. Both the Seventh and Eighth Frontier Wars were enthusiastically sanctioned by the settler farmers and their supporting press. The settler farmers profited amply from the money spent by the British government on the war effort. For them the outcome of both wars was a resounding victory for free enterprise and prosperity (see Crais 1992: 146).

The Eighth Frontier War was also an important turning point in the colonial history of the 19th century. For the first time since the rebellion of 1799–1803, the Khoisan in the Eastern Cape participated in a frontier war. What made the Khoisan Rebellion of 1851 so much more important is that, until then, they had fought in all the frontier wars on the side of the whites. The Khoisan participation in the Eighth Frontier War was triggered by the Cape legislative council's declared intention to enact a squatters ordinance in 1850. Ever since Ordinance 50 of 1828 the farming community in the Eastern Cape had been agitating for measures against those Khoisan living in small peasant communities outside white control. In areas of the Eastern Cape where land was more plentiful and the control of European colonists less secure, former serfs, slaves, and Xhosas established independent peasant communities, which complicated the labour problems of the colonists considerably (Crais, in Worden and Crais 1994: 278–80).

The agitation of settler farmers for the abolition of the Kat River settlement is a typical example of the interaction among land, labour, and capital in the emerging capitalist economy of the Eastern Cape. The productive wool farming activities required the proper combination of capital, land, and labour, and capital would not enter the colony unless ensured of adequate labour. The British settlers, who already owned much of the productive land in the 1840s, stood to profit by an inflow of capital. Consequently, they wanted to create the conditions for such an inflow, ie, by proletarianising the coloureds in the Kat River Settlement by abolishing it. From the farmers' point of view, settlements such as Kat River and other smaller ones were creating an unacceptable situation because they were giving sanctuary to many Khoisan (and some Xhosa) who could have been employed under the Masters and Servants Ordinance of 1841.

Shortly after the legislative council tabled the Squatters Ordinance in 1850, 80 per cent of rural workers – and inhabitants of the Kat River and other settlements in the districts of Albany, Fort Beaufort, and Somerset East – revolted.[28]

The creation in the 1830s and 1840s of small peasant societies outside white control by former serfs and slaves, and the Khoisan Rebellion of 1851, demonstrated how former serfs and slaves managed for some time and with reasonable success to resist their total proletarianisation.[29] This resistance was broken, however, when the Khoisan revolt was suppressed and many of their settlements – including the Kat River settlement – confiscated.[30] After the war the process of coloured proletarianisation in the Eastern Cape was accelerated.[31]

In 1846 the British parliament abolished the Corn Laws and embarked on a policy of international free trade. The triumph of free trade policy had important implications for Britain's colonial policy; *inter alia*, it implied that Britain should disengage itself partially from its colonies and its attendant financial burdens by granting 'responsible government' to the elites in those colonies. The idea of self-rule did not involve the dissolution of Britain's colonial bonds with its colonies; on the contrary, self-rule was regarded as perfectly compatible with the maintenance of colonial ties through economic interdependence and mutual goodwill (see Keegan 1996: 209).

Sir George Grey was governor from 1854 until 1861. Although perhaps the most able and sophisticated British governor at the Cape, he represented the 'Janus face'[32] of liberalism better than anybody else. He explicitly believed that only direct rule over non-European people could rid them of their 'barbarian' customs, and 'save' them for 'civilisation'. He went out of his way to curtail the authority of the chiefs by intervening directly in the structures of chieftainship and by undermining the social and material basis of their authority and power.[33] He started public works programmes for employing Xhosas with the purpose of inculcating a western work ethic in them. His road-building projects represented the most systematic effort yet made to draw the Xhosa into cheap labour. At the same time he established educational institutions for the children of Xhosa chiefs, as well as hospitals specifically for treating Xhosas.[34]

In line with the Victorian liberalism of the mid-19th century, the Cape gained a representative parliament in 1854 based on a 'colour-blind' franchise. Both houses of a two-chamber parliament were to be elected by males, irrespective of colour, who earned R100 a year and owned property with a rental value of R50. Despite the 'colour-blindness' of the new constitution, it actually enabled the dominant white minority – both English- and Afrikaans-speaking – to capture political power in the colony. Almost immediately, the colonial elite used their newly attained political power to pass the infamous

Masters and Servants Act of 1856, which tied employees to five-year labour contracts and stipulated severe punishments for desertion or breach of contract.[35] The act stood out for its severity, and also served as a 'vagrancy' act, which the settler elite had long called for.

Only three years after the destruction caused by the Eighth Frontier War, an even greater tragedy occurred in Xhosaland. In 1854 a form of bovine pneumonia known as lung-sickness had been introduced from Europe with a shipment of Friesian bulls. The disease, which the Xhosa had previously never encountered, struck their cattle at precisely the same time that Sir George Grey introduced his oppressive policies in western Xhosaland. The consequences were far-reaching; the destruction wrought by the war, the oppressive new policies, and the death of 5 000 head of cattle a month struck at the roots of Xhosa society. Grey regarded the situation as a godsend. He told London that the situation in Xhosaland was a 'most favourable opportunity' to lure the Xhosas into wage labour, and to destroy 'the Kaffir system of politics'. Grey's main purpose was to break down Xhosa society and to restructure it in a' way which he believed to be in their best interests.[36]

In a desperate reaction to the situation in Xhosaland, two Xhosa girls, Nongqawuse and Nombanda, prophesied that if Xhosas killed all their cattle, the sun would rise and set again on 18 February 1857 in the east, a whirlwind would sweep all white men and unbelievers into the sea, and all their cattle would be restored to them in great herds. After months of destroying stock and crops, the fateful day came without the the prophecy being fulfilled. In the 13 months during which the cattle-killing prophecies swept across Xhosaland, about 85 per cent of all Xhosa adult men killed their cattle and destroyed their corn. It is estimated that 400 000 head of cattle were slaughtered, and 40 000 Xhosas died of starvation. At least 40 000 left their homes and entered the colony as destitute people to find work; only 37 000 remained in British Kaffraria (see Mostert 1992: 1222).[37] What the missionaries and successive governments of the previous 30 years had been struggling to achieve – ie, to destroy the power of the chiefs, and the social structure of the Xhosa people – had suddenly come about. Grey's reaction was that 'great ultimate good would flow from it'. The settlers' reaction was that prospects for the colony were better than ever before. Grey also used the opportunity to bring a large number of chiefs before the courts. They were found guilty on charges relating to their behaviour during the period of cattle-killing, and sentenced to 'transportation' – ie, incarceration on Robben Island.

In 1857 the Cape parliament introduced the Kaffir Employment Bill to prevent the 'disgorging of Kaffirland', and enforced long-term (five-year) compulsory contracts of indentureship on Xhosa work-seekers. These contracts were drawn up by magistrates, while the destitute, desperate for relief, had no say over where they were to be employed or what the terms of the contracts would be. By the end of 1857 nearly 30 000 Xhosas had registered as labourers in the colony, with perhaps an equal number entering the colony unregistered. The vacuum created in British Kaffraria by the cattle-killing episode also enabled Grey to push forward earlier experiments in trust and individual land tenure for African farmers. It was mainly the Mfengu ('Fingoes') – a tribe that entered into alliances with the government and did not participate in the cattle-killing – who benefited from Grey's new schemes.[38]

6.6 The failure of the humanitarian movement, and the justification of a system of racial domination at the Cape

The evangelical humanitarian movement played a pivotal role – both in Britain and at the Cape – in the abolition of chattel slavery and Khoisan serfdom. It had served a profoundly instrumental purpose in transforming the feudal Cape society of the early 19th century – marked by corruption, despotism, slavery, and serfdom – into a post-Enlightenment and open society in which individual freedom, integrity, and civil rights were valued. Paradoxically enough, this period of individual freedom and legal equality lasted for only 13 years for the Khoisan, and for only three years for the former slaves. The Masters and Servants Ordinance of 1841 was the first of many repressive measures introduced by the Cape colonial authority to create a system of racial domination and racial capitalism that applied not only to former slaves and serfs, but also to Xhosas.

It remains one of the great riddles of South African history that a racially based repressive labour economy was introduced at the Cape immediately after the abolition of slavery. According to Nancy Stepan, 'a fundamental question about the history of racism in the first half of the 19th century is why it was that, just as the battle against slavery was being won by the abolitionists, the war against racism was being lost. The Negro was legally freed by the Emancipation Act of 1833, but in the British mind he was still mentally, morally and physically a slave' (1982: 1).

Any attempt to answer Stepan's question must address the issue of the failure of evangelical humanitarianism: why was a movement that had played such a crucial role in the abolition of serfdom and slavery unable to stem the expansionism and militarism of the British settlers? Given that it had the full co-operation and support of the colonial state, why could it not prevent the settlers' land grabs and the reduction of the Xhosa to unfree labour? The inability of the humanitarian movement to prevent the institutionalisation of racial domination at the Cape from 1840 onwards prompts Keegan to claim that, 'in the end, liberal humanitarianism turned out to be a shallow, tawdry, deceptive thing' (1996: 127). While, in the 1820s and 1830s, the London Missionary Society was the very seed-bed of humanitarian thought, its attempt to justify racially based settler capitalism in the 1840s and 1850s became 'infected with racial sentiment'. Although there is not much point in historical speculation, there is reason to believe that 150 years of racial capitalism in South Africa – from 1840 to 1990 – could have been avoided if liberal humanitarianism had not so easily been turned into a racially based liberal utilitarianism serving the interests of the emerging white capitalist class. South Africa's development could have been more humane and less exploitative if the British settlers had been less successful in their attempts to become a new gentry in Africa, and if they had not been supported by the British government and the colonial authorities in institutionalising a racially based agricultural capitalism (see Keegan 1996: 126–8, ch 8; see also Crais 1992: ch 7).

It is perhaps no accident that the humanitarian movement helped to destroy the remnants of feudalism, serfdom, and slavery in which Afrikaners of the Cape had a vested interest, but failed to stop the triumphal progress of the racist system of British settler capitalism; after all, neither the humanitarians nor their closest ally, the mercantile elite, had any vested interests in the former. The situation changed drastically after the Sixth Frontier War when not only the British settlers in the Eastern Cape but also the mercantile elite in Cape Town were deprived of opportunities for land-grabbing and land speculation when Lord Glenelg reversed the annexation of the province of Queen Adelaide. Moreover, the missionaries – especially those in Xhosaland after the Sixth Frontier War – played a rather dubious role as agents of British colonialism, and especially as the frontline 'troops' of imperial penetration. They corrupted the chiefs, consciously used policies of 'divide and rule', and were convenient instruments of domination (see Jaffe 1994: 60–2).

The superficiality and shallowness of evangelical humanitarianism probably stemmed from it being too closely associated with British liberalism in the late 18th and early 19th century. Both ideologies were based on the naïve belief that legal freedoms alone would be enough to develop both moral responsibility and economic progress. The missionaries were also naïvely optimistic about the ease with which the Xhosa would be assimilated into western and Christian civilisation. When D'Urban described the Xhosa as 'treacherous and irreclaimable savages', the scene was set for a fundamental reevaluation of the latter and their 'primitive culture'. Humanitarians' optimism about the potential of indigenous people for moral development and the assimilability of Africans into western culture were replaced by the obverse, and the need for prolonged domination to force them into disciplined and useful labour. It was in the crucible of the Sixth Frontier War and its aftermath that evangelical humanitarianism was 'transformed' into liberal utilitarianism, based on notions of the racial inferiority of indigenous people. The new ideas of liberal utilitarianism and racism were not only propagated by the settler bourgeoisie, but were also accepted by the colonial authorities – and especially by Sir George Grey – in in order to legitimise the new racially oriented labour and economic policies implemented from the 1840s onwards (see Crais 1992: ch 7; Mostert 1992: ch 22).

An interesting question is whether humanitarism was relatively easily defeated at the Cape because its roots in Britain were superficial. The economic system institutionalised in Britain in the 19th century was all but humane; on the contrary, until 1832 (when the first Reform Act was passed) British capitalism was an archaic system of gentry capitalism. From then on until World War 1 it was a system of bourgeois and *laissez-faire* capitalism which, in practice, was a repressive system of class capitalism.[39] In 1834 the British parliament (controlled by the industrialising bourgeoisie) abolished the Poor Laws enacted by Queen Elizabeth I in the 16th century, in order to force all able-bodied men and women to sell their 'free' labour in an unfree labour market. Because trade union rights were still denied in Britain, the playing field for employers and employees was all but level, and the labour market was still 'unfree'. One should perhaps not be surprised that the humanitarian movement was defeated at the Cape at exactly the same time when the working class in Britain was subjected to a repressive labour system. From, say, 1840 onwards the settler bourgeoisie in the Cape was imbued with the same entrepreneurial spirit as the industrial bourgeoisie in *laissez-faire* Britain.

As noted earlier, Worden and Crais blame the racist ideology that emerged at the Cape in the middle decade of the 19th century on the 'Janus face of liberalism'.[40] Watson blames the failure of South Africa liberalism on its inability to develop a systematic and comprehensive ideology of human rights, or a coherent movement to oppose the steady diminution of the rights of coloureds and Africans. For Watson, the weakness of the anti-slavery movement lies 'in the conflict within classical liberalism between two ideals, that of human freedom and that of property rights...the liberals had valued property more highly than liberty' (Watson 1990: 5.) As soon as property was valued more highly than liberty, it was only a small step towards enslaving the indigenous population groups in order to boost the wealth of the white property class.

Crais and Keegan take this argument further. For Crais, the transition from slavery to racial capitalism was not so much rooted in the 'failure' of liberalism, but in the ambiguous nature of liberalism itself. The racial forms of domination in the 19th-century Cape were not the antithesis of liberalism, but grew out of one part of its contradictory discourse. He then asks: 'What was this world which spoke of freedom and at the same time invented race?' (quoted in Legassick 1993: 337). Crais also believes that the colonial state played a decisive role in institutionalising racial capitalism in South Africa. Without this intervention, capitalism could, according to him, have taken a black peasant road.[41] Keegan is even more adamant that racism did not result from the attitudes and practices of *Trekboere* on the frontier in the 18th century, but was systematically institutionalised by the British colonial authority after the failure of evangelical humanitarianism. He believes it was the British and not the Boers who were responsible for the hierarchies of race, and the conquest of African societies.[42] We can draw the general conclusion that the failure of the humanitarian movement was not only the result of its own weakness, but also of the aggression of capitalist colonial expansionism – in Britain, and among British settlers in the eastern Cape – and of the replacement of liberal humanitarianism with utilitarian and racist ideologies in order to legitimise mid-19th century Victorian colonialism (see Legassick 1993: 329–68; see also section 8.4).

6.7 The rise of an African peasantry in the Cape Colony during the second half of the 19th century

Africans entered the colony from the 1820s onwards to seek wage labour. Ordinance 49 of 1828 provided for their employment on condition that they took out passes. When D'Urban announced his policy of 'total expulsion' after the Sixth Frontier War, not all Africans on the colonial side of the Kei River were expelled. The Mfengu, who did not participate in the war, were 'liberated', and 16 000 (who brought with them 22 000 head of cattle) were resettled near Grahamstown. The idea was that they should help fight the Xhosa and supply settlers with wage labour. In their privileged position *vis-à-vis* the Xhosa, the Mfengu quickly adapted to western ideas and western modes of production.

Their communal organisations and pastoralism gave way to independent tillage farming for the market. Their close contact with missionaries and traders hastened the commercialisation in their ranks. During the Seventh and Eighth

Frontier Wars the Mfengu remained loyal to the Cape government, and were generously rewarded with land grants.[43]

Through these events an African peasantry developed that no longer formed part of the communal system of land ownership, and was economically independent enough to resist employment as wage labourers. From the 1850s onwards different forms of peasantry developed, not only among the Mfengu but also among the Xhosa. Through this 'peasantisation' the communal organisation of Africans broke down and was replaced by a money economy and production for the market.

The development of a class of small freeholding African farmers was closely linked to the introduction of a qualified franchise system in the Cape in 1853. Two to ten acres of freehold land and house plots in villages enabled the owners to qualify for a vote in the Cape parliament. The scheme was supported by Sir George Grey and the missionaries who thought it would help facilitate the conversion of Africans to Christianity. Over the next 40 years the African peasantry in the Eastern Cape expanded, but never numbered more than 2 000 (see Rich 1996: 62).

During the second half of the 19th century the parallel and interrelated peasantisation and proletarianisation of Africans had the combined effect of *detribalising* Africans and integrating them into a western mode of production and western labour patterns. Colin Bundy distinguishes among three different kinds of peasants at that time: individual peasants who farmed on communally owned land, but produced and sold their own produce; squatter peasants living on land leased from mainly absentee proprietors and who either paid their lease in cash or by farming 'by the halves'; and peasants with individual land tenure who farmed as relatively independent, small-scale, commercial farmers.[44]

The rise of a relatively independent African peasantry in the Cape (and Natal) during the second half of the 19th century was an important and promising development. This also happened – if more slowly – in the Transorangia in the same period (see section 7.4). The peasantisation of Africans meant that a significant number of Africans became landowners and independent farmers, and therefore escaped – for 50 or 60 years – the humiliations and impoverishment caused by proletarianisation and repressive labour practices. Many white farmers, with their almost insatiable demand for cheap and bonded African labour, viewed the rise of an African peasantry with apprehension. Consequently, white landowners were responsible for an ongoing offensive against the peasantisation of Africans. Until 1890 this offensive did not succeed in halting this process, mainly because the coalition between the influential liberal mercantile elite and the missionaries was in favour of peasantisation (see Bundy 1988: ch 3).

After the discovery of gold, and the advent of New Liberalism, peasants' fortunes started to decline. From the early 1990s onwards a combined offensive by white landowners, the mercantile elite, and the gold mining industry resulted in legislation that in due course destroyed the African peasant class and forced them to join a wage-earning proletariat.[45]

Both the traders and the missionaries (ie, the champions of Cape liberalism) had a vested interest in breaking down the communal ownership of land and the distribution of the products of labour through kinship units in accordance with certain customary rules. By penetrating African culture through the buying and selling of goods, the mercantile elite in Cape Town built lucrative trade and speculation relationships with Africans. Peasants were usually exploited by white traders. As their need for cash increased, they had to accept depressed prices for their products.[46] The missionaries, in turn, could never understand the role of polygamy in Xhosa society and tried their best to break it by means of detribalisation and peasantisation (see Mostert 1992: 956–9, 1220–6). In due course, both the traders and the missionaries strongly favoured peasantisation because they regarded this as an effective method of detribalising Africans and drawing them into the sphere of influence of a western economy.[47] Those peasants who qualified to vote for the Cape parliament supplied the mercantile class with a buffer against the demands of the settler farmers – both Afrikaners and English-speakers.

In the 30 years from 1860 to 1990 the process of modernisation and detribalisation was always a double-barrelled and contradictory one. On the one hand, it promoted peasantisation on communal land, squatter farming on land leased from absentee farmers, and small-scale commercial farming by Africans with individual land tenure; on the other, thousands of Africans were proletarianised and forced to enter the labour market as cheap wage labourers. The Cape assembly, enjoying 'responsible government' from 1872 onwards, did its best to meet settler farmers' ever increasing demands for labour by enacting hut taxes, pass laws, and vagrancy laws, thus forcing 'idle squatters' on to the labour market. These laws did not always have the desired results. Although white farmers were agitating very strongly for a general anti-squatter act directed against Africans, such legislation was opposed by the mercantile elite and only enacted in 1892 when gold mining necessitated a new approach to proletarianisation (Bundy 1988: 134–48).[48]

The most common form of peasantry in this period was squatter peasants living on unalienated crown land and on white-owned land as labour tenants, rent tenants, or share-croppers. It is ironic that, during the years of economic depression and despair, white farmers were more prepared to allow Xhosa families to squat on their farms. The rent these so-called 'kaffir farmers' paid to white farmers was vital to the latters' economic survival.

From 1870 onwards the process of peasantisation was strongly promoted by the introduction of an important technological innovation: the ox-drawn plough. Bundy contends that 'the adoption of the ox-drawn plough...was undoubtedly the basic technological bridge from pre-colonial cultivator to peasant [farming, by the Africans]' (1988: 95). According to him the use of the plough shifted the balance from pastoralism to cultivation as the basis of subsistence; it decreased Africans' reliance on pastoralism, stimulated the use of animals for drawing ploughs rather than other purposes, and also made it necessary for Africans to earn a cash income to buy ploughs and oxen. By using the plough, as well as the labour of their extended families, African peasants often shifted from pastoralism to cultivation more successfully than their white counterparts did. An important reason for this was the greater supply of family labour available to African farmers.[49] Consequently, a pattern developed in several maize-producing areas in which white farmers remained *rentier* landlords and became involved in cattle farming and hunting, while African squatter tenants became involved in cultivation.

After the discovery of gold the liberal mercantile class revised its convictions about the congruence of proletarianisation and peasantisation. The increased demand for cheap and bound African labour on the gold mines made it necessary for the mercantile class to prefer proletarianisation to peasantisation. At the same time, the mining companies discovered that tribal chiefs and headmen were a more convenient collaborating class for 'controlled proletarianisation' than the modern class of propertied, Christian, progressive African peasants. Consequently an important ideological shift took place at the end of the 19th century away from assimilation through modernisation and peasantisation to a new policy of segregation, retribalisation, and increased proletarianisation.[50]

6.8 The rise of an African peasantry in Natal during the second half of the 19th century

In 1824 a small number of British traders and hunters settled at Port Natal and received land grants from Shaka and Dingane. In February 1838 Dingane gave land concessions to the Voortrekker leader Piet Retief, immediately before Retief and his commando were murdered. On the strength of these land concessions – and the defeat of the Zulus under Dingane – the Voortrekker republic of Natalia was established in the area south of the Tugela. The British annexed this republic in 1842, and turned it into a separate British colony in 1845.

When 6 000 Voortrekkers occupied Natal (ie, the area south of the Tugela) in the late 1830s, the area was substantially underpopulated as a result of the *mfecane*. After the defeat of Dingane, the African population increased from 10 000 in 1838 to 50 000 in 1843. While land was available in abundance to the Voortrekkers, they experienced problems in recruiting Africans as wage labourers. The Voortrekkers tried to solve their labour problems by 'apprenticing' children supposedly captured during 'legitimate' commando skirmishes with the Zulu and other African tribes. During their four years in Natalia the Voortrekkers depended either on barter or on raiding African produce for their subsistence. Military attacks on African villages enabled the Voortrekkers ('through God's guidance') to 'harvest and eat what others have planted' (quoted in Bundy 1988: 167). After Natalia was annexed by the British, about 4 000 Voortrekkers withdrew from Natal and trekked over the Drakensberg to the Transvaal and Orange Free State (OFS).[51]

In 1849–50 some 5 000 English and Scottish settlers were brought to Natal in terms of a scheme similar to that which had brought British settlers to the Eastern Cape in 1820. The white population increased steadily, and reached 18 000 in 1870. By that stage the African population had increased to more than 250 000.[52] By 1870 some 5 million of the 6 million acres of land owned by whites were in the hands of absentee proprietors or *rentiers*, and occupied by African squatters.[53] A sizeable portion of land – just less than 175 000 acres – was granted to various mission stations. More mission stations were active in Natal than in any other part of South Africa. By 1970, 3 million acres of Natal's total area of 12 million acres remained unalienated crown land.

More than 2 million acres were set aside as African reserves, called 'locations' by Theophilus Shepstone. He was a convinced and skilful paternalist and improvised a method of African control similar to the one that the British would later apply in colonial Africa, called 'indirect rule'. The key was the use of African chiefs (preferably not traditional rulers, but their own apprentices) as subordinate officials, made responsible not to their own people but to white magistrates and, in the last resort, to Shepstone as 'supreme chief' or lieutenant governor of Natal.[54] Shepstone's location system was the first government scheme to implement a grandiose system of territorial segregation.

When, in 1845, Natal became a British colony, the British government stipulated that its laws should be colour-blind. This stipulation was ignored by the mainly English-speaking whites in Natal who, until 1910, practised segregation and implemented blatantly racist policies. Although Africans could own land, very few obtained electoral rights. All Africans were obliged to pay hut taxes, excise duties, and other fees. They therefore needed to earn the cash necessary to pay these expenses.

One of the remarkable characteristics of Natal during the second half of the 19th century is that only small numbers of Africans were prepared to become wage labourers or labour tenants on white farms. This was because there were sufficient alternative means of subsistence for Africans in the locations, on absentee farms, on crown land, and on mission stations. With all these opportunities available, Africans attained a high degree of economic independence through their typical Zulu system of a lineage mode of production (see Slater, in Marks and Atmore 1980: 154–6).

From 1840 until 1893 a struggle continued in Natal between Africans who tried to maintain their economic independence by exploiting different forms of access to land and farming, and white commercial farmers, who tried to reduce the number of options open to Africans for maintaining their economic independence. The absentee farmers were quite content to allow large-scale squatting (or 'Kaffir farming') on their farms, and to extract rent from the squatters. Attractive farming opportunities were also available to African peasants on unalienated crown land, and in Shepstone's locations. Large numbers were also farming on mission land, but were required to obey religious prescriptions. A small number of Africans became landowners, and developed into successful peasant farmers.

Given the power relations in Natal during the second half of the 19th century, a relatively large surplus was extracted from Africans by white landowners and the colonial government. But owing to their modest living standards and satisfactory levels of productivity (especially after the introduction of the ox-drawn plough), African peasant farmers were able to pay taxes and rent without endangering their economic independence.

Throughout this period white commercial farming interests in Natal attempted to use the state apparatus to implement anti-squatting and other measures aimed at overcoming African resistance to proletarianisation. However, the absentee farmers (or *rentier* class) and missions stations strongly opposed this strategy. The commercial farmers were unsuccessful until 1893, when Natal was granted 'responsible government'. It was only when commercial farmers gained control of the Natal parliament that the state finally began to limit African alternatives to labouring for white employers. For most of the second half of the 19th century white commercial farmers complained bitterly about the severe shortage of labour and the 'unjustified' competition they experienced from African peasants (see Slater, in Marks and Atmore 1980: 158–9).

The Eastern Cape and Natal differed in an important way in the second half of the 19th century. In the Eastern Cape the proletarianisation and peas-antisation of Africans were parallel processes, with the result that large numbers of Africans became wage labourers or wage tenants on white farms. In Natal, Africans could access land easily enough to make it possible for almost all Africans to become peasant farmers, either on their own land, in locations, on crown land, at mission stations, or on the farms of absentee landlords.[55]

The seriousness of the labour problem experienced by commercial farmers in Natal is most clearly illustrated by the decision to import indentured Indian labourers to work on the sugar plantations from 1860 onwards;[56] African migrant labourers were also brought in from Mozambique (see Slater, in Marks and Atmore 1980: 168–9; Richardson, in Beinert *et al* 1986).

From 1870 until 1893 the African peasantry in Natal showed great progress, as opportunities to sell their produce improved considerably. Peasant production intensified, characterised by diversification and sensitivity to market opportunities. During this period white commercial farmers found it increasingly difficult – if not impossible – to compete with African agriculturists.

The discovery of gold in 1886 and the granting of 'responsible government' to Natal in 1893 changed the labour situation fundamentally. The absentee landlords started to shift their investments to the Witwatersrand in order to exploit the new profitable opportunities there. Under the new constitution the commercial farmers in Natal gained decisive influence in the colonial government. Owing to these two developments, the economic independence of African peasants was sharply attacked in the period 1893 to 1910. Although the existence of locations and the retention of access to other forms of land continued to benefit some of Natal's peasants, large numbers of them became proletarianised during this period, but not to the same extent as in the Eastern Cape (see Bundy 1988: 183–6).

Endnotes

1 From now on we can refer to the *Trekboere* as Afrikaners, so as not to confuse them with the British settlers who arrived from 1820 onwards.

2 Khoisan who wished to complain about low wages or bad treatment had to travel to the nearest magistrate and run the risk of being arrested for travelling without a pass.

Khoisan outside the borders could not enter the colony without running the risk of being arrested as vagrants (Le Cordeur, in Cameron 1986: 81–4).

3 In 1917 Lord Charles Somerset saw fit to prepare 'deeds of apprenticeship' for '*Bosjesnien*' children to protect them from 'savage parents', who might 'sell' them for a 'paltry bribe', as well as from persons bent on 'procuring children by plunder, depredation or fraud' (quoted in Malherbe 1991: 16).

4 In the almost 20 years from 1809 until 1828 – when Proclamation 50 was issued – most Khoisan had become the victims of a legal system of serfdom (or virtual slavery) that was even worse in many respects than the *inboekstelsel* of the 18th century. There is validity in the claim that 'by the 1810s Khoisan workers on settler farms were as firmly enchained as their slave counterparts' (Worden and Crais 1994: 18). The 1820 census in the Cape colony showed that almost 27 000 Khoisan were registered as contract workers. This figure implies that a very high percentage of Khoisan were trapped in a kind of legal subservience. The rest of the unfree labour force consisted of 32 000 slaves (see Elphick and Malherbe 1989: 35–43; Newton-King, in Marks and Atmore 1980: ch 7).

5 The intrusion of the British state into the private domain of Afrikaner patriarchs caused an ideological confusion among Afrikaners that lasted for the best part of the 19th century. When Proclamation 50 of 1828 again changed the master–servant relationship, and when slavery was abolished in 1838, Afrikaners again experienced these measures as an intolerable intrusion of the 'public' British state into their 'private' patriarchal domain.

6 When the abolition of serfdom and slavery did not bring about the expected moral reawakening among former serfs and slaves, humanitarian idealism evaporated and was replaced by a drive for new disciplinary measures directed at the former serfs and slaves to attain the economic results desired by the utilitarian liberals (see Keegan 1996: 75–82; see also section 6.5).

7 Philip found a strong ally for his humanitarian cause in his son-in-law, John Fairbairn, editor of the *Commercial Advertiser*. Thomas Pringle, Philip, Fairbairn, and Andries Stockenström put forward a strong humanitarian case for an entrenched and unchallengeable law that would give 'equal civil rights' to all 'persons of colour', ie, to the Khoikhoi and slaves. Their greatest accomplishment was the formal termination of Khoisan serfdom by persuading the then acting governor, Richard Bourke, to pass Ordinance 50 in 1828 (Mostert 1992: 547–89).

8 This settlement was established in 1829 on land from which the Xhosa had been expelled. It only lasted until 1851, when it was abolished as part of a new policy to proletarianise coloured people – ie, former slaves and serfs (see Keegan 1996: 116–28).

9 The reasons for this dramatic *volte-face* and its far-reaching implications for labour patterns in South Africa will be discussed in sections 6.5 and 6.6.

10 The British parliament decided to abolish slavery in 1833. Slavery at the Cape was supposed to be abolished on 1 December 1834, but a four-year transitional period was allowed until 1 December 1838.

11 The British government abolished the slave trade in 1807, but the abolition only took effect in the Cape in 1808.

12 Fairbairn was only concerned with the materialistic and pragmatic interests of the

entrepreneurial classes at the Cape. His main defence of the anti-slavery argument was purely economic. He believed that abolition would promote economic growth through a better motivation of labour and a better allocation of both labour and capital. His main concerns were the property rights of slave-owners, and how to abolish slavery without disrupting the labour situation at the Cape. Consequently, he strongly argued in favour of adequately compensating slave-owners, and the need to inculcate habits of 'diligence' and industriousness into slaves before abolition. Compensation for slave-owners was important to the mercantile class in Cape Town, because many of the slave-owners were heavily indebted to them (Meltzer, in Worden and Crais 1994: ch 7).

13 In September 1835 it was announced that the British government had awarded £1,2 million in compensation for the 38 000 slaves. The money was to be paid in 3,5 per cent government stock, and slave-owners had to collect their money in London. This caused great discontent among slave-owners because it made them dependent on merchants with British connections to collect their money. The mainly Afrikaner slave-owners were also not satisfied with the level of compensation. The main beneficiaries of compensation were both Afrikaans- and English-speaking merchants in Cape Town.

14 According to Depelchin, slavery was abolished by an 'abolitionist' movement, rather than an 'emancipationist' one. In the case of the latter, the slaves themselves would have been compensated. The same happened in the United States when slavery was abolished in 1863. Consequently, the abolition of slavery in South Africa – and the United States – did not set slaves free, but trapped them in new forms of labour servility and poverty (Depelchin 1996: 86–90).

15 Noël Mostert describes the frontier wars between the British and the Xhosa as the product of 'two of the greatest human odysseys and endeavours in history' (Mostert 1992: xvii–xviii).

16 Lord Charles Somerset's attempts to suppress freedom of the press brought him into sharp conflict with Thomas Pringle and John Fairbairn. Several of the victims of the governor's high-handedness gathered in London in 1825 and played an important role in Somerset's recall as governor (see Le Cordeur, in Cameron 1986: 85–6; Mostert 1992: ch 12).

17 The export of wool increased from 9 000 kilograms in 1822 to 90 000 kilograms in 1832, 5,5 million kilograms in 1855, and 8 million kilograms in 1860. By 1840 wool had become the most important colonial export. In 1840–4 annual average wool exports were valued at £73 000, and in 1855–9 at £984 000 (Keegan 1996: 158).

18 There was also something hypocritical about Ordinances 49 and 50. While Ordinance 50 deprived mainly Afrikaner farmers in the Eastern Cape of their subservient Khoisan labour, Ordinance 49 created the opportunity for mainly British settlers to tap the new source of unfree African labour (Keegan 1996: 104–6).

19 According to Bundy, the possession of cattle – which outnumbered the human population by at least two to one – affected the tribal economy, social customs, and legal system. The security of the Nguni family as an economic unit was bound up with milk-based products which were more easily stored than agricultural products (1988: 17). Life literally revolved around their cattle, since the huts of an extended family were grouped in a semi-circle around the cattle kraal. Cattle intricately and

indissolubly bound the material and sacred parts of their lives. Cattle were the medium of sacrifice to the ancestral spirits, linking the living with the dead. Cattle also represented the future, because they sealed marriage bonds through the *lobola* system (see Mostert 1992: ch 6).

20 In contrast with the San and Khoikhoi, the Xhosa – and other African tribes – were organised into centralised chieftains, ranging from a few thousand people to units as large as 40 000. They practised mixed farming. Besides owning sheep and cattle, hunting the abundant game, and gathering indigenous plants, farmers cultivated sorghum and made iron tools. They were generally healthy, and lived on well-balanced diets. African societies were not entirely egalitarian, but practised a redistributive economy (see Thompson 1990: 15–23).

21 If the British – at the zenith of their military power – had not arrived at the Cape, the Xhosa would probably have remained unconquered to this day. At the end of the 18th century close co-operation had developed among small groups of *Trekboere* who had allied themselves with some of the Xhosa tribes in clashes with other tribes. A process of racial integration between whites and Xhosas – as between white and Khoikhoi – was well under way in the Eastern Cape at the end of the 18th century. As Noël Mostert puts its: 'Without overseas intrusion upon them, the [Boers and the Xhosas] probably would have resolved their own contest along lines that already were discernible [at the end of the 18th century] . . . Xhosa society was so familiar [to the Boers], so close to their own way of life, that integration into it would have come naturally, their posterity would have been unaware of racial divide' (1992: 390).

22 See Crais 1992: ch 7; Keegan 1996: ch 9; Worden and Crais 1994: introduction; Mostert 1992: ch 21. See also section 6.6 for a detailed exposition of this new hegemonic order.

23 During the first half of 1838 a large group of Voortrekkers was murdered by Dingaan's Zulu impis in Natal. Afrikaners' feelings of bitterness over the abolition of slavery and the compensation paid for freed slaves reached a peak in 1838.

24 The masters and servants laws of 1841 and 1856 were colour-blind, and 'fair' in that they spelled out the obligations of both masters and servants. But since all masters were white, and almost all servants black or brown, 'an apparently race-free law consolidated rather than weakened race domination' (Bundy 1975: 38).

25 Trapido ascribes the large-scale social dislocation and severe poverty that have resulted from unfree labour in South Africa to four successive and overlapping phases of labour repression. Each phase was implemented by another modernising group in the white community with a vested interest in labour repression as well as the (political) power to implement it. The second phase of labour repression was implemented after the discovery of diamonds and gold. The main beneficiaries of this phase were British/English magnates and stockholders. The Glen Grey Act of 1894 and the Land Act of 1913 played important roles in intensifying the repression and exploitation associated with this phase. This second phase of labour repression was perpetuated until the mid-1970s, made possible by the third (from the 1930s) and the fourth (1948–74) phases of labour repression that created the legal shield for the mining industry to persist with labour repression and exploitation (Trapido 1971: 310–19). See sections 8.5 and 8.6 for a description of the second and third phases of black labour repression, and section 9.5 for a description of the fourth phase.

26 Harry Smith was D'Urban's military commander during the Sixth Frontier War, and was closely involved in proclaiming the Province of Queen Adelaide.

27 Despite his dramatic threats and use of force, Harry Smith failed dismally to impose order on the Xhosa. His actions were the direct cause of the Eighth Frontier War (see Mostert 1992: ch 21).

28 The Khoisan revolt of 1851 led to hysteria and fear throughout the colony, and convinced the legislative council to withdraw its Squatter Ordinance (see Kirk, in Marks and Atmore 1980: ch 9).

29 During the second half of the 19th century the majority of coloureds remained proletarianised and unfree labour, in accordance with the prescriptions of several masters and servants laws. But in due course an important bifurcation occurred in the coloured labour force; increasing numbers moved to the urban centres, where they became a free and skilled labour force.

30 In the Kat River Settlement the land of all those considered to be disloyal during the war was confiscated and the settlement was opened up to white land-grabbing. Plots fetching less than £20 before 1851 were changing hands for £1 000 and more. In the process the Kat River Settlement was decimated, and many of its inhabitants became proletarianised and dispersed through the colony (see Keegan 1996: 239).

31 The long struggle between white employers and coloureds in the Eastern Cape not only demonstrated the farmers' determination to nullify the effect of Ordinance 50 of 1828 and the abolition of slavery, but also the preparedness of the colonial state to implement measures to reinforce and extend the newly designed methods of racial oppression (see Crais 1992: 175–88; Crais, in Worden and Crais 1994: ch 10; Ross 1993: 102–10).

32 A term coined by Warden and Crais, who describe the middle decades of the 19th century as 'enormously Janus-faced', and personified by Sir George Grey. On the one hand he wanted to break down the tribal customs and structure of the Xhosa down to force them into useful labour. On the other, he built schools and hospitals for the Xhosa (see Warden and Crais, 1994: 23; Legassick 1993).

33 In accordance with his policy of 'assimilation', Grey urged that the Xhosa should be 'raised' to 'Christianity and civilisation, by the establishment among them and beyond our boundary, of missions connected with industrial schools, by employing them on public works' (quoted by Benyon, in Cameron 1986: 162).

34 Although his governorship was quite benevolent and significant in the long run, his seemingly philanthropical works were a deliberate attempt at the 'colonisation of the Xhosa mind' and the creation of a 'new identity' for the detribalised Xhosa – an identity that could be utilised by the European settlers. In Grey's philosophical orientation, utilitarianism had completely replaced evangelical humanitarianism (see Legassick 1993: 329–68; Crais 1992: 200–3). Benyon makes the interesting point that, 'while Grey's so-called "assimilationist" policy towards the Xhosa has drawn praise in the past, there are now historians who stress the more negative aspects of the "underdevelopment" of the Xhosa through the uncompetitive terms upon which the governor admitted them to a technological advanced society' (Benyon, in Cameron 1986: 163–4).

35 The English- and Afrikaans-speaking white elite co-operated in the new representative parliament to effect the new labour pattern. It is ironic that the

Voortrekkers left the Cape in 1836 because of the abolition of serfdom and slavery. If those who left had remained in the Cape for 20 years, they would have had access to labour that was as bonded as before 1828, and perhaps even more so.

36 The cattle-killing tragedy of 1857 gave him the opportunity to accomplish his purpose: to break traditional Xhosa society (see Crais 1992: 204–6; Mostert 1992: 1178).

37 For western people it remained a mystery why the Xhosa killed their sacred cattle to demonstrate their wrath against the whites. Benyon claims that recent studies among anthropologists in the western Pacific 'show that this phenomenon of "millenarianism", or a total belief in a supernatural route to the attainment of a better world in the future, is usually associated with the rapid disintegration of traditional society under severe pressure' (Benyon, in Cameron 1986: 164–5).

38 The Mfengu developed quickly into successful peasant farmers (Keegan 1996: 288–90; Benyon, in Cameron 1986: 162–6). See also section 6.7.

39 This system enabled the upper classes in Britain (about 25 per cent of the population) to empower themselves at the cost of the working class (about 75 per cent of the population). One can draw a remarkable parallel between the system of class capitalism in Britain in the 19th century and the system of racial capitalism in South Africa from 1840 until 1990. The Land Act (1913) played a similar role in South Africa as the repeal of the Poor Laws in Britain in 1834.

40 Crais, quoted by Legassick (1993: 330). According to Worden and Crais, 'the British colonial state and the liberal ideology that informed it was enormously Janus-faced. The ending of slavery was about human freedom, *but it was also about power and control*. The very era that ended bonded labour and, in 1853, established a non-racial franchise, also saw *the emergence of new forms of unfree labour and, perhaps more tragically, the emergence of modern racist ideologies in South Africa* ... The era that witnessed the ending of slavery in the Cape constitutes *a kind of connective historical tissue* uniting the beginnings of colonialism with the historical developments of the industrial era [after the discovery of gold]' (Worden and Crais 1994: 6, 23; author's emphasis).

41 Crais puts it as follows: 'The colonial state ... played a crucial role in the making of a colonial order in the Eastern Cape, as it did in much of settler Africa ... Capitalism ... [in South Africa] could have taken a black peasant road. But the [colonial] state supported white farmers and economic development followed ... the [black] "labour repressive" road in which massive state coercion went hand in hand with capitalist development' (1992: 173).

42 Keegan puts it as follows: 'The origins of the white supremacist state of the 20th century ... did not lie particularly in the attitudes spawned on isolated, backward frontiers, where Boers struggled for survival against harsh conditions and hostile indigenes. British influence tended to harden the hierarchies of race rather than dissolve them, and to strengthen the hegemony of white colonists rather than weaken it. *The permanent conquest of African societies was usually dependent on the exercise of [British] imperial power*' (1996: 292–3; my emphasis).

43 As part of Sir George Grey's policy of undermining African customs, he started to break up their communal ownership of land. After the Eighth Frontier War, Grey gave individual plots to the Mfengu in return for an annual payment. A proclamation

of 1858 permitted Africans (mainly Mfengu) to buy crown land at £1 an acre (Keegan 1996: 145–7; Bundy 1988: 44–60).

44 The three different kinds of peasants constituted not only an economic division, but also a social and cultural one. The first of the three categories was culturally 'more traditional', and the third 'less traditional' and more receptive to western culture (see Bundy 1988: 7–13).

45 The offensive against the African peasantry reached its high point when the Land Act of 1913 was passed in order to destroy the peasantry in the Transorangia and Natal. The destruction of the African peasantry was undoubtedly one of the saddest developments in South Africa's history, because African peasants were at the time considerably more successful at producing maize than their white counterparts (see sections 8.5 and 8.6).

46 Trapido describes the close co-operation between the mercantile elite and the missionaries in promoting peasantisation as follows: 'It is difficult to separate the expansion of the missionary frontier from that of the European merchants and trader, and the Christianity of free trade hastened the process of creating the market-orientated peasants which had begun with earlier settler conquests and economic expansion' (in Marks and Atmore 1980: 249).

47 The onslaught against Xhosa tribalism reached a high point after the cattle-killing episode of 1857, when Sir George Grey rounded up most of the chiefs and incarcerated them on Robben Island. The general policy of the *detribalisation* of the Africans was also the rationale behind the drive to create opportunities for the Mfengu – and later also for the Xhosa – to squat on white and missionary farms and to become landowners. While the process of peasantisation was limited to the Mfengu east of the Great Fish River until 1860, it expanded to the Ciskeian Xhosa during the 1860s and 1870s, and to the Transkeian Xhosa in the 1880s. The period from 1860 until the 1890s was not as prosperous for white farmers as the previous 30 years had been. Serious droughts were experienced in the 1860s, and from 1873 to 1896 Britain experienced its 'great depression' – a recession that adversely affected the economies of the advanced capitalist countries, but especially that of Britain. The decline in Britain severely affected the Cape (see Bundy 1988: 110–26).

48 One reason for the mercantile elite opposing a general squatting law until 1892 was the experience of 1850–1, when the tabling of a squatter ordinance led to the Khoisan Rebellion of 1851.

49 Extended families (even partially detribalised ones) were organised in such a way that their heads could command the involvement of almost all members in different aspects of cultivation. As soon as possibilities for selling part of their crops emerged, African peasants – given their strict control over the living standards of their extended families – could accumulate capital to buy more oxen and ploughs more easily than their white counterparts could (see Bundy 1988: 95–101).

50 As we will indicate in section 8.4, the ideological conviction of the New Imperialism about the justification of segregation, retribalisation, and increased proletarianisation of Africans became the basis for the social and economic policies of racial capitalism in South Africa during the first half of the 20th century (see Bundy 1988: 134–140; Keegan 1996: 290–3).

51 An important reason for this withdrawal was that the Voortrekkers were experiencing

the same delays over the registration of titles of the farms allocated to them as had been the case in the Eastern Cape. And, as had also been the case in the Eastern Cape, land speculators – mainly mercantile and financial groups in Cape Town and London – experienced no problems in obtaining titles for several farms (see Davenport 1991: 100).

52 The sharp increase in the African population was a result of faction wars between the supporters of the sons of Mpande (Dingane's successor), Cethwayo, and Mbuyazi. When Mbuyazi was defeated in 1856, thousands of his supporters fled across the Tugela into Natal.

53 A large portion of Natal property was concentrated in the hands of a relatively small group of absentee landlords. The Natal Land and Colonisation Company owned nearly a million acres. Until 1893 the small and well-organised absentee landlords were the most influential of several groups of whites who laid claim to controlling land and politics in Natal (see Bundy 1988: 168).

54 Shepstone also imposed a dual legal system: customary African law prevailed among Africans, and Roman Dutch law (taken over from the Cape) among whites. He persuaded large numbers of Africans to move and live in the designated locations. In 1851 two thirds of Africans lived outside the locations. In 1882 almost 60 per cent lived in the locations and on mission stations (see Bundy 1988: 170).

55 In contrast to the situation in the Transvaal and Orange Free State, share-cropping was not as prevalent in Natal. As was the case in the Eastern Cape, the introduction of the plough in the late 1860s led to a sharp increase in food production (see Bundy 1988: 170–4).

56 Indians were brought in on five-year contracts at agreed minimum wages. At the end of their contracts they were given the option of serving for another five years, obtaining their freedom, or returning to India. Since the law provided that at least 25 women should accompany every 100 men transported to Natal, it was inevitable that a permanent Indian population would emerge. The Natal legislature took special steps in 1872 to put right certain alleged abuses, including the flogging of workers, and excessive pay deductions for absenteeism. Provision was also made for allocating land to Indians who had completed their contracts. Indian immigration accelerated after 1872, and the population rose from 10 000 in 1875 to about 100 000 by the end of the century. The system continued until 1911, and resulted in the creation of a sizeable Indian population – one that would eventually outnumber the white population in Natal (Davenport 1991: 105–6).

Chapter 7

The systemic period of the two Boer republics (1850–1900)

7.1 The Great Trek and its causes

Between 1834 and 1840 about 15 000 Afrikaner frontier farmers left the Eastern Cape in a series of trek parties and established their own states north of the Orange River. This emigration of a large part of the Afrikaner population of the Cape became known as the Great Trek. It was an act of resistance against British colonialism and, in particular, against new British definitions of the way in which land and labour were to be 'owned' and used.

The Great Trek can be regarded as a deliberate attempt by the Voortrekkers to recreate in their new states the labour patterns, property relations, and patriarchal feudal order that prevailed at the Cape before the arrival of the British. They succeeded to a remarkable degree. The Voortrekkers did not experience serious problems in depriving the different African tribes in the Transorangia of large parts of their land, but found it difficult to turn Africans into a docile and subservient labour force. A protracted struggle – extending from 1850 to well into the 20th century – took place in the Transorangia during which Afrikaner farmers tried by various means to mould Africans into a useful and manageable labour force. Africans vehemently resisted these attempts.

The main reasons why Afrikaners found it so difficult to subjugate Africans in the Transorangia were the political and economic weakness of the Boer republics, and the relative success of African tenant farmers in producing foodstuffs for the emerging markets, especially after the discovery of gold. Africans in the northern provinces were only reduced to a wage-earning proletariat over a period of 30 years after the establishment of the Union of South Africa in 1910, when the new state, in collaboration with white farmers and the emerging corporate sector, used its considerable legal and administrative power to break African resistance.

The protracted struggle between Afrikaners and Africans – especially in the northern provinces – is an important element of South Africa's labour history.

During the process of modernisation initiated by the mineral revolution and the commercialisation of agriculture, many Africans as well as Afrikaners in the Boer republics became proletarianised. While the struggle between Afrikaners and Africans remained largely indecisive during the second half of the 19th century, during the first 40 years of the 20th century it took the form of a contest in the labour arena between an Afrikaner and an African proletariat.[1]

The Great Trek is a major theme in Afrikaner historiography. It is often interpreted as a quest for freedom from British domination, and is thus projected as an important event in the rise of Afrikaner nationalism. Economic and labour considerations probably played a more important role than ideological and political ones, but it would be wrong to claim that the latter did not play any role at all.[2] The anglicisation of administration and the courts by the colonial authority in the 1820s was symbolic of a larger process of disempowerment. While, in the 1820s, a remarkable alliance developed between Afrikaner and British elite groups in frontier districts – especially in respect of the Xhosa – this alliance broke down during the 1830s. Consequently the Great Trek represented a kind of rebellion not only against the British colonial authority but also against the British settlers.

During the 18th century the *Trekboere* became accustomed to a way of life in which they accumulated wealth through barter and trade with indigenous people. From trading they turned to raiding, particularly when indigenous people were not prepared to co-operate. After the arrival of the British, the opportunities for Afrikaners to maintain their hunter–trader–raider–pastoralist way of life was endangered in many ways. When the mercantile class in Cape Town started establishing trading centres, Afrikaners were deprived of an important source of income. We can regard the Great Trek as a desperate attempt by Afrikaners to perpetuate their traditional mode of existence in more distant venues. Although they succeeded in 'escaping' the British sphere of influence for a considerable period, they were closely followed by British financiers, traders, and land speculators.[3]

The main causes of the Great Trek were undoubtedly economic. The liberal reforms brought about by British colonialism, influenced by liberal humanitarianism, deprived Afrikaners of their easy access to labour and land.[4] Another important reason for the Great Trek was Cradock's abolition of the loan farm system in 1813. Farmers now had to apply for new title deeds, and the officials in Cape Town gave preference to requests for title deeds from British settlers. Often, Afrikaner farmers who had submitted land claims, had had the land surveyed, and had worked it for years were forced to make way for English-speaking claimants, some of whom owned far more land than they could use.[5]

The frontier conflicts with the Xhosa, and particularly the Sixth Frontier War (1834–5), inflicted heavy losses on frontier farmers. Farmers were required to use their own horses and equipment during punitive expeditions. They expected the colonial government to compensate them for losses during these expeditions, but none was forthcoming (Du Bruyn, in Cameron 1986: 129). To aggravate matters after the war, the British settlers and especially the *Grahams Town Journal* played a rather dubious, perhaps even treacherous, role in encouraging Afrikaners to trek.[6] The economic position of many Afrikaner farmers in the Eastern districts deteriorated dramatically during the 1830s.[7]

It is often asked whether the Voortrekkers subscribed to a particular racial ideology when they set out on the Great Trek. The fact that they trekked into an unknown interior populated with Africans with whom they were prepared to make treaties is sometimes used to argue that they were not necessarily racist. In section 5.6 we argue that the racial attitudes of the *Trekboere* had probably not crystallised into a conscious racial ideology by the end of the 18th century; however, in section 6.6 we argue that such an ideology did develop among British settlers during the two or three decades after the Sixth Frontier War. An important reason for the Great Trek was the great animosity that had developed between Afrikaners and the humanitarian evangelists.[8] The former regarded the way in which the evangelists challenged their ingrained racial assumptions and practices as unjustified, and lacking in sensitivity to their predicament. The Afrikaners who trekked were those who had been most negatively affected by the abolition of serfdom and slavery, as well as those who had experienced great losses during the Sixth Frontier War. There can therefore be no doubt that the bitterness and racial hatred that reached a high point among British settlers after the Sixth Frontier War were also prevalent in Afrikaner circles in the Eastern Cape.[9]

The *mfecane* or *difagane* (meaning 'smash in a total war', or 'hammering') also played an important role in the Great Trek, both directly and indirectly. Both the *mfecane* and the Great Trek caused large-scale movements of people in the 1820s and 1830s that transformed the eastern and northern parts of the later South Africa. These transformations set the scene for the power struggle between Afrikaners and Africans in the Transorangia in the second half of the 19th century. The *mfecane* erupted high up on the east coast at exactly the same time when the British settlers arrived in the Eastern Cape. This involved the Zulus under Dingiswayo and Shaka consolidating their empire by unleashing a genocidal attack on African tribes (mainly South Sothos) west of the Drakensberg. As in the case of other group conflicts, these wars were also triggered by economic considerations.[10]

It is often said that the *mfecane* created a vacuum west of the Drakensberg and in southern Natal that made it much easier for the Voortrekkers to occupy those areas. It is perhaps more accurate to claim that it seriously disrupted many African tribes, and that many were still busy re-establishing themselves when the Voortrekkers arrived in the Transorangia. This made it easy for the Voortrekkers to co-opt some of the disrupted tribes as labour tenants.[11]

7.2 The establishment by Afrikaners of semi-independent and vulnerable power constellations in the Transorangia

The Voortrekkers were not a single, well-integrated group. On the contrary, they consisted of several factions with a great variety of objectives. Most Voortrekkers were interested in establishing Boer republics in the north, but their attempts at state formation were disrupted by conflicts between the accumulating elite groups, the intervention of the British, and the resistance of African tribes.[12] At the Sand River Convention of 1852, Britain recognised the independence of a Voortrekker republic north of the Vaal River, but the different Voortrekker factions only succeeded in establishing a central state in 1860. This state – the Zuid-Afrikaansche Republiek (ZAR) – remained vulnerable due to internal strife as well as a lack of economic and public financial viability.

A smaller, more radical, group of Voortrekkers moved northwards with the intention of perpetuating the anti-statist tradition that had developed at the end of the 18th century in frontier districts of the Cape. The conflict between Boer and Brit over labour and land issues strengthened this tradition in some Afrikaner circles.[13] Because members of this group were neither interested in state formation nor in acquiring forced African labour, they caused a serious conflict among Voortrekkers. They were not prepared to conduct military campaigns against Africans, and continuously resisted the accumulative drive of Afrikaner 'notables' (larger and more prosperous landowners), who needed the protection and patronage of stable political institutions. The radical group also supplied African tribes with guns, much to the dismay of the 'notables'. Their recalcitrant attitude weakened the Voortrekker republics considerably (see section 7.4).[14]

One of the more remarkable accomplishments of the Voortrekkers was the relative ease with which they deprived Africans of land. As noted earlier, the *mfecane* had disrupted many tribes, and this enabled the Voortrekkers to occupy land before these tribes could reassert themselves. The Voortrekkers tried to negotiate treaties with some of the tribes, and offered to protect them against the stronger African kingdoms. The Voortrekkers encountered two powerful African kingdoms: the Ndebele kingdom in the Transvaal, and the Zulu kingdom in Natal. Well-organised and heavily armed Voortrekker commandos succeeded in driving the Ndebele into today's Zimbabwe, and in defeating the Zulus – in both cases before 1840. After the Ndebele had been expelled from their Transvaal empire (ie, the area between the Vaal and Limpopo rivers and between the Kalahari desert and the Drakensberg), the Voortrekkers claimed to have liberated all African tribes from Ndebele oppression. Consequently, they regarded those 'liberated' tribes as their vassals, who were now obliged to pay tribute to them.

Not all the African tribes living in the Transvaal acknowledged the Voortrekkers' claims. The Venda had never been effectively ruled by the Ndebele, while the Pedi claimed that they had been ruled only temporarily. Their capacity to resist the Voortrekkers' demands was strengthened by the arms and ammunition given to them by British traders and missionaries. The Pedi, under their king Shoshangane, provided the strongest challenge to Voortrekker land claims; they established a powerful and well-armed kingdom that ruled over much of north eastern Transvaal.[15]

The Voortrekkers in the OFS did not attempt to control the Griqua and African tribes in the area. In 1848 Sir Harry Smith annexed this territory, calling it the British Orange River Sovereignty, but in 1854 it was given back to the Voortrekkers at the Bloemfontein Convention. At that stage the British were convinced that their interests in the area had been secured, and that the new Boer government would be a trustworthy satellite state, enhancing the emerging capitalist interests of the British in the area. After independence the OFS government treated the Barolong tribe in a friendly way and received its assistance in its wars with the Basothos of Moshweshe. After several wars between the OFS and the Basothos, Britain resumed responsibility for (present-day) Lesotho in 1868.[16]

The relatively peaceful conditions prevailing in the ZAR after the flight of the Ndebele allowed its African population to increase rapidly.[17] But despite the small size of its white population *vis-à-vis* its African population, whites set aside only 1 million morgen for African occupation, and claimed 70 million morgen for themselves. The ZAR's coercive capacity, however, was so poor that many Africans continued to occupy, till, and graze white-owned land until the end of the first decade of the 20th century (Bundy 1988: 198–9).

For most of the second half of the 19th century the existence of the ZAR was threatened by conflicts between accumulating elite groups, and by the financial weaknesses of the new state. The hierarchy of *heemraden, landdrosten, veldcornetten,* and the commando system were reinstated in the Afrikaner republics. As in the Cape in the 18th century, these institutions played an important role in accumulation and social stratification in the new Afrikaner societies. It was mainly the *veldcornetten* – the pivotal officials of the burgher state – who were in powerful positions as far as the apportionment of land and African labour were concerned, and were therefore in strategic positions to enrich themselves and their close friends.[18]

The ZAR was incapable of collecting the revenue needed for its civil administration and military expeditions, and its poorly developed financial system worsened matters considerably. Because of a lack of funds, the salaries of administrators were often paid in land.[19] Another method of acquiring state revenue was to sell land to companies based outside the ZAR.[20]

The ZAR's financial position improved dramatically after the discovery of gold, and with it opportunities for corruption and patronage among the Afrikaner elite.[21] Owing to the poor administrative and financial position of the ZAR – and to a lesser extent the OFS – the state in both republics did not have the coercive power to intervene effectively in the relationship between white landowners and black tenants. As was the case in the Cape in the 18th century, labour relations became a private matter centred on the patriarchal household of the burghers.

7.3 Slave raiding and the indenturing of Africans in the Transorangia until the end of the 19th century

Slave raiding and turning Khoisan into indentured labour were common practices on the *Trekboer* frontier at the end of the 18th century (see section 5.4). During the last two decades of the 18th century, groups of *Bastaard-Hottentots*, escaped slaves, and convicted criminals – some of them European – migrated across the Orange River and settled on land occupied by Khoisan and Batswana. In the area north of the Orange River an intimate racial mix took place between the Khoikhoi, *Oorlams* (or 'tame') Khoikhoi, San, Batswana, and Boers. Out of this miscegenation a new population group emerged, christened by the missionaries as the Griqua. The Griqua groups were familiar with Dutch culture and economic activity; they forcibly dominated their African neighbours, and enslaved large numbers of African children and women as *inboekelinge*.[22]

One of the main purposes of the Great Trek was to perpetuate the labour patterns to which Afrikaners had become accustomed during the 18th and early 19th centuries. One way of doing this was to take large numbers of loyal black servants with them on the Trek. The Great Trek involved about an equal number of whites and blacks (ie, former serfs and slaves).[23] As soon as the

Voortrekkers had moved beyond British authority, they started slave raiding for African children.[24]

In 1840 the Natal Volksraad provided for 'native apprenticeship', and in 1851 the Transvaal Volksraad (in session in Lydenburg) passed the Apprentice Law. These laws also applied in the OFS. The employment of captured children was not legal unless the apprentices had been registered by a *veldcornet* or *landdrost*. The children were compelled to remain in the service of their masters until the age of 25, and the latter had to provide them with food, shelter, and clothing. They were also responsible for training the children in some useful occupation. But there was no method for establishing whether this ever happened. This was simply a perpetuation of the 'apprenticeship' system created by Cradock in 1812 and by the Cape government when slavery was abolished in 1834.[25]

Under its Apprentice Law, Transvaal burghers could indenture (*inboek*) 'any child, orphan, or orphans [who] were given as gifts or obtained in other legal or voluntary manner from Africans'. The attempt of the Voortrekkers to justify this practice with the humanitarian argument that the children were orphans was not convincing.[26] The Sand River Convention of 1852 stipulated that burghers in the Transvaal should not engage in slave raiding or slavery, and that firearms and ammunition should not be sold to Africans. Shortly after the convention the London Missionary Society alleged that the Voortrekkers were doing both. The society was promptly expelled from the Transvaal, and none of its members was allowed to settle in the area under Afrikaner control (see Thompson 1978b: 437–9).

The socio-political, economic, and legal framework in the two Boer republics in the second half of the 19th century differed radically from that in the Cape. While the Voortrekkers succeeded in recreating the feudal and patriarchal order of the 18th century, the British colonial authorities in the Cape succeeded – by working closely with both English and Afrikaans-speaking elites – in establishing a kind of bourgeois democracy, and a capitalist system in the agricultural sector.

While the labour system in the Cape was based on the proletarianisation of coloureds and Africans, and on contractual wage labour under masters and servants laws, the two Boer republics were not strong or progressive enough to bring about a similar proletarianisation of Africans in the Transorangia. The financial systems of the two Boer republics were also too undeveloped to enable the burghers to pay wages to contract labourers. Although the Voortrekkers deprived Africans of part of their land, and forced them to pay tribute to them, it was still possible for Africans to maintain their traditional independence. The ZAR government enacted several anti-squatter and masters and servants laws, but as long as Africans were not forcibly proletarianised they were also not prepared to become wage-earning labourers on a permanent basis. The inevitability of slave raiding and indentureship (*inboekelingskap*) in the two Boer republics in the second half of the 19th century must be understood (although not justified) against the background of the feudal and patriarchal order of the two Boer republics. For many burghers, *inboekelinge* were the only labourers they could effectively control.

The Boer republics saw the accusations by missionaries and other humanitarian groups in the Cape and in Britain that the Voortrekkers were involved in slave raiding and trading as a direct threat to their independence. Consequently, they enacted several anti-slavery laws. In 1866 the ZAR passed a new law which required people with destitute children to live up to their guardianship role, while the government would play the role of an upper guardian. But, despite the new law, allegations of the maltreatment of children continued unabated, and continued to embarrass the ZAR government.[27]

Slave raiding and the capturing of children in the eastern and northern Transvaal were linked to developments in Mozambique. From the end of the 1820s the Portugese ran a very profitable slave trade from Delagoa Bay for the Brazilian and American markets. It is sometimes said that this triggered the *mfecane* in Natal. There is, however, no evidence that Shaka took part in slave raiding. The increased export of slaves through Delagoa Bay only began at the end of the 1820s – after Shaka's death.[28] During the 1830s and 1840s it was mainly members of the radical Voortrekker group (such as the sons of Coenraad Buys) and the Griquas who participated in illegal slave raiding in the eastern and northern Transvaal.

In the period following the Sand River Convention of 1852, Voortrekkers dramatically stepped up their raids on African communities in order to capture children who could be 'apprenticed' in a presumably legal way. Although the convention prohibited slave raiding and trading, it was not taken seriously by the widely dispersed Voortrekkers. It was not only the poorer Voortrekkers who were involved in slave raiding. The 'notables' – and even the presidents of the two republics – were also actively involved, as were the *veldcornetten*, who had the task of distributing the captives after a cattle and slave raid (see Eldredge, in Eldredge and Morton 1994c: 114–21).

In the Zoutpansberg, the northernmost district of Transvaal, burghers actively participated in the smuggling of ivory and children during the 1850s and 1860s. While the Zoutpansberg was known as a major source of 'white ivory', it became known in burgher circles for its capacity to supply large numbers of '*Zwart Ivoor*' (black ivory, or black children) to the white and black smugglers (see Boeyens, in Eldredge and Morton 1994c: ch 8).

The Sand River Convention, which, as noted earlier, also prohibited Cape merchants from selling firearms to Africans, had the effect of encouraging some of the smaller tribes to obtain firearms and gunpowder from burghers in exchange for captured children. The fact that burghers claimed tribute from the tribes that remained in the Transvaal after the Ndebele had been driven out also created possibilities for slave raiding between African tribes. Some of the smaller tribes – which were on friendly terms with the burghers – were often involved in slave raids on other tribes in order to collect children. These children were then given to the burghers as their payment of tribute. Slave raiding was also used as a weapon of terror in order to discipline tribes that were not prepared to co-operate with the burghers, or were not inclined to pay their tributes.[29] One of the important aspects of the Apprentice Law of 1851 was the absence of an embargo on the acquisition of African children by means of barter. The Sand River Convention prohibited trading in slaves, but neither burghers nor Africans regarded barter as a form of trade. They were members of pastoral communities organised along patriarchal lines, whose economic life was marked by the absence of money. Africans probably saw nothing wrong in giving their own children (or captive children) in service to a white farmer and receiving compensation in kind, such as rights to squat on the farmer's farm.[30]

It is difficult to determine how many children and women were captured during commando raids, or 'purchased' from African and Griqua suppliers, because not all of them were registered as *inboekelinge*.[31] After their defeat in 1883, large numbers of Ndzundza, or south Ndebele, were indentured as apprentices in the ZAR.[32]

As in the Cape during the 18th and early 19th centuries, *inboekelinge* were integrated into patriarchal families in which they were 'repersonalised' and adapted to Afrikaner culture and religion. Until the 1870s stock farming and hunting remained the principal activities of Afrikaner landowners, who needed permanent, loyal, and mobile labourers on their farms. Like the 'tame' Khoikhoi in the 18th century, African *inboekelinge* were used on commando against other Africans. It is fascinating that commandos were used once again as instruments of white empowerment and black enslavement, and that *inboekelinge* again formed an indispensable part of the militia. It is claimed that a significant *inboekeling* element participated in the Anglo–Boer War as *agterryers* (auxiliaries.) According to Fransjohan Pretorius, the number of *agterryers* were about a quarter of the number of burghers on commando; many of them must have been *inboekelinge* (1991: 306–22).[33]

7.4 The rise of an African tenantry, and the deepening of class differentiation among Afrikaners in the Transorangia (1850–1910)

The Voortrekkers not only succeeded in depriving Africans in the Transorangia of a large part of their land, but also claimed tribute from them. It was, however, much more difficult for them to reduce Africans to a subservient labour force. Apart from those who became indentured as *inboekelinge*, the great majority of Africans maintained a high level of independence in their own areas or as tenant farmers on white-owned land. Owner–tenant relationships between Afrikaners and Africans were varied and complex. Although Africans in the Transorangia republics remained unproletarianised until the 1920s, the owner–tenant relationship was nonetheless an exploitative one that enabled the larger landlords to accumulate considerable wealth at the cost of the African tenantry. However, this feudal relationship was not as exploitative as the master–servant relationship between capitalist farmers and the wage-earning African proletariat in the Cape Colony during the same period. Most Africans in the Transorangia were only proletarianised when the Land Act of 1913 was implemented.

The fact that large-scale proletarianisation did not occur in the Transorangia from the 1850s onwards can be attributed to two factors: first, the state in both Boer republics was too weak to implement a coercive policy against Africans. And second, the agricultural economies in both republics retained their feudal character, with white farmers remaining pastoralists, while Africans practised tillage farming on their tribal land and as a tenants on white-owned farms.[34]

The ZAR found it quite difficult to exert its authority over the Tswanas in the west, the Vendas and Tsongas in the north, and the Pedi in the north east. The tribes living in these areas continued to practise their traditional agricultural methods, and remained self-sufficient. Owing to the influence of traders, they were active in mercantile activities, including the smuggling of ivory and children.[35]

When Britain annexed the ZAR in 1877 the latter's administration was still too weak to collect all the tribute or taxes payable to it in terms of the authority it claimed to exert over all African tribes. In 1877 only £3 000 in taxes were collected from more than 700 000 Africans living in the territory. Britain annexed the ZAR because it wanted more migrant labour for the Kimberley diamond mines. It believed this could be achieved by destroying Pedi autonomy and by alienating Africans generally from land, *inter alia* by forcing them to pay taxes. When, in 1881, the ZAR's independence was restored, the British were satisfied that they had secured a steady supply of migrant labour. The public administration developed by the British during this period was much better than its predecessor. From now on the ZAR could exert its authority over the African tribes far more efficiently, and could collect more taxes. Areas occupied by burghers increased considerably during the British annexation, and so did the number of Africans who squatted or farmed on white farms.

Apart from the gold mining industry, the political economy of the two Boer republics was characterised by a surplus of land, a shortage of labour, and a scarcity of capital. It is therefore not surprising that it retained its feudal character until after the Anglo–Boer War (see Trapido, in Beinart *et al* 1986: 339). Despite the primitive nature of this political economy, the situation was not static, but quite dynamic. In the 60 years from 1850 to 1910 the landlord–tenant relationship changed in important ways, which deepened the class stratification among Afrikaners. Remarkably, the competition between larger and smaller landowners for African labour played a decisive role in polarising a small group of 'notables' on the one hand, and a larger group of small landowners and landless *bywoners* (white squatters) on the other (see section 8.7).[36] While the 'notables' encouraged large-scale squatting (by rent-paying tenants) on their farms, the smaller farmers favoured anti-squatting laws and preferred to enter into partnerships with a few African families farming as sharecroppers (or 'on the halves'). The squatting opportunities offered by the former were mostly more attractive than the sharecropping contracts offered by the latter (see Trapido 1978: 34–5). While absentee landlords easily attracted squatter families, small landowners encountered serious labour problems. They closely supervised the activities of the sharecroppers, and were strict about obtaining their half of the crops. Both the larger landlords and smaller landowners tried to convince their tenants to work for a certain number of days a year as wage tenants. The landlords were also able to offer wage tenants better terms than the smaller ones. The rivalry between the big landlords and land companies on the one hand and the smaller landowners and *bywoners* on the other caused bitterness and animosity in Afrikaner ranks.[37]

Afrikaner landowners – both large and small – remained pastoralists until the end of the 19th century. They were mainly cattle farmers and hunters, and were continuing a tradition that had begun early in the 18th century. As soon as African tenants began to produce maize profitably by using family members as labourers, white landowners, who might have been inclined to become maize producers on their own land, were at a comparative disadvantage – they not only lacked the necessary knowledge and capital, but also the necessary labour. At that stage Africans were still independent enough to avoid seeking employment as wage labourers. If wage labour had been available to white maize farmers in the 19th century, it would have been too expensive for the poor Afrikaner farmers.[38]

In the years after gold was discovered, land was increasingly concentrated in the hands of Afrikaner 'notables' and in those of mining and land companies. As this tendency intensified, many of the poorer farmers lost their farms, and became impoverished. To stop this trend the smaller landowners convinced the *Volksraad* of the ZAR to pass the Squatters' Law of 1887, which stipulated that a farmer could not have more than five squatter families on his farm.[39]

While the discovery of gold intensified the struggle between larger and smaller landowners, it created much improved market conditions for African maize farmers.[40] The proportion of a crop a landlord could claim depended primarily on the balance of power between him and his African tenants. This power relation differed markedly from one district to another, and from one period to another. At the time, African tenants had considerable bargaining power, and their relative power *vis-à-vis* that of their landlords increased in the decade after gold was discovered, and even further in the first decade after the Anglo–Boer War.[41]

At the end of the 19th century two events negatively affected the economic position of both Afrikaners and Africans. The first was the the rinderpest epidemic of 1896, which killed about 2,5 million head of cattle, many of them owned by Africans. The second was the Anglo–Boer War, fought from 1899 until 1902.[42] During the war African peasants seized many Afrikaner farms, and many Africans believed that, after a British victory, they would have easy access to land. When these lands were reclaimed by white commandos – armed for the purpose by the British – the consequence was resentment and restlessness in African circles (O'Meara 1983: 24–6; see also section 8.2).

In the decade following the war the larger landowners attempted to move from pastoral to arable production. Many of their cattle had been killed, and they realised that arable maize farming offered better opportunities. However, these landlords could not transform their manorial estates from squatter or 'kaffir farming' into commercial or capitalist farming in one bound, with they themselves acting as as owners and maize producers. As a first step the wealthier landlords tried to enter into share cropping contracts with their rent-paying squatter tenants by offering them better contracts than the smaller landowners could. In many cases the landlords also got rid of their *bywoners*.[43]

In 1906 the Liberal Party of Henry Cambell Bannerman rose to power in Britain. This party was sharply critical of the British role in the Anglo–Boer War, and sent Lord Selbourne to South Africa as high commissioner to pursue a policy of reconciliation with the 'notables'. In 1907 the position of these wealthier landlords was considerably strengthened when Selborne granted 'responsible government' to the Transvaal.

The *Het Volk* party of Generals Louis Botha and Jan Smuts won the first election, which also placed the 'notables' in a stronger position. The symbiosis between Selborne and the 'notables' had a profound effect on the power struggle between the different elements of the land-owning class and between white landlords and African tenants.[44] The support given by Selborne to wealthy farmers convinced the latter that they could only make a successful transition from pastoral to capitalist farming if they could enlist the support of the state in their dual struggle against the smaller white landowners and against the African tenantry.[45]

In the decade following the Anglo–Boer War, the socio-economic position of Africans on the highveld improved considerably. The competition between larger landlords and smaller landowners resulted in more attractive contracts for many sharecropping tenants. More white farmers from Natal and the Cape moved to the Transorangia, and entered into sharecropping contracts with African tenants.[46] There were also better job opportunities for Africans in railroad building and in transporting goods by wagon.[47] Looking at the relative wealth and relative independence of Africans in the Transorangia in the first decade of the 20th century, it is tragic that this emerging entrepreneurial class was not given a chance to fulfil its promise after the Union of South Africa had been established in 1910. Their type of maize production – marked by a low input of capital, and a high input of family labour – was highly compatible with the uncertain weather conditions on the highveld.

The improvement in Africans' socio-economic position in the decade after the war happened in many respects to the detriment of smaller white landowners and the emerging landless Afrikaner proletariat.[48] Also, evidence suggests that African farmers were better maize farmers than whites, and in fact produced more maize than the latter.[49]

It is ironic that, while this was happening in the Transorangia, the status of African peasants (including tenant farmers) had already been under serious attack in the supposedly liberal Cape since 1890. On the eve of the Land Act of 1913, the position of Africans in the Transorangia contrasted sharply with that of Africans in the Cape. As we will show in the next chapter, the attack on the peasantry and tenantry in the Cape between 1890 and 1910 was repeated against independent Africans in the Transorangia in the decades after 1913 (see section 8.6).[50]

Endnotes

1 This contest between a white and black proletariat was 'resolved' in favour of Afrikaners and to the detriment of Africans, but in a way that reverberated politically and ideologically right through the 20th century (see section 8.7).

2 A patriarchal feudal order developed during the 18th century in which the *Trekboere* became accustomed to a high degree of individualism and self-rule. When the British started to intervene in the master–slave and master–serf relationships, Afrikaners experienced these interventions not only as an intervention in labour relations, but also an attack on their patriarchal cosmology. These tensions reached breaking-point in the 1830s when the boards of *heemrade* and *veldcornette* were abolished and the commando system (with its important hierarchies of privilege and patronage) subjected to British military authority.

3 The subordination of burghers in the ZAR and OFS by financial intermediaries will be discussed in section 8.7 (see Legassick, in Harris 1975: 240–5; Trapido 1978: 26–8).

4 Afrikaners experienced the abolition of Khoisan serfdom in 1828 and of slavery (with insufficient compensation) in 1838 as a serious and an unjustified material loss. The fact that many Khoisan succeeded in establishing themselves as vagrants in settlements outside white control after Ordinance 50 of 1828 created serious labour problems for Afrikaner farmers, especially those in the Eastern Cape. For them, the labour supply was never enough, or docile enough. When, in 1828, contractual serfdom was abolished, the labour force serving Afrikaner farmers not only became free, but also less exploitable and less obedient (see Crais 1992: 6).

5 While the Afrikaners were in effect deprived of their land rights, the British settlers and mercantile elite in Cape Town were given all the support they needed from the colonial authorities in Cape Town to engage in large-scale land speculation in the Eastern Cape and even in Natal. For many Afrikaners – still imbued with the *wanderlust* of the *Trekboere* – this 'closure' of their access to almost unlimited land must have been traumatic. Their decision to trek to the north was therefore a deliberate attempt to restore their easy access to land and labour (see Keegan 1996: 184–96).

6 For those British settlers who were interested in buying land evacuated by prospective emigrants, the *Journal* overemphasised the availability and quality of land in Natal on the one hand, and the bleakness of the situation in the Eastern Cape after the disannexation of the Province of Queen Adelaide on the other. By claiming that the Great Trek was the direct result of the Sixth Frontier War and its aftermath, the *Grahams Town Journal* did not have the Afrikaners' interests at heart, but (according to Keegan) was in fact advancing its own agenda – ie, provoking the imperial power into a policy of annexation and military advances (see Keegan 1996: 194–200).

7 Land for extensive farming was no longer available, and the British settlers drove land prices to unprecedented levels in their quest for additional land for their profitable sheep-farming activities. During a serious drought at the beginning of the 1830s, cattle raids by the Xhosa deprived Afrikaners of their cattle. Against this background, the abolition of the commando system by the British and the inability of

the latter to protect the frontier farmers against Xhosa invasions were for many farmers sufficient reason to trek to the north (see Du Bruyn, in Cameron 1986: 128–31.)

8 Mostert believes that religion did not play an important role among the *Trekboere* in the 18th century, but that Afrikaners became far more religious in the 19th century. When the Great Trek took place, 'the punitive, judgemental force of Voortrekker religion with its strengthened Calvinist affirmation of the elect became, in the face of new indigenous enemies, an unshakable faith'. Mostert agrees that the Sixth Frontier War caused 'newly sharpened states of mind on racial matters among all the frontier colonists, both British as well as Boer…[and that] the racial viewpoint of the frontier had never before been so equivocally articulated by either' (Mostert 1992: 781–2).

9 The fact that the Voortrekkers were completely opposed to any kind of *gelykstelling* (equalisation) between white and black, and did not allow Africans to own land, marry, or enjoy political rights in the Voortrekker states, is irrefutable evidence that they took a clear-cut racist ideology with them to the north. It is possible that their racist ideology and attitude of racial superiority hardened during their relative isolation in the second half of the 19th century (Mostert 1992: 778–83).

10 In the 18th century several northern tribes, in conjunction with European traders and whale hunters, were involved in the lucrative ivory, meat, and slave trade through Delagoa Bay. After the Portuguese closed Delagoa Bay in 1799 in order to monopolise all trade, the participating tribes were plunged into wars of survival. The Zulu were the ultimate victors. Among others, the *mfecane* drove the Mfengu tribe southwards to penetrate the Xhosa areas in the Eastern Cape. This was one of the reasons for the overpopulation that contributed to the Sixth Frontier War (see Edgecombe, in Cameron 1986: ch 9).

11 For many of the other tribes the arrival of the Voortrekkers was a serious shock. According to Thompson, 'the growth of Afrikaner settlement [in the Transorangia] following [shortly] upon the *difagane* wars, presented the African inhabitants of the high veld with their second massive challenge in a generation' (Thompson 1978b: 435).

12 A republic of Natalia was established in 1839, but annexed by Britain in 1843. In 1848 Harry Smith annexed the territory between the Orange and Vaal rivers.

13 According to Keegan, the more radical groups of Voortrekkers 'resisted the entrenchment of bureaucratic government, sought a more equalitarian, atomised and self-sufficient economic system' (1996: 280). In the 18th century this radical group lived in close co-operation with Xhosa tribes and trekked in order to establish similar relationships with African tribes in the Transorangia.

14 As the 'notables' succeeded in state formation and accumulation in the latter part of the 19th century, the 'outsiders' and landless Afrikaners increased and formed the core of poor white Afrikaners at the beginning of the 20th century. A H Potgieter is a typical example of the radical Voortrekkers. Rather than setting up satellite states which would co-operate with the British, his intention was to get as far away from British control as possible. He developed close relationships with African tribes in the Transvaal after the Ndebele had been expelled (see Keegan 1996: 204).

15 The Voortrekkers' attempts to subject the Pedi failed. In 1867 they had to abandon

the Zoutpansberg area to the Pedi and the Venda. The Pedi were only defeated by the British when the latter occupied the ZAR from 1877 until 1881. The tribes subjected by the Afrikaners in the Transvaal were ultimately forced to pay tributes in the form of taxes and labour (Thompson 1978b: 437–40). When, in 1881, the ZAR was given back to the Afrikaners as a suzerainty of Britain, Britain charged the cost of the military conquest of the Pedi to the ZAR, with the result that the republic's public debt rose from £257 000 to £426 000 (see Clark 1994: 15).

16 In 1861 the Griquas under Adam Kok sold their rights north of the Orange River to the OFS government and established themselves in Kokstad in East Griqualand. During the rest of the 19th century friendly relationships prevailed between the Afrikaners and the black communities in the OFS. The farmers employed coloured and African labourers, and many became sharecroppers and labour tenants (Thompson 1978b: 442–5).

17 In 1852 the African population was 100 000 and the white population 15 000; by 1880 these numbers were 800 000 and 43 000 respectively (see Heydenrych, in Cameron 1986: 152).

18 The unequal social stratification that developed in the Afrikaner republics had little to do with economic productivity, but largely depended on burghers' positions in the commandos and as official functionaries. In the period before the discovery of gold, some burghers became quite prosperous through land speculation, raiding African tribes, hunting and trading in ivory, and capturing children (Trapido, in Marks and Atmore 1980: 350–6).

19 When a military expedition was undertaken against an African tribe, it was often financed by issuing currency secured by the land that was to be taken during the expedition! This caused a continuous devaluation of both currency and land, with the consequence that many commercial transactions (also between employers and employees) took place through barter, while the system of tax collection became practically unworkable. In the long run, the devaluation of both currency and land set the ZAR off on a further quest for more land, continuing a vicious circle of conquest, greater debt, and increased insecurity and instability (see Arndt 1928: 94–121).

20 In 1899 more than 2 000 of 11 000 farms were owned by foreign companies, and almost 3 000 were registered in the name of the state (see Trapido, in Marks and Atmore 1980: 354–60). In 1872 the then president of the ZAR, Thomas Francois Burgers, negotiated a favourable loan with the Cape Commercial Bank, but the latter could not recover its funds. As a result, the bank and other creditors persuaded Britain to annex the ZAR in 1877. The bank was liquidated in 1881 (see Trapido in Marks and Atmore 1980: 353–4).

21 Whereas in the 15 years before gold was discovered the ZAR government's revenue had averaged £110 000 annually, this increased to £33 million in 1898 – a 30-fold increase in a decade (Clark 1994: 17). Immediately before the Anglo–Boer War, prominent Afrikaner leaders such as Paul Kruger, Piet Joubert, and Louis Botha each owned up to 40 farms. In the last two decades of the century the dominant group of Afrikaner landowners – the 'notables' – established an informal network which provided them with information and enabled them to accumulate profitable land holdings (Trapido, in Marks and Atmore 1980: 356–7).

22 Regular Griqua slave and cattle raids on San and Batswana groups affected the latter

to such an extent that they placed themselves under Griqua authority. The turmoil generated by slave raiding destabilised some of the tribes north of the Orange River to such an extent that there were severe famines during droughts in the first three decades of the 19th century. Breakaway Griqua groups – such as the Koras and Bergenaars – continued raiding African groups well into the 19th century, and sold the captives to Voortrekkers in the OFS and Transvaal (see Eldredge, in Eldredge and Morton 1994b: 93–114).

23 Thompson describes blacks on the Trek as 'the unregarded members of the movement' (1990: 88).

24 According to Elizabeth Eldredge, 'Boers in Natal in the 1830s readily admitted that battles were waged against the AmaZulus for the explicit purpose of capturing slaves as well as cattle ... Many Boers thought of the attacks on the AmaZulu "as simply a hunting expedition"' (Eldredge, in Eldredge and Morton 1994b: 114). Similar raids took place in the OFS and the Transvaal during the 1840s.

25 In both these cases very little, if any, training took place, and it was also not controlled. By naming their act the 'Apprenticeship Act', and by including the training condition, the Voortrekkers tried deliberately to create a system that would win the approval of the Cape government. It would have been more accurate if the Voortrekkers had enacted an indentureship or *inboekelingskap* law (see Malherbe 1991: 15–30).

26 While there was some validity in regarding displaced Khoisan children in the 18th century as orphans, there was, however, no justification for regarding African children without parents as orphans. In traditional African societies, children who had been orphaned or had lost one of their parents were sheltered by kin, and were subject to guardianship rules (see Boeyens, in Eldredge and Morton 1994c: 188–93).

27 The fact that burghers were scattered over an immense area with little means of communication and administration made it difficult for the government to act against slavery and misconduct. The continual strife between the followers of various Boer leaders weakened the control of the government, and made it relatively easy for irresponsible burghers to evade the anti-slavery and other labour laws. It is also possible that the government was inclined to turn a blind eye to malpractices, and use the convenient excuse that it did not have the administrative capacity to stamp out slave raiding and trading (see Kistner 1952: 242–3).

28 While only a few dozen slaves were exported through Delagoa Bay before 1825, this figure increased to an annual average of more than 3 000 from 1830 onwards. Elizabeth Eldredge claims that 'in the 1830s ... slave raiders supplying the Delagoa Bay slave trade began to operate in the northern and eastern Transvaal at the same time that the expanding Boer frontier brought raids and turmoil to the region' (in Eldredge and Morton 1994a: 129).

29 African auxiliaries were often willing to participate in these raids on recalcitrant tribes in order to protect their own positions. This pattern is reminiscent of the participation of 'tame' Khoikhoi in raids on the 'wild' Khoisan during the second half of the 18th century on the Cape frontier (see Kistner 1952: 232–3; Morton, in Eldredge and Morton 1994c: 262–3).

30 This procedure closely resembled the African marriage custom involving the payment of a *lobola* fee by the bridegroom. There are indications that the

apprenticing of bartered children was regarded as a normal and legal practice in the Transvaal (see Kistner 1952: 228–35).

31 Fred Morton claims that 'the number duly registered, together with those transferred extra-legally to new owners, range from several hundreds to 3 000 per annum' (in Eldredge and Morton 1994c: 173).

32 Some 10 000 Ndzundza were dispersed among the burghers, and indentured for a period of five years. Unpaid tribute was backdated and claimed from the Ndzundza. This taxation and debt bondage perpetuated their indentureship for several years (Malherbe 1991: 25).

33 Although it is sometimes claimed that slave raiding and the *inboekstelsel* were abolished when Britain controlled the ZAR from 1877 until 1881, the apprenticeship system was probably perpetuated by Sir Theophilus Shepstone, special commissioner in the Transvaal from 1877 until 1878, who assigned large numbers of African women and children to Transvaal farmers (see Morton, in Eldredge and Morton 1994c: 181, 256–61). *Inboekelinge* probably became a less important part of the labour force after 1877; however, there is reason to believe that the *inboekstelsel* was maintained until the end of the 19th century, and that some of the *inboekelinge* remained loyal members of Afrikaner households during the first decades of the 20th century.

34 The only capitalist sector that developed in the Transvaal was the gold mining industry, but until the end of the century it did not succeed in employing large numbers of Africans.

35 In the central and southern parts of Transvaal and the OFS, many Africans became tenants on white farms, where they produced maize as rent-paying squatters or as sharecroppers. Africans could not own land in the two Boer republics. To circumvent the prohibition on land ownership, prosperous African chiefs used missionaries as 'dummies' to buy farms on their behalf (see Bundy 1988: 200–2).

36 Wealthier farmers tried to free themselves from mercantile dominance by speculating in land and buying numerous farms. This speculative urge accounted for the fact that by 1900 more than one fifth of the total land area of the ZAR was claimed by land companies or absentee landlords. But despite their extensive land holdings, these landlords failed to free themselves from their feudal state and from mercantile dependency. Their chief source of income – often in kind – was the rent paid by the large numbers of Africans who squatted on their farms. But a continuing problem was that these landlords found it difficult to collect all the rent payable to them. Some of the land companies even experienced problems in gaining access to their land (see Trapido 1978: 26–34).

37 The fact that the 'notables' had access to the means of patronage and corruption – as officials in the government and the commandos – worsened relations between the two groups even further. In the decade after the discovery of gold the opportunities for land speculation improved, which caused additional tensions between the 'notables' and the rest (see section 8.7; see also Bundy 1988: 200–10).

38 This pattern of African tenants producing maize on white-owned land could only be broken by strong state intervention to stabilise maize prices at a higher level, and forcing African tenants to become a wage-earning proletariat. The state only became strong enough – and developed the necessary disposition – to intervene in the

landlord–tenant relationship and change it into a white master–African servant relationship *after* the Union of South Africa was established in 1910, and *after* political power was entrenched in white hands by the Act of Westminster (see section 8.1).

39 The purpose of the law was to prevent wealthy landlords from earning rent from large colonies of African squatters on their multiple farms, and growing rich from rent or 'kaffir farming'. The small landowners hoped the law would increase the numbers of sharecroppers on their farms (see Bundy 1988: ch 7; Trapido 1978: 42–6).

40 Keegan claims that 'the mineral discoveries...had profound effects on the agrarian formation of the highveld. From its inception with the opening of large urban markets, the South African maize revolution was in considerable measure predicated on black peasant enterprise...This enterprise largely took the form of sharecropping, a system in which surplus labour was expended on the tenant's plot, and the surplus extracted by the [white] landlord took the form of a proportion of the crop' (in Marks and Rathbone 1982: 195).

41 It has been calculated that a family unit using its own labour could subsist on a dozen bags of maize a year, while it could produce up to 300 bags on the 30 morgen cultivated (see Keegan, in Marks and Rathbone 1982: 195–8). Beinert *et al* are correct when they claim that, 'given the balance of power between landlords and tenants, it provided much of the terrain over which agrarian class conflict was fought' (Beinart *et al* 1986: 37).

42 About 40 000 Afrikaner homesteads were burnt down, and a large portion of the livestock and crops of Afrikaner and African farmers destroyed.

43 This intensification of the rivalry between landlords and smaller landowners – this time over the terms offered to African sharecroppers – caused an additional movement of poor whites into urban areas, where they swelled the ranks of unemployed Afrikaners (Trapido 1978: 46–52).

44 According to Keegan, 'the half-dozen years after 1907–8 were crucial in the process of capitalisation of settler agriculture and the transformation of productive relations on the farms in the maize belt of the highveld' (Keegan, in Marks and Rathbone 1982: 201–2).

45 The 'notables' in the Transvaal and OFS played a strategic role in the passage of the Land Act of 1913. This act enabled them to get rid of small landowners and *bywoners*, and transform the African tenantry into a wage-earning proletariat (see section 8.7).

46 The large demand for maize in urban areas and improved transport facilities made it possible for African tenants to sell their share of the crop far more profitably than before the war. After the war the ban on African land ownership was lifted, and many chiefs used the opportunity to buy some of the many farms that had come on to the market because of losses or death during the war. On these farms – and on the ones bought by missionary 'dummies' – an independent African peasantry emerged parallel to the tenantry class. Many of the African tenants also owned large herds of cattle and sheep.

47 In 1904 more than 80 per cent of the African population of 900 000 in the Transvaal still had access to land as a peasant and tenant class on terms more favourable than

the 123 000 on government locations or the 50 000 Africans in full-time employment. A similar situation prevailed in the OFS (see Bundy 1988: 208–10).

48 Bundy claims that 'the status of the white *bywoner* declined and his access to land became increasingly precarious as land became more commercially viable and as class differentiation in Afrikaner society deepened'. He quotes a report of 1910 in which fears were voiced that the black peasant 'with his more thrifty habits and small wants is gradually ousting the poor white' (1988: 210).

49 According to Keegan, in 1908 whites in favour of the maintenance of sharecropping in the OFS testified before a commissioner that 'some natives are as good or better farmers than some white men, and that unless the farmer has a direct interest in the crop, he will not exert his best endeavours towards its successful production' (in Marks and Rathbone 1982: 201).

50 While by 1910 large numbers of Africans in the Cape had been proletarianised and reduced to a subservient labour force subject to harsh master and servant laws, in 1912 Africans in the Transorangia were still a prosperous and independent tenantry. Only a small percentage were employed as wage labourers. But the Land Act not only proletarianises Africans in the northern provinces, but – in the political framework of white supremacy and the emerging system of racial capitalism – placed the new African proletariat in a highly disadvantageous position *vis-à-vis* white employers and the Afrikaner proletariat.

Chapter 8

The systemic period of British imperialism and the political and economic hegemony of the English establishment (±1890–1948)

8.1 The institutionalisation of a new power constellation in the late 19th and early 20th century

From about 1890 until 1924, South Africa experienced an economic and political 'revolution'. During this period various political units – controlled by the British, Afrikaners, and independent African tribes – were united into the Union of South Africa under the effective political control of whites. During the same period a mining and agricultural revolution took place in the northern provinces that not only extended the racially based system of agricultural capitalism first established in the Cape to the North, but also institutionalised a fully fledged system of racial capitalism in all sectors of the South African economy.

This period was not only one of state-building, during which white political domination was consolidated, but also one in which the state – on behalf of foreign-owned mining corporations – built the institutional and physical infrastructure of white supremacy. At the same time, it created a racially based socio-economic and labour structure aimed at supplying foreign corporations and white farmers with a cheap and docile labour force. Consequently, a symbiotic relationship developed between white political domination and racial capitalism that endured until the 1990s.

The active role of the state in facilitating the mining and agricultural revolutions and building racial capitalism can only be explained, firstly, in terms of the enormous influence exerted by the mining corporations; secondly, in terms of the political influences exerted by the well-organised, largely Afrikaner, agricultural sector; and, thirdly, by the power of certain key state departments that gave the state a strongly 'Bonapartist' character after 1910.[1]

The new power constellation – which was finally consolidated in the 1930s – was based on a close alliance between the British and local English corporations that controlled the South African economy, and the English-speaking electorate which, in collaboration with the Afrikaner agricultural elite (the 'notables'), controlled South Africa politically almost uninterruptedly until 1948.[2]

In the decades after union, the state emerged as a major actor in formulating the country's racist policies. Several government bureaucracies – especially the native affairs department (NAD) – acquired a great deal of power and independence, and effectively became 'states within a state'. According to Paul Rich, 'the NAD was not an institution that simply reflected class forces, but an independent agent in its own right which was crucial to the legitimisation of state authority during a period of major economic and social transformation [in the decades after 1910]' (1996: 157).

The new power constellation was legitimised by a new set of ideologies that were actively propagated from the start of British imperialism in the 1880s. Cultural and racial considerations may have played an equal – if not a more important – role than economic ones in motivating British imperialism in South Africa. Herbert Spencer's theory of Social Darwinism played a key role in justifying the alleged superiority of British civilisation to all others, but especially to African civilisations, and therefore deepened the racist ideology propagated by whites in the Cape and Natal since the 1840s. Victorian liberalism and its dogmatic optimism about the merits of liberal capitalism and a free market economy reached their zenith during the last quarter of the 19th century. It is therefore not surprising that British imperialism was permeated by the values of Victorian liberalism.

At the end of the 19th century the mining corporations launched an influential 'mining press', which, together with other British institutions, zealously propagated the alleged merits of British civilisation as well as the ideologies of racism and liberal capitalism. In the early 20th century the British authorities in South Africa – emulating segregationist policies and ideologies in the United States – started to propagate and practise *segregation* as the country's official 'native' policy. All three ideological strands – white superiority, liberal capitalism, and racially oriented segregation – played formative roles in constructing South Africa's political and economic system – and, more notably, its labour patterns – during the systemic period of British imperialism and the hegemony of the local English establishment (1890–1948). (All three ideological strands will be discussed in greater detail in section 8.4.)

The institutionalisation of racial capitalism not only required the state to proletarianise Africans more deliberately and completely, but also to create an even more comprehensive system of labour repression than before. While both the large corporations and the farming elite pressurised the colonial states – before and after 1910 – into proletarianising Africans, because they regarded this as indispensable for the mineral and agricultural revolutions, the process of modernisation (brought about by these revolutions) inadvertently also led to the proletarianisation of a large portion of the Afrikaner population. From the last quarter of the 19th century onwards, smaller Afrikaner farmers became landless for the first time in almost 200 years, and had no choice but to enter the labour market as members of an unskilled wage-earning proletariat. The competition between the Afrikaner and African proletariats for the same jobs in urban areas introduced a new element into the South African labour market. In the framework of the new power constellation – ie, a system of white political domination, and an almost exclusively white property and entrepreneurial class – this competition was 'resolved' in the period after Union by passing a battery of discriminatory laws applied – in addition to repressive labour legislation – to Africans and, to a lesser extent, coloureds and Indians, with the explicit purpose of protecting Afrikaners against black competition.

The labour patterns underpinning racial capitalism during most of the 20th century were a highly structured complex of exploitative measures. These included masters and servants laws, pass laws, laws aimed at proletarianising Africans, anti-tradesmen laws, the migrant and compound systems (on diamond and gold mines), influx control, and several segregationist and discriminatory laws aimed at protecting whites against black encroachment, and impoverished Afrikaners in particular against black competition in the labour market (see sections 8.5 and 8.7).

8.2 British imperialism, wars of conquest, and the 'alliance between gold and maize' (±1890–1910)

In the mid-19th century it seemed as if Britain might scale down its colonial involvement in South Africa, due to the high costs involved. But from the late 1880s onwards it embarked upon a new phase of aggressive imperialism in southern Africa that fundamentally changed the map of the region and institutionalised new patterns of political and economic power that shaped South Africa's development in the 20th century (Worden 1994b: 19).

The origins of this new phase of British imperialism lay partly outside and partly inside the region. Sharpened economic rivalry between the industrial countries of the west in the 50 years before World War 1 motivated them to gain political control over those parts of the developing world (mostly in Africa) that were not yet controlled by a country in the industrial core. When several European countries joined in the 'scramble for Africa', this prompted Britain to consolidate its grip on those parts of southern Africa within its sphere of influence.

Shortly after the discovery of diamonds in 1867, Lord Carnavon, the British colonial secretary, pushed for a federation of South African colonies and republics under British sovereignty. Besides infrastructural considerations, his idea was motivated by a desire to control the flow of African labour. It was strongly supported by officials on the diamond fields and by the Natal colonial authority. Many Pedis worked as migrant labourers on the diamond fields, and it became necessary to protect the migrant labour route from the north against the interference of burgher commandos of the ZAR.[3] Carnavon's ideas motivated the annexation of the ZAR in 1877. When, in 1880, the Liberal Party won a general election in Britain, its leader, William E Gladstone, expressed serious misgivings over British policy in the Transvaal. After the First War of Liberation (1881), the independence of the ZAR was restored. But despite this setback, Carnavon's idea of a South African federation lived on and gathered momentum. At the end of the century, Cecil John Rhodes and Alfred Milner considered it their mission to create a vast British state extending from the Cape to the Zambezi and even further. As in the case of Carnavon, their aim was not only to gain control over land, but to conquer the still independent African tribes and turn them into a subservient labour force (see Thompson 1990: 146–53; Worden 1994b: 25).

The discovery of gold in 1886 provided Britain with an even more compelling reason for expanding its interests in South Africa. The nature of the Witwatersrand gold mines, and particularly the low grade of the ore, meant that gold could only be produced profitably if production costs – and especially labour costs – could be minimised. During the 19th century two factors threatened to undermine the gold companies' ability to produce gold profitably – one had to do with the behaviour of Africans, and the other with the behaviour of Afrikaners in the ZAR (see Grundlingh, in Cameron 1986: 185; Thompson 1990: 120–2).

During the 1890s traditional and economically independent African communities were still not prepared to 'release' sufficient cheap labour for the mines. Africans in the Transorangia were successful maize and cattle farmers on white-owned land, and enjoyed a high level of economic independence. They were not prepared to work in the mines for the wages offered. By the end of the century almost 100 000 Africans worked on the mines, but most of them came from outside the ZAR. The mining companies became convinced that their labour problems would remain unresolved without a powerful and sympathetic state that would undermine the economic independence of Africans, thus creating the required volume of cheap labour (see Clark 1994: 22–5).

Afrikaners in the ZAR and their leader, Paul Kruger, had little sympathy for the gold mines and their quest to produce gold as cheaply as possible. Kruger adopted an adversarial stance towards the mine owners. He was hoping to bleed off a sizeable portion of the gold industry's profits and channel the money to local economic development, in order to increase the ZAR's economic independence from the British. However, despite the sharp increase in ZAR government revenue, the government failed to build the administrative and physical infrastructure the gold mines needed.[4]

The growing animosity between the ZAR and Kruger on the one hand and the gold mining industry and Alfred Milner, the British high commissioner for South Africa, on the other eventually led to the Anglo–Boer War (1899–1902). There can be little doubt that this was an imperialist war *par excellence* and, more specifically, a gold war.

At the end of the 19th century, economic conditions in Britain were rather bleak. Since the early 1870s Britain had experienced a 'long depression', and had lost economic and industrial ground to Germany and the United States (see Kennedy 1988: 288). In the late 19th century Britain's economy was characterised by sharp inequalities, widespread poverty and unemployment, and a chronic deficit in the current account. In a world based on the gold standard, Britain was losing gold. At that stage, gold was central to the fiscal stability of the capitalist world economy and, given London's position as the financial centre of the world, even more crucial to Britain. It was therefore not surprising that Britain saw the solution to its economic and trade problems in a greater and more profitable production of gold by the Rand gold mines. In a desperate attempt to protect its shrinking economic interests in large parts of the world, Britain conducted an increasingly more aggressive and ruthless policy of imperialistic conquest and capitalist exploitation of colonised people in an attempt to solve its internal socio-economic problems (see Worden 1994b: 26).

The factors that led to the Anglo–Boer War must therefore be seen in the wider framework of global capitalism at the turn of the century. On the surface, the war was a struggle between two white civilisations: the powerful British civilisation, marked by the arrogance of a world power, but caught in a downward spiral; and the emerging Afrikaner civilisation, still feudal in orientation and impudent in its challenge to a superpower.[5] At a deeper level the war was about the expansion of British corporate capitalism which was seriously constrained because it had to operate in the ZAR amid two kinds of feudalism: Afrikaner pastoral feudalism, led by a rather corrupt *nouveau riche* agricultural elite interested in primitive accumulation, and African maize-producing and cattle-farming feudalism (still maintaining its traditionalist redistributive economy), led by equally corrupt tribal chiefs who were also interested in primitive accumulation.

The British mining companies wanted to establish a capitalist mode of production throughout South Africa, but the Afrikaner elite was neither prepared nor able to create the social and physical infrastructure conducive to the accumulation Britain needed to compete against Germany and the United States. At the same time, the imperatives of capitalism dictated, at a crucial juncture in Britain's economic history, that gold could only be produced profitably if large numbers of Africans could be employed on the mines at extremely low wages. But the tribal and semi-feudalistic Africans were not inclined to become mineworkers, and the feudalistic Afrikaner elite was not prepared to use its political power to force Africans into wage labour. Therefore, the situation before the war was a stalemate between British corporate capitalism, with a relentlessly expansionist frame of mind, and two feudal civilisations locked in a strangely competitive and co-operative relationship with each other, but very much in the way of British imperialistic intentions (see Legassick 1975: 259–64; Halisi 1999: 34–7).

It was not possible for Britain to take on the Afrikaner and African feudal orders at the same time. When, after the two Boer republics had been defeated, but the mines' labour problems were still unresolved, the British became convinced that Africans could only be turned into a wage-earning proletariat with the co-operation of the defeated Afrikaner elite. To accomplish this, a remarkable *rapprochement* took place from 1906 onwards between the British and the Afrikaner elite in the Transvaal. From this perspective, the Anglo–Boer War can be seen as the essential prologue to the comprehensive onslaught against the economic independence of the African tenantry on the highveld by a formidable alliance of large British corporations and the Union of South Africa, led by two former Boer generals. Faced with this onslaught, Africans had no option but to be reduced to a wage-earning proletariat (see Legassick 1975: 244–51).

The Anglo–Boer War was undoubtedly the greatest tragedy in South Africa's history.[6] While the war was fought to consolidate and safeguard Britain's imperial interests in southern Africa, its high cost and the way in which it was conducted hastened Britain's economic and moral decline as an industrial and imperial superpower. From an economic point of view, the war was a disaster for Afrikaners as well as Africans. It not only brought about huge social dislocations, but also impoverished many people in both groups. It is estimated that 60 per cent of the assets of Afrikaners in the Transvaal and OFS – ie, houses, furniture, and livestock – were destroyed. The proletarianisation of Africans and Afrikaners, set in motion by the mineral revolution, was hastened by the war. Thus the end result of Britain's imperialist plundering was to create a large Afrikaner proletariat and an even larger African proletariat. The conflicting claims of these two proletariats were to dominate South African politics during the 20th century.

From the point of view of power relations and labour patterns, the Anglo–Boer War had devastating consequences for Africans. Shortly after the outbreak of the war in November 1899, Milner wrote a letter in which he clearly formulated his views on the political and economic status of Africans in a future South Africa: 'The *ultimate end* is a self-governing white community supported by *well-treated* and *justly-governed black labour* from Cape Town to Zambezi' (quoted by Thompson 1978a: 330; emphasis in the original). During the Anglo–Boer War the British colonial authority assured Africans that 'equal laws, equal liberty' would be granted to all population groups after a Boer defeat. But during the negotiations that led to the Peace of Vereeniging in 1902 the British imperial politicians reneged on these promises by making a crucial concession to the defeated Afrikaners. It promised them (in article 8 of the treaty) that the question of granting the vote to Africans (in the Transvaal and OFS) would be postponed until *after* self-government had been restored to the ex-republics.

This laid the foundation for a system of white political domination that endured for most of the 20th century. The South African Act of Westminster (1909) – the constitution of the Union of South Africa, passed by the British parliament, and based on a draft prepared by a South African national convention – honoured article 8 of the treaty by not extending the qualified voting rights of Africans and coloureds in the Cape to northern provinces. These events were no accidents, but formed part and parcel of the process of co-operation among the British government, the mining companies, and the Afrikaner elite aimed at assembling a white power bloc strong enough to attack the economic independence of the African tenantry (see Bundy 1993: 59–61).

Milner's labour policies during and after the war show clearly that the war was mainly fought to gain control over African labour. As part of his intended reconstruction programme, he envisaged an economic boom that would attract a massive influx of British immigrants. He hoped this would not only ensure that Afrikaners would become a minority among whites, but also that they would be swamped and denationalised. The key ingredient for bringing about the economic boom was cheap African labour. From 1901 the gold mining companies tried to get the gold mines going by employing Africans at wages about one third less than the pre-war rate, but did not succeed. Milner gave the CM permission to recruit African labour from as far afield as east and central Africa. When this also failed, Milner allowed the CM to import 64 000 Chinese workers. In 1903, in another attempt to solve the mines' serious labour problems, Milner appointed the South African Native Affairs Commission (SANAC), chaired by Sir Godfrey Lagden. Its report was published in 1905, but Milner was recalled to London before he could implement its recommendations. The SANAC report became, if not immediately, a major vehicle for the ideological justification of segregation, the proletarianisation of Africans in the northern provinces, and the principle of migrant labour with a subsistence base in the 'native reserves'.[7] Its approach was accepted unreservedly when the Land Act was promulgated in 1913 (see Cell 1982: 58–65; section 8.6).

Within three years after the Anglo–Boer War the British government had decided that socio-political stabilisation – indispensable for the mining industry – could only be achieved if Afrikaners, and especially the large landowners in the Transvaal (the 'notables'), were politically accommodated. This can be regarded as one of the most remarkable about-faces in the course of British policy towards South Africa. What brought it about? It was probably the mining companies and the 'notables' who convinced the Liberal government of Sir Henry Campbell-Bannerman that it would not be possible to turn Africans into a wage-earning proletariat without the co-operation of at least the 'notables'. In 1906 Lord Selborne was sent to South Africa to succeed Milner as high commissioner with the task of bringing about a *rapprochement* between the British government and the large landowners in the Transvaal and OFS (see Mostert 1992: 264–7).

In 1907 'responsible self-government' was given to the Transvaal and OFS, with constitutions that excluded Africans and coloureds from the franchise. In March 1907 General Louis Botha's *Het Volk* (The Nation) party won the elections in the Transvaal with considerable support from English-speakers who were concerned about the encroachment of Africans. Within the first three months an important event occurred that was destined to forge an alliance (or even a symbiosis) between the Afrikaner state and British capital. In May 1907 English-speaking (mainly British) miners staged the first major strike on the Witwatersrand gold fields in support of demands for higher wages. On 23 May

General Jan Smuts, the minister responsible, called in British imperial troops (still stationed in the Transvaal) to restore order on the mines.[8] This event forged a remarkably close and long-lasting alliance between the government (representing large Afrikaner landowners) and the gold mining industry (at that stage still very much under the control of British and Jewish magnates). In an apt phrase borrowed from the German 'alliance of iron and rye' in the 19th century, the new power elite has been described as 'the alliance of gold and maize' (see Yudelman 1983: 70–6).

This new alliance between the Afrikaner elite and the mining elite gave rise to a policy of 'reconciliation' between an important section of the Afrikaner community and the British authorities and interests. On this basis, Afrikaans and English-speaking elites agreed to unify the four British colonies into the Union of South Africa. In the preceding negotiations, parties easily agreed that white political power should be entrenched constitutionally.[9]

The Act of Westminster of 1909 enabled white settlers – both Afrikaners and English-speakers – to take over the unified state. An act of the British parliament was therefore the bridgehead that enabled whites in South Africa to perpetuate, for 84 years, the power relations of European colonialism. Coloureds and Africans retained their qualified voting rights in the Cape, but these rights were not extended to the Transvaal and Free State.[10] The qualified franchise of coloureds and Africans in the Cape and Natal could only be changed with a two-thirds majority of a joint session of both houses of parliament. The Africans' limited franchise rights were abolished by Hertzog and Smuts in 1936, and the coloureds' limited franchise rights by the NP in 1956. The Act of Westminster therefore institutionalised – for all practical purposes – a system of white political domination, and effectively disenfranchised blacks in South Africa. This system remained in place until 1984 when limited political representation was given to coloureds and Indians in the tricameral parliamentary system.

8.3 The Union of South Africa and state-building: the entrenchment of white power and racial segregation (1910–24)

From 1910 until 1948 South Africa was controlled by the predominantly English establishment, except for the nine years of the Pact government from 1924 to 1933. During the first half of the 20th century the English establishment was obsessed with two things: entrenching white political power, and entrenching racial segregation. We can regard these as the two pillars on which the edifice of the new state was assiduously built. Both the gold mining industry and the maize farmers had a vested interest in a strong state and in segregation as a method of controlling blacks.

According to Rich, segregation provided the white-controlled state

> with a strategy for developing social control mechanisms that would not depend simply on using its own policing powers to contain any threats to its own security. By developing the rural [African] reserves under the control and authority of tribal chiefs it was also hoped that relatively stable African communities could be established that would be able to control and discipline themselves (1996: 11–12).

The social control system that was institutionalised depended upon maintaining ties of political patronage and clientelism with rural Africans. A close relationship was built with obedient and often corrupt African chiefs who were prepared to act as clients of the white political authorities. In this way a system of indirect rule and white trusteeship was institutionalised that was built on an unequal distribution of power and status between whites and blacks, and echoed similar patterns of political patronage and clientelism in other British colonies.[11]

Through indirect rule in the 'native reserves', and with the co-operation of collaborating chiefs, successive white governments succeeded to a remarkable degree in defusing African radicalism until the 1970s. The system of white political domination – institutionalised by the Act of Westminster – could not have been maintained for 84 years were it not for the success of the doctrine of indirect rule by means of which essential colonial structures of political and social control were perpetuated.[12]

The South African state that came into being in 1910 was initially rather vulnerable. Despite being based on an alliance between an Afrikaner farming elite and a British/English business elite, and legitimised in terms of the segregationist ideology that was generally accepted in at least the British-American world, several problems remained unresolved, and threatened the stability and continued existence of the new state. The two most pressing problems concerned poor Afrikaners and poor Africans. The first was how to accommodate the Afrikaner and African proletariats, given the conflicting demands of capital *accumulation* and state (or political) *legitimisation*. The second was how to solve the serious labour problems of the mining industry and the maize farmers without endangering their alliance. Within 14 years after Union, 'solutions' were found to both these problems that enhanced the stability, viability, and profitability of the new state. Unfortunately, however, both 'solutions' were racist in nature, and very much to the detriment of Africans. The conflicting demands of the African and Afrikaner proletariats and the stress this placed on the new government's attempt to reconcile the accumulation and legitimisation imperatives were only 'resolved' when the interests of the marginalised white groups were entrenched in the consensual order created by the two white elite groups during the 1920s. The second problem was 'solved' when the Land Act was promulgated in 1913, and thousands of Africans were proletarianised and forced into wage labour. The act also prescribed a formula for distributing African labour between the gold mines and maize farmers, to the satisfaction of both groups (see section 8.6).

Marginalised Afrikaners – both the petit bourgeoisie and the proletariat – found a powerful leader in General J B M Hertzog who was excluded from the cabinet in 1912 because he had criticised Botha and Smuts for being too sensitive towards the interests of British capital and the empire. In 1914 Hertzog launched the National Party (NP), which over the next 10 years increasingly challenged the Botha and Smuts policy of 'reconciliation'. After Hertzog's defection from the South African Party, the majority of SAP supporters were English-speaking. The rest were the so-called *bloedsappe* ('blood' members of the SAP), mainly the larger Afrikaner landowners. From then on until 1948 the political hegemony of the English establishment was based on the English-speakers' control of the economy, their numerical majority in the SAP/UP,[13] the support they received from *bloedsap* Afrikaners, and the influence of the powerful English-oriented 'mining press'.[14]

A remarkable characteristic of the new state was the close collaboration between the government and the gold mining industry. In order to sustain its revenue, the state adopted policies that favoured the gold mining industry and protected the interests of British capital. This policy demonstrates the extraordinarily powerful position of the mining industry, and the symbiotic relationship between state and capital established in the Transvaal in 1907. Although this relationship was conducive to capital accumulation, the government's initial neglect of the interests of white workers and small farmers severely strained the legitimacy of the state (see section 3.2.1). A large portion of the white electorate rejected the validity of the post-union state, and challenged its authority through strikes and insurrections during its first two decades (see Yudelman 1983: ch 4; see also section 8.7).[15]

After the Rand Revolt of 1922, the Smuts government became convinced that conditions conducive to accumulation and legitimisation could only be guaranteed if the economic position of the white proletariat and the Afrikaner petit bourgeoisie could be secured. To accomplish this, the Smuts government passed the Industrial Conciliation Act early in 1924 (see Yudelman 1983: ch 6).

The power constellation – based on the 'alliance of gold and maize' – created in the years immediately before and after 1910 forged a symbiosis between the white-controlled state and British/English-controlled capital. In the period from 1910 until 1948 the terms of this symbiotic relationship sometimes came under strain, and small power shifts occurred, but they never threatened the symbiosis.[16] During the premiership of Botha and Smuts (1910–24), British-controlled mining capital (strongly supported by the English-speaking 'mining press') was the senior and the state the junior partner. After the strike of 1922 and the Pact victory of 1924, the balance tilted towards the state, now controlled by petit bourgeois Afrikaners and the white wage-earning class. This tilt was not as dramatic – or as disadvantageous to capital – as is often alleged (see section 8.8). Although the gold mining industry did not regain its extraordinary position of power and privilege after the strike of 1922, it remained a formidable pressure group for the greater part of the century.

A factor that contributed to the longevity of the symbiotic relationship between state and capital from 1910 until 1948 (and even until the 1980s) was the remarkable support given to the racist ideology of segregation and the system of black labour repression by both the Afrikaner and English establishments. The almost unanimous support in white circles for both these elements could only have occurred in an intellectual atmosphere in which South African (or Cape) liberalism declined dramatically (see section 8.4). Another contributing factor was the continuing and lucrative economic support of Britain and other industrialised countries such as Germany and the United States. It was only in the 1980s that the ANC-driven policy of disinvestment undermined both the accumulation and legitimation strategies. This led to a crisis of hegemony that proved to be irresolvable (see O'Meara 1996: 188–9).

To appreciate the true nature of the symbiosis between state and capital, and its remarkable staying power during the greater part of the 20th century, it is also necessary to emphasise the strategic role played by the NAD and its successors. The NAD was constructed in 1910 from separate provincial native affairs departments. It slowly became a bureaucratic empire with a high level of independence, and in due course became a 'state within a state'. This department played a decisive role in formulating and applying 'native policies' in accordance with segregationist ideology. The NAD (and its successors) was the main instrument with which successive white governments ruled the different African tribes as if South Africa were still a colony (see Rich 1996: 9–10).

8.4 The decline of Cape liberalism and the rise of racist ideologies (±1880–1948)

As noted earlier, the liberalism that developed in the Cape in the mid-19th century was 'Janus-faced'. Sir George Grey established a non-racial franchise in 1854, and gave property rights and educational institutions to a small African elite. At the same time, repressive labour legislation was enacted and several measures implemented to proletarianise large numbers of Xhosas. From 1860 until 1890 the torch of Cape liberalism was carried by the financial and mercantile elite in Cape Town and Port Elizabeth and to a lesser degree by the missionaries. This elite had an interest in maintaining the electoral rights of Africans and coloureds as a buffer against the Afrikaner vote. Consequently, Cape liberalism was strongly committed to creating and maintaining an African peasantry in the Eastern Cape (see Bundy 1988: ch 3).

After the discovery of gold and the advent of the New Imperialism, the mercantile and financial elite shifted their financial interests from the Cape to the Rand gold mines. This meant that the Cape liberals gained a vested interest in the mining industry, whose profitability depended on cheap African labour. On the basis of this material interest the elite changed its view on the economic and political role of the African peasantry. The mining revolution transformed the Cape economy quite drastically, and the growing demand for migrant labour undermined the peasant economy in the Eastern Cape and began to turn the Transkei into a labour reservoir (see section 5.5). At the beginning of the 1890s the mercantile elite – in coalition with the Afrikaner Bond – supported Cecil John Rhodes's Anti-squatting Act (1892), his Franchise and Ballot Act (1892), and his Glen Grey Act (1894) in the Cape parliament.[17] The purpose of the anti-squatting and Glen Grey acts was to hasten the process of proletarianisation in the Eastern Cape. At the same time the mining companies discovered that tribal chiefs and headmen were a more convenient collaborating class for the 'controlled proletarianisation' of Africans (needed by the gold mines) than the modern class of propertied, progressive, and secular African peasants (Bundy 1988: ch 4; Kuper 1978: 428).

From 1890 onwards, instead of remaining loyal to its liberal ideologies, the mercantile and financial elite became the champion of the retribalisation of the Africans in 'native reserves' under the control of mostly corrupt chiefs, who now had to fulfil the double function of social control in the 'reserves' and collaboration with white employers. The mid-Victorian objective of turning Africans into black Englishmen was given up at the end of the 19th century – by both the mercantile elite and the missionaries. With the bright side of the 'Janus face' of liberalism in eclipse, all that remained was the dark side – ie, the side that was prepared to rationalise the conversion of Africans into a poorly paid proletariat with the argument that such labour was essential for capitalist progress (see Rich 1984: 123; Trapido, in Marks and Atmore 1980: 247).

The outbreak of the New Imperialism and the decline of liberalism were closely associated with the rise of Social Darwinism. The British sociologist Herbert Spencer reinterpreted (and vulgarised) Charles Darwin's work on the survival of the animal world, and applied Darwinism to the economic and social life of humans. Spencer coined the phase 'struggle for life and survival of the fittest', and argued that the fittest must be 'selected' in order to enhance their 'generation'. His theory quickly attained cultural and racial connotations. In Britain and America his idea were regarded as divine revelations, and used by the rich to justify their wealth in the face of poverty (see Galbraith 1977: 44–50).

The 'individualistic' nature of Spencer's Social Darwinism – in which strong individuals survived, and weak individuals fell by the wayside – was quickly broadened into a struggle between strong (ie, rich) and weak (ie, poor) groups. This was subsequently broadened into a struggle between strong (eg, Britain) and weak nations, and ultimately to the struggle between the alleged natural superiority of white races and the alleged natural inferiority of non-white races. In this way Social Darwinism became the ideological justification for one of the worst forms of racism in recent history.[18] It is important to note that, in the late 19th and early 20th centuries, Britain and large parts of the English-speaking world were the pioneers of ideas of alleged racial superiority based on divine destiny. During the last quarter of the 19th century the attitudes and actions of the British elite were characterised by Victorian self-righteousness and the acceptance of British superiority as a self-evident truth. Both these characteristics played a dominant role in the aggressive and ruthless expansion of British imperialism, and in the exploitative nature of British capitalism in South Africa.

Cecil John Rhodes (1853–1902) personified notions of the superiority of the English perhaps more than anyone else (see Thomas, 1996: 8–9). Rhodes had a remarkable understanding of public relations and the power of the press. He acquired newspapers, both openly and secretly, in the belief that 'the press rules the minds of men'. In the 50 years after his death the so-called 'mining press' he had created continued to play a dominant role in propagating both the alleged superiority of English-speaking whites and the alleged merits of an unfettered system of liberal capitalism based on cheap African labour. In this way the ideological onslaught of Victorian complacency, the haughtiness of English-speaking whites, and the supposed merits of colonial and racial capitalism were perpetuated until deep into the 20th century. It is indeed difficult to properly evaluate the merits and demerits of British imperialism in South Africa, and the same is true of Rhodes's contribution. Although British imperialism in South Africa should be credited with several important accomplishments, perhaps its greatest negative legacy was to entrench racism as a structural element in mining capitalism for almost 100 years.[19]

The ideology of segregation (ie, segregationism) was formulated during the first decade of the 20th century to legitimise a variety of segregationist measures that were already in place. At that stage the ideology of segregation had already been propagated for two decades in the United States to legitimise similar segregationist measures. According to John Cell the origins and early development of segregation in South Africa and the American South were historically linked.[20] The system of segregation that developed in the American South after the Civil War was based on the conviction that African Americans were inferior to European Americans. When this idea crystallised, Social Darwinism had already become popular in the American South. The ideology of segregation in South Africa was formulated during Milner's 'reconstruction period', and immediately before and after the four British colonies were united into the Union of South Africa (see Dubow 1989: 52).

According to Beinart and Dubow, segregation as an umbrella ideology was 'more than a panoply of *restrictive* legislation: it refers as well to a composite ideology and set of practices seeking to *legitimise social differences and economic inequality in every aspect of life* [in South Africa]' (1995: 4; author's emphasis). Segregation as a socio-economic system comprised, *inter alia*, territorial segregation between white and black in rural and urban areas; segregation in political and educational institutions; and segregation in the workplace. As far as segregationist legislation applicable to black (but especially African) labour was concerned, we should distinguish carefully between segregationist practices and legislation as methods of labour *repression* aimed at guaranteeing an adequate supply of cheap black labour on the one hand, and those as methods of labour *discrimination* aimed at protecting white labour against competition from already cheap and docile black labour on the other. Discrimination in the labour market could either be statutory *job discrimination*, stipulating that certain jobs could only be occupied by whites, or statutory *wage discrimination*, stipulating that whites should be paid higher wages than blacks for the same job. Job and wage discrimination were often applied simultaneously. Segregation as a method of labour *repression* was important for the white employer class (in mining, farming, and industry) in its quest to keep production costs as low as possible. Segregation as a method of *discrimination* was important for the white working class (especially proletarianised Afrikaners) in its quest to protect itself against black labour.

Labour repressive measures were institutionalised in the Cape Colony from the 1840s onwards, when pass laws and masters and servants laws were passed and measures (eg, anti-squatting laws) implemented to proletarianise coloureds and Africans. These measures gained a specifically segregationist character when the Cape parliament enacted the Glen Grey Act in 1894. According to this act the Glen Grey district was demarcated as a 'tribal area' in which small plots were given to African farmers and where white employers could recruit Africans (without plots) as contract labourers.[21]

The first segregationist measures introduced to discriminate against black labour were applied in Kimberley in the 1870s and 1880s as part and parcel of the mining revolution. When gold was discovered in the ZAR in 1886, the gold mining industry followed the Kimberley precedent of a racially split labour force. On the Rand, as in Kimberley, African men were kept in all-male compounds owned and controlled by the mining companies, and severely disciplined by African foremen responsible to white managers. In 1889 white mineworkers struck successfully to protect their skilled positions and their rights to organise and maintain control over their working conditions. In the 1890s the ZAR government created colour bars and imposed a limit on the upgrading of African workers (see Thompson 1990: 115–22.)

Historians have disagreed over when and why segregation emerged, and who was responsible for segregationism as an ideology. The liberal view that it was a direct heritage of the 19th century Boer republics has been repudiated.[22] Dubow believes that English-speakers – rather than Afrikaans-speakers – were responsible for segregationist ideology (1989: 22). Legassick claims that the crucial formative period for the policy of segregation was that between the Anglo–Boer War and World War 1.[23] Milner and his *Kindergarten* (his inner circle of officials, many of whom were young Oxford graduates) not only created additional segregationist measures, but went out of their way to provide an elaborate ideological rationalisation for new and existing segregationist practices. Their ideological approach was distilled in the SANAC report of 1905, which was produced by British and English-speaking experts.[24] According to Rodney Davenport, the SANAC report 'introduced new rigidities into South African thinking about race relations which had an immense influence on later political debate ... It envisaged the territorial separation [segregation] of black and white as a permanent, mandatory principle of land ownership' (1991: 207). It also hoped to solve the labour problems of the mines by creating 'native reserves' which were too small to sustain their African populations and could therefore serve as 'reservoirs' for migrant labour. The report approved the systematic establishment of segregated locations for urban Africans, and urged the separation of blacks from whites in political life, with Africans represented by whites in parliament.

Those responsible for elaborating the ideology of segregationism were undoubtedly familiar with Social Darwinism, and convinced of the alleged superiority of whites, and especially Englishmen. Moreover, they were the champions of unrestrained capitalist progress, and obsessed with the idea that only the gold mining industry could drive such progress. Although the roots of segregationism undoubtedly lay in the racist attitudes and ideas of the previous three centuries, segregationism as a modernising ideology was qualitatively new and inextricably linked to the efforts to launch British imperialism and British capitalism during the first decades of the 20th century. As noted earlier, the NAD played a strategic role in rationalising and applying segregation during the first 14 years after unification (see Dubow, in Beinart and Dubow 1995: 153–7).

Concerned about the threat of African urbanisation, the Smuts government passed the Native (Urban Areas) Act in 1923. It was based on the following dictum enshrined in the 1921 Transvaal Local Government Commission, chaired by Colonel Frederick Stallard: 'The Native should only be allowed to enter urban areas, which are essentially the white man's creation, when he is willing to minister to the needs of the white man, and should depart therefore when he ceases so to minister.' For several decades, the Urban Areas Act – based on 'Stallardism' – was the main vehicle for administering 'influx control' and urbanisation (see section 9.5).

When segregationism was formulated in the period between the Anglo–Boer War and World War 1, the political authorities and gold mining corporations were collaborating closely. During this period the overwhelming concern was to secure an adequate supply of cheap African labour not only for the gold mines but also for white (predominantly Afrikaner) farmers who were becoming commercial maize farmers. There is little doubt that – as in the case of British imperialism – the motivation for segregationism should be analysed primarily in economic terms. The racial beliefs on which segregation was based should therefore be understood as a product or rationalisation of economic and capitalist imperatives (see Beinart and Dubow 1995: 7–8).

According to Marks and Trapido, the reason why unification in 1910 did not lead to 'a single pan-South African, pan-ethnic nationalism' was because it was 'the outcome of a history of regional divisions, the racism and social Darwinism of the late 19th century, and the specific political-cum-class struggles which were being legitimised by the discourse of nationalism [in Afrikaner and African circles]' (1987: 103). For English-speakers – who dominated South Africa politically and economically during the first half of the 20th century – nationalism was an alien and perhaps unnecessary ideology. Both the Afrikaners and the Africans saw their 'salvation' in nationalism, but these were two different versions of nationalism. While the exclusiveness of Afrikaner nationalism had its roots in late 19th-century European nationalism, black nationalism – despite its Africanist underpinnings – was strongly influenced by 19th-century liberal values originally propagated by English-speakers and missionaries. As the struggle between the Afrikaner and African proletariats intensified from the 1930s onwards, both Afrikaner and African nationalisms gained a new content. In the 1930s Afrikaner nationalism was 'derailed' into an aggressive version of 'Afrikaner Christian nationalism', accompanied by an insulting version of racism. African nationalism, in turn, became much more Africanist from the 1940s onwards and replaced its liberal orientation with a militant aggression against Afrikaner nationalism and against the economic domination and alleged superiority of the British/English (see Marks and Trapido 1987: ch 1; see also sections 9.1 and 9.7).

In the years immediately after Union important segregationist legislation was enacted by parliament to complement the 'segregationist principles' already entrenched in the Act of Westminster.[25] Although the ANC was established in 1912 as a protest movement against the disenfranchisement of Africans in the northern provinces, segregationist legislation was not strongly opposed before the end of World War 1. Between 1917 and 1922 black political awareness sharpened significantly when black political leaders were radicalised (see section 8.10).

8.5 The assault on the peasantry in the Eastern Cape and Natal, and the proletarianisation of growing numbers of Africans (1890–1913)

In the quarter century between the discovery of gold and the adoption of the Land Act, South Africa experienced revolutionary changes in social, economic, and political relationships. The emerging capitalist nature of gold and agricultural production generated a fundamental change in the nature of the demand – by white employers – for African labour. Both the gold mining companies and white farmers claimed that they could only operate profitably if enough cheap and docile African labour was available. In their quest for profits, both the gold mines and the large farmers convinced the relevant governments – ie, the colonial governments in the Cape and Natal, and the

Union government after 1910 – to use extra-economic coercion to deliver cheap and docile African labour. Through a comprehensive process of political engineering, the relative economic independence of Africans (in and outside the 'native reserves') was reduced to structural underdevelopment *vis-à-vis* the developed and modernising gold and agricultural sectors.

From 1890 onwards the fortunes of African peasant farmers in the Cape and Natal declined. The mercantile or *rentier* landlords – who for decades had had a political and material interest in the peasantisation of Africans – shifted their investments from the Cape and Natal to the gold industry of the Witwatersrand, and developed a material interest in the adequate supply of African mine labour. While the mercantile elite previously favoured peasantisation, it now supported the 'retribalisation' and 'controlled proletarianisation' of Africans. As the gold mines intensified its recruitment of migrant labour, through the monopsonistic CM established in 1889, white farmers experienced an increasingly severe shortage of African labour. Consequently, it became expedient for the white employer class – farmers, mining, and construction companies – to agitate jointly for extra-economic pressures (or legal measures) to break down African peasants' economic independence, and coerce them into becoming a wage-earning proletariat. This was a huge task that necessitated active state involvement in the labour markets of the Cape and Natal from 1890 to 1910, and even more aggressive state intervention in the labour market in the three northern provinces in the five decades after 1913. The resistance of Africans to this assault on their economic independence was perhaps as courageous (although less organised) than the 'struggle' for political independence during the last quarter of the 20th century. Although the extra economic pressures exerted on Africans were not necessarily bloody, they were nonetheless experienced as violent and disruptive.

The 1890s can be regarded as the period in which the governments of the Cape and Natal – now firmly in the hands of the white agricultural class – experimented with various 'anti-squatting' measures in an attempt to find effective instruments to break down the peasants' independence, and induce them to become wage-labourers. At the same time, a series of events made the African peasantry more vulnerable to this assault on its independence. Firstly, after the railway line from the Cape reached the Vaal River in the early 1890s, large quantities of cheap maize were imported from the American mid-West, which undermined the profits made by African peasants. Secondly, in the same decade, traders in predominantly African areas started to change the terms of trader–peasant relationships in such a way that a greater surplus could be extracted from peasants. The fact that members of the mercantile elite – who owned most of the trading centres – shifted their interest to the Rand's mines could have induced them to exert greater pressure on their peasant clients. Most traders became recruiting agents for the gold mines, and were empowered to pay lucrative cash advances to labourers to be repaid either by remittance or when the latter returned from the mines. This procedure amounted to the deliberate and systematic 'debt enslavement' of migrant workers (see Bundy 1988: 130–1; Wilson 1978: 113–26).

A third series of events that made African peasants more vulnerable to the 'legal assault' against them was a population increase that put pressure on the limited areas allocated to them, the severe drought in the early years of the 1890s, and the rinderpest epidemic of 1896–7.[26] As all these events impoverished the smaller peasants, more successful and moderately well-to-do peasants used the predicament of the smaller peasants to gain control of their land. This in turn stratified the peasantry more sharply (see Bundy 1988: 120, 241).

When, in 1890, Rhodes became prime minister of the Cape (he was in office until 1896) with the support of the Afrikaner Bond, he united all the interest groups in the colony – ie, the white farmers (both English- and Afrikaans-speaking), the mercantile elite, and even the missionaries – in an 'employers' offensive' against the African peasantry. Many of the Bond's supporters were commercialising Afrikaner farmers who were anxious to dispense with the quasi-feudal relationships on their farms. To enable the farmers to get rid of squatters on their farms, an 'anti-squatting' or Location Act was passed in 1892. Additional location acts were passed in 1899 and in 1909 in which loopholes in the first act were closed. These acts were so effective that the Cape, according to Bundy, 'already possessed and employed [by 1910] a formidable battery of anti-squatter laws, and had already done [by that time] much to undermine the position of the squatter-peasant in the Eastern Cape' (1988: 137).

In 1894 the Glen Grey Act – Rhodes's great contribution to the employers' 'onslaught' on the economic independence of Africans – became law.[27] This was a deliberate – and indirect – attempt to force Africans on 'tribal' as well as 'white' land to become a proletariat. Glen Grey was an overpopulated district south of the Kei River in the former Kaffraria. The act turned this into the first 'native reserve' in the Cape, and can be regarded as the prototype for the Land Act of 1913. While whites were prohibited from acquiring land or property in the Glen Grey area, some blacks would receive eight-acre allotments which they were forbidden to subdivide, sell, or add to. The land in possession of one holder would in most cases be insufficient to provide a living for the whole family, and so some males from each family would have to seek work. Every family would be compelled to pay a hut tax, and every male (whether landowner or landless) who did not sell his labour outside the area within a 12-month period would be compelled to pay a labour tax (see Bundy 1988: ch 4).

Apart from the 'employers' offensive' against the independence of Africans, the Cape government also launched, in the 20 years from 1890 to 1910, a massive programme of subsidies, grants, and other forms of assistance to promote the commercialisation of white agriculture. The Cape government used a sizeable part of the income it received from the gold mining industry to subsidise almost every aspect of white farming, but none of these subsidies was available to African farmers. While, until 1980, the predominantly African areas in the Cape could not have been regarded as underdeveloped appendages in a 'dual' model of South African economic development, the double-barrelled effect of the legal onslaught against the independence of Africans and massive state support for white agriculture degraded the predominantly African areas to such an extent that they became underdeveloped backwaters, which they have remained to this day.

Developments in Natal from 1893 (when 'responsible government' was granted) until 1910 were in many respects similar to those at the Cape. As was the case in the Cape, the influence of the mercantile elite was neutralised and the government used its power and increased indirect income from the gold mines to support the commercialisation of white (predominantly English-speaking) farmers. Many absentee or *rentier* landlords sold their estates at exceptionally low prices to commercial farmers. The area cultivated by white farmers increased from 85 000 in 1891 to 541 000 acres in 1909. As was the case in the Cape, African peasant agriculture deteriorated after 1890 because of severe droughts and the devastating effect of the rinderpest epidemic. But the peasantry in Natal was economically more independent that that in the Cape, while a small percentage of Africans was already proletarianised in 1890. Consequently, the struggle between white farmers and African peasants in Natal was more relentless than in the Cape. When commercial farmers attempted to transform the 'kaffir farming' on estates bought from *rentier* landlords into commercial farming with labour tenants, the African squatters resisted this vehemently (see Bundy 1988: 125–85).

The struggle between commercial farmers for supremacy over the African peasantry centred on two issues: African 'squatters', and African land purchases. In 1891 the Natal Native Code was streamlined and consolidated, giving the authoritarian Lieutenant-Governor Sir Theophilus Shepstone almost unlimited power over matters concerning Africans. White farmers (who now controlled the Natal executive council) continuously pressurised the governor into using his extraordinary power against 'squatting' and African land purchases. A great deal of the pressure to open Zululand to white settlement came from the prosperous sugar industry (see Richardson, in Beinart *et al* 1986: 129–36).[28]

In 1910 Africans in Natal had not been dispossessed and proletarianised to the same extent as those in the Eastern Cape. It was only following concerted action by the Union government in the five decades after the adoption of the Land Act – with its provisions against African land purchases, rent tenancy, and sharecropping – that predominantly African areas in KwaZulu-Natal also degenerated into an underdeveloped appendage of the economy (see Slater, in Marks and Attmore 1980: 162–4).

8.6 The Land Act of 1913 and the proletarianisation of Africans in the three northern provinces

One of the main problems that confronted the new government after Union was that Africans in the three northern provinces were still engaging in semi-feudal production activities. Consequently, not enough Africans were prepared to become wage labourers in the mines and on farms at the wages offered. Botha and Smuts's SAP and the Unionists who represented financial and mining interests largely agreed on the issue of a 'native policy'. As a result, in an effort to solve the labour problems of both the gold mining industry and maize farmers, the Union parliament passed the Native Land Act in 1913.[29] This act was based on an 'ideal formula' aimed at simultaneously satisfying the demands of both white farmers and the mining industry. It stipulated that Africans could no longer own land outside the 'native reserves', which made up 8,3 per cent of South African territory. The purpose was to allay the fears of white farmers – especially in the Transvaal and OFS – about the amount of land purchased by Africans, and to protect them against the competition of successful African peasants (see Bundy 1988: 213–14). The act also stipulated that white farmers could employ pass-carrying Africans outside the 'native reserves', while the CM was given the right to recruit migrant labourers in the reserves and in high commission areas (ie, the then Bechuanaland, Swaziland, and Basotholand).

The Land Act was extraordinarily successful in proletarianising the great majority of Africans and creating large reservoirs of cheap and docile African labour for white farmers and the mining industry. It was truly the rock on which not only the political alliance between a section of the Afrikaner farming elite and the British/English business elite was built, but also on which the ultra-exploitative system of racial capitalism was built and maintained until the 1970s.

In 1905, after an exhaustive investigation, the SANAC concluded that South Africa's mines, farms, and industries were short of about 300 000 workers. To explain the lack of African labour, the commission gave specific attention to the anthropological and/or cultural peculiarities of Africans. It assumed that, because of their traditional attitudes, their supposed undisciplined nature, and their attachment to extended families, Africans would always remain marginal participants in the economy. The commission concluded that Africans would stay in white areas for short periods only, and that their families would continue to be based in the 'native reserves'. SANAC also concluded that higher wages for Africans would not end the labour shortages, because they would merely shorten Africans' temporary sojourn in white areas. On the strength of these dubious assumptions and conclusions, SANAC recommended that Africans' access to land in tribal and white areas should be drastically curtailed, thus inducing adequate numbers to become wage labourers. Although the commission did not favour directly 'forcing Africans into wage labour, it was in favour of attempts "*to compel indirectly*" in order to create a voluntary supply' – in other words, to proletarianise (see Legassick, in Beinart and Dubow 1995: 48).

SANAC realised that, in order to secure the migrant labour required, a 'delicate equation' would have to be maintained between land and labour.[30] Lagden wanted the 'reserves' to be organised in such a way that they would support migrant labourers *before* and *after* their spell of migrant labour, thus bearing part of the cost of gold production. This is exactly what happened after 1913.[31] The Land Act authorised the CM to recruit migrant labour in the 'native areas' and in high commission areas,[32] and also entrenched the principle of migrant labour based on subsistence in the rural areas. The fact that the African 'reserves' and foreign southern African countries originally bore part of the cost of gold production made it possible for the gold industry to create an extremely successful system of plundering not only African men but also African land (Wolpe, in Beinart and Dubow 1995: ch 3; Cell 1982: ch 8).

The migrant labour system would not have been as 'successful' if it had not been complemented by the labour compound system. This system was originally developed for health and safety reasons (ie, to prevent theft) at the Kimberly diamond mines, but it soon became apparent that the system had other advantages for gold mining. It enabled the mines to impose a quasi-military discipline upon African workers, thus further restricting their freedom in the labour market. Throughout their working lives, migrant workers oscillated between their rural families and the all-male mining barracks, simultaneously hindering them from acquiring urban political and organisational (eg, trade union) skills, and undermining the social structure of rural society (Trapido 1971: 312).

Under the Land Act, more than a million African were abruptly proletarianised. At that stage, the African population was about 5 million. The structural domination of whites over blacks created by the Land Act is clearly demonstrated by the fact that the real wages of African workers in mining and agriculture did not increase between 1910 and 1972. The migrant labour system made it possible for the mining industry to justify average wages below the bare subsistence level on the grounds that jobs in white areas were merely supplementing Africans' basic economic life in the 'native reserves'.[33]

Table 8.1:	African wages as a percentage of white wages, 1911–1990	
	*Mining**	*Manufacturing and construction*
1911	8,6	–
1930/1	8,8	19,7
1940/1	8,3	18,6
1944/5	8,6	24,0
1950/1	7,4	21,5
1955/6	7,0	18,5
1960/1	5,9	18,6
1970/1	4,8	16,7
1975/6	12,0	20,7
1980	17,0	21,0
1985	19,0	22,0
1990	–	29,5

* Cash wages only.

Sources: Lipton 1986: tables 10.11 and 12; Fallon 1992: table 7; css 1995; Davies 1979: table 30; Crush et al 1991: table 4.2.

The Land Act also stipulated that Africans could not be involved in share-cropping, tenant farming, and squatter farming in 'white' South Africa. Although it took decades to fully implement this provision, it was an enormous setback for the economic independence of many Africans. When the Land Act was promulgated, share-cropping and 'kaffir farming' were still the dominant relationships of production in many farms in the 'maize triangle'. Farmers who were becoming commercialised wanted wage labour or labour tenants, and the only way of obtaining such labour was via the *active* intervention of the state.[34] The act also laid down that all African tenants (and not only contracted wage earners) in the OFS, although not elsewhere, would be defined as servants under the Masters and Servants Act, and therefore guilty of a criminal offence if they broke their contracts.[35]

The Land Act further institutionalised the close relationship between collaborating tribal chiefs and white employer groups. With the support of the NAD, the CM's administrators built up personal relationships with chiefs of specific tribes, who benefited from a lucrative system of patronage (see section 8.3).[36]

The Land Act laid down the terms in which the rural struggle between white landowners and African tenants would ultimately be resolved in favour of the white farmers. It did not immediately transform the countryside. It not only proletarianised African tenants, but also large numbers of *bywoners*, and small and vulnerable white farmers. Many poorer farmers on the highveld could not afford wage labour, and could not buy the implements needed for maize farming. Many of them continued illegal sharecropping agreements with African tenants. In the Transvaal, parts of the OFS, and Natal, African tenants continued to live on land owned by large companies.[37] The Land Act enabled farmers on the highveld to destroy sharecropping and to change rent tenants into labour tenants, but it took the best part of 50 years before more or less all Africans on white farms were forced into the wage-earning proletariat (see Morris 1976: 334–8).

In assessing the struggle between white landowners and the African tenantry in the 50 years after the promulgation of the Land Act, the support given by the Union government to maize farmers should not be underestimated. Apart from the 'legal assault' on the independence of the tenantry, the government tried to strengthen the economic position of maize farmers by adopting a series of 'farm' acts and large-scale subsidies, mainly financed with tax revenue from the gold mines. According to Legassick, the Union parliament enacted 87 bills relating to land between 1910 and 1935. The railway system was also developed in a way that benefited agriculture at the expense of the rest of the economy.

The Land Bank was established in 1912 to provide white farmers with both short-term loans for crop harvesting and long-term loans for capital improvements. This policy culminated in the Marketing Act of 1937, whereby the marketing of the bulk of South Africa's farm produce were brought under the control of a series of producer-friendly control boards.[38]

By depriving African farmers of much of their land, and ending sharecropping and tenant farming on white-owned land (if not immediately, then in due course), an important agricultural and entrepreneurial tradition and store of indigenous farming knowledge were destroyed.[39] It is difficult to determine the value of this tradition, but it was probably considerable, because it was well adapted to South Africa's weather, land, and labour peculiarities. If this African agricultural tradition had not been destroyed, but given more or less the same government support (both financially and technologically) given to white farmers, South Africa's agricultural and economic history could have been radically different.[40]

The South African Native National Congress (later the ANC) was founded in 1912 to protest against the disenfranchisement of Africans by the Act of Westminster. Soon after its foundation the ANC found that the passage of the Native Land Act necessitated a national protest campaign. Sol Plaatje wrote that the act made the South African black 'not actually a slave, but a pariah in the land of his birth'. During World War 1 the ANC refrained from criticising the act. In 1916, in testimony before the Beaumont commission on the act, the leader of the Congress in the Transvaal, S M Makgaltha, described it as 'fraught with the most momentous issues, as it infringes upon the common rights of the people [which were] recognised as resting upon the elementary principle of justice and humanity which are the heritage of a free people' (quoted in Rich 1996: 18). Thus the Land Act served to radicalise African politics (see section 8.10).

8.7 The proletarianisation of Afrikaners, and its political and economic ramifications (±1870–1924)

As long as land for occupation by white farmers remained scarce – as was the case in the second half of the 17th century – whites imported by the VOC as *knechts* remained wage-labourers and were used by the company and white landowners in tandem with chattel slaves. As soon as Willem Adriaan van der Stel made loan farms easily accessible, almost all the *knechts* opted to become pastoral farmers, or *Trekboere*. With land available in abundance – or relatively easily conquered – during the 18th and 19th centuries, all the members of the white master class remained landowners and used their political and military power to turn indigenous people into an unfree and exploitable labour force. This led to the extraordinary state of affairs that for almost 200 years – from ±1700 to ±1880 – a white wage-earning class did not exist. Such a class only emerged at the end of the 19th century when almost all the land suitable for farming had been occupied, and when the modernisation brought about by the mineral revolution had made it impossible for those white farmers (predominantly Afrikaners) living on small uneconomical units to persist with subsistence farming (see section 5.2).

In the mid-20th century Afrikaner populists claimed that, until the end of the 19th century, Afrikaner society had been egalitarian, without hierarchies or social strata. This is a myth. A Cape gentry class emerged during the 17th and 18th centuries in the wine-producing districts of the Cape whose members were far wealthier than the *Trekboere*. Both the *Trekboere* and the Voortrekkers used commandos as instruments of social stratification. Although the abundance of land until the end of the 19th century allowed almost all Afrikaners to become landowners, some smaller landowners were existing precariously as subsistence farmers on much-divided farms (according to the precepts of Roman Dutch law) or on farms that were unworkable. One of the most inhibiting factors for successful white farming was the scarcity of cheap black labour. This factor also inhibited larger landowners, but affected smaller landowners far more.

A white wage-earning class only emerged from 1860 onwards. The indigenous pool of white wage earners was considerably swollen by policies favouring the import of unskilled labourers from Europe. There were two waves of immigrant labourers: from 1857 to 1863, and from 1873 to 1883.[41] At the same time, particularly after the severe droughts of the 1860s and 1870s, many Afrikaners moved off the land.[42]

An important factor that impoverished many Afrikaners from 1880 onwards was the dubious role played by mercantile intermediaries, not only in the Cape and Natal but also in the two Boer republics. White agriculture in South Africa developed as a by-product of European mercantile activity.[43] The interaction over a period of more than 200 years between mercantile intermediaries and the tradition-bound white farmers was complex. If anything, the mercantile intermediaries did not promote modernisation, but tended to maintain agriculture in its semi-feudal and dependent state of affairs – at least until the end of the 19th century. Due to the chronic lack of both working and investment capital, farmers mostly bought on credit, and paid in product. The farmers' mercantile 'enslavement' not only hampered the transition to commercial agriculture, but also helped to bankrupt smaller farmers on uneconomical units. From 1870 onwards the state became an important player in agricultural transformation throughout South Africa. The combined effect of modernisation and state involvement consolidated the domination of larger, wealthier landowners to the detriment of smaller ones. Consequently, many smaller farmers were reduced to the status of *bywoners* on the farms of wealthy landlords (see Trapido 1978: 26–34; Legassick, in Harris 1975: 247–9).

In Afrikaner folklore the emergence of the so-called 'poor white problem' is often ascribed to colonial exploitation and other factors beyond Afrikaners' control. Consequently, the intense struggle that developed between wealthier farmers (supported by the state) and the more numerous smaller landowners during the process of modernisation and commercialisation is normally not acknowledged in Afrikaner historiography. But in reality a relentless struggle to gain control over land and labour and so produce successfully for the market took place between larger and smaller Afrikaner landowners.[44]

From 1880 onwards the rapid capitalisation and accumulation of some Afrikaner farmers contributed directly to' the proletarianisation of other Afrikaners. Because of the concentration of land in the hands of larger landlords and land companies, and the easy access of African squatters to this land, smaller landowners were placed in an awkward position, facing a severe shortage of both land and labour. From 1880 to 1910 many smaller farmers went bankrupt, but remained in the agricultural sector as *bywoners*. It was only after the passage of the Land Act and the acceleration of commercialisation that most *bywoners* were forced to urbanise. Paradoxically, the continuing process in which larger landowners used dubious methods to swallow up smaller landowners reached its peak in the 20 years after the adoption of the Land Act (see Trapido, in Marks and Attmore 1980: 357; Bundy, in Beinart *et al* 1986: 108).

Although the 'poor white problem' among Afrikaners had already assumed serious dimensions in the 1870s and 1880s, it was only publicly recognised by the broader Afrikaner community from the 1890s onwards. It was only then that a major shift in ruling class perceptions of the nature of poverty made it possible to regard the poor whites' unfortunate fate with a measure of sympathy. It was only when large numbers of Afrikaners were impoverished by the Anglo–Boer War that the poverty and dislocation of 'poor white' Afrikaners became an ideological issue used for political mobilisation. During the period when the predicament of poor whites was neglected, ethnic identities were blurred. Poor whites were employed alongside black workers, and intermarriages and sexual liaisons between white and black rural and urban poor were quite common.

The proletarianisation of a large portion of the Afrikaner community in the late 19th and early 20th century was closely linked to a parallel proletarianisation of coloured people. During the 18th and 19th centuries, the social and economic history and vicissitudes of Afrikaners and coloureds were intertwined. There was no clear line between them, and what line there was shifted with changing circumstances. In many cases the determining factor was not colour, but the ownership of land. Brown Afrikaner landowners were gradually incorporated into white Afrikaner circles, while many whites who lost their farms were incorporated into the ranks of coloured people. When many small and subsistence farmers went bankrupt and were proletarianised at the end of the 19th century, their coloured workers were also uprooted and driven to urban areas as a hopelessly impoverished proletariat. By the late 19th century a large portion of the coloured proletariat in cities such as Cape Town and Port Elizabeth was regarded as 'a dangerous class'. Part of the rising Afrikaner consciousness about the 'poor white' Afrikaners at the beginning of the century and steps taken towards Afrikaner upliftment were stimulated by a desire to protect them against impoverished coloureds. Unfortunately, no steps were taken to similarly uplift 'poor brown' people who were already exhibiting the syndrome of chronic community poverty (Marks and Trapido 1987: 26–31; see also section 10.3.1).

While coloured people's rights deteriorated dramatically *vis-à-vis* those of whites in the early decades of the 20th century, when the 'upliftment' of the Afrikaner proletariat became a priority, coloureds were nevertheless in a relatively advantageous position in relation to Africans. In 1930 they were exempted from influx control, pass laws, and legislation governing urban segregation. But after the NP had taken office in 1948 and again emphasised the need for Afrikaner upliftment and 'purity', the position of the coloureds was again degraded through a rigid definition of coloured ethnicity and by making numerous apartheid laws applicable to them.

The proletarianisation of Afrikaners was strongly stimulated by the rinderpest of 1896–7 and by the social dislocation and destruction of property during the Anglo–Boer War. After the war, many landless and impoverished Afrikaners had no choice but to move to towns and cities where they found it extremely difficult to find jobs.[45] The war also exacerbated the hostile relationships between larger Afrikaner landlords and Afrikaner *bywoners*. After the war many *bywoners* who had become *hensoppers* ('hands-uppers') and *joiners* ('sell-outs') during the war were rejected by other Afrikaners, and this aggravated their impoverishment (see Grundlingh, in Cameron 1986: 217). [46]

After the war the Transvaal 'notables' tried to change from pastoral to arable production. This also aggravated the already deteriorating relationships between Afrikaner landlords and their *bywoner* tenants. Many of the modernising landlords preferred African tenants to *bywoners*, because they were more likely to provide wage labour. The arrival of Lord Selborne as high commissioner for South Africa in 1905 improved the conditions of Afrikaner landlords quite dramatically (see section 7.4). The commercialisation of the larger estates in the three northern provinces and the consequent proletarianisation of white and African tenants received its final push with the passage of the Land Act.[47]

It is difficult to determine the severity of white poverty in the first third of the century, and to meaningfully compare Afrikaner and African poverty. The methods of measurement were unreliable, and the value judgements involved were laced with the racial prejudices of the time.[48] In 1932 the white population was 1,8 million, of which more or less 1 million were Afrikaners. About a third of Afrikaners was classified by the Carnegie commission as 'very poor' at the beginning of the 1930s, and another third classified as poor. Those who migrated to the cities lacked the necessary skills to compete with black labour. They also found it very difficult to adapt to the unfriendly, English-dominated cities (Le Roux 1984: 2; Grosskopf 1932: part 1, Joint findings, para 9).

Although, in 1932, white poverty was not nearly as serious as African and coloured poverty, the Carnegie report placed 'white poverty' in the limelight and dramatised it in a way that gave the Purified NP the opportunity to stir up Afrikaner nationalism into an aggressive movement. However, the commission never intended its findings to be used for party-political or ethnic mobilisation (see section 9.1). It did not blame poverty among Afrikaners exclusively on environmental and/or systemic factors, but also on characteristics such as a lack of industry (see Grosskopf 1932: part 1, Joint findings, paras 12–64).

Poverty among Afrikaners became critical immediately after the Anglo–Boer War. At a time when Afrikaner political and religious organisations became highly conscious of the predicament of poor whites, the gold mines were unwilling to employ landless Afrikaners despite the fact that the mines were – by their owners' own reckoning – suffering from an acute shortage of unskilled labour. The reasons offered by the mines was that these Afrikaners, having themselves employed subservient African labour, were unsuitable to arduous underground work (see Trapido 1978: 50–4).

According to Merle Lipton, the colour bar – the prime instrument of exclusion in the workplace – emerged in the course of the bitter struggle for jobs in the mining industry and state sectors. The discrimination against Afrikaners by mining companies and British mineworkers contributed significantly to Afrikaner poverty.[49] To solve this 'awkward' problem, the colour bars introduced by the ZAR government in the 1890s were reintroduced after the Anglo–Boer war. During and after the miners' strike of 1907, Afrikaners were employed for the first time in skilled and semi-skilled positions previously occupied by British mineworkers. The percentage of South African-born whites (predominantly Afrikaners) employed on the mines increased from 17,5 per cent before the strike of 1907 to 24,6 per cent during the strike – an increase of about 1 250 men (see Yudelman 1983: 75).

The Botha/Smuts government which assumed office in 1910 faced the difficult task of creating conditions conducive to accumulation (for mining and agriculture) on the one hand, and having to pamper the white electorate (especially mineworkers and poor Afrikaners) to prevent them from endangering the legitimacy of the new state on the other. By intensifying repressive measures in respect of African labour, the aim of accumulation was promoted, but insofar as employers chose to employ cheap African rather than poor white workers, the aim of legitimising the white-controlled state was put at risk. In 1911 two important segregationist laws were passed which created a pattern that would last for decades: the one was a *repressive* measure aimed at making African labour cheaper and more docile, and the other a *discriminatory* measure aimed at protecting white miners against competition from Africans. The Native Labour Regulation Act (1911) extended the criminal sanction against contract-breaking contained in masters and servants acts[50] to African mineworkers, and prohibited them from striking. The Mines and Works Act (1911) protected white mineworkers in various ways, *inter alia* by reserving certain jobs on the mines for whites only.[51]

Another factor that influenced the position of poor Afrikaners on the mines was the tense relationship that had existed since the strike of 1907 between the gold companies and British artisans. In a deliberate attempt to move towards Africanisation, mining employers changed the structure of the white workforce by fragmenting jobs. This was done from 1907 onwards through increased mechanisation and electrification, and by creating semi-skilled supervising jobs for Afrikaners rather than employing British artisans. These changes helped to trigger off the strikes of 1913 and 1914, which were harshly suppressed by the Botha/Smuts government. Davenport and Saunders claim correctly that 'much was done during the Botha/Smuts era, before and after Union, to lay down a legislative colour bar; but it became increasingly evident that the manner in which this was done was more to the advantage of white management [ie, mine owners and the notable farmers] than of white labour' (2000: 634).[52]

Thus the African proletariat was deliberately created by a series of repressive labour measures, institutionalised on behalf of white employers. These repressive measures included masters and servants laws, pass laws, measures that deprived Africans of their access to land and farming opportunities, and measures that denied them political bargaining power. The Afrikaner proletariat, however, was not deliberately created but emerged largely inadvertently, mainly because of modernisation and the Anglo–Boer

War. While repressive labour measures were institutionalised on behalf of white employers and the mainly English-speaking capitalist class, discriminatory measures were institutionalised mainly on behalf of the Afrikaner proletariat or working class. While the repressive measures saved costs for capital, the discriminatory measures increased them.

Consequently, a protracted struggle developed between the English-speaking capitalist class, emerging Afrikaner capitalists, and large Afrikaner landlords with a vested interest in cost-saving repressive measures on the one hand, and the mainly Afrikaner petit bourgeoisie and Afrikaner employee class with a vested interest in discriminatory measures on the other. Those who favoured repressive measures mainly supported the SAP and UP, while those who favoured discriminatory measures mainly supported the NP and Labour Party (LP).

It is not surprising that the most intensive attempts to introduce repressive segregationist measures were made (on behalf of the mainly English-speaking electorate) by the SAP government of Botha and Smuts, while the segregationist measures introduced by the Pact government of Hertzog (1924–33) were not primarily repressive (perhaps because the necessary repressive measures had already been adopted), but rather discriminatory ones aimed at protecting white, predominantly Afrikaner, employees (see Davenport 1991: 233–6, 518–19).[53]

Gold mines' profits declined steadily from 1910 to 1920. The rate of inflation outstripped the increase in the sterling price of gold by more than 25 per cent.[54] At the same time the wage ratio between white and black mineworkers increased from 11.7:1 in 1911 to 15:1 in 1920.[55] The decline in the real wages of African mineworkers led to an ANC-organised strike by Africans in 1920 that was again suppressed harshly by the Smuts government. When, in 1920, the price of gold declined sharply, it forced the CM, in 1921, to announce plans to employ fewer whites and more Africans, *inter alia* by abandoning the *status quo* agreement of 1918 and by eliminating the colour bar for semi-skilled work.[56] The chamber's plans threatened the jobs of 15 000 white workers.

This triggered off the 1922 strike by white mineworkers (mainly poor white Afrikaners), under a 'Red flag' and with the slogan: 'Workers of the world unite and fight for a white South Africa'. Smuts used the South African air force to suppress the strike. After the strike, it was agreed that the ratio between African mineworkers and white supervisors would be maintained at 9:1. The harsh suppression of the strike (resulting in more than 200 casualties) featured prominently in the consciousness of the Afrikaner working class. It also led to a class-based white 'pact' between the mainly English-speaking LP (led by Col F P H Cresswell) and Hertzog's NP. By mobilising the mineworkers' anti-capitalist and the Afrikaners' anti-imperialistic sentiments, the Pact won the election of 1924 (see Lipton 1986: 114; see also section 8.8).

The most important effect of the Rand revolt of 1922 was that it demonstrated to the government that it could only gain legitimacy (within the parameters of white supremacy) if the position of white workers on the gold mines (now predominantly Afrikaners) could be secured.[57] The Smuts government also realised that the state had to intervene even more actively in South Africa's industrial order to protect white workers against black competition.

To accomplish this, it passed the Industrial Conciliation Act early in 1924 – ie, before the Pact government took over. This act was supported by a broad spectrum of political interests, the white bureaucracy, and a united front of mining, industrial, and agricultural employers and white trade unions. Its most important stipulation was that 'pass-carrying' black men could not become members of trade unions, and were thus excluded from the official labour relations system. This was a *repressive* measure with far-reaching implications for the bargaining power of Africans, and also a *discriminatory* measure, because Africans could no longer participate in wage negotiations alongside white workers.[58]

The strike of 1922 therefore turned into a victory for white (and especially Afrikaner) mineworkers insofar as it led to the entrenchment of the colour bar and the exclusion of Africans from trade union rights. But, as was the case after the strikes of 1907 and 1914, the bargaining power of white mineworkers was considerably reduced. As a result, their wages fell by 18 per cent, and remained at this lower level until the 1940s.[59] Although white mineworkers had won the battle for statutory protection against African competition, they had to pay a price in terms of their bargaining power as employees.[60] For African mineworkers the events of 1922 and 1924 (the latter when the Industrial Concilliation Act was passed) were disastrous.

When the Union was established, the Botha/Smuts government accepted the ideology of liberal capitalism propagated so strongly by British capital. However, in the decade after World War 1, it adopted an increasingly interventionist approach to the structural imbalances in the economy and the crisis of legitimacy caused by disgruntled and unemployed white workers and petit bourgeois Afrikaners. An important result of this interventionist approach was the establishment, in 1922, of the Electricity Supply Commission (ESCOM) as the first state corporation (see section 9.6).[61]

8.8 The Pact government and the 'civilised labour policy' on behalf of poor white Afrikaners (1924–33)

When the Pact government of Hertzog and Cresswell assumed power, the process of state formation was – for all practical purposes – completed. The government, based on an electoral union formed by the NP and LP after the 1922 strike, won the June 1924 election after a bitter campaign that strongly emphasised the need for greater state protection of white workers, and particularly unemployed and poor Afrikaners. The Pact victory can therefore be regarded as a victory for the consolidation of white supremacy. Those marginalised white communities – primarily white workers, small businessmen, and the petit bourgeois – now controlled the government. Given that Hertzog represented white interests to a far greater extent than Smuts did, the Pact strengthened the legitimacy of the white-oriented state founded in 1910.[62]

Given its strong hostility to British imperialism and foreign capitalism, it was feared in 1924 that the symbiosis between state and capital might be endangered. During the election campaign the Pact called for far-reaching changes in economic policies in order to empower impoverished whites. The Pact was relentlessly critical of 'Hoggenheimer' – the caricature of a foreign Jewish capitalist greedily exploiting South Africans. It contrasted the economic problems of many white South Africans with the enormous profits of the gold industry (dividends in 1923 and 1924 were almost as high as the record amounts paid in 1909; see Clark 1994: 60–2).[63] However, the Pact's hostile rhetoric against the gold mines during the election campaign did not translate into hostile policies. Its apparent *volte-face* must be judged against events during the two years before its election victory. The defeat of the miners in 1922 and the adoption of the Industrial Conciliation Act by the Smuts government in 1924 co-opted the previously militant white labour force into the white-controlled consensual order. Consequently, it was no longer necessary for the Pact to be concerned about the legitimisation imperative, and it was therefore free to devote more attention to the accumulation imperative (see Yudelman 1983: 215–23).

In its attempt to evolve a new approach, the Pact was hampered by the English- and business-oriented bureaucracy inherited from the SAP government. As regards its 'native policy', it could hardly ignore the 'expert' advice of senior officials in the NAD. While the Pact government perpetuated almost all the segregationist measures adopted during the Botha/Smuts years, it has subsequently become notorious for four policy initiatives: the 'civilised labour policy', the Wage Act of 1925, the Mines and Works Amendment Act of 1926, and the Native Administrative Act of 1927.

The Mines and Works Amendment Act introduced a 'colour bar' on the mines in favour of white and coloured workers. This measure was not entirely new. A 'colour bar' had in fact been introduced in the Mines and Works Act of 1911, but in 1923 the Supreme Court had declared this to be *ultra vires*. The amendment act of 1926 restored the 'colour bar' – this time simply by reserving certificates of competency in skilled trades in the mining industry for whites and coloureds, thus excluding Africans and Indians. It is estimated that between 1924 and 1933 the Hertzog government transferred about 8 000 jobs from blacks to whites. While the Pact government was less concerned about the supply and cost of African labour than its predecessors, it was more concerned about white *unemployment*. Consequently, the segregationist measures it enacted were mainly *discriminatory*, aimed at protecting whites (predominantly Afrikaners) against competition from blacks in the labour market.

The Wage Act of 1925 closed certain loopholes in the Industrial Conciliation Act's protection of white employment. It empowered the minister to appoint a wage board, and to prescribe the same minimum wages for white and black labour. The purpose of this was to eliminate the economic incentive to employ black miners.[64] The Pact government's main initiatives to solve the white unemployment problem were the 'civilised labour policy', and the promotion of industrial development. To create jobs for white unemployed was very difficult. In effect, the policies involved paying 'civilised labour' (mainly whites and some coloureds) a 'civilised rate' (ie, higher wages) for doing the same jobs as blacks. The government applied this policy in the public service and on the South African Railways,[65] and also put pressure on industries protected by tariffs to do so. In its attempt to stimulate employment (for whites), 'civilised wages' were pegged at relatively low levels. Thus minimum wage rates for whites in 1933 were 23 per cent lower than they had been in 1920.[66]

The Native Administration Act of 1927 significantly advanced the NAD's influence and power, and consolidated its 'colonial' policy of indirect rule in the 'native reserves'. It enhanced the authority of co-opted tribal chiefs, and revived African customary law as a means of maintaining state authority over the disintegrating African society in the reserves, and controlling the rate of African proletarianisation. This act also advanced the NAD's efforts to distribute cheap African labour to various economic sectors (see Rich 1996: 10, 35).

In the mid-1920s the Industrial and Commercial Workers' Union (ICU) – a union of African and coloured workers which organised the strike of black workers in 1920 – transformed itself into a mass movement, voiced a broad range of popular grievances, and established branches throughout the Union.

By 1927, its peak year, the ICU had some 100 000 members and had become quite radical in its demands. But after the adoption of the Native Administration Act, which also contained strictures against black trade unions, the movement declined rapidly. Apart from the mineworkers' strike in 1946, in which 70 000 black workers participated, black trade unionism was only rekindled in the 1970s (see Murray, in Cameron 1986: 253).

Contrary to expectations, the Pact government did not tax the mines more heavily. Hertzog – concerned about the mines' capacity to employ poor white Afrikaners – went out of his way to promote the industry. However, the renewed entrenchment of the 'colour bar' in 1926 contributed to significant disinvestment of foreign shareholders in the gold mines from 1924 to 1932 (see Lipton 1986: 114). Remarkably, the earnings gap between white and black wages declined from 15:1 in 1921 to 11.3:1 in 1931 (see Yudelman 1983: 228).

The main question in respect of the Pact government is whether, and to what extent, it initiated industrialisation. According to Tom Kemp, it 'did not have a consciously worked-out policy of industrialisation, nor would it be correct to see it as a representative of industrial capital as opposed to mining capital'. The government's comprehensive tariff protection was not primarily intended to stimulate industrialisation, but to assist those industries using mainly white labour.[67] Its inward industrialisation policy was clearly meant to stimulate white employment, and numerous government contracts were granted with the same objective in mind (1993: 182).[68]

Although many historians regard the Pact victory of 1924 as a crucial turning point in South Africa's racial history, the Pact government in fact perpetuated the Smuts/Botha government's racial policy. However, during the period of the Pact government, the 'whiteness' of white supremacy and the 'racial' character of racial capitalism were undeniably strengthened – if not the actual policies, then at least on the rhetorical or ideological level. What is perhaps more important is that the power constellation on which the Union of South Africa was based was not endangered when the capitalist-oriented SAP of Botha and Smuts was replaced in 1924 by the Afrikaner petit bourgeois and white worker parties of Hertzog and Cresswell.[69] At the same time, the policies of the Pact government strikingly illustrate the widepread agreement among whites of the importance of perpetuating segregationism and exploiting blacks on behalf of the profitability of British/English capital and the creation of jobs for poor Afrikaners. Although many poor whites were employed 'artificially' at the cost of blacks, the Pact strategy did not succeed in solving the poor white unemployment problem. This only happened after the sharp increase in the price of gold in 1932, the enlistment of Afrikaners in the South African forces that participated in World War 2, and the creation of many additional jobs in the industrial sector during the war.

8.9 The English establishment regains political hegemony in 1933, and maintains it until 1948

The years 1933 and 1934 were watershed years in South Africa's political and economic history; in that period its political and economic structures and power relations were significantly restructured. The context of power created by the events of 1933–4 and its ramifications in white – and especially Afrikaner – society was exceptionally detrimental to Africans. It not only prolonged their subjugation, but also intensified it.

In the early 1930s the great world depression that followed the collapse of the New York stock exchange in October 1929 made itself felt in South Africa, presenting the Pact government with a serious and seemingly insoluble economic crisis. GDP declined by 6 per cent a year between 1929 and 1932, and unemployment rocketed in all sectors of the economy. In September 1931 Britain suspended the gold standard and depreciated the pound sterling by more than 40 per cent. The South African government made the costly mistake of not following suit.[70] Amid political turmoil – which threatened the leaderships of both Hertzog and Smuts of the NP and SAP respectively – South Africa left the gold standard in December 1932, and devalued its currency, thus boosting the income of the gold mines by some 45 per cent.

Early in 1933 the Pact government announced proposals to tax most of this bonanza and use the income to support other sectors in the economy – especially the farming sector – in an attempt to solve the serious unemployment problem among Afrikaners. Under pressure from the CM (which was distressed by the prospect of higher taxes) Smuts entered into a coalition with Hertzog in March 1933. During the preceding negotiations, both Hertzog and Smuts had hidden agendas. Hertzog's was to gain Smuts's support for removing Africans from the common voters' role in the Cape. This was in fact accomplished in 1936, with Smuts's support. Smuts's hidden agenda was to stop Hertzog from taxing the gold bonanza. The fact that Smuts was prepared to engage in 'ugly horse-trading' and allow the abolition of the African franchise in the Cape in exchange for lower taxes on gold revenues demonstrates the power of the mining industry. It also demonstrates that Smuts (and most members of the old English-oriented SAP) were prepared to sacrifice the entrenched political rights of Africans on the altar of economic and political expediency (see O'Meara 1983: 43–6).[71] Under the so-called '50/50 arrangement', Hertzog agreed to tax only 50 per cent of the bonanza. This arrangement was extremely advantageous to the state as well as the private sector.[72] A mining house historian later acknowledged that, after 1993, it had made 'profits beyond the dreams of avarice' (Potts, quoted in Yudelman 1983: 252).

When, in 1934, Hertzog and Smuts decided on *Samesmelting* (Fusion), and launched the United Party, a section of Afrikaners led by D F Malan decided to break away and establish the *Gesuiwerde* (Purified) NP. These two political events had a profound effect on South Africa's economic and political history. The first (ie, the alignment of Hertzog and Smuts) heightened the symbiosis between state and capital, and created conditions that were highly conducive to accumulation and growth. The second (ie, the formation of the Purified movement) presaged the upsurge of a radical version of Afrikaner nationalism that led to the victory of Malan's NP in the election of 1948, and the subsequent intensification of the repression of and discrimination against blacks. Neither the heightened symbiosis between state and capital nor the upsurge of Afrikaner nationalism was good news for Africans, already beleaguered by segregation and a repressive labour system. Both trends subjected them to new types of deprivation and plunder (see Murray in Cameron 1986: 256–60; see also section 9.1).

The new relationship of co-operation between state and capital was a white and business alliance *par excellence*. Its explicit purpose was to promote the social (or developmental) interests of white Afrikaners (in their capacity as farmers and workers), and the *economic* (or accumulative) interests of mainly English-speaking whites. In the period until 1948 the symbiosis between the state and capital solved the poor white problem, and launched an industrial revolution.[73] When, in 1939, Smuts succeeded Hertzog as prime minister on the issue of participation in World War 2, state policy was even more strongly oriented towards business and the English establishment.

The 1932 increase in the effective price of gold and the regaining of political hegemony by the English establishment laid the basis for a period of unprecedented growth that lasted for 40 years. In this period the state contributed significantly to the development of manufacturing by creating the iron and steel industry. High duties on imported machinery also encouraged and in effect subsidised local industry. The most remarkable feature of the gold boom of the 1930s was that it did not result in any meaningful increases in the wages of either the white or black labour force.

In 1936, amid riches 'beyond the dreams of avarice', the real wages of both white and African mineworkers were lower than they had been in 1911, and remained at that low level until 1946 (see Yudelman 1983: 253–7). The huge profits of the gold industry and the sharp increase in government income – used to 'create' the industrial take-off – were therefore attained at the cost of both white and black labour. How could the wages of white and black workers increase only slightly from 1932 until 1940, while the economy grew at a rate of almost 6 per cent a year? As regards white labour, the Industrial Conciliation Act of 1924 had 'co-opted' and 'depoliticised' it so effectively that it had lost not only its militancy but also its industrial bargaining power. At the same time, it was as important for the Fusion government (1934–9) as it had been for the Pact to look after the interests of unskilled urbanised poor white Afrikaners.[74]

The heightened symbiosis between state and capital under the Fusion government was a huge setback for Africans. Both the state and capital regarded themselves as strong enough to proceed with the final consolidation of segregationist legislation. While Hertzog was in a position to extend discriminatory legislation on behalf of poor and unemployed Afrikaners, Smuts and the corporate sector were responsible for several measures intensifying labour repression in what Trapido identifies as the third phase of black labour repression (1971: 313). The relative cheapness of African labour was sustained by the persistence of such extra-economic coercion as the prohibition of African strikes, the control of labour through the NAD and collaborating chiefs, the modified pass laws, the migrant system, and so on, as well as the perpetuation of institutions that 'separated' white and black workers (see Legassick, in Harris 1975: 257).[75]

What made the structural exploitation of migrant labour by the gold mining industry so much more problematic was that the gold mines continued to pay low wages (in real terms) despite the deterioration of economic conditions in the 'native reserves'. The gold mines justified the low wages paid to migrant workers with the argument that part of the 'reproduction' cost of labour was carried by the reserves. After exhaustive investigations, the Landsdowne commission concluded in 1943 that the idea that the reserves could supply a part of the migrant workers with subsistence was a 'myth' because of the growing poverty in the reserves. It concluded that the CM had an obligation to pay migrant workers a 'living wage'. The chamber rejected this recommendation, provoking protests from African workers organised by the African Mine Workers Union (AMWU). This culminated in the 1946 African miners' strike, which was violently supressed. The chamber also vigorously resisted any move from a migratory to a stable urban labour force, arguing that such a 'disastrous' policy would force the closure of the mines.[76]

Proponents of liberal capitalism often claim that the low level of African wages was a precondition for the mineral and agricultural revolutions in the early 20th century. Trapido makes the important point that 'even if we accept the imperative of the Chamber of Mines cost structure... *it would have been possible to raise African wages significantly some time between 1935 and 1950*. The raising of wages might in its turn have suggested that the extreme control of labour was not essential. In practice, the opposite occurred' (see Trapido 1971: 315; author's emphasis).[77]

Segregationist legislation reached a high water mark with the Representation of Blacks (Native) Act (1936), the Development Trust and Land Act (1936), and the Black (Native) Laws Amendment Act (1937). The first removed African voters in the Cape from the common roll, and placed them on a separate roll.[78] The second authorised the government to expand the 'native reserves' to a total of 13,6 per cent of South African land. The third prohibited Africans from acquiring land in urban areas, thus extending the Stallardist legislation of 1923, and taking a more aggressively Stallardist line in its quest to control the influx of Africans to urban areas.[79] The inability of the Smuts government to control African urbanisation in the 1940s played an important role in the NP's election victory in 1948.

Chapter 4 of the Land Act (1936) was designed to transform the remnants of labour tenancy on white farms into wage labour, in order to finally end African squatting and give farmers greater control over African labourers. However, it was not implemented immediately; fearing black unrest, the Smuts government dragged its heels on this issue during the war years, to the dismay of white (predominantly Afrikaner) farmers. As a result, Africans continued to migrate from white farms to urban areas, thus intensifying the labour problems of white farmers. However, despite the scarcity of labour, white farmers were not prepared to increase African wages. In 1947 the average annual wage of African males on white farms, including the cash value of food, was a mere R64 (see Posel 1991: 30).[80]

World War 2 established conditions for a full-scale industrial boom to continue the gold boom of the 1930s.[81] A war industry was established to produce a considerable proportion of the Union Defence Force's requirements. The sharp decline in imports from Britain and other countries strongly stimulated local industries. The Industrial Development Corporation (IDC) was established in 1940 to promote and help finance new industries, and build closer relations between government and privately owned industry. Mass production in wartime factories created new 'semi-skilled' positions which fell outside the racially defined legal classification of 'skilled' and 'unskilled' labour previously used in South Africa. If racial stratification was to be continued, these new jobs would have to be classified as either exclusively for blacks or for whites, with serious ramifications for production costs.[82] Fearing repercussions from white voters and white businessmen, Smuts was not prepared to address the *legal* definition of semi-skilled work in manufacturing industries. To alleviate the serious shortages of skilled and semi-skilled labour, Smuts allowed the colour bar to be diluted, masked under emergency war measures; unqualified black workers were allowed to do skilled work under supervision in the engineering and other industries. In the process, Smuts merely postponed addressing a sensitive labour issue to the post-war period, when white soldiers would return to take up many of the skilled and semi-skilled jobs occupied by blacks during the war years. In all the industries in which African workers were drawn into semi-skilled operators' positions, at wage rates considerably lower than those of skilled whites, labour costs fell markedly.[83] But as manufacturing production expanded rapidly throughout the country – the value of manufacturing output jumped by 53 per cent between 1939 and 1945 – it became apparent that old labour policies, based on strict race and skills differentiation, would not sustain such dramatic growth (see Clark 1994: 107–10, 118). Without acknowledging it openly, the Smuts government actively encouraged the 'rationalisation' and mechanisation of industry on the basis of low-paid African labour during the war years (see O'Meara 1983: 227).

The ambiguous situation concerning 'skilled' and 'unskilled' jobs in manufacturing gave rise to increased industrial and political conflicts between employers and black workers.[84] After the war, the English mining and industrial corporations began to realise that growing African militancy threatened the profitability of their enterprises and their political control, and therefore began to favour a relaxation of the colour bar. It was at this time that the Fagan commission (1946–8) recommended that certain limited concessions be made as far as the urbanisation of Africans and labour patterns were concerned. If these recommendations had been implemented, they would have resulted in higher wages and improved economic conditions for Africans, which would have either reduced the profits of the English-dominated corporate sector, or employment opportunities for and the real wages of Afrikaner employees. The Smuts government accepted most of the commission's recommendations, but before they could be properly implemented, the UP was defeated in the election of 1948. The growing dissatisfaction among Afrikaner workers about job and wage security played an important role in the NP's victory (See Wolpe, in Beinart and Dubow 1995: 78–80).

The large influx of Africans into urban areas during the war, their poor living conditions, and the coercive mechanisms used by the state and municipalities to control Africans in the new urban squatter settlements created a serious moral dilemma for those 'liberals' who had, before the war, favoured 'protectionist segregationism' and the 'retribalisation' of Africans. For the first time, the ideology of segregationism and economic progress proved to be irreconcilable for the English-speaking entrepreneurial class. This moral dilemma led to a split between the humanitarian liberals and a liberal-capitalist school that emphasised economic determinism. The humanitarian liberals began to advocate the abolition of segregationism, and founded the Liberal Party in 1953. The economic determinists – mainly mining and manufacturing entrepreneurs – argued that the expanding economy still needed more African workers, but that the industrial colour bar and repressive economy would be dismantled, and the wages of Africans improved, at some stage in the future. These sorts of arguments might have been partly valid earlier in the century; however, they were entirely invalid after the sharp increase in the price of gold from 1932 onwards.[85]

Black trade unions were active in the 1920s, but were then suppressed. By the 1930s African workers, realising they could expect little support from white artisans, formed their own African Federation of Trade Unions, which was incorporated in a Council of Non-European Trade Unions (CNETU) in 1941. The CNETU soon launched several strikes. War Measure 145 of 1942 was introduced to prohibit strikes, but was not effective. In 1943 the African Mine Workers' Union (AMWU) was formally constituted. It campaigned energetically, and claimed to have 25 000 members in 1944. At the time the social upheavals of the war led to a radicalisation of black politics that caused great concern in government circles. The ANC Youth League (ANCYL), which was formed in 1944, adopted a more radical position than senior members of the organisation. When the government and the CM did not accept all the recommendations of the Landsdowne commission about increasing mineworkers' wages, the AMWU organised a strike in 1946 in which 70 000 workers participated. The Smuts government suppressed it with a contingent of 16 000 policemen. Production stopped completely on ten mines, and was seriously affected on many others. The strike leaders were tried under War Measure 145.[86]

The manner in which the Smuts government suppressed the strike and passed legislation in 1943 and 1946 to curtail the land rights of Indians in Natal and the Transvaal shows clearly that it was still committed to segregationism and labour repression, notwithstanding its pragmatic concessions on the colour bar and influx control. Basil Davidson argues that 'systemic discrimination' was well entrenched when the NP assumed power in 1948.[87] Although Smuts did not remove a single segregationist law from the statute books, his relaxation of the implementation of many racist measures was nonetheless meaningful. Given the extent to which these measures were relaxed during the 1940s, few would have foreseen that the most comprehensive and cruel phase of racist legislation would occur during the next 25 years (see ch 9).

8.10 Black protest in the first half of the 20th century: its weakness, ineffectiveness, and ideological orientation

The weakness and ineffectiveness of black protest against the segregation policy of the mainly English establishment in the first half of the 20th century is puzzling. The ANC was established in 1912 in protest against the disenfranchisement of Africans in the northern provinces, and it opposed much of the segregationist legislation (especially the Land Act of 1913) until the late 1940s. However, it remained a moderate organisation favouring gradual reform, and did not question the basic legitimacy of the segregationist South African state. Until the 1940s the ANC was very careful not to act in ways that would enable the white government to brand it as an organisation that acted illegally or unconstitutionally.

During the segregationist period there were periodic signs of more radical black resistance, but the government suppresssed these easily, although often in a harsh and authoritarian manner. Between 1917 and 1922 black political awareness sharpened distinctly when black political leaders were radicalised by the government's commitment to persist with its segregationist policies. But, because of disagreements among key ANC leaders, the protest petered out. The ANC organised the mineworkers' strike of 1920, but this was harshly suppressed by security forces. A second example of the radicalisation of black (and especially coloured) resistance came in the 1920s when the ICU became a nation-wide and regional black movement, embracing both urban and rural workers. Its membership increased from 39 000 in 1926 to 100 000 in 1927. The aggressive attitude of the ICU and the close links between it and the Communist Party of South Africa (CPSA) were sufficient reason for the government to regard the former as a dangerous organisation, and legislation was enacted to neutralise it. The Native Administration Act of 1927 contained in its 'hostility' clause tough provisions for exiling political leaders considered to be politically subversive. When this clause proved impossible to implement, amendments to the Riotous Assemblies Act of 1930 enabled the minister to deport several ICU leaders. This led to the demise of the ICU (see Davenport 1991: 270–3; Rich 1996: ch 3; Dubow, in Beinart and Dubow 1995: 164–5).

In the late 1920s the CPSA became active in protest politics. When, under its influence, the then ANC president, James Gumede, adopted rather radical views, others in the ANC reacted against this, and in 1930 the moderate Pixley Seme was elected president. After this, co-operation between the ANC and the CPSA was suspended. For the best part of the 1930s both the ANC and the CPSA declined, and exerted little influence over public affairs. This ideological division created the opportunity for D D T Jabavu to create the All African Convention (AAC) in 1935 as a united front of the ANC, CPSA, and ICU. However, the divisions within the AAC prevented it from becoming an effective protest movement (see Rich 1996: ch 3).

One would have expected the Hertzog 'native' bills of 1936 to provoke a sharp reaction from the African elite. The Representation of Blacks (Native) Act of 1936 removed African voters in the Cape from the common roll, and placed them on a separate roll. All Africans in the Union were represented by four white senators. At the same time a Native Representative Council (NRC) with 16 African members (of whom 12 were elected and four appointed by the government) was created. The Development Trust and Land Act (1936) further entrenched territorial segregation by establishing a South African Native Trust tasked with increasing the size of the 'native reserves' to 13 per cent of South Africa's territory.

The ANC, and more specifically the AAC led by Jabavu, protested vehemently but peacefully against the Hertzog bills. Jabavu described the African franchise in the Cape as a 'treasured gift of justice inherited from Queen Victoria', and 'nothing less than the noblest monument of the white man's rule'. In the end African leaders accepted the Hertzog bills, and some ANC members (though not Jabavu) fought for and obtained seats on the NRC. By reluctantly accepting the new system of representation, the African leadership agreed, albeit implicitly, with the principle of white trusteeship, and strengthened the ties of patronage between African leaders and the system of white political domination (see Davenport 1991: 284–7; Rich 1996: ch 4, 6).

When, in 1940, Dr A B Xuma became president of the ANC, black political opposition to segregation revived. Despite strong resistance from the CM, the AMWU was established in 1941 under the auspices of the Transvaal African Congress. In 1943 the ANC published *African claims* in which it rejected the principle of 'trusteeship' and indirect rule, and demanded incorporation into white structures. When its attempts to improve the wages and working conditions of African mineworkers failed, the AMWU declared a strike in August 1946.[88] The strike drove the frustrations of African leaders with the NRC to breaking point, and, during the strike, they voted to suspend this body.

Perhaps one of the most important events in African politics in the 1940s was the formation of the ANCYL in 1944. The radicals in this new organisation (in which Nelson Mandela played a strategic role) renewed the co-operation with the CPSA that had been suspended during the 1930s. The ANCYL was committed to transforming the ANC from a moderate political elite into a more militant movement prepared to mobilise popular support under a vigorous African nationalism. The ANCYL soon dominated the formulation of ANC ideology and strategy, and was instrumental in the ANC's adoption of its *Programme of action* in 1949. This was the first attempt by the ANC to formulate a common strategy against white political domination. It is remarkable that the ANC only succeeded in formulating an aggressive and comprehensive strategy against the segregationist regime at the very end of its rule (see Posel 1991: 36–9; Rich 1996: 157–67). In 1948 the ANC called for universal suffrage – the first time it had done so – and demanded that all racial discrimination be abolished (Bundy 1993: 64–5; O'Meara 1996: 26–7).

Several reasons can be advanced for the weakness and ineffectiveness of black protest during the first half of the 20th century. Apart from the enormous political and economic power the Act of Westminster had concentrated in white hands, many black leaders simply did not understand state power and the important role the ideological rationalisations of white pressure groups played in consolidating and perpetuating the power of the white-controlled state.[89]

A very important factor was the strong reformist outlook inculcated in black leaders by the Cape liberal tradition in the second half of the 19th century.[90] The golden age of Cape liberalism only stretched from ±1850 to ±1890, but during that period a small African elite enjoyed the privileges of participating in the Cape legislature, and the Christian mission stations convinced the African elite of the virtues of Christian humanism. The Cape liberal tradition was maintained in the second half of the 19th century (until 1890) by the mercantile elite and by the mission stations. After the discovery of gold, the white champions of liberalism in the Cape gained a vested interest in the gold industry, whose profitability depended on cheap labour. From then on the liberal tradition declined, creating the space for the rise of racist ideologies, of which segregationism was the most important. It is a huge irony that, in the period from 1890 to 1950, when Cape liberalism among whites was suspended by the ideology of segregationism (in order to justify repressive labour practices), the African elite remained devoted to liberal values and to the idea of parliamentary government.[91]

On the strength of their devotion to Cape liberalism and parliamentarian government, the African elite did not appreciate the full meaning of the British betrayal when the Act of Westminster placed political power almost exclusively in the hands of the two 'settler communities'. This betrayal must be understood against the assurance given to Africans during the Anglo–Boer War by the British colonial authority that all population groups would enjoy 'equal laws, equal liberties' after a Boer defeat. For more than 40 years, the African elite's loyalty towards parliamentary processes and the rule of law prevented them from questioning the legitimacy of the state created by the Act of Westminster.

Apart from the weakness and ineffectiveness of black protest during the segregationist period, another remarkable phenomenon was the preparedness of especially African leaders – mainly tribal chiefs – to co-operate with white politicians and white public servants in their own governance, and to enter into a discourse with whites about the supposed 'reformist' intentions of segregationism. During the segregationist period the NAD was remarkably successful in containing and even defusing black radicalism and black unrest. Many NAD officials were recruited from missionary families, and, although they enthusiastically accepted the ideology of segregationism, their discourse with African leaders was reminiscent of the rhetoric of the missionaries and Cape liberals (See Rich 1996: 11).

In accordance with the principle of white *trusteeship*, the majority of chiefs of various African tribes were 'co-opted' as a collaborating class during the first half of the 20th century. Many chiefs were corrupted by white authority with generous forms of patronage. Until the 1940s the 'reformist' leadership core of the ANC could not escape the moderate 'advice' given to it by the English-speaking bureaucrats in the NAD. At the same time the NAD acted as a 'clearing house' for employers of cheap African labour (especially the gold mines and white farmers), and a sounding board for political and ideological trends in African society. The information the NAD gave the government was crucial to maintaining the authority and sovereignty of the state. The NAD was therefore strategically placed in the white power constellation, not only to 'develop' the repressive African labour patterns on behalf of white employers, but also to convince an important (and mainly rural) elite core of Africans that segregation was a 'reformist' policy applied in the best interests of the African community. Through its activities the NAD succeeded in putting Africans 'outside' the range of the South African state. This enabled the white-controlled state to carry on with its business as if the Africans belonged to another 'country' or another realm (see Rich 1996: 7, 157–67; see also section 9.7).

Endnotes

1 The large British corporations involved in gold and diamond exploration were new players in South Africa. From the beginning of the mineral revolution until 1910 a close partnership developed between these corporations and the British government, and then between them and the South African government. While, in the mid-19th century, the sheep-farming British settlers – and the settler press in Grahamstown – succeeded in 'co-opting' both the colonial administration in Cape Town and the colonial office in London in support of their territorial expansionism, the maize farmers in the northern provinces succeeded – in close co-operation with the mining companies – in 'co-opting' the Transvaal and South African governments, before and after 1910, in solving their land, labour, and marketing problems.

2 The manner in which the *racially* based South African economic and political systems were 'constructed' from ±1890 to 1924 will be discussed in greater detail in section 8.3.

3 Between 1871 and 1875 about 50 000 Africans from the interior entered and left Kimberley annually as labourers. Most of these were Pedi from the north eastern Transvaal, who were drawn to the area by wages higher than those elsewhere. The Pedi largely used their cash income to buy rifles, which they regarded as essential for ensuring the continued political existence of independent African tribes (Heydenrich, in Cameron 1986: 155).

4 Whereas in the 15 years before the Rand gold discoveries ZAR government revenue had averaged £110 000 a year, this figure increased to £3,3 million a year – a 30-fold increase in little over a decade. The ZAR government was also not prepared to intervene in the labour situation on behalf of the gold mines. The burghers were also experiencing labour problems on their farms, and put pressure on Kruger to peg African mineworkers' wages at a much higher level than the mining companies wanted to pay. On the eve of the Anglo–Boer War, the gold companies strongly favoured the idea that Britain should annex the ZAR and turn it into a colony that could create social and economic conditions conducive to producing gold more profitably (see Clark 1994: 17–21; Grundlingh, in Cameron 1986: 184–6).

5 Robinson and Gallagher conclude that the '[British] empire went to war in 1899 for a concept [the restoration of supremacy] that was finished, for a cause that was lost, for a great illusion' (quoted by Atmore and Marks 1974: 128).

6 Britain expected the war to last three months, and budgeted £20 million to conduct it. It lasted almost three years, and cost Britain more than £220 million. It has been estimated that about 90 000 men fought on the republican side, accompanied by about 30 000 African *agterryers* (auxiliaries). Almost 500 000 men fought on the British side – 365 000 from Britain, 30 000 from British colonies (Canada, Australia and New Zealand), 50 000 from the South African colonies, and at least 50 000 Africans (see Thompson 1990: 141–2). It was a brutal war; an estimated 35 000 Afrikaners died (27 000 of them women and children in concentration camps), as well as an estimated 22 000 British soldiers and at least 20 000 Africans (many of them in concentration camps in which conditions were appalling). In a desperate attempt to stop the guerrilla phase of the war, Lord Kitchener launched a 'scorched earth' policy by burning down more than 40 000 Afrikaner homesteads and putting

the women and children into concentration camps. This strategy provoked a worldwide outcry (see Pakenham, in Cameron 1986: 217–18).

7 The SANAC report concentrated on the situation in the northern provinces. At that stage the Cape already had legislation to undermine the position of the squatter peasants in the Eastern Cape.

8 Lionel Phillips, a mining magnate, described the events of May 1907 as follows: 'The whole position is getting topsy-turvy; a Boer Government calling out British troops to keep English miners in order, while Dutchmen are replacing them in the mines' (quoted by Yudelman 1983: 75).

9 Although it was mainly Afrikaner leaders who lobbied for the entrenchment of the white franchise, Leonard Thompson acknowledges that 'the race attitudes [of Afrikaners] were [in the early 20th century, when Social Darwinism enjoyed prominence in the culture of the Western world] not fundamentally different from the attitudes that prevailed in Europe and the United States' (1978a: 342–3).

10 About 14 000 coloured people and 6 000 Africans in the Cape Province were qualified to vote. In 1910 some 85 per cent of Cape voters were white, 10 per cent coloured, and only 5 per cent African. The total coloured population was half a million, and the total African population more than 4 million. Political power was vested almost exclusively in the hands of 1,1 million whites. In 1906 only three Africans had acquired the vote in Natal. Coloureds and Africans in the Cape and Natal could not become members of the Union parliament.

11 Rich comes to the important conclusion that the white-controlled state that emerged in South Africa after Union 'proved to be a resilient instrument in entrenching white domination by modernising structures of control and peripherilising black political demands away from the control of echelons of policy making... What was unique about the South African state was the way it developed and rationalised what were *essentially colonial structures of political and social control*' (Rich 1996: 157; author's emphasis).

12 There is indeed merit in the claim that segregationism (1910–48) and apartheid (1948–94) were the perpetuation of colonialism of a special type. For millions of Africans there was indeed no difference between colonialism, segregation, and apartheid (see Rich 1996: 157–61).

13 Herzog and Smuts – the leaders of the NP and the SAP respectively – decided on a coalition government in 1933. In 1934 they 'fused' their two parties into a new party: the United Party (see section 8.9).

14 The English establishment's political, economic, and ideological power was formidable during the first half of the 20th century, when it was responsible for a battery of segregationist legislation. This belies the popular myth in English-speaking circles that discriminatory and repressive policies were only institutionalised under the Afrikaner-oriented NP government.

15 Early in 1914 a general strike by mainly English-speaking skilled workers seriously threatened the accumulation function of the state, to the dismay of British/English capital. The Botha/Smuts government used 60 000 government troops to smash the strike. In the later half of 1914 Afrikaner small farmers in the Transvaal and OFS (supporters of Hertzog's newly established NP) staged a rebellion against the government's decision to participate in World War 1 on the side of Britain. This

threatened to deteriorate into a civil war that could have undermined the political legitimacy of the new state. It was fiercely repressed by Botha and Smuts. Botha led an army of 40 000 soldiers – mainly Afrikaners – against the Afrikaner rebels. The even more damaging Rand Revolt took place in 1922, when most white mineworkers were already Afrikaners.

16 An important power shift took place when the NP assumed power in 1948; during its 46 years in government the symbiosis between state and capital was occasionally also severely stressed, but remained intact until 1994.

17 The Franchise Act excluded tribally owned property from the property qualification, raised the property qualification from R50 to R150, and included an education test, in order to increase the number of poor white farmers on the list and decrease the number of non-whites. The effect of the bill was to remove 3 348 non-white voters from the electoral roll in the first year, and add 4 506 whites (Thomas 1996: 268). In the ten years before the Franchise Act and Ballot Act were passed, the African vote in the five Eastern Cape seats of King Williams' Town, Queenstown, Victoria East, Aliwal North, and Woodhouse rose from 14 per cent in 1882 to 47 per cent in 1886. Franchise qualifications for Africans were first tightened in 1887 (Rich 1996: 63, 196). These acts set an early precedent for the progressive diminution of African political rights by constitutional measures. Many such measures were to follow until the Africans were deprived of their parliamentary rights in 1936 (Kuper 1978: 428).

18 Relevant examples are British notions of racial superiority and divine election in the 19th century; Aryan superiority as proclaimed by Hitler in the 1930s; and the idea that Afrikaners were a people chosen by God and destined to play a dominant role in South Africa during the second half of the 20th century (see section 9.1).

19 In such an evaluation we must take into account that Britain and its imperialist entrepreneurs had the necessary political, military, economic, and financial power to subjugate all the local population groups, succeed in large-scale imperialist plundering, and justify all their actions in terms of a highly deplorable racist ideology. At the same time they launched a mineral revolution that was crucial to the South African economy. In the process they extended the system of racial capitalism in the agricultural sector to the mining sector.

20 He puts it as follows: 'The evolution of segregation in South Africa ran a decade or so behind that of America... Several English-speaking South Africans... studied the extensive American literature on the subject... So did... influential members of the British High Commissioner Sir Alfred Milner's 'kindergarten'... who tried to reconstruct the former Afrikaner republics after the Boer War' (Cell 1982: 192).

21 The Glen Grey Act became the prototype of a multitude of segregationist laws, of which the Land Act of 1913 was the most important (see Bundy 1988: ch 4). A similar form of territorial segregation was also introduced in Natal when Shepstone created his 'location' or 'reserve' system (see sections 6.8 and 8.5).

22 Worden alleges that the Transvaal and OFS 'were [in 1900] less racially segregated in terms of land settlement and economic activity than were Natal and the Eastern Cape' (1994b: 73).

23 Legassick also claims that 'during [the] six years [from 1900 to 1905] Milner and his administrative appointees had... the opportunity to 'reconstruct' the institutions of South Africa with a power greater than that wielded before and since by Britain...

British power...was called in to destroy a state based on feudal relations of production in the Transvaal, and to create throughout South Africa *the conditions for securing a sufficiency of black labour at a suitably low price*' (in Beinart and Dubow 1995: 45–6).

24 The word 'segregation' occurred for the first time in paragraph 90 of the report. In many ways, it systematised thinking about segregationist 'native policy' for the future South Africa, as envisaged by Milner and his *Kindergarten*.

25 The most important of these were the Mines and Works Act (1911), which imposed the colour bar; the Natives Land Act (1913), which segregated land ownership and prohibited squatting and sharecropping; and the Native (Urban Areas) Act (1923), which provided for residential segregation in towns. The full implications of these laws will be discussed in sections 8.6 and 8.7.

26 This disease destroyed almost 80 per cent of cattle in South Africa and had a catastrophic impact on smaller peasant farmers. It liquidated much of their capital, adversely affected their creditworthiness, and made ploughing more difficult and transport facilities rarer and dearer.

27 When the act was debated in parliament, Rhodes said the following about African labour: 'When I see the labour troubles that are occurring in the United States, and when I see the troubles that are going to occur with the English people in their own country...I feel rather glad that the labour question here is connected with the native question...*If the whites maintain their position as the supreme race, the day will come when we shall all be thankful that we have the natives with us in their proper position*' (quoted in Thomas 1996: 271; author's emphasis).

28 The government's actions against Africans early in the 20th century was so aggressive that it sparked the Bambatha rebellion in 1906. In 1905 the Delimitation Commission set aside 2,6 million acres for white settlement in Zululand, leaving only 3,9 million acres in tribal hands. To counteract 'squatting', the government imposed a poll tax of R2 on every male not liable for hut tax in 1906. The Bambatha unrest continued until 1907, claiming the lives of almost 4 000 Africans. It was the last 'Anglo-African war', and undoubtedly the result of white land grabbing and systematic attempts to turn African peasants into a wage-earning proletariat (see Davenport 1991: 208–9).

29 The original Land Bill was drafted in 1912 by Hertzog, then minister of native affairs. His bill was modelled on the Glen Grey system, since it provided for the extension of individual land tenure for Africans in segregated areas. He also planned to allocate substantially more land to Africans than eventually occurred. Before Hertzog's bill could be enacted, he was dropped from the cabinet because of his complaint that the Botha government was too sensitive to Britain's imperial interests. The final bill was far more sensitive to the needs and demands of white farmers. At that time Botha and Smuts had a political incentive to introduce stricter measures against Africans in order to pacify white farmers (in especially the OFS) and prevent them from defecting to Hertzog (see Rich 1996: 18).

30 If the land and farming opportunities granted to Africans were generous enough for them to be self-sufficient, they would not come out to work. If the land granted was too little, and farming opportunities too restricted, the 'native reserves' would not be in a position to support the migrant workers partially while they were employed, and

fully when they returned to their families. This meant that, if not enough land was granted, wages would have to be set at higher levels than employers in the white economy were prepared to pay.

31 The land set aside as 'native reserves' perhaps accorded in the short term with Lagden's 'delicate equation'. But, in a longer-term perspective, even the larger allocation of 1936 was too small to support migrant labourers before and after their spell on the gold mines.

32 By giving this monopsonistic privilege to the chamber, the state legitimised and formally sanctioned the extra-exploitative African labour system on the gold mines that was to remain in place until the 1970s.

33 The number of foreign African migrants on the gold mines oscillated between 50 per cent and 60 per cent from 1911 until 1961, and increased to 80 per cent in 1973 before dropping to 42 per cent in 1982 (see Lipton 1986: 407).

34 The act was immediately applied in the OFS. It laid down that, from then on, the only legal way in which African tenants could pay rent to white landlords was to work for them. Rent in the form of a share of the crop or cash was illegal due to the powerful influence of land-owning companies in the Transvaal and Natal, existing share-cropping contracts remained in force in these two provinces. The act was only applied in the Transvaal and Natal after the Beaumont Commission (1916) had recommended how this should be done.

35 This stipulation had considerable implications for the legal status of tenants and for the coercive apparatus that the farmers could summon to their aid against recalcitrant and unwilling workers. The extension of the Masters and Servants Act to tenants effectively stripped tenant families of their defence against landlords (see Keegan, in Marks and Rathbone 1982: 205–7).

36 In his autobiography, Nelson Mandela gives a personal account of the co-operation between the authorities at Crown Mines and the ruling regent in his native Transkei (see Mandela 1994b: 55–8).

37 According to Bundy, 'share-cropping persisted in South Africa, despite its contravention of the law, in pockets of the Eastern Cape and the of OFS, and in a broad swathe of the south eastern Transvaal [until the 1940s]' (1988: 231; see also Beinart, in Beinart et al 1986: 38–40).

38 Although subsidies to maize farmers declined during the war years, they increased sharply during the first 30 years of NP rule (ie, from 1948 to 1978; see Legassick, in Harris 1975: 251).

39 According to Davenport and Saunders, 'the story of independent African entrepreneurship had been short and unhappy. Those who succeeded [in the late 19th century and early 20th century] succumbed partly from plagues (like the rinderpest of 1896–7), or drought, or lack of access to loans or easy transport to good markets – but most decisively from legal restrictions' (2000: 598). The African peasantry dwindled from 2,5 million in 1936 to 832 000 in 1946 (Marais 2001: 9).

40 Both Bundy and Wolpe emphasise that, for many decades, the underdeveloped 'native reserves' subsidised the gold mining industry by absorbing part of its production costs. Bundy concludes that the *underdevelopment* of the African reserves can only be understood in the framework of the *development* of agrarian, mining, and industrial capital (see Bundy 1988: 223–4; Wolpe, in Beinart and Dubow 1995: 68–70).

41 About 10 000 immigrants arrived between 1857 and 1863, and nearly 23 000 between 1873 and 1883.

42 The diamond mines and the construction of the Cape rail system in the 1870s absorbed large numbers of unskilled white workers. It is estimated that almost 21 000 whites were employed as wage labourers in 1875 in the Cape (see Bundy, in Beinart *et al* 1986: 111–15).

43 Until diamonds and gold were discovered, South Africa's only economic value, from a foreign perspective, was its mercantile value and the small wine industry in the Western Cape.

44 In this struggle little love was lost between the larger and smaller landowners. According to Trapido, 'the dominant group of Afrikaner landowners [in the ZAR] had established [in the last two decades of the 19th century] an informal network [between *landdrosten* and *veldcornetten*] which provided them with information and enabled them to accumulate profitable land-holdings' (in Marks and Attmore 1980: 357).

45 The percentage of the white population in urban areas increased from 36 per cent in 1891 to 53 per cent in 1904. Many of the new arrivals in urban areas were Afrikaners (Welsh 1978: 173).

46 After the fall of Pretoria in June 1900, no fewer than 14 000 burghers voluntarily laid down their arms. Many of these *hensoppers* ('hands-uppers') were *bywoners* who had no land to defend. Some of them even fought actively on the British side, and became 'joiners'. When hostilities ceased in May 1902 there were 17 000 *bittereinders* (bitter-enders) and 5 500 'joiners' in the field (see Grundlingh, in Cameron 1986: 217).

47 The Carnegie report (1932) on the 'poor white question' refers to 'a considerable decrease in the number of white rural inhabitants... between 1911 and 1921', adding that this could not, 'be treated as a fairly harmless and normal process' (Grosskopf 1932: Part 1, Joint findings, para 21).

48 The Indigency Commission in the Transvaal estimated that in 1906 there were 10 000 white indigents in the Transvaal alone. Estimates of the 'very poor' in South Africa as a whole increased from 106 000 in 1916 to about 300 000 by 1929. If the effect of the Great Depression is included, the number may even have increased to 330 000 in 1933.

49 Lipton contends that 'the struggle over jobs was [originally] not only between whites and blacks, but [also] between local whites (mainly Afrikaners) and immigrants (mainly British.) Initially, the skilled trades were dominated by the [British] immigrants... They established exclusive craft unions and tried to limit competition from their jobs by agitating further immigration [from Britain] and by excluding Afrikaners from skilled jobs and from their unions' (1986: 186).

50 It also instituted a very low standard wage rate for African mineworkers. By making African miners cheaper to recruit and retain, they became more accessible to the mines, and thus accentuated the threat to white miners.

51 These two acts were the first comprehensive statutory codifications of labour discrimination on the mines. Attempts by the Chamber of Mines to prevent the introduction of this colour bar were successful, but it was finally defeated by the Mines and Works Amendment Act of 1926 (see Yudelman 1983: 87–9; Davenport and Saunders 2000: 634).

52 According to Johnstone, the collective restrictions on Africans in the labour market made it possible to force the wages of Africans down to such a low level that poor whites could not compete with them in an 'open market' for unskilled jobs. It was precisely because African workes were made 'ultra-exploitable' by repressive measures that they threatened the job security of unskilled Afrikaner workers. Consequently, the government used its political and bureaucratic power to protect the Afrikaner proletariat against the competition of the 'ultra-exploitable' African proletariat. At the end of the 1910s the 'exploitation colour bar' was a class as well as a racial matter: employers justified extraordinarily low wages for an already proletarianised *class* of workers on the additional grounds of *racial* inferiority (see Johnstone 1976: 26–49; Davenport 1991: 506).

53 After 1948 the NP government became notorious for stricter repressive and *discriminatory* legislation (see sections 9.4 and 9.5).

54 The working cost of the gold mines increased from R1,81 per ton milled in 1911 to R2,58 in 1920 (see Horwitz 1967: 237).

55 In 1920 the 21 455 whites employed on the mines earned a total of £10,64 million, whereas the 179 000 blacks employed earned only £5,96 million (see Davenport 1991: 254).

56 The 'status quo' agreement of 1918 stipulated that the number of blacks in mining should be frozen at a ratio of 7,4 Africans for every one white supervisor. In 1921 the CM announced that the ratio would be increased to 11.4 Afrcans to 1 white – ie, by almost 50 per cent (see Lipton 1986: 14).

57 The percentage of Afrikaners among white mineworkers increased from 24 per cent in 1907 to 51 per cent in 1920, 65 per cent in 1930, and 86 per cent in 1945 (see Yudelman 1983: 132).

58 According to Yudelman, the Industrial Conciliation Act was one of the most important events in the process of state formation and, specifically, the final consolidation of the symbiosis between white supremacy and racial capitalism. By co-opting white labour, the act comprehensively institutionalised the principle that justified state intervention to enforce industrial peace in a system of economic segregation and black exploitation. By passing the act, the Smuts government finally chose in favour of the Afrikaner proletariat and against the African proletariat, and set a pattern that lasted until the 'reformist' industrial relations legislation of 1979 and 1981 (see Yudelman 1983: ch 7).

59 White earnings as a percentage of total gold revenue fell from 24,8 per cent in 1921 to 18 per cent in 1922 (see Yudelman 1983: 190).

60 According to Yudelman, in the new industrial order organised white labour was effectively co-opted into the leadership structure of white supremacy in order to avert threats to the stability of that structure. By co-opting white labour, the white trade union movement was *depoliticised* and an important section of the marginalised whites (mainly the proletarianised Afrikaners) incorporated into the political and administrative structures of the white-controlled state (see Yudelman 1984: ch 6).

61 This interventionist policy was perpetuated by the Pact government when the Iron and Steel Corporation (ISCOR) was established in 1928. When the NP came to power in 1948, several other state corporations were created. The NP used the state corporations as important instruments in its comprehensive interventionist policies,

and to implement its discriminatory and repressive policies (see Clark 1994: 43; see also section 9.6).

62　O'Meara makes an important point: 'The creation of a central South African state in 1910 rested on a tenuous compromise between competing colonial elites rather than on a broad consensus of the overwhelming white...electorate. Between 1910 and 1922 this absence of a consensual order pushed various elements of the white population into two serious armed rebellions [in 1914 and 1922] and a number of violently contested strikes, all of which were suppressed militarily. Only after the election of the so called "Pact" government...in 1924...*was a fragile "South Africanist" consensual order forged around the notion of an interventionist state securing institutionalised minimum privileges for all whites regardless of their class position*' (1996: 471; author's emphasis).

63　At this stage 80 per cent of the shares in the mining corporations were still owned by foreigners, most of them Britons. In 1918 the proportion of mining dividends paid abroad was 82 per cent. This declined to 47 per cent in 1945, and 29 per cent in 1964 (Lipton 1986: 258). Another criticism of the gold mining industry was that only a tiny part of its huge profits was invested in South Africa.

64　It operated on the principle of the 'rate for the job', which gave the appearance of complete fairness, but was in fact a powerful and subtle colour bar. The act also empowered the government to determine wage rates in non-unionised industries (thereby setting higher rates for whites), and to restrict skilled jobs to white workers. The Chamber of Mines was strongly opposed to the powers given to the Wage Board, because it feared the board might raise mine wages. But the board never made a determination for the mining industry. This is another example of the Hertzog government's sensitivity towards the interests (and profitability) of the mining industry (Davenport 1991: 509).

65　According to Sheila van der Horst, between 1924 and 1933 the number of whites employed by the railways rose from 4 760 to 17 783, while the number of blacks fell from 37 564 to 22 008. Likewise, in central and local government the proportion of whites rose from 45 per cent to 64 per cent (1942: 251, 264). In the public sector the 'civilised labour policy' was made compulsory, resulting particularly in the displacement of Indians and coloureds, who had moved into such jobs from the agricultural forced labour system.

66　Yudelman concludes that 'the increased employment of whites was paralleled by a decrease in white wages in real terms, suggesting that the more skilled workers, in particular, paid part of the price for the employment of their lesser skilled white colleagues' (1983: 238).

67　This strategy operated through the reconstituted Board of Trade and Industries which selectively encouraged local industry via substantial increased tariffs. The number of items on the tariff schedule jumped from 192 to 371.

68　An issue that caused considerable tension between the Pact government and the corporate sector was the former's legislation to create a local steel industry. Despite strong resistance by the English establishment, the legislation establishing ISCOR was eventually passed in 1928 by a combined session of both houses of parliament.

69　Yudelman regards this as 'a striking illustration of the strength of the structural factors shaping the development of the increasingly interventionist South African state' (1983: 243).

70 The government based its case on the conservative, fundamentalist viewpoint that gold convertibility was an unmistakable symbol of stability, discipline, and financial probity, and that South Africa – as the main gold producing country in the world – should demonstrate its confidence in the metal. The government's retention of the gold standard triggered off large-scale speculation against the South African currency, and aggravated the already serious economic situation.

71 Eleven members of the old SAP (including F S Malan and J H Hofmeyr) voted against the 1936 act. They were bitterly critical of Smuts's betrayal of the entrenched principles in the constitution of 1910.

72 The price of gold increased from R12,48 in 1932 to R16,90 in 1940 and R25 in 1950. Despite the higher taxes on the gold industry, the mining companies made extraordinarily large profits (in both working capital and shareholder profits) in the decades after 1933. The revenue from the gold mines (as a percentage of ordinary state revenue) increased from 5,8 per cent (or R3,2 million) in 1930 to 33,6 per cent (or R21 million) in 1935, and remained at that level until 1940 (see also Hancock and Van der Poel: 1973.)

73 The acceleration of economic growth from 1934 onwards created thousands of new jobs for white and black workers. The employment of jobless Afrikaners went a long way towards solving the 'poor white' problem. Young Afrikaners who 'joined Jan Smuts's war' were also, in effect, profitably employed.

74 The Fusion government maintained its commitment to the 'civilised labour policy' in order to create more jobs for whites at relatively low wages. As in the days of the Pact, the public sector and subsidised manufacturing industries were pressurised into giving preference to 'civilised labour'. The uneconomic protection of local manufacturing and agriculture meant that these sectors were unable to compete in world markets. At the end of the 1930s the manufacturing sector was an especially weak sector of the economy.

75 In 1934 the CM rejected the Mine Natives Wages Commission's recommendation that the wages of Africans be raised by 4 cents a shift. The real wages of Africans on the gold mines remained exceptionally low until 1960. In this period the government provided the gold mining industry with all the help it needed to establish the monopsonistic migrant labour system that covered almost half of Africa south of the Sahara. In 1931 migrant workers constituted 50 per cent of the total migrant labour force, rising to 60–80 per cent a year in 1950–73 (see Lipton 1986: 407). In the 1930s, the use of foreign migrants not only kept wages low on the gold mines, but also in other sectors of the economy. In the late 1930s the ANC requested the government and the Chamber of Mines to curtail the use of foreign labour, hoping that this would lead to an increase in wages, but the request was rejected. To keep African mine workers subservient, the gold mines proceeded with mechanisation.

76 When rejecting the proposal of the Lansdowne Commission that the migrant labour system should be suspended, the chamber alleged that the 'Natives themselves would be the first to oppose it'. Presumably the Gold Producers' Committee had not even read the demands of the AMWU before the 1946 strikes, which in effect called for the migrant labour system to be ended (see O'Meara 1983: 230, 264).

77 In 1933–73 – when the economic growth rate averaged 4,5 per cent, and both local and foreign investors made huge profits – African workers were so cruelly exploited that even the staunchest proponent of liberal capitalism should not try to justify this. According to Legassick, what neo-classical economists euphemistically describe as 'self-financing' and 'high rates of profit retention' in fact represent the 'reinvestment of capital accumulation from the forced African labour economy' (in Harris 1975: 256–7).

78 The NAD policy of indirect rule over Africans reached its zenith when the Native Representative Council (NRC) was created by the 1936 Representative of Black (Native) Act. The department's ability to dispense patronage helped it to involve African political leaders in a dialogue about 'native policy', and blunt more radical demands. Within a few years the NRC proved to be a disappointment, and in August 1946 it decided to suspend itself (Rich 1996: 12, 163; see also section 8.10).

79 While the legislation was being drafted a rift developed between pro- and anti-Stallardist factions in the NAD. The former regarded African urbanisation as a serious threat to white political supremacy, while the latter regarded African urbanisation as essential for economic growth. Although the pro-Stallardists won the argument in 1937, the extraordinary wartime demand for African labour brought the long-standing conflicts between pro- and anti-Stallardist factions within the NAD to a head, plunging the department's policy into ambiguity and incoherence (see Posel 1991: 43–4).

80 At this stage African migrant labourers on the mines earned R100 a year, and those in manufacturing R250. The figures for white workers were R1 600 and R918 respectively (Lipton 1986: 409–10.)

81 The contribution of manufacturing increased from 13 per cent of GDP in 1936 to 27 per cent in 1951. During the same period the contribution of agriculture increased from 15 per cent to 19 per cent, while the contribution of mining declined from 19 per cent to 13 per cent (see Lipton 1986: 402).

82 At that stage, manufacturing was an especially weak sector of the South African economy. Its most striking features were low average productivity per worker – the value of production per head of employees was about half that of factory workers in Australia, Canada, and New Zealand – and an artificial wage structure that resulted in white workers earning the bulk of wages or salaries (see Clark 1994: 105).

83 The sharp increase in demand for African labour narrowed the gap between white and African wages in manufacturing. While, in 1940, African wages were less than 20 per cent of white wages, this figure increased to 24 per cent in 1945, but declined sharply after the NP assumed power in 1948 (table 8.1). In the mid-1930s the number of blacks employed in manufacturing was about 100 000 – little more than the number of whites. Most of the 1 million Africans in urban areas were employed in mining and domestic service. By the end of the war the number of blacks in the manufacturing industry had increased to 250 000. Much of the increase may have been among coloureds and Indians (rather than Africans), who were not subject to the same forms of extra-economic coercion (Legassick 1974b: 268).

84 In 1940–9 (which included the massive strike of African minewokers in 1946) 1 684 915 African man-hours were lost, against 171 088 in 1930–9. The years 1939–45 also saw a record number of 304 strikes, involving 58 000 Africans, coloureds and Indians (Posel 1991: 38).

85 During the 1950s and 1960s – when apartheid was in its heyday – the argument for economic determinism was propagated as the 'Oppenheimer thesis'; ie, the English-speaking corporate sector (especially the mining industry) was formally opposed to apartheid and discriminatory legislation, but nevertheless maintained the repressive labour economy based on the legally entrenched and ultra-exploitable migrant labour system. In real terms, the wages of migrant workers on the gold mines were lower in 1971 than they had been in 1911, while the wages of Africans in manufacturing in 1970 were only 17 per cent of those of whites (table 8.1).

86 This was the first time black workers had seriously challenged the industrial relations system since 1920 (Stadler, in Cameron 1986: 266; Davenport and Saunders 2000: 357–8). Rising class struggles in a racially divided society led to a 'progressive paralysis' of UP government policies in the years immediately after the war. According to O'Meara, the 'UP government was able neither to defuse strident African demands for change and restore stability through reform, nor to reimpose ideological control [on behalf of its white (and predominantly English-speaking) constituency'. O'Meara also claims that the UP itself was deeply divided. The wartime restructuring of South African capitalism and the intensified class struggles which this provoked produced growing conflict within the capitalist class itself, not only on the question of African political rights but also on fundamental questions on economic policy. The result was an escalating political crisis (O'Meara 1983: 229–30).

87 He puts it as follows: 'The history of South Africa since the 1880s... is that of the dispossession and eventual destruction of ancient and stable rural communities, and the transformation of their people into the helots and servants of a white minority, whether English-speaking or Afrikaner... When the NP came to power in 1948 on a program of full-blooded apartheid, its task was in no way to install systemic discrimination, but only to complete what already existed of that kind, while taking additional measures to repress a growing volume of non-white protest' (Davidson 1994: 114–17).

88 According to Marais, 'the 1946 miners' strike is commonly portrayed as a landmark event, announcing a crisis in South African capitalism... Worker militancy in support of higher wages and better working conditions challenged the basic system that pivoted on an abundant supply of very cheap, controlled labour'. Marais quoted O'Meara's remark that, 'the violence of the state's response not only indicated the degree to which it felt threatened, but forshadowed the extreme repression after 1948' (2001: 12).

89 Rich puts it as follows: 'Black political leaders at the time of Union had a number of different conceptions of the way the political terrain in South Africa was formed. Some leaders, trained in missions in the late 19th and early 20th century, looked for the ultimate source of political authority overseas in the imperial "mother country" of Britain... For others [like the CPSA]... the real terrain lay in the field of international class conflict that also extended beyond the confines of the South African state' (1996: 10).

90 According to Rich, this tradition 'provided the basis for a benign faith in parliamentary gradualism, and was undoubtedly a major reason for the failure of many [black] leaders to understand the nature of state power after Union' (1996: 61).

91 Rich puts it as follows: 'Missionary-educated Africans in the Cape enthusiastically embraced parliamentary government and continued to assume well into the 20th century that racially discriminatory legislation would be ultimately reversed through [parliamentary] means. Many also believed that the British parliament would intervene if necessary to protect the rights secured under the 1854 constitution [of the Cape]...The tenacity of this commitment [by the African elite] indicates that the roots of the 19th century Cape liberal tradition did not only lie in the sphere of economic processes, but also in a fundamental restructuring of African society as a result of missionary evangelisation' (1996: 62).

Chapter 9

The systemic period of the political hegemony of the Afrikaner establishment (1948–94)

9.1 Three major paradigm shifts in South African history

South African history is marked by three major ideological paradigm shifts, each of which hardened racial attitudes towards blacks. The first occurred from ±1840 onwards, when evangelical humanitarianism was replaced by Benthamite liberal utilitarianism and notions of racial superiority. The second occurred during the last quarter of the 19th century, when the upsurge of British imperialism was legitimised by the racial ideologies of Social Darwinism and white superiority.

In due course, this ideology was supplemented by segregationism and liberal capitalism, in a period when Cape liberalism declined. The third – and perhaps most regrettable – shift involved the rise of an aggressive and religiously oriented Afrikaner Christian Nationalism from the 1930s onwards, and the hardening of racist ideology during the NP's implementation of apartheid after 1948.

The rise of Afrikaner Christian Nationalism will be discussed in section 9.2. The manner in which the NP government institutionalised a new power constellation will be discussed in section 9.3, and the crisis of the apartheid regime in section 9.4.

Because of the intensification of both repressive and discriminatory measures by the apartheid regime, a discussion of these two unfree labour patterns follows in section 9.5 and 9.6 respectively. The important role played by state corporations in 'manufacturing' and perpetuating apartheid will be discussed in section 9.7. The radicalisation of black protest in the second half of the 20th century – as a prelude to the implosion of the apartheid regime – will be discussed in the final section.

9.2 The rise of Afrikaner Christian Nationalism, and the hardening of racist ideology

When, in 1934, Hertzog and Smuts decided on *Samesmelting*, Dr D F Malan and a section of the NP broke away to form the *Gesuiwerde* (Purified) National Party (G/NP). This caused a sharp division in Afrikaner circles between the so-called *Hertzogiete* and *Malaniete* (Herzogites and Malanites), which triggered off an unprecedented debate about the true nature or soul of Afrikanerdom. The polemic in the ranks of the G/NP was very intense. A new group of young urban intellectuals emerged which guided the party towards a far more aggressive and exclusive version of nationalism, which they referred to as 'Afrikaner Christian Nationalism' (see O'Meara 1996: ch 2).

The stratification of Afrikaners into a small elite of 'notables' and a relatively large underclass (comprising at least two thirds of Afrikaners in the 1930s) was largely the result of a protracted *internal* struggle between larger and smaller landowners over control over land and black labour. This struggle began in the 18th century and was particularly intense during the last quarter of the 19th century and the first quarter of the 20th – ie, during the process of modernisation when some larger landowners consolidated their economic position to the detriment of smaller ones, leading to the latter losing their land and becoming an urbanised proletariat (see section 7.4). Certain 'external' factors such as pests, droughts, and especially the Anglo–Boer War also helped to impoverish predominantly rural Afrikaners. During the mobilisation of Afrikaner ethnic power in the 1930s and 1940s, the prior conflicts within Afrikaner society and their role in impoverishing a section of Afrikaners were deliberately obfuscated by Afrikaner propagandists.

By overemphasising the alleged injustices done to Afrikaners by British imperialism and foreign capitalism, and exaggerating the dangers of *swart oorstroming* ('black swamping'), Afrikaner ideologues succeeded in creating a 'syndrome of victimisation' – ie, the idea that the existence and interests of the Afrikaner volk were endangered by other population groups. In this way the NP succeeded in mobilising Afrikaner ethnic power by portraying Afrikaners as the wrongful victims of a double onslaught: the first was their exploitation 'from above' by British colonialism and foreign capitalism, and the second the danger 'from below' of Afrikaner culture being swamped by an 'uncivilised' African majority.[1]

In the 1940s, as growing African urbanisation fuelled fears of *oorstroming*, it became expedient for Afrikaner ideologues to emphasise the ethnic 'purity' of Afrikaners and the imperative of protecting this purity against miscegenation with ostensibly inferior indigenous races. Consequently, as the reverse side of the coin of aggressive Afrikaner nationalism, NP ideologues formulated an explicit and insulting version of racism, which crystallised into the policy of apartheid. The NP regarded the different African ethnic groups as heathen nations to be Christianised and civilised by Afrikaners. White English-speakers were portrayed as people with dubious moral standards, permeated by the materialistic and egotistic values of capitalism.

Economic factors played a major role in the crystallisation of Afrikaner Christian Nationalism, and its accompanying version of racism. Some 'backward' Afrikaners felt deeply inferior to other whites. Not only were their educational levels and per capita income lower than those of other whites; they also played a lesser role in the economy than English-speakers, for example. NP propaganda incited hostility between Afrikaners and English-speakers, and blamed the former's economic backlog on injustices meted out by the British and English-speakers. Consequently, the ideology of Afrikaner nationalism was really a means to an end, namely the mobilisation of ethnic power to attain political power, and especially greater wealth. The racism accompanying this ideology was also a means to an end, namely maintaining the subordination of allegedly inferior indigenous races in order to create the 'space' for Afrikaners to attain their political and economic aims, and their promised land. Many Afrikaners envied English-speakers for their wealth, and realised that the latter had become wealthy by using extra-economic measures to turn blacks into a cheap and docile labour force. After Afrikaners had captured political power, many believed their turn had come to benefit from exploiting blacks.

The Afrikaner *volksbeweging* ('people's movement') played an important role in the NP's election victory of 1948, and in the perpetuation of NP rule. This was the first time that an exclusively Afrikaner party had risen to power. Without any experience of the proper use of political power, and carried away by the emotional *élan* of the *volksbeweging*, the NP misused its political power on a grand scale; it manipulated the constitutional system to perpetuate NP rule, and passed a plethora of racist laws to suppress and exploit blacks to an ever greater degree than the white governments that had preceded it. For many Afrikaners the *volksbeweging* became an all-embracing movement (see Moodie 1975: ch 1).

With the NP in power, and its political and bureaucratic power harnessed to promote the sectional interests of Afrikaners, the *volksbeweging* went seriously wrong. *Inter alia*, the Afrikaner establishment became notorious for its uncritical self-righteousness; it was this 'sick' society that uncritically institutionalised and defended apartheid. The conversion of Afrikaners from a relatively poor group into a relatively wealthy one happened in the surprisingly short period of 25 years. It has been claimed that Afrikaner business was largely responsible for uplifting Afrikaners economically – ie, that Afrikaners had pulled themselves up 'by their own bootstraps' before the NP's election victory of 1948. There is a degree of truth to this.[2]

The NP's victory of 1948 was unexpected. During the elections of 1938 and 1943, the UP retained its strong support in the rural constituencies in the Transvaal and OFS. However, it neglected the interests of farmers during the war in favour of the new generation of urban industrialists.[3] The support given to the G/NP in 1948 by prosperous farmers represented a historic shift in Afrikaner circles. It was the first time that wealthy farmers in the Transvaal (the 'notables') associated themselves with smaller Afrikaner farmers and the Afrikaner petit bourgeoisie (see O'Meara 1996: 27–37).

The other major issue during the election was rapid black urbanisation, which widened the already deep differences within the UP and among the social forces that supported it. While the industrialists favoured a further relaxation of influx control and job reservation (as a means of lowering their production costs), those in favour of 'protective segregation' were shocked by the poor living conditions of Africans in the mushrooming urban shanty towns. However, both Afrikaner farmers and urban workers were distressed by the economic implications of black urbanisation, and the NP was horrified by the alleged dangers of *oorstroming*. When, in 1948, the Fagan commission emphasised the inevitability of African urbanisation, and recommended a policy of 'facilitating the stabilisation of [African] labour' in urban areas, it provoked a strong reaction from the NP. The Sauer commission, which formulated the NP's apartheid programme as a 'solution' to the growing racial conflict inherent in the UP's 'native policy', published its report in 1947 (see section 9.5).[4]

At the end of the 1950s, Dr Hendrik Verwoerd – who had become prime minister in 1958 – was astute enough to realise that the notion of the upliftment of poor Afrikaners – as the alleged victims of British imperialism and foreign capitalism – was no longer an adequate justification for the system of Afrikaner power and privilege. Consequently, he announced that the policy of apartheid would be replaced with the 'non-racist' policy of separate development. According to Verwoerdian ideology, 'national' sovereignty and political freedom would be granted separately to each of the nine African ethnic groups. This ideology was propagated with evangelic zeal. It is a prime example of an ideological travesty, and represented the pinnacle of Afrikaner self-delusion (see section 9.5.2).

In the late 19th century the British tried to legitimise the advent of the New

Imperialism in terms of Social Darwinism and their alleged superiority over people of other races, as well as a segregationism based on the supposed inferiority of indigenous people. Both these ideological strands were maintained and propagated by the local English establishment during the first half of the 20th century. The similarities between the ideologies with which the British/English tried to legitimise their imperialism and their economic plunder on the one hand, and those with which Afrikaners tried to legitimise their sectionalism and economic plunder on the other, are perhaps greater than the differences. But the differences are nonetheless important. We can identify at least four.

First, the propaganda surrounding British/English superiority was far more sophisticated and subtle than the blatant and almost crude propaganda of the Afrikaner establishment. While Afrikaners undoubtedly imitated English ideas in respect of Afrikaner superiority and black inferiority, they did so in a rather clumsy way. The fact that some of the key ideologues of Afrikaner nationalism – Dr Nic Diederichs, Dr Piet Meyer, and Verwoerd – were exposed to German philosophy and Nazi propaganda during the 1920s and 1930s helps to explain the influence of *herrenvolk* ideas on Afrikaner political thinking.

Second, while religious considerations played a role in the British belief that they were a divinely chosen people, these considerations were not nearly as explicit as the claim of Afrikaners (supported by Afrikaner churches) that *they* were a divinely chosen people with the task – prescribed by Providence – of promoting Christian civilisation and instilling high moral values into the members of all other population groups (including the English).

Third, we can regard the British ideological onslaught as a typical response of a great world power in a downward spiral. By contrast, the Afrikaner ideological onslaught was typical of a petit bourgeoisie trying to attain political and economic power for the first time.

Finally, the British formulated and propagated their double-barrelled ideology about British superiority and indigenous inferiority before World War 2, while Afrikaners formulated their ideologies about Afrikaner superiority and aborigine inferiority during and after it. Perhaps one of the most important result of the war against Hitler's Nazism was that it brought ideas about racial superiority into disrepute. When the NP launched its ideological propaganda in the 1940s, and institutionalised its racist policies in the 1950s and 1960s, it went completely against the grain of post-war world opinion. What is remarkable is that the NP and Afrikaners got away with their crude and unwarranted ideological propaganda for so long. Needless to say, if it were not for the large-scale economic and cultural support the great powers such as

Britain, the United States, Germany, and Japan gave South Africa during the second half of the century, the apartheid regime would not have lasted for 46 years.

9.3 The NP government and the institutionalisation of a new power constellation

The NP's agenda before the 1948 election was to create a new socio-economic order. This agenda had three main items. The first was to restructure the economy so as to free Afrikaners from 'foreign' capitalism, and adapt it to the needs of the Afrikaner *volk* – ie, creating a system of Afrikaner *volkskapitalisme* ('national capitalism'). The second was to implement the policy of apartheid as a solution to the 'native problem', in order to ensure the purity of the Afrikaner *volk* and defuse the conflict inherent in a process of racial integration. The third was to solve the problem of poor white Afrikaners and remedy the alleged injustices of the past by implementing a comprehensive welfare policy for uplifting Afrikaners. Two groups of Afrikaners – farmers and urban workers – were identified for special governmental support programmes.

This threefold agenda should not be taken to mean that the NP had a 'grand plan' for attaining its aims. According to Deborah Posel, 'the notion of a single master plan fundamentally misrepresents the political processes whereby apartheid was built, greatly exaggerating the extent of the continuity, control, and long-term planning involved'. Nevertheless, she notes, there was 'some method in the madness of apartheid' (1991: 4–5).

Once in government, the NP failed conspicuously to replace the 'foreign' system of capitalism with a new socio-economic order. It was mainly the secret Afrikaner Broederbond (AB) that was originally responsible for the anti-capitalist (and even pro-socialist) attitude of the NP. During the war, NP spokesmen put forward the idea of an 'Afrikaner socialist order', and toyed with radical ideas about nationalising the gold mines and introducing a statutory system of profit-sharing. It is therefore understandable that the English establishment – then almost completely in control of the non-agricultural economy – was in a state of panic after the NP victory. Although the relationship between the NP government and the English business sector remained tense (especially on the rhetorical level) and occasionally hostile until the 1960s, the fear of the English establishment that the Afrikaner government would create a new economic order and nationalise the gold mining industry proved to be unfounded. On the contrary, the NP did not 'restructure' or 'capture' the capitalist system. The symbiosis between state and capital was maintained with little adaptation after 1948.

How should we explain the NP's *volte-face* on this key issue? Firstly, it is perhaps another example of the strength of the structural and racist factors underpinning the symbiosis between the white Afrikaner state and white English capital. As soon as the NP was confronted with the responsibility of government, it realised that the maintenance of the white hegemonic order – which entailed the structural subjugation of Africans – was more important than the 'Boer/Brit' squabble. Once in government, the NP discovered that the racial character of South African capitalism was far more advantageous to Afrikaners than its supposedly 'anti-Afrikaner' nature. The NP's insight demonstrates the staying power and dynamic momentum of racial capitalism. Secondly, the policies of the new government were probably not shaped by the firebrand ideologues in the AB (mainly from the Transvaal), but by the more pragmatic (and already capitalist-oriented) farmers and Afrikaner corporations in the Western Cape. The fact that the capitalist-oriented economy was growing strongly may also have convinced the NP to use that system to advance its Afrikaner agenda instead of 'restructuring' it.

Within ten years, almost all state departments – including the security departments and the NAD – were brought under the strict control of the NP, and 'Afrikanerised' and politicised at the same time. The NP's drive towards statism involved the stimulation of the private sector and the creation of a multitude of new state and semi-state bodies and institutions. The bureaucracy was also enlarged by the welfare system developed to uplift Afrikaners. The lucrative employment opportunities created in the public sector and parastatals not only wiped out almost all the remnants of the 'poor white' problem, but also contributed considerably to the rapid (probably too rapid) embourgeoisement of Afrikaners in the third quarter of the 20th century. Afrikaners were taken to their 'promised land' in two vehicles: a dynamic and growing system of racial capitalism (controlled by the English corporate sector and a growing Afrikaner-controlled corporate sector), and an expanding Afrikaner state bureaucracy (controlled by the NP).

In the course of implementing its apartheid policy, the NP built a mammoth organisational structure in order to control not only the movement of Africans, but also their living and working patterns and their intellectual lives. A plethora of segregationist and discriminatory laws was put on the statute books (see sections 9.5 and 9.6). Much of the political legislation was aimed at controlling black labour in order to meet the demands of agriculture and the emerging Afrikaner industrial sector. While the system of *segregation* (mainly based on migrant labour and the compound system) was well adapted to labour needs during the mining revolution, the system of *apartheid* (with its comprehensive control over Africans in urban areas) was developed to suit the interests of the industrial revolution. Verwoerd developed the abortive system of border industries from the 1960s onwards in a desperate attempt to 'reconcile' territorial segregation with industrialisation, but this was doomed from the very beginning.[5]

A very high rate of economic growth was maintained in the 1950s and 1960s.[6] During the heyday of state and racial capitalism the racial disparity ratio between white and African incomes became much larger (see table 10.8). Apartheid undoubtedly reached its zenith in the early 1970s. The concentration of economic and bureaucratic power in the hands of Afrikaners in this period played a decisive role in the embourgeoisement of Afrikaners, and the further proletarianisation and impoverishment of Africans (see sections 10.3 and 10.4).

The third item on the NP's agenda was to solve the poor white problem and remedy the alleged injustices done to Afrikaners in the past. In implementing its policy of 'affirmative action', or social upliftment, the NP used its fiscal powers to tax wealthier English-speakers and increase social spending on Afrikaners. This kind of redistributive policy significantly improved the economic position of the Afrikaner petit bourgeoisie – ie, the poorer two thirds of Afrikaners.

However, the NP policy of Afrikaner 'favouritism' was even more advantageous to the upper layers of Afrikaners, whom it enriched and empowered in a spectacular manner. In a curious twist of fate, in the late 1950s the NP's emphasis shifted away from the ideological aim of uplifting poor Afrikaners towards helping richer farmers and emerging Afrikaner entrepreneurs.[7] Through extraordinarily generous types of favouritism, an Afrikaner haute bourgeoisie was created which quickly became the champion of a system of unbridled Afrikaner capitalism.[8] Examples of Afrikaner favouritism were the allocations of fishing quotas, mining and liquor concessions, government contracts, and all sorts of valuable inside information.[9]

It was, however, not only Afrikaner business that profited in the 1950s and 1960s. Apartheid proved to be good for all white business. O'Meara has made the important point that although English-speakers may have had 'moral and theoretical qualms about the NP racial policy, [he] know[s] of no anglophile liberal businessman who declined to profit from [the] NP "interference" in the "free market" and raise their [black] workers' wages' (1996: 81). The hypocrisy displayed by the English establishment in criticising the 'ugly system' of segregation and apartheid – partly created by itself – while continuing to benefit handsomely from it was an important cause of continued friction between Afrikaners and English-speakers.[10] During the 1950s and 1960s South Africa was strongly supported by the large industrialised countries despite its racist policies. The intensified exploitation of African workers, high profit levels, and the rise of the gold price all contributed to a large and sustained inflow of foreign capital in the third quarter of the century.[11] FDI more than doubled between 1960 and 1972.

The shift in NP policy from helping the poor towards favouring the rich can partly be explained in terms of the growing capitalist orientation of the NP in office, and partly in terms of the strong bargaining power of the emerging Afrikaner corporate sector (both public and private), Afrikaner business organisations such as the AHI, and the strongly Afrikaner-oriented South African Agricultural Union (SAAU). Despite popular opinion to the contrary, the NP remained very sensitive to the demands of the English corporate sector, ie, the mining industry, the Federated Chamber of Industries (FCI), and the Association of Chambers of Commerce (ASSOCOM).[12]

The decisive role played by the maize farmers in the NP election victory of 1948 placed them in an extremely powerful position. After taking office, the NP almost immediately reorganised the labour bureaux to prevent African farm workers from migrating to the cities. The NP implemented the Agricultural Marketing Act of 1937 in such a way as to secure higher prices for agricultural produce – between 1950 and 1954 the maize price, for example, rose by almost 50 per cent. But in applying its policy of favouritism – ie, subsidies, Land Bank loans, and so on – the NP explicitly favoured the larger and more efficient farmers.[13] In this way an economic culture of favouritism was nurtured in the ranks of Afrikaner agricultural capitalism. Although their ideological orientation became as haute bourgeois as those of their industrial counterparts, most 'capitalist farmers' remained vulnerable due to their dependence on credit, subsidies, and cheap African labour. The low interest rates introduced as part of Verwoerd's programme to create a 'white economy' stimulated an unhealthy process of mechanisation in agriculture.[14] Despite all this support, the agricultural sector did not become independent or self-sustainable.[15]

The symbiosis of state and capital attained its purpose of accumulation in a spectacular manner during the third quarter of the century. However, success in terms of legitimacy was mixed. Although the NP succeeded in increasing its parliamentary majority, the racist character of the political system was increasingly questioned by broader civil society and especially by liberation organisations such as the ANC and PAC. Protest against the apartheid system became violent at times, but was effectively suppressed by a harsh and effective security system. Consequently, the viability of white supremacy was never seriously endangered until the mid-1970s. In those years the NP was far more concerned about its own power base among white voters than about protests brewing in the ranks of people other than white, or in international organisations such as the United Nations and the Organisation of African Unity (OAU) (see section 9.8).

Owing to the NP's small majority in the 1948 election, the party developed an obsession about consolidating its grip on white political power. A first step in this direction was to give parliamentary representation to whites in Namibia, and to lengthen the period before immigrants could attain citizenship. Its attempt in 1951 to remove coloured people living in the Cape from the common voters' roll was halted by the Appeal Court. In 1956, after a long constitutional struggle, and after the enlargement of the senate, coloureds were finally deprived of their political rights in a morally deplorable, if not unconstitutional, manner. Numerous laws were passed aimed at gaining stronger control over civil society and extra-parliamentary groups.[16]

The NP was also bolstered by the ideological support it received from the three Afrikaans churches. Given this, it was easy for the NP to consolidate the great majority of Afrikaners (at least until the early 1980s) into a *volksbeweging* with a religious purpose – ie, to realise the lofty aims of 'Christian Nationalism'. Another method used by the NP to mobilise electoral support was to capture part of the media. These and other means – typically undemocratic and morally questionable – enabled the NP to win 11 successive general elections and three referendums between 1948 and 1992.[17] The parliamentary system in which only whites (of which 60 per cent were Afrikaners) could vote was used cleverly (but in diabolical ways) to perpetuate NP control within the system of white political supremacy for a period of 46 years.

9.4 The intensification of the liberation struggle, the survival crisis of white supremacy, and the transition to a negotiated settlement (1974–94)

The most serious crisis of legitimacy in the Verwoerdian period was triggered off by the Sharpeville unrest. In March 1960 police shot dead 69 people in Sharpeville, an African township near Vereeniging in the Vaal triangle, during an ANC/PAC (Pan-Africanist Congress) campaign against the pass laws. In response to the nationwide protest, the government cordoned off townships, banned the ANC and the PAC, and arrested thousands of people. Once underground, the ANC set up a guerrilla wing, Umkhonto We Sizwe (the Spear of the Nation), which committed various acts of sabotage until its leaders were rounded up at their headquarters in Rivonia, and incarcerated for life in 1964 (see section 9.8).

In 1966, following Verwoerd's assasination in parliament, John Vorster became prime minister. Vorster created a web of security legislation that turned South Africa into a 'police state' by the end of the 1960s.[18] As minister of police, Vorster had built the security police into a formidable political force which was used not only to suppress black protest, but also his own nationalist opponents. Vorster's security system was highly authoritarian and employed brutal methods; it succeeded in suppressing almost all African protest in the decade from 1963 to 1973.[19]

A series of dramatic events in the mid-1970s plunged the white hegemonic order into a survival crisis. This caused a profound paradigm shift in the ideological thinking of both whites and blacks, and dramatically changed power relations within white political supremacy and racial capitalism. The crisis also tilted the broader balance of power towards blacks. Although it took a power struggle stretching two decades before blacks emerged as the victors, the events of the mid-1970s were nonetheless decisive. In the early 1970s the white hegemonic order seemed invincible; it was based on well-structured and well-integrated political, economic, and ideological power, and enjoyed the support of all the major western countries. During the next 20 years, facing a mounting offensive from the liberation movement, the white regime managed to ward off its survival crisis by shoring up its political and economic power – but failed to maintain its legitimacy. Desperate attempts to provide new ideological justifications for white rule all failed dismally. Without the necessary legitimacy, the white hegemonic order collapsed like a pack of cards in the early 1990s.[20]

The cluster of events (from 1973 to 1976) that precipitated the white hegemonic order's survival crisis included the 'unlawful' strike by black trade unions in 1973, the OPEC oil crisis of 1973, the downturn in the economy from 1974 onwards, the *coup d'état* of General Spinola in Lisbon in April 1974, and the Soweto uprising of June 1976. In 1973 South African industry was shaken when large numbers of African workers in Durban struck illegally in support of demands for higher wages and the right to organise. The protracted nature of and wide support for the strikes demonstrated the nascent strength of African 'labour power' in a way that surprised even Africans. The 1974 *coup* in Lisbon and the subsequent independence of Angola and Mozambique broke the *cordon sanitaire* of white colonial regimes to the north of South Africa, and exposed the white minority regimes to the rest of *uhuru* Africa and communist penetration of the continent. The abortive invasion of Angola by P W Botha's army in 1975 and the resultant deployment of Cuban troops in Angola complicated the situation rather seriously from the NP point of view. In the second half of the decade, the critical attitude of the Carter administration in the United States and the increased hostility of the OAU and the Group of 77 succeeded in putting the 'immorality' of the apartheid regime in the international limelight.

Even before the Soweto uprising of 1976 the economy had moved into a serious recession, caused by the OPEC oil price hikes and a downturn in the international economy. The South African recession turned into prolonged stagflation that lasted until the 1990s. The deteriorating economic situation and the intensifying liberation struggle reinforced each other, and nullified all attempts by the white hegemonic order to create conditions conducive to accumulation.[21] The long period of stagflation cannot be regarded as a long and normal cyclical downswing, but represented a deep-seated structural crisis for the system of racial capitalism (Smit, in Schrire 1992: ch 2; see also sections 3.2.2 and 10.2.3).

The Soweto uprising in June 1976 was partly caused by deteriorating economic circumstances. This must be regarded as one of the most decisive events in South Africa's political and economic history in the 20th century (see section 9.8). The reaction it unleashed from the 'frontline' states in southern Africa and the international community generally was as damaging (if not more so) for the white hegemonic order than the awakening of a militarist culture of resistance in African circles in South Africa. The liberation organisations' programme of disinvestment took off after Soweto.[22]

During the 1960s, when the threat to the white hegemonic order was identified as an internal one, the police budget and security legislation enjoyed preference. Early in the 1970s the NP realised that external forces might be the real menace. This insight was confirmed by the Angola debacle of 1975. The defence budget increased from R345 million in 1971/2 to R1701,9 million six years later (see Calitz 1986: table 15.6).[23] It was in this period that the defence establishment devised the ideology of 'total strategy' to counteract the alleged 'total onslaught' against South Africa.

In contrast to Verwoerd's ideology of separate development, 'total strategy' not only functioned as an ideology, but also became the key mobilising element of the apartheid state's attempt during the P W Botha regime to ward off it's survival crisis. It also supplied an ideological and economic pretext for redefining the symbiosis between state and capital, turning it into an 'unholy' coalition in which the 'normal' dividing line between the two domains became blurred. As noted earlier, the NP commonly mobilised electoral support by inciting fear about one peril or the other. The ideologues of the 'total strategy' cleverly characterised the anti-apartheid movement as a 'total onslaught' on the continued existence of white civilisation, Christianity, western values, and the capitalist system. The 'total onslaught' was presented as part of the Cold War and as a high-profile project of the Soviet Union – said to be organised, financed, and orchestrated from Moscow. In a well-executed propaganda campaign, the Soweto crisis was 'internationalised' and 'militarised', and thus deprived of any racial connotations.[24]

'Total strategy' also meant that the main aim of the NP had shifted from promoting the sectional interests of Afrikaners (as in the days of Malan and J G Strydom), through promoting the interests of white South Africans (as in the latter days of Verwoerd, and during the Vorster period), to protecting the continued existence of all South Africans against the dark forces of communism. This widening of the 'common interest' to give greater substance to the 'total strategy' was far more important for the eventual transition towards a non-racial dispensation than the strategy's architects realised in the early 1970s. Also, by presenting the 'survival struggle' as the overreaching purpose of government, the NP, for the first time, justified its existence without falling back on racial and weighty moral arguments.[25]

Shortly after Botha became prime minister in 1978, a comprehensive new policy agenda was implemented in an attempt to ensure the survival of the white hegemonic order. This 'neo-apartheid' policy was a rather odd – but nonetheless well-integrated – mixture of three ingredients. The first was the 'total strategy', aimed at counteracting the alleged 'total onslaught', and meeting the security interests of the military and security establishments. The second was a new accumulation strategy, formulated on behalf of the corporate sector. The third was a policy of 'centralised managerialism', aimed at meeting the ambition of the government and its loyal bureaucracy to maintain a strong managerial grip on the process of reform. Each of the three partners – the securocrats, the business sector, and the government and its bureaucracy – was mainly interested in a specific aspect of the policy package, but also had vested interests in each of the other two. Surprisingly, the securocrats became staunch supporters of 'free market reforms', hoping that reformist policies would remove the grievances that (communist) revolutionaries could exploit, and also that neo-apartheid concessions would convince urban blacks of the merits of capitalism. A large part of the business community developed a direct vested interest in the expansion of ARMSCOR.[26]

Owing to the close co-operation between and overlapping interests of the main partners in Botha's policy agenda, state and capital began to collaborate in a rather artificial manner. Close 'interaction' between the private and public sectors became an everyday phenomenon. The different kinds of interconnections between the government, key sections of the bureaucracy, the parastatals, and a significant number of monopolistic businesses raises questions about who was co-opting whom, and at what price. These are difficult questions to answer. Perhaps the best answer is that every one of the main players in this 'compact of power' believed that it was co-opting the others.[27]

Botha's policy agenda represented a shift away from the NP's traditional rural and Afrikaner constituency towards an urban constituency comprising both the Afrikaner and the English haute bourgeoisie. This shift had important implications for agriculture, and especially for maize-producing farmers. The shrinking tax capacity of the sluggish economy, together with increased spending on defence and black education after the Soweto uprising, created serious budget problems. In these circumstances, something had to give.[28]

The protracted power struggle between the liberation organisations and the white establishment took another decisive turn in 1985 in favour of the former. Shortly after the introduction of the tricameral parliament in September 1984, unrest erupted in African townships throughout the country, and escalated hugely during the first half of 1985. Botha deployed the South African Defence Force (SADF) in the townships in a desperate attempt to smash the uprising. In July 1985 a partial state of emergency was declared. On 15 August 1985 Botha made his infamous 'Rubicon' speech that resulted in a large outflow of foreign investment. In the ten years after 'Rubicon', no less than R50 billion was disinvested.[29] When Chase Manhattan and other American banks refused to renew short-term loans, South Africa was plunged into its worst ever financial crisis.[30]

Between 1985 and 1989 Botha's policy approach was one of 'co-optive domination', in close collaboration with the SADF. The state security council (SSC) effectively governed the country. Due to the additional power given to Botha as executive state president by the tricameral constitution, the drive towards centralised managerialism reached its zenith. In May 1986 Botha used his extraordinary powers to reject the proposals of an Eminent Persons Group of the Commonwealth, and ordered the bombing of Lusaka. In June 1986 a comprehensive state of emergency was declared, and additional security legislation adopted. However, the strategy of 'co-optive domination' became a pretext for adopting a system of structural corruption. This can be regarded as an important episode in the long drama (or tragedy) of white plunder.[31] However, this method of plunder did not benefit all whites, but only those members of the elites (of all populations groups) willing to be co-opted.[32]

While this was not realised at the time, this development hastened the downfall of the old order (see Davenport 1991: 437–45).

From 1985 to 1987 the government made several important policy announcements under severe internal and external pressure. These concessions were important, not because they were valuable contributions to reform, but because they clearly indicated the extent to which power had already shifted from the NP government towards the liberation organisations – both their external and internal wings. The overall effect of the concessions was to boost the moral stature, and intensify the 'onslaught', of the liberation movement.[33]

At the end of the 1980s the white hegemonic order was in an almost unmanageable state of crisis from a security, international, and economic point of view. In 1988 the Botha government deemed it necessary to enact additional security legislation, ban several organisations, and restrict COSATU. COSATU nonetheless mobilised a successful boycott against the municipal elections of 1988. The extra-parliamentary opposition regrouped itself into the Mass Democratic Movement (MDM), which organised several defiance campaigns. Internationally, South Africa was extremely isolated. A hostile block of third-world countries had forced South Africa out of almost all international political forums. Even the 'friendly' governments of the United States, Britain, and West Germany exerted strong pressure on South Africa. After 16 years of stagflation, the economy was in a deep structural crisis. Unemployment reached record levels, and government spending was at an unhealthily high level.[34]

On 2 February 1990, F W de Klerk – who had succeeded a faltering Botha as state president in August 1989 – stunned the world with his announcement that the liberation organisations would be unbanned, that Nelson Mandela and other political prisoners would be set free, and that the NP government was prepared to enter into negotiations with all political parties to seek a peaceful transition to a democratic political system. The true reasons for the NP government's unexpected *volte-face* are still shrouded in mystery.[35]

By the end of the 1980s the South African state could still mobilise the power needed to maintain the *status quo*. However, it was unable to restore stability, or the system's internal and external legitimacy. At the same time, it had, for almost two decades, failed to maintain conditions conducive to accumulation. The symbiosis of the white-controlled state and white-controlled capital was experiencing a serious survival crisis. It was indeed remarkable that the symbiosis still existed, given that it had failed for so long to attain the objectives of legitimation and accumulation. In the prevailing social, economic, and political situation, South Africa was extremely vulnerable to any further initiatives to exclude it from international markets. During 1989 rumours were rife that Margaret Thatcher's Conservative government were finding it increasingly difficult – mainly due to pressure from the Commonwealth, the United Nations security council, and the European Union – to maintain its policy of not applying sanctions to South Africa (see section 3.2.2).

The political 'revolution' that took place in South Africa in 1990 should not be seen and judged in isolation. It should be seen as part and parcel of the global power shift during the last few years of the 1980s, which culminated in the fall of the Berlin Wall in November 1989 and the implosion of the Soviet Union in 1991. Different scenarios have been constructed of the chain of external events that played a causal role in the NP government's *volte-face*.[36]

When tentative negotiations began in May 1990, they quickly developed into a new kind of power struggle between the predominantly white bourgeois establishment and the predominantly black liberation alliance of the ANC, COSATU, and SACP. The differences between the white establishment and the black alliance were striking. While the white establishment could command considerable 'structural' power – in the form of economic, bureaucratic, securocratic, media and professional resources – the alliance could only count on *people's power* – in the form of mass demonstrations or votes in an election – and on *ideological power*, in that it held the moral high ground as the organised voice of the disadvantaged majority.

In May 1992 negotiations broke down over the issue of an entrenched (white) minority veto. When, after the Boipatong massacre on 17 June 1992, the liberation alliance withdrew from the negotiations, the situation in the country became very tense. In early August 1992 COSATU organised a peaceful mass demonstration at the Union Buildings to demonstrate the alliance's huge 'street' power. Following the Bisho massacre on 7 September 1992, the country was hovering on the brink of civil war. In this extremely tense and volatile situation the NP government and members of the alliance signed key Minutes of Understanding on 26 September 1992. In doing so the NP abandoned its demand for a statutory minority veto, and accepted the idea of democratic majoritarianism. The De Klerk government, in a situation of severe crisis, was prepared to dilute the demand for a minority veto in favour of sharing power for five years, in a rather limited manner, in a government of national unity.

9.5 The apartheid system, labour repression, and influx control (1948–86)

The NP coined the term 'apartheid' during the 1948 election campaign, in order to distinguish its 'native' policy from the segregationist policy of the UP. However, apartheid was not as new or as different from segregation as is often alleged. It built scrupulously on the foundation laid by the English establishment's segregationist regimes of the previous 50 years. Ideologically, the apartheid regime was as segregationist as its predecessors, but in practice it intensified both the *repressive* and the *discriminatory* character of segregation. This means that long-standing state controls over the African labour market were restructured and intensified, and made partially applicable to coloureds and Indians as well.

Although the differences between labour patterns under the segregationist and apartheid regimes are important, they probably constitute only a difference in degree and not a qualitative one. However, in due course the term *apartheid* was associated not only with the NP's 'native' policy, but also with the powerful arsenal of security laws enacted by the NP government to suppress black protest. If we take apartheid to mean not only the NP's segregationist legislation (including its repressive, discriminatory, and social engineering programmes) but also the draconian security system used to perpetuate white political domination, then apartheid, especially in 1964–94, did differ qualitatively from the segregationist regime of the mainly English establishment during the first half of the 20th century.[37]

The architects of apartheid were confronted with the same challenge faced by the architects of segregation: how to develop a black labour policy that would encourage white capital accumulation without endangering the legitimacy and stability of white political domination (see Posel 1991: 8). The dilemma the NP government faced in 1948 was not new. The Native Urban Areas Acts of 1923, 1937, and 1945 were designed (in close co-operation with the business sector) to control African urbanisation in accordance with Stallardism.[38] The sharp increase in demand for African industrial workers during the war years created the opportunity for the anti-Stallardists in the NAD to relax influx control.

When the Fagan commission (1946–8) stated that the continuing expansion of urban industries and the growth of a permanent African population was inevitable and desirable, and that they should be regulated but not inhibited, it took the side of the anti-Stallardists. When the report of the Sauer commission – the NP's 'blueprint for apartheid' – was published in 1947, it took a strong Stallardist position. Despite these differences, the Fagan and Sauer reports were both ambiguous on the issues of influx control and African urbanisation. While the former remained thoroughly committed to white political supremacy, the latter acknowledged that some African urbanisation was inevitable. Also, while the former did not call for unrestricted urbanisation, the latter did not advocate the complete withdrawal of African labour from urban areas.[39]

The growing urbanisation of Africans was probably the most contentious issue during the 1948 election.[40] In the run-up to the election the NP regarded growing African urbanisation with horror, and presented it as a diabolical formula for the 'swamping' of white civilisation. The NP's persistent beating of the *'swart gevaar'* ('black peril') drum probably played a decisive role in its victory.

The new NP government was confronted with serious social, economic, and racial problems. It decided that the contradictions and potential conflicts it had inherited from the UP government required a comprehensive statist approach, with a much greater degree of planning and control. In implementing its approach the NP government was torn apart by powerful pressure groups in its own constituency, while the resistance and opposition of blacks set limits to what it could achieve with its comprehensive programme of social engineering.

'Apartheid' is the catch word for the multitude of racially based control measures implemented and regularly amended by the NP government to resolve the contradictions inherent in South Africa's modernisation process, and to perpetuate white political domination. With the benefit of hindsight, one can see that the NP's comprehensive statism did not resolve the structural contradictions, but accentuated them. From the early 1960s onwards the multitude of administrative and legislative control measures were complemented by the institutionalisation of a police state, which was developed into a securocratic state with a militant orientation in the 1970s and 1980s. All these repressive measures were challenged by both organised and unorganised black 'struggle' groups over a period of more than 40 years. It is important to understand that apartheid was not only shaped by government intervention from above, but also by popular struggles from below.[41]

When the NP assumed power, it did not have 'a grand plan' for solving the problems it had inherited from the Smuts government. Its supporters shared a commitment to the sanctity of white supremacy, but had conflicting ideas about how it could best be preserved.[42] At the end of the 1940s there were two schools of thought on what apartheid ought to be: the 'purist' school saw it as a policy of total segregation between white and black, and the 'practical' school saw it as a policy intended to maintain white supremacy, but in a way that would not hamper Afrikaner business interests.

The 'purist' conception of apartheid was propagated by cultural organisations such as the AB, the South African Bureau of Racial Affairs (SABRA), and the Dutch Reformed Church (DRC). The 'practical' conception of apartheid was propagated by emerging Afrikaner entrepreneurs (ie, those in the Afrikaner *volksbeweging*, and those organised into the AHI), and the Afrikaner farming community (organised into the SAAU). The AHI argued that business profits depended on uninterrupted access to an abundant supply of cheap African labour. It also stated that it preferred a permanently urbanised African labour force to migrant labour.[43] The SAAU, in turn, was not opposed to African urbanisation as long as this took place from the 'native reserves' and not from white-controlled rural or farming areas.[44]

According to Posel, both the 'purist' and the 'practical' conceptions of apartheid were contained in the Sauer report. Consequently, as Posel puts it,

> the Sauer report did not bear the imprints of a single hegemonic conception of apartheid. It was rather an internally contradictory and ambiguous document – contradictory, because it wove together strands from mutually exclusive conceptions of apartheid, and ambiguous, because it did not finally choose between [the 'purist' and the 'practical' conceptions of apartheid]' (1991: 60).

The contradictions in the Sauer report set the scene for an ongoing battle in Afrikaner and NP circles over what the NP's 'native policy' (and especially its influx control policy) should be. From the 1940s onwards the NP was obsessed with the supposed dangers of economic integration, and the 'flooding' of Africans into urban areas. For almost 40 years – from 1948 until 1986 – influx control was the core of the NP's 'native policy'. Although influx control was also practised before 1948, the NP government became notorious for its zeal in designing stricter and more efficient influx control measures in an almost desperate attempt to stop African urbanisation, while still allowing a sufficient supply of cheap African migrants.[45]

These measures did not succeed in arresting African urbanisation.[46] The large migrant labour force created by the battery of influx control measures enacted by Verwoerd in 1952 was a wage-earning proletariat which – like the migrant mineworkers – was supposed to subsist on the pre-capitalist economies of the 'native reserves'.[47] What was frightening was the dynamic and ever-changing character of the final phase of African labour repression. As Africans in the reserves increased rapidly from 1950 onwards, and deteriorating conditions in those areas drove them to the urban areas in increasing numbers, the NP government regularly redesigned influx control measures to ensure that only enough – but not more – African migrants were available for manufacturing employment. Due to Verwoerd's stricter influx control measures, migrants became increasingly more vulnerable and more exploitable (see section 9.4.1).[48]

The deteriorating position of African migrants can be demonstrated by identifying five phases of influx control measures during 40 years of NP rule.

i   The 1950s were the years of Verwoerdian pragmatism, when an exploitative African migrant system was designed for the manufacturing sector.

ii The 1960s were the years of growing Verwoerdian dogmatism, when 'territorial apartheid' or 'separate development' became official NP policy.

iii The 1970s were the years in which influx control was applied increasingly rigidly by post-Verwoerdian ideologues.

iv The 1980s were the years of P W Botha's reform initiatives, when a distinction was drawn between African 'insiders' and 'outsiders'.

9.5.1 Verwoerdian pragmatism in the 1950s, and the design of a migrant labour system for the manufacturing sector

The first four years of NP rule can be regarded as the gestation period of its African labour policy. During this period a relentless battle took place behind the scenes between supporters of the 'purist' and the 'practical' conceptions of apartheid. In 1952 the NP's native policy gained a legal foundation when both the Black (Natives) Laws Amendment Act and the Black (Abolition) of Passes and Co-ordination of Documents Act were promulgated. The debate on the contradictory and ambiguous formulations of the Sauer report continued unabated in the NP and the NAD until, in 1950, Verwoerd presented these two conceptions of apartheid as two separate phases of the same blueprint. In what Posel describes as 'a shrewd ideological device', Verwoerd presented the 'purist' conception of total segregation as the morally desirable and long-term ideal, and the the 'practical' conception as a short-term 'exception' dictated by 'economic realities' (1991: 66–7).[49] This approach also enabled him to claim that the NP's native policy and the existing reality of white domination was morally justified, because the *final* result of the policy – ie, complete political and economic segregation – would create a 'moral' situation.[50] In a final attempt to allay fears among NP supporters about the large number of Africans that would still work in the urban areas, Verwoerd promised in 1953 that all these problems would be solved by means of effective 'control'.[51]

The two native affairs acts of 1952 differentiated between two categories of Africans: a minority who were 'detribalised', and thus permanently urbanised, and the majority, who retained their 'tribal' identities and should only be allowed temporarily into urban areas. The purpose of the new legislation was to get rid of the vagaries of the African labour market, which gave rise to the problem of urban labour surpluses and unemployment, and labour shortages in white agricultural districts. This labour market was to be replaced with state labour bureaux tasked with rationally allocating labour to different sectors (see Bonner *et al* 1993: 30–1).

The scarcity of African labour in the 'maize triangle' was one of the main issues during the 1948 election. Given the decisive role played by the white rural vote in swinging the election in the NP's favour, the new government wasted no time in addressing the labour problems of white farmers. Organised agriculture was invited to participate in all the activities of the NAD affecting the agricultural labour supply. It was the only capitalist lobby that enjoyed routine and institutional links with the NAD. The idea of a national labour bureau that could allocate African labour to urban and rural employers was proposed by the SAAU. In due course, local labour bureaux were created in agricultural districts, in order to restrict and control the movement of farm labourers to urban areas. This imposition of 'efflux control' at the 'source' was quite successful in constraining African urbanisation.[52]

The Native Laws Amendment Act (1952) amended the previous Stallardist legislation by applying influx control to African women as well. The announcement that African women had to carry 'passes' (identity documents) provoked great discontent, and led to the Defiance Campaign of 1952.[53] Section 10 restricted Africans with permission to live in urban areas to a small percentage. After taking account of 'economic realities', Verwoerd – who supported the 'purist' conception of apartheid – made several concessions about who could become permanent city dwellers.[54]

When the NAD planned the 1952 legislation, it wanted an influx control system that would only allow 'tribal' Africans to enter urban areas as migrant workers after all the 'detribalised' Africans with urban residence rights had been fully absorbed in employment. The NAD was adamant that influx control should be based on an Urban Labour Preference Policy (ULPP) which should specify categorically that 'until all permanent urban labour resources had been utilised, the further influx [of Africans] was undesirable'.[55] When the 1952 legislation was finally enacted, Verwoerd made the important concession to the business lobbies that 'section 10' Africans could remain in urban areas *even when unemployed*. This concession had the ostensibly unintended effect of creating a small, urbanised African elite with considerable bargaining power.[56]

Several reasons can be advanced for Verwoerd's pragmatic concessions to the business lobbies. Apart from the pressures from the influential AHI and the English-oriented business organisations, the NP was not certain in the early 1950s of its parliamentary majority, and was careful not to enact legislation that could lead to defeat in the 1953 election. But despite the concessions, the 1952 acts succeeded in creating a migrant labour system for industrial employment that was not only harsher and more repressive than those that had preceded it, but also supplied urban employers with as many tribal workers as they demanded (see Hindson 1987: 64–8).

The Abolition of Passes and Co-ordination of Documents Act (1952) repealed previous laws relating to the carrying of passes by Africans. Under the act, reference books were to be issued (to men and women) to enable the labour bureaux – created by the NAD – to control and channel African labour. The act authorised the creation of a network of labour bureaux at the 'local', 'district', and 'regional' levels. Through these labour bureaux a system was established for exercising an unprecedented degree of control over the distribution and allocation of African labour.[57]

Tribal Africans could enter urban areas to seek work as migrant workers – with the prior permission of their local labour bureau – but were only given 72 hours to do so; if they could not find work within that period they had to leave. Exceeding this limit – or being in an urban area without permission for other reasons – was a criminal offence, and the police were tasked with monitoring this. While thousands of pass law offenders were sent to prison, many more were 'endorsed out' of the urban areas to work for a set period on white farms (see Posel 1991: 120–8).

Organised industry and commerce – both English- and Afrikaans-speaking – were rhetorically very critical of the labour bureaux and influx control. Their argument was that they needed Africans as semi-skilled workers, and that Africans could only acquire the necessary skills if they lived permanently in the urban areas. In order to allow employers the benefits of skilled African labour without antagonising the hostile white trade unions, the state permitted some skilled jobs to be performed by semi-skilled African workers. Although the percentage of Africans employed as 'skilled' and 'semi-skilled' workers increased steadily, the overwhelming majority of Africans employed in manufacturing – 84 per cent in 1960 – remained unskilled. Despite the fact that organised business formally opposed influx control, most urban employers actually preferred to employ 'tribal' African migrant workers in the large number of unskilled jobs available. They were much cheaper, and also far more docile (see Posel 1991: 155–60).

Owing to the deteriorating socio-economic conditions in the 'native reserves', it became urgently necessary for 'tribal' Africans to find jobs in urban areas. Given that those who received permission from a labour bureau to enter an urban area had to find employment within 72 hours, their position was exceptionally vulnerable. Many – driven to the cities by poverty – often had no choice but to remain there illegally, and for them the need to find employment was even more pressing. Government officials were aware that most Africans forcibly removed to the Bantustans would return to the urban areas, and would then be prepared to accept lower wages. The crushing of African rural resistance in the early 1960s and the banning of the liberation organisations in 1961 enabled the NP government to put 'tribal authorities' – who were prepared to help administer the government's influx and migrant policies – in charge of the Bantustans. As a result, migrant labour became even more disciplined, and even cheaper (see Marks and Trapido 1987: 22).

Those looking for employment illegally depended upon employers' preparedness to flout the regulations, and were vulnerable to the threat of exposure to the authorities. 'Tribal' or migrant workers – and especially 'illegal' migrant workers – were not only prepared to work at exceptionally low wages, but were also prepared to perform unpleasant jobs. In contrast with 'urbanised' Africans with permanent residence rights, 'tribal' workers could not afford to be 'choosy', 'lazy', or 'cheeky', and had to perform heavy industrial work. Consequently, despite their public complaints about the system, many urban employers preferred to employ migrant workers (see Hindson 1987: 64–8; Halisi 1999: 37–43).

The Smuts government's *laissez-faire* approach to urban development during the 1940s created an untenable problem of urban decay, large-scale squatting, overcrowding, and growing poverty and unemployment among members of the urbanised white, coloured, and African proletariat. From the point of view of the NP, the most pressing 'urban problem' was looming racial conflict and the threatened swamping of whites – especially poorer Afrikaners who were also living in semi-squatter conditions. Consequently, the NP government embarked on a strategy of urban 'stabilisation' designed to bolster the state's control over the living and working conditions of predominantly Africans in urban areas. The shanty towns in larger centres were replaced by neatly laid-out 'locations' or 'townships', comprising well-built houses for 'detribalised' Africans with residential rights, and hostels for migrant workers.[58]

Influx control deprived millions of Africans of the barest minimum of social citizenship. Government spending on education, health, housing, and social security for urban Africans was deliberately minimised, so as not to 'attract' more Africans to the cities. As in the case of the mining industry, the migrant system for employment in the manufacturing sector was also based on the supposition that 'welfare services' for migrants were supplied in the 'reserves' (see Posel 1991: 123). The fact that African wages as a percentage of white wages declined from 1950 to 1970 in both the manufacturing and mining industries (despite the economic deterioration in the 'native reserves') shows clearly that the migrant labour systems – in both industries – became considerably more exploitative during the first 25 apartheid years.[59]

When the influx control legislation of 1952 was adopted, Verwoerd went out of his way to ensure that it would not hamper the gold mines' ability to recruit migrant workers in the 'native reserves' and other African countries, but would make it even easier for them to do so. While the legislation explicitly prohibited the employment of foreign Africans in secondary industry and commerce, the gold mines were given the rights to continue doing so. The gold mines were also excluded from the scope of the labour bureau system in the course of recruiting Africans in South Africa (see Bonner *et al* 1993: 8). The special treatment of the gold mining industry by the NP government is yet another example of the extraordinary bargaining power of the gold mines, not only during the hegemonic periods of the English establishment but also during the hegemonic periods of the Afrikaner establishment – ie, by the Pact government in the 1920s, and the NP after 1948.[60]

If the support given to the CM by successive governments (including the NP) to recruit migrant labour in foreign countries is also taken into account, there can be no doubt that, from 1910 until 1972, the mining industry was fully in cahoots with the segregationist and apartheid regimes in their systemic exploitation of local and foreign African labour.[61] The real wages of migrant workers in mining remained unchanged from 1932 until 1960, despite several increases in the price of gold and the serious deterioration of economic conditions in the 'native reserves'. The gold mines stubbornly continued to pay low wages to Africans on the grounds that they had a subsistence base in the 'native reserves' and in foreign countries, even when this was clearly no longer the case (see Wolpe, in Beinart and Dubow 1995: ch 3).

9.5.2 *Verwoerdian dogmatism and the acceptance of 'territorial apartheid' as official government policy in the 1960s*

At the end of the 1950s important shifts occurred in apartheid policy. These coincided with important events in the Afrikaner political arena, and with a new realisation that the influx control measures of 1952 were too flexible and had not succeeded in stopping the growing economic integration of whites and Africans. Renewed concerns over the growing numbers of Africans in white urban areas caused not only an ideological shift towards the 'purist' conception of apartheid, but administrative measures were also adapted in order to curtail the flow of migrant labour to the urban areas.

The struggle in Afrikaner circles between those favouring the 'purist' conception of apartheid and those favouring the 'practical' conception continued unabated during the 1950s. At the same time, English business organisations increased their attacks on influx control measures, but continued to employ large numbers of migrant workers (both legally and illegally) at extremely low wages. Certain events at the end of the 1950s strengthened the 'purist' position, the most important being the Treason Trial (1956–61) and the escalation of African resistance that culminated in the Sharpeville protest of 1960.[62] In an atmosphere of growing hostility between whites and Africans, the liberation organisations were banned, and from 1961 onwards an authoritarian security system was created in order to suppress black unrest more effectively. This system forced the black opposition movements underground, with the consequence that open resistance to apartheid declined in the second half of the 1960s.

Verwoerd was always inclined towards the 'purist' rather than the 'practical' conception of apartheid. However, economic and political conditions in the early 1950s had forced him to apply influx control measures in a more pragmatic manner. When he was elected as prime minister in 1958, it became possible for him to show his true colours and favour a more dogmatic application of influx control. (The NP's electoral position was vulnerable at the beginning of the 1950s, but improved dramatically in the early 1960s.)[63] In 1958 the NAD was renamed the bantu affairs department (BAD), as part of a restructuring exercise aimed at implementing influx control more effectively. Until that time local authorities had played an important role in applying influx control measures. Many local authorities (including Johannesburg's, for example) were still controlled by the UP, and did not always co-operate with the NAD. From the outset, the BAD tried to deprive local authorities of their responsibilities for 'native affairs'. This caused a long and protracted struggle that culminated in the creation of the bantu affairs administration boards (BAABs) in 1971.[64]

Perhaps the most important policy shift in NP policy after 1948 was Verwoerd's announcement in 1959 that the policy of apartheid was to be replaced with the supposedly 'non-racist' policy of *separate development* – also known as 'grand apartheid'. In terms of this new package, independent homelands', or Bantustans, would be created for different African ethnic groups, based on the 'native areas' comprising 13 per cent of South Africa's territory, (according to the Development Trust and Land Act of 1936); urbanisation would be stemmed; and decentralised industries created on the borders of the Bantustans. The Bantustan scheme rested on the convenient proposition that there was no African majority in South Africa. It held that

'Bantu' were not South Africans, but belonged instead to a multitude of 'national/ethnic groups', and should exercise their citizenship in their own 'homelands'.[65] Although this ideological edifice was propagated with evangelical zeal, and was accepted by the majority of Afrikaners (and by some English speakers) as a morally justifiable 'solution' to the African problem, it impressed only a small number of co-opted and corrupted African leaders, and was never accepted in the outside world.

During the 1960s the policy of 'separate development' and the idea of ethnicity were used as an excuse for a renewed attack on the residential rights of Africans with 'section 10' rights. In sharp contrast with the pragmatic approach of the 1950s, the government now claimed that 'section 10 Africans' could not claim guaranteed residential rights. It now used the idea of the fundamental ethnic unity of Africans in the urban and rural areas to reject the idea that there were 'two kinds of Africans', ie, those who were urbanised, and those who retained ties with the reserves. In accordance with the new approach, the BAD regularly disclaimed the residential rights of 'section 10 Africans'.[66]

The first of BAD's attacks on these rights came via its urban removal policy. Initially, the authorities emphasised the relocation of communities living in 'black spots' in rural white areas to the homelands. However, in the mid-1960s they also began to remove Africans with section 10 rights. In 1964 the government amended legislation concerning the movement, settlement, and employment of Africans. The Black Labour Act (1964) enabled the government to embark on a policy of large-scale social engineering, with devastating effects on the lives of millions of black people. Under this legislation, the BAD started to remove individuals declared to be 'non-productive' or 'idle and undesirable' from urban to rural areas. The definition of an 'idle' person was widened to include section 10 Africans who refused three jobs offered by a labour bureau, and thousands were removed as a result. The 1964 legislation also strengthened influx and efflux control, and streamlined registration procedures for migrants. At the same time the regulations controlling the entrance of women and children were made much stricter.[67]

One of the main characteristics of the 1960s was the intensified struggle between the government and its main administrative arm (the BAD) on the one hand, and those opposed to influx control on the other. At a time when the ideological obsession with influx control and the administration's capacity to administer it grew stronger, both white employers and African migrants experienced strong economic motivations to oppose it. The high average annual economic growth rate of 5,5 per cent increased the demand for African labour in urban areas at the same time that the deteriorating situation in the Bantustans forced increasing numbers of Africans to migrate to the urban areas – either legally or illegally. Agricultural production per capita in the Bantustans fell dramatically from the late 1950s onwards.

In 1954 Verwoerd – then minister of native affairs – announced that part of the Cape Province below a line between Humansdorp and Colesburg would become a 'coloured preference area', and that African migrant labour and the settlement of African families in this region would be more severely discouraged there than in the rest of the province. In 1961 the authorities decreed that migrant workers' contracts in the western part of the Cape Province could only last for a year, and in 1966 African labour on farms in this part was frozen at the number employed on 31 August 1966 (see Van der Horst, in Truu 1976: 114).

During the 1960s the demand for and supply of African migrants was so strong that, according to Posel, 'the expansion of BAD's bureaucracy, and the general hardening of attitudes, were insufficient to deter resistance from large numbers of employers and work-seekers' (1991: 253). Throughout the decade the BAD experimented with new measures to combat the illegal employment of migrants, and improve influx control. In a desperate attempt to stop the inflow of migrant workers and others, the government introduced two drastic measures that set the scene for the 1970s. The first was the Physical Planning and Utilisation of Resources Act of 1967, which introduced labour quotas for urban manufacturing. The second was the creation of the BAABs in 1971, which took over the task of controlling the movements and rights of Africans at the local level, thus depriving municipalities of their control over African labour (see section 9.5.3).

Although the NP government did not succeed in arresting the flow of Africans from the Bantustans to the urban areas, it did succeed in stopping the efflux from the white agricultural sector in the 1960s. Coincidental with the destruction of the labour tenant and squatting systems, the government passed the Bantu Laws Amendment Act of 1964 which stipulated, *inter alia*, that all farm labourers had to be registered in Pretoria. This meant that, as soon as a farm labourer was employed in an urban area, the records would show that he was a farm labourer and therefore not eligible for urban employment (Bundy 1975: 44–5).

It is difficult to determine the relative costs and benefits of stricter influx control and the mass removals of 'surplus' people in the 1960s. For some capital-intensive industries – mainly controlled by the English-speaking business sector – the high turnover of 'tribal' or migrant workers was undoubtedly a serious obstacle to improving labour productivity. For employers lacking the motive or capital to mechanise their operations, this instability was, according to Posel, 'a small price to pay for the ways in which influx control cheapened the price of labour by undermining the bargaining power of illegal workers' (1991: 269).

We can come to the general conclusion that the different stages of black labour repression (that began in 1841 and continued until the 1980s) were functional for capitalist accumulation until more or less the end of the 1960s. During this decade, the very high economic growth rate and need for technological modernisation on the one hand, and stricter influx control measures on the other, began to create major bottlenecks in the supply of specific categories of labour. These were so serious that the low cost of African migrant labour could no longer compensate for its detrimental effects. There can be little doubt – as we will show in the next section – that the labour quota system introduced at the end of the 1960s and the obstructive role played by the BAABs from 1971 onwards created a labour pattern that was dysfunctional for continuous capital accumulation and economic growth.

It is ironic that, precisely when the government began to succeed in its attempts to prevent the flow of African workers to the urban areas, the demand for such labour started to decline sharply, with growing structural unemployment in the Bantustans the unfortunate result.

The 1960s were one of the most prosperous decades in South Africa's history. On average, the economy grew at 5,5 per cent a year (Mohr 1994: 46). While the per capita income of whites (in constant rand terms) increased by 46 per cent, that of Africans increased by only 23 per cent. The ratio of white to African per capita income rose sharply during the decade (see table 10.8). This was not because Africans benefited less from the rapid economic growth than whites did, but because many of them experienced entirely new forms of repression and exploitation. This was also the decade in which millions of Africans were relocated under the Group Areas Act.

In the 1960s, migrant workers in the mining industry were an impoverished proletariat suffering from chronic health problems. Many migrant workers in the manufacturing industry were also an impoverished proletariat, but with impressive petty crime records rather than chronic health problems. The inability of the ULPP to channel African youths born in the cities into the formal labour market (given job reservation) set the scene for their mounting unemployment and the spread of juvenile delinquency, youth gangs, and urban crime. The cumulative effect of this criminalisation of a large part of the African population in urban areas is perhaps one of the most unfortunate legacies of apartheid. As criminal activity became a part of the everyday existence of millions of Africans during the 1960s and 1970s, many people were not only criminalised but brutalised to such an extent that it became difficult for many of them to act in a lawful and civil manner after the apartheid system had been abolished (see Bonner *et al* 1993: 34–5; see also section 10.5).

The 1960s was also the decade in which the NP government embarked on a policy to develop the 'native reserves' (now referred to as 'homelands', or 'Bantustans'). The Tomlinson commission of inquiry into socio-economic conditions in the 'native reserves' published its report in 1956. The commission confirmed the appalling socio-economic conditions in the reserves that other government commissions and committees had documented since the 1920s: malnutrition, stark poverty, overstocking, denuding of land, and so on. The commission also found that only a small and relatively prosperous portion of African peasants had escaped the ravages of extreme poverty; it estimated that 46,3 per cent of the income earned in the reserves in the early 1950s was concentrated in the hands of a small and often corrupt elite comprising only 12,7 per cent of the population. The commission's central finding was that R204 million should be spent during the following ten years to develop the reserves, and to create urgently needed employment opportunities.[68] If these funds were not spent, the commission warned, 'the inevitable consequences of the integration of the Bantu and European populations into a common society must be endured' (see Davenport 1991: 368–74).

Although Verwoerd was initially very critical of the commission's recommendations, he nonetheless decided in 1959 that the political and economic solution to the 'African problem' lay in the 'underdeveloped' reserves, and declared that these areas should in due course accommodate 75 per cent of the African population. The commission recommended that industrialists be attracted to the periphery of the reserves by cheaper power, water, housing, and transport for their workers, who would commute from their homes nearby. It took Verwoerd until 1964 to realise that Tomlinson had underestimated the difficulties of economic development in the Bantustans and border areas.[69] The government then tried to speed up industrial decentralisation, but by the end of 1966 fewer than 45 000 new jobs for Africans had been created in the border areas and reserves.[70]

9.5.3 The increasing rigidity of post-Verwoerdian ideologues in the 1970s, and the creation of a system of commuter migrancy

John Vorster, elected as prime minister after Verwoerd's assassination in 1966, remained in office until 1978. His election had two important consequences. Firstly, by electing the minister of police as prime minister, the NP endorsed a further entrenchment of the authoritarian police state which Vorster had already begun to create. Secondly, the 'purist' conception of apartheid was now applied with increasing rigidity by 'smaller prophets' on whose shoulders the Verwoerdian mantle had fallen.[71]

As noted earlier, in the late 1960s the government took a first step towards introducing a labour quota system in urban areas by passing the Physical Planning and Utilisation of Resources Act, which gave the minister of planning the authority to restrict the use of land in designated controlled areas for industrial purposes. The act deprived local authorities of their responsibility for regulating the rate of industrial development and growth of the industrial African workforce in their areas of jurisdiction. In 1970 the government published a white paper in which it authorised the implementation of labour quotas. The maximum ratio of white to African industrial workers on the Witwatersrand was to be 1:25 until 1973, and only 1:2 thereafter. Any industry exceeding the quota would be compelled to decentralise to a border area or a Bantustan.[72]

The second drastic step taken by the Vorster government to improve influx control was the creation of the BAABs in 1971. By 1975 22 BAABs had been set up, each responsible for regions comprising a few municipalities and the surrounding farming districts. The task of administering Africans in 'white' areas, previously performed by white local authorities, now fell to these boards. This was a resounding victory for the BAD, which had campaigned from its inception in the late 1950s for full control over the application of influx control.

Despite these measures the authorities were still unable to stem the increase in the illegal employment of migrants in urban areas.[73] As influx control measures became more efficient in the 1970s, it became increasingly necessary for poor people in the Bantustans to violate them. By the 1970s the Bantustans had become repositories of fully proletarianised surplus people. At the end of the 1970s it was estimated that a person who could find work in a 'white' urban area for nine months and then spend three months in jail would still be better off than if he/she had remained in a Bantustan (see Savage 1986: 201–5; Hindson 1987: 68–74, 80–3).

When the BAABs took over the administration of African townships, they also gained control over the provision of housing for Africans in urban areas. They immediately started to use the availability of housing as an instrument of influx control. Adequate housing for Africans in urban areas had been a serious problem from the beginning of the century, but especially after the adoption of the Stallardist legislation in 1923. The big growth in urbanisation in the 1940s resulted in large-scale squatting. As a result, in the 1950s and 1960s the NP launched an energetic slum clearance and housing programme. But in the late 1960s the government decided to slow down the construction of houses for Africans in 'white' urban areas and concentrate on building houses in the Bantustans, in order to encourage the growth of commuter migrancy. Bantustan borders were redrawn to include urban areas near East London, Durban, and Pretoria.[74] By shifting home-building for Africans from 'white' to African urban areas, the housing shortage in 'white' urban areas became more acute. Instead of addressing this shortage, the government only built hostels or 'bachelors' quarters' in the urban areas in order to make it even more difficult for families to move to 'white' urban areas. The result of this policy of 'deliberate deprivation' was that slum conditions began to reappear in many urban areas.[75] A new decree that Africans could only gain permission to work in 'white' urban areas if housing was available was another powerful – albeit cruel – deterrent (Davenport 1991: 526–7).

By creating a scarcity of housing, by industrial licensing, and by developing black dormitory areas in Bantustans near major industrial centres, the government succeeded in the 1970s in creating a wholly new form of African migrancy: a system of *commuter migrancy*. African workers were forced to travel daily – often over considerable distances – from their homes in a Bantustan to a 'white' industrial area, and back again.[76]

A third drastic step taken by the Vorster government was to change the citizenship rights of Africans. The Bantu Homelands Citizenship Act of 1970 attached the citizenship of *all* Africans to one of the homelands, even if they had never lived outside the 'white' areas. In 1971 the Bantu Homelands Constitution Act empowered the president to confer self-government on any of the eight territorial authorities. As several Bantustans became self-governing, and after a while also supposedly 'independent', migrants from these areas who were illegally in 'white' urban areas were now regarded as 'foreigners'. As a result, they could now be deported, and these deportations were no longer subject to legal appeal. In this way even the limited legal rights granted to African migrants under the pass laws were removed.[77]

To justify its policy of industrial licensing, the Vorster government stepped up industrial decentralisation to areas bordering on the Bantustans, and also allowed white entrepreneurial activity in the Bantustans on an agency basis. Decentralisation was encouraged by offering industrialists incentive packages including five years' income tax exemptions, favourable loan rates, road and tariff rebates, and other concessions. The direct and indirect cost to taxpayers of industrial decentralisation during the 1970s and 1980s amounted to billions of rands. Although thousands of new jobs were created in the Bantustans and in border industries, their cost per capita was far higher than could be regarded as economically justifiable.[78]

The high level of economic growth in the 1960s changed the structure of, and capital accumulation in, the industrial sector. These changes caused a greater demand for skilled workers than could be filled by whites. Consequently, the Vorster government was forced to relax job reservation and allow semi-skilled African operatives to perform skilled work, not only in border areas but also in white urban areas. Therefore, in the early 1970s, the strange situation existed that, while large numbers of Africans were drawn into skilled jobs, even larger numbers of unskilled African migrant workers were made redundant and forced back to the poverty-stricken Bantustans by stricter influx control measures.

The Vorster government's policy of decentralising industrial development to border areas, together with its resettlement policy, caused the populations of the Bantustans to increase sharply, from 4 million in 1960 to 11 million in 1980. In an almost desperate attempt to improve the carrying capacity of the Bantustans, the amount spent on Bantustan development also increased sharply, from R18,38 per head (in 1978 prices) in 1961 to R89,64 per head in 1979. But much of the money was spent on costly government buildings rather than on developing infrastructure and subsistence mechanisms. Ironically, the socio-economic situation in the Bantustans and their ability to produce a subsistence base for their inhabitants declined dramatically during this period, mainly as a result of the sharp population increase (see Davenport 1991: 368–74, 403–5; Lipton 1986: 402).

The migrant labour system in the gold mining industry also changed in the early 1970s. The wages of migrant workers started to rise as a result of the rise in the price of gold and the suspension of migrant labour from Mozambique after this territory had become independent under a Marxist regime in 1975. As a result, an important shift towards using domestic labour took place in the mining industry. In 1973 almost 80 per cent of its workforce consisted of foreign migrants; by 1982 this figure had dropped to less than 40 per cent. The mines also tried to stabilise their migrant workforce by guaranteeing jobs to workers who returned within a specified period. In 1982 the real wages of African mineworkers were almost four times higher than in 1971. While African wages in mining as a percentage of white wages were only 5,9 per cent in 1971, they increased to 19 per cent in 1985 (Hindson 1987: 88; Crush *et al* 1991: 104–10; table 8.1).

The 1970s was the decade in which influx control was improved, and its effects on a large part of the African population became more destructive than ever before. While, for more than a century, labour repressive measures had decreased costs by supplying white employers with cheap and docile African labour, the new measures increased the costs of many white employers, thus further depressing the already declining economy. The Vorster government started, hesitantly, to relax some of the costly discriminatory measures in the 1970s.

In 1974 the masters and servants laws, which made it a criminal offence for an employee to break his/her contract, and had been part and parcel of repressive labour systems since 1841, were repealed. However, this did not stem from Vorster's reform initiatives but was prompted by legislation in the United States that prohibited the import of goods produced by indentured labour (Dugard, in Hellman and Lever 1980: 47).[79]

9.5.4 P W Botha's reform initiatives, and the distinction between African 'insiders' and 'outsiders' (1978–89)

The stricter influx control policies of the Vorster government caused widespread controversy during the 1970s. As the downturn in the economy from 1973/4 onwards caused sharp declines in corporate profits, organised industry and commerce in especially the English-oriented business sector called for the relaxation of influx control, in order to increase the size of the urban African workforce, and the liberalisation of urban labour markets, so as to increase the mobility of workers in the urban areas. Although the downturn in the economy was universal, the English-oriented corporate sector believed that improved access to African labour would solve their accumulation problems. Deteriorating economic conditions, together with the political vacuum created by Vorster's indecision after the *coup d'état* in Portugal in 1974, also prompted Afrikaner capitalists to criticise the government's economic and labour policies for the first time.[80]

The clash between the Vorster government and almost all sectors of organised business on economic and especially labour policy was the most serious confrontation between government and business in South African history. It threatened to destroy the symbiotic relationship that had existed since Union between the government of the day and a least some sections of organised business. Vorster reacted furiously to the pressures from the business community, and denounced its requests as unjustified interference in the realm of government.

When, in 1978, P W Botha succeeded Vorster as prime minister, the 'total strategy' formulated by Botha's generals became not only his main propaganda tool, but also the cornerstone of his political agenda. The pronouncement that the 'total onslaught' was Soviet-inspired and designed to destroy the capitalist or free enterprise system in South Africa created the space for a remarkable collaboration between apartheid and capitalism. The 'total strategy' became a comprehensive policy framework in terms of which the government and the business sector (both white and black) could join forces to save the capitalist system and white civilisation from the communist threat. The FMF was established in 1976 by all major business groupings to 'spread the message of free enterprise among young urban blacks'. The business community – spearheaded by the UF and FMF – easily convinced the Botha government of the need to improve the 'quality of life' of urban blacks, and to cultivate a black urban middle class as a bulwark against a communist or Soviet-inspired revolution. Business leaders, particularly those linked to the government via ARMSCOR, also persuaded the Botha government to dismantle the interventionist policies the NP had followed since 1948, and accept the free enterprise approach.[81]

Elements of Botha's reformist policy was formulated by the Riekert and Wiehahn commissions (both of whose reports were published in 1979) and by the Carlton (1979) and Good Hope (1981) conferences. The conferences were held to enhance agreement between the government and the business sector on policy issues, and to 'institutionalise' a role for the private sector in the growing bureaucratic state. Owing to the strategic role played by the white business community in formulating and legitimising the Botha reforms, the serious flaws in these initiatives cannot only be blamed on the Botha government. As we will indicate below, the Botha reforms did not resolve either the legitimacy or the accumulation crisis, but intensified them by creating various structural contradictions. The business community must bear some responsibility for the ensuing fiasco (Davenport 1991: 397– 403).

The government was quite optimistic that its new co-operative relationship with the corporate sector and its reform initiatives would stimulate entrepreneurship. The Wiehahn commission's brief was to investigate labour legislation and to make recommendations that would stimulate productivity. In line with the commission's recommendations, statutory job reservation in the manufacturing sector was abolished, and restrictions on the mobility and training of African labour eased. The Labour Relations Amendment Act (1981) extended formal trade union rights to Africans, and attempted to institutionalise and regulate industrial conflict (O'Meara 1996: 272–7; see also section 9.6).

The Riekert commission concentrated on 'the improvement, modernisation, and reform of the existing official institutional and statutory framework of the labour market in South Africa, with a view to the better utilisation of black manpower' (Manpower Utilisation Commission 1979: para 18). Its main focus was the African labour market – excluding the mines – and the living conditions of Africans in urban areas. The commission reiterated that separate development was non-negotiable, but argued – against the grain of NP orthodoxy – that the de facto permanence of urbanised Africans should be acknowledged. In the process, the Riekert commission at long last acknowledged the correctness of the view of the Fagan commission more than 30 years earlier.

Perhaps the most important of the Riekert commission's recommendations was that Africans should be divided in two groups: urban 'insiders' on the one hand, and rural 'outsiders' on the other. Urban 'insiders' were those with section 10 rights in 'white' urban areas whom, the commission said, should be granted unrestricted freedom to move to and work in any urban area, and 'whose quality of life' should be improved through property rights, better housing, better training, and higher wages. Rural 'outsiders' were to be kept out of the 'white' urban areas with even stricter influx control measures. This division of the African population into 'insiders' and 'outsiders' was based on the supposition that a dualistic economy was still in place, and that it was possible to separate the modern capitalist sector in the white areas and the pre-capitalist sector in the Bantustans by means of control measures. Paradoxically, the free market approach – now accepted by both the corporate sector and the government – was to be applied to'insiders' only, while the movement of 'outsiders' was to be restricted to an even greater extent than before (see Davenport 1991: 379–400).

In applying the Riekert recommendations, the government encountered several problems. While it was now possible for 'insiders' with 'section 10' rights to move from one industrial area to another, all sorts of red tape prevented them from doing so. On the positive side, the government accepted Riekert's recommendations on urban renewal. This was urgently needed because of the way in which African townships had been allowed to run down during the Vorster period, when home-building was shifted to the Bantustans. In 1980 a plan was announced for upgrading greater Soweto by introducing 99-year leasehold ownership and launching a massive electrification project (see Hindson 1987: 83–5).

The Riekert commission's recommendations had important political implications. While the government was still convinced that the Bantustans were an adequate vehicle for the political rights of 'outsiders', the acknowledged permanence of 'insiders' presented it with a difficult political challenge. To 'solve' this problem it decided in the early 1980s to allow 'insiders' to elect their own 'community councils' in urban African townships. It envisaged a process in which the BAABs would gradually be replaced by black local authorities. In its 1981 election manifesto the NP suggested that these black local authorities (BLAs) could also eventually be tied to the Bantustans, thereby providing the basis for a political settlement in terms of the Verwoerdian doctrine.[82]

The recommendations of the Wiehahn and Riekert commissions as applied by the government went a long way towards meeting the demands of the corporate sector for a more flexible labour force in urban areas. But the recommendations of both commissions led to a sharp increase in the wages of 'insiders', and a further decline in the income of 'outsiders' (see table 10.4). Taken together, the Wiehahn and Riekert reforms also facilitated the reorganisation of production on a more capital-intensive basis (O'Meara 1996: 274; see also section 9.6).

Riekert's intention to barricade the already impoverished rural 'outsiders' in the Bantustans was defeated by millions of squatters who simply moved illegally to the periphery of 'white' urban areas, and vehemently resisted attempts to send them back. The squatters' struggle against forced removals started in the late 1970s and escalated into an aggressive movement in the 1980s. The government's attacks on squatters gave rise to explosive situations that received considerable international coverage and put the government under severe international pressure. It was especially the situation in the Western Cape, and particularly at Crossroads, that received the most attention, because the larger Western Cape was supposed to be a coloured preference area. In a protracted battle of wills, thousands of African women were sent back to the Transkei, but most of them returned within two weeks. When, in 1985, the government finally accepted the permanence of large informal African settlements in 'Soweto-by-the-sea' at Crossroads, and started to build new African townships with leasehold rights in the Cape Peninsula, the squatters attained a resounding victory of immense symbolic importance. In 1986 – under pressure from the corporate sector – the government abolished influx control thus acknowledging the failure of its cherished policy of territorial apartheid (Hindson 1987: 83–5; Cobbett et al 1986: 137–45; see also section 3.2.3).

A second structural contradiction was created when, in 1984, representation in the so-called tricameral parliament was extended to coloureds and Indians, but not to urban Africans with voting rights in the new BLAs. From the perspective of urban Africans, there was no logic in not extending parliamentary rights to them. Dissatisfaction with Botha's restricted reform programme was expressed in the formation of the United Democratic Front (UDF) in August 1983, as well as the low turnout of voters in the BLA elections of 1983. The UDF came to play a key role in co-ordinating the internal struggle of the liberation movement during the 1980s.[83]

A third structural contradiction of the Botha reforms arose from the Wiehahn proposals to extend formal trade union rights to Africans in a political vacuum. Although the Labour Relations Amendment Act of 1981 abolished all racial distinctions in respect of trade union membership, and permitted the formation of mixed trade unions, it also laid down strict rules to prevent any direct association or financial links between political parties and trade unions. In the absence of any meaningful vehicle to express their political grievances, black trade unions, and especially those affiliated to the Congress of South African Trade Unions (COSATU), founded in December 1985, established close ties with the UDF and became part of the internal wing of the liberation struggle. Renewed attempts by the government in the late 1880s to prevent COSATU and other black trade unions from participating in protest and political movements were in vain. At that stage the black trade union movement was already entirely politicised, and fully involved in the liberation struggle (see Davenport 1991: 401–2, 500–3).

9.6 The apartheid system and discriminatory legislation, with special reference to the black labour market (1948–90)

Discriminatory practices and legislation have been an integral part of South African society since the 18th century. Discriminatory practices were legitimised in the late 19th century and early 20th century by the racist ideologies of Social Darwinism and segregationism. During the first half of the 20th century, various governments tried, in a somewhat unsystematic manner, to divide the population into different racial groups and to legally sanction social conventions. Besides health considerations, the main motivation for this racist and discriminatory legislation was to protect 'poor whites' (or the Afrikaner proletariat) against competition from the coloured and African proletariat. Before World War 2 neither civil society nor the legal profession was particularly critical of discriminatory practices and legislation, despite the fact that they increased employers' costs. It is indeed strange that, during the first half of the 20th century, the English establishment displayed few scruples over repressive and discriminatory practices.[84]

In 1948 the NP began to entrench racial discrimination in a far more comprehensive and systematic way, at a time when thinking in the western world about the advancement of human rights and the elimination of racial discrimination was changing fundamentally. The UN charter adopted in 1945 committed that organisation to working for 'universal respect for, and observance of, human rights and fundamental freedoms for all without distinction as to race, sex, language or religion'. This was followed, in 1948, by the Universal Declaration of Human Rights, which contains a detailed code of freedoms to which states are expected to aspire. The movement away from discrimination and towards human rights and fundamental freedoms was enhanced by the process of decolonisation that had gathered momentum after the war. There can be no doubt that the reaction against racism and discrimination after the war was a reaction against the blatant racism of Hitler's Nazism (see Dugard, in Hellman and Lever 1980: 82–3).

When the NP came to power, it was obsessed with the dangers of racial swamping and racial mixing. Whites, especially Afrikaners, felt increasingly threatened by black social mobility and advancement. To address the alleged dangers of black swamping, the NP embarked on a 'politicisation of racism' and on the restructuring of the entire society along racial lines (Bonner *et al* 1993: 28–30). For this purpose, besides the influx control mechanisms described earlier, the NP placed a plethora of segregationist and discriminatory legislation on the statute books. In order to maintain racial 'purity', the Prohibition of Mixed Marriages Act (1949) and the Immorality Amendment Act (1950) were introduced to forbid marriages between black and white people as well as extramarital sexual relations between whites and blacks. The Population Registration Act (1950) required people to be identified and registered from birth as members of one of four racial groups. This act caused severe hardship, especially in the coloured community. In 1950 the piecemeal, regional attempts in the pre-apartheid period to secure residential and occupational segregation were replaced by a uniform scheme contained in the Group Areas Act which provided for areas to be declared for the exclusive use of one particular racial group.[85]

An important part of the discriminatory legislation was the creation of separate education systems for the four population groups. As chairman of the Bantu Education Commission appointed in 1949, Dr Werner Eiselein, secretary of the NAD, recommended that control over African schooling be taken away from the Christian missions that had controlled it for more than a century. The Black Education Act (1953) formalised the segregation of black education, and laid the foundations for 'Bantu education'. The Extension of University Education Act (1959) empowered the minister to designate colleges for specified African ethnic groups.[86] African education was taken over by the state in an attempt to gain ideological control over the black intelligentsia who were the product of a mission-based educational system still imbued with assimilationist ideals (Marks and Trapido 1987: 21). Although the system of 'Bantu education' greatly extended the reach of primary education, it remained vastly inferior to white education.[87]

Other discriminatory laws that had a very negative effect on not only Africans but also on coloureds and Indians were the Separate Representation of Voters Act (1951), which removed coloured people from the common voters' roll, and the Reservation of Separate Amenities Act (1953), which allowed for public facilities and transport to be reserved for particular race groups, although there were large differences in quality between the public and transport facilities allocated to the different population groups.[88]

When the NP rose to power, it faced an explosive labour situation.[89] Owing to the increase in industrial production during the war, new 'semi-skilled' jobs were created for Africans who fell outside the racially defined legal classification of 'skilled' and 'unskilled' jobs. To meet the serious shortages of skilled labour, the Smuts government allowed a 'dilution' of the colour bar, and masked these steps under emergency war measures. After the war Smuts refrained from addressing the contradictions created by these 'dilutions'. Blacks had advanced into more skilled jobs, the formerly sharp division between white skilled and black unskilled workers had been blurred, and a racially mixed area of semi-skilled jobs had emerged. Many ex-servicemen were Afrikaners who were not only concerned about their own economic prospect, but were also alarmed by the advancement of black workers into industrial jobs during the war.[90]

In 1948 the NP appointed the Industrial Legislation Commission (ILC) to report *inter alia* on 'whether or not the existing wage-regulating legislation operates as an adequate protection for all races and if not, the steps to be taken to ensure the desired protection' (Van der Horst, in Truu 1976: 103–5). Even before the commission could complete its report, the government – under pressure from the white trade unions – endorsed job reservation by introducing the Black Building Workers Act (1951). This act prohibited blacks from performing skilled work in the building industry in white urban areas. But to increase the supply of housing for Africans in urban townships, the act permitted and encouraged the training and use of Africans in urban townships.[91] It continued the ban on African trade unions.

The NP's policies on labour discrimination can be divided into four phases, in the four decades from 1950 to 1990:

i   In the 1950s the legal framework for grand apartheid and more comprehensive job reservation was created.

ii In the 1960s the implementation of the policy encountered stiff opposition; employers complained vociferously about the 'shortage' of skilled workers, while growing concern was expressed over the low level of wages of most blacks.

iii In the 1970s the government backtracked on many policies in an attempt to break the grip of stagflation. This culminated in the Wiehahn reforms.

iv During the 1980s the implementation of the Wiehahn reforms led to unforeseen labour instability and militancy.

9.6.1 The legal framework for grand apartheid, and the introduction of more comprehensive discriminatory measures in the 1950s

The scene for the first phase of the NP's discriminatory policies was set when the ILC tabled its report in 1951. It recommended that African trade unions should be recognised, and concluded that a colour bar was an 'obstacle to the further progress of non-European workers, as they had not the same opportunities as Europeans'. The government immediately rejected the recommendation that African trade unions should be recognised. The Black Labour Relations Regulation Act (1953) amended the definition of 'employee' to exclude African men and women from becoming members of registered trade unions.[92]

After lengthy deliberations the government introduced the Industrial Conciliation Act of 1956 to replace those of 1924 and 1937. It ignored the ILC's conclusion that a colour bar was an 'obstacle' to the further progress of 'non-European workers'. In the new act the legal job bar, which previously had only applied to the mining industry and to Africans, was extended to manufacturing, construction, and commercial employment, and also (in some cases) to coloureds and Indians.[93] Section 77 of the new act provided for job reservation and for the creation of an industrial tribunal of five members to investigate and issue orders concerning job reservation.[94] The act gave the minister of labour blanket powers to safeguard the economic welfare of employees of any race in any industry or trade by requiring an industrial tribunal to reserve particular kinds of work for members of particular race groups in particular areas.[95]

Between 1956 and 1971, 27 job reservation investigations were conducted, and orders issued. According to Sheila van der Horst, they were far more important than their number, or the number of people directly affected, indicate. According to her, these orders were not only designed to maintain the *status quo*, but also to turn back the clock in respect of the employment of members of different racial groups in occupations and industries in which changes were taking place. Many of the orders stipulated that the percentage of whites (or whites and coloureds) should not decline below a certain level (Van der Horst, in Truu 1976: 102–8; Davenport 1991: 512; see also Clark 1994: ch 6 for job discrimination in public corporations).[96]

Job Reservation Determination no 3 of 1958 reserved 15 different operations for whites. The reason given was that some firms were threatening to replace their white workers 'because of the competition experienced from firms who employed Bantu [at lower wages than were paid to Whites] on such manufacture'. When the industrial council, representing both employers and trade unions, vetoed the determination, the government amended the Industrial Conciliation Act in 1959, enabling it to overrule council decisions.[97]

However, there was an important difference between the motivation for the industrial conciliation acts of 1924 and 1937 on the one hand, and that of 1956 on the other. While the first two were passed to protect large numbers of unemployed 'poor whites' against black competition, white unemployment was not an issue in 1956. At that stage the Afrikaner trade unions were using their considerable bargaining power to entrench their petit bourgeois privileges in the face of black competition. At the end of the 1950s, the positions of white and African workers differed starkly. In contrast with the statutory privileges enjoyed by white workers, Africans – even those with 'section 10' rights – entered the labour market with much less education and training, and were further disadvantaged by job reservation. In addition, their opportunities for advancement and mobility were seriously curtailed and their bargaining power reduced by their exclusion from trade union membership, and therefore their right to participate in legal strikes. Many African workers were rendered virtually rightless *vis-à-vis* employers, the bureaucracy, and the police by the masters and servants laws and the Native Service Contract Act (1932). The last-named act made breaches of contract by African farm and mineworkers a criminal offence – which meant they could not legally leave their jobs without their employers' consent.[98]

9.6.2 The 'reformist' implementation of job reservation in the 1960s amid increasing complaints from employers about the growing scarcity of skilled labour

The second phase of discriminatory legislation and practices introduced by the NP government coincided with the prosperous 1960s, when serious shortages in skilled labour occurred in all sectors of the economy. During this decade, South Africa's economy grew by 5,5 per cent a year. During this economic boom, white employers intensified their pressure on the government to allow them to employ urban Africans in greater numbers, and at higher skills levels. Successive economic development programmes (EDPs) quantified and made explicit the notion that coloured, Indian, and African workers would have to work at higher levels if the government's growth targets were to be attained. The EDPs also indicated that the white community was incapable of supplying the personnel required for the type of work legally reserved for it, and predicted an increase in African unemployment and underemployment, especially in the Bantustans. In a unilateral attempt to solve the problem, the government resorted to encouraging immigration, upgrading the skills of employed whites, and enticing women into the labour market. As the pressures mounted, the government allowed the colour bar to become a 'floating bar', which allowed traditionally white jobs to be fragmented and/or reclassified. This occurred on condition that no white worker would be replaced by a black worker, and that no white person would work under a black person. But despite these concessions the Bantu Laws Amendment Act (1970) demonstrated the government's determination to keep Africans out of skilled jobs.[99]

From the 1890s onwards the mining industry strongly supported labour repressive measures. These enlarged the supply of cheap, unskilled African labour, and ensured that it was docile and exploitable. After an intense struggle in the 1920s the colour bar became more strongly entrenched in mining than in any other sector of the economy. In no other industry were the cost-decreasing effect of repressive measures and the cost-increasing effect of discriminatory measures so clearly visible. There was a sharp conflict between mine owners' *benefits* from their monopsonistic power in the unskilled African labour market (in which Africans were deliberately proletarianised and also subjected to the migrant and compound systems), and the high *cost* of white labour in the skilled labour market, in which white interests were entrenched. According to Merle Lipton, this conflict lay at the heart of ambivalence and divisions among mine owners over segregation and apartheid. A strange love–hate relationship existed between the gold mining industry and the NP government. According to Lipton, the industry was opposed to some of the NP's discriminatory measures, but until the 1980s supported many of its racist policies and, as its attitude to black unions showed, were hardly out of step with many of the Nationalists' repressive policies (1986: 132).

By 1960 gold mining was a declining industry, with many mines kept open with subsidies amounting to R30 million in 1970. These problems led to renewed pressures to substitute African workers for whites, or to increase mechanisation. It was estimated that the replacement of 70 per cent of white workers with Africans could save the industry R30 million a year. At the same time, the mines were badly affected by a growing shortage of white skilled workers. In 1964 the mines took the initiative to relax job reservation; the owners of 12 gold mines reached an agreement with the white unions to allow black workers to fill jobs legally reserved for whites. The experiment resulted in increased productivity, but white miners on other mines objected, and the government blocked the experiment. After several white strikes in 1966, a compromise agreement was reached that allowed blacks to do some 'white' jobs, but in return the whites obtained guarantees against retrenchment, as well as the lions' share of the proceeds of the increase in productivity (See Crush *et al* 1991: 86–90).

The steel and engineering sector also experienced a severe shortage of skilled workers in the 1960s. From 1968 onwards this sector followed the example of the gold mining industry in negotiating a 'productivity bargain' with the white trade unions. In return for 'rationalisation' – ie, the reorganisation, fragmentation, and reclassification of jobs – white workers received higher wages, fringe benefits, and retraining schemes. The preparedness of white workers and white trade unions to participate in 'productivity bargains' and to agree to black advancement deals from the mid-1960s onwards is surprising, given their unyielding attitudes at the end of the 1940s and during the 1950s.[100]

As Bantustan and border area development became an important priority of the NP in the 1960s, the government announced that there would be no 'ceiling' on the skills Africans could acquire in the border areas. As part of the lucrative incentives offered to entrepreneurs to establish factories in the border areas, the government pledged itself to maintain lower wages in these areas, on the strength of the alleged lower cost of living of Africans in these areas (see Van der Horst, in Truu 1976: 112).

In section 8.6 we described the 'ultra-exploitability' of African labour in 1918. F A Johnstone uses this term to describe the position of Africans whose personal power had been destroyed by the collective effect of political, legal, educational, and residential measures institutionalised by white political domination and racial capitalism. If we consider the collective effect of the repressive influx control legislation in the 1950s and 1960s; the discriminatory measures in respect of job reservation and trade union rights enacted in the 1950s, and implemented (with only a few concessions) in the 1960s; and the fact that Africans were still deprived of political rights in the 1950s and 1960s, and were far more proletarianised than in 1918, it becomes evident that Africans were far more exploitable in the 1950s and 1960s than in the 1910s (see tables 8.1 and 10.8).

9.6.3 The gradual dismantling of job reservation in the 1970s in a desperate attempt to create conditions conducive to economic growth, and the acceptance of the Wiehahn recommendations in 1979

Apart from the highly discriminatory Bantu Laws Amendment Act (1970), job reservation was not extended in the 1970s. While black labour repression was intensified by attacks on 'section 10' rights and by more efficient influx control measures (such as the quota system and the creation of the BAABs in 1971), job reservation was gradually dismantled in the 1970s under immense pressure from not only English and Afrikaner business organisations, but also from some of the '*verligte*' ('enlightened') white trade unions. In the first half of the decade the authorities allowed several exemptions from job reservation determinations, but did not dismantle the discriminatory labour machinery.[101]

The scarcity of skilled workers became critical at the beginning of the 1970s. This and the growing gap between the wages of skilled white workers and unskilled black workers became a strong incentive for employees to use black workers illegally to do skilled work. As a result it became increasingly difficult for the authorities to enforce job reservation. Their inability to maintain the job bar in the building industry illustrates the point. In 1970 almost 40 per cent of white construction workers were in jobs reserved for them. Many skilled African construction workers were available in the urban areas, but could not be appointed legally to jobs for which whites were unavailable. The Black Building Workers Act (1951) prohibited blacks from performing skilled building work in white areas, but allowed them to be trained for building work in black townships. Many of these trainees and skilled Africans were employed illegally in white areas at wages lower than those of the white skilled workers.[102]

In 1973 Vorster announced that blacks, including Africans, would be allowed to perform skilled work in white areas as long as the white unions agreed. The sacred rule that blacks had to work under whites was eventually abandoned. In 1972/3 the government also acknowledged the need for training facilities for blacks, established several government-run industrial training centres, and announced its preparedness to subsidise the industrial training of blacks by the private sector. In 1972 the Verwoerdian principle that expenditure on African education should be pegged to direct African taxation was also abolished. Henceforth, finance came from general revenue and expenditure, and African education started to improve. Business organisations that had made poor profits due to the stagflation that had begun in 1974 renewed their pressure on the government to relax job reservation.[103]

The widespread outbreak of unofficial black strikes in Durban in 1973 drew attention to the lack of effective consultative mechanisms for African labour. Several new African trade unions were formed after the strikes, but the government remained adamant in its refusal to recognise African trade unions. At that stage many employers and some white trade unions declared themselves in favour of granting Africans formal trade union rights.[104]

In 1979 the government accepted the recommendation of the Wiehahn commission that Africans be admitted to the official labour relations system, and built this into the Industrial Conciliation Act of 1979. Black trade unions were allowed to register for the first time, provided they excluded Bantustan citizens. The implication was that job reservation along racial lines was abolished in principle, but that existing determinations had to be explicitly repealed before they would lose force (Davenport 1991: 512–17).

9.6.4 The unintended consequences of the Wiehahn reforms, increased labour instability, and growing trade union militancy in the 1980s

From the mid-1970s onwards most white business people, given their accumulation crisis, believed Africans should be granted some form of trade union rights, and that job reservation should be relaxed. Their demands were largely met when the government accepted the Wiehahn recommendations. The main purpose of these recommendations was to promote labour stability, and improve the living conditions of urban blacks. Contrary to expectations, the Wiehahn reforms led to unprecedented labour instability and industrial conflict due to the full-scale politicisation of the African labour movement.[105]

Black workers and their trade unions reacted in conflicting ways to the new rights extended to them. In 1982 the National Manpower Commission reported that African membership of registered trade unions had risen from 56 700 in 1980 to 260 000 in 1981 – almost a quarter of the total membership. However, in 1983 less than 20 per cent of African workers belonged to any union at all. At the end of the 1970s politicised workers increasingly regarded registered trade unions as part of the apartheid system, to be avoided for that reason.

Most white trade unions supported the recommendations for trade union rights for Africans, but the more *verkrampte* unions fought a bitter rearguard battle against the reform measures. White mineworkers struck in 1982 against the repeal of job reservation, but found their employers unyielding. Owing to the hostility of white mineworkers, the CM was the last of the major employers' organisations to extend recognition to African unions in 1982. The National Union of Mineworkers (NUM) grew very rapidly, and organised a strike by African mineworkers in 1984. After extensive negotiations between the CM and NUM, the colour bar in the industry was finally abolished in August 1987.[106]

The main source of industrial unrest in the 1980s was African workers. They were not satisfied with the stipulations of the Industrial Conciliation Act (1979) that Bantustan citizens and migrant workers could not become members of registered trade unions.

Moreover, while the right to join or form registered unions had been extended to Africans, the rights of registered unions had simultaneously been circumscribed; as a result, black workers and their (unregistered) trade unions felt that, rather than a genuine attempt to empower them, the labour reforms represented an attempt to subject them to state control. In the highly charged atmosphere surrounding labour relations, black unions proliferated; many of them opted to demand direct recognition from employers outside the statutory industrial relations system.

In April 1979 numerous militant trade unions – formally non-racial, but with largely black memberships, and most of them eschewing the newly opened formal industrial relations system – formed the Federation of South African Trade Unions (FOSATU).[107] It was subsumed into COSATU, which was formed in December 1985.

The number of strikes and working days lost increased considerably from 1980 onwards and reached a new high point in 1982, when almost 400 strikes took place and 365 000 working days were lost (compared to 230 000 working days lost in 1973). In 1981 the government redefined the definition of 'employee' in the Labour Relations Amendment Act to cover all black workers, including local and foreign migrants and commuters. It gave all black workers the right to organise, and abolished remaining job reservation. However, strict rules were laid down to prevent any association or financial links between political parties and trade unions. All these attempts were in vain. It was completely unrealistic of the government to give full trade union rights to Africans in a political vacuum and think that they would not use these powers to exert political pressure on it (Davenport 1991: 402–3).

From its formation in December 1985 onwards, COSATU was deeply involved in the unrest that had started in the Vaal Triangle at the end of 1984 and rapidly spread through the entire country. From its inception COSATU had a strong political agenda, and acted in an openly militant way. It became, with other black trade unions, a member of the UDF and as such part of the internal wing of the liberation movement. It is ironic that, far from taming or stabilising the African labour movement, the Wiehahn reforms politicised it, with devastating results for the white hegemonic order. During 1987 more strikes took place than ever before. Most of these were openly politically motivated, and formed an integral part of the struggle against the white regime. In a last, almost desperate, attempt to counter the politicisation of black trade unions, the government tightened up the Labour Relations Act in 1987/8. But this was too late, and it only intensified the militant actions of trade unions. At the end of the 1980s the apartheid government was almost completely beleaguered by the black trade union movement (Davenport 1991: 401–2 , 515–17; Worden 1994b: 126–8).

9.7 State corporations and the 'manufacturing' of apartheid[108]

In her seminal work *Manufacturing apartheid*, Nancy Clark analyses the strategic role played by state corporations in South Africa's industrial development, and more specifically in 'manufacturing' the labour policies of the apartheid period. According to her, the labour pattern in state corporations was not only moulded on the labour pattern of the gold mining industry, but 'state corporations have [also] grown and developed throughout the 20th century with due attention paid to the needs of the dominant mining industry, the vocal [and powerful] white working class, and [the powerless, disenfranchised and] potentially volatile African workers' (1994: 11).

As indicated in section 8.6, ESKOM (1922) and ISCOR (1928) were created to gain access to markets dominated by foreign companies, and solve the white (and especially the Afrikaner) unemployment problem. It was not easy for ESKOM or ISCOR to compete with foreign corporations, or to increase their market shares in order to expand their operations and lower the cost of their products. To complicate matters, the foreign corporations had access to far cheaper European capital. The only way to compensate for their higher capital cost was for the state corporations to use highly mechanised production methods, a small elite of skilled white workers, and large numbers of unskilled, disenfranchised, and cheap African workers. In doing this the state corporations perpetuated the production and labour patterns already in place in the gold mining industry. This 'duplication' had already given a unique character to racial capitalism when the NP came to power. The IDC was established in 1939 to attract FDI in local ventures. Its original task was to fund the establishment of public corporations in partnerships with private business. In 1942 the Industrial Development Corporation Act was amended to allow it to establish undertakings on its own, rather than simply assist private enterprises (Clark 1994: 130, 160).

During the 46 years of NP rule, state corporations became a far more

important – and even strategic – instrument, not only for industrial development in general but also for increasing the share of Afrikaner capital and
Afrikaner entrepreneurship in the industrial sector. Consequently, the 'skewed'
character of the South African manufacturing sector – ie, highly mechanised
production methods and a small elite of white workers, together with a large
complement of cheap and unskilled African workers – became far more
institutionalised. The state corporations concentrated on what Clark has called
'upstream, key, or produce goods… such as steel, chemicals, electricity… [and
produced these products] through processes not unlike the production of gold
or diamonds' (1994: 10).

In the period before World War 2 ESKOM and ISCOR succeeded in achieving
a significant measure of control over both their market and labour costs.
Despite this success a sizeable part of the local market for electricity and steel
was still in the hands of foreign corporations. Although the creation of job
opportunities for whites was an important justification for launching ESKOM
and ISCOR, both deviated from this intention. Even before World War 2 both
corporations were increasingly replacing whites with blacks, gaining
significant control over their workforce and their ability to make profits.

During the war the demand for electricity and steel increased sharply. To
meet the demand, the colour bar was 'diluted' and large numbers of Africans
were employed in semi-skilled and skilled work. During the war both ESKOM
and ISCOR learnt that their private partners in the production and marketing of
electricity and steel were making huge profits, and that this was depriving them
of the revenue they needed to expand their production. Anticipating continued
growth in demand for their products after the war, both state corporations
decided to move towards a monopolisation of their markets and a further
fragmentation of jobs to enable them to employ more Africans in skilled and
semi-skilled work.[109]

After 1948 the state corporations became a very important tool of the new
government's economic and racial policies. Both ISCOR and ESKOM's
partnerships with the AAC proved to be extremely valuable, and the NP
maintained these partnerships despite its suspicion of mining capitalists. The
NP government was eager to gain control over strategic industries, and to create
state corporations in which a new generation of Afrikaner businessmen could
gain entrepreneurial experience in a protected environment.[110]

In the early 1950s the NP government used the IDC as a vehicle for creating
SASOL and FOSCOR, and channelled huge amounts of public money via the
IDC to finance the two new state corporations. In all the state corporations the
NP reversed the 'dilution' of the colour bar after strikes by white steelworkers

before and after 1948. The Industrial Conciliation Act of 1956 amply protected white skilled workers in state corporations. In 1960 the IDC was made responsible for the the Border Areas Development Scheme, and in 1963 the Armaments Corporation (ARMSCOR) was established following the announcement of an international arms embargo. ARMSCOR played a hugely important role in protecting and perpetuating the apartheid regime during the 1970s and 1980s. The public sector's share of the economy almost doubled during the first 25 years of NP rule.[111]

While state corporations played a far greater role during the NP's rule, they continued to operate largely according to the economic precepts developed during earlier years. The new corporations were mainly patterned on ESCOM, but continued to reflect the investment and labour patterns of the gold mining industry. To keep production costs low, all the state corporations concentrated on the production of less finished products. By producing 'upstream' – or producer – goods, relatively large capital investments were made, while the labour force was split into a protected white elite and large numbers of cheap African workers. Where possible, the plants of state corporations were shifted to remote rural areas in which African workers could openly be employed as operatives. The NP government's border policy and industrial decentralisation of the 1970s were in fact an extension of the experience gained by state corporations in the 1940s in decentralising plants to rural areas and to the 'native reserves'.

By developing a variety of state corporations, and by modelling their production on the gold mining industry, the South African economy attained a unique character. From the mineral revolution onwards, its system of racial capitalism rested on capital intensity on the one hand, and large numbers of unskilled and easily controllable African workers on the other. By modelling the state corporations on the pattern of the gold mines, the high capital intensity of the economy was significantly increased. Mechanisation proved to be a powerful instrument in the hands of both the gold mining industry and the state corporations to create 'upstream' production conditions in which large numbers of unskilled African workers could be employed at low wages. When, in the 1970s and especially the 1980s, the wages of African workers started to increase, the old formula ceased to be cost-effective. Consequently, both the gold mining industry and the state corporations were forced to take mechanisation to a far higher level, substituting machines for unskilled workers on a grand scale. This second phase of capital intensity from the 1970s onwards had a devastating effect on the employment of unskilled migrant labour. While large numbers of semi-skilled African operatives were drawn into employment from the 1970s onwards, even larger numbers of unskilled African migrant workers were made redundant by capital deepening in the gold mining industry and in the state corporations (also see section 10.2.2 for the unemployment effect of this growing capital intensity).

9.8 The growing radicalisation of black protest in the second half of the 20th century

At the end of the 1940s important shifts took place in the ideological orientation of blacks and whites that set the scene for a protracted and relentless confrontation along racial lines in the second half of the century. The NP won the 1948 election on the basis of a manifesto that promised intensified segregationist measures to protect whites, and especially Afrikaners, against the 'uncivilised' African majority. At the same time the ANCYL and CPSA started to question the legitimacy of the white-dominated 'parliamentary democracy', and began to talk of overthrowing the existing system by means of a revolutionary struggle. When the ANC accepted its militant *Programme of action* in 1949, the ANCYL gained an important victory. The programme demanded 'freedom from white domination', and the rights of Africans to self-determination. It rejected the principle of white 'trusteeship', and urged the use of boycotts, strikes, civil disobedience, and non-cooperation. African political movements after 1948 should be understood in the context of the apartheid counter-revolution, and the NP government's reaction to it (Kuper 1978: 459–70).

Verwoerd's 'native laws' of 1952 applied extended influx control measures to African women. This provoked the Defiance Campaign of 1952, the first head-on confrontation between the more radical Congress Alliance (of the ANC and CPSA) and the NP government. During this civil disobedience campaign, selected discriminatory laws were openly violated with the aim of getting transgressors arrested. The government silenced these protests with threats and violence. To counter the growing militancy in black circles – and especially the influence of the CPSA – the latter was banned under the Suppression of Communism Act of 1950. In 1954, after the Defiance Campaign, the Riotous Assemblies and Suppression of Communism Amendment Act was passed to enable the government to suppress extra-parliamentary opposition more effectively. The 1954 act was one of a series of measures introduced over the next few years which, in the interests of 'national security', ignored the principles of civil liberty on which the public law of South Africa had been based until then (see Davenport and Saunders 2000: 383 –7; Lötter 1997: 43; Lodge 1983: ch 6).

After the defeat of the Defiance Campaign, and after the NP's victory in the 1953 election, black leaders were forced to rethink their strategy. For this purpose several opposition movements organised a Congress of the People, held at Kliptown, south of Johannesburg, in June 1955.[112] The congress adopted a Freedom Charter which, *inter alia*, called for equal rights for all ethnic groups, and declared that South Africa belonged to all its inhabitants. Certain 'socialist' principles such as state ownership of minerals, banks, and industries were also adopted. To those African nationalists with an Africanist perspective, the Freedom Charter, with its goal of racial co-operation between Africans, coloureds, and Indians, represented a betrayal of African nationalism. The ideological rift between the exclusive 'non-racialism' of the Africanists and the 'multiracialism' of the ANC and Congress Alliance came to a head in 1958/9 when the Pan-Africanist Congress (PAC) was established under the leadership of Robert Sobukwe. The independence of Ghana in 1957 and the Conference of Independent African States and the All African People's Conference in 1958 were inspirational events for the PAC. The pan-Africanists were not committed to non-violence, and projected an image of being resolute and courageous people who would take whatever steps were necessary for African liberation (see Coetzer, in Cameron 1986: 283; Halisi 1999: 52–4).

The NP government responded to the Freedom Charter by arresting 156 black leaders and charging them with treason. Their trial, which lasted until March 1961, marked a more active strategy by the state against black protest, aimed at seeing to what extent it could clamp down on extra-parliamentary opposition without alienating itself from the mainstream of western political opinion. With this consideration in mind, the state's case was built mainly on the allegation that the Freedom Charter was inspired by communism.[113]

Even before the Sharpeville unrest erupted in March 1960, the NP government started moving towards a more radical version of indirect rule by tribal chiefs. The Bantu Authority Act (1951) enhanced the authority of tribal chiefs, and with it the patronage and corruption that were part and parcel of the policy of indirect rule since its introduction by the Native Administration Act of 1927. After Verwoerd had announced his separate development policy in January 1959, the Promotion of Bantu Self-Government Act (1959) was passed in order to 'co-opt' the conservative rural elite and drive a wedge between them and the more militant black urban intelligentsia. While the English-speaking officials of the NAD had been exceptionally successful in convincing many rural and urban African leaders of the supposed developmental merits of segregation, the Afrikaner officials of the 'new' NAD of the 1950s and 1960s could not establish the same rapport with the urban African intelligentsia. They did, however, succeed in convincing many tribal and Bantustan leaders of the supposed merits of separate development, mainly because of the lucrative patronage on offer.

When, in 1957, Ghana became independent, with '*uhuru*' as its clarion call, it opened up a new prospect of the rapid decolonisation of Africa. When Verwoerd announced his Bantustan policy two years later, he was hopeful that this would help the NP government to rebuild its international relations, and that the 'independence' of the Bantustans would be accepted internationally as South Africa's version of 'decolonisation'. From the early 1960s it became evident to the black protest movements that the NP was extremely concerned about its own legitimacy – both internally and externally. When the treason trial did not succeed in legitimising the NP government internationally, the Bantustan policy was offered instead. However, it impressed neither the black urban intelligentsia nor the international community. From about 1960 onwards the struggle between the white regime and the black protest movement was largely an ideological one in which the white regime tried to gain legitimacy and the black protest movement tried to undermine it, gaining growing international recognition in the process (Davenport 1991: 352–6; Halisi 1999: ch 4).

In March 1960 the PAC launched an anti-pass campaign, which led to the massacre at Sharpeville on 21 March 1960 when the police fired on unarmed demonstrators and killed 69 people. On 30 March 1960 Philip Kgosana led a march of 30 000 Africans to the centre of Cape Town. After these events Sobukwe and other PAC leaders gave themselves up at the Orlando police station in Soweto, and were arrested. With the PAC's leaders in prison, it ceased to be an effective protest movement. The Sharpeville massacre was nonetheless a huge ideological setback for the NP government. It provoked widespread unrest, and caused a flight of foreign investment and a storm of international protest. On 8 April 1960 the government passed the Unlawful Organisations Act, declaring the ANC and the PAC to be prohibited organisations. Consequently the ANC and the PAC went underground and increasingly advocated violent measures to oppose the state. In 1961 the ANC and CPSA launched Umkhonto we Sizwe, or MK ('Spear of the Nation') as their military wing, while the PAC launched Poqo for the same purpose. In July 1963 police raided the MK headquarters in Rivonia and detained the leadership of the ANC. In 1964 these leaders – Nelson Mandela, Walter Sisulu, Govan Mbeki, Ahmed Kathrada, and Lionel Bernstein – were sentenced to life imprisonment for sabotage after the state had withdrawn charges of treason (Coetzer, in Cameron 1986: ch 18; Lodge 1983: ch 10).

After the banning of the ANC and PAC, and the imprisonment of their key leaders, the liberation movements and protest organisations were largely inactive for more than ten years. During the 1960s John Vorster, then minister of police, created a set of security laws that turned South Africa into a comprehensive 'police state'. This security system was highly authoritarian, and allowed black protest to be suppressed with inhumane methods (see section 9.4). *Inter alia*, the coercive apparatus institutionalised by the NP government gave the police broad powers to arrest people without trial and hold them indefinitely in solitary confinement.[114] With the wisdom of hindsight, the seemingly peaceful period of the 1960s and 1970s was a hugely important one, serving to gestate new radical ideas and nurture a new generation of revolutionary leaders.

Three strands of thought were prevalent among blacks in this period. The first was liberalism, whose popularity declined dramatically among the new generation of African intellectuals. Secondly, radicalised black middle-class students were inspired by the New Left student movements in the United States and Europe. And, thirdly, again influenced by American trends, the black consciousness movement (BCM) formulated a race consciousness in which the term 'black' signified an explicit and radical rejection of apartheid in all its forms (Thompson 1990: 198–200).

The African elite educated by the missionaries associated liberal thought with humane treatment, human rights, parliamentarianism, and European cultural and religious values. The ANC's founders were Christian democrats, and as long as democracy remained an option they favoured a non-violent liberal democratic path (see section 8.10). From the late 1940s onwards liberalism lost its appeal to African intellectuals, and increasingly came to be associated with both colonial and capitalist exploitation. The growing acceptance of Marxist ideas in the black protest movement sparked off a fierce debate between black nationalists or Africanists on the one hand, and the ANC and SACP on the other. While the former insisted that the communists had 'captured' the ANC, the latter insisted that, while the two organisations had enjoyed a long and fruitful fraternal relationship, neither movement had ever controlled the other (Halisi 1999: ch 3).

In the 1950s the NP government took over African education in order to gain ideological control over the black intelligentsia, who had until then been produced by the mission-based education system and were therefore still imbued with assimilationist ideas. The creation of several ethnic universities by the department of Bantu education resulted in a considerable increase in the number of black tertiary students. But the whole system was designed to structure the market for educated black labour along racial lines, and to channel the emerging black middle class into segregated institutions. What the government apparently did not realise was that it was creating an explosive situation by increasing the number of black graduates whose upward mobility was blocked by apartheid.

At both ethnic and English universities, small groups of radical students played an important role in student activities and organisations in the 1960s. At a time when New Left students were causing havoc at universities in Europe and the United States, South Africa's indigenous New Left – consisting of black and white students and organisations – received ideological and intellectual support from foreign student bodies. While the New Left in the United States was protesting against the all-embracing character of consumerist capitalism and the influence of the military industrial complex during the Vietnam War, radical black students had similar experiences of the all-embracing character of racial capitalism and the multitude of apartheid rules and regulations.

In the late 1960s and early 1970s the growing rejection of liberalism and enthusiasm for the New Left in black circles resulted in the black consciousness movement (BCM), in which Steve Biko played a strong intellectual and leadership role. The purpose of the BCM was to create an awareness of the merits and dignity of black people, and to encourage them to take credit for their own achievements. The banning of the ANC and PAC in the early 1960s had left Africans relatively voiceless and vulnerable to the large-scale social engineering and propaganda of the NP government. In 1967, 90 segregated 'white' and 'black' delegates founded the University Christian Movement (UCM) at Rhodes University. Black delegates formed a black caucus which developed into the South African Student Organisation (SASO). In 1968 SASO broke away from the formally non-racial but white-dominated National Union of South African Students (NUSAS) to provide black students with a vehicle of their own. The Black People's Convention (BPC) was formed in 1972 to operate on the political front, while the Black Community Programme (BCP) was set up to promote black health and welfare initiatives. When SASO and the BPC supported the Durban strikes of 1973, and welcomed the installation of a Frelimo government in Mozambique in September 1974, many of their leaders were tried on charges under the Terrorism Act and sent to prison. Their defiant attitude in the dock was widely publicised, and stimulated a similar attitude among black youths during the Soweto uprising two years later. Biko's death in September 1977 – from injuries sustained while being held by the security police – sent shock waves through South Africa and not only stimulated the philosophy of black consciousness, but also gave the movement greater credibility (see Davenport and Saunders 2000: 434–7).

Biko's most important contribution was his attempt to construct a new political consciousness for black South Africans. He believed that a transformation of consciousness was a necessary precondition for mass action. Consequently, he stressed the responsibility of revolutionary intellectuals to emancipate themselves psychologically *before* they could steer a mass cultural movement with an effective revolutionary programme (see Lodge 1983: 323–6).

Black consciousness was strongly influenced by the black theology and black power of Afro-Americans during the civil rights struggle in the 1960s. SASO and the American Student Non-Violent Coordinating Committee (SNCC) shared a similar commitment to the 'subjective dimension' of liberation and populism. Biko and other members of the BCM encouraged a dialogue between intellectuals in Africa and the Africa diaspora, particularly in the United States. While the idea of 'black power' had not been part of the liberation organisations' discourse until then, the BCM was the first organisation to raise this idea in South Africa. In section 8.6 we discussed the way in which the early development of the ideology of segregationism during the first two decades of the 20th century was strongly influenced by segregationist practices and ideology in the American South (see Cell 1982: 192–6). It is remarkable that notions of black theology and black Power in the American South exerted a similarly strong influence on anti-segregationist and anti-apartheid thinking some 70 years later.

Although SASO launched the BPC in 1972 to replace or rival the ANC, PAC, and other liberation organisations, and although it was strongly committed to revolutionary action, it could not sustain its own armed struggle. The strong emphasis of the BCM (and especially Biko) on the 'subjective dimension of violence' as a necessary precondition for mass action could be the reason for its revolutionary failure. After the 1976 Soweto uprising thousands of young black people formerly associated with the BCM left the country to join the military wings of the ANC and PAC. It is not possible to determine the extent to which the BCM brought about the 'subjective transformation' of consciousness in black circles that Biko regarded as a precondition for mass action – or the 'objective dimension of violence'.[115]

On 16 June 1976 Soweto erupted into violence, irrevocably changing the South African political landscape.[116] Early in 1976 the government had stipulated that certain subjects in African schools should be taught in Afrikaans, despite the fact that there weren't enough teachers to teach in

Afrikaans. This was the direct cause of an illegal march by thousands of school children in Soweto that ended in a bloody confrontation with the police. Disturbances broke out throughout the country, which continued sporadically until 1980.[117] The compulsory use of Afrikaans was not the only cause of the uprising. The downturn in the growth performance of the economy since 1974 had caused increased unemployment and poverty in black townships. Harsher influx control measures had caused great discontent, and a BAAB had taken over the administration of Soweto from the relatively benign Johannesburg City Council. It immediately increased rates payable by residents, *inter alia* to pay higher salaries to mainly white officials. Moreover, from the early 1970s the government had shifted home-building for Africans from 'white' urban areas to the Bantustans. This resulted in a serious housing shortage, which led to the re-emergence of slum conditions in Soweto and other townships. The BAABs also took over the implementation of the pass laws, and did so with increasing rigidity. The defeat of the South African army in Angola at the end of 1975 was also, from a psychological point of view, a great setback for white power. It destroyed the myth of the invincibility of white military power in the minds of black South Africans (see Davenport and Saunders 2000: 449–54).

Following its banning in 1960 the ANC was relatively ineffective, and played only a marginal role in the Soweto uprising of 1976–7. But many of the young people who left South Africa after Soweto joined the ANC, and not only gave it a new lease of life, but transformed it into a truly militant liberation movement. The ANC started a well-organised guerrilla campaign against the apartheid regime, and attacked strategic targets such as a SASOL oil refinery and various power stations. When the UDF was launched in August 1983, in protest against the exclusion of Africans from the new tricameral parliament, the ANC acquired a powerful internal wing. The same happened when COSATU and other trade unions with close links with the ANC and other liberation organisations were launched in the early 1980s (Davenport and Saunders 2000: 458–78; Thompson 1990: 228–30; see section 9.6.4 for an account of the growing militancy in the trade union movement).

The NP government introduced its 'total strategy' in the mid-1970s to counteract the alleged 'total onslaught' against South Africa. The draconian measures used by the securocrats to suppress black insurrection provoked more terrorist attacks on strategic targets, and during the latter part of the 1980s the struggle and the state's resistance to it developed into a vicious circle that threatened to plunge the country into open war. Despite belated reforms, the apartheid regime was on a slippery slope that undermined its trustworthiness and bargaining power. Although economic and political power was ostensibly still in white hands, the intensification of the struggle had already caused a substantial 'power shift' from white to black that brought about a redistribution of income (see section 10.4.1).

What hastened the eventual collapse of white supremacy was perhaps not the military campaign of the liberation organisations, or the disinvestment campaign of the international community, but the efficacy of the propaganda war that disputed the legitimacy of the apartheid system as well as the authoritarian methods used by the security forces to defend it against the legitimate claims of black South Africans. At the end of the 1980s the crises of accumulation and legitimacy became a crisis of hegemony that could not be remedied. By the end of the 1980s the liberation organisations and the large variety of protest movements associated with them had succeeded in creating an almost unmanageable economic and security situation. This crisis of hegemony forced the NP government to announce, in 1990, its preparedness to enter into negotiations with the liberation movement over a new political dispensation (see O'Meara 1996: 183–9; see also section 9.3. For the activities of the liberation movement from 1960 to 1990, see TRC 1998l: vol 2, ch 4).

Endnotes

1 Each of the six prime ministers (and later state presidents) of the NP, from 1948 until 1994, misled his supporters with misguided ideologies about Afrikaner victimisation, placing the prospect of unattainable 'promised lands' before them, and instilling a comprehensive false consciousness in their minds. A rather peculiar characteristic of many of the NP's ideologies was the inclination to evade hard reality and to blame problems and/or deficiencies in the ranks of its supporters (mainly Afrikaners) on some scapegoat – ie, on evil forces *outside* the Afrikaner volk or society. The inclination of Afrikaners not to face harsh realities but to 'escape' to a make-believe world of self-delusion was not only extremely damaging for them, but for all the people of South Africa.

2 Afrikaner ownership of the South African economy (excluding agriculture) increased from ±5 per cent in 1938/9 to 9,6 per cent in 1948/9. The economy maintained a high growth rate in the 1940s as a result of World War 2. Consequently, it is difficult to determine to what extent the larger share of Afrikaner business resulted from the *reddingsdaadbeweging* ('salvation movement'), emanating from the formation of the *Reddingsdaadbond* (Salvation League') during the 'economic congress of the people' in 1938, and to what extent it resulted from the war effort. In fact, Afrikaners' 'great leap forward' came after the election victory of 1948, when political power fortified the economic movement. After the NP assumed office, Afrikaner corporations became influential pressure groups in the new power constellation. Afrikaner business leaders strongly supported the

'practical' conception of apartheid, and favoured stricter measures to supply emerging Afrikaner industrialism with cheap, docile, mainly migratory African labour (see section 9.4).

3 Throughout the 1940s, organised agriculture fought in vain for major policy changes. First, farmers wanted the immediate implementation of the anti-squatting provisions of the Native Trust and Land Act (1936), designed to give white farmers greater control over African labour tenants. Implementation of chapter IV of the act would have forced African labour tenants to work as wage labourers. Fearful of black unrest, the Smuts government dragged its heels on this issue. Second, the farmers wanted pass laws to be strictly applied to prevent the migration of farm workers to urban areas. Third, organised agriculture strove to persuade the government to implement the 1937 Marketing Act in a way that would ensure higher prices for agricultural produce. As part of the government's cheap food policy during the war, the price of maize was maintained at relatively low levels. When the cheap food policy was maintained after the war, Afrikaner farmers were profoundly alienated (O'Meara 1996: 22–3).

4 During the election campaign the NP used a double-barrelled strategy: on the one hand, it presented Afrikaners as 'victims' of British imperialism and capitalism, and on the other it exploited the 'black peril' argument. This dual 'syndrome of victimisation' proved to be a winning formula – also in future elections. The NP won the first 'apartheid election' with six seats, but only 40 per cent of the total vote. At that stage rural seats were 'deloaded' to the advantage of the NP. The NP built on its 40 per cent support in 1948 in a clever but questionable way to stay in power for the next 46 years (Davenport 1991: 320–4).

5 Despite the NP's indignation about African urbanisation before the 1948 election, it never succeeded in stopping the flow of black people to the cities. During the 1950s and 1960s Afrikaner entrepreneurs succeeded with their own industrial revolution with lucrative government support – initially in the public sector, but in due course also in the private sector. Afrikaner industrialists convinced the NP government to maintain the supply of African migrant labour in urban areas (see section 6.4).

6 From 1947 to 1974 gross domestic product grew at an average of 4,8 per cent a year (Mohr 1994: table 1). We should, however, remember that the economic growth rate of the OECD countries during the 'golden age of capitalism' (1950–73) was even higher. The white hegemonic order and its repressive labour system created lucrative opportunities for foreign investors, and South Africa enjoyed a large influx of foreign investment during this period. Terence Moll claims that the growth rate during the 1950s and 1960s could have been much higher if it were not for apartheid. His argument is interesting, but based on doubtful suppositions (see Moll 1991: 271–91).

7 During the 1940s Prof C G W Schumann of Stellenbosch already favoured a policy to promote the wealthier component of the Afrikaner community instead of concentrating on the 'poor white' problem (see Sadie 2002: 21).

8 Largely as a consequence of NP policies, Afrikaner control of private industry (excluding agriculture) rose from 9 per cent in 1948 to 21 per cent in 1975. If the state corporations are included, industrial output under the 'control' of Afrikaners rose to 45 per cent of the total in 1975 (O'Meara 1996: 80).

9 While ethnic favouritism was part of NP policy from 1948 onwards, Lodge observes that, 'as the NP administration matured it became more degenerate. By the 1980s political corruption was common in both central government and in homeland administration. It was especially entrenched in those domains of government activity which one might term "strategic" and which expended secret funds... Quite aside from the mysterious world of covert operations [several] central government departments had a history of routinised corruption' (Lodge 1999: 9–60).

10 Marais observes correctly that the contradictions inherent in the South African political economic system at the end of the 1940s 'were resolved by the apartheid state [on behalf of the English-controlled capitalist system] with comparative ease and little disruption... from capital's point of view... The costs were visited upon the black, particularly African, population' (Marais 2001: 19).

11 The average rate of return on foreign capital invested in apartheid South Africa after 1964 (ie, after investor fears had been allayed by the post-Sharpeville crackdown) was among the highest in the world. As late as 1974 the average American corporation received an 18 per cent return on South African investments, as against a return of only 8 per cent in Britain (see O'Meara 1996: 174).

12 The NP government's preparedness to create conditions conducive to capital accumulation not only by the Afrikaner-controlled corporations but also by the far more prominent English-controlled corporations was acknowledged and rewarded by the English business sector. The best example of this was when, in the late 1960s, the AAC practically handed over its General Mining and Finance Corporation to a subsidiary of the Afrikaner-owned insurance giant Sanlam. Slowly but surely, the Afrikaner-controlled corporations were co-opted – especially ideologically – by the English-controlled corporations. According to Marais, 'Afrikaner capitalists were propelled into the upper reaches of the economy and integrated into the steadily evolving web of conglomerates... [In 1970] the graduation of Afrikaner capital as a junior partner in the (still English-dominated) economy was in full swing' (Marais 2001: 21).

13 The policy of favouring the larger farmers led to a continuous outflow of whites from agriculture. The number of whites in agriculture, forestry, and fishing fell from 180 000 in 1936 to 96 000 in 1970. Similarly, the number of white farms declined from 120 000 in 1950 to 75 000 in 1976 (O'Meara 1996: 143).

14 It is estimated that more than 50 per cent of all the money spent by the government on research in the 1950s and 1960s was related to agriculture. The government also took all the steps demanded by farmers to control African farm workers more strictly. The wages of farm workers were exceptionally low (see section 9.5).

15 Total state subsidies for white farmers amounted to R66,8 million in 1967, or almost double the state spending on black education. The output on white-owned farms increased by 47 per cent from 1949 until 1959. Although the average real income of white farmers grew by 7,3 per cent a year between 1960 and 1975, most white farmers were virtually totally dependent on state support. A commission reported in 1972 that state assistance provided 20 per cent of an average white farmer's income. This situation prevailed despite the fact that black agricultural wages barely increased from 1866–1966 (Wilson 1978: 160–74).

16 One of the most effective methods used by the NP to consolidate its power was to

build up its Afrikaner constituency through every possible form of patronage and favouritism. In the long run the favouritism turned into large-scale corruption. By beating the ideological drums of Afrikaner nationalism and republicanism, enough support was mobilised in 1960 to change South Africa into a republic in 1961.

17 Freund makes the important point that the English establishment 'lost the political battle but on terms that encouraged their continued prominence in many key areas of "civil society"... [when they] protested against the political order [of the apartheid state] [they] tended to be against abuses to the legal structures [and] violations of the Rechtstaat' (in Hyslop 1999: 439). This protest against the apartheid state was valuable during the final and repressive phase of the apartheid regime.

18 In 1962 the powers of the police were extended with regard to interrogation procedures, and detention without trial for 12 days was permitted. This was extended to 90 days in 1963 and to an indefinite period if authorised by a judge in 1965.

19 The only important development in African resistance in the later 1960s was the emergence of the powerful new ideology of black consciousness. At that stage, however, black consciousness was more of a philosophical movement than an active political programme (Thompson 1990: 198–200; see also section 9.8. For the actions of the state against the liberation movements from 1960 to 1994, see TRC 1998: vol 2, ch 3).

20 Although the collapse of the white regime was sudden and dramatic, the bargaining position of blacks increased gradually during the 20 years from 1974 until 1994. The main reason for this was that the white hegemonic order increasingly found itself on a slippery slope, from an economic, moral, and ideological point of view. Consequently, during these 20 years it made more and more concessions to blacks in a vain attempt to pacify them.

21 The only two exceptions were in 1980/1, when the gold price increased to R900, and the economic revival of 1994/5. From 1974 to 1994 real GDP only increased by 1,7 per cent a year, while real per capita income declined by 0,7 per cent a year, amounting to a quarter century of creeping poverty and rising unemployment (see section 10.2).

22 The Vorster government was paralysed and displayed an astonishing inability to grasp the true meaning of the crisis. Vorster was clearly unable to reorient himself to the new regional situation created by the independence of Mozambique and Angola. The political vacuum created by Vorster's lack of leadership gave unexpected moral encouragement to the liberation organisations.

23 Defence spending as a percentage of GDP doubled from 2,4 per cent to 4,8 per cent in these six years. It remained at this high level until 1989. This was a clear indication that the minster of defence, P W Botha, and the military establishment used the 'lame duck' period of Vorster's government to strengthen their position, not only in the government and in the bureaucracy, but also in the business sector (through a substantial expansion in production by ARMSCOR).

24 From a propaganda point of view, this was a rather astute twist, because the real struggle was against the *racist* character of white supremacy, and it was not only supported by communist countries but by almost all countries in the world. However, the Botha government could not have maintained its 'total strategy'

against the 'evil empire' without the comprehensive ideological and material support of Reagan and Thatcher in the 1980s (O'Meara 1996: 224–8, 258–69).

25 Since the formation of the G/NP in 1934, Afrikaner nationalism – as a typical petit bourgeois phenomenon – was essentially a moral and religious crusade. The fact that the 'total strategy' was now presented as a *survivalist* ideology, deprived of any moral considerations, could be the reason why the beleaguered white establishment employed (especially during the 1980s) such ruthless and even immoral methods not only against its enemies, but also against those political opponents who did not agree with the methods of the 'total strategy'. The absence of a moral content in the ideology of 'total strategy' could also be the reason why the NP and the bureaucratic establishment descended into such widespread 'structural corruption' during the 1980s (O'Meara 1996: ch 13; Van Aswegen, in Cameron 1986: 298–300).

26 During the time of stagflation, ARMSCOR was one of the few profitable concerns, and the continued expansion of this parastatal was crucial for its 5 000-odd subcontractors. P W Botha used his close co-operation with the securocrats and the business community to consolidate his own (rather vulnerable) political position. To consolidate his power even further, Botha created the state security council (SSC), not only to manage the reform process and 'total strategy', but also to neutralise ministers in his cabinet whom he did not like or trust. Botha's policy agenda was therefore an attempt to reconcile the economic interests of business, the political interests of his administration, and the security interests of the military and security forces. O'Meara states correctly that the 'total strategy' reforms also led to an *intensification* of political repression, strengthened security legislation, and sanctioned even more ruthless levels of violence against the liberation organisations and their supporters (1996: 321–3, ch 14).

27 It was not surprising that the overt and covert 'agreements' between private and public sector institutions and the lucrative 'transactions' between ARMSCOR and its multitude of subcontractors set the scene for all sorts of corrupt wheeling and dealing that eventually turned into structural corruption. This happened especially when, after Botha's 'Rubicon' speech of 1985, his reforms degenerated into a 'co-optive domination' (Terreblanche 1989).

28 Spending on agriculture was cut by more than half between 1971/2 and 1978/9 – ie, from 1,5 per cent to only 0,6 per cent of GDP. This low level of spending was more or less maintained during the remainder of the Botha years, despite the serious drought in the early 1980s. The fact that the Botha government was unable (and perhaps also unprepared) to maintain high agricultural subsidies was an important reason for the split in the NP in February 1982 and the defection of Dr Andries Treurnicht and his supporters (Calitz 1986: table 15.6).

29 Disinvestment by foreign firms was considerable. One fifth of British firms had withdrawn from South Africa by 1988. By April 1989, 184 American corporations had left South Africa. Of the 114 American firms which withdrew between January 1986 and April 1988, most sold their assets at bargain prices to South Africans (mainly whites) who could raise the finance to buy them (Davenport 1991: 464).

30 This crisis had many ramifications, both internally and externally. It enabled the ANC to consolidate the mounting external pressures on South Africa. From now on it was clear that disinvestment was a far more effective punitive measure than trade

sanctions. Internationally, the 'Rubicon' crisis aggravated South Africa's already parlous economic situation. In the week after 'Rubicon', the rand lost one third of its already declining value. The political effect of 'Rubicon' was devastating for Botha.

31 With the wisdom of hindsight we now realise that the structural corruption that took hold in the public sector and in dealings between the public and private sectors in the 15 years before 1994 was far more serious than was appreciated at the time, and its long-term effects were extremely damaging. When the democratically elected government assumed power in 1994, corruption in the public sector proved to be really 'structural' or 'endemic'. Despite the miraculous political transformation, structural corruption continued unabated, and has perhaps become even more comprehensive and more structurally entrenched (see Terreblanche 1989).

32 Those prepared to co-operate with Botha's bureaucratic state – including sections of the bureaucracy, business, sections of the media, and co-opted Africans (especially in the Bantustans), coloured and Asian leaders – were handsomely rewarded, while every form of opposition was mercilessly suppressed. While the main purpose of the 'total strategy' reforms in the early 1980s was to restore the legitimacy of the system, the only purpose of 'co-optive dominance' was the survival and perpetuation of the white hegemonic order at any price. At the end of the 1980s the NP had lost its purpose and direction, and found itself in a 'desert of disillusionment'.

33 In May 1985 the NP admitted that the homelands policy had failed and that a different way of incorporating the African population politically had to be found. In 1986 the NP's federal congress endorsed the principle that Africans were to be incorporated into 'all levels of decision-making at the highest level'. The NP also committed itself to 'the principle of a united South Africa, one citizenship, and a universal franchise', but without indicating how this principle would be implemented. In 1986 the system of influx control was abolished. All these concessions were too little, too late.

34 During the 11 years of P W Botha's term, government spending increased by an annual average of 18,5 per cent, rising from 25,1 per cent to 27,3 per cent of GDP. A 'conservative' estimate of real 'security' spending puts the figure at 20 to 25 per cent of the 1987/8 budget, or 8 to 9 per cent of GDP. The ratio of gross domestic fixed investment to GDP fell from 27,7 per cent in 1982 to 18,7 per cent in 1987. Net savings dropped from 14 per cent in 1982 to 7 per cent of GDP (see Smit 1992).

35 De Klerk's speech was the more unexpected because he had been associated with the right wing of the NP before his election as its leader. However, by 1989 – after 16 years of stagflation and rising unemployment – the economy was in a parlous state. The large outflow of foreign investment – which accelerated after P W Botha's 'Rubicon speech' in 1985 – continued unabated. At the same time the MDM had succeeded in making many African and coloured townships ungovernable.

36 The most credible of these takes the summit between presidents Ronald Reagan and Michael Gorbachev in October 1986 at Reykjavik in Iceland as decisively important. They reached remarkable agreements, and it was decided *inter alia* to seek jointly for negotiated solutions to regional conflicts such as those in Namibia and Angola, South Africa, the Middle East, Afghanistan, and so on. One of the first results of this joint agenda of the two superpowers was a peaceful settlement of the Namibian and

Angolan problems. As part of the new working relationship between the United States and the Soviet Union, the great powers – including the United Kingdom, West Germany, France, Canada and Italy – decided that Margaret Thatcher was the best placed head of state to renew discussions with the NP government on a negotiated solution for the South African problem. According to this scenario, Thatcher exerted strong pressure on De Klerk during the second half of 1989.

37 Beinart and Dubow are correct when they claim 'that apartheid [in the wider sense of the word] purported to be a rigorous and totalizing ideology in a way that segregation had never been' (Beinart and Dubow 1995: 12).

38 For Stallard, all Africans would *always* be merely 'temporary sojourners' in the urban areas. The 1937 Native Laws Amendment Act took a far more aggressive Stallardist line than the original 1923 act. When the act was drafted, sharp differences developed in the NAD between pro-Stallardists (in favour of stricter influx control) and anti-Stallardists (in favour of African urbanisation to fuel growing industrialisation).

39 For the differences and similarities between the Fagan and the Sauer reports, see Posel 1991: ch 2; and Hindson 1987: 59–64.

40 Between 1936 and 1946 the urban African population grew by 57 per cent from 1,1 million to 1,8 million, outstripping the urban white population, which increased by 31 per cent from 1,3 million to 1,7 million. According to Posel: 'These demographic changes had two principal economic determinants: expanding avenues of urban African employment (largely due to the growth of manufacturing), and widespread rural impoverishment' (1991: 24).

41 An important facet of this protracted drama was the influx control measures designed and regularly redesigned by the NP government – mostly in close co-operation with the white employers in mining, agriculture, and industry – to control not only the flow of cheap migrant labour, but also the struggle of millions of migrant workers against them. While the liberation movement's organised struggle against apartheid has been well-documented, the role of the unorganised struggle of millions of migrant workers against influx control and the *dompas* has not been sufficiently appreciated.

42 Posel correctly observes that 'the term *apartheid* won the support of Afrikaner nationalists across the board, because it successfully described and legitimised the Afrikaner cause in an ideological discourse *sufficiently ambiguous to accommodate these conflicting versions of apartheid policy*' (1987: 123).

43 In Afrikaner business circles the conviction was nurtured that greater economic 'integration' was not necessarily irreconcilable with white economic and political supremacy as long as the state could effectively control African urbanisation.

44 The SAAU was, however, strongly opposed to SABRA's proposal that the government should develop the economic potential of the 'native reserves', because it feared increased competition from African farmers. The 'practical' conception of apartheid was also strongly supported by the business organisations of the English establishment, which were concerned about the availability of cheap African labour, and less concerned about the political implications of economic integration (see Posel 1991: ch 2).

45 While 4 million Africans were arrested and prosecuted under pass laws and influx

control regulations from 1916 to 1950, almost 13 million prosecutions took place from 1950 to 1980. The manner in which the NP government stepped up influx control becomes evident if we compare the number of pass law prosecutions in successive decades: 1,9 million Africans were prosecuted in the 1940s, 3,5 million in the 1950s, 5 million in the 1960s, and 4,2 million in the 1970s. The decline in prosecutions in the 1970s is deceptive, because the newly introduced BAABs dealt with technical pass offenders directly so that the number of court prosecutions declined. The number of Africans prosecuted during the 1970s declined, but not the number arrested (Hindson 1987: 81; Savage 1986: 181–205).

46 Africans living in urban areas increased from 27,2 per cent in 1951 to 31,8 per cent in 1960 and 33,1 per cent in 1970, and declined slightly to 32,9 per cent in 1980. But, without the formidable battery of pass and influx control laws the rate of African urbanisation would have been much higher, due to the deteriorating socio-economic conditions in the 'native reserves' (see Lipton 1986: 401).

47 From the 1930s onwards economic conditions in the 'native reserves' deteriorated to such an extent that increasing numbers of migrants were driven to the urban areas to earn not a part of, but their total, subsistence via low-paying urban jobs.

48 The population of Africans in the 'native reserves' or Bantustans increased from 3 million in 1946, or 40 per cent of the total African population, to 11 million in 1980, or 53 per cent of the total African population (see Lipton 1986: 402).

49 This two-phase formulation of Verwoerd's is remarkably reminiscent of Lenin's two-phase programme for communism and the two-phase programme of the SACP propagated by Joe Slovo. It is the device of every tyrant who wishes to control his constituency with a grand vision, however unattainable this vision is.

50 It is remarkable how susceptible the Afrikaners were, during their period of political hegemony, to being deceived by arguments such as Verwoerd's that the NP's native policy could be morally legitimised by the long-term intention to segregate blacks and whites politically.

51 Verwoerd promised 'better control, better influx control, better control of the people there [in the towns], better order, [and] better combating of frustration' (quoted in Posel 1991: 68).

52 To solve farmers' serious labour problems, the NAD also channelled large numbers of foreign work-seekers (with the exception of those in the mining industry) to farm work. In addition, those Africans who were convicted of petty offences (those without identity documents or without the necessary permission to be in urban areas) were also sent for fixed periods to agricultural districts as farm labourers. But the biggest service rendered to white farmers by the NAD (in conjunction with the department of prisons) was to put convict labour at farmers' disposal. This system of forced labour enabled the farmers to pay extraordinarily low wages to African labourers (see Posel 1991: 125–6, 136, 260–1).

53 African women resisted the carrying of passes for several years. In 1959 native labour regulations made it obligatory for women to register contracts with employers. Resistance against the carrying of passes continued in 1959, the Anti-Pass Year, but was finally broken in 1960 with the shooting at Sharpeville (Hindson 1987: 64).

54 In terms of section 10(1)(a & b) of the act, Africans born in urban areas, and Africans with ten years' continuous employment with one employer or 15 with

several employers, were entitled to remain permanently in urban areas *even if unemployed*. And in terms of section 10(1)(c), African women living in rural areas married to men with 'urban' status could join them and become permanent city dwellers. Despite these concessions, the act excluded many thousands of Africans who had settled in urban areas but had not been continuously employed in formal jobs. A large portion of these people were women who were only doing casual work in the cities (see Dugard, in Hellman and Lever 1980: 84–5).

55 The NAD also wanted the ULPP to be applicable irrespective of the type of labour demanded by urban employers. The proposal for an ULPP was strongly opposed by organised commerce and industry. Although these organisations sang the praises of a 'stable' and permanent workforce, many employers (both English and Afrikaans-speaking) preferred to employ migrant workers not only because they were much cheaper, but also because they were more 'docile' than 'detribalised' workers (see Posel 1991: 82–5).

56 Verwoerd's concession seriously undermined the NAD's ability to control the influx of Africans to urban areas. It created a loophole that licensed the continuous growth of the African urban population irrespective of whether or not the labour requirements of a particular urban area justified such a large number of Africans. Those urban employers who wanted to employ Africans with the required 'skills' and 'permanence' had to pay the section 10 Africans much higher wages. Many of them, however, opted not to enter into wage employment, but to become petty entrepreneurs. The aversion of section 10 Africans to wage labour – and the concession that such labourers could remain in urban areas, even if unemployed – made industrialists not only more dependent on migrant labour, but also made the migrants more vulnerable.

57 The system of influx control required an enormous bureaucratic machinery. A range of permits had to be issued, renewed, or cancelled by the labour bureaux. The first reference books were issued in 1952. By the end of 1954 some 800 000 African men had been issued with the new pass books. By 1959 the number had risen to 3,6 milion (Hindson 1987: 64).

58 Until the mid-1950s real wages for urban workers declined as both the government and employers sought to crush African trade unions and buy off white workers' discontent by granting them wage increases to the detriment of African workers. At the same time, the rents and transport costs of African residents in the new urban townships soared as the NAD insisted that the former should carry the full costs of urban housing and township development. This part of Verwoerd's social engineering programme was an important reason for the urban unrest among both 'urbanised' Africans and migrant workers in the late 1950s and early 1960s (see Bonner *et al* 1993: 23–8).

59 The wages of Africans in manufacturing and construction in the 1950s and early 1960s were twice as high as the wages of Africans in mining. But we must take into account that those Africans with residential rights and in semi-skilled jobs received a much higher wage than the migrant workers in mining and in manufacturing (Lipton 1986: 409–10). We must also take into account that more than 60 per cent of the migrants in gold mining were foreigners who were prepared to work for exceptionally low wages.

60 The labour market privileges granted by successive governments to the gold mines enabled the latter, as late as 1961 and 1971, to pay their migrant workers real wages that were respectively 20 per cent and 8 per cent lower than those paid in 1911. (Lipton 1986: tables 10, 11).

61 The percentage of foreign migrants employed on the gold mines increased from 61 per cent in 1951 to 79 per cent in 1973 (Lipton 1986: 407). While, from the 1930s onwards, agriculture in the 'native reserves' was too unproductive to help sustain mineworkers, it is difficult to establish whether agriculture in foreign African countries was productive enough to help sustain foreign migrants. However, there is reason to believe that agricultural conditions in some of these foreign countries (and especially in Mozambique) were even worse.

62 Between 1955 and 1958 the number of industrial disputes and strikes were nearly double that of the early 1950s.

63 While the NP received only 40 per cent of the popular vote in 1948, and 44,5 per cent in 1953, this figure increased to 48,5 per cent in 1958 and 53 per cent in 1961.

64 In the meantime, the staff of BAD was not only increased, but also loaded with loyal Nationalists who favoured the 'purist' conception of apartheid. The shift of the government and BAD towards the 'purist' conception set the scene for a relentless struggle in the 1960s between those who favoured stricter influx controls, and those who wanted the policy to be applied more flexibly, or abolished (Posel 1991: 227–35).

65 In keeping with Afrikaner nationalism's emphasis on the realisation of ethnic identity (*the volkseie*), each of these 'national/ethnic' minorities was to be given the right to realise its divinely ordained 'national calling' – and its political and economic independence – in its own 'homeland' or Bantustan. While the reserves were treated in the 1950s as reservoirs of migrant labour, they now gained a completely new character. They became the 'geographical space' in which the different African ethnic groups were supposed to exercise their political sovereignty. Verwoerd had hoped that separate development – as a policy of decolonisation within South Africa's borders – would bring South Africa ideologically in line with western countries' anti-colonial (or *uhuru*) policies of the time. (Ghana became independent in 1957, and in the following ten years almost all the colonies of European countries were granted independence.)

66 This led to a sustained struggle between BAD and those with a vested interest in maintaining section 10 rights. Although BAD did not succeed in removing the residential rights of section 10 Africans, and put ULPP firmly in place, it did succeed in depriving many 'urbanised' Africans of their residential rights (Posel 1991: 227–35).

67 While the ratio of men to women in urban areas increased in the 1950s, it declined in the 1960s. In its notorious 1967 circular, BAD defined 'surplus people' as the aged, unfit, widows, and women with dependent children, and promised to leave no stone unturned in making the Bantustans the rural receptacles of the nation's unemployed. From 1968 Africans could no longer own their own houses on 30-year leasehold plots, but could only rent them. Forced removals assumed massive proportions in the 1960s. From 1960 to 1970 the Bantustans' population increased from 4 million to 7,4 million (Hindson 1987: 68–70). According to Bundy, 3,5

million people were relocated between 1960 and 1982, representing '*some of the most dismaying pages in the entire history of South Africa* ... In them may be learned the details of broken promises, naked force, shattered communities, desolated camps, and shallow graves' (in Schrire 1992: 34).

68 R204 million in 1956 prices would be about R9 billion in 2002 prices.

69 The money spent by the government on 'developing' the Bantustans during the 1960s and 1970s had the effect of mainly improving the economic base of the small Bantustan petit bourgeoisie, and did little for the already proletarianised majority. If we consider all the ideological, political, economic and demographic forces at work, it is ironic that the most prosperous decade in South Africa's history sharply increased the standard of living of whites, but further impoverished and disrupted the lives of the majority of Africans. There is little doubt that influx control played a decisive role in this contradictory outcome.

70 Tomlinson had recommended that 45 000 new jobs be created every year. If we take into account the fact that the government spent only a fraction of the sum recommended by Tomlinson on development in and around the Bantustans during the first ten years, the fact that Tomlinson seriously underestimated the development needs of the homelands, and the growth of the African population, it is clear that socio-economic conditions were much worse during the 1960s than they had been at the beginning of the 1950s when the Tomlinson enquiry took place. The commission projection was that the total African population would increase from 8,5 million in 1951 to 16,3 million in 2000. It actually increased to 35 million (see Davenport and Saunders 2000: 426–8). The population of the Bantustans increased from 3 million in 1946 to 7,4 million in 1970 (Lipton 1986: 402).

71 Verwoerdian influx control was scrapped in 1986. In the 20 years after Verwoerd's death, almost every NP leader continued to pay homage to the Verwoerdian idea of territorial apartheid in order to ensure his/her legitimacy in the NP. The Vorster government was obsessed – more so than any NP government before it – with the flow of Africans to urban areas, and was prepared to take direct coercive measures to stop this flow irrespective of its negative effective on job creation and economic growth in urban areas.

72 The task of administering the Physical Planning Act was given to the BAD. This gave the department the power to prohibit the building and expansion of factories in designated areas. During the 1970s BAD used this power to prohibit industrial expansion and turn down applications for the employment of thousands of Africans.

73 The decline in pass law prosecutions from 5 million in the 1960s to 4,2 million in the 1970s should not be interpreted as a decline in pass law infringements. On the contrary, in the 1970s the BAABs largely took over the enforcement of the pass laws from the police. They introduced centres for dealing with technical pass offenders directly, so that the number of court prosecutions declined. The number of Africans prosecuted was reduced, but not the number arrested. Instead of sending culprits to jail, many were simply deported to the Bantustans.

74 Large housing schemes were developed in these Bantustan urban areas. While, as in the 1960s, African migrants were still forcibly removed from the 'white' urban areas, the provision of housing and employment in or near the Bantustans was now also used to draw Africans back to the Bantustans.

75 According to Bundy the NP government already began in the 1960s with a policy of 'deliberate deprivation' in the large townships as part of the effort to relocate Africans to rural areas. Bundy quotes a deputy minister who warned the local authorities in 1967 not to provide 'bigger, better, more attractive facilities' in case these should compete with 'the Bantu's own homeland and accustom the Bantu to a foreign taste' (Bundy 1993: 70).

76 Some of this new generation of 'migrant' workers had to travel as far as 80 kilometres twice a day, rising at 3 am and returning home at 11 pm. This kind of migrancy became so thoroughly institutionalised that it remains part of the South African labour pattern to this day (see Savage 1986: 197–205).

77 It was estimated that, in the late 1970s, half of the urban African population in some towns could be classified as either illegal or 'foreigners'. Granting independence to some of the Bantustans therefore had the important implication that being illegally in 'white' areas became a far more serious criminal act. In this way the criminalisation of increasing numbers of Africans was augmented considerably (see Savage 1986: 201–5). In 1970 a national survey found that 30 per cent of registered workers in urban areas found and accepted jobs without registering as work-seekers, and only registered their contracts later. A study in the early 1970s, based on information from labour bureaus, found that, in the case of 46 per cent of registered industrial workers, no vacancies had been registered prior to employment (Hindson 1987: 69–70).

78 The NP's policy of industrial licensing and labour quotas in urban areas on the one hand, and its policy of subsidising industrial decentralisation on the other hand, were both ideologically driven and responsible for serious economic wastage –for white employers as well as potential African employees – during the period of serious economic decline that started in 1974.

79 According to Bundy, the policies of the NP government made the masters and servants laws increasingly anachronistic. A barrage of new laws that controlled, directed, and disciplined the black labour force had by then been rationalised and strengthened to such an extent that the masters and servants laws had become redundant (1975: 43).

80 Within the Afrikaner establishment a serious 'breakdown' developed between the *verligtes* ('enlightened' – those who, *inter alia*, favoured more pragmatic influx control measures) and the *verkramptes* ('constricted/cramped' – those who favoured the 'purist' concept of apartheid and wanted stricter influx control). After the Soweto unrest of 1976 both the English and Afrikaner business sectors expressed concern about the living conditions of urban Africans, and tried to incorporate a black middle class into the 'white' capitalist economy. At the initiative of the AAC and the Rembrandt group, the UF was established in 1977 to improve the living conditions of urban Africans (O'Meara 1996: ch 9).

81 Even the Defence Force generals – who played such a key role during the Botha regime – now claimed that the only recipe for victory against the alleged Soviet onslaught was to win the 'hearts and minds' of the people through an 80 per cent political reform programme and a 20 per cent military approach (see O'Meara 1996: 182–6, 323; see also section 3.2.3.1 for the first phase of the search for a new accumulation strategy during the first period of the Botha government).

82 The first BLAs were elected in 1983, but only 16 per cent of potential voters went to

the polls. BLAs were introduced in 1983 with powers equal to those of the white municipalities. Although the BLAs were supposed to be financially self-sufficient, this was not the case, because the Group Areas Act precluded them from gaining access to rateable commercial and industrial property. To improve the financial self-sufficiency of the BLAs, it was accepted that the wages of the 'insiders' should be markedly increased, and it was for this reason that Riekert recommended that the 'insiders' should be protected against competition for employment and housing from migrant workers by means of stricter influx control.

83 Intended to satisfy 'the political aspirations' of urban Africans, the hated BLAs sparked the uprising that started shortly after the introduction of the tricameral parliament in 1984. These uprisings reached a high point in 1986 when a comprehensive state of emergency was announced. The main targets of these uprisings were the BLAs, African policemen and informers, all seen as 'agents' and 'stooges' of the apartheid regime. Instead of defusing African anger, the new constitutional dispensation and the BLAs provoked uncontrollable black protest. When the UDF was banned in 1988, leadership of the internal liberation struggle passed on to the MDM, which, *inter alia*, made many townships ungovernable (Davenport 1991: 428–45).

84 John Dugard observes that 'there was little concern over the use of the legal process to achieve a discriminatory order as, in the pre-Second World War era, law was seen essentially as a mechanism of control by lawyers and politicians reared in the positivist legal tradition, which denies the importance of legal values' (in Hellman and Lever 1980: 82).

85 The implementation of this law resulted in large-scale social engineering and population removals that caused immense disruption and distress. Under this law it became compulsory for people to live in an area designated for their classification group. The significant erosion of economic segregation during World War 2 was energetically reversed by the NP after 1948. The emerging black middle and skilled working classes were pushed back. The NP government stopped all trading by Africans outside the reserves and townships, and discouraged trading within the latter in the hope of encouraging businessmen to return to the reserves. The Group Areas Act further restricted the residential rights of blacks and, for the first time, those of coloureds (Dugard, in Hellman and Lever 1980: 84–5; Lipton 1986: 23).

86 Black students were prohibited from attending the Universities of Cape Town and the Witwatersrand without permission.

87 As an auxiliary to job reservation, the Bantu Education Act (1953) required that African education be largely self-funded. Expenditure on African education was pegged to the level of African taxation. As a result, expenditure on African education fell in per capita terms from 13 per cent of white levels in 1953 to 10 per cent in 1961, and to only 4 per cent in 1975 (De Villiers 1996). It increased sharply after the Soweto unrest, and reached 22 per cent of white levels in 1990 in per capita terms (see Bonner *et al* 1993: 25–6; Van der Berg and Bhorat 1999: 9; see also section 10.4 on racial inequalities and systemic injustices).

88 The Separate Representation of Voters Act was declared illegal by the appellate division, and only became law in 1956 after the senate had been enlarged to give the government a two-thirds majority.

89 In 1946 Smuts suppressed the strikes of Africans on the mines for higher wages and better job opportunities by deploying 16 000 policemen. After the war, 106 000 ex-servicemen returned and demanded preferential jobs and training. The definition of 'skilled' and 'unskilled' jobs was a burning issue. As indicated in section 8.7, numerous discriminatory laws were enacted during the first half of the 20th century in this area. The most important was the 'civilised labour policy' of the Pact government to create protected employment opportunities in the industrial sector for the large number of 'poor whites' who were moving into the urban areas.

90 After long years of seemingly fruitless struggle, Afrikaner Nationalist-orientated trade unions finally captured control of the white Mineworkers Union after the 1947 strike, and also made important breakthroughs in the steel industry. The NP won a critical number of predominantly working class seats on the Rand in the 1948 general election, and was therefore sensitive to an electorate which regarded black competition with great fear (O'Meara 1996: 36; Lipton 1986: 38–40, 140–7).

91 By the end of 1974 almost 8 000 Africans had been registered as skilled building workers (Van der Horst, in Truu 1976: 111).

92 The act totally prohibited Africans from striking. In addition, it made lock-outs of blacks, the instigation of strikes and lock-outs, and sympathetic strikes illegal. African workers were provided with a separate system of plant-level 'works' and 'liaison' committees within which management and African workers were meant to negotiate terms of employment (Dugard, in Hellman and Lever 1980: 85; Horrell 1978).

93 Under the IC Act of 1956, all non-whites in the Transvaal and OFS were excluded from skilled and many semi-skilled occupations, as well as apprenticeships, but this did not apply to all industries in the Cape Province and Natal. The building and furniture trades, especially in the Wetern Cape, were open to coloured persons (Van der Horst, in Truu 1976: 104).

94 When Ben Schoeman, then minister of labour, introduced the Industrial Conciliation Bill in parliament in 1954, he said: 'Section 77 will be the Sword of Damocles that will hang over the head of the (white) employer, so that he will not dare to exploit the non-European worker at the expense of the European worker' (Hansard 17, 31 May 1954, col 5852).

95 At first the minister only used these powers to protect white workers. In 1957 skilled work in the clothing industry was reserved for whites, but the determination was withdrawn when it was declared invalid by the courts and replaced in 1960 by a new determination designed to stabilise racial percentages. The act prohibited the establishment of any further mixed trade unions – ie, unions of white, coloured, and Asian workers. Africans had previously been excluded. African trade unions were not illegal, but could not be registered under the act (Davenport 1991: 505–12).

96 In the clothing industry the percentage of white employees had fallen from 62 per cent in 1938 to 24 per cent in 1955. It was stipulated that the percentage should not fall further. In respect of motor vehicle assembly it was stipulated that the percentage of whites should not fall below 65 per cent in Uitenhage, 45 per cent in Bellville and Port Elizabeth, 25 per cent in East London and on the Witwatersrand, and 20 per cent in Durban (Van der Horst, in Truu 1976: 104).

97 It was claimed that only 2,9 per cent of jobs in the industrial sector were formally

reserved for whites. But, according to Merle Lipton, this translated into 217 500 jobs in 1970, or 15 per cent of the 1,5 million employed whites. If the effects of the colour bar and the 'civilised labour policy' in the public sector (which employed one third of whites in 1970) are also taken into account, the number affected must have been substantial. As the result of the 1924 election was decisive in determining the labour structure of the gold mining industry for the next 50 years, so the result of the 1948 election was decisive in determining the labour structure of secondary and tertiary industries for the next 30 years (Lipton 1986: 38–41, 142).

98 In 1960 and 1970 African wages in manufacturing and construction were 18,6 per cent and 16,7 per cent of white wages respectively, compared to 24 per cent in 1945 (table 8.1). While the additional discriminatory measures of the 1950s had an important cost effect on employers, their negative effect on the socio-economic conditions of blacks was enormous. They not only impoverished urbanised blacks, but also criminalised many youths because it was not possible for them to make occupational advancement (see Lipton 1986: 20, 409).

99 This act was the most far-reaching job reservation measure ever introduced. It made possible the prohibition of the employment of a 'Bantu' in any job, in any area, or in the service of any employer. The act coincided with the government's drive at the end of the 1960s to divert economic activities from white urban areas to the border areas (see Lipton 1986: 33; Van der Horst, in Truu 1976: 101–3).

100 Several reasons can be given for the more accommodating attitudes of white workers. By the mid-1960s the high unemployment and poverty of the pre-war period in Afrikaner circles had given way to security and prosperity. The white workers who agreed to black advancement and the fragmentation of jobs were initially handsomely compensated. The leadership core of white trade unions also started to understand that the scarcity of 'skilled' labour hampered economic growth. Despite an intensive campaign to persuade all the trade unions about the necessity of black advancement, the concessions made to black people in the late 1960s and 1970s nevertheless led to a bitter struggle between *verligtes* and *verkramptes* in the white, and especially Afrikaner, trade union movement.

101 Given the strength of the right wing in the NP and in the Afrikaner trade union movement, the government did not dare dismantle the discriminatory machinery. But it is also possible that the government kept the legislation on the law books in the event of prolonged and serious depression and white unemployment. In 1971 the government accepted recommendation of the Economic Advisory Council concerning the reclassification of jobs in order to permit less skilled work to be done by semi-skilled workers. The council also advocated the increased use of white female labour to release male labour for more productive use, and the training of coloured and Indian workers for both skilled and semi-skilled work. Africans were to be trained for employment in the Bantustans and border areas. In 1971 the government issued a white paper on the decentralisation of industry which contained a section on the better use of African labour in these areas (Van der Horst, in Truu 1976: 108; O'Meara 1996: 172–8).

102 It was almost impossible to police labour practices on thousands of building sites. In the building and engineering industries unskilled and semi-skilled black workers were also used illegally by skilled workers to do skilled work, to the enormous

financial benefit of white workers. These blacks were often paid the wages of unskilled or semi-skilled workers. This was an illegal and crude version of black exploitation (Lipton 1986: 205–10).

103 By the end of 1977, 18 of the 25 work reservation orders in force had been cancelled, and a further two (in the metal and engineering industries) suspended, with the concurrence of the trade unions concerned. In 1977 the UF published a code of employment practice in which it pleaded for the elimination of discrimination based on race or colour in all aspects of employment. This code was accepted by 90 per cent of organised industry and commerce (Lipton 1986: 59–60; Van der Horst, in Hellman and Lever 1980: 118–20).

104 The most important was the Trade Union Council of South Africa (TUCSA), representing a quarter of a million members, of which 28 per cent were white and 72 per cent coloured and Indian. The pressure to acknowledge African trade unions escalated considerably with the Soweto stay-at-home in August 1976. Almost all business organisations made renewed requests that African trade unions be recognised. Piet van der Merwe, director-general of manpower and a member of the Wiehahn commission, played a major role in persuading the state and big business to accept the need for black organisations and black unions. First, he argued that by 1979 economic and workplace changes had made existing industrial law an anachronism which failed to recognise that blacks were already dominating many skilled and semi-skilled labour categories. Second, many employers and particularly companies exposed to foreign markets were becoming increasingly aware of the urgent need to accommodate black labour. Thirdly, there were already about 50 black trade unions operating outside the statutory framework, and the number was growing fast (see Crush, et al 1991: 26–7; Mamdani 1996: 243–6).

105 Morris and Padayachee put the reasons for the failure of the Wiehahn reforms as follows: 'Instead of allowing for the co-option of the "insiders" working class, as Wiehahn intended, [his proposals] rather provided a vehicle of political protest; instead of facilitating the depoliticisation of industrial relations, [his proposal] fostered the radical and overt politicisation of working class economic struggle' (Morris and Padayachee 1989: 67).

106 But this did not stop the NUM from continuing to bargain over important issues, notably wages and safety conditions. In the 1990s Africans held 8,8 per cent of the skilled and 36,4 per cent of the semi-skilled jobs in mining (Lipton 1986: 170, 204–6; Davenport and Saunders 2000: 616–17).

107 The 12 unions which formed FOSATU were reluctant to become embroiled in overt politics, and were adamant about restricting their struggles to the workplace. This approach was contested by a variety of 'community unions' which believed it was impossible to separate workers' factory and political demands. The tension between black and non-racial trade unions persisted in the early part of the 1980s until FOSATU and several 'community unions' joined forces in 1985 when COSATU was founded. The joint purpose linking COSATU and organisations such as the UDF was to fight apartheid and capitalism. Inkatha, by contrast, set up its own rival trade union, UWUSA in 1986, consistently opposed sanctions and disinvestment, and sought the support of business interests (Davenport and Saunders 2000: 486–94).

108 This section is based mainly on Clark 1994 and Clark, in Bonner et al 1993: 65–95.

109 As a result of close co-operation between H J van der Bijl of ESKOM and Ernest Oppenheimer of the AAC, the privately owned Victoria Falls Power Company was expropriated early in 1948 with huge financial support from the AAC. As the major mining house and consumer of electricity, the AAC benefited enormously from the cheaper electricity supplied to it by ESKOM. With the support of Ernest Oppenheimer, ISCOR also made headway towards a steel monopoly before 1948 (Clark, in Bonner *et al* 1993: 77–86).

110 It is ironic that many of the Afrikaner entrepreneurs, nurtured in the protective environment of state corporations, later became outspoken supporters of an unbridled free market capitalist system. Hardly any English-speakers were initially appointed to the managements of state corporations (Lipton 1986: 283).

111 Between 1946 and 1973 the share of state corporations in gross fixed investment rose from 6,2 per cent to 11,5 per cent, while that of the private sector declined from 63,5 to 53 per cent (O'Meara 1996: 79). The state sector became the largest employer in South Africa, accounting in 1980 for 34 per cent of economically active whites (and an even larger percentage of Afrikaners), 16 per cent of coloureds, 12 per cent of Asians, and 14 per cent of Africans, including employment in the state corporations such as ISCOR (Lipton 1986: 235).

112 The Congress of the People, which accepted the Freedom Charter, consisted of the ANC, the Indian Congress, the South African Coloured People's Organisation, and the South African Congress of Trade Unions (SACTU).

113 The NP government hoped that if it could prove, at the height of the cold war, that the main black protest movement was on the side of the communists, the west would be more sympathetic towards apartheid. However, it failed to make a convincing case against the accused, all of whom were acquitted on 29 March 1961 (Rich 1996: 167–71).

114 Looking at the 1960s and early 1970s from the point of view of the liberation struggle, Jaffe observes that 'it was a prolonged period of darkness, which [was] momentarily "moonlit" by workers' strikes in Natal in the early 1970s' (1994: 182).

115 There are, however, reasons for believing that the BCM infused blacks with a kind of radicalism without which the liberation organisations could not have succeeded in their struggle against the apartheid regime. The BCM inspired blacks not only to achieve a high degree of solidarity, but also to develop an awareness that the path to fundamental reform in South Africa could not be gradual, but was destined to be apocalyptic and violent. In this way an ideological orientation was inculcated that was completely different to that of the black protest movements in the first half of the 20th century (Halisi 1999: 117–21).

116 O'Meara describes the importance of Soweto as follows: 'Soweto regenerated a deep sense of pride in much of the black population. *It was a key catalyst of the psychological liberation which the Black Consciousness movement had worked so hard to produce* ... The vast courage of the young rebels defying the might of the apartheid state helped to generate a revolutionary élan which transfigured the politics of black liberation in the 1980s. Its major beneficiary was a rebuilt ANC, which emerged as the dominant force in South African politics ... Soweto was thus also a crucial moment which significantly shaped an emerging militarist political culture throughout the whole of southern Africa – a culture which was to play a

crucial role in the unfolding regional tragedy of the 1980s' (1996: 181–2; author's emphasis).

117 During the first year after the Soweto uprising an estimated 600 people died, and almost 6 000 were arrested (Davenport and Saunders 2000: 453).

Chapter 10

The legacy of colonialism, segregation, and apartheid

10.1 The legacy of the pre-1994 period in historical perspective

The purpose of this chapter is to summarise the dismal socio-economic legacy of five systemic periods of white political domination and economic exploitation. We can regard 1994 as the biggest turning point in the 350 years of modern South African history. For many years to come, social historians and social scientists will distinguish between what happened before and after that year.

However, in doing so, we should not lose sight of the contribution of the extended colonial period to contemporary socio-economic problems. As we have already indicated in section 2.2, social disruption and abject poverty gained an endogenous dynamic long before 1994. All attempts at relieving the terrible predicament in which the poorest half of the population finds itself today will fail if the legacy of the pre-1994 period is not thoroughly recorded and studied.

A thorough study of the past is also necessary if justice is to be restored, and lasting reconciliation achieved. The fact that the TRC failed to investigate systemic exploitation during extended colonialism places a huge responsibility on social historians and social scientists to do so. The TRC not only interpreted its mandate too narrowly, but also compromised truth-seeking, because it was established as a result of the compromises forged between ANC leaders and the corporate sector in the early 1990s. According to Mamdani, this constrained its search for the truth about the causes of the plight of so many black South Africans. Notably, it prevented the TRC from identifying the business sector as one of the main players in, and beneficiaries of, systemic exploitation. In accepting the political constraints imposed by the compromise between the ANC and the corporate sector, the TRC turned a political compromise into a moral one, obscuring the truth in the process (see Mamdani, in Amadiume and Abdullahi 2000: 177–8).

As noted earlier, the TRC's short life span may be a reason for its inability (or unwillingness) to investigate the social injustices inherent in white political domination and racial capitalism. Before and after the appointment of the TRC, Mamdani and others (including the author of this book) proposed that the TRC should be complemented by a Justice and Reconciliation Commission (JRC) with a longer life span and an open mandate. Such a JRC was regarded as essential for educating whites about how white-controlled systems had impoverished blacks and enriched whites. Such an investigation could also have sensitised whites to their responsibility for restitution and nation-building. Unfortunately, neither the new government nor the TRC could be convinced of the need for a JRC.

If such a commission had been appointed, it would certainly have embarrassed the managerial elite of the corporate sector. By opting to leave the business sector 'uninvestigated', the ANC chose short-term expediency above justice and restitution.

The analysis in this chapter is not the first attempt at uncovering the truth about South Africa's ugly past, and will certainly not be the last. However, it will hopefully contribute to a better understanding of the dismal socio-economic situation that existed in 1970, when apartheid reached its zenith, and its further deterioration from 1970 to 1994. Hopefully, this overview will also stimulate debate on the nature of the five systemic periods of white domination and the exploitation of black labour before 1994.

10.2 Unemployment and underemployment

The extent of unemployment in 1994 has been hotly debated. In this study we are mainly concerned with structural unemployment: the overall inability of an economy to provide employment for the total (or potential) labour force, even at the peak of its business cycle. Structural employment is contrasted with cyclical unemployment – ie, the extent to which employment fluctuates with business cycles. Unemployment in South Africa is mostly structural rather than cyclical.[1] While more than 20 per cent of the potential labour force were already unemployed in 1970, this rose to almost 40 per cent in 1995.[2]

Fortunately, those who could not find jobs in the formal sector could find some kind of 'employment' in the informal sector or in subsistence agriculture. It is estimated that, in 1995, between 15 and 20 per cent of the total labour force (or at least 40 per cent of the 'unemployed', according to the extended definition of unemployment)[3] were 'underemployed', involved in various kinds of *ad hoc* informal or casual employment, or 'employed' in subsistence agriculture. The growth of the informal sector has accelerated since the 1980s because of the rapid increase in urbanisation after influx control was abolished, and the slow increase in the demand for labour in the formal sector.

Table 10.1: Labour supply, formal sector employment, and unemployment[1] in 1970 and 1995

Population group	Category	1970 (000)	1995 (000)	Change, 1970–95 (000)	Change, 1970–95 (%)
Africans	Labour supply	6 943	9 397	+2 454	+35.4
	Employed[2]	5 277	5 074	-203	-3.8
	Unemployed[1]	1 666	4 323	+2 657	+159.5
	Unemployed (%)	24	46	–	–
Coloureds	Labour supply	774	1 380	+606	+75.3
	Employed	642	1 063	+421	+65.5
	Unemployed	132	317	+185	+140
	Unemployed (%)	17	23	–	–
Asians	Labour supply	177	379	+202	+114
	Employed	165	331	+166	+100.6
	Unemployed	21	48	+27	+128.6
	Unemployed (%)	12	13	–	–
Whites	Labour supply	1 551	2 269	+718	+46.3
	Employed	1 458	2 117	+659	+45.2
	Unemployed	93	152	+59	+63.4
	Unemployed (%)	6	6,7	–	–
Total	Labour supply	9 445	13 425	+3 980	+42.1
	Employed	7 542	8 585	+1 043	+13.8
	Unemployed	1 903	4 840	+2 937	+154.3
	Unemployed (%)	20.2	36.1	–	–

1 Unemployment according to the expanded definition of the labour force outside the formal sector.

2 Employment in the formal sector.

Source: Bhorat and Hodge 1999: table 7; Barker 1999: table 7.1; CSS 1970; CSS 1995.

From 1970 to 1995 – ie, during the last 25 years of apartheid – unemployment worsened considerably.[4] The number of unemployed increased from 1,9 million in 1970 to 4,8 million in 1995. While, from 1970 to 1995, the potential labour force increased by almost 4 million (or 42 per cent), employment increased by only 1 million (or 13,8 per cent). But what is really shocking is that, from 1970 to 1995, the number of African workers employed in the formal sector *decreased* by 203 000, or 3,8 per cent. During the same period the number of non-African workers employed *increased* by 1,3 million (or 45 per cent).[5] In 1995, female unemployment among all racial groups was substantially higher than male unemployment, and unemployment among African women was estimated at 60 per cent. Unemployment is also higher among those younger than 25 years; in 1995, no fewer than 65 per cent of Africans between the ages of 16 and 24 were unemployed. Unemployment was also much higher among the poor.

The high levels of unemployment in 1994–5 can be attributed to a number of interrelated factors. Some of them were beyond government control, while others were strongly linked to the liberation struggle and the policies of the NP government and its predecessors. In our attempt to unravel the role played by these factors, we will also concentrate on those responsible for the sharp increase in African unemployment *vis-à-vis* that of non-Africans. Although the next four factors are closely interrelated, we can attribute the sharp increase in unemployment since 1970 to:

i   the slow growth of the economy since 1974;
ii the growing capital-intensity of the economy, which has changed production methods;
iii structural shifts in production, as reflected in a decline of the primary sector and a sharp increase in the service sector; and
iv the sharp increase in the rate of growth of the African population group since 1960.

The first three factors are mainly responsible for the slow increase in the demand for labour, and the increase in demand for some categories of labour and the decline in demand for others. An important interaction took place from 1970 to 1995 between the changes in demand for different categories of labour as a result of changes in the method and structure of production on the one hand, and the different levels of literacy and schooling of the different population groups on the other. The segregated system of education for different population groups, and the large qualitative differences between these different systems of education, should be blamed for the undersupply of certain categories of skilled and professional labour as well as the oversupply of other categories. The sharp increase in the total population – especially its African component – also contributed to the increase in the supply of labour.

10.2.1 The sustained decline in economic growth since 1974

South Africa's economy grew at the relatively high rate of at least 5 per cent a year in the post-war period from 1947 to 1974. This high rate of growth was attained by means of a large inflow of foreign investment, foreign entrepreneurship, and foreign technology. Measured in 2000 prices, FDI in 1974 totalled almost R175 billion.[6] Many of the foreign corporations that invested in South Africa exploited cheap and docile African labour to make very big profits.[7] When the oil crisis of 1973 slowed down economic growth elsewhere, South Africa also experienced a severe recession. But, in contrast with most other countries, the recession deteriorated into chronic stagflation that coincided with a period of political instability and black unrest, culminating in the collapse of white political domination in the early 1990s.[8]

The repressive black labour system that began in 1841 and continued until the 1980s contributed to capitalist accumulation until the end of the 1960s or early 1970s, but became dysfunctional from then on (see section 9.5.3). The very high economic growth rate during the 1950s and 1960s, and the need for technological modernisation, created a demand for skilled labour that could not be supplied by the white population group only. The NP, however, continued with its costly discriminatory policies for another decade (see section 9.6).

According to Stephen Gelb, the economic crisis developed from 1970 onwards when the Verwoerdian accumulation strategy reached its limits. This strategy was based on the effective control of cheap and docile African labour, and on an industrialisation policy of inward substitution (see section 3.2.2). At the end of the 1960s socio-economic conditions in the Bantustans had deteriorated to such an extent that they could no longer supply migrant workers with a subsistence base. As the productivity of migrant workers declined, it became necessary to invest in sophisticated machinery in order to improve productivity. This caused a sharp increase in the capital–labour ratio, and a decline in especially African employment (Gelb 1991: 19–20).

In the 'golden age' from 1950 to 1973, the economies of OECD countries grew by almost 5 per cent a year, but by less than 3 per cent a year since 1973. While South Africa benefited from a large demand for its primary products in the third quarter of the century, it was negatively affected by a decline in the demand for these products after 1973.[9] FDI also declined sharply from 1974 to 1984 as a result of political instability and black unrest. The current account was kept roughly in balance during this period, but this could only be achieved by deliberately curtailing domestic spending and by importing fewer capital goods.[10] After P W Botha's notorious 'Rubicon speech' in August 1985, a serious debt crisis developed. From 1985 to 1992 the average annual outflow of foreign capital was equal to 4,1 per cent of GDP a year. This outflow made the constraint of the balance of payments on the growth potential of the economy far more serious. This became evident from the steady decline in domestic investment after 1980. Whereas gross domestic investment was 30 per cent of GDP in 1972, it stood at only 16 per cent in 1993. This low level of investment can be attributed – directly and indirectly – to the sanctions and disinvestment campaigns directed at the apartheid regime, and South Africa's political and social instability.

The decline in the inflow of foreign investment and technology caused a decline in productivity.[11] Economic sanctions against the apartheid regime involved retricting international trade opportunities, and limiting access to international loans and foreign technology. All these anti-apartheid measures deliberately 'exploited' the vulnerability of South Africa's balance of payments. The continuing balance of payments problem and the high level of inflation (partly due to a sharp increase in black wages) caused several devaluations of the South African rand.

The decline in South Africa's economic performance from 1974 to 1994, and the parallel increase in socio-political instability during the same period, did not happen by accident. The perpetuation of black poverty in the 1950s and 1960s, together with the stricter influx control measures of the 1970s, helped to fuel black unrest from the early 1970s onwards. This unrest, and the government's attempts to suppress it, led to an intensification of the liberation struggle, and created socio-political conditions that were no longer conducive to foreign investment and domestic capital accumulation.

The 'low-level war' between the liberation organisations (and their allies in the international community) on the one hand and the NP government and its securocracy on the other was mainly fought in the economic arena, where it caused irreparable harm. If we take into account the fact that the NP was defending an immoral and discredited system, the harm done to the South African economy should largely be blamed on the short-sightedness and recalcitrant attitude of the NP government and its supporters. During the latter part of the 1980s the NP government was prepared to 'go it alone' economically irrespective of the cost involved.[12] The sharp increase in structural unemployment since 1974 was largely caused by the NP government's attempts to cling to political power and economic privilege at almost any cost. But the destructive methods used by the liberation movement also helped to damage the South African economy from 1974 to 1994.

10.2.2 The high and growing capital intensity of the economy after 1970

The capital intensity (or capital–labour ratio) of the South African economy has always been relatively high compared with other developing countries (and even some developed countries), and has increased considerably over the past

30 to 40 years.[13] This has weakened the job-creating capacity of the economy – especially since 1970. South Africa's job-creating capacity is much poorer than that of other developing countries with lower levels of capital intensity.

The gold mining industry needed high levels of investment from its inception, especially in exploiting deep-level mines. Although a high capital intensity or an increase in capital intensity tends to lower the demand for unskilled labour and increase the demand for more skilled labour, the pace at which this occurs is strongly influenced by relative factor prices. In 1911 the wages of unskilled African mineworkers were 8,6 per cent of those of white mineworkers, and in 1971, only 4,5 per cent of those of white mineworkers (table 8.1). Given the nature of gold production, and the large gap between the wages of skilled and unskilled workers, the capital intensity in the gold mining industry did not necessarily disadvantage unskilled workers until 1970.[14]

The production methods of several state corporations were modelled on those of the gold mines. The state corporations were also relatively capital-intensive, but by concentrating on producing 'upstream' or producer goods instead of finished production, their labour force was also split between a small and highly paid white skilled labour force and a large, cheap, and unskilled African labour force (section 9.7). When wages for Africans began to increase sharply from the 1970s onwards, the gold mining industry, the state corporations, and the private manufacturing industry changed their methods of production quite drastically and moved to a level of capital intensity that clearly damaged the employment of unskilled African labour.[15] This dramatically increased unemployment among Africans (see section 11.1).

The factors responsible for the high capital intensity of the economy and its increase since 1970 are complex, and their relative contributions difficult to determine.[16] In the 1960s the NP government embarked on a labour and economic policy that seriously distorted price relations. Over the next three decades this resulted in a skewed development of the economy. Verwoerd's policy of creating a white or 'European' economy at the southern tip of Africa had far-reaching effects on the South African economy. His policies for creating a capital-intensive first-world economy on a third-world continent not only weakened the employment capacity of the economy, but did so in a way that was highly detrimental to African workers.[17]

In the 1960s and early 1970s, rapid economic growth resulted in a serious shortage of skilled labour in all sectors of the economy. The supply of white (and even coloured) workers was simply not large enough to meet the increasing demand for skilled workers. During the 1960s job discrimination was maintained quite rigidly, and it was only during the 1970s that Africans were allowed to move into skilled and semi-skilled jobs. Influx control became much stricter during the 1970s and early 1980s. We can therefore say that the *non-availability* of different kinds of African labour (both skilled and unskilled) in the 1960s and 1970s provided a strong incentive to industrialists to substitute capital for labour. This incentive was reinforced by the sharp increases in African wages from 1975 onwards.[18]

During the 1980s Africans used their new trade union and strike rights to increase their real wages. From the Durban strikes in the early 1970s onwards, Africans ceased to be a docile and manageable work force, and continuing labour and township unrest in the 1970s, but especially in the 1980s, may have been an even stronger incentive to employers to substitute capital for labour.[19]

In the agricultural sector the capital–labour ratio increased by 168,8 per cent from 1970 to 1995, while the employment of unskilled workers declined by 16 per cent. The increase in the capital–labour ratio in the agricultural sector was largely the result of distorted factor prices. The NP government continued to supply farmers with low-cost capital (at least until 1978), while African and coloured labour became scarcer and more expensive in agriculture from 1980 onwards, when influx control started to break down (Bhorat and Hodge 1999: 352–9).

10.2.3 Structural shifts in production: a decline in the primary sector, and an increase in the tertiary sector

The economy changed in important ways from 1970 to 1995.[20] The significant decline in the contribution of the primary sector – traditionally an employer of mainly unskilled African and coloured workers – caused a significant decline in the employment of African and coloured workers generally. Although all four racial groups benefited from increased employment in the services sector, it was, according to Bhorat and Hodge, mainly whites and Asians who benefited from this shift. In the case of Africans, the gain in employment was not large enough to compensate for the general loss of employment resulting from the slowdown in economic growth, and the growing capital intensity of the primary sector.[21]

At first glance, it seems contradictory that, after 1970, the South African economy should have become more capital-intensive while gross domestic investment declined from 30 per cent of GDP in 1972 to only 16 per cent in 1993. This apparent contradiction can be explained by overinvestment in capital-intensive activities, and underinvestment in labour-intensive activities.[22]

Another reason for the high levels of unemployment among Africans and coloureds was the relative underdevelopment of the informal sector and the low level of investment in informal manufacturing. For many years the informal sector was relatively unknown, partly because it was illegal for Africans to head their own enterprises or to engage in manufacturing activities.[23]

The 'skewed' development of the South African economy over the past 30 years – characterised by overinvestment in capital-intensive activities in the private and public sectors, and underinvestment in labour-intensive activities and in the informal sector – was not only the result of a distorted capital–labour ratio (caused by Verwoerdian separate development), but also of large public sector investment on behalf of the 'total strategy' against the 'total onslaught'.[24] The large-scale government intervention in the economy from 1960 onwards was strongly driven by ideology – by Verwoerdianism in the 1960s and 1970s, and by 'total strategy' in the 1970s and 1980s – and not only undermined the growth potential and job-creating ability of the economy, but also contributed to its distorted development.

The ANC acknowledged in its RDP that serious *structural* problems had become built into the South African economy during segregation and apartheid, and especially during the liberation struggle. For more than a century, South Africa's economic development was shaped by political, economic, and ideological forces aimed at serving the interests of the white core by exploiting the black periphery. During the past 40 years this twist in favour of the first world-oriented modern sector became much stronger, and, as a result, a large part of the unskilled periphery was declared redundant.

Looking at the African unemployment problem from a broad historical perspective, from 1841 until 1970 the freedom and economic independence of Africans were deliberately undermined in order to force them into the unfree labour market, thus satisfying the seemingly insatiable demands of white employers for unskilled labour. In 1970, just when this process had been completed, the white-controlled economy was modernised and structurally transformed. When that happened, a growing number of already proletarianised Africans became unemployed. By then the economic independence of Africans had already been destroyed. Black poverty worsened spectacularly after 1970 because those whose economic independence had been destroyed during the previous 130 years had no capacity to protect themselves against the pauperisation effects of the period of stagflation (see section 11.1 for a description of the tendency of the South African economy to develop into an open, first-world, capitalist enclave).

After the black population groups had been defeated and subjugated in colonial wars, they were effectively deprived of all forms of political representation, and also 'enslaved' economically through an elaborate system of proletarianisation, repression, and discrimination. We can regard the Durban strikes in the early 1970s as one of the most important turning points in South Africa's racial history, with contradictory effects on the political system of white domination and the economic system of racial capitalism. From a political point of view, the Durban strikes set in motion a protracted process of black unrest that ultimately led to the breakdown of white political domination in the 1990s. From an economic point of view, they spelled the end of black subservience in the labour market. As soon as this happened, the white entrepreneurial class and white bureaucracy deliberately set in motion socio-economic processes to marginalise the black labour force as effectively as possible.

While the black protest movement that got under way during the Durban strikes ultimately succeeded in ending the political 'enslavement' of blacks, it provoked a powerful protective reaction among whites, aimed at safeguarding their endangered economic interests. After centuries of political and economic subservience, black people ultimately succeeded in liberating themselves politically, but at a huge economic price – ie, the inheritance of a 'skewed' economic structure, and the 'enslavement' of a large part of the black population in the miserable situation of seemingly insoluble structural unemployment and abject poverty. We can say that the liberation organisations succeeded in winning the political battle, but lost the economic war – at least for the time being (see table 10.4, and figure 2.1).

10.2.4 The high rate of growth of the African population

The high growth rate of the African population has also contributed to African unemployment, and will do so to an even greater extent over the next 25 years. The percentage share of the total population of each of the four population groups remained remarkably stable from 1910 to 1960 (table 10.2).[25] However, from 1960 to 1996 the percentage contribution of Africans and whites changed significantly. The share of Africans increased by 7,5 percentage points, from 69 per cent to 76,5 per cent, that of whites declined by 6,5 percentage points from 19 per cent to 12,5 per cent, and that of coloureds and Asians declined only marginally.

According to Professor Jan Sadie, each population group has moved, or is moving, through five demographic phases. The first phase of the cycle is characterised by almost uncontrolled fertility and mortality, and a growth rate of about 2 per cent. During the second, or explosive phase, mortality declines more rapidly than fertility, with the result that population growth starts to

Table 10.2:	The share of the total population of various population groups (%)			
	African	White	Coloured	Asian
1910	67	22	9	2
1925	68	22	8	2
1946	69	21	8	2
1960	69	19	9	3
1970	70	18	9	3
1980	72	16	9	3
1991	75,2	13,5	8,7	2,6
1996	76,5	12,5	8,6	2,6

Source: Sadie 1989: table 1; Whitefield and Van Seventer 1999: table 2.1.

increase. During the third, or transitional phase, population growth peaks. During the fourth phase, population growth starts to decline, and during the fifth and final phase, fertility drops below replacement level.

The white and Asian population groups were in their transitional phases from 1946 to 1951, when their population growth rates were 2,2 per cent and 3,69 per cent respectively. Their population growth rates declined to only 0,49 per cent and 1,28 per cent respectively in 1990–6. The coloured population group reached its transitional phase in the 1960s, when its growth rate was 3,21 per cent, declining to only 1,68 per cent in 1990–6. The growth of the African population group started to accelerate from 1950 onwards, and reached its transitional phase in 1980–5 with a growth rate of 2,96 per cent. Africans have been in a declining phase of the population cycle since 1985, with an average growth rate of 2,73 per cent.[26]

The supply in African labour increased from 68 per cent of the total in 1970 to 70 per cent in 1995, or from 6,9 million to 9,4 million. In 1970 Africans' share of the total population was 70 per cent, and Africans constituted 70 per cent of the employed workforce, as against 76,5 per cent and only 59 per cent in 1996.

According to projections made by Sadie, the supply in African labour will increase to 76 per cent of the total in 2020. The large numbers of Africans that will enter the labour market during the next 20 years will undoubtedly contribute considerably to African unemployment until 2020. At present 37,4 per cent of Africans are younger than 14 years, compared to only 20,9 per cent of whites. When the generation younger than 14 years reaches working age, the African labour force will increase dramatically, and aggravate the already high unemployment in their ranks. A high percentage of Africans presently younger than 14 years will probably never have formal jobs in their lifetimes (see Sadie 1999: tables 1.1, 1.2).

However, the effect of HIV/AIDS[27] on the population growth rate and on employment/unemployment rates needs to be taken into account. According to the BER (2000) a number of factors have been identified that have made, and continue to make, South Africans highly susceptible to HIV/AIDS.[28] It is estimated that between 4 million and 6 million people (about 11 per cent of the population) were HIV-positive at the end of 2000. HIV prevalence is most acute in the 15–49 age group. The high incidence of HIV among the young makes the potential economic impact of HIV/AIDS quite serious, as working people are disproportionately affected. It is estimated that the total population will be 18 per cent smaller by 2015 than it would be if AIDS were not a factor – ie, 50 million instead of 61 million. Arguably the most serious threat of HIV/AIDS to the economy is its impact on skills.[29] It is likely that semi-skilled and skilled workers lost to AIDS can be replaced by the unemployed, countering the negative impact on the labour supply. However, the relatively high prevalence of HIV among skilled and highly skilled workers has serious implications not only for labour productivity, but also the demand for labour. While, by 2015, the population and labour force will be reduced by 18 per cent and 21 per cent respectively compared to a non-AIDS scenario, the decline in economic production, employment, and income will be substantially less. According to the BER, it is not entirely clear that economy-wide unemployment will decline as a result of HIV/AIDS.

Overall, real GDP growth is projected to be 1,5 per cent lower by 2010 and 5,7 per cent lower by 2015 compared to a non-AIDS scenario. The projected decline in GDP is significantly less than the decline in the overall population (18 per cent), which suggests that per capita GDP will increase. Over the complete projection period real per capita GDP growth is 0,9 per cent higher a year on average (BER 2001). This will, of course, have a negative effect on the demand for labour. From an unemployment point of view, the pandemic will probably neither 'relieve' nor aggrevate unemployment in a meaningful manner. Its human and social impact is likely to be far more serious than the economic one, even though the former has implications for the latter. The socio-political climate could deteriorate, which will impact negatively on the economy.

10.3 Poverty and deprivation

A very high percentage of the South African population are abjectly poor. As in the case with unemployment, poverty affects mainly Africans and, to a lesser degree, coloured people. In 1996 the monthly expenditure of the poorest 81,4 per cent of African households was as follows: 21,5 per cent spent R600 or less, 32,4 per cent spent R601–R1 000, and the next 27,5 per cent spent R1 001–R1 800 (at constant 1996 prices). In the case of coloured households, monthly expenditure of the poorest 47,6 per cent was as follows: 7,8 per cent spent R600, 13,6 per cent spent R601–R1 000 or less, and 25,8 per cent spent R1 001–R1 800 (table 10.3).

According to Statistics South Africa, households that spent R600 or less a month in 1996 could be regarded as very poor, whereas households that spent R601–R1 000 a month could be regarded as poor (2000: 59). Even those households that spent R1 001–R1 800 a month can be regarded as relatively poor and vulnerable.[30]

Table 10.3: Monthly household expenditure by population group, 1996

Households '000	R0–600 %	R601–R1 000 %	R1 001–1 800 %	R0–1 800 %	R1 801–R3 500 %	R3 501 or more %
African	6 534	21,5	32,4	27,5	81,4	14,2	4,4
Coloured	741	7,8	13,6	25,8	47,2	32,7	20,2
Asian	244	0,8	1,7	9,3	11,8	37,0	51,1
White	1 483	1,4	1,3	5,8	8,5	20,4	71,1
Total	9 001	16,5	24,9	23,3	64,7	17,4	18,0

Source: SSA 2000: table 5.

Several measurements are used in South Africa to determine the extent of poverty.[31] According to Leibbrant and Leibbrant, 'the nature of South African poverty [among Africans and coloureds] is so clear-cut and pervasive that, for any reliable data, the application of an array of appropriate technical tools will produce very similar poverty pictures' (2000: 6). Irrespective of what measurement is used, between 50 and 60 per cent of Africans and between 22 and 32 per cent of coloureds were living in poverty in 1993 and 1995.[32]

Apart from the close correlation between race and poverty, other correlations are also conspicuous. Levels of poverty are much higher in rural than in urban areas. According to one measurement, the poverty 'rate' in rural areas is 63 per cent, compared with 22 per cent in urban areas. Many of the rural poor live in the erstwhile Bantustans, where many households are headed by women. There is also a strong correlation between educational achievement and poverty. Individuals with no education or less than seven years of primary education are more likely to be poor than individuals with higher levels of education.[33] Poverty and unemployment are also closely linked. The unemployment rate among members of poor households is almost double the overall national rate. Women, children, the elderly, and those with disabilities bear the greatest burden of poverty. According to a 1995 survey, the poverty rate was 60 per cent among female-headed households compared to 31 per cent among male-headed households. It is estimated that 61 per cent of all children live in poverty. It is also estimated that between 2 and 3 million South Africans are malnourished (Leibbrant and Leibbrant 2000: 6–11, tables 8–14; see also section 11.3.3 for South Africa's position on the UNDP's human development index).

It is not easy to describe or define poverty – especially poverty amid plenty. Poverty is normally a lifelong experience of *multiple deprivation*, and is accompanied by pain, destitution, humiliation, and squalor.[34] For most of the 28 million South Africans (of whom 25 million were Africans) who in 1996 belonged to households that spent R1 800 or less a month, poverty was not a new phenomenon but had been their destiny for many generations.[35] The impoverishment and proletarianisation of the Khoisan and the different African tribes was a long and relentless process that began in the late 17th century and continued uninterruptedly and with increasing intensity until the 1980s.

The difficult question arises whether the economic subjugation of indigenous people over the past 350 years was historically inevitable. If political power had been less unequally distributed, the economy would undoubtedly have developed in a less exploitative and less humiliating manner for the indigenous population groups. Given the power relations on which colonialism, segregation and apartheid were based, the empowerment and enrichment of whites were one side of the colonial coin, and the exploitation and impoverishment of Africans and coloureds the other.

We can arrange the factors that contributed to poverty under the following headings:

i   land deprivation and the deliberate proletarianisation of the Khoisan and the different African tribes in order to institutionalise repressive black labour systems;

ii discriminatory measures to protect the white (and predominantly Afrikaner) proletariat against competition from the black proletariat;

iii official discrimination in social spending (especially on education and training); and

iv stagflation since 1974, and a further pauperisation of two thirds of the population.

10.3.1   Land deprivation, proletarianisation, and repressive labour systems

The seizure of the ancestral lands of the Khoisan and different African tribes during Dutch and British colonialism and the hegemony of the English establishment in the period of segregation is a very sensitive cultural issue. It is not specific to South Africa, but to all the so-called 'New Europes' colonised by Europeans from the 16th to the 20th centuries. In North and South America and in Australasia, it was easier for European colonists to seize land because the indigenous peoples were so vulnerable to European diseases. In the case of South Africa the Khoisan were vulnerable to smallpox and other diseases, but African tribes were immune to them. Even in those countries where millions of indigenous people died of foreign diseases, the European colonisers still used their monopoly over gunpowder to conquer the indigenous populations and deprive them of their land. This was also true of the Dutch colonists who conquered the Khoisan. But in the case of the African tribes in South Africa, it was mainly the British colonisers – equipped with superior military power, and obsessed with expansionism and domination – who did the conquering. However, the British had to use considerably more military aggression to conquer the Africans and deprive them of their land than was the case in most other European colonies (see Diamond 1997: ch 11; see also section 6.4).[36] It must be emphasised that, in the South African case, land was not always seized for the sake of land *per se*. As De Kiewiet remarked: '...the land wars were also labour wars' (1941: 180). Perhaps it would be more correct to claim that in large parts of South Africa the land wars were more often than not labour wars – ie, land was seized to gain access to cheap black labour.[37]

During the last two decades of the 17th century Simon van der Stel used the VOC garrison as an official commando to destroy the socio-economic and political structures of the Khoikhoi in the vicinity of Cape Town. In 1713 the Khoikhoi in the Western Cape were decimated by a smallpox virus and, for the rest of the 18th century, it was relatively easy for the *Trekboere* to deprive the Khoisan of the greater part of their land and cattle.[38] During the three frontier wars in the Eastern Cape between 1835 and 1853, the social structures of the Xhosa were disrupted, their chieftainships undermined, large parts of their land seized for sheep farming by British settlers, and thousands of Xhosa impoverished and driven into the colony to search for employment as contract workers. During the colonial conquest, the cosmology and physical and cultural existence of the Xhosa were assaulted so relentlessly that the Xhosa sought their 'salvation' in the cattle killing movement of 1856–7. A similar process of colonial conquest and land seizure occurred in the northern provinces at the end of the 19th and in the early 20th century, but not in such a dramatic and bloody way as in the Eastern Cape.

The onslaught on the economic independence of Africans assumed a more systematic and aggressive character after the discovery of diamonds and gold.

The Glen Grey Act (1894) was a deliberate attempt to turn African peasants – who had until then maintained a relatively independent existence on 'tribal' as well as 'white' land – into an impoverished proletariat. The Land Act (1913) was the most notorious, but also the most successful, measure for impoverishing and proletarianising Africans.[39] From 1936 to 1994, Africans were prohibited from owning land in 87 per cent of the country.

As noted earlier, more than 70 per cent of households that spent R1 000 or less a month in 1996 were living in rural areas. Most of the rural poor were living in the erstwhile Bantustans. For many decades, the underdeveloped 'native reserves' subsidised gold mining and industrial development in white urban areas by absorbing (on dubious moral grounds) a part of their production costs. Although the NP government spent billions of rands from 1970 on Bantustan 'development', only a small part of this expenditure benefited the poor. Most of the money was spent on government buildings, and used to bribe corrupt Bantustan leaders. The underdevelopment of the Bantustans and the wealth in white urban areas are therefore structurally linked.[40]

Colonialism during the Dutch and British periods (1652–1910) severely disrupted and impoverished indigenous population groups, but the range and penetration of exploitation during the periods of segregation (1900–48) and apartheid (1948–94) were undoubtedly more severe from a social and cultural point of view, and caused more alienation and poverty – at least in the ranks of the lower 70 per cent of Africans and, say, the lower 40 per cent of coloureds. The poorest half of the population was poorer and socially more dislocated in 1994 than in 1950, and probably also more so than in 1900.[41] The sharp increase in the growth of the African and coloured population groups – especially during the second half of the 20th century – undoubtedly played an important role in aggravating black poverty. But we can also argue that chronic community poverty and the social and cultural disruption of African and coloured communities contributed to the increase in their population growth rates.

10.3.2 Discriminatory measures to protect the white (and mainly Afrikaner) proletariat against black competition

Discriminatory practices have been an integral part of South African society since the 18th century, and were legitimised by the racist ideology of Social Darwinism at the beginning of the 20th century. The real motivation for discrimination – especially in the labour market – was to protect poor white Afrikaners against competition from cheap black (and especially African) labour. One of the most serious problems that confronted the Union government from 1910 onwards was the dual proletarianisation unfolding as part of the process of modernisation and industrialisation. While the African proletariat was largely deliberately 'created' by a series of repressive measures, the white proletariat emerged almost inadvertently as a result of modernisation (see sections 8.6 and 8.7).

The 'struggle' between the Afrikaner and African proletariats for a place in the South African sun dominated political and economic policies in the 20th century. What made dual proletarianisation such a thorny problem – with the potential for escalating conflict – was the fact that the two proletariats were in a 'zero-sum relationship' with each other. Given South Africa's economic capacity as a mineral-based developing country in the first half of the century, and given the power structure in place, it was apparently not possible to adequately address the poverty of both proletariats at the same time. What exacerbated the 'unequal struggle' between the two proletariats was the vested interest of the white employer class in keeping the African proletariat in place as a source of cheap and docile labour. While Afrikaners had strong bargaining power by virtue of their participation in the predominantly white parliamentary system created by the Act of Westminster (1909), the Africans had for all practical purposes been disenfranchised by the same act, and were therefore politically powerless.

A multitude of discriminatory laws prevented Africans from doing skilled and highly paid jobs. They were paid lower wages even if they were employed in the same job categories as whites. Moreover, they were prevented from joining recognised trade unions, and therefore deprived of the opportunity to participate in industrial action and wage negotiations. Discriminatory legislation also deprived Africans of the opportunity to gain skills and undergo professional training, with the consequence that they were, for all practical purposes, condemned to low-paid and unskilled work. While several discriminatory laws were enacted before the NP rose to power in 1948, this legislation was considerably extended and intensified during the first 30 years of NP government, and also applied to coloureds and Indians.[42] The NP government's policy of forced removals caused immense disruption and pauperisation in the ranks of Africans (see sections 9.5 and 9.6).

Both repressive and discriminatory measures degraded Africans. Many of these measures were closely interrelated, and reinforced the exploitative character of the others. The low wages of Africans, as a percentage of white wages, in mining and manufacturing during most of the 20th century are a good indication of African exploitation *vis-à-vis* white privilege (see table 8.1). The racial disparity between the per capita income of whites and Africans also increased sharply during the halcyon years of apartheid (see table 10.1).

The increase in African wages in mining and manufacturing as a percentage of white wages, and the narrowing of the per capita income gap between whites and Africans since 1970, are deceptive. From 1970s onwards a small elite of Africans advanced to more skilled and better-paid jobs, but most Africans either experienced a decline in their real wages, or became unemployed. The impoverishment of the African workforce in the 20th century occurred in three phases: during the first half of the century, African wages in all sectors were less than one fifth of white wages, and the gap grew, except in the manufacturing sector during World War 2; during the third quarter of the century, African wages declined to less than one sixth of white wages in all sectors; and in the last quarter, the wages of about 20 per cent of Africans increased considerably *vis-à-vis* those of whites, while the other 80 per cent of the African workforce either experienced a decline in wages *vis-à-vis* white wages, or became unemployed.

Job reservation and discrimination in the labour market were abolished in 1979, but unofficial discrimination and cultural barriers still made it difficult for blacks to compete with whites on an equal footing. According to Van der Berg and Bhorat, racial and gender wage differentials within a given job grade have

---

Table 10.4: Percentage changes in per household income class in 1975–91 and 1991–6, and the main household income per income class in 1996 (constant 1996 prices)

Population group	Period	Poorest 40%	Next 20%	Next 20%	Top 20%
Africans	1975–91	-42%	-26%	-10%	+38%
	1991–6	-21%	-4%	+4%	+15%
	Income 1996	2 383	9 120	19 183	72 780
Whites	1975–91	-40%	-26%	-7%	0%
	1991–6	-16%	-13%	-13%	-3%
	Income 1996	29 549	83 506	134 821	306 662
Coloureds	1975–91	-4%	+23%	+19%	+20%
	1991–6	0%	+6%	+8%	+14%
	Income 1996	8 214	25 967	46 463	122 935
Asians	1975–91	+29%	+36%	+36%	+31%
	1991–6	-5%	+5%	+13%	+25%
	Income 1996	17 878	49 569	80 882	192 103

Source: Estimated from Whiteford and McGrath 1994: table 7.1; Whiteford and Van Seventer 1999: table 3.6 and Appendix C.

declined considerably since the mid-1970s, but had not been wiped out by 1989.[43]

10.3.3 Discrimination in social spending on the four population groups

Reliable statistics on social spending on the four statutory population groups during the first half of the 20th century are not available. There is, however, little doubt that social spending on blacks was even lower during the first half than during the second half of the century. It is alarming that per capita social spending (including spending on education) on Africans until 1975 was less than 12 per cent of that on whites, and that on coloureds less than 40 per cent of that on whites (table 10.5; see also section 10.4.3).

Earlier, we referred to poverty as a lifelong experience of multiple deprivations. The poor in South Africa have been singularly deprived of adequate educational opportunities. Consequently, they have owned very little human capital, and the little they own is constantly undermined by the lack of proper job opportunities.

Sadie's classification of the labour force into four categories is a useful barometer of educational distortions. Category 1 represents the executive category (entrepreneurs, managers, and directors); category 2 the highly skilled category; category 3 the lesser skilled category; and category 4 the unskilled category. While, in 1985, only 5 per cent of Africans and 13,6 per cent of coloureds had the educational and skills qualifications to be classified into the first two categories, 50 per cent of whites were classified in that category. While only 1,2 per cent of whites were classified as unskilled workers, almost 65 per cent of Africans and 43 per cent of coloureds were classified as unskilled. The classification of the labour force was not substantially different in 1994 (table 10.6).[44]

Table 10.5: Estimated real per capita social spending on whites (in 1990 rands) and social spending on non-whites as a percentage of spending on whites (1949–93)

	Whites 1990 rands	Whites %	Africans %	Coloureds %	Asians %	All groups %
1949	978	100	12,0	42,0	35,6	32,3
1969	1 511	100	10,8	39,6	46,1	29,8
1975	2 033	100	11,8	39,5	43,8	29,6
1986	1 972	100	20,9	54,1	62,9	36,1
1993	1 475	100	50,9	69,3	100,8	72

Source: Van der Berg and Bhorat 1999: table 9.

Table 10.6: The skills composition of various South African population groups versus that of the entire population of the United States (1985)

Categories	US %	Whites %	Asian %	Coloureds %	Africans %
I	12,6	13,1	4,2	0,6	0,1
II	29,4	36,8	18,4	12,6	4,9
III	51,0	48,9	63,4	44,2	30,2
IV	7,0	1,2	14,0	42,6	64,8
	100	100	100	100	100

Source: Sadie 1991: ch 7.

At the end of the apartheid period a large percentage of Africans were either unemployed, or employed in low-paying jobs, mainly as a result of low levels of education. The cumulative effect of the inadequate opportunities for Africans (and to a lesser extent for coloureds) to accumulate human capital during the 20th century has burdened them enormously (see section 10.4.3).

10.3.4 Stagflation, unemployment, and the further pauperisation of the poorest two thirds of the population from 1974 to 1994

The economic crisis from 1974 to 1994 sharply increased especially African unemployment. This, in turn, was an important reason for the further pauperisation of the poorest two thirds of the population. The mean household income of the poorest 40 per cent of African households (equal to 50 per cent of the African population) declined by 42 per cent from 1975 to 1991, and by a further 21 per cent from 1991 to 1996. The mean household income of the next 20 per cent of Africans declined by 26 per cent and 4 per cent respectively over these two periods. The household income of 60 per cent of Africans (almost 70 per cent of the African population) was therefore considerably lower in 1996 than in 1975 (see table 10.4).

Although most the repressive and discriminatory measures were abolished during the last quarter of the 20th century, no compensation was paid to the worst victims of systemic exploitation. On the contrary – owing to the structural movements in the South African economy towards greater capital-intensity and post-industrial production from 1960 onwards – a very large part of the erstwhile unskilled African labour force became redundant and structurally unemployed. African unemployment increased from 24 per cent in 1970 to 46 per cent in 1995 (table 10.1).[45]

It is not difficult to explain why the poorest 70 per cent of Africans and 25 per cent of coloureds were so dramatically impoverished during the last 20 years of apartheid. By 1975 almost two thirds of the total population were already so abjectly poor that they had very little material or human capacity to withstand the pauperisation effects of the droughts of the 1980s, growing unemployment, and the socially disruptive effects of the liberation struggle.[46]

The only other population group that experienced, from 1975 to 1996, a decline in household income comparable to that of Africans was whites (and mainly Afrikaners).[47] The decline in the income of the poorest 40 per cent of white households can perhaps be explained in terms of the rapid (and perhaps too rapid) embourgeoisement of Afrikaners in the third quarter of the century, and the inability of many of the Afrikaner *nouveau riche* to maintain their income levels when economic conditions deteriorated – when, for example, the agricultural sector was burdened by serious droughts, high indebtedness, high interest rates, and a decline in government subsidies. The NP government could not maintain the high levels of favouritism for Afrikaners after 1974, when government income declined and expenditure on defence and black education increased sharply.

It would, however, be a mistake to underestimate the traumatic experiences of many Afrikaners who had progressed from relative poverty in the first half of the 20th century to substantial wealth during the third quarter, and then regressed to substantially lower standards of living in the last quarter. Also, of the 28 million members of households with a monthly income of less than R1 800 in 1996, no fewer than 500 000 were white.

10.4 Racial inequalities and systemic injustices

Racial inequality and social injustices are writ large in South Africa's history. These inequalities are often characterised as the 'inequalities of apartheid', but this is an oversimplification. Many reasons of a historical, cultural, and demographic nature can be given for any number of these inequalities. The theme of this study is, however, that racial inequalities should largely be understood in systemic terms, ie, in terms of deeply ingrained white power and black powerlessness.[48]

We can distinguish among four different levels or types of racial and class inequalities:

i   racial inequalities in the share of income and per capita income of the different population groups;

ii racial inequalities in the distribution of political, military, economic, and ideological power and the ensuing unequal power struggles in South African history;

iii racial inequalities in the distribution of economic, entrepreneurial, and educational opportunities; and

iv the highly differentiated class structure that has emerged among blacks, and the rise of a black elite.

10.4.1 Racial inequalities in the distribution of income

Both the percentage share of each of the four population groups of the total population and the percentage share of each of total income remained remarkably constant during the first 70 years of the 20th century. We can simplify the relative share of Africans and whites of population and income during this period as follows: while whites constituted about 20 per cent of the population during these 70 years, they constantly received more than 70 per cent of the income, and while Africans constituted 70 per cent of the population, they received only about 20 per cent of the income (see tables 10.2 and 10.7)

Table 10.7: Share of income by population group			
	African	White	Coloured	Asian
1925	18	75	5	2
1946	22	71	5	2
1960	21	71	6	2
1970	19,5	71	7	2,5
1980	25	65	7	3
1991	29,9	59,9	6,8	3,8
1996	35,7	51,9	7,9	4,5

Source: Whiteford and McGrath 1994: table 5.1; Lipton 1986: table 9; Whiteford and Van Seventer 1999: table 2.1.

From 1970 to 1996 the percentage share of Africans of the total population increased from 70 per cent to 76,5 per cent, and their share of total income from 19,5 per cent to 35,7 per cent. In the case of whites, their share of the total population declined from 18 per cent to 12,5 per cent, and their share of total income from 71 per cent to 51,9 per cent (see tables 10.2 and 10.7). These opposed shifts are significant, and result from an equally remarkable shift in the relative bargaining power of Africans *vis-à-vis* that of whites since 1970. (This shift in relative bargaining power during the liberation struggle will be discussed in section 10.4.2.) Although the improvement in the share of income of Africans *vis-à-vis* that of whites is meaningful, it is deceptive.[49]

Estimates of per capita income by race groups in 1995 rands for the period 1917 to 1995 are given in table 10.8. The very large inequalities in the

Table 10.8: Estimated per capita personal incomes by race group relative to that of whites, 1917–95

	Whites	Coloureds	Asians	Africans	Average
Per capita income (in constant 1995 rands)					
1917	9 369	2 061	2 075	849	2 829
1936	13 773	2 151	3 185	1 048	3 842
1946	18 820	3 068	4 238	1 671	5 417
1960	22 389	3 568	3 828	1 815	6 006
1970	32 799	5 684	6 630	2 246	7 986
1980	34 655	6 623	8 821	2 931	8 472
1995	34 689	6 931	16 793	4 678	9 013
Relative per capita personal incomes (per cent of white level)					
1917	100	22.0	22.1	9.1	
1936	100	15.6	23.1	7.6	
1946	100	16.3	23.0	8.9	
1960	100	15.9	17.1	8.1	
1970	100	17.3	20.2	6.8	
1980	100	19.1	25.5	8.5	
1995	100	20.0	48.4	13.5	
Racial disparity ratios: number of times whites per capita income was higher than that of other races					
1917		4.6	4.5	11.0	
1936		6.4	4.3	13.2	
1946		6.1	4.3	11.5	
1960		6.3	5.8	12.3	
1970		5.8	5.0	14.6	
1980		5.2	3.9	11.8	
1995		5.0	2.1	7.4	

Source: Van der Berg and Bhorat 1999: table 6.

distribution of per capita income during the 20th century become clear when the per capita income of the non-white groups is expressed as a percentage of white per capita income (see middle part of the table).[50]

10.4.2 Racial inequalities in the distribution of political, military, economic, and ideological power, and the ensuing unequal power struggles

Many reasons can be given for the racial inequalities discussed above. But the factors that have contributed most, both directly and indirectly, to the inequalities in income distribution are undoubtedly racism and racial inequality in the distribution of political, economic, and ideological power. During the systemic period of Dutch colonialism, the Cape was not a colony of Holland but a colony of the VOC. The Dutch government granted the company extraordinary powers and privileges. In accordance with the doctrine of mercantilism, the VOC used its power in a reckless manner to promote its narrow commercial interests. In the 17th century the company's garrison was used as an official commando to subjugate the Khoikhoi, and in the 18th century the commando – now controlled by *Trekboere* – was used to dispossess and subjugate the Khoisan.

When the Cape became a British colony at the end of the 18th century, Britain was not only the leading industrial country, but also one of the strongest military powers in the world. In the 19th century British colonial power in all its manifestations – from its political and economic institutions to its *Weltanschauung* – was imprinted on every corner of the country and on each of its great variety of population groups. The power shift caused by British colonialism had devastating effects on the feudal and tribally oriented social orders of the Afrikaner, Khoisan, and African population groups. But the real victims of the British colonial onslaught were the Xhosa and the Zulu, who were defeated in bloody wars and dispossessed of a large part of their land, while many of them were forced to turn into an unfree proletariat. In the middle decades of the 19th century a humiliating racist ideology was formulated by predominantly British settlers to legitimise the emerging system of racial capitalism and labour repression.

In the last decades of the 19th century Britain's colonial policy was transformed into an aggressive type of exploitative and expansionist imperialism. This was partly the result of intensified rivalry between the large industrial countries of the western world, and partly of the lucrative economic opportunities offered to Britain when gold was discovered in the ZAR to solve its chronic economic and balance of trade problems. The exploitation of gold ore necessitated the introduction of new organisations to South Africa – ie, the large mining corporations, with predominantly foreign shareholders. Those capitalist corporations played a dominant role in the history of South Africa in the 20th century.

Almost all the repressive and exploitative legislation in the period after 1890 was introduced at the request and on behalf of the influential mining and manufacturing corporations. To serve the interests of the gold mining industry, the British government fought the Anglo–Boer War, and subordinated several African tribes to British rule. In order to perpetuate socio-political stability on behalf of the gold mining industry, and find a formula for turning Africans into a wage-earning proletariat, the Afrikaner 'notables' in the Transvaal were co-opted into a white elite in 1907. This led to the Act of Westminster of 1909, the constitution of the Union of South Africa, which – for all practical purposes – created a system of white political domination and, with few exceptions, disenfranchised blacks. Expansionist imperialism and racial capitalism were legitimised in terms of the racist ideologies of Social Darwinism and segregation at a time when Cape liberalism was eclipsed. During the hegemony of the English establishment in the first half of the 20th century, racially based segregation became the official policy, and both repressive and discriminatory labour patterns were institutionalised. Both these measures were exploitative and repressive, and not only perpetuated but also increased socio-economic inequalities between whites and blacks.

It is important to realise that the unequal distribution of power between white and black not only benefited whites to the detriment of blacks; it also had an international dimension. In the first 60 years after the discovery of gold, economic power was mainly concentrated in the hands of foreign corporations and foreign shareholders who profited hugely from the low wages paid to (local and foreign) migrant workers in the gold mines. During the third quarter of the 20th century multinational corporations made extremely large profits in mining and manufacturing by exploiting the Verwoerdian labour laws. After the Sharpeville unrest of 1960, numerous foreign – and mainly American – financial institutions became involved in South Africa and also made very large profits under apartheid until they decided to disinvest after the 'Rubicon speech' of 1985.

The power shift that occurred in the decades after 1948 was initiated by Afrikaners, who portrayed themselves not only as a divinely elected people, but also as the wronged victims of British colonialism and a group threatened by the allegedly uncivilised African majority. Many Afrikaners envied the wealth of the English, and were aware of the fact that the latter had become wealthy by exploiting indigenous people. Once the Afrikaners had gained political power, many of them regarded this as their turn to benefit from exploiting blacks. Consequently, a plethora of additional repressive and discriminatory laws was enacted in accordance with apartheid policy.

To counteract black protest movements, and to perpetuate black powerlessness, the NP government, in the 1960s, enacted numerous authoritarian security laws, and turned South Africa into a police state – while claiming that their policy was based on the democratic and Christian values of the western world. With repressive, discriminatory, and authoritarian measures at its disposal, the apartheid regime succeeded in suppressing black protest until the mid-1970s on the one hand, and bringing about a fairly rapid embourgeoisement of the Afrikaners during the third quarter of the 20th century on the other. The comprehensive and rigid manner in which oppressive, repressive, and discriminatory measures were implemented during the third quarter of the 20th century increased the inequalities between whites and blacks considerably (see table 10.8; sections 9.5 and 9.6).

An important paradigm shift took place during the first half of the 1970s. As the liberation struggle intensified from the early 1970s onwards, the balance of power started to shift slowly but surely from whites to blacks, despite the desperate attempts by the apartheid regime to retain its grip on the levers of power. It launched a 'total strategy' to counteract the alleged 'total onslaught' against South Africa, but even this could not stop the internal and external groundswell of protest against apartheid. In belated attempts to meet black grievances, the Botha government made a series of concessions to blacks. Perhaps the most important of these was the abolition of discriminatory labour legislation in the late 1970s and early 1980s. This constituted a strategic economic power shift that enabled the upper ±20 per cent of blacks to make enormous progress (see table 10.4).[51]

It is ironic that, at a time when the apartheid regime – and more specifically its securocracy – was responsible for all sorts of atrocities and human rights violations in combating the liberation struggle, the NP government also made concessions that in effect undermined its own authority and control. Even before the elections of 1994 a meaningful power shift took place from whites to blacks, and, as a result, some of the glaring inequalities of apartheid were removed.

10.4.3 Racial inequalities in the distribution of economic, entrepreneurial, and educational opportunities

One of the most tragic features of South African history is the variety of ways in which whites used the political and economic power at their disposal to deprive indigenous groups of reasonable opportunities for social, economic, and entrepreneurial development. Although indigenous people were not deprived of all opportunities, the opportunities allocated to them were far fewer and usually far inferior to those available to whites.

The seizure of the land of indigenous population groups during the extended colonial period was not only a powerful instrument for enriching whites, but also for impoverishing and proletarianising indigenous people and deliberately turning them into a dependent and subservient labour force. Although, in 1936, 13 per cent of South Africa's land surface was reserved for African occupation, most of this land was communal property, controlled by tribal chiefs. Only a small elite owned private property in the Bantustans.[52]

Africans living outside the Bantustans were (with a few exceptions) propertyless; they were almost completely deprived of the opportunity to own farms, their own dwellings, or other tangible property. More than 90 per cent of Africans therefore did not own the kind of property that could protect them against the impoverishing effects of inflation.[53] As late as 1980, 99-year leasehold was announced for urban Africans. For most of the 20th century almost the entire African population was a disenfranchised and propertyless proletariat with few citizenship rights.[54]

The rise of an African peasantry in the Cape and Natal in the second half of the 19th century and of tenant farming in the Transorangia in the same period represented a very promising form of petty entrepreneurship for Africans. The peasant and tenant farmers produced large quantities of maize by using family instead of wage labour. By keeping their production costs relatively low, their production methods were well adapted to the climatic conditions of the 'maize triangle'. Unfortunately, this promising version of agricultural entrepreneurship was deliberately destroyed as the gold mining industry and modernising white farmers displayed an almost insatiable demand for cheap African labour. In order to supply these two white sectors with the required volume of cheap African labour, the white political authorities passed the Land Act of 1913 in an attempt to destroy all forms of share-cropping and squatter farming. As a result of this legislation, and additional laws that prohibited Africans from conducting business in white areas, Africans were, before 1980, almost completely deprived of the opportunity to legally accumulate capital and entrepreneurial skills outside the Bantustans, and to develop a capitalist class.[55]

During the 20th century governments throughout the world accepted responsibility for social spending to improve the health, welfare, and education of their populations. In South Africa per capita social spending on the four statutory population groups was very unequal, with the result that opportunities for social and intellectual development were far more limited for blacks than for whites (table 10.5). Consequently, the opportunities for accumulating human capital were also far more limited for blacks than for whites. Discriminatory legislation and practices, and the restrictions placed on the participation of coloureds, Asians, and especially Africans in skilled, professional, and entrepreneurial activities, further limited the opportunities of these indigenous population groups to accumulate human capital (see section 10.3.3). This kind of inequality, for which the government was responsible, boils down to a very crude form of social injustice.

Governments worldwide spend about half their social budgets on education, and this is decisively important for human capital formation. This was especially true during the second half of the 20th century, when proper scholastic and professional training – especially in the developed world – became an important determinant of economic growth. In South Africa, however, spending on education was very unequally divided among the different racial groups in the apartheid period.

In 1953 African education was transferred from the mission schools to the department of bantu education. The new system greatly extended the reach of primary education, but remained significantly inferior to white education. As noted earlier, expenditure on African education was pegged in the 1950s at the level of African taxation. As recently as 1982, total spending on African education was less than half that on white education, despite the fact that the African population was more than 4,5 times larger than the white population. In 1992 it surpassed that of whites for the first time (Van der Berg and Bhorat 1999: 17).

Despite the narrowing of the spending gap on education since 1976, the quality of African education remains far inferior to that of whites and Asians, owing to the large sizes of classes in African schools, the inadequate training of African teachers, and the absence of a culture of learning in African schools. After generations of neglect, African education has fallen so far behind that a vicious circle of inferiority has been established. It will not be easy to turn it into a virtuous circle.

Most job opportunities created since 1970 have been in the services sector, but, because of their low levels of education, Africans have not been able to compete for these jobs to the same extent as other population groups. The effect of the relative low levels of spending on African education and of the inferiority of the African education system on the accumulation of African human capital is immeasurable. Since the abolition of job discrimination in 1979, and the political transition of 1994, many lucrative job opportunities have become available to Africans. But, owing to their inadequate education and professional training, many Africans are not in a position to make full use of these new opportunities. As a result of inferior training, the productivity of many Africans is very low. It will take decades before the educational backlog is eliminated.

10.4.4 The highly differentiated class structure that has emerged among blacks, and the rise of a black elite

One of the most remarkable characteristics of the African community until the 1960s was its lack of class differentiation. This was the result of the oppressive measures implemented in accordance with colonial, segregationist, and apartheid policies. The state had closed off blacks' access to the most accumulative activities, and used the Group Areas Act to drive African business people out of central business districts. The only wealthy Africans were collaborating Bantustan leaders and/or chiefs who were co-opted and corrupted by the CM and the NAD. Some of these African leaders succeeded in accumulating considerable wealth. Apart from the rich chieftainship class, a small professional class emerged before 1960 as an urban elite.

The social stratification among coloureds and Asians had a more normal profile. Coloureds and Asians were always allowed to own property and perform skilled and professional jobs, and their opportunities for entrepreneurship and accumulation were therefore more lucrative. Both these groups were also negatively affected by the Group Areas Act, but showed exceptional ingenuity in overcoming statutory stumbling blocks. Asian entrepreneurs in particular have been extremely successful over the past 40 years, largely as a result of effective 'networking' among members of their two dominant religious groups.

Africans with permanent residence rights in urban areas succeeded, from the 1960s onwards, with covert entrepreneurship, including organised crime and other activities regarded as 'illegal' under apartheid laws. They also began to accumulate in their capacity as shacklords and semi-skilled and skilled labourers. This process gathered momentum in the 1970s and 1980s when discriminatory legislation was abolished, and Africans emerged as successful entrepreneurs with the support of the corporate sector. As several of the Bantustans became 'independent', the NP government allocated lucrative favours to political and bureaucratic leaders in an attempt to ensure the 'success' of the new 'states'.

Ample opportunities were therefore created for the emergence of a rich African rural elite. Many African political representatives and bureaucrats used their powerful positions in or links with Bantustan government structures to build up lucrative and often corrupt business ventures. At the same time, a new generation of African entrepreneurs emerged in urban areas. Many of them had no option – given the restrictions of the apartheid structures – but to build business empires through dubious and illegal activities.[56] The income of the top 20 per cent of African households increased by an impressive 38 per cent from 1975 to 1991, and by a further 15 per cent from 1991 to 1996.[57]

The rise of a black elite and the emergence of a highly differentiated class structure in the black population groups over the past 30 years have been, in the last resort, the result of formal and informal power shifts from whites to blacks. The NP government's reform policies were mostly a euphemism for the allocation of more power and privileges to the leadership core of the three black population groups.

The best examples are the 'independence' granted to Bantustans, the Wiehahn and Riekert legislation from 1979 to 1981, the tricameral parliament of 1984, the unbanning of the liberation movements in 1990, and the transition to a majoritarian democracy in 1994. Unfortunately, the rise in income of the top 20 to 30 per cent of black households occurred at a time when the income of the poorest 60 per cent of black households declined sharply. These trends were strongest among Africans.[58] As a result, in 1995 the inequality in the distribution of income *within* the African population group was considerably larger than the inequality within each of the other three population groups (see sections 2.2.3 and 4.7).[59]

An important result of the rise of an elite within each of the three black population groups is that South Africa's skewed distribution of income has shifted, over the past 30 years, from a race-based to a class-based one.[60] While the skewed distribution of income between white and black has decreased considerably since 1974, it remains a matter of concern. But what gives greater cause for concern is the sharp increase in inequality *within* the three black population groups.[61]

10.5 Violence and criminality

South Africa's history over the past 350 years has been exceptionally violent. During the periods of colonialism and white political supremacy, violent methods were used to dominate indigenous people politically, exploit them economically, and oppress them socially. Colonial authorities and white governments constantly attempted to justify the extraordinary use of political, military, and economic violence. In western political theory it is normally accepted that a legitimate government can use state violence to restore or maintain law and order, and counteract insurrection. But when a government is ilegitimate, and is not trusted by its people, the use of state violence becomes controversial. According to John Locke, a government can be violently opposed if it acts against the will of the people, or if it has lost their trust. To what extent the colonial governments – in all the 'New Europes' – were illegitimate is a contentious matter that has not been addressed sufficiently in colonial historiography. What is beyond dispute, however, is that colonial authorities and white governments in South Africa constantly used their undemocratically acquired political power, their extensive (and often foreign) military power, and their control over labour patterns to institutionalise and perpetuate the exploitation of indigenous people. Not surprisingly, the social injustice enforced and maintained by violent measures regularly provoked fierce resistance and counterviolence from the oppressed indigenous groups. It is against this background that we should understand that South Africa's history is one of *institutionalised* or *systemic* violence (see Lötter 1997: 21–31).

This systemic violence has caused irreparable harm to the social and cultural structures of indigenous people over a period of almost 350 years. We can say that systemic violence has been responsible for nurturing not only a subculture of poverty, but also a subculture of criminality. Although whites have been mostly responsible for systemic violence, many of them have also become contaminated by it. The mutually reinforcing interaction between systemic violence and the subcultures of poverty and criminality is a part of South Africa's hidden history that has yet to be explored.

One reason for the durability of the syndrome of violence, poverty, and criminality is the extent to which children – and especially black children – are exposed to it. Apart from the physical neglect of poorer children, it is especially the spiritual, psychological, and moral neglect of children during their pre-school years that helps to perpetuate the mentality of poverty from one generation to another.[62]

In a countrywide survey of crime perceptions in 1995 (quoted by Budlender 2000), half of those in the 'very poor' group reported assault as 'the most important crime' committed against them, as opposed to one in ten in the highest income category. While the wealthy are victims of property crime, poor people – largely black, and many women – are at risk from personal crime. According to Debbie Budlender, poor women are often trapped in abusive relationships because they depend on their partners for food, shelter, and money. She also claims that 'extreme levels of inequality and the political conflict both contributed to high levels of crime...Crime levels in black townships have been high for years, but racial segregation largely insulated whites [from the high levels of crime]' (quoted in May 2000: 134).

South Africa has among the highest rates of violent crime in the world. More than 16 per cent of all deaths in South Africa occur as a result of trauma, compared to a global figure of 5 per cent calculated by the World Health Organisation (WHO). Not all trauma is the result of crime, but in South Africa crime is the leading cause of injury and death (SA Medical Research Council 1993). May *et al* report that post-apartheid South Africa enjoys the dubious distinction of experiencing some of the highest rates of violence and crime found anywhere in the world. According to them, recorded levels of almost all forms of crime rose dramatically between 1990 and 1994, with serious crimes increasing by between 18 and 42 per cent (assault and rape respectively). A much higher proportion of those in the lowest income brackets reported falling victim to violent crimes, with African women accounting for 95 per cent of reported rapes (in May 2000: 254). According to the Institute of Security Studies (ISS), violent crime in 2000 increased by 21,6 per cent, while 32,6 per cent of all reported crime was violent, compared with 15 per cent in the United States and 6 per cent in Britain. The ISS believes that the culture of violence and criminality will not decline during the next ten years (2000).

We should understand that the subculture of criminality is an integral part of both systemic violence and the syndrome of chronic community poverty. The inclination towards violent and criminal behaviour has become deeply ingrained among impoverished Africans and coloureds – especially during the 46 years of apartheid. While state violence and the resistance to it were comparatively well organised, the inclination towards criminality was initially less well organised. It was only when the struggle – and state attempts to suppress it – intensified from the 1970s onwards that subversive and criminal activities were organised on a large scale by organisations involved in the struggle. The lawlessness of that period created the opportunity for those who had already been marginalised and criminalised by poverty and coercive labour patterns to become involved in organised violence and criminality.[63] By the time the apartheid regime ended, this subculture had become thoroughly entrenched.

Systemic violence and the subculture of criminality should be regarded as two of the ugliest legacies of colonialism, segregation, and apartheid. Although these phenomena should be denounced in the strongest terms, and although every effort should be made to eradicate them, it is important to realise that both are so deeply embedded in South Africa's violent history that it will probably take generations to get rid of them.

During the period of Dutch colonisation, both the colonial authority and slave owners used violence to keep slaves in a subservient position. When the conditions of slavery or the nature of violent punishment became unbearable, many slaves became *drosters* who lived in small outcast communities in mountainous areas. During the 18th century, *Trekboer* commandos were increasingly used to break the ferocious resistance of the Khoikhoi and the San to the expansion of the colony. The violent clashes between the *Trekboere* and Khoisan culminated in the bloody Khoisan Rebellion of 1799–1803. After this war, and after the Khoisan had been further humiliated for two decades by Caledon's labour regulations, their resistance was completely broken, and many of them became an underclass inclined to violence and criminality (see section 6.3).

During their 'long 19th century' of colonialism and imperialism, the British used superior military power to defeat not only the different African tribes, but also the two Boer republics in a series of bloody and violent wars. The Xhosa were so badly affected by the British onslaught during the frontier wars that they sought their salvation in the cattle-killing episode of 1857. From the mid-19th century onwards the Cape government – now in the hands of white settler groups – enacted masters and servants laws and started to criminalise labour relations on behalf of white farmers and the mining companies. Based on the twin pillars of proletarianisation and masters and servants laws, the repressive labour system was a violent one that remained in place for almost 150 years (see sections 6.4, 8.5, and 9.5).

The bloody wars that formed an integral part of South Africa's violent colonial history since the 17th century ended with the Anglo–Boer War. During the first three quarters of the 20th century, smaller skirmishes took place, including the Bambatha Rebellion of 1906, the Afrikaner Rebellion of 1914, and the violent strikes of 1913–4, 1920, 1922, and 1946. During the last quarter of the 20th century South Africa experienced the struggle against apartheid, and the state's resistance to it. For all practical purposes, this was a protracted low-level war in which systemic violence turned into open political violence between the white regime and the oppressed. It would, however, be wrong to think that South African society was less violent during the first three quarters of the 20th century.

On the contrary – when, in 1910, all the dispersed groups had been defeated and a strong and centralised white government put in place, the nature of the violence against the indigenous population groups changed drastically. In the Cape Colony, open warfare had already been replaced by institutionalised violence when the Glen Grey Act and several anti-squatting measures were enacted in 1894–1909 to destroy the independent peasantry. This process continued when the Land Act of 1913 and similar measures were adopted to destroy the economic independence of Africans in the northern provinces. Africans vehemently opposed this onslaught.

But, given the seemingly insatiable demand for cheap and docile African labour, the violent onslaught on Africans' economic freedom and independence was institutionalised in a plethora of laws that became more subtle and comprehensive after the NP assumed power in 1948. In the 1960s the heroic resistance of the African peasantry to this onslaught was finally defeated (see section 9.5.2).

A large part of the African population was not only deprived of its land and economic independence by institutionalised or systemic violence, but also degraded by being further reduced to an ultra-exploitable proletariat. During the first 75 years of the 20th century, many members of this proletariat became migrant workers on the gold mines, where they were exposed to degrading living conditions in the compounds, dangerous and unhealthy working conditions, and extraordinarily low wages. In the 1950s, the institutional violence to which millions of Africans were exposed by unfree labour patterns became far more violent and exploitative when Verwoerd designed a migrant system for employment in the manufacturing sector in white urban areas. Under this system only a small percentage of Africans could obtain permanent residential rights in urban areas.

Impoverished 'tribal' Africans could work in urban areas only with permission (which was not easily obtained), and if they could find temporary jobs. Many – driven to the cities by desperate poverty – often entered the urban areas illegally. Millions were prosecuted under the pass laws, and sent back to the Bantustans. Government officials were well aware that most unemployed African migrants who were forcibly removed from the urban areas would return, either legally or illegally, and would be prepared to accept even lower wages and poorer working conditions.

The combined effect of the Land Act and deteriorating socio-economic conditions in the Bantustans on the one hand, and strictly enforced influx control measures on the other, created a situation of systemic violence that deliberately or inadvertently criminalised many migrant workers. The inevitable result of this inhumane situation was that millions of Africans were drawn into a vicious circle of violence, lawlessness, and criminality. It is ironic that the strong inclination towards criminality was not restricted to migrants. Many African youths with residential rights in urban areas were also criminalised.

In their case, this was not the result of influx control but of discriminatory measures. As the educational levels of urban African youths rose, and their job advancement opportunities were blocked, many opted to make a living from crime. While 'Bantu education' was aimed at stabilising the urban situation, its eventual effect was to promote a gang culture and a tradition of violent criminality. It was these urban African youths who were responsible for the Soweto uprising and for the campaign of 'liberation before education' in the 1980s. Many urban youths left South Africa after Soweto to be trained as freedom fighters (see Bonner et al 1993: 25–6).

South Africa's violent history entered a new phase when the struggle intensified during the Soweto uprising, and with it also the violent reaction from the NP government and its securocrats. During the almost 20 years from 1976 to 1994, political violence escalated to unprecedented levels. The TRC was burdened with the task of establishing as complete a picture as possible of the causes, nature, and extent of the gross violations of human rights committed during the period 1 March 1960 to 10 May 1994. The TRC defined 'gross violations of human rights' mainly in an individualistic and legalistic sense, and did not investigate the violation of human rights by structural or systemic violence. In accordance with its rather narrow approach, the TRC nonetheless published a list of names of 18 000 persons who had fallen victim to gross violations of human rights (TRC 1998: vol 5, ch 2). To this list should be added those who fell victim to 'non-gross' violations of human rights, as well as structural or systemic violence, not only after 1960 but throughout South Africa's violent history.

When influx control was applied very strictly during the 1970s and 1980s – at a time when the economy was in a downturn – both white employers and predominantly black employees were criminalised by the 'system' (see section 9.5.3). If we also take into account the corrupt wheeling and dealing between the private and public sectors in the 1980s and early 1990s as part of the 'survival struggle', we can argue that the crisis of the apartheid regime' ($\pm 1974 - \pm 1990$) was also a crisis of racial capitalism and the white corporate sector. In their struggle to survive, both the white political establishment and a large part of the white business establishment became involved in all sorts of criminal and corrupt activities.

As indicated in section 9.4, the 'structural corruption' during the period of 'co-optive domination' ($\pm 1984 - 94$) can be regarded as the final episode in the long drama of white plunder. When reflecting on the violent nature of South Africa's history over the past 350 years, we are left with the disturbing conclusion that systemic violence and criminality left their ugly marks not only on blacks but also on whites. As Lötter observes, 'apartheid did major moral harm to white people, a harm that seriously affected the core of their humanity' (1997: 36).

Vivian Taylor observed in 1993 that the struggle for democracy and social justice in South Africa was, by its very nature, rooted in opposition to the apartheid state. Therefore, political violence could not be assumed to be irrational and senseless, because 'the discourse of the struggle [could] only be generated in the process of violent struggle itself. The struggle . . . could thus be said to be underpinned by a culture of violence'. She makes the important point that the struggle, like apartheid, 'dehumanised both the perpetrators and the victims of violence. For this reason neither the perpetrators nor the victims can afford to take the morally high ground on the issue of violence and yet ignore its structural and political roots.'

She reaches the following conclusion: 'The painful reality is that the sustained level of violence has had a physical, psychological, and structural impact on both the victims and the agents of violence. That it has its basis in and is reinforced by the social, economic and political inequalities that are a legacy of apartheid and is part of the crisis of capitalism, makes the problem of political violence a lot more complex' (1993: 187).

An unfortunate aspect of the political violence during the last quarter of the 20th century was the 'black-on-black' violence in which the ANC and the Inkatha Freedom Party (IFP) were centrally involved. This reached its zenith during the negotiations from 1990 to 1994. The extent to which the (predominantly white) security forces played a role in instigating the violence remains a controversial issue that has not yet been fully clarified.

The violent character of the 'total onslaught', and the 'total strategy' used to counteract it, created a space for lawlessness and criminality. With the police mainly involved in a desperate attempt to protect an illegitimate political system, opportunities were created for already sizeable criminal elements in the black community to wreak havoc with their lawlessness and violent gang activities. The struggle and the resistance to it gave people on both sides of the great divide ample opportunities to find all kinds of moral, religious, and ideological justifications for violent and criminal activities. This tendency to act in an anti-social manner and to find easy ideological justification for such behaviour has become internalised in large sections of the South African population, both black and white. After centuries of colonialism, segregation, and apartheid, and the struggles against them, South African society is fractured and divided not only along racial lines, but also moral and attitudinal ones.

One of the most disconcerting aspects of violence and criminality is that it became deeply institutionalised in especially the black community during the long period of extended colonialism. As we saw in section 2.2.4, a mutually reinforcing dynamic exists today between crime and violence on the one hand and the process of pauperisation on the other. In this way crime, violence, and poverty are not only being intensified, but also perpetuated.

Endnotes

1 Unemployment is often measured in 'narrowed' or 'broad' (or expanded) terms. The 'broad' definition includes all people of working age who cannot find jobs in the formal sector of the economy irrespective of whether they have actively been searching for a job.

2 The Bureau of Economic Research (BER) at the University of Stellenbosch has estimated that, while 19,1 per cent of the labour force was outside the formal sector in 1970, this figure had risen to 49,1 per cent in 1995. Although there is much uncertainty about the extent and definition of unemployment, it undoubtedly presented a major challenge in 1994, and attained crisis dimensions during the last 25 years of apartheid.

3 The extent of 'employment' in the informal and subsistence sectors is very difficult to measure. Although those involved in this 'hidden' economy cannot be classified as formally employed, the income earned in these sectors makes a valuable contribution to the living standards of the people and families involved. The implications of unemployment for poverty and criminality would have been much more serious, if (as was the case in 1995) it wasn't possible for up to 20 per cent of the workforce to make a living in the informal sector and in subsistence agriculture.

4 Bhorat and Hodge chose this period, ie 1970–95, for several reasons. The census of 1970 was the last that included all the Bantustans (ie, before some of them became 'independent'), and the 1995 October Household Survey was the first to include these territories once again as part of a unified South Africa. Shortly after 1970 an important paradigm shift took place in South African affairs, and another shortly before 1994. The period from 1970 to 1995 roughly covers the crisis phase of apartheid.

5 While, in 1995, only 517 000 of non-Africans (or 12,8 per cent) were unemployed, no less than 4,3 million (or 46 per cent) Africans were unemployed. In 1970 the African population was 70 per cent of the total, and Africans constituted 70 per cent of the employed workforce. In 1995 the African population was 76,5 per cent of the total, but Africans constituted only 59 per cent of the employed workforce. While almost 5,3 million Africans (or 34,2 per cent) of the total African population of 15,5 million was employed in the formal sector in 1970, only 5,1 million Africans (or 16 per cent) of a total African population of 32 million were employed in the formal sector in 1995. While one in three Africans was employed formally in 1970, only one in six was thus employed in 1995. Although a larger percentage of the African population in 1995 was younger than 15 years in 1970, the above figures nonetheless demonstrate dramatically that unemployment has become an African problem par excellence.

6 In the 30 years after World War 2, foreign investment contributed significantly to South Africa's economic growth. A net foreign inflow was registered in 24 of the 31 years from 1945 to 1976. During this period 13,5 per cent of GDP was financed by FDI (Smit 1991: 4).

7 It is estimated that as late as 1974 the average American corporation received an 18 per cent return on its South African investment, compared with a return of 8 per cent on its investment in Britain (O'Meara 1996: 174).

8 From 1974 until 1994 the annual growth rate was only 1,7 per cent, while the inflation rate oscillated between 11 and 15 per cent in 1974–92.

9 This is illustrated by the fact that the contribution of gold export earnings to total export earnings declined from 64,8 per cent in 1969 to only 24,3 per cent in 1990. The change in the international economic environment also increased the vulnerability of the South African balance of payments to social and political instability. Between 1946 and 1974 South Africa could afford to run large balance of payments deficits because they were financed by net inflows of foreign capital. During this period the annual inflow of foreign investment (mostly FDI) was equal to 2,5 per cent of GDP (13,5 per cent of gross domestic investment was financed by foreign investment). See Mohr 1994: 50–2.

10 South Africa's capacity to import was severely hampered by balance of payments constraints. From 1970 to 1990 its capacity to import rose from only 74 to 96 (1980 = 100). For new industrial countries, it rose from 60 to 176 (Kaplinsky 1995: 179).

11 The inadequate educational system during apartheid should also be blamed for the decline in productivity. In 1972–90 total factor productivity *declined* at 1,02 per cent a year (Mohr 1994: 50–2; Kaplinsky 1995: 179; and SAF 1996).

12 When, in 1987, a group of professors from the University of Stellenbosch told a cabinet committee that South Africa could not 'go it alone economically' they were told that, if necessary, it would.

13 According to Kaplinsky, the South African economy is very capital-intensive compared to developed countries with similar levels of per capita income. It is also higher than the capital intensity of developing countries. In general the capital intensity is more like Latin American countries than newly industrialised Asian countries. Over the past 30 years the growth in capital intensity has been higher in middle-income countries than in South Africa. This can partly be explained in terms of the higher economic growth rate of these countries compared to South Africa over the past 30 years (Kaplinsky 1995: 182–3).

14 During the first three quarters of the past century, gold mining was characterised by its relatively high capital intensity, and a labour force divided between a small group of, and highly paid skilled white workers on the one hand, and a large group of unskilled and poorly paid African workers on the other. The gold mining industry used the threat of electrification and mechanisation to discipline its unskilled workers and to keep their wages at exceptionally low levels. The cheapness and easy manageability of the African labour force made it unnecessary for the gold mines to become significantly more capital-intensive until the beginning of the 1970s.

15 To create employment opportunities, the Pact government started a protection policy in the 1920s. By restricting competition, the government encouraged the emergence of large monopolistic firms in mining and manufacturing, and in banking and finance. In 1983 it was estimated that seven companies controlled 80 per cent of the value of the shares listed on the JSE. These firms displayed a strong tendency towards capital intensity. The growth of these conglomerates was stimulated by the deeply institutionalised repressive labour system and the extremely low wages paid to African workers until the early 1970s. According to Lipton, the South African development path has been one of harsh extraction of a large surplus from the African majority. This surplus was mainly used for capital accumulation and for

expanding the conglomerates. As the employers of large numbers of white and black workers, these conglomerates gained huge power to influence the government's economic and labour policies in their favour. What neither these conglomerates nor the government realised was that their ability to accumulate large amounts of capital in due course created contradictions that undermined apartheid and the possibility of employing high levels of cheap African labour (see Lipton 1986: 242–54).

16 According to Bhorat and Hodge, the overall capital–labour ratio (in R1 000 per worker, in constant 1990 rands) of the South African economy increased by 142 per cent from 1970 to 1995. The sectors that experienced the greatest capital deepening were the primary sectors – mining (416 per cent) and agriculture (168,8 per cent) – followed by construction (160,1 per cent) and manufacturing (157,3 per cent). By contrast, the increase in the service sector was modest. From 1970 to 1995 the capital–labour ratio increased from 40,1 to 97,4 for the economy at large, from 10 to 27 for agriculture, from 29,3 to 151,3 for mining, from 30,8 to 79,3 for manufacturing, and from 466,5 to 712,9 for electricity (1999: 352–9, tables 1, 2, and 3).

17 Verwoerd implemented measures to marginalise Africans in the modern sector of the economy. He implemented a comprehensive system of social engineering (which continued under Vorster and Botha) to deliberately increase the capital intensity of the economy in an attempt to make its modern sector less dependent on African labour. The idea was that Africans should become unemployed in white urban areas, and that they would then have no choice but to move back to the Bantustans and seek employment there. To attain this aim, the exchange rate was kept at high levels during the 1960s and 1970s in order to ensure that imported capital goods would remain relatively cheap. To stimulate capital accumulation, interest rates were kept at a very low level. At the same time, large tax concessions were granted to investors, while businesses were allowed accelerated capital write-offs. The state corporations – which had been built on comparative advantages in capital-intensive natural resource beneficiation – were supplied with further capital at low prices through the IDC (see Bhorat and Hodge 1999: 354–5).

18 In 1975 to 1990, the real wages of Africans in the non-primary sectors of the economy rose by 2,9 per cent a year, while those of whites actually dropped during the same period. The increase in African wages is, however, deceptive. From 1975 to 1985, the real wages of unskilled African workers in the manufacturing sector in Johannesburg dropped by more than 3 per cent a year on average. Hofmeyr concludes that the increase in average wages of (skilled and semi-skilled) Africans resulted from the advance up the occupational ladder of a small African elite after job discrimination was first relaxed and finally abolished in 1979 (Hofmeyr 1994: 198–213; Mohr 1994: 51).

19 Capital intensity in the mining industry increased by 416 per cent from 1975 to 1995. This dramatic increase should largely be attributed to the labour turmoil at the beginning of the 1970s. After the *coup d'état* in Portugal, led by Spínola in 1974, and the subsequent independence of Angola and Mozambique, the gold mines experienced serious problems in recruiting foreign migrant workers. The component of foreign migrants declined from 79 per cent in 1973 to 48 per cent in 1978. To recruit more South African migrants, the nominal wages of unskilled labour were increased by almost 38 per cent from 1974 to 1976, and thereafter continued to keep

pace with the rate of inflation amid increased unionisation. The scarcity of foreign migrant workers and the sharp increase in wages were perhaps the stimulus for the unprecedented leap towards increased mechanisation in the mining industry. The employment of unskilled workers – ie, production workers and operatives – in the mining industry declined by 37 per cent from 1970 to 1995, mainly because output also declined, especially that of gold mines.

20 The *primary* sector saw its share of GDP declining from 18,6 per cent in 1970 to 11,7 per cent in 1995. The share of the mining industry increased from 10,3 per cent in 1970 to 21,7 per cent in 1980, but then declined to only 7,5 per cent in 1995. This can be attributed to the rise in the price of gold early in the 1970s, and its sharp decline from 1980 onwards. South Africa's remaining gold reserves lie at very deep levels, and have become very expensive to mine. While agriculture's share of GDP was 18,3 per cent in 1970, it declined to only 4,3 per cent in 1995. The share of the *secondary* sector remained almost stable, declining from 31,1 per cent in 1970 to 30,4 per cent in 1995. The decline in the primary sector was compensated for by a rise in the services sector: this sector increased its share of GDP from 50,2 per cent in 1970 to 57,9 per cent in 1995. The largest group of services is producer services (transport, communication, financial, and business services). The share of this group of services increased from 35,2 per cent of GDP in 1970 to 42,7 per cent in 1995. This shift was mainly driven by information technology. A significant component of the service sector is final demand social services, whose share increased from 14,7 per cent to 18,5 per cent (Bhorat and Hodge 1999: 359–63).

21 An important reason why Africans could not benefit more from the shift from the primary to the services sector is that this shift also implied a movement from unskilled jobs (in the primary sector) to skilled jobs (in the services sector). But owing to the large percentage of Africans without the necessary levels of education and skills, it was not possible for them to benefit to the same extent as other population groups (Bhorat and Hodge 1999: 363–79). (In section 10.4.3 we discuss the low level of human capital accumulation among Africans due to the low per capita spending on African education during apartheid.)

22 According to Kaplinsky, the capital stock of labour-intensive activities – such as textiles, furniture, leather, footwear and clothing – declined by 19 per cent from 1972 to 1990. Kaplinsky argues that the underinvestment in labour-intensive activities was the consequence of the prevailing political climate in the dying years of apartheid, in which private sector capitalists were reluctant to invest in these activities. The decline in investment in labour-intensive activities undoubtedly had a very negative effect on the job-creating ability of the economy. It is quite possible that investment in labour-intensive activities was 'crowded out' by heavy investment in certain capital-intensive sectors. During the 1980s the NP government drastically increased investments in SASOL, MOSSGAS, and ARMSCOR. These increases were not driven by economic logic, but by strategic, political, and ideological considerations at a time when the NP government was domestically and internationally under siege. In a desperate attempt to shore up apartheid, the NP government embarked on investments that were clearly economically unviable. If the sums invested in those 'strategic' industries in the late 1970s and the 1980s had been invested in labour-intensive activities, many additional jobs would have been created (Kaplinsky 1995).

23 For many decades Africans were prohibited by law from acquiring artisanal, financial or managerial skills, as jobs in these fields were reserved for whites. Moreover, Africans could not own property in white urban areas, and were also not allowed to launch their own corporations. Infrastructure in African and coloured townships was poor, and sometimes non-existent. While criminality and gangsterism were the order of the day in these townships, policing was poor. The political uncertainty and disruptions caused by the struggle militated not only against the development of manufacturing in the African and coloured townships, but also against the development of services and other micro enterprises. Consequently, the creation of highly needed job opportunities in the informal sector was highly constrained (Kaplinsky 1995: 188–90).

24 The defence budget increased from 2,4 per cent of GDP in 1972 to 4,8 per cent in 1980, and remained at that high level until 1989.

25 The share of Africans over this period increased by only 2 percentage points from 67 per cent to 69 per cent; that of whites decreased by 3 percentage points from 22 to 19 per cent; that of coloureds remained at 9 per cent; and that of Asians increased by 1 percentage point from 2 to 3 per cent.

26 Statistics show that public health methods, the availability of modern medicine, and better diets started to reduce the mortality rates of coloureds and Africans from the 1950s onwards. Improved medicines and diets also led to an increase in the life expectancies of the various population groups. From the late 1930s to the 1990s, the life expectancy of whites rose from 61 years to 73 years; of Asians from 51 years to 68 years; of coloureds from 43 years to 62 years; and of Africans from 40 years to 63 years (Sadie 1989: 3–6; Sadie 1991: fig 1.4).

27 HIV is the acronym for the Human Immunodeficiency Virus, a virus which leaves sufferers open to secondary illnesses and eventually mutates into AIDS (Acquired Immune Deficiency Syndrome).

28 These are: (i) the prevalence of other epidemics, and other sexually transmitted diseases; (ii) disrupted family and communal life due to apartheid, migrant labour, and extensive poverty; (iii) good transport infrastructure and high mobility, allowing for the rapid spread of the virus; (iv) resistance to the use of condoms, based on cultural and social norms; (v) the low status of women in society, and the high prevalence of violence against women; and (vi) social norms that allow men in particular to have large numbers of sexual partners. Ironically, South Africa's developmental edge over other African countries may be a disadvantage with regard to HIV/AIDS (BER 2001).

29 From 2000 to 2015, HIV prevalence rates among highly skilled workers are projected to increase from 7,2 per cent to a peak of 18,3 per cent; among skilled workers from 12,1 per cent to 25,4 per cent; and among unskilled workers from 14,3 per cent to 27,6 per cent. The total labour force is projected to contract by 21 per cent by 2015 compared to a non-AIDS scenario, with the overall size of the labour force remaining almost static for the next 14 years.

30 In 1996, 81,4 per cent of African households and 47,2 per cent of coloured households spent less than was R1 800 a month. This implies that the daily expenditure of 25 million Africans and 1,6 million coloureds was $2 or less a day.

31 The most common criteria are: per capita consumption, household consumption, per

capita income, per capita food expenditure, and so on (Leibbrandt and Leibbrandt 2000: 6).

32 According to Statistics South Africa (2000), 3,99 per cent of African households, 21,4 per cent of coloured households, and 41,4 per cent of all households were living in poverty in 1996. May *et al* contend that levels of poverty are even higher; according to them, 60,7 per cent of Africans, 38,2 per cent of coloureds, 5,4 per cent of Asians, and 1 per cent of whites lived in poverty in 1995 (May *et al*, in J May 2000: fig 3). This implies that 50 per cent of the total population of 41 million lived in poverty in 1996. This estimate is somewhat conservative if we compare it with McGrath and Whiteford's 1994 estimate of the percentage of households with an income below the Minimum Living Level (MLL) calculated by the Bureau of Market Research. Their estimate was that, in 1991, 50,8 per cent of households (or 60 per cent of the total population) were living in poverty (ie, below the 'poverty line'). Of all the households with a monthly expenditure of R1 000 or less in 1996, 94,7 per cent were African, and 4,2 per cent coloured; ie, almost 99 per cent of households spending R1 000 or less a month were African and coloured (SSA 2000: table 5).

33 According to May *et al*, of those with no education, 69,1 per cent are living in poverty; of those with only primary education, 54,3 per cent are living in poverty; and of those with secondary education only 26,7 per cent are living in poverty (in J May 2000: fig 5).

34 According to May, poverty is 'characterised by the inability of individuals, households, or entire communities to command sufficient resources to satisfy a socially acceptable minimum standard of living... Poverty was seen to include... alienation from the community... food insecurity... crowded homes... fragmentation of the family, etc' (2000: 5).

35 In the pre-colonial period, the living standards of the Khoisan and the different African tribes had been meagre in modern terms, but they could not be described as poor. The social and economic lives of the indigenous population were organised on a communal basis and, although famine occurred from time to time, these people did not experience the multiple deprivation and the humiliation associated with poverty in the modern world.

36 The cultural, moral, and ideological issues involved in the seizure of the land of indigenous people by colonial intruders from Europe are still largely unresolved in European historiography. They are, however, issues that cannot be ignored in a study such as this – especially when we try to give plausible explanations for the widespread and deep-rooted poverty among Africans and coloured people.

37 More correctly, land was seized by military and legal means from 1890 (ie, after the discovery of gold) because land deprivation proved to be a powerful and effective instrument for depriving Africans of their traditional livelihood and economic independence, thus 'coercing' them indirectly into becoming an impoverished and easily manageable and exploitable proletariat.

38 When, in 1828, the Khoisan were 'liberated' and granted legal rights to own land they were already – after decades of violent oppression, exploitation, and humiliation – such an impoverished and demoralised proletariat that they neither had the capacity nor the inclination to adopt a different lifestyle. This was also the case with the ex-slaves when slavery was abolished in 1838. The freedom of the coloureds (ie, the

Khoisan and ex-slaves) was short-lived. In 1841, the first of a long series of masters and servants ordinances and laws was adopted.

39 Besides depriving Africans of much of their land, the act also prohibited share-cropping and squatter farming by Africans. Although it took 50 years to implement all the provisions of the act, and wipe out share-cropping and squatter farming, its purpose was to destroy the African peasantry and with it the promising petty entrepreneurship in African circles.

40 According to Bundy, 'the development of capitalism always proceeds unevenly, but in the South African case *the skewing of its costs and benefits was markedly increased along a racial axis*. Here [in South Africa]... racial capitalism intensified inequality [and poverty]' (1993: 68). 'In South Africa we can regard [black] poverty as the carcass left over from [white] wealth acquisition' (Kurien 1978, quoted by Bundy).

41 The per capita income of Africans increased from R1 671 to R3 075 (in 1995 rands) from 1946 to 1975, but the income of the poorest 40 per cent declined from R1 001 in 1975 to R586 in 1991; the income of the next 20 per cent declined from R2 231 in 1975 to R1 643 in 1991; and the income of the next 20 per cent declined from R3 707 in 1975 to R3 528 in 1991 (in 1995 rands; tables 10.4 and 10.8).

42 Most discriminatory labour legislation was abolished in 1979 when the government accepted the recommendations of the Wiehahn commission (see section 9.5.3). Many of the discriminatory measures became known as 'petty apartheid'. These measures were not introduced to protect whites against black competition in the labour market, but to create a more convenient living 'space' for whites – especially in urban areas. They nonetheless created discomfort for blacks and seriously harmed their dignity.

43 African wages were 43 per cent lower than those of whites in similar job grades in 1976, but only 15 per cent lower in 1989. Coloured wages for similar job grades were 37,8 per cent lower in 1976, and 21,1 per cent lower in 1989. Indian wages were 33 per cent lower in 1976, and only 10,6 per cent lower in 1989 (Van der Berg and Bhorat 1999: table 5).

44 The extent to which whites have been privileged by educational spending during apartheid becomes evident when we compare the percentage of whites in the four skilled categories, with those of a highly developed country such as the United States. While, in 1985, 42 per cent of the labour force in the United States fell in the two top categories, 50 per cent of whites in South Africa fell in those two categories.

45 In terms of 1996 prices the annual mean household income of the poorest 40 per cent of African households (50 per cent of the African population) declined from ±R5 000 in 1975 to less than R2 400 in 1996, while the annual household income of the next 20 per cent declined from R11 000 in 1970 to R9 120 in 1996. The poorest 40 per cent of coloured households also became poorer from 1975 to 1996, but not to the same extent as the poorest 60 per cent of African households (table 10.4).

46 Almost all of them were relatively uneducated and unskilled, with almost no property and no reserve sustenance at their disposal. They were powerless and unorganised. After generations of systemic exploitation and suppression, the poorest two thirds of the population were extremely vulnerable to additional socio-economic shocks. Until 1986, many of the poorest were restricted to the Bantustans by stricter

influx control measures. Living conditions in those areas deteriorated as a result of droughts, overpopulation, and decades of predatory cultivation.

47 The mean household income of the poorest 40 per cent of white households declined by 40 per cent from 1975 to 1991, and by a further 16 per cent from 1991 to 1996 (table 10.4). This group's mean household income declined from almost R63 000 in 1975 to less than R30 000 in 1996 (at 1996 prices.) Although the percentage decline in the household income of the poorest 40 per cent of Africans and the poorest 40 per cent of whites was more or less the same, the household income of the poorest 40 per cent of white households was in 1996 still 12 times higher than that of the poorest 40 per cent of Africans (table 10.4).

48 Bundy claims that 'the very high levels of... inequality in South Africa are deeply embedded in its history. They will not easily be cut back, let alone uprooted. *South Africa's modern capitalist economy was profoundly shaped by the institutions and timing of colonial conquest.* Racist ideologies and racially discriminatory institutions were central to the creation of the social relations of capitalist production' (1993: 77–8).

49 The income of the poorest 80 per cent of African households declined substantially from 1975 to 1996, while the income of the top 20 per cent increased sharply (table 10.4). In the case of whites, the income of the lower 80 per cent declined in that period. The only other population group whose share of income has changed substantially since 1970 are the Asians. Their share of household income increased from 2,5 per cent in 1970 to 4,5 per cent in 1996 (table 10.7).

50 From 1917 until 1946 the per capita income of Africans remained at about 9 per cent of white per capita income, but declined to only 6,8 per cent in 1970. This resulted from the increased exploitation of Africans during the first 25 years of NP government. From 1970 to 1995 the per capita income of Africans increased from 6,8 per cent to 13,5 per cent of white levels. But this improvement was mainly restricted to the top 20 per cent of Africans at a time when the per capita income of the poorer 80 per cent declined sharply (table 10.4). Moreover, the per capita income of whites was 11,5 times higher than that of Africans in 1946, and 14,6 times higher than that of Africans in 1970 (see bottom part of table 10.8). These racial disparities in the distribution of income clearly reflect the uneven patterns of economic development of the four population groups during the 20th century.

51 The ill-conceived tricameral parliament of 1984 also represented a political 'power shift' to the advantage of coloureds and Asians, which remarkably improved their socio-economic position.

52 In 1950 a small elite of 13 per cent of the population in the Bantustans (comprising the chiefs and the landowner class) received almost 50 per cent of income earned in those territories.

53 Property – a house, farm, or other tangible property – worth R1 000 in 1910 could be sold for more than R100 000 in 2000 owing to inflation (BER).

54 In the early 1980s, the top 5 per cent of the population (almost exclusively white) owned 88 per cent of all private property, and with it all the advantages attached to property. Such a 'skewed' accumulation of property would not have been possible without white political domination and racial capitalism, and the power relations on which those systems were based.

55 The income of Africans from non-labour factors of production (capital, land, and entrepreneurship) and from government transfers was exceptionally low during the greater part of the 20th century. The informal sector and the entrepreneurial activities in it were also underdeveloped when compared with the informal sector in other developing countries in the 1990s.

56 In due course, sophisticated criminal enterprises intersected with legitimate business empires that enjoyed the support of the corporate sector and the NP government. One of the most important areas of African entrepreneurship was the legal and illegal taxi industry. All these activities were responsible for the rise of an African elite from the early 1970s.

57 The income of the top 40 per cent of coloured households increased by 20 per cent and ±10 per cent in the two periods, and that of the top 60 per cent of Asian households by ±35 per cent and more than 10 per cent (table 10.4; Marais 1998: 29, 106–7).

58 According to McGrath and Whiteford, 'the interplay of decreasing incomes as a result of rising unemployment and drought on the one hand, and rising incomes of upwardly mobile, professionals, skilled workers and entrepreneurs on the other hand, has resulted in a vast increase in the level of inequality of African household income' (1994: 18).

59 In 1995 the Gini coefficient for the pay of Africans, coloureds, and whites was 0,70, 0,57, and 0,55 respectively (SSA 2000: 88).

60 According to McGrath and Whiteford, the 'inequality within population groups [in 1991] is by far the biggest contributor to all inequality, its relative contribution increased from 75 per cent to 77 per cent between 1975 and 1991' (1994: 19).

61 Bundy already warned in 1993 'that a new axis of inequality will solidify between a minority of unionised skilled and semi-skilled black workers and a majority of unskilled, unemployed and unemployable (black) urban poor' (1994: 78).

62 In a report for the United Nations Children's Fund, Wilson and Ramphele have written that 'children may be socialised into vandalism or find themselves having to adopt violent measures as a matter of survival and, in the process, lose any sense of right and wrong. The impact on children's minds and values of the physical violence that they witness and experience, not least at the hands of the police, is a matter of great concern' (quoted by Thompson 1990: 201–2).

63 Dume Nkosi, secretary general of the ANC's Thokoza branch, had this to say in 1992: 'Political violence and crime sleep under one blanket! It's easy for anyone to employ criminals to carry out acts of violence for political motives. The desire is for our people to be governed by fear, to become inactive, and so not participate in the peace process' (quoted by Taylor 1993: 196).

PART 4

An incomplete transformation: what's to be done?

Chapter 11

Working towards a social democratic version of democratic capitalism

11.1 The apparent dysfunctionality of South Africa's version of neo-liberal democratic capitalism

Eight years after the transition from white political domination to a representative democracy, South Africa is faced with serious political, social, and economic problems. The new governing elite is struggling to consolidate the multiracial democratic system, and exert its authority in matters of state. The viability of the new democracy is threatened by bureaucratic incapacity, the inability of the state to make meaningful progress in deracialising the economic system, and its failure to alleviate the widespread poverty and social deprivation inherited from apartheid.

As indicated in chapters 2 and 10, apartheid has left a worse legacy than was realised in 1994. During the past eight years the social distortions and destructive dynamics introduced by apartheid have reproduced and augmented poverty, and perpetuated inequality. The four poverty traps to which the poor are exposed have been discussed in section 2.2. Increased spending on social services and the redirection of social spending from whites to blacks are laudable, but when the structural dynamics surrounding the poor are taken into account, it becomes apparent that the new government is not doing nearly enough to alleviate poverty.

What complicates matters is the seeming inability or powerlessness of the new government to address these problems effectively. Its ability to implement comprehensive programmes for alleviating poverty and redistributing wealth is clearly constrained by its elite compromises with the corporate sector and its global partners. Thus the terms of the negotiated transition have trapped the poor in a situation of systemic exclusion, and left the government with no choice but to ignore their terrible plight (see sections 4.2 and 4.4). It is therefore hardly surprising that poverty has worsened over the past eight years. The accumulation crisis experienced during the chronic stagflation in the 20 years from 1974 to 1994 has also not been resolved to the necessary degree, and this has also complicated matters for the new government (see section 10.2.3).

Given the severity of these political, social, and economic problems eight years after the political transition, we should reconsider the appropriateness not only of the new government's social and economic policies, but also of the liberal capitalist version of democratic capitalism introduced after 1994. It can be argued that eight years are far too short a period for judging a new politico-economic dispensation, or a negotiated settlement. Although we are aware of this, and as well as the enormity of the reconstruction and development task after centuries of extended colonialism, we nonetheless believe we have ample reason for questioning the appropriateness of not only the new government's neo-liberal economic policy, but also the liberal capitalist version of democratic capitalism in a situation such as South Africa's.

South Africa's political and economic systems have changed in important ways over the past 30 years. All these changes have not been benign. To understand and evaluate the appropriateness of our version of democratic capitalism, it is necessary to compare the current politico-economic system with that of 1970 when apartheid reached its zenith. The system of the early 1970s was one of white political domination, and colonial and racial capitalism. It had been in place for almost a century. A close symbiotic relationship existed between the white political class and the white economic class. The racist character of both the political and economic components of the politico-economic system accentuated its general racist and exploitative character (see ch 8, 9).

The literature on the changes in South Africa's politico-economic system since 1970 has largely focused on the many dramatic events in the political arena. Consequently, the equally important changes in the economic system and its relationship with the political arena have largely been neglected. Until the 1970s the economic system of colonial and racial capitalism was based on the availability of docile and exploitable black (and especially African) labour. It is not incidental that colonial and racial capitalism grew most vigorously from 1934 to 1974 when predatory labour patterns were in place that enabled the white employer class – both local and foreign – to make very big profits. Owing to the fact that the economic system thrived – for more than a century – on the *exploitation* of natural resources (especially in mining and agriculture), and of black (and especially African) labour, the system had a conspicuously *colonial* character.

When, in the 1970s, black labour ceased to be docile, cheap, and easily exploitable, the white employer class lost one of the pillars of its colonial plundering. The non-availability of exploitable black labour from the 1970s onwards created an accumulation crisis for the corporate and farming sectors. To complicate matters further, the non-availability of exploitable black labour coincided with 20 years of stagflation caused by the mounting liberation struggle, and the state's response to it. In almost desperate attempts to solve its accumulation crisis, the corporate sector has – over the past 30 years – taken several defensive steps.

First, it has changed its production methods by substituting capital for labour. In the process, technology has been modernised, and methods of production geared to the first world. These changes have substantially increased the capital intensity of the modern sector of the economy. At the same time, the employment of black labour has declined sharply, dramatically increasing black unemployment. As a result, the labour-absorptive capacity of the South African economy is far weaker than those of many other developing countries (see section 10.2.2).

A second defensive strategy has been to reorganise the corporate sector. Corporations have increased their size and influence through mergers, takeovers, minority shareholdings in other companies, indirect controls over other companies, and, lately, 'globalisation', and moving their primary listings offshore. These changes have given the modern sector an oligopolistic character which belies the notion that South Africa has a free market economy. As a result of all these changes, the mining, industrial, financial, and tertiary sectors of the economy have been artificially integrated in a way that has further enhanced the excessive first-world orientation of the corporate sector. The alliance between industry and finance explains the substantial share of services in the economy. The contribution of the tertiary sector to GDP rose from 50,6 per cent in 1960 to 64,3 per cent in 1998, while the financial system is unusually sophisticated for a developing country (see Cling 2001: 54).

Thirdly, the English-controlled corporate sector has become overtly liberal capitalist and globally oriented, as if South Africa was a member of the Rich North. With its strong propensity for myth-making, the English corporate sector has succeeded in convincing not only the Afrikaner-controlled corporate sector but also the NP and ANC governments of the alleged virtues of a neo-liberal and globalised approach, even for a developing country such as South Africa. The AAC and its affiliates have taken the initiative in introducing many of the changes in the private sector, and have also forged a powerful and prescriptive relationship with both the old and the new political sector. We have labelled the growing ideological and political influence of the corporate sector the *Anglo-Americanisation* of not only the South African economy, but also the modern part of South African society. But the new government's acceptance of a neo-liberal and globally oriented approach has not only resulted from pressure from the local corporate sector, but also from the global corporatism of the British-American (or Anglo-American) world. Consequently, South Africa has been exposed over the past 10 years to the dual influence of corporate and global *Anglo-Americanisation.* This has significantly enhanced the power and wealth of the local corporate sector, the more so since it is now embedded in a highly favourable politico-economic system whose legitimacy is unquestioned – at least for the time being. The regular summits of government and business leaders (both local and global) provide the latter with strategic opportunities for prescribing their policy agenda, and prioritising the interests of the capitalist class. In these 'think-tanks on building sustainable partnerships', the dual *Anglo-Americanisation* of South Africa has become even more deeply entrenched, to the detriment of the population as a whole.[1]

As a result, the economic system has been changed over the past 30 years from one of colonial and racial capitalism to a neo-liberal, first-world, capitalist enclave that is disengaging itself from a large part of the black labour force. In the process, part of the black labour market and the black consumer market – ie, the consumer market of the lumpenproletariat – has been made irrelevant to corporate operations and profitability.[2] Although the black elite – both the bourgeoisie and petit bourgeoisie – has been adopted as a junior partner, the new system has retained a racist character: it is still a white-controlled enclave in a sea of black poverty (see Mhone 2000).

The transformation of colonial capitalism into a first-world capitalist enclave has coincided with the introduction of a system of representative democracy which is effectively controlled by a black, predominantly African, elite. As we indicated in chapter 4, the new governing elite became 'systemically trapped' when it reached several elite compromises with the corporate sector and its global partners. When the new governing elite agreed to these compromises, it effectively sanctioned the trend towards first-world capitalist enclavity. Given that the poorer 60 per cent of the black population are a loyal part of the ANC's constituency, we might have expected the government to counteract the capitalist enclavity's inclination to detach itself from a large part of the black labour force. The fact that, over the past eight years, the corporate sector has continued undisturbed to turn the modern sector into a first-world capitalist enclave is an indication of how thoroughly the ANC government has been co-opted by the local corporate elite and its global partners.[3]

The politico-economic system that has replaced white political domination and colonial and racial capitalism is a liberal capitalist version of democratic capitalism, that can best be described as a system of *African elite democracy cum capitalist enclavity*.[4] A new symbiotic relationship has been forged between the mainly white corporate elite and the black governing elite in which the former is very much the senior partner and the latter very much the junior and dependent partner. We need to ask whether this new politico-economic system serves the needs of the entire South African population.

It is beyond dispute that the old politico-economic system – in place from 1870 to 1970 – was highly dysfunctional, certainly from the perspective of the majority of black people who comprised more than 80 per cent of the population. The current system is also dysfunctional, again from the perspective of at least the poorer 60 per cent of the black population. Capitalist enclavity is detaching itself from a large part of the black labour market and a part of the black consumer market, while the new government seems unable or unprepared to stop this tendency.

It is in this sense that the socio-economic problems facing South Africa eight years after the political transition have attained an ominous systemic character. Neither the political nor the economic part of the new politico-economic system is geared to effectively addressing the predicament of the poorest half of the population, or regard poverty alleviation as a priority. What complicates matters is that the unequal power relations between the two parts of our new politico-economic system strongly favour the mainly white economic (or corporate) part, which militates against a comprehensive policy of socio-economic upliftment.

In the new politico-economic system, individual members of the upper classes (comprising one third of the population) profit handsomely from mainstream economic activity, while the mainly black lumpenproletariat (comprising 50 per cent of the population) is increasingly pauperised. Ironically, individual members of the black and white upper class in the new system seem as unconcerned about its dysfunctionality as individual members of the white elite were about that of the old. The common denominator between the old and the new systems is that part of society was/is systemically and undeservedly enriched, while the majority of the population were/are systemically and undeservedly impoverished – in the old system through *systemic exploitation*, and in the new system through *systemic exclusion* and *systemic neglect*. While the politico-economic system of 2002 is a marked improvement on that of 1970, poverty is worse than in 1970, and probably also more deeply institutionalised.

11.2. Questioning the premises on which the corporate and governing elite's neo-liberal policy approach are based

The economic and social policy approach of the new government was formulated under strong pressure from the corporate sector and its global partners, and was based on several contentious premises. Eight years into the post-apartheid period, neither its economic nor its social policy programmes has delivered the promised outcomes. It is therefore essential to reappraise the premises on which they rest. We can identify the following five:

i   *South Africa has a high economic growth potential.*
   The South African economy had a high growth potential that was strangled by apartheid, but its full potential can be realised in the post-apartheid period if the white-controlled modern sector remains intact or 'un-restructured', and if the free market economy is given the required 'space' and freedom via a policy of neo-liberalism.

ii   *Integration into the benign global economy will enhance economic growth.*
   The international community – which played such a pivotal role in South Africa's democratisation – will be well-disposed towards post-apartheid South Africa, and the country's economic growth potential can be enhanced by integrating the modern sector as fully and as rapidly as possible into the benign system of global capitalism, by lifting all restrictions on the movement of capital and goods.

iii   *A high economic growth rate will unlock the labour-absorptive capacity of the economy.*
   If the high growth potential of the economy can be realised through a policy of neo-liberalism and globalisation, the labour-absorptive capacity of the modern sector will be unlocked, which will create enough additional job opportunities to resolve the problems of structural unemployment and underemployment.

iv   *The benefits of a high economic growth rate will 'trickle down' to the poor.*
   A high economic growth rate, achieved via a competitive free market and integration with the global economy, will generate a large enough 'trickle-down' effect from the modern or first-world sector to the informal or third-world periphery to narrow the income gap, alleviate poverty, and resolve the social crisis inherited from apartheid.

v *The restructuring of the economy should be entrusted to market-led economic growth.*
Achieving a high economic growth rate is the most effective – and the least painful – method of 'restructuring' the South African economy, and resolving, at least in the long term, its dualistic character and structural anomalies after centuries of colonialism and apartheid. Or, to put it differently, the task of 'fundamentally restructuring' the economy as envisaged by the RDP should be entrusted to free market capitalism, neo-liberalism, globalisation, and a high rate of growth.

With the benefit of hindsight, we have good reason to reject all five of these premises. All five are either false, or do not apply under South African circumstances. All five have their roots in the naïve optimism of the managerial elite of the corporate sector and its global partners about the benefits of the free market. All five are propagated by the corporate sector and its global partners in order to protect their vested interests, enhance their position of power and privilege, and promote their sectional and short-term financial interests. All five premises incorrectly regard economic growth, neo-liberalism, and globalisation as the panacea for South Africa's social crisis.

If we consider the relatively low economic growth rate and the further intensification of the social crisis over the past eight years, we have reason to reject the new government's economic policies and the premises on which they are based as nothing but corporate myths and wishful thinking. Those responsible for these premises and the government's approach were highly unrealistic, and did not take into account the following three defining characteristics of the South African economy:

- its *dualistic* character; after 350 years of unequal power relations, unfree labour patterns, and uneven socio-economic development, it is divided into a mainly white-owned and white-controlled modern sector, and a black underdeveloped non-formal sector;
- the deeply institutionalised *inequalities* in the distribution of income, socio-economic power, and property and opportunities; and
- the emergence – over the past 30 years – of a modern, first-world, capitalist enclave that is detaching itself from the black labour market and the lumpenproletariat because they are regarded as irrelevant to the enclave's operation and profitability.

All three of these characteristics overlap and accentuate the 'two worlds' character of the economy: one modern, smart, professional, efficient, and globally oriented; the other neglected, messy, unskilled, downtrodden, and thriving on crime and violence. To complicate matters, political and economic developments over the past 30 years have increased the distance between these 'two worlds', and destroyed what beneficial interaction might have previously existed between them.

South Africa is *en route* to a situation in which the only interaction between the 'two worlds' will be at the level of crime, violence, and contagious diseases, that will be 'exported' daily from the third-world periphery to the first-world enclave.

In an attempt to bring about the urgently needed paradigm shift in the minds of those who make socio-economic policy, and choose the appropriate version of democratic capitalism for South Africa, it is necessary to refute each of the five premises on which the current policy approach is based.

11.2.1 Questioning the premise about South Africa's high economic growth potential and the appropriateness of a policy of neo-liberalism

South Africa's medium- to long-term growth potential is not nearly as high as the protagonists of growth claimed in the early 1990s. It was predicted at the time that, as soon as the shackles of apartheid had been thrown off and South Africa became a constitutional democracy, it would experience sustainable economic growth of more than 6 per cent a year, and even as high as 12 per cent a year. These predictions were clearly not based on facts, but on the need of the corporate sector and its global partners to convince the government-to-be of the alleged virtues of an unbridled free market. These predictions did not take account of the damage done to the South African economy during the liberation struggle and the period of disinvestment. It also underestimated the effects of the outflow of highly skilled and professional people during the 1990s.

The outflow of R50 billion at current prices (or ±R150 billion at 2002 prices) of previous FDI during the 1980s and early 1990s seriously harmed the South African economy, not only because of the loss of capital but also because of the loss of foreign entrepreneurship, technology, and networking. It also restricted South Africa's opportunities for international trade, as well as its access to foreign loans. The outflow of capital made the constraints of the balance of payments on internal growth far more serious. These sorts of setbacks cannot be easily or quickly rectified. We must consider the fact that FDI by the Rich North in a developing country such as South Africa is always conditional, and that these conditions were considerably stricter in the 1990s – when the power of global capitalism was consolidated – than in the 1960s and 1970s, when these funds were originally invested in South Africa.[5]

The lack of skilled and professional labour – including imaginative entrepreneurship – imposed even greater constraints on economic growth than the lack of capital. Although the economy has been freed from the shackles of apartheid, it is still constrained by the poor education of blacks during apartheid. Despite the new government's increased spending on education, low productivity will continue to constrain South Africa's growth potential for a long time to come. The shortage of skilled personnel needed to sustain a high economic growth rate was seriously aggravated during the 'transitional' period in the 1990s, when an estimated 250 000 skilled and professional people left the country.

Instead of the economic growth rate of 6–12 per cent a year predicted so confidently in the early 1990s, economic growth since 1994 has only averaged 2,7 per cent a year. A sense of realism demands that economic and social policy-makers abandon their naïve optimism and scale down estimates of South Africa's growth potential to an average rate of 3 per cent – or at best 4 per cent. Given the constraints of inadequate savings, capital, and skilled labour, as well as our location in the Poor South and in Africa, it is simply not possible to attain a higher growth rate over the next 10 to 20 years. As soon as this is accepted, it will no longer be possible to present a growth rate of 6–12 per cent as the panacea for South Africa's problems. Policy-makers will have to face harsh reality and search for other and more direct remedies for the inhumane conditions of unemployment, poverty, and social and moral decay in which half the population has been trapped.

In the early 1990s the protagonists of growth argued that a neo-liberal economic policy would unlock the high growth potential of the economy. As indicated in chapters 3 and 4, the free market approach was misguided. If ever there was a time in South Africa's history for an interventionist and government-led developmental policy, it was in the post-apartheid period.

What South Africa has needed since 1994 is a developmental policy for integrating the peripheral sector into the mainstream of economic activity, and turning around the tendency towards capitalist enclavity. With the benefit of hindsight, we now realise that, although the campaign for a free market approach did not lead to high economic growth, it was designed to enable the corporate sector to proceed with the process of Anglo-Americanisation in order to transform the modern sector of the economy into a first-world capitalist enclave. Although the ideological and systemic trends towards Anglo-Americanisation and capitalist enclavity benefited the bourgeoisie, both trends strongly disadvantaged the lumpenproletariat.

In the early 1990s the protagonists of growth and neo-liberalism warned that increased government investment would not only 'crowd out' the private sector, but also undermine macroeconomic stability. Although it was important to maintain macroeconomic stability and fiscal balance, it was nevertheless possible to finance a government investment programme in a non-inflationary way. Larger government investment could have 'crowded in' private investment, and could also have helped to bridge the still growing gap between the capitalist enclave and the lumpenproletariat. But to accomplish these goals would have required higher taxes than the 24 per cent of GDP agreed on when the corporate sector and core ANC leaders reached their elite compromises in the early 1990s.

11.2.2 Questioning the premise that integration with the 'benign' system of global capitalism will enhance the growth potential of the economy

After almost two decades of sanctions, disinvestment, and isolation from the global economy, it was certainly necessary, from 1994 onwards, for the South African economy to re-engage with global capitalism. But the new government should have realised that the global economy had changed a great deal during those 20 years. By 1994 the multinational corporations of the Rich North had significantly consolidated their power. Moreover, at the end of the 20th century, developing countries of the Poor South found themselves in an unenviable position: they were dependent on the investments and technology of the Rich North, but this simultaneously exposed them to the risk of being destabilised by the erratic global movement of capital and global currency speculation, and of being exploited by global corporatism (see Rupert 2000: ch 2). It would have been advisable for South Africa to weigh the benefits and risks of globalisation very carefully, and to adopt a strategic and differentiated approach to opening up its economy.

Unfortunately, in the early 1990s the corporate sector and its global partners considered it necessary to force the ANC as comprehensively and quickly as possible into the framework of global capitalism, in order to prevent it from implementing a redistributive social policy once it was in power. Given the socialist orientation of the ANC Alliance during the liberation struggle, the perceived need to 'box in' the ANC is partially understandable. However, the corporate sector used its extraordinary power to co-opt the ANC's core leadership into pursuing a liberal capitalist version of democratic capitalism, thus depriving the new government of the sovereignty to formulate and implement an independent socio-economic policy.

The new government was pressurised into aligning the economy with global capitalism with lofty promises that the benign system of global corporatism would richly reward South Africa for its peaceful democratisation. But the Asian crises of 1998 and the spectacular decline of the rand in 2001 have shown that there is no charity in the global village. Global capitalism is a ruthless and cruel system for those who are not independent, fit, and shrewd enough to play the global game. Despite the relentless propaganda about the benefits of global capitalism with which countries in the Poor South are bombarded, these countries – and especially those in Africa – should be alive to the fact that the power vested in these corporations is so great and so deeply entrenched that countries in the Poor South can only benefit from the global game at the price of becoming dependent on their new masters in the Rich North.

According to Jean-Pierre Cling, 'the warnings of some foreign and local economists regarding the risks linked to [the opening up of the South African economy]... and its uncertain benefits have been largely ignored'(2001: 104).[6] Over the past eight years neither the liberalisation of capital movements nor the liberalisation of trade has improved economic growth. Both versions of liberalisation have, however, enabled individual corporations to accelerate their own internationalisation and to spread their corporate risk, thereby augmenting the dysfunctionality of the new politico-economic system.

Whether dropping its trade barriers was in South Africa's best interests is a highly controversial issue. As a developing country, South Africa traditionally exports raw materials and semi-manufactured goods, and imports the capital goods needed to make the economy function. It has developed a dichotomy in its relations with developed countries in the Rich North to which it exports mainly intermediary goods, and the countries in Africa to which it exports manufactured products. South Africa cannot be compared to the newly industrialised countries of south east Asia which have major comparative advantages in that they export labour-intensive manufactured products to large foreign markets nearby.[7]

The biggest problem surrounding South Africa's exports is its inability to increase the share of its labour-intensive manufactured products. It is therefore unlikely that increased exports will solve the unemployment problem. From an employment point of view, it would rather have been advisable to continue protecting labour-intensive industries such as textiles and clothing, and subsidise these and other labour-intensive products for export. Instead, South Africa has committed itself to reducing tariffs to the point where it has exceeded the targets demanded by the General Agreement on Tariffs and Trade (GATT). According to Cling, South Africa cannot be compared with countries with low labour costs – such as China and India – even if its wage levels are similar. This is because, given the lower productivity and inferior education levels of South African workers, wage costs per unit produced are higher than those in other developing countries. Exports of manufactured goods have increased, but mainly as a result of the declining rand. At the same time, imports of capital goods have also increased sharply, and will have a strong inflationary effect (Cling 2001: 114).

The liberalisation of capital flows has produced even fewer advantages for all sectors of the South African economy (including the informal sector) than the liberalisation of trade. The former has enabled corporations – especially the large globalised corporations such as the AAC, Old Mutual, and SA Breweries – as well as wealthy individuals to move a huge amount of capital, and thus South African wealth, out of the country. These amounts are considerably larger than FDI. In 'disinvesting' voluntarily from South Africa, these corporations and individuals have increased the global orientation of the capitalist enclave. This overhasty internationalisation of South African corporations also demonstrates a lack of confidence in the country's long-term growth potential.[8] In the early 1990s the corporate sector promised ANC leaders that South Africa's financial liberalisation was a precondition for a large inflow of both short-term portfolio capital and long-term FDI. This promise has not materialised. Financial liberalisation has, however, enabled many corporations and individuals to 'escape' to foreign financial markets. This has intensified the trend towards a first-world, globally oriented, capitalist enclave. Although the inflow of portfolio capital has increased, the disinvestment by South African corporations since 1994 has outstripped FDI (see section 4.5).

The purpose of almost all the elite compromises between core ANC leaders and the corporate sector was to create fiscal and macroeconomic conditions that would be conducive to FDI. Perhaps the biggest misjudgement of the new government and the corporate sector was to underestimate the negative impact of the social crisis and the high levels of crime and violence on potential foreign investors. If the government and corporate sector were really serious about attracting foreign investment, it should have done far more to alleviate poverty and stabilise society.

Given the large outflow of capital since 1994, it is hardly surprising that FDI since then has only amounted to 1 per cent of GDP a year. Foreign investors' lack of confidence in South Africa and their hesitation to take risks in this country mirror the attitudes displayed by prominent South African businessmen who have opted to 'disinvest'. The large-scale integration of South Africa's perhaps too modern and too sophisticated financial institutions with global financial institutions – with the blessing of the new government –

has created a systemic situation in which corporations and individuals can participate in financial manipulation and speculation to their own advantage. The chronic problems surrounding the value of the rand should not be blamed on the unlawful or irregular actions of individuals or corporations, but on the undue 'openness' of the South African economy. The real culprits are probably those who pressurised the government into exposing the vulnerable and relatively powerless South African economy to the chill winds and powerful forces of global capitalism. As Guy Mhone argues:

> With the introduction of *openness* the [modern sector of the South African] economy is able to escape the internal barriers to growth by resorting to external markets for investment funds, investment opportunities, effective demand and innovation, without requiring the growth process to be *inclusive and integrating* of the non-formal sector...*Essentially, openness accentuates the enclavity, and by the same token the marginalisation of the non-formal sector.* In the context of openness, the formal sector begins to have a momentum of its own quite independent of the non-formal sector, which now becomes economically irrelevant (2000: 17; author's emphasis).

South Africa's economic problems are far more serious in 2002 than they were in 1994. The capitalist enclavity and global orientation of the economy are far more developed than in 1994, and the marginalisation of the lumpenproletariat in the informal sector far more complete. Many corporations and individuals have 'escaped' into global capitalism, and can no longer be regarded as being fully part of the South African economy. Ironically, some of the corporations that have won permission to move their main listings offshore are among those which accumulated their wealth by plundering both South Africa's natural resources and its black labour force during the period of colonial and racial capitalism. It seems as if, since the early 1990s, at least some corporations have followed a clever 'master plan' that has enabled them to detach themselves from South Africa and from possible intervention by the new government. If this has indeed been their secret strategy, they have succeeded spectacularly – but once again to the detriment of the victims of the systemic exploitation in which the corporate sector played a central role for so many years.

11.2.3 Questioning the premise that a high rate of economic growth will unlock the labour-absorptive capacity of the modern sector

The GEAR strategy of 1996 is the best example of the naïve optimism about the large labour-absorptive capacity that would be unlocked if an economic growth rate of 6 per cent could be attained by 2001. This rate of growth was not nearly achieved. Instead of the additional 1,3 million job opportunities supposed to be created by 2001, more than 1 million jobs have been destroyed in the modern sector, including the agricultural sector, since 1996. The important question is how many new job opportunities would have been created during the past six years if GEAR's growth target had in fact been achieved. It is quite possible that very few – if any – new job opportunities would have been created. What might have happened is that fewer jobs would have been lost.

The GEAR strategy was built on the supposition that the growing unemployment during the two decades from 1974 to 1994 was mainly the result of low economic growth during the period of stagflation. Although this factor undoubtedly contributed to the loss of job opportunities, these losses must be attributed mainly to the sharp increase in the capital intensity of the modern sector, and to the structural shift in production that was responsible for a decline in the primary sector and an increase in the tertiary sector (see sections 10.2.1; 10.2.2; 10.2.3). According to the South African Reserve Bank, 'a given rate of economic growth [in the last 10 years] has become associated with a considerably smaller change in formal sector employment growth [than in the 1970 and 1980s]' (2001: 22). It should be remembered that the increase in the capital intensity of the modern sector was triggered off when the black labour force became less docile and cheap in the 1970s, and was no longer as exploitable as it had been in the heyday of apartheid.

Mhone contends that the poor labour-absorptive capacity of the modern sector of the economy should be attributed to the premature and disproportionate expansion of the tertiary sector *en route* towards capitalist enclavity before the labour-absorptive capacities of the primary and secondary sectors had been fully developed. This tendency to develop the tertiary sector at the cost of the primary and secondary sectors has been strongly stimulated over the past eight years by 'opening up' the economy, and by the continuing trend towards capitalist enclavity. The inability of the secondary sector to mature and retain its labour-absorptive capacity was caused by the small and shrinking demand for industrial production by consumers in the informal sector, and the failure of the manufacturing sector to export more labour-intensive products. This latter inability is largely the result of the low productivity of the poorly educated African workforce (see Mhone 2000: 13–15).

The structural transformation of the modern sector of the economy from a system of colonial capitalism in 1970 to a capitalist enclave in 2002 has considerably reduced its labour-absorptive capacity at a time when the African population group in particular has grown at a relatively high rate, and the potential workforce has increased by 200 000–300 000 workers a year. As the trend towards capitalist enclavity has reduced the demand for labour, demographic trends have increased the supply of African labour at a faster rate than that of other population groups. While colonial capitalism thrived on exploiting African labour in mainly the primary sector (agriculture and mining), the trend towards capitalist enclavity has significantly reduced the employment of Africans in the primary sector at a time when the additional jobs that have been created have been in the tertiary sector, for which many Africans have not qualified because of their inadequate education under apartheid. The combined effect of the tendency towards capitalist enclavity, the sharp increase in the supply of African labour, and the legacy of poor education is that only 13 per cent of the total African population are currently employed in the modern or formal sector of the economy, as against 34 per cent in 1970 (see table 2.1; figure 2.1; table 10.2).

It is often said in government circles that unemployment is not caused by incorrect policies, but by the fact that most unemployed South Africans are unskilled and therefore unemployable. It is undoubtedly true that if the African workforce were better schooled, and equipped with better skills, unemployment would not have been as high as it is. It is also true that the domestic impact of FDI increases significantly as levels of education increase. The poor labour-absorptive capacity of the economy will certainly improve with higher levels of education. But to claim – as government spokespersons do – that higher levels of spending on education will create jobs for 6 to 7 million people clearly indicates that the complexities of the unemployment problem are not fully appreciated in government circles. Although the inadequate supply of different categories of labour inhibits growth, the inadequate demand for labour in a sluggish economy, by employers obsessed with first-world efficiency and high capital intensity, is a far greater constraint on the job-creating capacity of the economy.

While unemployment among Africans was already serious in 1995 (when 46 per cent were unemployed), it has become far more serious over the past six years. It is estimated that almost 55 per cent of the potential African labour force cannot find jobs in the modern or formal sector of the economy. Although the tendency towards capitalist enclavity and the concomitant decline in the labour-absorptive capacity of the modern sector were in full swing during the last decades of apartheid, these tendencies have continued unabated in the post-apartheid period. The new government is currently confronted with the awful predicament that even if a higher economic growth rate can be attained as a result of greater foreign investment, it will probably not result in more job opportunities. It is quite possible that an economic growth rate of, say, 4 per cent a year will not only mean 'jobless growth' – as is the case in some first-world countries – but may in fact be 'job-destroying growth' because of the declining labour-absorptive capacity of the first-world capitalist enclave.[9]

The flip-side of the strong trend towards first-world capitalist enclavity is the marginalisation of large numbers of the former working class to the third-world informal sector. Over the past eight years many women have been shifted from the formal to the informal sector.

At the same time, many male workers have been turned into casual and contract labourers – ie, a process of 'casualisation' – without the benefits and security of full-time employment. These workers are 'rightless' and unorganised, and are often badly exploited – even more so than workers in the formal sector under apartheid. It is ironic that new labour legislation has strengthened the tendencies towards the 'peripheralisation' and 'casualisation' of formerly fully employed workers, especially in the agricultural sector. But what is even more ironic is that the new labour legislation does not protect people against the often inhuman exploitation in the peripheral and 'casual' sector.[10]

Hard statistics on the additional 'employment' opportunities created in the informal sector over the past 30 years are not available. The size of the workforce in this sector is estimated at several million. Unfortunately, the informal sector is chronically depressed. We have reason to believe that a higher economic growth rate in the modern sector will have a positive 'spin-off' effect on the informal sector, and that a thriving informal sector will not only increase levels of informal 'employment', but will also improve the content or quality of those job opportunities. It should, however, be noted that all kinds of 'self-exploitation' are occurring in the predominantly black informal sector. Under conditions of abject poverty, contagious diseases, and violent criminality, many of the 'workers' in the informal sector are exceptionally vulnerable to exploitation by the ruthless employer class in this sector.[11]

One of the main themes of this book is the multiplicity of the unfree labour patterns to which millions of black people were subjected during South Africa's extended colonial history. We can identify structural unemployment and underemployment in the informal sector – and the 'self-exploitation' in this sector – as the most recent versions of 'unfree' labour. In South Africa's dualistic economy, unemployment and underemployment are complex phenomena with social, cultural, educational, demographic, political, and economic dimensions.

The new government hopes to solve these problems through high and sustainable rates of economic growth. It is, however, not realistic or humane to concentrate almost exclusively on a *single* remedy for this complex malady and, what is more, one that will probably not be effective. If a high economic growth rate is achieved, it will probably not create jobs but destroy them, or at best further 'peripheralise' and 'casualise' a part of the workforce. Instead of concentrating exclusively on economic growth in the private sector as the remedy for unemployment, the government should launch comprehensive labour-intensive development programmes, and search for a version of democratic capitalism that will be more sensitive to the creation of job opportunities for the unemployed, and less sensitive to the creation of extravagant wealth and luxury for the elite.

The unemployment rate, as a percentage of the total labour force, has increased during each of the past 30 years, with a huge pauperisation effect on the unemployed. If we are unable to solve the unemployment problem, we should at least be sensitive to its dehumanising effects, and search for methods to restore the dignity and humanity of those caught in the terrible grip of life-long structural unemployment over which they have little, if any, control.

11.2.4 Questioning the premise that high economic growth will generate a large enough 'trickle-down' effect to narrow the income gap and alleviate poverty

The GEAR strategy of 1996 is also the best example of the naïve optimism about the spontaneous 'trickle-down' effect of a high economic growth rate on the poor. In the GEAR strategy, the redistribution of income is of secondary importance, as is indicated by its position in the acronym. The advocates of the 'trickle-down' approach regard job creation as the main mechanism for transmitting the additional income created by high economic growth rates to the poor. But if it is unlikely – as argued earlier – that higher economic growth will create additional jobs, it is even more unlikely that a meaningful part of the additional income will reach the poor. It is important to realise that the 'distance' – both literally and figuratively – between the modern first-world enclave and the third-world periphery has become so great that a declining portion of the income generated in the capitalist enclave has reached the poorest half of the population over the past 30 years (see section 2.2.1; table 2.2; figure 2.1).

In the early 1990s there was a lively debate over whether preference should be given to 'growth through distribution' or 'distribution through growth'. The corporate sector lobbied aggressively for the latter, and won the day. At that stage the corporate sector was optimistic about the growth potential of the economy, and its positive job-creating and 'trickle-down' effects. Its optimism was unfounded on all three counts. If it is indeed unlikely that a high rate of economic growth will be achieved and that it will have positive employment and 'trickle-down' effects, what other 'mechanism' is available for transferring income from the wealthy modern sector to the impoverished informal sector? The only other 'mechanism' available is a comprehensive and government-led redistribution programme.

A relatively large transfer of income has taken place through the national budget over the past eight years. This redistributive effect has, however, not been large enough to make a difference to the lives of those trapped in the vicious circle of growing unemployment, violent criminality, and contagious diseases (see section 2.2). If we could achieve a higher rate of economic growth, the tax capacity of the economy would increase. This would enable the minister of finance to use the 'growth surplus' to alleviate poverty. But there is no guarantee that this would happen; it depends on the distribution of power in society. In each of the three budget years from 2001 to 2003 the minister did have a 'surplus' at his disposal – mainly as a result of improved tax collection – but chose each time to use a large part of the 'surplus' to reimburse relatively wealthy taxpayers.[12]

These decisions were not surprising. As indicated in section 2.2.2, a new 'distributive coalition' has been forged over the past decade between the old white elite and the new black elite. If this coalition insists that total state revenue should be pegged at 24 per cent of GDP, a comprehensive redistribution programme on behalf of the poor is not possible (see National Treasury 2001; table 3.3). As long as the ideological cement that binds the two elite groups holds, it is unlikely that redistribution via the budget will be stepped up – even if a higher economic growth rate is attained. The extremely strong anti-tax lobby of the corporate sector and predominantly white taxpayers makes it unlikely that the minister of finance will agree to implement a comprehensive poverty alleviation programme. Before this can happen, not only is an ideological paradigm shift in the thinking of the elite essential, but also an economic power shift in favour of the impoverished majority (see sections 11.3 and 11.4).

The highly unequal distribution of socio-economic power, property, and opportunities between the upper class (comprising one third of the population) and the middle and lower subclasses (comprising 50 per cent of the population) is a very worrying feature of South African society. What complicates matters is that the democratic transition and other developments since then have not improved the socio-economic bargaining power of the poor in any meaningful way – at least not in the 'distribution struggle' between the bourgeois elite operating in the capitalist enclave and the lumpenproletariat relegated to the third-world periphery. Without an economic power shift, and without a new 'distributive coalition' that includes representatives of the lumpenproletariat, the poorer half of the population will remain poor.

11.2.5 Questioning the premise that market-led economic growth is the most effective way of restructuring the South African economy

The RDP claimed in 1994 that 'the South African economy is in a deep-seated structural crisis, and as such requires *fundamental restructuring*' (ANC 1994: 75; author's emphasis). It based its conclusion on the fact that the white minority had used its monopoly over political and economic power to promote its sectional interests at the expense of blacks; on the unequal power relations inherent in the South African version of capitalism, and its strong tendencies towards capital intensity and a further concentration of economic power in the hands of the 'commanding heights'; and on the fact that the distribution of income, opportunities, property, and wealth in South Africa is among the most unequal in the world.

We can identify three approaches to the 'restructuring' of the South African economy over the past eight years. However, they do not add up to the 'fundamental restructuring' envisaged by the RDP. First, the new government has committed itself to 'restructuring' – ie, privatising – certain state-owned assets in order to attract much-needed foreign investment and foreign technology. But according to COSATU – which strongly opposes the government's privatisation policy – this form of 'restructuring' does not resolve the 'deep-seated structural crisis' and the unequal distribution of economic power, but augments them instead.

Second, the government's policy of black empowerment is aimed at 'restructuring' the economy in such a way that the participation of blacks in entrepreneurial and highly skilled jobs as well as their 'entitlement' to property will increase. This policy has achieved only limited success over the past eight years. Consequently, the plea of the Black Empowerment Commission (BEECom) for 'a national integrated black economic empowerment strategy' should be regarded as a timely and important document that deserves the enthusiastic support of the new government (see BEECom 2001; Black 2002). In implementing the recommendations of this commission, the government should, however, be careful not to restrict empowerment to a privileged minority and in so doing neglect the more urgent economic empowerment and upliftment of the impoverished and unemployed majority. If empowerment only involves transferring wealth to a small number of black entrepreneurs, the objective of social transformation will not be achieved. Instead of promoting the further enrichment of the existing small black elite, the government ought to give preference to the empowerment and 'entitlement' of large numbers of small black business people and farmers (see section 11.5.3).

The third form of 'restructuring' is the continuation of the trend towards establishing a globally oriented and first-world capitalist enclave. The liberalisation of capital and trade by the new government has created conditions that have encouraged this trend. This is certainly not the 'fundamental restructuring' envisaged by the RDP. If anything, it has aggravated the 'deep-seated structural crisis' in so far as it has enhanced the power of globally oriented corporations, and enabled many corporations to detach themselves further from unskilled black labour, thereby continuing the destruction of black (and especially African) job opportunities in the modern sector of the economy.

These three forms of 'restructuring' are either inadequate or misguided. The 'fundamental restructuring' to which the new government committed itself in the RDP has clearly been neglected. It seems as if the corporate sector and the government have tacitly agreed that the 'restructuring' of the economy should be entrusted to the supposedly *neutral* forces operating in South Africa's free market system. They seem to have agreed that it would be expedient and less painful if the 'restructuring' were to take place through market forces, while the economy was growing rapidly. The 'common wisdom' about the desirability of market-led 'restructuring' in a fast-growing economy was expressed in the maxim that it is easier to 'turn a moving tanker than a stationary one'. This 'wisdom' is usually complemented by the 'market wisdom' that it is not advisable to act against the grain of local and global market forces, and that those who do so will be duly penalised. This, in a nutshell, is the core of the free market propaganda that was accepted uncritically by the new government. But by doing so the new government in effect agreed that the unequal distribution of economic power and property would be left intact, and that the skewed economic system – ie, the first-world-oriented capitalist enclavity – would be perpetuated.

The main flaw of the free market propaganda lies in its claim that economic forces operating in domestic and global markets are *neutral*. The huge power and influence of the big corporations and their global partners are deeply institutionalised, structurally entrenched, and contrast sharply with the socio-economic powerlessness and dispossession of the lumpenproletariat. The acceptance of the idea that market forces will 'restructure' the South African economy in the long run and move it in the desired direction boils down to giving a blank cheque to the most powerful economic players to reshape the economy in a way that serves their sectional, selfish, and myopic interests. It is therefore no wonder that the strong tendency towards capitalist enclavity has continued unimpeded over the past eight years. The South African economy has not only remained 'fundamentally unrestructured', but has in fact become even more distorted and dysfunctional – certainly from the point of view of the impoverished majority.

11.3 Why a paradigm shift towards social democracy is necessary

A first, indispensable step out of the present *cul-de-sac* is for the governing elite to change its thinking about the nature of the South African problem and about possible solutions to that problem. It has to change its *weltanschauung*. We are convinced that a decisive paradigm shift from the *liberal capitalist* ideology of the British-American world (BA) towards the *social democratic* ideology of continental Europe (CE) can contribute meaningfully to solving South African's most pressing problems over a period of, say, two decades (see appendix for a description of the social democratic ideology of CE).[13] If ANC leaders were to initiate such a paradigm shift, they would have to reject all five of the premises on which the present policy approach is based.

The last 15 years have perhaps been the most momentous period in the history of the core leadership of the ANC. As the Cold War ended unexpectedly in 1989, and the Soviet Union's ideological and financial support for the liberation struggle suddenly ended, the ANC was challenged by a new constellation of world power – dominated by the United States and Britain – to change its strategy. When, in the late 1980s, it became apparent that the apartheid regime could not be defeated militarily, and that it would no longer be possible to simultaneously take political *and* economic control of South Africa, the leadership core was obliged to make certain strategic concessions in order to attain at least its first prize: the transfer of *political* power from the apartheid regime to the liberation movement. One of the strategic concessions wrung from the ANC by the corporate sector was the acceptance of the neo-liberal and globalised economic ideology prevalent in the British-American world. The domestic corporate sector and key international institutions took the initiative in convincing ANC leaders of the alleged virtues of the liberal capitalist approach. Although the ANC leaders were late converts to this ideology, they have clung to this approach over the past eight years as if they believed in it all along. But there's the rub. Whatever the merits of this ideological approach for highly developed and powerful first-world countries may be, it is not appropriate for a dualistic and developing country such as South Africa in which economic power, property, and opportunities are as unequally distributed as they are.

Although South Africa was decolonised in 1910, the powerful English-oriented business sector remains a colonial extension of Britain to this day. Over the past 20 years the English-controlled corporate sector has succeeded in convincing the Afrikaner-controlled corporations and core ANC leaders of the alleged virtues of liberal capitalism. This ideology enjoys such unanimous and widespread support in both white and black elite circles that it seems as if that part of the South African population is indeed living behind an Iron Curtain. We can call it the London–Washington wall of liberal capitalism. Being trapped behind it, South Africans have little knowledge and even less understanding of the true nature of the social democratic approach of CE countries. Many South Africans – and almost all whites – are indeed so right-wing when judged in terms of the ideological spectrum of CE countries that the terms 'left' and 'right' have lost their normal meaning. It will therefore be necessary to revive the true meaning of 'left of centre'.

To change gear from a liberal capitalist to a social democratic approach is something that cannot happen easily or quickly. It will require a huge adult education campaign. The first prerequisite is that the new government should become thoroughly convinced of the merits of a social democratic approach – or of an adapted version of it – in the post-apartheid period of healing and reconstruction. If the new government could be persuaded to embark on a social democratic route, this would go against the grain of the influential and neo-liberal business sector with which the government has forged a symbiotic relationship over the past 10 years. Freund claims correctly that:

> the forces of the *status quo* within the economy are powerful. The South
> African state will be afraid of antagonising the business world and may be
> unable to intervene efficiently or effectively in the economy, even if it
> would like to do so. Current signs do not suggest that the ANC has any real
> commitment to structural change or is taking chances that would involve
> confrontation with capitalists on economic issues (in Hyslop 1999:
> 440–1).[14]

Although it will be difficult for the ANC government to change its approach to economic policy and economic systems, it must do something meaningful – even drastic – to relieve poverty. The momentous political transformation should be urgently complemented by an equally momentous *socio-economic transformation* in order to deracialise the economy, get rid of the ugly remnants of racial capitalism, and end poverty and destitution. It is indeed unacceptable that such a large percentage of black people, who were exploited and humiliated for so long, should still be doomed to live under such appalling conditions at a time when the wealth of whites remains largely intact, and when members of the new black elite also live in extravagant wealth and luxury. Against this background it ought to be the government's highest priority to find a new ideological approach to economic development, not only to end the systemic exclusion of the poorest half of the population, but also to democratise South Africa in the socio-economic sense of the word.

A first step towards ending systemic exclusion would be to replace the ideology of neo-liberalism with a truly developmental policy based on social capitalism and on the social democracy of CE countries. This would imply a new vision of:

i human beings and their relationship with society;

ii sound social relations and the importance of restoring social justice;

iii the role the state and its bureaucracy in the post-apartheid economy;

iv the relevance of a well-developed civil society in a social democratic system; and

v what constitutes (or defines) social welfare.

11.3.1 A new vision of the dignity and humanity of all South Africans

South Africa is in the unfortunate position that the dignity and humanity of more than 80 per cent of its population were not sufficiently acknowledged by the white minority during racism and apartheid. Following the political transformation, and the adoption of the new constitution, the human rights of every South African are now formally acknowledged and protected. This is especially true of first-generation human rights, but unfortunately not necessarily true as far as a second generation of economic and social rights is concerned. Although the constitution prescribes 'that the state must take reasonable legislative and other measures, *within its available resources*, to achieve the progressive realisation of each of these [social] rights', they have not been realised to the necessary degree as far as the poorest half of the population is concerned. It is debatable whether the state is legally and constitutionally obliged to realise these social rights. But if we take into account that the top 20 per cent of households (±17 per cent of the population) receive more than 70 per cent of the national income, and the poorest 40 per cent of households (±50 per cent of the population) less than 3,5 per cent of the national income, there can be no doubt that the necessary resources are available, or can be made available (see table 2.2; figure 2.1).

If South Africans are really concerned about the dignity and humanity of those living in abject poverty, in disrupted communities, amid contagious diseases, and amid criminality and violence, they ought to be prepared to mobilise more resources for restoring the dignity and humanity of the poor. Unfortunately, the population – and especially its wealthy part – will not readily agree to a greater mobilisation of resources for poverty alleviation. This is an unsavoury state of affairs. It prevents the government from restoring social justice, and can endanger the stability and viability of the new democratic system. We claim to have a modern and people-centred constitution. If this is indeed the case, a huge responsibility rests on the Constitutional Court to educate the public at large about the constitutionality of social rights. If the Constitutional Court is truly elevated above party politics, and unconstrained by the elite compromises agreed to by the ANC and the corporate sector, it will hopefully be brave enough to interpret social rights as entrenched rights which the government is obliged to realise.

On 24 May 1994, during his first speech in the new representative parliament, then president Nelson Mandela declared that the restoration of the human dignity of the poor and destitute would be the centrepiece of the new government's social policy:

> Our single most important challenge is to help establish a social order in which the freedom of the individual will truly mean the freedom of the individual. We must construct that people-centred society of freedom in such a manner that it guarantees the political liberties and the human rights of all our citizens ... Our definition of the freedom of the individual must be instructed by the fundamental objective to restore the human dignity of each and every South African. This requires that we speak not only of political freedoms ... My government's commitment to create a people-centred society of liberty binds us to the pursuit of the goals of freedom from want, freedom from hunger, freedom from deprivation, freedom from ignorance, freedom from suppression and freedom from fear. These freedoms are fundamental to the guarantee of human dignity. They will therefore constitute part of the centrepiece of what this government will seek to achieve, the focal point on which our attention will continuously be focused ... When we elaborated [the RDP] programme, we were inspired by the hope

that all South Africans of goodwill could join together to provide a better life for all (Mandela 1994b: 3–15).

The harsh reality eight years later is that the ANC government has failed dismally to create a people-centred society, despite president Thabo Mbeki's claim to the contrary.[15] Who is to be blamed? Has the government lost its commitment to this noble goal, or has it encountered severe resistance from mainly white taxpayers and the predominantly white corporate sector to releasing the funds needed to create a people-centred society? Or are both the government and those with large vested interests to be blamed? Whoever the culprit, it is really disconcerting that not enough South Africans are prepared to work together to provide a better life for all, and to provide to the poor those basic social rights needed to create a civilised society.

In section 3.1.1 we discussed the unsympathetic attitude of both the white and black elites towards the poor, and their unwillingness to acknowledge the structural nature of poverty. This indifference towards the poor – and the continuing violation of their dignity and humanity – are ultimately based on racial and/or class prejudices that are deeply embedded in South Africa's unfortunate history. We cannot make progress if South Africans are not prepared to drastically change their view of the humanity of fellow compatriots. The NGO forum at the conference on racism held in Durban in 2001 described the attitudinal changes required as follows:

> Racism exists in our minds and hearts. Changes of attitudes on social transformation will happen only if we can open our minds and hearts through education and consciousness. This transformation within ourselves is the first and vital step. This will enable us to positively influence the communities we live in, in order to bring about tolerance, respect, and appreciation (NGO Forum Mission 2001).

A fundamental change in the way in which South Africans view their fellow compatriots is therefore a *sine qua non* for building a better South Africa. It is important that every South African – and especially every white South African – should cleanse him/herself of any residual racial, class, and group prejudices. Many whites were sceptical about the world conference against racism, racial discrimination, xenophobia, and related intolerances held in Durban in September 2001. But these kinds of conferences are urgently needed to confront those who still covertly harbour racist convictions. It is equally important that the black and white elites rid themselves of their reductionist materialism, their possessive individualism, and their class prejudices, and accept their patriotic responsibility towards all South Africans. But what is necessary above all is that the privileged part of the population should regard the poor with empathy and compassion, and should acknowledge that the terrible plight of the poor is the result of factors largely beyond their control.

11.3.2 A new vision for sound social relations and social justice

Currently, South Africa's population does not constitute a society. After centuries of group conflict and group plundering, and after a century of systemic exploitation and violations of the human rights of the majority, the population is still divided into seemingly irreconcilable groups. These groups do not share the same values, and do not have the cross-cutting interests needed to cement them into a single community.

The RDP acknowledges that 'central to the crisis in our country are the massive divisions and inequalities left behind by apartheid... Nation-building is the basis on which to build a [new] South Africa... [It] is also the basis on which to ensure that our country takes up an effective role in the world economy' (ANC 1994: 5–6). Nation-building and reconciliation were the hallmarks of Mandela's presidency. He was remarkably successful in these spheres during a very sensitive stage in South Africa's history. Unfortunately, many whites regarded Mandela's accommodating attitude towards them as a sign of weakness, and became even more recalcitrant towards the new government. Mandela nonetheless succeeded in laying the foundation for a new society.

As a part of a process of facilitating reconciliation, the TRC was saddled with the task of uncovering the truth about gross violations of human rights from 1960 to 1994. Although the TRC's investigation helped to make whites aware of the atrocities committed during the final phase of apartheid, the commission unfortunately interpreted its mandate too narrowly, and ignored the important dimension of systemic exploitation (see section 4.6).

The TRC explicitly decided that not all the laws that together constituted the system of racial capitalism were part of its mandate (see TRC 1998: vol 5, ch 1, par 48). Because of this unforgivable decision not to investigate a crucially important aspect of South Africa's history, the task of society-building and reconciliation is now far more difficult. Other opportunities now have to be devised for educating whites about the devastating effects of racial capitalism – and the insatiable need of white employers for cheap and docile black labour – on social structures and on the behaviour of a large section of the black population.

It has become customary to refer to South Africa as a country of 'two nations' – one rich and white, and the other poor and black. Although there is still merit in focusing attention on racial divisions, the class division has become more relevant because of the important distributive shifts that have occurred over the past 30 years. South Africa is a 'two-nation' country because it is sharply divided between a non-racial upper class of about one third of the population, and a mainly black lower class of about two thirds (table 2.2; figure 2.1). Almost all property – physical and human – and almost all opportunities and socio-economic power are concentrated in the hands of the upper class, while the lower class experiences all kinds of deprivation and destitution. This deep class division – which has deepened even further over the past eight years – has the potential to destabilise South African society. It is not possible to base a system of democratic capitalism and a prosperous South Africa on such sharp inequalities in the distribution of income, power, property, and opportunities.

Distributing income, power, property, and opportunities more equally for the sake of greater social justice is a value in its own right that ought to enjoy a very high priority. But a more equal distribution of income, power, and property between the upper and lower classes also has an important *instrumental* value: to create the social preconditions for deepening our nascent democracy, and for giving credibility – or a human face – to capitalism. To think that economic growth will bridge the gap between the upper and lower classes is not only wishful thinking, but puts the cart before the horse in a rather dangerous way. In sharp contrast to a liberal capitalist approach to South Africa's problems, a social democratic approach would certainly give preference to a redistribution of income, power, property, and opportunities, and to society-building, as undeniable preconditions for sustainable economic growth and the maintenance of a humane system of democratic capitalism.

The strongest argument for compelling the ANC government to accept a social democratic and interventionist approach is the need to address poverty and inequality. Even if we consider the conditions under which the poorer half of the population have to live in a historical vacuum, the social democratic argument for a more comprehensive redistribution programme and for better funded poverty alleviation is still compelling. But if, as we have done in this book, we take into account the unequal racial distribution of power that has characterised South Africa's extended colonial history, the argument in favour of a more comprehensive redistribution programme becomes far more convincing.

A plea for *restitutive* justice is not a plea for *retributive* justice. The latter will be destructive, while the former can – and probably will – help to restore the disrupted social structures and the dignity and humanity of blacks. It is perhaps expecting too much of South Africans to accept the notion prevalent in CE countries that society is an organic whole. But we can expect South Africans to acknowledge that the economic well-being of each of the different groups in society is – and always has been – inextricably linked to the economic well-being of other groups. During South Africa's long colonial history the wealth of the predominantly white group was structurally linked to the poverty of blacks. Wealth and poverty were – and still are – two sides of the same structural coin. The link between white wealth and black poverty was a very unfortunate one. But we share the same future, and the same destiny. We, as a democratic people, should ensure that our interdependent future is one of social justice and mutual respect.

11.3.3 A new vision of the role the state has to play in post-apartheid South Africa

The RDP stated quite categorically that 'neither a commandist central planning system nor an unfettered free market system can provide adequate solutions to the problems confronting [South Africa in the post-apartheid period]. Reconstruction and development will be achieved through the *leading* and *enabling* role of the state, a thriving private sector, and active involvement by all sectors of civil society which in combination will lead to sustainable growth' (ANC 1994: 78–9).

This statement cannot be faulted. The government, however, made a huge mistake by not assuming the role the RDP envisaged for it and instead allowing the powerful corporate sector to co-opt it as the junior partner in implementing a liberal capitalist version of democratic capitalism, in which the role and sovereignty of the democratic state has been severely restricted and in which the enormous task of 'solving' the legacy of apartheid and 'reorganising' the economy has been entrusted to 'free market mechanisms'. Given the serious market failures, power and income inequalities, and informational deficiencies that have become the outstanding characteristics of South African capitalism, and the inability of the government and corporate sector to implement a successful accumulation strategy after all the predatory labour patterns have been abolished, it has become crucially important to realise that the economic destiny of South Africans can no longer be entrusted as exclusively to the so-called free market economy and to the powerful domestic and global corporations as it has been over the past 100 years, and particularly over the past eight years. In any democratic country with a social democratic orientation in which the 'performance' of the capitalist sector and its 'outcome' are as unsatisfactory and as 'unequal' as in South Africa, the democratic state would have decided long ago to play a far more interventionist and *dirigiste* role in the economy in an attempt to ensure a more balanced and more moral outcome for the sake of the social welfare of the total population.

According to Harrop and Dyson, France and several other European countries are 'state' societies in the sense that they regard state-building and the bureaucratic capacity of the state as crucially important. These countries do not trust the 'invisible hand' of the market as dogmatically as BA countries do. They allocate great responsibility to their bureaucracies, and both France and Germany possess a corps of civil servants which is efficient, professional, and imbued with a strong culture of service and loyalty. By contrast, the BA countries are regarded as 'stateless' societies that are inherently sceptical of the state's right and ability to lead society. These countries are dogmatic believers in free marketeerism (see Harrop 1992: 9–12; Dyson 1980; appendix).

South Africa is currently a 'stateless' society typical of liberal capitalist countries. It is also a 'stateless' society in that the balance of power between the capitalist sector and the democratic state in the new system of democratic capitalism is significantly tilted towards the former. As originally a part of the British colonial world, the South African corporate sector was always very strong in relation to the colonial state, and always 'spoilt' with all sorts of 'free market' favours.[16]

South Africa is not only a 'stateless' society, but also a country with a weak state. From the outset the new government was hesitant, and lacked confidence and experience. It took several years before government leaders started to believe in their own autonomy, legitimacy, and authority. The fact that they had to operate in the shadow of the powerful, capable, overly self-assured, and dogmatic managerial elite of the corporate sector did not help to build up their self-esteem. But the real weakness of the new state lies in the conspicuous lack of capacity in the bureaucracy at all three levels of government. There are several reasons for this. The affirmative action programme to replace white bureaucrats with blacks was perhaps driven too vigorously. Although it was necessary to get rid of *verkrampte* and racist white bureaucrats, those retrenched included many less *verkrampte* senior officials who could have made a valuable contribution to the bureaucratic efficiency of the new government. But, as a result of poor black education under apartheid, the pool of black people with the necessary education and professional training for appointment to the public sector was too small. Consequently, many positions in the higher echelons of the bureaucracy – at all three administrative levels –

were filled with black people who did not have the experience, professionalism, commitment, or culture of service needed to be productive and loyal civil servants. To complicate matters further, many of the new appointees are – like their white predecessors – indulging in nepotism, corruption, and careerism. It will be extremely difficult to purge the bureaucracy of incompetence so that a culture of service can take root.

The organisational and bureaucratic capacity of the corporate sector is incomparably stronger than the capacity of the public sector. But this is not an argument for leaving things that ought to be done by the democratic state – especially alleviating poverty – to the market. As indicated in section 1.4, the 'logic' and functions of the state and capitalist sectors are very different, and these differences should be respected. The efficiency of the corporate sector can, however, be used as an argument in favour of entrusting certain state functions to 'smart partnerships' between the private and public sectors. In such cases the government must be aware of the danger that both private and public partners are often strongly inclined to misuse these partnerships for rent-seeking. The government will then have to decide between the disadvantages of bureaucratic inefficiency and the disadvantages of 'crony capitalism'. In a situation where the corporate sector is as powerful and persuasive as it is in South Africa, the disadvantages of 'crony capitalism' can easily be greater.

The weakness of the state and the lack of capacity of the bureaucratic sector will seriously impede any government effort to embark on a social democratic approach and start implementing a truly developmental state policy. Luiz observes that when the new government became aware of 'its own limitations as a result of the RDP experience, [it] seemingly decided that state-led development was inappropriate and that since the state could not restructure the economy, the market would have to' (1998: 264). Whether this is true or not, the democratic state cannot shrink from its responsibilities towards its citizens merely because it lacks capacity. It is therefore a great tragedy that the new government did not identify building the capacity of the public sector as a priority from 1994 onwards. Numerous south east Asian countries have shown that state capacity can be built. The government ought to spend much more on training public servants, assisted by the bureaucracies of some of the social democratic countries in CE. At the same time, it ought to take strong steps to root out the nepotism, corruption, and careerism that are rife in the political, public, and private sectors. These phenomena are a malignant growth that can destroy the country. Unfortunately, the widespread white-collar corruption and careerism in the private sector are often used to justify corruption and careerism in the public sector. If the government embarked on a truly developmental state policy, it would have to spend much more on the security and judicial systems needed to root out corruption.

South Africa is indeed confronted with an awkward dilemma. On the one hand, the capitalist enclave is clearly dysfunctional and cannot solve the problems of the poorer half of the population because its growth and job-creating abilities are highly questionable. The growth performance of the capitalist enclave over the past eight years has been disappointing despite all the privileges conferred on it. But what is really disconcerting is that, even if the capitalist enclave could attain higher economic growth, it is unlikely that this would create employment, and even more unlikely that it would generate a 'trickle-down' effect. The democratic state, on the other hand, is inexperienced, without the necessary capacity, and seemingly without the will to live up to the goals spelled out in the RDP and mandated by its constituency in two general elections.

Looking at the South African economic situation from the perspective of the poor, it is not only hortatory but also absurd to think that the capitalist enclave will ever 'rescue' the lumpenproletariat from poverty, unemployment, violent criminality, and contagious disease. Given the system's strong tendency towards Anglo-Americanisation and capitalist enclavity, the market-oriented system has – despite its narrowly defined efficiency – neither the inclination nor the motivation to 'rescue' the poor. Its systemic orientation simply militates against 'serving' the poor. It will never be profitable for the corporate sector to be the champion and the servant of the marginalised majority, because the latter are too unproductive and their 'spending power' too small – less than 3,5 per cent of GDP, and mainly spent in the informal sector.

The state sector, on the other hand, lacks the capacity and seemingly also the will to 'rescue' the poor. But if the political elite in control of the democratic state can be convinced of the dysfunctionality of the capitalist enclave, it can hopefully be awakened – despite all attempts by the corporate sector to prolong its slumber – to its huge responsibility to seek *non-market* solutions to poverty and unemployment. A clear understanding of the public sector's undeniable responsibility for changing the devastated social and economic landscape – after centuries of colonialism and apartheid – will hopefully prompt the government to become more sensitive to the predicament of the poor, and more assertive about the huge socio-economic role it has to play in the post-apartheid period.

11.3.4 A new vision of the role of civil society in a social democratic system

Another matter of great concern is South Africa's poorly developed civil society. During the liberation struggle a very strong civil society emerged in the form of the MDM. According to Marais, the 1980s 'represented perhaps the heyday of South African civil society... The variety and sweep of initiatives, broadly gathered under the canopy of the anti-apartheid struggle, offered hints of... a flowering of autonomous activities, linked laterally and not subjugated to hierarchical ideological and strategic conformity' (2001: 62). Mike Morris claimed in 1991 that 'the mass of the population had recently embarked on the process of spontaneously gaining an angry consciousness of their potential power' (in Gelb 1991: 49). The predominantly black organs of civil society – ultimately organised under the umbrella of the MDM – played a strategic role in preparing the way for the negotiated political settlement of the 1990s. Unfortunately, these civil society organisations collapsed after the 1994 election, especially among the poor. This was because they had lost their central focus: the abolition of the apartheid regime. The poorer part of civil society took it for granted that the new government would automatically be its agent, and did not realise that any civil society has the continuing function of monitoring the government of the day and playing a strategic role in defining what the 'general will' is or ought to be. Perhaps the biggest setback for civil society was that many of its leaders left to occupy senior positions in government, the bureaucracy, and the corporate sector. This created administrative and leadership problems that were aggravated when many organisations encountered serious financial problems, partly because foreign donors diverted funds to the newly democratic – and legitimate – government. But the main problem was that the broader and poorer part of civil society had lost its focus, and was unable to find a new unifying purpose.

The paralysis of a large part of civil society is to be deplored from both a society-building and a social democratic point of view. A well-organised and vibrant civil society should have contributed towards building post-apartheid society, and restoring social justice. It should have conducted a lively debate on the new government's priorities and approach. The vacuum that developed as a result of the disintegration of a large part of civil society in the post-apartheid period enabled the leadership core of the ANC and the new government to enter into elite compromises with the corporate sector without justifying this to civil society. When GEAR was announced, government spokespersons stated repeatedly that the strategy was 'non-negotiable'. In this way the umbilical cord between the new government and the civil society of the struggle period was cut. From a social democratic point of view, this is a distressing state of affairs. If we want to nurture a social democratic tradition in South Africa, it is necessary to reactivate a civil society that includes the poorer half of the population, and creates the capacity it needs for its own development and critical functioning. Only then can it play its indispensable role in defining the 'general will' as a directive for social policy. Whether the new elite – and especially the intellectuals in its ranks – will be prepared to take the initiative in reactivating a broadly based civil society, in giving it consciousness, purpose and courage, and in restoring its role in society-building and in the democratic discourse, is uncertain.

Over the past year or two there have been signs of a revitalisation of civil society. In the fields of education, HIV/AIDS activism, and gay and lesbian rights, and among civil associations, youth groups, church groups, community self-help groups, societies for women, and so on, promising signs of a reawakening of civil society are visible. Unfortunately, this is occurring mainly among the petit bourgeoisie and the upper lower class, and does not really include the lumpenproletariat. This reawakening must be broadened, and should target the inadequacy of the government's poverty programmes. Given the gravity and extent of the poverty problem, and the inadequacy of the government's upliftment programmes, white and black civil society organisations among the most prosperous sections of the population ought to take the initiative in empowering the poor. Given the misdeeds committed by whites during apartheid, a special responsibility rests on their shoulders to mobilise civil society organisations among the poorer half of the population, and support them with their organisational and professional skills in the fight against poverty.

11.3.5 A new vision of what constitutes or defines social welfare

In a typically liberal capitalist country such as South Africa there is a strong tendency – especially in business circles and in the media – to equate economic growth with social welfare. It often happens that when GDP grows by, say, 3 per cent, the claim is made that 'welfare has increased by 3 per cent'. Those inclined to equate economic growth and social welfare are guilty of 'growthmanship', ie, the tendency to regard economic growth as the highest purpose of economic activity.[17] Elliot warns against this fetish as follows:

> By making the rate of growth of income per head a fetish or a talisman, we are in danger of making it also the ultimate criterion by which everything else is judged... To evaluate every part of society by its contribution to increasing the rate of growth of real income per head is to confuse means with ends... One may ask oneself whether economic growth and economic development are not becoming a new golden calf. The hysterical fascination

that the rate of growth of income per head exerts ... is infectious ... There is a danger that economic growth ... is becoming increasingly regarded as the end of economic activity (in Munby 1966: 339–40).

Paul Streeten claims that the emphasis usually put on economic growth is not justified 'without sufficiently looking at the *content* of growth, its *quality* and *composition*, the kind of things we should wish to do with the growing production, the conditions in which growth occurs, and its non-economic costs' (in Henderson 1966: 34).[18]

South Africa's GDP per capita was $3 160 in 1999, making it one of the wealthiest countries in Africa. While South Africa's population comprises only 6 per cent of that of sub-Saharan Africa, its GDP is 42 per cent that of sub-Saharan Africa. These averages mean little when we take into account the scope of *inequality* in the distribution of income in both South Africa and sub-Sahara Africa.[19] The United Nations Development Programme (UNDP) has developed a human development index by adding a certain number of socio-demographic indicators (including life expectancy, the percentage of children in full-time education, and literacy) to income indicators. In 1999 'white' South Africa was classified in 19th position (out of 173 countries), close to Germany, Italy and Denmark. By contrast, 'black' South Africa was ranked much lower, and South Africa as a whole in 110th position (see Cling 2001: 56–7). In 2002 South Africa was ranked in 107th position (out of 173 countries) – 19 positions lower than in 1990 (out of 135 countries), and 15 positions lower than in 1975 (out of 100 countries; UNDP 1999, 2002).

The great emphasis the new government has placed on economic growth as the panacea for South Africa's unemployment and poverty problems creates the impression that it has uncritically accepted the 'growthmanship' fetish and 'reductionist materialism' typical of neo-liberalism in BA countries. In questioning the government's obsession with economic growth, we are not downplaying the important contribution that a high and sustained economic growth rate *can* make – under strictly defined conditions – to South Africa as a developing country of the Poor South. On the contrary. But we have reason to be sceptical, because the 2,7 per cent GDP growth attained annually during the past eight years has not been translated into job creation, poverty alleviation, or a more equal distribution of income. It has been mainly the top 30 per cent of the population that have benefited from economic growth. Must we bargain on similar 'outcomes' of economic growth – even if a GDP growth rate of, say, 5 per cent a year is achieved – over the next eight years? If we consider the unequal distribution of power, property, and opportunities among the different classes in society, and the possibility that the government will persist dogmatically with its neo-liberal policies, this is highly likely. As long as the government remains an ideological proselyte of the corporate sector, it is unlikely that it will create socio-economic conditions in which economic growth will benefit the population at large.

We should take to heart the warning of two American economists, Stein and Denison, that:

> the importance of more rapid [economic] growth depends *critically* upon how well we allocate our output among our needs ... If our national product is *wisely* used, the contribution of a higher rate of growth would be the satisfaction of less critical needs, not of the most critical ... If [we] do not allocate [our] output to the most important uses, [we] cannot be sure that any specified rate of [economic] growth or level of output will satisfy [our] critical needs ... If we are not wise in the use of our resources we cannot expect the abundance of our resources always to compensate (in Phelps 1969: 53).

If this statement is valid for a rich country such as the United States, it is much more valid for a developing country such as South Africa.

The main thrust of Stein and Denison's argument is that any country has to decide what its most important needs are, and how it should distribute its output among its needs. These decisions cannot be exclusively entrusted to the market. The slogan that 'the market knows better' does not apply in South Africa. Many decisions currently entrusted to the dysfunctional market ought to be taken collectively through the democratic process and through continuing public discourse about what our national interest is, or what will best promote the social welfare of the society at large in the long run.

The crux of a social-democratic and humane system of democratic capitalism is that, on the one hand, the capitalist sector should allocate scarce resources as efficiently as possible and attain reasonable rates of economic growth; and on the other, the democratic sector should decide collectively – in the full glare of public scrutiny – how this output should be allocated, what society's most important needs are, and what goods and services should be provided by the government. But if, as we argue below, the capitalist sector is too strong and too influential *vis-à-vis* the democratic state, there is a real danger of it usurping the functions of the latter (in all kinds of covert ways) in deciding how our output should be allocated, and what our most important needs are.

From a social welfare point of view, this is an unsavoury state of affairs. It is quite possible that South Africa's real socio-economic problem is not the size of our GDP, but how we as a nation are using it. This, of course, was also the problem in apartheid South Africa. But at that time we did not have a democratic process and an open discourse that allowed us to reflect on the general interest and our social welfare. During the apartheid period, about three quarters of the black population was systemically exploited due to the dysfunctionality of the politico-economic system at that time. At present about three fifths of the black population are systemically neglected owing to the dysfunctionality of the politico-economic system in place since 1994.

In the last resort, a plea for a social democratic approach in South Africa is a plea for a new evaluation of and a new discourse on what defines – or what ought to define – our social welfare in a 'two world' country at a delicate stage of the transitional process. Considerations that are crucially important in this discourse are our notion of what determines the dignity and humanity of human beings; notions about the relationships between individuals and society, and what constitutes a healthy society; notions about the cultural, educational, and social values our society wishes to maintain and strengthen; notions about material wealth, how it should be used, and how the 'outcomes' of the production process should be allocated between the different groups and classes; and notions about employment opportunities in a modern society, and what the absence of such opportunities implies. When a society is as multicultural and multi-ethnic as ours, when the different groups and socio-economic classes 'share' a divided and conflicting history, and when society is divided between such a variety of groups – some rich and others desperately poor, some powerful and others hopelessly powerless, some highly developed and educated, others undeveloped and uneducated, some employed and many unemployed, some law-abiding, and many inclined towards criminality and violence – then the decision about what is and what is not in society's interest is extremely difficult. In such a situation, decisions on what constitutes or defines social welfare cannot be based on slogans or vague promises about the relationships between economic growth and poverty alleviation, and can certainly not be left to the alleged 'wisdom' of the free market. These decisions can only be taken by the democratically elected government responsible for deciding what is in the interests of society at large, and what is affordable and what isn't.

From time to time, all democratic states are confronted with the need to make *zero-sum trade-offs*. These trade-offs are particularly difficult in developing and divided societies. They are also invariably painful, and in our case exceptionally so – especially when they involve the interests of the powerful and spoilt bourgeois elite on the one hand, and those of the powerless and neglected lumpenproletariat on the other. But a democratic government cannot shy away from them.

The government will have to make the desired – ie, desired from a social democratic perspective – trade-offs between *equality* and *efficiency* (or between social justice and economic growth), and between the *social rights* of all and the *property rights* of the few. It would, however, be helpful if the democratic state were always explicit about the social values in terms of which these trade-offs are made, because only then will it be possible to know whether the trade-offs are based on value judgements or whether they are made under pressure from hidden and sectional power groups such as the corporate sector.

In a society such a ours, the discourse on the values that define our social welfare ought to be extremely vigorous. It is a discourse in which the old white intellectual elite and the new black intellectual elite should endlessly debate what the soul of the 'new South Africa' ought to be. Sadly enough, this discourse is not taking place – not nearly at the level which we so desperately need. Can it be that the intellectual elites – both the old and the new – have let down the new government and the people of South Africa in the discourse on values?

11.4 Why another power shift is necessary, this time towards a social democratic system of democratic capitalism

Eight years after the political transition of 1994, the South African version of democratic capitalism is in crisis. The most important challenge facing South Africa at this stage is to bring about yet another structural power shift in order to deepen our embryonic democratic system, and empower the government and the bureaucracy to act as effective countervailing forces against the all-powerful capitalist system. In the previous section we argued that a paradigm shift towards a social democratic ideology is a necessary, but insufficient, step in the right direction.

An ideological paradigm shift without the necessary empowerment of the democratic state would be meaningless, because the government and its bureaucracy would still be incapable of implementing an effective policy agenda along those lines. A comprehensive or structural power shift to empower the government in its relationship with the corporate sector and its global partners is a *sine qua non* for this urgently needed socio-economic transformation. The corporate sector has succeeded in prescribing the rules of the economic game in the 'new South Africa'. The government now needs to suspend this excessive concentration of power in the hands of the corporate sector.

Colin Stoneman draws an ominous parallel between Zimbabwe and South Africa, arguing that, in both cases, the transfer of political power to the majority was not accompanied by an equivalent transfer of economic or structural power to the democratic state:

> When the whites indicated willingness to surrender their monopoly of [political] power – from 1979 in Zimbabwe and from 1990 in South Africa – most international pressure seems to have been immediately redirected to ensuring that blacks did not gain a monopoly of power, *and that white economic interests should survive the loss of political power largely intact.* Herein lies the relevance of Zimbabwe's experience, because the survival of white economic power meant the closing of the hopes of the black majority, and the imposition of a range of constraints against redistribution, causing disillusion with the new government and making it ever more repressive (in Simon 1998: 91; author's emphasis).

We describe South Africa's new politico-economic system as a liberal capitalist version of democratic capitalism. The democratic part of the system (controlled by the leadership core of the ANC) is too weak, too constrained, too underdeveloped, too hesitant, and too uncertain of itself when compared with the capitalist part (controlled by the managerial elite of the corporate sector), which is too strong, too developed, too modern and sophisticated, too globalised, and too dominant.

. Our politico-economic system is an *African elite democracy cum first world capitalist enclavity.* This system cannot rectify the repression, social destruction, exploitation, neglect, and maladministration of the past 350 years. It cannot bring about the sorely needed socio-economic transformation, and cannot guarantee the long-term stability and legitimacy of South Africa's new democracy.

The hesitation and lack of confidence in the ranks of the ANC are deeply rooted in this organisation's history. During the first half of the 20th century many ANC leaders, trained in the missionary tradition of the late 19th century, looked towards the imperial 'mother country' and to the British parliament for the 'salvation' of blacks (see section 8.10). In the second half of the 20th century the ANC (together with the SACP) hoped that the Soviet Union would liberate blacks from apartheid (see section 3.3). Since the early 1990s core ANC leaders have been pressurised by the local corporate sector into accepting a collaborative relationship with the neo-liberal British-American world as the only strategy that will place the South Africa economy on a high growth path, and relieve unemployment and poverty (see section 4.2). It is, however, crucially important for the ANC to mature, and suspend its inclinations to wait for a foreign country (or group of countries) to come to South Africa's rescue. As the government of the most developed and wealthiest country in Africa, the ANC should rely on South Africa's own human and natural resources, and regard foreign aid as a bonanza.

South Africa faces a serious systemic dilemma. Its liberal capitalist version of democratic capitalism is dysfunctional because – despite its power and its privileged position – the white-controlled capitalist enclave is unable and unwilling to serve all sections of the population, unable to create enough job opportunities, and unable to alleviate poverty. Our dual politico-economic system is also dysfunctional because the African elite democracy is too unassertive; it is doing too little to create additional job opportunities, and transfer enough income from the middle classes (with 89,4 per cent of total income) to the lower classes (with only 10,6 per cent total income; see table 2.2). South Africa needs another power shift to enable the democratic government to gain enough control over the capitalist enclave to appropriately redirect economic resources and bring about the necessary redistribution of income, property, and opportunities.

It is reasonable to expect that, if the ANC government were to embark on a social democratic approach and start implementing a comprehensive redistribution programme and a truly developmental state policy, the corporate sector (and its global partners) will oppose this change in direction with all the economic, organisational, ideological and propaganda power at their disposal. The corporate sector's first line of defence may be that such a policy approach would be impractical and costly, and would not achieve the government's goals. This will be a hollow defence, because the policy approach proposed by the corporate sector has failed dismally to achieve what it promised. Whether the corporate sector and its global partners are strong enough to orchestrate a global 'crisis' for South Africa should the government decide to change ideological 'gear' is uncertain. Should such an attempt be made, it would be a serious indictment of the corporate sector's lack of patriotism, sincerity, and trustworthiness.[20]

It is quite possible that the trend towards turning the modern sector of the South African economy into a globally oriented first-world capitalist enclave has already proceeded to the point where it is no longer possible for the government to disengage from the grip of global corporatism. If South Africa has indeed become a dependent and powerless entity in the web of what Thabo Mbeki himself has referred to as 'global apartheid', the prospects for another power shift must be regarded as very slim. Then we will have to acknowledge the awful truth that South Africa was liberated from apartheid at the beginning of the 1990s with the support of the domestic and foreign corporate sectors only to become a helpless captive of global apartheid. If this is the case, it is highly unlikely that the democratically elected government will regain the political sovereignty it needs to implement a policy of social upliftment and poverty alleviation.

The second line of defence of the corporate sector may be that the neo-liberal and globally oriented approach has provided the basis for increasing the productive capacity of the economy. It could also counter a more comprehensive redistribution policy with the argument that such a policy will 'kill the goose that lays the golden eggs'. What is at stake when these kinds of defensive arguments are raised are the terms on which the trade-off between the short-term interests of the privileged minority and the long-term interests of the majority ought to take place. The corporate sector is inclined to take a myopic view of the future, and therefore inclined to 'twist' the trade-off over time in favour of its short-term vested interests. But when we consider the inhuman conditions under which the poor have to live, the urgency of addressing their predicament becomes all the more pressing. We can ill afford postponing the solution to the problem of poverty to an unspecified future date. As Keynes observed, 'in the long run we will all be dead'.

As a third line of defence, the corporate sector may claim that the elite compromises concluded between it and the ANC are sacrosanct. It may argue that these compromises saved South Africa from a bloody revolution, and that they are therefore inviolable. This is an important argument, but one that can – and should – be challenged. As we argued in detail in section 4.2, the corporate sector (with its global partners) used its extraordinary power in dubious ways to convince, coerce, or co-opt hesitant ANC leaders into accepting agreements that were not in the long-term interests of all the people of South Africa. But, more importantly, the corporate sector ought to acknowledge that these agreements – irrespective of their importance at the time – are not cast in stone. It is almost nine years since the ANC and the corporate sector entered into the first elite compromise in November 1993. The momentous consequence of that compromise was an economic policy and system that could only propose a '50 per cent solution' to South Africa's socio-economic problems. The agreement of 1993 and the GEAR strategy of 1996 laid the foundation for the systemic exclusion of the poorer half of the population. Through these elite compromises the ANC government was co-opted as a junior partner of the powerful corporate sector and its global partners, without the political sovereignty and structural power to remedy the social injustices resulting from centuries of repression and exploitation.

Another reason why the corporate sector and global corporatism cannot claim sanctity for the elite compromises is that the managerial elite has clearly ventured into the political arena without being prepared to take responsibility for what has gone wrong as a result of its ill-advised interference in economic policy. One of the core principles of a truly democratic system is that those who are responsible for wrong policy decisions have to face the music in the electoral arena. What the corporate sector has attempted over the past eight years is what Noreena Hertz calls the 'silent take-over' of the democratic state by global corporatism, on the tacit assumption that the corporate sector will remain invisible and will not be called to account for the improper political game it is playing (Hertz 2001). In the early 1990s the corporate sector and its global partners were responsible for what we can call a 'secret take-over' of the political independence of the democratically elected government, and they are neither prepared to acknowledge this 'take-over' nor to accept any responsibility for the harmful results of their deeds.

The corporate sector's excessive and unhealthy participation in economic policy formulation and implementation, and its propaganda for a free market capitalist system for South Africa should be suspended, and with it also the elite compromises on which its participation is based. Should the government succeed in disentangling itself from the ideological and structural stranglehold of the corporate sector, this should not preclude healthy co-operation between them. It is only the dominating, prescriptive, and pedantic interference of the managerial elite and its corporate economists that should be terminated. When the government becomes empowered enough to take an independent stand against the corporate sector, this should in no way imply that the corporate sector should not be given the opportunity to fulfil its proper corporate functions. As Arthur Okun has correctly stated: 'The market [or the private sector]...must be given enough space to accomplish the many things it does well' (1975: 119). If the government succeeds in 'liberating' itself from the undue influence and prescriptions of the corporate sector, it should be careful in turn not to interfere unduly in the proper affairs of the corporate sector.

South Africa needs a further power shift not only to empower the government in its interaction with the domestic corporate sector, but also to empower it in its interaction with global corporatism, and especially with institutions such as the World Bank and the International Monetary Fund (IMF). The liberalisation of South Africa's financial markets and trade, in line with global capitalism, has not been nearly as advantageous as promised by the corporate sector and its global partners at the beginning of the 1990s. On the contrary, South Africa might well have been better off if its re-engagement with global capitalism happened in a more measured and differentiated manner. The reason why globalisation has not been as advantageous as expected is the presence of unequal power and property relations in global capitalism that places a developing country such as South Africa in a rather vulnerable and exploitable position.

President Thabo Mbeki has begun to use the term 'global apartheid' – first coined by the eminent African scholar Professor Ali Mazrui – to refer to the extremely unfavourable balance of forces in global capitalism between the Rich North and the Poor South. Mbeki has described global·apartheid as 'barbaric' because of the extent to which it enriches a minority (say 20 per cent of the world's population) while impoverishing the majority. But if this is indeed the case, we must also ask serious questions about the true nature of South Africa's new politico-economic system in which only a few (say 20 per cent) live in extravagant wealth and the majority in abject poverty. (As long as the government maintains its neo-liberal approach, it is unlikely that the gap between the rich and the poor will be narrowed.) It seems as if Mbeki prefers to 'reform' global apartheid instead of reforming South Africa and its relations with global capitalism. If Mbeki can succeed in his endeavour to change the world, we will certainly inhabit a better world. But this project is too ambitious. Instead, he should concentrate his energies on changing South Africa and its relationship with global capitalism (see Bond 2001: ch 7).

11.5   An agenda for socio-economic transformation

To achieve the urgently needed socio-economic transformation over the next 10 to 20 years, the governing elite should take the initiative and accomplish the following three closely related goals:

i   It should initiate a paradigm shift by rejecting the liberal capitalist and free market ideology of the BA world as inappropriate for South Africa, and instead accept the social democratic ideology of the CE countries.

ii   It should engineer another power shift by asserting itself *vis-à-vis* the corporate elite and by implementing measures to change the power relations in our politico-economic system from a distorted and neo-liberal system of democratic capitalism into a well-balanced, social democratic, and humane system of democratic capitalism.

iii It should effect enough of a distributive shift to bring about the necessary redistribution of income, opportunities and property – over a reasonable period of time – to alleviate the worst poverty, restore social justice, and narrow the huge income and property gaps.

It is crucially important for the government to succeed at once with the paradigm shift, the power shift, and the distributive shift. Succeeding with only one or two will not be sufficient to attain the necessary socio-economic transformation. All three shifts are integral parts of a new holistic policy approach. To bring about small adaptations in, for example, the poverty upliftment policy in the absence of the much-needed paradigm and power shifts will boil down to 'playing the fiddle while Rome burns'.

11.5.1 Initiating a paradigm shift towards a social democratic ideology

The initiative for rejecting the liberal capitalist ideology and accepting an appropriate social democratic ideology as the *leitmotiv* for a new policy approach has to be taken by the governing elite. There are, unfortunately, several reasons why the governing elite may be reluctant to change its ideological approach. Understandably, it does not want to lose face, power and privilege. A long-standing debate has been raging in ANC Alliance circles over ideological and economic issues, and the governing elite will be reluctant to admit that it has been wrong all along. What is more, it is generally acknowledged that an ideological gap has opened up between the governing elite and the rest of the ANC.[21] The ideological gap between the governing elite on the one hand and COSATU and the SACP on the other is causing growing tensions in the alliance. It seems as if the governing elite has become accustomed to operating within the 'broad ideological church' of the alliance. It continues to pay lip-service to the RDP, although this programme has been sidelined – except at election times. There are, however, many points of contact between the ANC's traditional social philosophy and the ideology of social democracy, and also between Mandela's people-centred speech of May 1994 and the ideology of social democracy.

An ideological 'change of gear' by the governing elite is so important that we need to ask under what circumstances it might be persuaded to accept and implement a social democratic approach. A change in conviction can be triggered off by mounting pressure within the 'broad church' of the ANC Alliance and its supporters. There are signs that growing poverty is creating grave dissatisfaction at the grass roots and in civil society organisations. We also have reason to expect that concerted pressure will be exerted at the national conference of the ANC in December 2002 for a change in socio-economic policy, and for a further – and even dramatic – improvement in the delivery of services to those in dire need of those services. We have reached a point where the non-delivery of services should not be blamed on bureaucratic inefficiency alone, but also on the inadequacy of socio-economic policy and the amounts budgeted for poverty relief and socio-economic upliftment. In an extreme case, the government could be forced to reconsider its policy approach if the alliance breaks up or if the ANC experiences a substantial setback during the 2004 election. An important opportunity – and perhaps the last peaceful one – for the ANC to decide on a new (and hopefully social-democratic) ideological approach will be its national conference of 2007, when a new leader will be elected. For the time being, the position of the government seems entrenched owing to the loyalties forged during the liberation struggle. But blind loyalties are not worthy of a system of multiparty democracy.

The ANC could also be convinced to change its ideological orientation if its close allegiance to the corporate sector – or at least a part of the corporate sector – is soured by serious disagreements. To understand the ideological orientation of the governing elite, it is necessary to consider the nature of the ideological and structural stranglehold of the corporate sector and its global partners over the ANC's core leaders since the early 1990s. As we have shown, over the last two decades a remarkable unanimity has developed among almost all members of the corporate fraternity and its global partners about the advisability of a neo-liberal and globalised approach. But, following the dramatic decline in the value of the rand in December 2001, it seems as if a fault-line is opening up between some of the smaller corporations and some Afrikaner-controlled corporations on the one hand, and the 'commanding heights', mainly controlled by English-speakers, on the other. The first group is uncomfortable with the permission granted to some corporations to shift their main listings offshore, and have started to question the advisability of exposing the South African economy to global influences in a too undifferentiated way. It will, indeed, be much easier for the ANC to change its policy approach if important sections of the corporate sector realise that a free market approach is not the appropriate policy for addressing the inequities inherited from the extended colonial period.

11.5.2 Engineering another power shift to change the power relations in the current politico-economic system

It will certainly not be easy to change the power relations between the democratic state (controlled by the weak and hesitant governing elite) and the capitalist enclave (controlled by the powerful and arrogant corporate elite). But because of the dysfunctionality of the liberal capitalist version of democratic capitalism in South Africa, the system cannot remain the way it is. As soon as the governing elite has disentangled itself from the ideological and structural stranglehold of the corporate sector and its foreign partners, it should reclaim its sovereignty over socio-economic policy and exercise the mandate given to it by the electorate to govern the country on behalf of its impoverished and victimised constituency. The ANC's core leaders effectively 'sold' its sovereign freedom to implement an independent and appropriate socio-economic policy for a 'mess of pottage' when it entered into several elite compromises with the corporate sector and its global partners. Those unfortunate 'transactions' must now be either retracted or renegotiated. But before this renegotiation can take place, ANC leaders must re-evaluate the power relations within the ANC Alliance. As we indicated in sections 4.2 and 4.4, the leadership core of the ANC drew on international power relations and processes to shift the balance of domestic power to the right of centre. This shift will have to be reversed before the desired structural power shift in our new politico-economic system can be achieved.

It could well be easier said than done to expect the leadership core to reclaim its sovereignty, and exert its mandate. Yet this may be the only way out of the impasse. To do what has to be done will require courage and determination. The South African state is weak. It is crucially important for the ANC's core leaders to strengthen the state without making it undemocratic or authoritarian. This leadership will have to rid itself of its inferiority complex on economic matters. It is time for core ANC leaders to realise that the managerial elite and its global partners are not as knowledgeable on economic issues as they claim to be. Perhaps the most important lesson the ANC can learn from having been exposed to the 'propaganda machine' of the corporate sector is that this sector seldom has the general interest in mind, but that it is often clever enough to dress up its sectional interests in the trappings of the long-term interests of society at large. The responsibility for defining the common good cannot be left to the corporate sector and to market forces; it rests squarely on the shoulders of democratically elected political leaders. The sooner the ANC realises this basic precept of democracy, the better.

As a first step in asserting itself, the governing elite needs to rediscover its own roots and its true purpose. It must gain confidence in itself, and in its decision-making capacity. This implies that it must cleanse itself of all forms of corruption and arrogance, and account as effectively as possible to the electorate for its policies and actions. Only after improving the quality of its own governance can it build the capacity of the bureaucracy. These tasks will not be easy, but good governance and a bureaucracy with the necessary capacity are essential for the much-needed developmental state policy. Special attention needs to be paid to the inconsistencies, inefficiencies, and corruption which are rife at especially the second and third tiers of government. These malpractices are responsible for a massive waste of public funds, and a culture of non-delivery of essential services.

Secondly, the governing elite must commit itself to a truly developmental state policy. A key element of this policy must be to implement measures to reverse or counteract the strong tendency towards large, capital-intensive enterprises as well as the strong inclination towards capitalist enclavity, and the latter's tendency to detach itself from a large part of the unskilled black labour market and from a part of the black consumer market. The purpose of these measures should be to create a well-balanced and humane social democratic system of democratic capitalism. In building a truly developmental state to address the dismal legacy of colonialism and apartheid, the government will have no choice but to assume control over a far larger part of the South African economy.

It will, of course, not be easy to reverse or counteract the strong tendencies towards Anglo-Americanisation, internationalisation, globalisation, and capitalist enclavity. It will also not be possible to achieve success in these endeavours over a short period of time. It would have been much easier to counteract these trends in 1994 than in 2003. Ironically enough, the new government has – under pressure of the corporate sector – created an environment that has been exceptionally friendly to the unimpeded proliferation of these tendencies. The privilege given, for example, to some of the largest corporations to 'escape' to foreign share markets can probably not be undone. Unfortunately, it will not be possible to unscramble these – and other – scrambled eggs. Another serious problem is that the corporate sector might argue that most of these tendencies form part of global capitalism and should still be pursued in order to achieve greater efficiency – narrowly defined – and profitability in the modern world. The counter-argument is that if we allow the tendency towards capitalist enclavity to continue unimpeded, we are heading for disaster. If the trend towards a first-world capitalist enclave continues unabated for another 30 years, it is almost too ghastly to contemplate how much smaller and how much richer the bourgeoisie of the capitalist enclave will be, and how much bigger and how much poorer the lumpenproletariat on the periphery will be.

Of course, in counteracting the drive towards capitalist enclavity, the government must be careful not to compromise macroeconomic stability. But the trend towards enclavity cannot be countered without controlling the financial sector, without a savings and investment policy, and without redirecting investment in ways that will be strategically important for relieving unemployment and poverty. These measures should include far greater labour-intensive public investment that could have the additional advantage of 'crowding in' private sector investments. It should also include giving the emerging entrepreneurial class access to the capital market. To counteract the trend towards globally oriented capitalist enclavity would also require a fundamental revision of the government's liberalisation and globalisation policies. If the New Partnership for Africa's Development (NEPAD) succeeds in convincing the countries of the Rich North to supply countries in Africa with Marshall Aid – something for which a strong case can be put forward – the government ought to use these resources for developmental purposes in the true sense of the word.[22]

An important part of the strategy for reversing the tendency towards capitalist enclavity is to formulate and implement a comprehensive and appropriate employment policy. Employment in labour-intensive economic activities – especially the production of export goods – ought to be subsidised. But the government will have to become a far larger entrepreneur in public sector enterprises that are labour-intensive, and produce goods and services for the poor at affordable prices.

To counteract uneven socio-economic development, which has characterised South African history over the last 350 years, the government should spend considerably more on public works and infrastructural development in impoverished rural and urban areas by employing workers at low wages. These projects should be as labour-intensive as possible. In an attempt to increase the labour-absorptive capacity of the economy, extravagant salaries in especially the higher echelons of the private and public sectors ought to be reduced, and the inflexibilities in the labour market removed. In as far as affirmative action and equal opportunity legislation are hampering the creation of permanent job opportunities, such legislation should be revised. The government also has a large responsibility to counteract the 'peripheralisation' and 'casualisation' of a large part of the labour force, and to protect workers in the informal sector against the extreme exploitation found in this sector. To improve the productivity of the workforce, the amount spent on skills, in-service, and professional training should be increased considerably in both the private and public sectors, in a planned project to meet the demand for highly skilled and professional labour.

The strong tendency of the production processes in the modern sector to become more capital-intensive and less labour-intensive should be counteracted. This is such an important issue that the government needs to consider the appointment of a commission to investigate how rewards and penalties can be used to induce both labour and capital to reverse these trends. The tendency towards capital intensity is also linked to the rise of large conglomerates. The government should therefore formulate a comprehensive policy for counteracting the oligopolistic nature of the corporate sector. If the collusion between a few corporations that control economic activity in a multitude of economic sectors is allowed to continue, the South African economy will remain fundamentally unrestructured, and with it also the unacceptable inequalities in economic power, property, and control institutionalised during the period of extended colonialism.

Attempts to counteract the strong tendency towards capitalist enclavity will be incomplete without reconsidering the policy of overhasty liberalisation in the international flow of capital and trade. When the government embarked on globalisation, it did not properly consider the great risks involved in global capitalism's distorted power structures in favour of the Rich North, or the erratic swings in global financial and currency markets that are so harmful to developing and vulnerable countries in the Poor South such as South Africa. The government should consider the possibility that the dramatic devaluation of the rand at the end of 2001 is *systemic* in nature – ie, a problem inherent in the 'international system' in which South Africa became an exploitable entity when its foreign exchange market was 'opened up' without the necessary circumspection and differentiation.

11.5.3 Effecting a distributive shift to restore social justice

An agenda for socio-economic transformation would be incomplete without a comprehensive policy for redistributing income, property, and opportunities from the rich middle classes to the impoverished lower classes. We have explained in section 3.1.4 that a distributive shift will probably not occur spontaneously through market-led economic growth. The two distributive shifts that took place in the third and fourth quarters of the 20th century were induced by political power shifts in favour of Afrikaners and the black elite respectively. If the strong 'distributive coalition' forged between the old 'capitalist' elite and the new 'political' elite in the early 1990s remains intact, it will not be possible to effect a third politically induced distributive shift on behalf of the mainly black lower classes. The additional power shift discussed in the previous subsection should therefore be such that a new 'distributive coalition' is forged between the governing elite and representatives of civil society concerned with poverty and unemployment problems. The economic empowerment of the impoverished part of the population and the distributive shift should occur simultaneously and interdependently, and should be enthusiastically supported by the new governing elite.

A distributive shift cannot take place to the necessary degree as long as the current ideological orientation and policy approach remain in place. As in the case of unemployment, there is no point in waiting for higher rates of economic growth – in the capitalist enclave – to generate a strong enough 'trickle-down' effect to the poorer half of the population. If higher growth does materialise – in mainly the capitalist enclave – the rich will probably become even richer, and the poor even poorer. Although many corporations have social programmes, they are often limited to improving the living conditions of their employees and their families, or are used for corporate image-building. It is not realistic to think that the social programmes of all the corporations put together can ever · succeed in alleviating the dismal socio-economic conditions of the lumpenproletariat. Consequently, it is inevitable – if we are serious about the restoration of social justice – that a larger transfer of income and property will have to take place at the initiative of the government through the budget, and through land reform and property reform measures.

If the government can be persuaded to embark on a social democratic and redistributive approach, the restriction on the percentage of GDP that can be taxed – agreed to in the elite compromise of November 1993 – will have to be abolished. Lowering the budget deficit of 9 per cent of GDP in 1994 to ±2 per cent in the budget of 2002 is – from a purely fiscal point of view – a major achievement. It is, however, highly doubtful whether the implementation of such a strict or conservative fiscal policy was justifiable from a socio-economic perspective. The strict control over government spending – and especially social spending – had a very negative affect on the delivery of social and economic services to the impoverished majority.

As soon as the government accepts a social democratic approach, it will have to re-evaluate the zero-sum trade-off between *efficiency* and *equality* that is, according to Okun, the 'Big Trade-off' – not only in developed but especially in developing countries (1975). The government will have to make a new trade-off between *efficiency* (ie, leaving the capitalist enclave intact, and with it also the largely undeserved and extravagant wealth and property of the rich) and *equality* (ie, implementing measures to restore social justice to those who were victimised by exploitative systems, and held captive in the formidable grip of structural unemployment and abject poverty). In terms of this new trade-off, a larger transfer of income should take place through the budget to alleviate poverty and to narrow the alarming gap between the richest 20 per cent of households (receiving 72,2 per cent of income) and the poorest 40 per cent of households (receiving only 3,3 per cent of income; see table 2.2; figure 2.1).

But a larger transfer of income will neither address the poverty problem nor sufficiently narrow the large income and property gaps. The redistribution of income will have to be complemented by additional measures to create employment and educational opportunities, improve the 'entitlement' of the disadvantaged majority, and transfer productive property and assets from the relatively small and privileged proprietor class to the relatively large, disadvantaged, and propertyless classes in accordance with well-structured 'property reform' programmes. The lesson to be learnt from Zimbabwe is that the distribution of property and wealth – to remedy the dismal remnants of colonialism and apartheid – cannot be ignored or postponed to an unspecified date. Consequently, the government should speed up all its programmes related to education, housing, land reform, black economic empowerment, and small business development to enhance the transfer of 'entitlement' and property to blacks. It is, however, crucially important that property should not only be transferred to a small black elite. South Africa's new political democracy should be deepened by a broadly based democratisation of property and 'entitlement' rights.

The limited tax capacity of the South African economy – as a dualistic economy with a highly modern and developed capitalist enclave and a large undeveloped periphery – and the strong anti-tax culture of wealthy taxpayers (both white and black) will present the government with a difficult task in mobilising enough additional resources for a larger distributive shift. The danger that the government can 'over-tax' the economy and harm the growth and employment capacity of the capitalist enclave is a real one. The danger that higher taxation and additional property reform measures will have a disruptive effect will be greater if whites remain unconvinced of the heavy social responsibility resting on their shoulders to compensate the impoverished majority for the grave injustices committed against them (or against their ancestors) during the long period when the exploitative systems of white political domination and racial capitalism were in place. An increase in taxation and property reform programmes should be accompanied by a programme of adult education to educate whites about the true nature of South African history, and their responsibility towards the impoverished and victimised majority. Those who are opposed in principle to additional taxation and property reform should realise that the growing inequalities in these areas cannot be left unattended. It is essential for these gaps to be narrowed, not only from a social justice and a democratic perspective but also from the perspective of the legitimacy, stability, and proper functioning of the capitalist system.

It is also important that the new black elite – whose enrichment is largely artificial, and often undeserved – should realise that they too have a huge responsibility to make sacrifices for the sake of the still impoverished majority of blacks. Prominent black elite organisations ought to take the initiative in forging a new 'distributive coalition' on behalf of the poor. It would also set an important precedent if the black elite were to show greater compassion for the predicament of the impoverished black majority. It should, however, be acknowledged that the economic position of many members of the new black elite is still rather fragile, and that their extravagant lifestyles are often based on high levels of debt. But this can in the last resort not be an excuse for the indifferent attitudes of some members of the black elite towards the impoverished majority.

It is part of the harsh reality in present-day South Africa that income is being wrongly and unlawfully redistributed by means of crime, violence, and corruption. Given that fewer than 10 per cent of serious crimes are successfully prosecuted and punished, crime and corruption are paying handsomely for many criminals. These are versions of 'redistribution' that should be rooted out with an improved judicial and criminal system. Ironically, the poor are the main victims of criminality and violence. Therefore, rooting out crime and violence will – oddly – have a positive 'distributive effect' on the poor.

If the government embarks on more comprehensive redistribution and poverty alleviation programmes, it should take all the necessary precautions to ensure that redistributive spending is as effective as possible, and benefits those who need it most. Given the complexity of the problem of poverty, it will be difficult to decide on the most effective methods for transferring resources to the poor. An improvement in the existing social security system (ie, spending on welfare, health, and housing, including improvements in delivery) – along with an increase in the amount budgeted for social spending, is one possibility. It is inexcusable that almost 50 per cent of the people who qualify – or ought to qualify – for social assistance are not receiving assistance at present. If the plans to supply every household in urban areas with some free water and electricity can be fully implemented, it will indeed make a meaningful difference to the lives of the poor. Widely spread contagious diseases (and especially HIV/AIDS) are causing havoc among the poor. Improved health services and particularly food security for those affected ought to be a high priority.

Given that the monthly expenditure of 41,4 per cent of households (or 50 per cent of the population) was less than R1 000 in 1996, the government ought to seriously consider – as an urgent short-term programme – the feasibility of a basic income grant (BIG) of R100 per capita a month to at least the poorest half of the population (see table 10.3).[23] The prospects of many unemployed people finding jobs and thus wage income in the formal sector in the foreseeable future is very slim. The argument that a BIG programme is morally questionable is fallacious; to argue that the poor will become dependent and morally degraded by such a programme is an expedient excuse of the wealthy middle class. Most poor people are already morally fractured by the heavy burden of poverty and destitution, and by the absence of a better future. The argument that South Africa cannot afford the BIG or a dramatically improved social welfare and social insurance system to supply the impoverished majority with a safety net is also fallacious. What South Africans cannot afford is the coexistence of the conspicuous consumption of the few and the destitution of the many.

Endnotes

1 The International Investment Council was established in 2000 at the initiative of president Thabo Mbeki 'to draw upon the wisdom and insights of distinguished international business leaders on how to meet the challenges of economic growth and development in South Africa'. Most of the business leaders serving in the council are from highly developed countries in the Rich North. It is doubtful whether they possess the wisdom and insight needed to address economic issues in a developing and dualistic country such as South Africa.

2 Consumer spending of the poorer half of the population is less than 3,5 per cent of total spending, and a large part of this expenditure is in the informal sector.

3 We have reason to believe that, during the negotiations, some ANC leaders – especially some of those who had been exiled for a long period in first-world countries – already favoured the trend towards first-world capitalist enclavity. Having being exposed to the production and consumption patterns of highly developed countries, some of these 'exiles' may have been inclined to romanticise the developed first world. Consequently, it may have been difficult for them to appreciate the harsh reality that South Africa is a typical developing country in the Poor South with developmental problems that require a fundamentally different policy approach to those adopted in first-world countries.

4 The proportional system of parliamentary representation places the elite in control of the ANC in an extraordinarily powerful position to determine the ideological orientation and decisions of both the caucus of the ANC Alliance and the ANC's national executive committee (NEC).

5 Whereas gross domestic investment (GDI) was 30 per cent of GDP in 1970, it was 16

per cent of GDP in 1993, and has increased only marginally since then. Gross domestic savings (GDS) averaged 27 per cent of GDP in the 1960s and 1970s, dropped to an average of only 14 per cent of GDP in 1980–94, and increased only slightly to about 16 per cent of GDP in 1994–2002 (Smit, in Schrire 1992: 49–50; SARB 2002: s127). A country with such low levels of GDS and an inflow of FDI equal to only 1 per cent of GDP since 1994 cannot expect to achieve the high economic growth rate predicted by the protagonists of growthmanship and globalisation.

6 Krugman observed in 1995 that 'trade liberalisation and other market liberalisation measures are certainly good, but the idea that they are going to generate an economic take-off represents a hope rather than a well-founded anticipation'.

7 South Africa's main exports are mining and agricultural products, and semi-manufactured products in the metal and wood subsectors. Its main comparative disadvantages are in energy (petrol), and in complex industrial products: transport equipment, capital goods, and intermediary goods. South Africa demonstrates an absence of specialisation in products that are most dynamic in global trade, such as those related to information technology, machinery, and transport equipment (see Cling 2001: 109–12).

8 These corporations have justified their internationalisation by claiming that it is easier for them to finance expansion – which, they say, will also benefit the South African economy – if their main listings are moved offshore. But these corporations will inevitably reduce their investment in and commitment to South Africa. Before the new government gave in to corporate pressure to liberalise the movement of capital, it should have taken note of the fact that 40 per cent of Africa's private wealth is kept outside Africa, compared to 17 per cent in the case of Latin America, and only 3 per cent in the case of Asia.

9 According to the *Financial Mail* (Thomas 2002), job losses in manufacturing have accelerated from 1,2 per cent a year in 1992–6 to 2,65 per cent a year in 1997–2001. Given their increasing exposure to global competition, South African companies have to match global prices, volume, and quality. Consequently, they have swung strongly towards mechanisation. This trend is strikingly illustrated by the fact that, over the past 10 years, the volume of goods produced in South African factories has increased by 26 per cent, but employment has slumped by 18 per cent. There are also indications that financial institutions will retrench large numbers of staff over the next five years.

10 In a publication of the Central Committee of the SACP, 'employment' in the peripheral sector is described in the following terms: 'The unemployed are largely concentrated in the periphery of our urban areas, in informal settlements, as well as in the former Bantustan areas. They constitute the reserve army of labour that seems to be permanently reserved in the light of growing joblessness and absence of other economic opportunities. In the former bantustans they are under the rule of chiefs, therefore highly susceptible to political manipulation and are vulnerable to patronage. In the informal settlements there is a growing phenomenon of shacklords who carry out all forms of extortion against the unemployed and vulnerable workers who are seeking to retain a place to live closer to potential areas of employment or informal self-employment. It is this section of the working class that is forced to live a parasitic type of a relationship to the main urban economies of our country, thus

being highly vulnerable to criminality and all other forms of social ills of society' (SACP 2002).

11 Mhone puts this as follows: 'The self-exploitation [in the non-formal sector] is reflected in the long hours of work for low returns, in the use of child labour and women...and in the widespread depreciation of the human being as an economic asset, and in the collapse of the non-formal sector household and communal infrastructure in the face of indomitable odds against survival' (2000: 21).

12 The net effect of these reimbursements is that the predominantly white taxpayers are paying more than R60 billion less in taxes from 1 March 2000 until 28 February 2003. This amount would have made a substantial difference to poverty relief measures.

13 The acceptance of the social democratic approach does not imply that social spending as a percentage of GDP should be increased to the same level as those in CE countries. It does, however, imply higher levels of spending than that in South Africa at present (see table A.1 in appendix).

14 The resistance to change towards a more progressive approach may be less marked in Afrikaner and black business circles than in English-oriented business circles. Afrikaner and black businesses are less inclined towards 'globalisation'. In contrast with the English-speaking community, both the Afrikaner and the black communities have been exposed to poverty, and may therefore be more sympathetic towards a comprehensive poverty alleviation programme.

15 In August 2002, Mbeki commented as follows on the 51st national conference of the ANC, to be held in December 2002: 'The national executive committee took the view that the essential pillars of our (ie the ANC's) policy as decided by the 1997 and 2000 conferences remain valid and correct...An important feature of the ANC over time has been the stability of its policy position...At the heart of these is the commitment to achieve people centred development and build a caring society...This entails not only freedom from want. It also includes the critical right of the citizen to safety and security and the inviolability of every person. It also includes access to knowledge, to banish ignorance, and freedom to enjoy one's culture and language and to develop one's identity' (Mbeki 2002b). Given high and rising employment, the abject and worsening poverty of the poorest half of the population, the high levels of crime and violence, the widespread abuse of children and women, and the rapid increase in HIV infection rates, these remarks are rather puzzling. Mbeki's unwillingness to acknowledge the severity and (worsening nature) of poverty was again evident in his response to a speech by Dr Lionel Mtshali, premier of KwaZulu-Natal, in the National Council of Provinces (NCOP) in November 2002. Responding to Mtshali's concern that 'the situation in our country is rapidly deteriorating, as proven by rising unemployment, inflation, and crippling economic recession', Mbeki declared: 'I do not think it is particularly brilliant leadership to be communicating to the people a sense of gloom.' He added: 'To create something (ie, a worsening poverty situation) that does not exist and then communicate it to the people in order to project a future which is terrible and horrible, I do not think that it is a proper exercise of leadership. And I really do not think any one of us should take pride in that kind of behaviour' (Mtshali 2002; Mbeki 2002b).

16 At least three events have enabled the corporate sector to further consolidate its

position of power and privilege *vis-à-vis* the state over the past 25 years. During the last 20 years of the apartheid regime, the NP government's crisis of legitimacy enabled the corporate sector to 'sell' liberal capitalism to the beleaguered NP. This considerably enhanced the power and influence of the corporate sector *vis-à-vis* the state. The rise of global capitalism and global corporatism over the past 25 years has given the South African corporate sector a golden opportunity to use its close relationship with its global partners to further diminish the sovereignty of not only the NP but especially the ANC government. Thirdly, and perhaps most importantly, the corporate sector succeeded in the early 1990s in taking the hesitant and inexperienced ANC leadership core in tow, and concluding several elite compromises with it that have significantly diminished the new government's sovereignty.

17 Ezra Mishan claims that the tendency to identify an increase in per capita income with an improvement in social welfare is based on such precarious suppositions that it is easy to prove that 'economic growth per se is a component of policy on which the least emphasis should be placed if we are interested primarily in social welfare'. If all the tangible and intangible and all the hidden and indirect costs of economic growth are taken into account, then 'the adoption of economic growth as a primary aim of policy ... seems on reflection as likely to add at least as much "ill fare" as welfare to society' (1967: 35–7).

18 Alvin Hansen is also convinced that economists should justify economic growth in terms of social priorities: 'Economics must concern itself with something more than merely maximum output and employment. It must also concern itself with social priorities. In other words, it must, in a sense, become a branch of moral philosophy ... This is an area in which economists have been, I feel, neglectful of their duty. We need more study of social priorities' (in Phelps 1965: 1, 10). Even a growth-oriented economist such as James Tobin warns that 'economic growth has become a good word, and the better a word becomes, the more it is invoked to bless a variety of causes and the more it loses specific meaning' (1964: 1).

19 Sub-Saharan Africa has a population of 645 million people, but received only 1,1 per cent of world income in 1999. South Africa, with a population of 45 million, receives 0,46 per cent of world income, or 42 per cent of that of sub-Saharan Africa. The richest 15 million people in South Africa receive 89,4 per cent of South African income and 37 per cent of the income of sub-Saharan Africa, while the other 630 million in the latter territory receive only 63 per cent of its income (see World Bank 2000b; figure 2.1).

20 The ability and inclination of the corporate sector to hold the democratic state 'hostage' should not be underestimated. Mark Rupert describes the power of the capitalist sector *vis-à-vis* the democratic or state sector as follows: 'If a [modern] state fails to maintain conditions of "business confidence" ... investors ... may decline to invest there. In effect, they may subject the state to a "capital strike" ... depressing levels of economic activity ... and endangering the popular legitimacy of the incumbent government ... The disciplinary power [of the capitalist class] has the effect of prioritising the interests of investors, who are as a class effectively able to hold entire states and societies hostage. Moreover, the particular interests of ... [this capitalist] class are represented as if they were the general interests of all' (2000: 78–9).

21 Prof Ben Turok, an ANC MP, said in February 1999 that 'we must distinguish between the ANC as a liberation movement and the ANC in government... The ANC [in government] is [ideologically] centre right, and [the] ANC [as liberation movement] is centre left' (1999: 96).

22 Although this has not been explicitly acknowledged, NEPAD can only be in the long-term interest of African countries if it enables democratic governments to empower themselves and exert their sovereignty on behalf of their impoverished majorities. It would be tragic for Africa if NEPAD turns out to be nothing but a formula for the 'recolonisation' of Africa. The architects of NEPAD should realise that it is, in the last resort, not the inequality in the distribution of income between the Rich North and the Poor South that is decisively important, but the unequal distribution of political, military, corporate, economic, and ideological power that has 'trapped' Africa in a situation of dependency *vis-à-vis* the Rich North in the system of global apartheid. The Rich North is in a position to promote its own interests with little concern for the interests of the impoverished and powerless in Africa. Perhaps the best example of this is the fact that the Rich North spends huge amounts on internal agricultural subsidies, while Africa primarily exports agricultural products. If NEPAD fails to convince the Rich North of the need to restructure global economic relations, it is doomed to mean little to Africa's upliftment. Another deficiency of NEPAD is that it is based on the same neo-liberal principles and the same naïve optimism as the GEAR strategy. When GEAR was announced, it was presented as a panacea for South Africa's unemployment and poverty problems. Following the failure of GEAR, NEPAD is now presented as the panacea for Africa's unemployment and poverty problems.

23 Shortly before going to press, SSA released new figures showing that the deterioration in the position of the poor since 1994 is even more severe than reflected by the earlier figures used in this book. According to these latest statistics, the monthly income of the poorest 20 per cent of households declined from less than R660 in 1995 to less than R620 in 2000 (in 2000 prices), and that of the next 20 per cent of households from R660–R1 103 in 1995 to R628–R1 025 in 2000. Moreover, the monthly per capita income of the poorest 20 per cent of the population declined from less than R200 in 1995 to less than R181 in 2000, that of the next 20 per cent from R200–R393 in 1995 to R181–R336 in 2000, and that of the next 20 per cent from R392–R803 in 1995 to R336–R626 in 2000 (SSA 2002: tables 3.1, 3.2). According to SSA, these figures indicate that the poorest 50 per cent of the population were 'even poorer in 2002 than in 1995' (ibid: 28).

Appendix

The history of democratic capitalism in the liberal capitalist British-American (BA) world, and in social democratic continental European (CE) countries

Since decolonisation, and the collapse of the Soviet Union, most countries have adapted to the dual politico-economic system of democratic capitalism. It is, however, necessary to distinguish among different versions of democratic capitalism. For our purposes it is sufficient to distinguish between the version prevalent in the British-American (BA) world, based on and legitimised by the ideology of *liberal capitalism*, and the version prevalent in continental European (CE) countries, based on and legitimised by the ideology of *social democracy*.

Most of the developing countries in the Poor South (as well as countries previously part of the Soviet Union) are imitating the BA model. It is, however, debatable whether this model really suits the developmental needs of those countries. A strong case can be made that, if these countries – including South Africa – were to adopt the social democratic version of democratic capitalism, their developmental needs would be far better served.

In any country with a system of democratic capitalism, citizens are linked to the state in three ways. First, they help to create state authority. Second, they are potentially threatened by the immense power wielded by the state in maintaining order; consequently, their freedom and property have to be protected by law against the state's possible misuse of its power. Third, citizens depend on the social services provided by the state (see Offe 1996: 147–9).

We call the procedures and institutions in terms of which citizens jointly 'create' government, and 'transfer' political power and legitimacy to it, a system of representative democracy. This 'transfer' of authority by citizens (or the electorate) to the state's rulers is achieved via periodic elections in which parliaments with legal authority are elected. During an election an electorate chooses among different political parties or elite groups, and the elite group that gains the most votes is made responsible for, and given the authority to, rule the country for a certain period.

The laws and traditions in terms of which citizens are protected against the potential misuse of state power, and in terms of which freedom, security, and economic opportunity are created for them, are referred to as the legal system, or the rule of law. These laws and traditions include property and contract rights which provide the foundation for market-oriented or capitalist economic systems. While state power is indispensable for preventing social chaos, the legal order created in the western world after a long and difficult evolution is one that gives individuals and private organisations – including corporations – considerable freedom to promote their own interests within the framework of the law.

Before the rise of modern economies (ie, before 1800), individuals and households often practised isolated subsistence economies. Extended and often paternalistic families established welfare communities in miniature, which offered their members a degree of security and a minimum standard of living. However, the processes of industrialisation and urbanisation, and the rise of the modern labour market, eroded the economic independence of households to such an extent that it became necessary in the 20th century for the 'welfare state' to provide social security, particularly to those members of society at risk of becoming poor. Therefore, all modern states accept responsibility for creating and maintaining not only the legal framework that makes capitalism possible, but also the welfare system needed to maintain a healthy, just, and productive society.

T H Marshall claimed in 1949 that every person in a modern, civilised state was entitled to certain social rights, and that the state was responsible for providing them. This responsibility was only recognised fully in the first half of the 20th century. Just as, for centuries, the liberal state had assumed responsibility for protecting the *property rights* of the small propertied class, the democratic state has, since the early 20th century, assumed responsibility for providing all its citizens with *social rights*. According to Marshall, every individual has an undeniable claim to certain basic social rights for no other reason than that s/he is a human being. In a system of democratic capitalism, the state is, according to this argument, morally responsible for countering excessive individualism, greed, and the abuse of economic power – which often emerge in capitalism – by taxing the 'winners' in order to provide the 'losers' with basic social rights. Property rights can therefore not be regarded as absolute. The democratic state is responsible for bringing about a 'fair trade-off' between the 'property rights' of the minority and the 'social rights' of all (Marshall, in Held *et al* [1949] 1983: 248–59).

The tripartite link between citizens and the political, economic, and welfare components of the total social system crystallised over time into what we can call the *democratic capitalist welfare state system*. It is interesting to note that this occurred during the 18th, 19th, and 20th centuries respectively. The 18th century witnessed long struggles in western countries for equal legal rights for all citizens. This struggle was largely won by 1800, and the legal system has since then created the space for the rise of capitalism. During the 19th century a struggle took place in western countries over equal political rights for all citizens. In 1918 – after World War 1 – democracy triumphed in the west. The 20th century has witnessed the gradual rise of the welfare state in terms of which certain basic social rights are provided to all citizens.[1] The welfare state began to flourish during the third quarter of the 20th century (see Marshall, in Held *et al* [1949] 1983).

The relationship between democracy, capitalism, and the welfare state in the 'total system' of democratic capitalism is not 'fixed', but is subject to continuous change and adaptation. In our dynamic world – characterised by technological, organisational, and ideological change – the power of the capitalist sector can become too great *vis-à-vis* the other two sectors, and hence disturb the 'balance of power' to the detriment of society at large. It can also happen that the power of the democratic or welfare sectors become too great *vis-à-vis* the capitalist sector, also with negative consequences. As a result, society is continuously faced with the challenge of 'repackaging' power (in all its forms) and redefining institutions so that a sound balance of power is maintained.

We can identify four systemic periods during the past 130 years when the three components of the 'total system' – democracy, capitalism, and the welfare state – were 'institutionalised' or 'repackaged' in different patterns. We can also identify important differences among the BA and CE models.

The four successive systemic periods in the history of democratic capitalism since 1870 are:

i   the period of *laissez-faire* capitalism from 1870 to 1914, during an early phase of global capitalism;

ii the period of instability from 1914 to 1950 coinciding with two world wars, political revolutions, the rise of representative democracy, the early emergence of the welfare state, and the Great Depression;

iii the golden age, or the period of high economic growth from 1950 to 1973, comprising the first phase of the Cold War, the expansion of the welfare state, and exchange rate and employment stability under the Bretton Woods system; and

iv the period since 1973, which has witnessed the rise of global capitalism, the 'crisis' and retreat of the welfare state, and the end of the Cold War.[2]

During the first period, the system of democratic capitalism was strictly speaking not yet in place, because the franchise right was still limited to people who could meet the property qualification. The propertied classes that controlled parliament in western countries used their parliamentary power to promote the sectional interests of the upper classes to the detriment of the lower classes. Except for Germany, no western country created a welfare state in this period. Consequently, no other country, except Germany, had a social policy for alleviating the appalling poverty of many members of the lower class, and for addressing social instability and unrest. The gold standard was still in place, and in the framework of the global economy of the time, individual countries did not have the economic sovereignty, fiscal space, or political will to create a state welfare system.

The ideological approach during this period (and especially in the BA world) was that of *laissez-faire* capitalism based on a dogmatic belief in the doctrines of the neoclassical school of economics. According to these doctrines, the free market was a self-regulating system in which price adaptation would create not only microeconomic equilibrium in every individual market, but also macroeconomic equilibrium and full employment in the economy at large. Consequently, it was thought unnecessary for the state to have a social and economic policy, or to be concerned with poverty and inequalities in the distribution of income. The general ideological consensus was that the state should leave the economy to its own devices and should practise economic liberalism, or *laissez-faire* capitalism. However, unrestrained and cut-throat competition between industrialising countries played an important role in the outbreak of World War 1.[3]

The second period from 1914 to 1950 was one of relatively low economic growth owing to the disruptions caused by the two world wars, political revolutions, the Great Depression, and exchange rate instability after the abolition of the gold standard. After World War 1 most western countries accepted a system of representative democracy. The parliaments in which the lower classes gained representation started to establish welfare systems for the first time. Owing to depressed economic conditions, levels of social spending were still relatively low, except in the Scandinavian countries in which 'green–red coalitions' (between small farmers and trade unions) were responsible for higher levels of social spending. This period was nonetheless one in which all western countries experimented with a radical new relationship (or 'social contract') between democracy, capitalism, and the emerging welfare state. The role of the state – and government spending as a percentage of GDP – grew constantly as a result of the increase in social spending, and because governments accepted responsibility for providing infrastructural facilities to deal with stagnant economic conditions and the problem of cyclical unemployment (see table A.1).

In the United States, *laissez-faire* capitalism remained in place until the Great Depression (1929–33). That country only began to experiment with a new 'mix' of democracy, capitalism, and the welfare state when president Franklin Roosevelt launched his New Deal in 1933. From an ideological point of view, the second period is characterised by a multitude of conflicting ideological currents such as socialism, communism, fascism, Nazism, central planning, and statism. It was a time when serious doubts existed about the appropriateness of the political and economic systems of the time, and when each of the multitude of competing ideologies offered a different solution for the depressing social and economic problems of the inter-war period. An interesting example of the ideological turmoil of the time was Joseph Schumpeter's prediction that democratic capitalism would not survive, and would be replaced by democratic socialism ([1943] 1950).

During the third period, from 1950 to 1973, the industrialised countries experienced a golden age of high and sustained economic growth within the framework of the Bretton Woods system, with its fairly stable exchange rates. During this period the welfare state assumed its final shape, and also experienced its greatest growth.[4] This meant that the mutual relationships between democracy, capitalism, and the welfare state were 'repackaged' in such a way that considerably greater power and 'space' were allocated to the democratic and welfare states *vis-à-vis* the capitalist sector. Consequently, the state became far more involved in the 'production' and 'provision' of goods and services. The new approach was justified in terms of Lord John Maynard Keynes's persuasive arguments that *laissez-faire* capitalism should be replaced by a system of 'mixed' capitalism in which the democratic state should play a more interventionist role, that the ideology of liberalism should be replaced by a more caring one of social democracy, and that the welfare state should, *inter alia*, address the inequalities in the distribution of income that had – according to him – become an impediment to economic growth.[5]

During the third period, living standards increased dramatically in industrialised countries, income and opportunities were distributed more equally, poverty was largely eliminated, employment was maintained at high levels, and prices were kept relatively stable. Because of the success of the new 'mix' of democracy, capitalism, and the welfare state, a remarkable ideological consensus was reached on the merits of what is referred to as the Keynesian social-democratic synthesis. In sharp contrast with the previous period of conflicting ideological currents, the industrialised countries became convinced that they had found the correct 'mix', and had at long last found a formula for organising political, economic, and social life in a proper and just manner.

The sociologist S M Lipset was so impressed with this 'social contract' and with the Keynesian social democratic synthesis – on which the new system was based – that he claimed in 1963 that the western world had reached 'the end of ideology'.[6] The crux of the new approach was that a well-developed welfare state and large-scale anti-cyclical fiscal and monetary policy were regarded as indispensable for compensating not only for cyclical instability, unemployment, and market failures, but also for structural flaws, uncertainties, and unequal power and property relations endogenous to the capitalist system.

Another remarkable characteristic of this period was that, for the first time ever, the lower classes attained – within the broader framework of a politico-economic system – a bargaining position more or less equal to that of the upper classes. They did so not only through parliament and the welfare state, but also through the strong bargaining position of the trade union movement during a time of high economic growth. The strong (and perhaps too strong) bargaining position of the lower classes – as institutionalised via *mitbestimmung* (co-determination) agreements, and via wage indexing – made the system vulnerable when an economic downturn was experienced. This happened after the Egypt–Israel war, the oil crisis, the formation of OPEC in 1973, and the collapse of the Bretton Woods system.

The economic crisis of stagflation after 1973 brought the 'great ideological consensus' and the general acceptance of the Keynesian social democratic synthesis to an end. Instead of consensus, a sharp ideological polarisation developed between the neo-liberal New Right and the social democratic New Left. The New Right blamed economic stagflation on excessive government intervention, the power and lack of responsibility of the trade union movement, the 'overdevelopment' of the welfare state, and bureaucratic failure. The New Left blamed the crisis on structural factors, and claimed that the huge power in the hands of the corporate sector deprived the system of its ability to adapt to changing circumstances. The New Left continues to emphasise market failures and structural flaws in the capitalist system which, it says, make it difficult for the latter to promote social welfare in a just and balanced way.

The stagflation of the 1970s, the high levels of unemployment, wage increases that outstripped increases in productivity due to *mitbestimmung* agreements, and the sharp increase in unemployment benefits paid to the unemployed necessitated an increase in taxation in a declining economy. These circumstances created the opportunity for a popular 'revolt' against the welfare state, the power of the trade unions, statism, bureaucratic inefficiency and waste, and taxation. The ensuing ideological battle was won by the New Right, which engineered an ideological swing to neo-liberalism and anti-statism that reached its zenith during the terms of president Ronald Reagan in the United States and prime minister Margaret Thatcher in Britain. The end result of the New Right's victory and the freeing of financial markets – supported by the electronic revolution in communication – gave rise to the emergence of global capitalism. There is little doubt that the 'right-wing backlash' was excessive. Government failures and the bureaucratic waste of the welfare state were overemphasised at a time when market failures and the skewed power relations in the capitalist sector were glossed over, and, instead, highly theoretical but unrealistic models of the mainstream (or neoclassical) school of economics were presented as proof of the alleged efficiency of the free market.[7]

The ideological victory of the New Right was, and still is, sustained with evangelic zeal by the powerful corporate sector in industrialised countries, with their huge vested interest in anti-statism. The propaganda of the free marketeers, together with the rise of global capitalism after the abolition of the Bretton Woods system, enabled the higher classes – and especially the managerial elite of the multinational corporations – to consolidate their power dramatically *vis-à-vis* that of the democratic state, the lower classes, and the trade union movement. This happened to a far greater degree in BA countries than in CE countries. All these events brought about yet another 'repackaging' of democracy, capitalism, and the welfare state. In the new 'mix' the power and 'space' of the capitalist sector increased considerably *vis-à-vis* those of the democratic state and the welfare state.

As all countries became far more exposed to the relentless discipline of global markets in this period, the democratic state lost much of its sovereign power to implement an independent social policy. In all industrialised countries, these developments created a crisis for the welfare state. Most attempted to retrench the welfare state, but BA countries were more determined in these attempts than CE countries. In sharp contrast with the third quarter, the last quarter of the 20th century was a period of lower growth, chronic unemployment (especially in continental Europe), higher levels of inflation, and a sharp increase in the unequal distribution of income (especially in BA countries). While unemployment stubbornly remains at levels higher than 10 per cent in CE countries, the unequal distribution of income has increased sharply in BA countries to levels of inequality higher than those in 1950.

What is even more important is the clear difference between the way in which CE countries 'packaged' the relationship between democracy, capitalism, and the welfare state over the past 130 years, and the way in which BA countries did so. The former consistently gave the democratic state a larger, more active, and more interventionist role. CE countries consistently tend to emphasise social democratic ideology (even during systemic periods when the liberal capitalist ideology has been in the ascendant), while BA countries tend to emphasise liberal capitalist ideology (even during the systemic periods when the social democratic ideology has been in the ascendant). From 1890 to 1999, government spending as a percentage of GDP in CE countries was 7 to 12 percentage points higher than in BA countries (see table A.1). From 1890 to 1999, social spending as a percentage of GDP averaged 50 per cent or more of total government spending in CE countries, but considerably less than 50 per cent of total government spending in BA countries.[8]

Table A.1: Government spending in BA and CE countries as a percentage of GDP

	1890	1910	1930	1950	1970	1980	1992	1999	Av
Liberal capitalist countries									
UK	9,0	12,7	24,7	32,0	37,8	44,3	43,0	37,8	30,1
US	6,5	7,1	12,2	22,4	33,7	35,3	34,4	32,7	25,7
Social democratic countries									
France	14,3	15,0	21,9	29,4	37,7	43,3	52,3	48,5	33,4
Germany	12,1	15,1	29,4	29,2	36,9	46,5	48,5	44,8	33,0
Sweden	–	10,4	14,0	35,0	42,8	60,9	67,2	55,1	41,0

Source: World Bank 1997, World Development Report, Washington: table 14; oecd, Economic Outlook (62), December 1997; Cusack 1992: tables 1 and 29; oecd 2001: 36.

The differences in size of both the public and welfare sectors in CE and BA countries are not incidental, but linked to differences in the conception of the state and the market in these two worlds. According to Harrop and Dyson, France and other European countries are 'state' societies that regard state-building and the bureaucratic capacity of the state as crucially important. These countries defer to state authority, and regard state intervention in many sectors of the economy as legitimate. By way of contrast, Harrod and Dyson see BA countries as 'stateless' societies that are inherently sceptical of the right, ability, and legitimacy of the state to lead society. The corporate sector in BA countries is often even hostile towards the state, and regularly questions the latter's right to intervene in the economy. As far as the BA countries are concerned, the state is regarded as an indispensable annoyance (see Harrop 1992: 9–12; Dyson 1980).

Not surprisingly, CE and BA countries have very different views of human beings, society, the state's responsibility for supplying welfare services, the merits of the market mechanism, and what defines social welfare. According to the 'corporatist' approach of CE countries, society is regarded as an organic whole. Individuals are regarded as subordinate components of this organic entity, and their well-being depends on the well-being or health of society as a whole.[9] To complement this corporatist conception of society, France maintains an *etatistic* and Germany a *paternalistic* conception of the state. In the former approach the task of finding solutions for the social problems caused by industrialisation and urbanisation is entrusted in the first instance to the state (*etât*). The latter flows from the Prussian tradition, in which the king (or head of state) was seen as the 'father' who had a special responsibility to maintain the well-being and development of his 'children', or citizens.[10]

The contribution of the etatistic and paternalistic conceptions of the state to the rise of the welfare state in CE countries contrasts sharply with the role of the liberal or *laissez-faire* conception of the state. The BA world also maintains a different view of individuals and their relation to society. A British author, David Marquand, is concerned about what he calls the 'crisis of maladaptation' in Britain, which he ascribes to the 'possessive individualism' and 'reductionist materialism' of the British people, and their inability to conceptualise the 'common good'.[11] The atomistic view of society in Britain was neatly encapsulated when Thatcher famously declared: 'There is no such thing as society.' As far as she was concerned, all social or public issues should be reduced to the level of individuals; ie, a reductionist individualism. In the United States – with its multi-ethnic and multinational population – the notion of society is often as individualistic and as 'non-organic' as in Britain, except in time of war.

The fact that the BA countries are classified as 'anti-state' societies can be blamed partially on John Locke and partially on the popular (but incorrect) interpretation of the work of Adam Smith.[12] According to Locke, the state has only a 'night-watch' task to protect the property of the propertied class. According to the *laissez-faire* interpretation of Adam Smith, the economic activities of a market-oriented or capitalist economy will be 'organised' automatically to the benefit of all by the 'invisible hand' of the free market. The proponents of the liberal capitalist approach in BA countries are opposed to state interference in the 'automatic' or 'perfect' operation of the free market. They claim this hinders the tendency of the market – in accordance with its 'innate wisdom' – to achieve the beneficial equilibrium achieved by supply and demand. During the 19th and early 20th centuries – and again in the last quarter of the 20th century – the economic liberals claimed that, should governments introduce poverty relief programmes, they would not eliminate unemployment and poverty but in fact aggravate them. It is, however, wrong to claim that Smith advocated a political economy in which the state withholds all forms of social protection, or that he was unconcerned about the health and stability of society. The blame for dogmatic free marketeerism should be placed on the shoulders of David Ricardo, some neoclassical economists, and the protagonists of neo-liberalism.[13]

In sharp contrast to BA countries, CE countries were never enthusiastic about the liberal capitalist conception of an unrestrained market economy and its allegedly beneficial effects. Flowing from their notion of the moral well-being of society, they believe unbridled competition in 'free' markets may harm society, human relations, and moral standards. CE countries are familiar with what Schumpeter has described as the 'process of creative destruction' in capitalist countries. This process produces many winners but also many losers, and threatens traditional social values, beliefs, and institutions. The more successful an unrestrained capitalist economy is, the more destructive its social and moral implications are, and the stronger its tendencies towards concentrating wealth, power, and influence. It is for these reasons that CE countries regard the democratic and welfare states as indispensable countervailing forces against the disruptive effect of unrestrained markets.

It is illuminating to compare the circumstances under which the welfare state was introduced in CE and BA countries. The social democratic welfare state in CE countries was established on the basis of moral, social, and political considerations – ie, to protect individuals against the moral corruption accompanying industrialisation and urbanisation, and to protect society – as an organic whole – against the detrimental effects of economic progress. At the time, political authorities accepted paternalistic responsibilities for promoting social welfare. While the introduction of the welfare state in CE countries during the first half of the 20th century did not provoke strong resistance, this did occur in both Britain and the United States; in these countries the introduction of the welfare state was seen as an attack on property rights.

The idea that the government should constrain the property rights of the propertied class to enable it to provide certain basic social rights to all citizens was originally unacceptable to the propertied classes in the liberal capitalist BA world. The welfare state was introduced belatedly in BA countries, and only when widespread poverty and mass unemployment began to threaten the survival of the market-oriented capitalist system.[14] The BA countries therefore introduced the welfare state not for moral, social, and political reasons, but mainly for economic reasons, and to perpetuate the free market. The implication is that, as soon as a reasonable rate of growth is attained, and the survival of capitalism is no longer threatened, strong forces are unleashed to roll back the welfare state, as happened in Britain and the United States under Thatcher and Reagan.

Current conceptions of society and state are no longer as 'organic' and etatistic in CE countries as they were in the 19th and early 20th centuries. This can be explained by the Americanisation of the world, and the strong ideological influence exerted by the United States during the second half of the 20th century. But despite the increased influence of the liberal capitalist approach of the BA world in CE countries, it is not possible to explain the present differences of approach to economic systems and policies between CE and BA countries without taking into account the traditional differences between these two 'worlds'. It is because of these different conceptions that the welfare state is larger and more developed in CE than in BA countries. The governments in CE countries play a more interventionist role in their economies, and assume greater responsibility for the victims of structural unemployment and structural poverty, and their taxpayers are more prepared to carry the burden of unemployment insurance.

The persistent belief in the BA world in the efficiency of the market, and the persistent hostility to the state, is puzzling. The dogmatic belief in the merits of the market during the first and fourth quarters of the 20th century was based on the neoclassical doctrine that competitive markets not only 'clear' all markets (ie, automatically harmonise supply and demand via price adjustments), but also allocate resources efficiently. Despite the huge legitimacy crisis experienced by this school of thought in the middle two quarters of the 20th century – ie, during the Great Depression and the early years of the Cold War – the alleged efficiency of the market was 'rediscovered' in the BA world in the 1970s and 1980s, and enthusiastically propagated by multinational corporations in particular in order to legitimise their power and influence, and to foment distrust in 'wasteful' state intervention. The World Bank and IMF used their strategic position as purveyors of development assistance to developing countries to give almost sacrosanct status to the alleged efficiency and growth-promoting capacity of free market capitalism; their combined stance became known as the 'Washington consensus'. With the co-operation of the Washington institutions, the corporate sector in the United States succeeded in exporting not only the free market ideology but also a highly idealised (and therefore unrealistic) version of the American economic model to Europe and the developing world, irrespective of its relevance for those countries.

The large gap between the myth of the free market and its workings in reality – even in the United States – can only be explained by the fact that neo-classical economics has exchanged its analytical thrust for an ideological one.[15] While it pretends to be concerned with efficient allocation and choice, it uses the 'beauty' of its theoretical model to legitimise the limitless accumulation, power, and prestige of the corporate sector in developed countries. Instead of continuing the quest for knowledge, neoclassical economics have begun to market the liberal capitalist economic system as some kind of 'perfect construct', propelled by natural laws.

Several economists have argued convincingly that competitive markets are not necessarily efficient, and may not necessarily optimise economic growth. But the main defect of a purely competitive market (assuming that this can ever be realised) is its moral weakness. For even if entirely free markets were to produce efficient outcomes (which is highly unlikely), these outcomes would probably not be socially justifiable, and also fail to coincide with the definition of social welfare expressed through the democratic process. Przeworski is correct when he claims that 'the present state of economic theory does not support the conclusion that competitive markets are sufficient either to allocate resources efficiently or to generate growth... The notion that the market by itself can efficiently allocate scarce resources is purely hortatory' (1992: 49).[16] Given the limits of the market – which is obviously far less efficient in developing countries – there is indeed merit in Okun's balanced statement on democratic capitalism:

> The market needs a place, and the market needs to be kept in its place. It must be given enough scope to accomplish the many things it does well. It limits the power of the bureaucracy and helps to protect our freedoms against the transgression of the state... most importantly, the prizes in the market place provide the incentives for work effort and productive contribution... But the market needs to be kept in its place... [because] given the chance, it would sweep away all other values, and establish a vending machine society. The rights and powers that money should not buy must be protected with detailed regulation and sanctions, and with countervailing aids to those with low income... In a democratic capitalist society... we need democracy and capitalism... [and] they need each other to put some rationality into equality and some humanity in efficiency' (1975: 119–20).

Closely connected with the liberal capitalist belief that free market capitalism allocates scarce resources efficiently and that it promotes economic growth is the liberal capitalist notion that economic growth – or, more correctly, the level of per capita GDP – is a good (or even a satisfactory) index of the level of social welfare of a country. This disposition betrays a blatant materialistic and individualistic notion of what constitutes the social welfare or the general interest of a country. An important difference between the liberal capitalist approach of the BA world and the social democratic approach of CE countries is the inclination of the first to translate every dimension of social progress or retrogression into measurable money terms. In turn, CE countries strongly favour *multidimensional* – and often not quantitatively measurable – indicators of social welfare. Those who believe in the 'collective wisdom' of the market are satisfied that market prices represent true values and that the 'sum' of all market prices and goods represents 'social value' as expressed in GDP.[17] This approach is also visible in what Marquard calls the 'reductionist materialism' and 'possessive individualism' in Britain.[18] The crux of the social democratic approach in CE countries is that the market cannot be trusted to promote all the indicators that collectively determine the 'multidimensional' entity that represents or defines the social welfare of society at large. In line with this approach, the state has the essential task of defining, via the democratic process, what the common purpose of society is, and which collective goods, services, and non-marketable rights it has to supply to promote the social welfare in as balanced a way as possible.

In fulfilling its task, neither the state nor the democratic process is perfect. As the market is prone to 'failures', the state and the democratic process are also prone to all sorts of 'democratic' and 'bureaucratic failures'. But these failures can never be an excuse for substituting the market for the state or the democratic process. As indicated in section 1.5, the democratic state and the capitalist system are based on conflicting 'logics', and each has its own function to fulfil. Given these conflicting logics, the market cannot do what the state is supposed to do, and the state cannot do what the market is supposed to do – with some grey areas in between. The power of each has to 'counteract' that of the other. The state and the market can also act – as far as this is desirable – to compensate for 'market' and 'bureaucratic failures'. But this does not imply that the capitalist system can be substituted for the state, as liberal capitalists often propose. Whenever the functions of the state are transferred to the market – with its different 'logic' – the 'outcome' will almost certainly be an even greater failure.

As noted earlier, the remarkable feature of the golden age (1950–73) was that all the industrialised countries benefited from *positive-sum trade-offs*: economic growth rates were high; prices, exchange rates, and societies were relatively stable; full employment was maintained; income was distributed more equally; and poverty was largely eradicated. In sharp contrast, the era since 1973 has been one of stagflation (until the mid-1980s), growing unemployment, and widely fluctuating exchange rates, while income has become distributed more unequally in mainly the BA world.[19] In these circumstances all industrialised countries were confronted with having to make *negative-sum* trade-offs.[20] Perhaps the most important influence on the ability of individual countries to implement independent social security and redistribution programmes is the rise of the global economy.

The way in which the liberal capitalist BA and social democratic CE countries have managed both the negative-sum trade-off problem and their diminished sovereignty within the framework of global capitalism over the last 25 years clearly reveals their different values and ideological orientations. In the trade-off between economic growth and job creation on the one hand, and the maintenance of social rights (including the right to unemployment insurance) on the other, CE countries have consistently chosen the latter, and the BA countries the former.[21] Consequently, during the past 25 years, the income has been distributed fairly equally in CE countries, but far more unequally in BA countries.[22] While CE countries realise that the glory days of high growth, extravagant welfare benefits, and lifelong jobs are probably gone for ever, they are nonetheless not prepared to accept the American model with its economic brutalities and social fractures. Because of these countries' more humane view of labour, they regard the low wages and poor conditions under which Americans must perform their 'junk' or 'lousy' jobs as undignified. The United States – and, to a lesser extent, Britain – are prepared to 'buy' job creation with lower wages, lower social expenditure, and growing inequalities.[23] In 1997, *Time* reported that 'Europeans remain convinced that the welfare state is the right path for them. Europeans are not about to trade in their hard-won model of social justice for the hazards and inequalities of the US-style free market'.[24]

Przeworski comes to the important conclusion that

> statistical analysis of OECD countries [comprising BA and CE countries] has shown repeatedly that lower income inequality, more extensive welfare services, a more favourable trade-off between employment and inflation, and a more favourable trade-off between growth and social policies are to be found in countries that combine strong unions with social democratic control over the government...The only countries in the world in which almost no one is poor after taxes and transfers are those that pursue social democratic policies (1992: 54).

We can therefore conclude that in developed countries with a strong social democratic approach, the 'democratic' part of the system of democratic capitalism will be well developed and relatively strong *vis-à-vis* the 'capitalist' part; the welfare state will be more developed, and income more equally distributed; and their levels of social welfare will probably be higher than those in liberal capitalist countries with the same – and even higher – levels of per capita GDP.

Endnotes

1 It is disturbing to note that, before 1990–4, South Africa still did not have a fully representative democratic system (with political rights for all), a legal system that guaranteed property and contract rights for all, or a fully fledged welfare system that supplied basic social rights to all. While political, judicial, and social rights for all developed in the western world over more than 300 years, South Africa faces the enormous task of developing these three rights for all after 1994.

2 Economic growth per capita of 16 leading member countries of the OECD averaged 1,6 per cent a year in the first period, 1,2 per cent a year in the second, 3,8 per cent a year in the third, and 2,5 per cent a year in the fourth (see Maddison 1989: 32).

3 Keynes put it as follows: 'Under the system of domestic laissez-faire and an international gold standard [in the late 19th and early 20th century] ... there was no means open to a government whereby to mitigate economic distress at home except through the competitive struggle for markets [as was experienced before the First World War]' ([1936] 1949: 382).

4 The social expenditure of 21 OECD countries rose from 12,3 per cent of GDP in 1960 to 24,6 per cent of GDP in 1985. Even after the decline of GDP after 1973, social expenditure continued to rise primarily because of the higher unemployment insurance that had to be paid out. Although social expenditure (expressed as a percentage of GDP) peaked in 1985, the idea of the welfare state peaked in the early 1970s.

5 Keynes put it as follows: 'In contemporary conditions the growth of wealth, so far from being dependent on the abstinence of the rich, as is commonly supposed, is more likely to impede. One of the chief [economic] justifications of great inequalities is therefore removed' ([1936] 1949: 473).

6 The policies of political parties to the left and right of the ideological spectrum (for example, the Labour and Conservative parties in Britain) were so similar that it was pointed out in jest that both of them were guilty of 'me-too-ism' on almost every policy issue.

7 According to Heilbroner and Milberg, 'the mark of modern-day economics [ie, the neo-classical school] is its extraordinary indifference ... [to] the connection between theory and "reality" ... The "high theorising" of the present period attains a degree of unreality that can be matched only by medieval scholasticism' (1996: 3–4).

8 Since 1960 government expenditure in the United States has been 3–7 percentage points lower than the average for OECD countries. If we also take into account that

American spending on defence (primarily to maintain its nuclear capability) has been ±7 per cent of GDP, while the average spending on defence of 15 industrialised countries has only been 3,1 per cent of GDP, then government expenditure in the United States (excluding expenditure on defence) has been 7–11 percentage points lower than most EC countries. The lower level of government expenditure in the United States must be ascribed in the first instance to the fact that the liberal capitalist ideology is particularly strong in that country, and that its welfare system is weakly developed compared to those of other western countries. In the second place it must be ascribed to the fact that 55 per cent of welfare in the United States is financed by the public sector, and 45 per cent by the private sector, while the public sector in Europe bears 80 per cent of the burden and the private sector only 20 per cent.

9 This kind of corporatist or 'organic' view of society was accepted as natural in the feudal and medieval period dominated by the church. The mutual societies formed by the guilds were also based on this view. The conception of society of the Roman Catholic Church is also that society is an organic whole in which all members owe one another mutual loyalty and moral responsibility, and in exchange for this can claim certain social rights and privileges. In terms of this approach, all forms of excessive individualism and materialism and relentless competition are see as a threat to the 'health' and 'coherence' of the organic or corporate 'body', and hence as a threat to the (moral) well-being of the individuals concerned (see Esping-Andersen 1990: 89).

10 It is therefore not surprising that Germany already launched its welfare state in the 1880s. It is also not surprising that the paternalistic Prussia instituted compulsory state education in 1806, while in liberal Britain a system of compulsory education was only introduced in 1902.

11 Marquand also states: 'If we [in Britain] are told repeatedly that society is made up of atomistic individuals driven by self-interest, and pursuing individually chosen goods – that the notion of a common good is a sentimental fantasy, and the notion of politics as a process of deciding what should count as the common good, either absurd or potentially tyrannical – we may come to believe it; and if we believe it, we may start to behave, in some small but destructive degree, as though it were true' (1988: 214–18).

12 According to Przeworski et al, 'the principal mistake of neo-liberal prescriptions is that they underestimate the role of the state institutions in organising both the public and the private life of groups and individuals. If democracy is to be sustained, the state must guarantee territorial integrity and physical security, it must maintain the conditions necessary for an effective exercise of citizenship, it must mobilise public savings, co-ordinate resource allocation and correct income distribution' (1995: 12).

13 Esping-Andersen puts it as follows: 'It was among Ricardo and other *laissez-faire* popularisers that the pure commodification form [of labour] was sanctified. From a welfare perspective, their argument was a double one. First, they held that a guaranteed social minimum [for the poor] would cause poverty and unemployment, not eradicate it – an argument that has found new life in recent neo-liberalism [cf Milton Friedman]. Second, to them social protection caused moral corruption, thriftlessness, idleness, and drunkenness' (1990: 41).

14 The first (limited) social legislation was enacted in Britain in 1909. The welfare system grew very slowly until 1945, when Attlee extended it considerably. Thatcher tried her best to reduce the welfare state to pre-World War 2 levels. In the United States a 'welfare state' was only introduced in 1933 amid mass unemployment. The New Deal was extended by president Lyndon Johnson's Great Society in 1965, but the welfare state in the United States today is not nearly as well developed as it is in CE countries.

15 Michael Ignatieff says correctly that 'Europeans like to think of the American model as *laissez-faire*, red in tooth and claw, but it is actually a form of state capitalism in which the great corporations of the military-industrial complex fatten on the largesse of the state, while the poor and disadvantaged [in the USA and in the rest of the world] get a firm dose of *laissez-faire*' (*The Observer*, 15 September 1991).

16 Stiglitz puts it as follows: 'Externalities (such as associated with pollution or innovations) and public goods are not the only factors that create stumbling blocks for an otherwise market efficient economy. Imperfect information and incomplete markets – an extremely common condition – have been added to the list of factors which give rise to problems in the market economy' (1998: 3).

17 According to Alex Rubner, there is no such a linear link between the size of GNP and the utility or welfare people derive from it, as is conventionally believed: 'A fundamental appraisal of the conventional GNP must centre on its divergence from the *social product*, ie, the failure of the GNP tool to draw a comprehensive picture of the total human happiness generated by the efforts of a given society within a stated time span. The conventional GNP is, however, also open to the prosaic criticism that it fails to provide accurate welfare measurements for even those human endeavours the output of which it purports to record. The (money) values of which the GNP is made up are not uniformly oriented links with the utilities people derive from them' (1970: 61).

18 Marquand claims that 'the notion that politics is, or should be, a process through which a political community agrees on its common purposes is nonsensical [in the British approach as moulded on the ideas of Jeremy Bentham]. The community, in Jeremy Bentham's cutting phrase, is a "fictitious body". Politics is about reconciling conflicts between individually chosen purposes... [Consequently] it has no business with the choice of [the public] purposes' (1988: 214).

19 While the average rate of GDP growth in OECD countries in the 1960s was 5 per cent, it was 3,6 per cent in the 1970s, 2,8 per cent in the 1980s, and 2,0 per cent from 1990 to 1995 (Thurow 1996: 1).

20 The transition of the so-called industrial to the post-industrial society in highly industrialised countries that took place from 1960 onwards further complicated the trade-off problem. With the rise of post-industrial society and the changing nature of job opportunities, the fear has arisen 'that high-technology economics can satisfy our wants, but not our need to work' (Esping-Andersen 1990: 191–2).

21 Despite an unemployment rate higher than 10 per cent, the taxpayers in CE countries remain prepared to pay the taxation necessary for unemployment benefits. In sharp contrast, almost all such benefits have been abolished in the United States.

22 According to Thurow, the benefits of the higher growth rate in the United States went mainly to the richest 20 per cent of the American population. During the 1980s

the richest 1 per cent pocketed no less than 64 per cent of the greater earnings. The net result of this is that not only income but also property was distributed far more unequally in 1995 than in 1973. The net wealth of the richest 0,5 per cent of the American population rose from 26 per cent in 1983 to 31 per cent in 1989. The net wealth of the richest one per cent in 1920 was about 44 per cent of total wealth. In 1975 it dropped to 22 per cent and in 1990 rose once again to 44 per cent (Thurow 1996: ch 1).

23 Social security and health expenditure in Germany as a percentage of GDP has decreased from 25,4 per cent in 1980 to 23,5 per cent in 1990, but remains less than 15 per cent in the United States (Esping-Andersen 1996: 71).

24 *Time* quotes Andreas Schockenhoff, a member of the German Bundestag, as saying: 'Nobody in Germany would seriously propose abolishing the welfare state. This is a model not of our economy, but of our very society. We don't want to abolish it; we want to bring it up to date. The problem (according to *Time*) is that, while Americans are used to performing with the flimsiest of social safety nets, Europeans have grown accustomed to – and some argue, unhealthily dependent on – the providential hand of government' (8 December 1997).

References

References

Adam, H. 1971. *Modernizing racial domination: South Africa's political dynamics.* Berkeley: University of California Press.

Adam, H; Slabbert, F Van Z; and Moodley, K. 1997. *Comrades in business: post-liberation politics in South Africa.* Cape Town: Tafelberg.

Adelzadeh, A. 1996. From the RDP to GEAR: *the gradual embracing of neo-liberalism in economic policy.* Occasional Paper No 3. Johannesburg: National Institute for Economic Policy (NIEP).

African National Congress. 1992a. *Negotiations: a strategic perspective.* Johannesburg. November.

———. 1992b. *Ready to govern.* Johannesburg.

———. 1994. *The Reconstruction and Development Programme: a policy framework.* Johannesburg: Umanyano.

Amadiume, I; and Abdullahi, A (eds). 2000. *The politics of memory: truth, healing and social justice.* London: Zed Books.

Archives yearbook for South African history, vol 2. 1939. Pretoria: Government Printers.

Armstrong, J C; and Worden, A. 1989. The slaves, 1652–1834. In Elphick and Giliomee (eds). *The shaping of South African society, 1652–1840.*

Arndt, E H D. 1928. *Banking and currency development in South Africa, 1652–1927.* Cape Town: Juta.

Atmore, A; and Marks, S. 1974. The imperial factor in South Africa in the nineteenth century: towards a reassessment. *Journal of Imperial and Commonwealth History,* 3.

Barchiesi, F. 1999. Socio-economic exploitation, meaning contestation, and the TRC: problematic foundations for a discourse of social citizenship in post-apartheid South Africa. Paper presented to the international conference on the TRC: commissioning the past, University of the Witwatersrand, 11–14 January 1999.

Barker, F. 1999. *The South African labour market, a critical issue for renaissance.* Pretoria: J L van Schaik.

Baskin, J (ed). 1996a. *Against the current: labour and economic policy in southern Africa.* Johannesburg: Ravan Press.

———. 1996b. The social partnership challenge. In Baskin (ed), *Against the current: labour and economic policy in southern Africa.*

Beinart, W; and Delius, P. 1986. Introduction. In Beinart *et al* (eds). *Putting a plough to the earth: accumulation and dispossession in rural South Africa.*

Beinart, W and Dubow, S (eds). 1995. *Segregation and apartheid in twentieth-century South Africa.* London: Routledge.

Beinart, W; Delius, P; and Trapido, S (eds). 1986. *Putting a plough to the earth: accumulation and dispossession in rural South Africa.* Johannesburg: Ravan Press; London: James Currey.

Benyon, J. 1986. The Cape Colony, 1854–1881. In Cameron (ed). *An illustrated history of South Africa.*

Bhorat, H; and Hodge, J. 1999. Decomposing shifts in labour demand in South Africa. *The South African Journal of Economics,* 67 (3).

Black, P. 2002. On the case for black economic empowerment in South Africa. Presidential address to the Economic Society of South Africa, September.

Black Empowerment Commission (BEECom). 2001. *A national integrated black economic empowerment strategy.* Johannesburg: Skotaville.

Blumenfeld, J. 1997. *From icon to scapegoat? The experience of South Africa's Reconstruction and Development Programme.* London: Brunel University.

Boeyens, J C A. 1994. Black ivory: the indenture system of slavery in Zoutpansberg, 1848–1869. In Eldredge and Morton (eds). *Slavery in South Africa: captive labor on the Dutch frontier.*

Bond, P. 1999. *Elite transition: from apartheid to neoliberalism in South Africa.* Pieter-maritzburg: University of Natal Press; London: Pluto Press.

——. 2001. *Against global apartheid.* Cape Town: University of Cape Town Press.

Bonner, P; Delius, P; and Posel, D. 1993. *Apartheid genesis: 1932–1962.* Johannesburg: Ravan Press.

Bornstein, L. 2000. Institutional context. In May (ed). *Poverty and inequality in South Africa.*

Boucher, M. 1986. The Cape under the Dutch East India Company. In Cameron (ed). *An illustrated history of South Africa.*

Bredenkamp, H C. 1986. The pre-colonial and colonial Khoikhoi. In Cameron (ed). *An illustrated history of South Africa.*

Budlender, D. 2000. Human development. In May (ed), *Poverty and inequality in South Africa.*

Bundy, C. 1975. The abolition of the Masters and Servants Act. *South African Labour Bulletin,* 2 (1).

——. 1986. Vagabond Hollanders and runaway Englishmen: white poverty in the Cape before poor whiteism. In Beinart *et al, Putting a plough to the earth: accumulation and dispossession in rural South Africa.*

——. 1988. *The rise and fall of the South African peasantry.* 2nd edition. London: Heinemann.

——. 1992. Developments and inequality in historical perspective. In Schrire (ed). *Wealth and poverty? critical choices for South Africa.*

——. 1993. Challenging the past: South Africa in historical perspective. In Gentili (ed). *Sudafrica: processi di mutamento politico & constituzionale.*

Bureau of Economic Research (BER), 2000. Research Note 8. University of Stellenbosch.

——. 2001. *The macroeconomic impact of HIV/AIDS in South Africa.* University of Stellenbosch.

Caldwell, D. 1989. *South Africa: the new revolution.* Saxonwold: Free Market Foundation of South Africa.

Calitz, E. 1986. Aspekte van die vraagstuk van staatsbestedingsprioriteite met spesiale verwysing na die Republiek van Suid-Afrika: 'n funksionele ekonomiese ondersoek. Unpublished DPhil thesis, University of Stellenbosch.

Cameron, T (ed). 1986. *An illustrated history of South Africa.* Johannesburg: Jonathan Ball.

Cawker, G; and Whiteford, A. 1993. *Confronting unemployment in South Africa.* Pretoria: HSRC.

Cell, J. 1982. *The highest stage of white supremacy: the origins of segregation in South Africa and the American South.* Cambridge: Cambridge University Press.

Central Statistical Services. 1995. *South African Labour Statistics.* Pretoria.

Clark, N L. 1994. *Manufacturing apartheid: state corporations in South Africa.* New Haven: Yale University Press.

Cling, J P. 2001. *From isolation to integration: the post-apartheid South African economy.* Pretoria: Protea Book House and Institute Francais á Africa du Sud (IFAS).

Cobbett, W; Glaser, D; Hindson, D; and Swilling, M. 1986. South Africa's regional political economy: a critical analysis of reform strategy in the 1980s. In *South African Review* no 3. Johannesburg: Ravan Press.

Coetzer, P W. 1986. The end of apartheid, 1948–1961. In Cameron (ed). *An illustrated history of South Africa.*

Cole, K; Cameron, J; and Edwards, C (eds). 1991. *Why economists disagree: the political economy of economics.* London: Longman.

The Commission of Inquiry into Matters Concerning the Coloured Population Group (the Theron commission). 1976. RP38/1976. Pretoria.

Congress of South African Trade Unions (COSATU). 1996. Social equity and job creation. Johannesburg.

Crais, C. 1992. *The making of the colonial order: white supremacy and black resistance in the Eastern Cape, 1770–1865.* Johannesburg: Witwatersrand University Press.

——. 1994. Slavery and emancipation in the Eastern Cape. In Worden and Crais (eds). *Breaking the chains: slavery and its legacy in the nineteenth century Cape Colony.*

Crush, J; Jeeves, A; and Yudelman, D. 1991. *South Africa's labor empire: a history of black migrancy to the gold mines.* Boulder: Westview Press.

Cusack, T R. 1992. *The changing contours of government.* Berlin: The International Relations Research Group.

Dahl, R A. 1956. *A preface to democratic theory.* Chicago: University of Chicago Press.

——. 1985. *A preface to economic democracy.* Cambridge: Polity Press.

——. 1992. Why free markets are not enough. *Journal for Democracy,* 3 (3).

Davenport, T R H. 1991. *South Africa: a modern history.* London: Macmillan.

Davenport, T R H; and Saunders, C. 2000. *South Africa: a modern history.* London: Macmillan.

Davidson, B. 1994. *The search for Africa.* London: James Currey.

Davidson, B; Slovo, J; and Wilkenson, A (eds). 1976. *Southern Africa: the new politics of revolution.* London: Penguin.

Davies, R H. 1979. *Capital, state and white labour in South Africa.* Brighton: Harvester Press.

De Bruyn, J T. 1986. The Great Trek. In Cameron (ed). *An illustrated history of South Africa.*

De Kiewiet, C W. 1941. *A history of South Africa, social and economic.* Oxford: Clarendon.

De Kock, V. 1950. *Those in bondage.* Cape Town: Allen & Unwin.

De Schweinitz, R. 1964. *Industrialisation and democracy.* London: Free Press of Glencoe.

De Villiers, A P. 1996. *Effektiwiteit van Suid-Afrika se onderwysstelsel: 'n ekonomiese analise.* Unpublished PhD thesis, University of Stellenbosch.

De Villiers, R. 1978. Afrikaner nationalism. In Wilson and Thompson (eds). *The Oxford history of South Africa,* vol 2.

Department of finance. 1993. *The key issues in the Normative Economic Model.* Pretoria.

——. 1996. *Growth, employment and redistribution: a macro-economic strategy.* Pretoria.

——. 2000. *Budget Review.* Pretoria.

Department of trade and industry (DTI). 2000. Database. South Africa.

Depelchin, J. 1996. From the end of slavery to the end of apartheid: towards a radical break in African history. In *Comparative studies of South Asia, Africa, and the Middle East,* XVI (1).

Diamond, J. 1997. Guns, germs and steel: the fate of human society. New York: W W Norton and Co.

Domar, E D. 1970. The causes of slavery or serfdom: a hypothesis. *Journal of Economic History,* 30 (1).

Du Plessis, L J. 1964. *'n Volk staan op.* Cape Town: Human and Rousseau.

Dubow, S. 1987, Race, civilisation, and culture: the elaboration of segregationist discourse in the inter-war years. In Marks and Trapido (eds). *The politics of race, class and nationalism in twentieth century South Africa.*

——. 1989. *Racial segregation and the origins of apartheid in South Africa, 1919–1936.* London: Macmillan.

——. 1995. The elaboration of segregationist ideology. In Beinart and Dubow (eds). *Segregation and apartheid in twentieth-century South Africa.*

Dugard, J. 1980. Racial legislation and civil rights. In Hellmann and Lever (eds). *Race relations in South Africa, 1929–1979.*

Dyson, K H F. 1980. *The state tradition in western Europe.* Oxford: Robertson.

Economist, The. 2001. South Africa sets a stable, but in some ways disappointing, example. 24 February.

Edgecombe, R. 1986a. The Mfecane or Difagane. In Cameron (ed), *An illustrated history of South Africa.*

——. 1986b. Natal: 1854–1887. In Cameron (ed), *An illustrated history of South Africa.*

Eldredge, E A; and Morton, F (eds). 1994a. Delagoa Bay and the hinterland in the early nineteenth century: politics, trade, slaves and slave raiding. In Eldredge and Morton (eds), *Slavery in South Africa: captive labor on the Dutch frontier.*

——. 1994b. Slave raiding across the Cape frontier. In Eldredge and Morton (eds), *Slavery in South Africa: captive labor on the Dutch frontier.*

——. 1994c. *Slavery in South Africa: captive labor on the Dutch frontier.* Pietermaritzburg: University of Natal Press.

Elliot, C. Ethical issues in the dynamics of economic development. In Munby (ed). *Economic growth in world perspective.*

Elphick, R. 1985, Kraal and castle: *Khoikhoi and the founding of white South Africa.* New Haven: Yale University Press.

Elphick, R; and Giliomee, H (eds). 1989. *The shaping of South African society 1652–1840.* Cape Town: Maskew Miller Longman.

Elphick, R; and Malherbe, V C. 1989. The Khoisan to 1828. In Elphick and Giliomee (eds). *The shaping of South African society 1652–1840.*

Elphick R; and Shell, R. 1989. Intergroup relations: Khoikhoi, settlers, slaves and free blacks, 1652–1795. In Elphick and Giliomee (eds). *The shaping of South African society 1652–1840.*

Esping-Andersen, G. 1990. *The three worlds of welfare capitalism.* Cambridge: Polity Press.

——. (ed). 1996. *Welfare states in transition: national adaptations in global economies.* London: Sage.

Fallon, P R. 1992. *An analysis of employment and wage behavior in South Africa.* Washington: World Bank, Southern African Department.

Fernández-Armesto, F. 1997. *Truth, a history.* London: Black Swan.

Fine, B. 1994. Politics and economics in ANC economic policy: an alternative assessment. *Transformation,* 25.

——. 1995. Privatisation and the RDP: a critical assessment. *Transformation,* 27.

Franzsen, D G. 1983. Monetary policy in South Africa, 1932–82. *The South African Journal of Economics,* 51 (1).

Freund, B. 1999. The weight of history: the prospects for democratisation in South Africa. In Hyslop, J (ed). *African democracy in the era of globalisation.* Johannesburg: Witwatersrand University Press.

Freund, W M. 1989. The Cape under the transitional governments, 1795–1814. In Elphick and Giliomee (eds), *The shaping of South African society 1652–1840.*

Galbraith, J K. 1977. *The age of uncertainty.* London: BBC, André Deutsch.

Gelb, S (ed). 1991. *South Africa's economic crisis.* Cape Town: David Philip.

——. 1999. The politics of macroeconomic policy reform in South Africa. Paper presented to the conference on democracy and the political economy of reform, Cape Town, 16–18 January.

Gentili, A M. 1993. *Sudafrica: processi di mutamento politico e constituzionale.* Rimini: Maggiole Editore.

Giliomee, H. 1989. The eastern frontier, 1770–1812. In Elphick and Giliomee (eds), *The shaping of South African society 1652–1840.*

Greenberg, S B. 1987. *Legitimating the illegitimate state, markets and resistance in South Africa.* Los Angeles: University of California Press.

Grosskopf, J F W. 1932. *The poor white problem in South Africa.* Report of the Carnegie Commission. Part I. Economic report: Rural impoverishment and rural exodus. Stellenbosch: Pro Ecclesia.

Grundlingh, A M. 1986a. The 'handsuppers' and 'joiners'. In Cameron (ed), *An illustrated history of South Africa.*

——. 1986b, The prelude to the Anglo-Boer War, 1881–1899. In Cameron (ed), *An illustrated history of South Africa.*

Guelke, L. 1989. Freehold farmers and frontier settlers, 1657–1780. In Elphick and Giliomee (eds), T*he shaping of South African society 1652–1840.*

Halisi, C R D. 1999. *Black political thought in the making of South African democracy.* Indianapolis: Indiana University Press.

Hancock, W K; and Van der Poel, J (eds). 1966–1973. *Selections from the Smuts papers,* (7 volumes). Cambridge: Cambridge University Press.

Hansen, H A. 1965. Standards and values in a rich society. In Phelps (ed). *Private wants and public needs.*

Harrington, M. 1962. *The other America.* New York: MacMillan.

Harris, L. 1993. South Africa's social and economic transformation: from no middle way to no alternative. *Review of African Political Economy,* 57. Sheffield.

Harris, R (ed). 1975. *The political economy of Africa.* New York: John Wiley & Sons.

Harrop, M (ed). 1992. *Power and policy in liberal democracies.* Cambridge: Cambridge University Press.

Heilbroner, R; and Milberg, W. 1996. *The crisis of vision in modern economic thought.* Cambridge: Cambridge University Press.

Held, D. 1987. *Models for democracy.* Cambridge: Polity Press.

Held, D *et al* (eds). [1949] 1983. *States and societies.* Oxford: Martin Robertson.

Hellmann, E; and Lever, H (eds). 1980. *Race relations in South Africa, 1929–1979.* London: Macmillan.

Henderson, P D (ed). 1996. *Economic growth in Britain.* London: Weidenfeld and Nicolson.

Hertz, N. 2001. *The silent takeover: global capitalism and the death of democracy.* London: Arrow.

Heydenrych, D H. 1986. The Boer republics, 1852–1881. In Cameron (ed). *An illustrated history of South Africa.*

Hindson, D. 1987. *Pass controls and the urban African proletariat in South Africa.* Johannesburg: Ravan Press.

Hobson, J A. 1902. *Imperialism: a study.* New York: James Pott.

Hofmeyr, J F. 1994. The rise in African wages: 1975–1985. *The South African Journal of Economics,* 62 (3).

Horrell, M. 1978. *Laws affecting race relations in South Africa (to the end of 1976).* Johannesburg: South African Institute of Race Relations.

Horwitz, R. 1967. *The political economy of South Africa.* London: Weidenfeld and Nicolson.

Houghton, D H. 1978. Economic development, 1665–1965. In Wilson and Thompson (eds), *The Oxford history of South Africa,* vol 2.

Hyslop, J (ed). 1999. *African democracy in the era of globalisation.* Johannesburg: Witwatersrand University Press.

Ignatieff, M. 1996. Articles of faith. *Index of Censorship* (5).

Iliffe, J. 1987. *The African poor: a history.* Cambridge: Cambridge University Press.

International Monetary Fund (IMF). 1995. *South Africa: selected economic issues.* Washington: IMF.

Jaffe, H. 1994. *European colonial despotism: a history of oppression and resistance in South Africa.* London: Kamak House.

James, W G and Simons, M (eds). 1989. *The angry divide: social and economic history of the Western Cape.* David Philip: Cape Town.

Johnson, R W. 1977. *How long will South Africa survive?* London: Macmillan.

Johnstone, F. 1976. *Class, race and gold: a study of class relations and racial discrimination in South Africa.* London: Routledge and Kegan Paul.

Kaplinsky, R. 1995. Capital intensity in South African manufacturing and unemployment. *World Development,* 23 (2).

Keegan, T. 1982. The sharecropping economy, African class formation and the 1913 Natives' Land Act in the highveld maize belt. In Marks and Rathbone (eds). *Industrialisation and social change in South Africa.*

——. 1986. White settlement and black subjugation on the South African highveld: the Tlokoa heartland in the north eastern Orange Free State ca 1850–1914. In Beinart *et al* (eds). *Putting a plough to the earth: accumulation and dispossession in rural South Africa.*

——. 1989. The origins of agrarian capitalism in South Africa. *Journal of Southern African Studies,* 15 (4).

——. 1996. *Colonial South Africa and the origin of the racial order.* Cape Town: David Philip.

Keegan, W. 1992. *The spectre of capitalism: the future of the world economy after the fall of communism.* London: Radius.

Kemp, T. 1993. *Historical patterns of industrialization.* London: Longman.

Kennedy, P. 1988. *The rise and the fall of great powers: economic change and military conflict.* New York: Random House.

Kentridge, M. 1993. *Turning the tanker: the economic debate in South Africa.* Johannesburg: Centre for Policy Studies.

Keynes, J M. [1943] 1949. *The general theory of employment, interest and money.* London: Macmillan.

Kindleberger, C P. 1996. *World economic primacy: 1500–1900.* Oxford: Oxford University Press.

Kirk, T. 1980. The Cape economy and the expropriation of the Kat River settlement, 1846–1853. In Marks and Atmore (eds). *Economy and society in pre-industrial South Africa.*

Kistner, W. 1952. The anti-slavery agitation against the Transvaal republics, 1852–1868. In *Archives yearbook for South African history.*

Klein, N. 2000. *No logo: taking aim at the brand bullies.* New York: Picador.

Kuper, L. 1978. African nationalism in South Africa. In Wilson and Thompson (eds). *The Oxford history of South Africa,* vol 2.

Kurien, C T. 1978. *Poverty, planning, and social transformation.* Bombay: Allied.

Lamar, H; and Thompson, L (eds). 1981. *The frontier in history: North America and southern Africa compared.* New Haven: Yale University Press.

Lawton, T C; Rosenau, J N; and Verdun, A C (eds). 2000. *Strange power: shaping the parameters of international relations and international political economy.* Hampshire: Ashgate, Albershot.

Le Cordeur, B. 1986. The occupation of the Cape, 1795–1854. In Cameron (ed), *An illustrated history of South Africa.*

Le Roux, P. 1978. The poor white problem: an economist's perspective. *Social Worker,* March and June.

——. 1984. *Poor whites.* Second Carnegie Inquiry into Poverty and Development in Southern Africa. Cape Town.

Legassick, M. 1974a. Legislation, ideology, and economy in post-1948 South Africa. *Journal of Southern African Studies,* 1 (1).

——. 1974b. South Africa: capital accumulation and violence. *Economy and Society,* 3 (3).

——. 1975. South Africa: forced labour, industrialisation, and racial differentiation. In Harris, R (ed). *The political economy of Africa.*

——. 1980. The frontier tradition in South African historiography. In Marks and Atmore (eds). *Economy and society in pre-industrial South Africa.*

——. 1989. The Northern Frontier to ca 1840. In Elphick and Giliomee (eds), *The shaping of South African society, 1652–1840.*

——. 1993. The state, racism, and the rise of capitalism in the nineteenth-century Cape Colony. *South African Historical Journal,* 28.

——. 1995. British hegemony and the origins of segregation in South Africa, 1901–1914. In Beinart and Dubow (eds), *Segregation and apartheid in twentieth-century South Africa.*

Leibbrant, S; and Leibbrant, M (eds). 2000. *Labour markets and the challenge of poverty and inequality in South Africa.* University of Cape Town, Development Policy Research Unit.

Leipoldt, C Louis. [1938] 1999. *Jan van Riebeeck: die grondlegger van 'n blanke Suid-Afrika.* Kaapstad: Nasionale Pers.

Lewis, J D. 2001. *Policies to promote growth and employment in South Africa.* Washington: The World Bank.

Lipton, M. 1986. *Capitalism and apartheid: South Africa, 1910–1986.* Cape Town: David Philip.

Lipset, S M. 1963. *Political man.* New York: Doubleday.

Lodge, T. 1983. *Black politics in South Africa since 1945.* London: Longman.

——. 1999. *South African politics since 1994.* Cape Town: David Philip.

Lonsdale, J. 1983. From colony to industrial state: South African historiography as seen from England. *Social Dynamics,* 9 (1).

Lötter, H P P. 1997. *Injustice, violence, and peace.* Amsterdam: Rodopi.

Louw, A; and Shaw, M. 1997. *Stolen opportunities: the impact of crime on South Africa's poor.* Johannesburg: Institute for Security Studies.

Lowenstein, A D. 1997. Why South Africa's apartheid economy failed. *Contemporary Economic Policy,* XV.

Luiz, J M. 1998. Political regimes and the conditions for development-orientated state intervention: a theoretical and comparative perspective with reference to South Africa. Unpublished PhD thesis, University of Stellenbosch.

Macmillan, W M. 1927. *The Cape coloured question: a historical survey.* London: Faber.

Macro-Economic Research Group (MERG). 1993. *Making democracy work, a framework for macro-economic policy in South Africa.* Bellville: Centre for Development Studies.

Maddison, A. 1986. *Phases of capitalist development.* Oxford: Oxford University Press.

——. 1989. *The World Economy in the 20th century.* Paris: OECD Development Centre.

Malherbe, V C. 1991. Indenture and unfree labour in South Africa: towards an understanding. *South African Historical Journal,* 24.

Mamdani, M. 1996a. *Citizen and subject.* Cape Town: David Philip.

——. 1996b. Reconciliation without justice. *Southern African Review of Books,* November, December.

——. 2000. The truth according to the TRC. In Amadiume and Abdullahi (eds). *The politics of memory: truth, healing and social justice.*

Mandela, N. 1994a. Address to joint session of both houses of parliament. First session, first parliament, RSA.

——. 1994b. *Long walk to freedom.* Boston: Little Brown.

Manuel, T A. 1996. Speech by the minister of finance to the Bureau of Economic Research Conference, Cape Town, 8 October.

Marais, H. 1998. *South Africa: limits to change – the political economy of transition.* 1st edition. Cape Town: University of Cape Town Press.

——. 2001. *South Africa: limits to change – the political economy of transition.* 2nd edition. Cape Town: University of Cape Town Press.

Marks, S. 1995. Natal, the Zulu royal family and the ideology of segregation. In Beinart and Dubow (eds), *Segregation and apartheid in twentieth-century South Africa.*

Marks, S and Atmore, A (eds). 1980. *Economy and society in pre-industrial South Africa.* London: Longman.

Marks, S and Rathbone, R (eds). 1982. *Industrialisation and social change in South Africa.* London: Longman.

Marks, S and Trapido, S. 1979. Lord Milner and the South African state. *History Workshop Journal,* 2.

——. (eds). 1987. *The politics of race,class, and nationalism in twentieth century South Africa.* London: Longman.

Marquand, D. 1988. *The unprincipled society.* London: Jonathan Cape.

Marshall, T H. [1949] 1983. Citizenship and social class. In Held, D *et al* (eds). *States and societies.*

Mason, J E. 1994. Fortunate slaves and artful masters: labor relations in the rural Cape Colony during the era of emancipation, ca. 1825–1838. In Eldredge and Morton (eds), *Slavery in South Africa: captive labor on the Dutch frontier.*

May, C. 2000. *A global political economy of intellectual property rights: the new enclosures?* London: Routledge.

May, J. 1998. *Experience and perceptions of poverty in South Africa.* Durban: Praxis.

May, J (ed). 2000. *Poverty and inequality in South Africa.* Cape Town: David Philip.

May, J; Rogerson, C; and Vaughan, A. 2000. Livehoods and assets. In May (ed). *Poverty and inequality in South Africa.*

May, J; Woolard, I; and Klasen, S. 2000. The nature and measurement of poverty and inequality. In May (ed), *Poverty and inequality in South Africa.*

Mbeki, T. 1998. Address to NUM congress. 28 March. Johannesburg.

——. 2002a. Address in the Council of Provinces. 12 November. Unedited transcript.

——. 2002b. A congress of cadres united in action for change. Editorial. *Umrabulo*, 16. 6 August.

McCarthy, C. 1991. *Stagnation in the South African economy: what went wrong?* University of Stellenbosch, Centre of Contextual Hermeneutics.

McGrath, M; and Whiteford, A. 1994. *Inequality in the size distribution of income in South Africa.* University of Stellenbosch, Stellenbosch Economic Project.

Meister, R. 2000. Ways of winning: the cost of moral victory in transitional regimes. Unpublished paper, University of California.

Metzer, L. 1994. Emancipation, commerce and the role of John Fairbairn's Advertiser. In Worden and Crais (eds), *Breaking the chains: slavery and its legacy in the nineteenth century Cape Colony.*

Mhone, G. 2000. *Enclavity and constrained labour absorptive capacity in southern African countries.* Geneva: International Labour Organisation (ILO).

Michie, J and Padayachee, V (eds). 1997. *The political economy of South Africa's transition: policy perspective in the late 1990s.* London: Dryden.

Mishan, E J. 1967. *The cost of economic growth.* London: Staples Press.

Mohr, P J. 1994. Restructuring the South African economy: some pertinent issues. *Journal for the Study of Economies and Econometrics* (SEE), 18 (7).

Moll, P G. 1991. *The great economic debate.* Johannesburg: Skotaville.

Moll, T. 1991. Did the apartheid economy 'fail'? *Journal of Southern African Studies,* 7 (2).

Moodie, T D. 1975. *The rise of Afrikanerdom: power, apartheid, and the Afrikaner civil religion.* London: University of California Press.

Moore, B. 1966. *Social origins of dictatorship and democracy.* Boston: Beacon Press.

Moosa, E. 2000. Truth and reconciliation as performance: spectres of Eucharistic redemption. In Villa-Vicencio and Verwoerd (eds). *Looking back, reaching forward: reflection on the TRC in South Africa.*

Morris, M. 1976. The development of capitalism in South African agriculture: class struggle in the countryside. *Economy and Society,* 5.

——. 1991. State, capital and growth: the political economy of the national question. In Gelb (ed). *South Africa's economic crisis.*

——. 1993. Who's in, who's out? Side-stepping the '50 per cent solution'. *Work in Progress,* 86. Johannesburg.

Morris, M; and Padayachee, V. 1989. Hegemonic projects, accumulation strategies, and state reform policy in South Africa. *Labour, Capital and Society,* 22 (1).

Morton, F. 1994a. Captive labor in the eastern Transvaal after the Sand River Convention. In Eldredge and Morton (eds). *Slavery in South Africa: captive labor on the Dutch frontier.*

——. 1994b. Slavery and South African historiography. In Eldredge and Morton (eds), *Slavery in South Africa: captive labor on the Dutch frontier.*

——. 1994c. Slavery in South Africa. In Eldredge and Morton (eds), *Slavery in South Africa: captive labor on the Dutch frontier.*

Mostert, N. 1992. *Frontiers: the epic of South Africa's creation and the tragedy of the Xhosa people.* London: Pimlico.

Mtshali, L. 2002. Address in the National Council of Provinces. 12 November. Unedited transcript.

Müller, A L. 1981a. The economics of slave labour at the Cape of Good Hope. *The South African Journal of Economics,* 49 (1).

——. 1981b. Slavery and the development of South Africa. *The South African Journal of Economics,* 49 (2).

Munby, D (ed). 1966. *Economic growth in world perspective.* New York: Associated Press.

Murray, B K; and Stadler, A W. 1986. From the Pact to the advent of apartheid, 1924–1948: the period 1924–1939. In Cameron (ed), *An illustrated history of South Africa.*

Murray, M J. 1989. The origins of agrarian capitalism in South Africa: a critic of the social history perspective. *Journal of Southern African Studies,* 15 (4).

Myers, M L. 1983. *The soul of the modern economic man: ideas of self-interest, Thomas Hobbes, and Adam Smith.* Chicago: University of Chicago Press.

Mytelka, L K. 2000. Knowledge and structural power in the international political economy. In Lawton *et al* (eds). *Strange power: shaping the parameters of international relations and international political economy.*

Nash, M D. 1986. The 1820 Settlers. In Cameron (ed). *An illustrated history of South Africa.*

National Treasury, South African Government. 2001. *Budget Review,* 2001. RP 27/2001.

Nattrass, N. 1994a. Politics and economics in ANC economic policy. *African Affairs,* 93.

——. 1994b. South Africa: the economic restructuring agenda: a critique of the MERG report. *Third World Quarterly.* 15 (2).

——. 1996. Gambling on investment: competing economic strategies in South Africa. *Transformation,* 31.

——. 2001. High productivity now: a critical review of South Africa's growth strategy. *Transformation,* 45.

Nattrass, N and Ardington, E (eds). 1990. *The political economy of South Africa.* Cape Town: Oxford University Press.

Newton-King, S. 1980. The labour market of the Cape Colony, 1807–1828. In Marks and Atmore (eds). *Economy and society in pre-industrial South Africa.*

——. 1994. The enemy within. In Worden and Crais (eds). *Breaking the chains: slavery and its legacy in the nineteenth century Cape Colony.*

Nürnberger, K. 1998. *Prosperity, poverty and pollution.* London: Zed Books.

Offe, C. 1996. *Modernity and the state.* Cambridge, Massachusetts: The MIT Press.

Okun, A M. 1975. *Equality and efficiency: the big trade-off.* Washington, DC: The Brookings Institute.

O'Meara, D. 1983. *Volkskapitalisme: class, capital and ideology in the development of Afrikaner nationalism, 1934–1948.* Johannesburg: Ravan Press.

——. 1996. *Forty lost years: the apartheid state and the politics of the National Party, 1948–1994.* Athens: Ohio University Press.

Organisation for Economic Cooperation and Development (OECD). 1997. *Economic Outlook* (62). Paris: OECD Publications.

——. 2001. *OECD in figures.* June.

Pakenham, T. 1986. The Anglo-Boer War, 1899–1902. In Cameron (ed). *An illustrated history of South Africa.*

Peires, J B. 1989. The British at the Cage, 1814–1834. In Elphick and Giliomee (eds). *The shaping of South African society 1652–1840.*

Penn, N. 1989. Labour, land and livestock in the Western Cape during the eighteenth century. In James and Simons (eds). *The angry divide; social and economic history of the Western Cape.*

——. 1994. Drosters of the Bokkeveld and the Roggeveld, 1770–1800. In Eldredge and Morton (eds). *Slavery in South Africa: captive labor on the Dutch frontier.*

Perkin, H. 1989. *The rise of the professional society, England since 1880.* London: Routledge.

Phelps, E S (ed). 1965. *Private wants and public needs.* New York: W W Norton.

——. (ed). 1969. *The goal of economic growth.* 2nd edition. New York: W W Norton.

Posel, D. 1987. The meaning of apartheid before 1948: conflicting interests and forces within the Afrikaner nationalist alliance. *Journal of Southern African Studies,* 14 (1).

——. 1991. *The making of apartheid,* 1948–1961. Oxford: Clarendon Press.

Pretorius, F. 1991. *Kommandolewe tydens die Anglo-Boereoorlog,* 1899–1902. Cape Town: Human and Rousseau.

Przeworski, A. 1992. The neoliberal fallacy. *Journal of Democracy,* 3 (3).

Przeworski, A *et al.* 1995. *Sustainable democracy.* Cambridge: Cambridge University Press.

Republic of South Africa (RSA). 1996. *Constitution of the Republic of South Africa.* Act 108 of 1996, as amended on 11 October 1996.

Rodrick, D. 1997. Sense and nonsense in the globalisation debate. *Foreign Policy,* Summer.

Rich, P B. 1984. *White power and the liberal conscience.* Manchester: Manchester University Press.

———. 1993. *Hope and despair: English-speaking intellectuals and South African politics, 1989–1976.* London: British Academic Press.

———. 1996. S*tate power and black politics in South Africa, 1912–1951.* London: Macmillan.

Richardson, P. 1986. The Natal sugar industry in the nineteenth century. In Beinart *et al* (eds). *Putting a plough to the earth: accumulation and dispossession in rural South Africa.*

Rix, S; and Jardine, C. 1996. Privatisation: the debate over restructuring of state assets. In Baskin (ed), *Against the current: labour and economic policy in southern Africa.*

Ross, R. 1983. *Cape of torments: slavery and resistance in South Africa.* London: Routledge and Kegan Paul.

———. 1986. The origins of capitalist agriculture in the Cape Colony: a survey. In Beinart *et al* (eds). *Putting a plough to the earth: accumulation and dispossession in rural South Africa.*

———. 1989. The Cape of Good Hope and the world economy, 1652–1835. In Elphick and Giliomee (eds). *The shaping of South African society 1652–1840.*

———. 1993. *Beyond the pale: essays on the history of colonial South Africa.* London: Wesleyan University Press.

———. 1994. Rather mental than physical: emancipation and the Cape economy. In Worden and Crais (eds). *Breaking the chains slavery and its legacy in the nineteenth century Cape Colony.*

Rubner, A. 1970. *The sacred cows of economics.* London: MacGibson.

Rupert, M. 2000. *Ideologies of globalisation; contending visions of a new world order.* London: Routledge.

Sadie, J L. 1975. Die ekonomiese faktor in die Afrikanergemeenskap. In Van der Merwe (ed). *Identiteit en verandering: sewe opstelle oor die Afrikaner vandag.*

———. 1989. *The South African population into the twenty-first century and its environment.* Paper delivered at University of Cape Town, Cape Town.

———. 1991. *The South African labour force, 1960–2005.* Navorsingsverslag 178, Buro van Marknavorsing, Pretoria: UNISA.

———. 1992. Unemployment in South Africa: its nature and origins. *Journal for Studies in Economics and Econometrics* (SEE), 16 (1).

———. 1999. *A projection of the SA population.* Buro van Marknavorsing, Pretoria: UNISA.

———. 2002. The fall and rise of the Afrikaner in the South African economy. *Annale,* 1. University of Stellenbosch.

Samuelson, P A (ed). 1970. *Readings of economics.* 6th edition. New York: McGraw-Hill.

Samuelson, P A; and Nordhaus, W D. 1985. *Economics.* 12th edition. New York: McGraw-Hill.

Saul, J and Gelb, S. 1981. *The crisis in South Africa: class defence and class revolution.* New York: Monthly Review.

Saul, J S. 1993. *Recolonization and resistance: southern Africa in the 1990s.* New Jersey: Africa World Press.

Savage, M. 1986. The imposition of pass laws on the African population in South Africa, 1916–1984. *African Affairs,* 85.

Schrire, R (ed). 1992. *Wealth and poverty? Critical choices for South Africa.* Cape Town: Oxford University Press.

Schumpeter, J A. [1943] 1950. *Capitalism, socialism, and democracy.* 3rd edition. London: Allen & Unwin.

Schusster, M. 2001. COSATU Newsletter. 5 November.

Schutte, G. 1989. Company and colonists at the Cape, 1652–1795. In Elphick and Giliomee (eds). *The shaping of South African society 1652–1840.*

Seligman, B B. 1968. *Permanent poverty, an American syndrome.* Chicago: Quadrangle Books.

Shampande, Y K. 1998. Gears in shift. *UN Chronicle,* 35 (1).

Shaw, M. 1995. *Partners in crime? Crime, political transition and changing forms of policing control.* Research Report No 39. Johannesburg: Centre for Policy Studies.

Shell, R C-H. 1989. The family and slavery at the Cape, 1680–1808. In James and Simons (eds). *The angry divide: social and economic history of the Western Cape.*

——. 1994a. *Children of bondage: a social history of the slave society at the Cape of Good Hope, 1652–1838.* London: Wesleyan University Press.

——. 1994. The Tower of Babel: the slave trade and creolization at the Cape, 1652–1834. In Eldredge and Morton (eds). *Slavery in South Africa: captive labor on the Dutch frontier.*

Simon, D (ed). 1998. *South Africa in southern Africa: reconfiguring the region.* Cape Town: David Philip.

Skidelsky, R. 1994. *John Maynard Keynes: the economist as saviour, 1920–1937.* New York: Viking Penguin.

Slater, H. 1980. The changing pattern of economic relationships in rural Natal, 1838–1914. In Marks and Atmore (eds). *Economy and society in pre-industrial South Africa.*

Slovo, J. 1976. South Africa: no middle road. In Davidson, Slovo, and Wilkenson (eds). *Southern Africa: the new politics of revolution.*

——. 1992. Negotiations: what room for compromise?' *African Communist,* 130. Third quarter. Johannesburg.

Smit, B. 1991. Foreign capital flows and economic growth in South Africa. Paper presented to the Conference of the Economic Society of South Africa, Stellenbosch, 2–3 October 1991.

——. 1992. Secular trends in South Africa's macroeconomic data. In Schrire (ed). *Wealth and poverty? Cricital choices for South Africa.*

Smuts, J C. 1942a. Native policy in Africa: Rhodes Memorial Lectures at Oxford, 1929. In Smuts. *Plans for a better world.*

——. 1942b. *Plans for a better world.* London: Hodder & Stoughton.

South Africa Foundation (SAF). 1996. *Growth for all: an economic strategy for South Africa.* Johannesburg.

South African Communist Party (SACP). 2002. Information Bulletin of the Central Committee, 2. March.

South African Medical Research Council. 1993. National Trauma Research Unit.

South African Reserve Bank (SARB). 2000. *Quarterly Bulletin.* September.

——. 2001. *Quarterly Bulletin.* September.

——. 2002. *Quarterly Bulletin.* September.

Spies, S B. 1986a. Reconstruction and unification, 1902–1910. In Cameron (ed). *An illustrated history of South Africa.*

——. 1986b. Unity and disunity, 1910–1924. In Cameron (ed). *An illustrated history of South Africa.*

Stadler, A W. 1986. From the Pact to the advent of apartheid, 1924–1948: the period 1939 to 1948. In Cameron (ed). *An illustrated history of South Africa.*

Standing, G; Sender, J; and Weeks, J. 1996. *Restructuring the labour market: the South African challenge.* Geneva: International Labour Organisation (ILO).

Statistics South Africa (SSA). 2001. *Measuring poverty in South Africa.* Pretoria.

——. 2002. Earnings and spending in South Africa: selected findings and comparisons from the income and expenditure surveys of October 1995 and October 2000. Pretoria.

Stepan, N. 1982. *The idea of race in science.* London: Macmillan.

Stiglitz, J A. 1991. Whither socialism? Perspectives from the economics of information. Wicksel Memorial Lecture, unpublished manuscript.

——. 1998. Redefining the role of the state. Paper presented on the tenth anniversary of the MITI Research Institute, Tokyo, 17 March.

Stoneman, C. 1998. *Lessons unlearned; South Africa's one-way relationship with Zimbabwe.* In Simon (ed). *South Africa in southern Africa: reconfiguring the region.*

Strange, S. 1994. *States and markets.* Cambridge: Cambridge University Press.

——. 1996. *The retreat of the state: the diffusion of power in the world economy,* Cambridge: Cambridge University Press.

Streeten, P. 1966, The objectives of economic policy. In Henderson, P D (ed). 1966. *Economic growth in Britain.*

Stein, H; and Denison, E F. 1969. Economic growth as a national goal. In Phelps (ed). *The goal of economic growth.*

Sunter, C. 1992. *The new century; quest for the high road.* Cape Town: Human and Rosseau.

Taylor, V. 1993. The problem of political violence in South Africa. In Gentili (ed). *Sudafrica: processi di mutamento politico e costituzionale.*

Terreblanche, S; and Nattrass, N. 1990. A periodisation of the political economy. In Nattrass and Ardington (eds). *The political economy of South Africa.*

Terreblanche, S J. 1977. *Chroniese gemeenskapsarmoede.* Kaapstad: Tafelberg .

——. 1980. *Die wording van die westerse ekonomie.* Kaapstad: Academica.

——. 1988. The dream fades. *Leadership,* 7 (2).

——. 1989. Structural corruption in the National Party. IDASA lecture at the University of Cape Town, 12 April.

Theron Commission. 1976. See *The Commission of Inquiry into Matters Concerning the Coloured Population Group.*

Thomas, A. 1996. *Rhodes.* Johannesburg: Jonathan Ball.

Thomas, S. 2002. Another jobless boom as SA companies turn to machines. *Financial Mail,* 8 November.

Thompson, L. 1978a. The compromise of union. In Wilson and Thompson (eds). *The Oxford history of South Africa,* vol 2.

———. 1978b. Co-operation and conflict: the Zulu kingdom and Natal. In Wilson and Thompson (eds). *The Oxford history of South Africa,* vol 1.

———. 1978c. Great Britain and the Afrikaner republics. In Wilson and Thompson (eds). *The Oxford history of South Africa,* vol 1.

———. 1990. *A history of South Africa.* London: Yale University Press.

Thurow, L C. 1996. *The future of capitalism.* London: Nicholas Breadley.

Tobin, J. 1964. Economic growth as an objective of government policy. *American Economic Review,* May 1964.

Toffler, A. 1990. *Powershift.* New York: Bentham.

Townsend, P (ed). 1970. *The concept of poverty.* London: Heinemann.

Trapido, S. 1971. South Africa in a comparative study of industrialisation. *Journal of Development Studies,* 7 (3).

———. 1978. Landlord and tenant in a colonial economy: the Transvaal, 1880–1910. *Journal of Southern African Studies,* 5 (1).

———. 1980a. The friends of the natives: merchants, peasants and the political and ideological structure of liberalism in the Cape, 1854–1910. In Marks and Atmore (eds). *Economy and society in pre-industrial South Africa.*

———. 1980b. Reflections on land, office and wealth in the South African Republic, 1850–1900. In Marks and Atmore (eds), *Economy and society in pre-industrial South Africa.*

Truth and Reconciliation Commission of South Africa. 1998. Final report (five volumes). Cape Town: Juta.

Truu, M L (ed). 1976. *Public policy and the South African economy.* Cape Town: Oxford University Press.

Turok, B. 1999. On RDP and GEAR: governing under contraints. In Religion in Public Life, Multi-Events 1999, conference proceedings.

United Nations Development Programme (UNDP). 1999. *Human development report.* New York, Oxford: Oxford University Press.

———. 2002. *Human development report.* New York, Oxford: Oxford University Press.

Van Aswegen, H J. 1986. South Africa and Africa, 1961–1984. In Cameron (ed). *An illustrated history of South Africa.*

Van Beek, U J (ed). 1995. *South Africa and Poland in transition.* Pretoria: HSRC.

Van der Berg, S. 1991. Prospects for redistribution of primary and secondary income in the transition to democracy. Paper presented to the Biennial Conference of the Economic Society of South Africa, University of Stellenbosch.

Van der Berg, S; and Bhorat, H. 1999. *The present as a legacy of the past: the labour market, inequality and poverty in South Africa.* University of Cape Town, Development Policy Research Unit.

Van der Horst, S T. 1942. *Native Labour in South Africa.* Oxford: Oxford University Press.

———. 1976. Labour policy in South Africa (1948–1976). In Truu (ed). *Public policy and the South African economy.*

———. 1980. The changing face of the economy. In Hellmann and Lever (eds). *Race relations in South Africa, 1929–1979.*

Van der Merwe, H W (ed). 1975. *Identiteit en verandering: sewe opstelle oor die Afrikaner vandag.* Cape Town: Tafelberg.

Villa-Vicencio, C; and Verwoerd, W (eds). 2000. *Looking back, reaching forward: reflections on the Truth and Reconciliation Commission of South Africa (TRC).* Cape Town: University of Cape Town Press.

Waldmeir, P. 1997. *Anatomy of a miracle: the end of apartheid and the birth of the new South Africa.* London: Viking.

Watkins, K. 1997. *Globalisation and liberalisation: implications for poverty, distribution and inequality.* Occasional Paper 32.

Watson, R L. 1990. *The slave question: liberty and property in South Africa.* London: Wesleyan University Press.

Welsh, D. 1978. The growth of towns. In Wilson and Thompson (eds). *The Oxford history of South Africa,* vol 2.

Whiteford, A; and McGrath, M. 1994. *The distribution of income in South Africa.* Pretoria: HSRC.

———. 1998. *Income inequality over the apartheid years.* Working Paper 6. Cape Town: South African Network for Economic Research.

Whiteford, A; and Van Seventer, D E. 1999. *Winners and losers: South Africa's changing income distribution in the 1990s.* Menlo Park: WEFA Southern Africa.

Whiteford, A; Posal, D; and Kelatwang, T. 1995. *A profile of poverty, inequality and human development.* Pretoria: HSRC.

Wilson, F. 1978. Farming, 1866–1966. In Wilson and Thompson (eds). *The Oxford history of South Africa,* vol 2.

Wilson, M. 1978. Co-operation and conflict: the Eastern Cape frontier. In Wilson and Thompson (eds). *The Oxford history of South Africa,* vol 2.

Wilson, M and Thompson, L (eds). 1978. *The Oxford history of South Africa (OHSA),* vols 1 and 2. Oxford: Oxford University Press.

Wolpe, H. 1995. Capitalism and cheap labour power in South Africa: from segregation to apartheid. In Beinart and Dubow (eds). *Segregation and apartheid in twentieth-century South Africa.*

Worden, N. 1989. Adjusting to emancipation: freed slaves and farmers in the mid-nineteenth century south-western Cape. In James and Simons (eds). *The angry divide: social and economic history of the Western Cape.*

———. 1994a. Between slavery and freedom: the apprenticeship period, 1834–1838. In Worden and Crais (eds). *Breaking the chains: slavery and its legacy in the nineteenth century Cape Colony.*

———. 1994b. *The making of modern South Africa: conquest, segregation, and apartheid.* Oxford: Blackwell.

Worden, N and Crais, C (eds). 1994. *Breaking the chains: slavery and its legacy in the nineteenth century Cape Colony.* Johannesburg: Witwatersrand University Press.

World Bank. 1996. *World development report.* Washington.

———. 1997. *World development report.* Washington.

———. 2000a. *Attacking poverty, opportunity, empowerment and security.* Washington.

———. 2000b. *Selected world development indicators.* Washington.

Yudelman, D. 1983. *The emergence of modern South Africa: state, capital, and the incorporation of organised labour on the South African gold fields.* Cape Town: David Philip.

Index

Index